The

PASSION

of

MICHEL

FOUCAULT

James Miller

HARVARD UNIVERSITY PRESS
Cambridge, Massachusetts

First Harvard University Press paperback edition, 2000

Library of Congress Cataloging-in-Publication Data is available

ISBN 0-674-00157-5

Parts of "Be Cruel!" first appeared as "Carnivals of Atrocity: Foucault, Nietzsche, Cruelty" in *Political Theory*, Copyright © 1990 Sage Publications, Inc., reprinted by permission. Parts of "The Secrets of a Man" first appeared in *Salmagundi*, Copyright © 1990 by Skidmore College, reprinted by permission. Parts of "The Heart Laid Bare" first appeared in *Grand Street*, Copyright © 1991 New York Foundation for the Arts, Inc., Grand Street Press, reprinted by permission.

The excerpts from "Le mortel partenaire" and from "Partage formel," #XXII, both by René Char, from Char's *Seules demeurent* and *La parole en archipel*, are reprinted by permission of Editions Gallimard. Copyright © Editions Gallimard 1945 and 1962.

The excerpt from "To Be Done with the Judgment of God" by Antonin Artaud, from Artaud's *Selected Writings*, is reprinted by permission of Georges Borchardt, Inc. Copyright © Editions Gallimard 1956, 1961, 1964, 1966, 1967, 1969, 1970, 1971, 1974; translation Copyright © 1976 by Farrar, Straus and Giroux.

CONTENTS

PREFACE

This book is not a biography, though in outline it follows the chronology of Michel Foucault's life; nor is it a comprehensive survey of his works, although it does offer an interpretation of a great many of his texts. It is, rather, a narrative account of one man's lifelong struggle to honor Nietzsche's gnomic injunction, "to become what one is."

Through a blend of anecdote and exegesis, I have approached Foucault's writing as if it expressed a powerful desire to realize a certain form of life; and his life as if it embodied a sustained and partially successful effort to turn this desire into a reality. In the spirit of an investigative journalist, I have gathered information about various aspects of Foucault's life that have been hitherto undocumented and, therefore, largely unexamined. In the spirit of an intellectual historian, I have sketched the broader cultural and social context within which this life unfolded. And in the spirit of a literary critic, I have highlighted a handful of recurrent fantasies and imaginative obsessions that gave a characteristic color and mood to both Foucault's composed texts and everyday life. My aim has been to conjure up "neither the pure grammatical subject nor the deep psychological subject," as Foucault himself once put it, "but rather the one who says 'I' in the works, the letters, the drafts, the sketches, the personal secrets."[1]

When I started to work on this book in 1987, three years after Foucault died, I was warned by one expert that my time would be wasted. His papers were inaccessible; his friends would not talk; my inquiry would prove futile.

Since then, one useful biography of Foucault, by Didier Eribon, has already appeared, and still another, by David Macey, was being prepared as I wrote. To my own surprise, I was able to talk to a great many of Foucault's friends; I have learned a good deal about his life, and been able to consult more than one rare document. I do not feel my time has been wasted.[2]

Still, in one sense, the expert who warned me was right. The time is not ripe for a definitive biography. Too many witnesses have yet to share all that they know. Even worse, too many documents remain unpublished.

Before his death in 1984, Foucault destroyed a great many of his personal papers; in his will, he prohibited the posthumous publication of any papers he might have overlooked; and so far, Foucault has yet to find his Max Brod. Though a center for researchers has been established in Paris, its holdings are incomplete. At the time I was writing, his various essays and interviews were widely scattered in a number of different languages in publications that were sometimes hard to locate. The promised French publication of Foucault's complete shorter works and interviews in chronological order will eventually transform the understanding of his work. But even then, more material will remain to be studied. His longtime companion, Daniel Defert, has Foucault's notebooks and journals, and also his personal library. At least one person has a partial manuscript of the volume on perversion that Foucault drafted for the original version of his History of Sexuality; but he has not shown it to me for the good reason that Foucault explicitly asked him to promise never to show it to anyone. And there is more: every year that I was at work, I discovered new documents, some of them illicit and unauthorized. I know of no other contemporary philosopher whose work has prompted such a flourishing black market in bootleg tape recordings and freelance transcriptions of public lectures, many hoarded jealously by collectors.

The secondary literature on Foucault is, by contrast, altogether too extensive. Anyone tempted to master it would doubtless soon give up, out of a combination of boredom and fatigue altogether at odds with the impact left by Foucault's work itself. In order to move forward, I found it useful to adopt a kind of studied ignorance. I was inclined to approach the lifework as naively as possible, deliberately withholding judgment and taking nothing for granted.

There were a number of other obstacles and potential pitfalls, which it is just as well to point out. Consider, for example, the dilemma of trying to write a narrative account of someone who questioned, repeatedly and systematically, the value of old-fashioned ideas about the "author"; someone who raised the gravest of doubts about the character of personal identity as such; someone who, as a matter of temperament, distrusted prying questions and naked honesty; someone, finally, who was nevertheless inclined to see his own work as, on some level, autobiographical.

A preface is not the place to grapple with the many complex issues raised by Foucault's views on such matters. It is enough to say that, in the end, I was forced to ascribe to Foucault a persistent and purposeful self, inhabiting one and the same body throughout his mortal life, more or less consistently accounting for his actions and attitudes to others as well as to himself, and understanding his life as a teleologically structured quest (or, in French, recherche).

It may be that telling Foucault's story in this way betrays his deepest teachings; it may be, as the philosopher Alasdair MacIntyre recently argued, that the apparent need to approach even Foucault by ascribing to him a persistent and purposeful self, behind all his masks and outward changes of belief and behavior, reveals a crucial limitation of his philosophy; or it may be—as I believe—that Foucault himself never held the ultimately incoherent kind of views about the death of the author and the disappearance of the self that MacIntyre rightly rejects.[3]

The issue of personal identity does not, alas, exhaust the methodological conundrums facing anyone who writes about this most unyielding of modern skeptics. For Foucault also called into question the concept of "truth" itself, suggesting that all of his own historical studies were, in some sense, works of "fiction."[4]

This, again, is not the place to address the many interesting and perhaps intractable issues posed by Foucault's own approach to historiography. But it is wise to state explicitly what "game of truth," to borrow Foucault's phrase, I think I am playing.

In what follows, I have adhered to the conventions of modern scholarship, checking my hunches and leaps of imagination against the available evidence. I have included an extensive apparatus of endnotes, documenting the source of every citation and every anecdote, exploring uncertainties and elaborating qualifications where appropriate. At every step, I have prized simplicity and struggled to achieve clarity of expression, even though I am often dealing with complex ideas and sometimes hermetic practices. Above all, I have tried to tell the truth.[5]

The truth, indeed, has presented me with my most difficult problems. As readers will soon enough discover, the crux of what is most original and challenging about Foucault's way of thinking, as I see it, is his unrelenting, deeply ambiguous and profoundly problematic preoccupation with death, which he explored not only in the exoteric form of his writing, but also, and I believe critically, in the esoteric form of sado-masochistic eroticism. Though Foucault himself spoke frankly about this aspect of his life, I sometimes had to wonder, while I was writing my book, whether I was behaving like some not-so-Grand Inquisitor. As an American critic has acutely remarked, "in a culture that without ever ceasing to proliferate homosexual meaning knows how to confine it, as well in collectivities as individuals, to a kind of false unconscious, there is hardly a procedure for bringing out this meaning that doesn't look or feel like just more police entrapment."[6]

And that was not the end of the problems raised by telling the truth. To make matters worse, AIDS entered into the story, casting a pall over every page I wrote, giving this life a twist that was not at all the twist that I would have hoped for. The fact that my book was written, and will at first be read, in the shadow of a plague, makes it all too easy to discount the possibility that Foucault, in his radical approach to the body and its pleasures, was in fact a kind of visionary; and that in the future, once the threat of AIDS has receded, men and women, both straight and gay, will renew, without shame or fear, the kind of corporeal experimentation that formed an integral part of his own philosophical quest.

Still, no profession of good faith can defuse what is volatile and perhaps tragic in the life that follows. Yet despite the many dangers, of scandal and reductionism, of unconscious stereotyping and prurient sensationalism—and last but not least, of offering fresh ammunition to critics hostile to everything Foucault fought for—I have gone ahead, and tried to tell the whole truth, as best I could.

Part of my purpose is old-fashioned: telling the truth is what writers of history are supposed to do.

Another part is equally straightforward, though a little harder to justify—the justification in many ways is the book as a whole. For better or worse, Michel Foucault is one of the representative men—and outstanding thinkers—of the twentieth century. His life and the texts he wrote are intricately intertwined in ways that prove mutually illuminating. Therefore, a recounting of his life in all of its philosophical dimensions, however shocking some of these may seem, is not only warranted, but essential.

Still another part of the reason for this book is more personal. I am someone who holds the not entirely happy conviction that there is no Aristotelean mean, no Platonic idea of the good, no moral compass implicit in our ability to reason, and no regulative ideal of consensus that could help us to smooth away the rough edges of competing forms of life and enable us to reconcile their incommensurable claims. Therefore, Nietzsche's philosophy has always been for me a puzzle and a provocation, if only because, in terms of its inner logic, which I have yet to see refuted,

I can find no easy way to rule out the sort of cruel and murderous practices embraced by some of his followers.

What it might mean, after Auschwitz, to live a life thoughtfully "beyond good and evil" is, in short, worth finding out. And what better way than to study the life of the most revolutionary—and deeply serious—of postwar Nietzscheans?

This, of course, is by no means the only way to approach Foucault's work. His books long ago made their way into the world, coming into contact with other fields of experience, other types of intelligence, to flourish or fall in the clash of ideas. As is true of any fashionable figure, a great deal of nonsense has been said, and done, in his name. But he equally deserves some measure of credit for informing, if nothing else, an impressive variety of pathbreaking historico-philosophical studies: for example, Peter Brown's great reexamination of sexual renunciation in early Christianity, The Body and Society; Paul Veyne's account of classical Roman institutions in Bread and Circuses; Ian Hacking's history of statistical styles of reasoning, The Taming of Chance; François Ewald's study of workman's compensation and health insurance in nineteenth-century France, The Provident State. And this is just the beginning of a long and growing list.

But such studies, despite demonstrating the power of Foucault's texts to inspire exciting and original scholarship, do not, finally, put us in touch with what is most singular—and perhaps most disquieting—about the philosopher's work as he himself, at the end of his life, invited us to understand it.

"At every moment, step by step," he remarked in 1983, "one must confront what one is thinking and saying with what one is doing, what what one is." And this requires examining the fusion, or perhaps confusion, of concept and existence, of dream and reality, just as Foucault himself suggested: "The key to the personal poetic attitude of a philosopher is not to be sought in his ideas, as if it could be deduced from them, but rather in his philosophy-as-life, in his philosophical life, his ethos."[7]

This book, then, is a "philosophical life"—dedicated to the memory of Michel Foucault.

Certain beings have a meaning that
eludes us. Who are they? Their secret
resides in the depths of the very secret of
life. They approach it. Life kills them.
But the future which they have thus
awakened with a murmer, divines them,
creates them. Oh labyrinth of extreme
love!

— RENÉ CHAR

No one converses with me beside myself
and my voice reaches me as the voice of
one dying. With thee, beloved voice, with
thee, the last remembered breath of all
human happiness, let me discourse, even
if it is only for another hour. Because of
thee, I delude myself as to my solitude
and lie my way back to multiplicity and
love, for my heart shies away from believing love is dead. It cannot bear the icy
shivers of loneliest solitude. It compels
me to speak as though I were Two.

— FRIEDRICH NIETZSCHE

1

THE DEATH
of
THE AUTHOR

AT THE TIME OF HIS DEATH on June 25, 1984, at the age of fifty-seven, Michel Foucault was perhaps the single most famous intellectual in the world. His books, essays, and interviews had been translated into sixteen languages. Social critics treated his work as a touchstone. In a variety of academic fields, scholars were grappling with the implications of his empirical research and pondering the abstract questions that he had raised: about the reach of power and the limits of knowledge, about the origins of moral responsibility and the foundations of modern government, about the character of historical inquiry and the nature of personal identity. For more than a decade, his elegant shaved skull had been an emblem of political courage—a cynosure of resistance to institutions that would smother the free spirit and stifle "the right to be different." In the eyes of his admirers, he had replaced Jean-Paul Sartre as the personification of what an intellectual ought to be: quick to condemn, determined to expose abuses of power, unafraid to echo Émile Zola's old battle cry, "*J'accuse!*"[1]

His death came as a shock. He had collapsed in his Paris apartment earlier in June, but was widely assumed to be on the road to recovery. He was in the prime of life, at the peak of his powers. Just days before he died, two more volumes of his eagerly awaited History of Sexuality had appeared.

In France, he was regarded as a kind of national treasure. After his death, the prime minister issued a memorial tribute. *Le Monde*, *Libération*, and *Le Figaro* all bannered the news on page one. For its weekend edition, *Libération* rushed out a special twelve-page supplement detailing the great man's life and works. From all corners of the country, eulogies flooded the media.

In the newsweekly *Le Nouvel Observateur*, editor Jean Daniel celebrated "the breadth, the vastness, the insolent force of his intelligence," "the sometimes cruel strictness of his judgment." Paul Veyne, the renowned classicist, proclaimed his work to be "the most important event in the thought of our century." Fernand Braudel, perhaps France's most eminent living historian, stiffly saluted "one of the most dazzling minds of his era." And so the testimonials went, from scholars and artists, cabinet ministers and aging ex-Maoists, trade union leaders and former prisoners, sincere and patently false, the sheer range of the tributes striking evidence of Foucault's impact on his own society.[2]

His fame, as the obituaries recalled, began with the work that he produced in the 1960s. In *Madness and Civilization,* published in 1961, he argued that the perception of insanity had changed dramatically after 1500: in the Middle Ages, the mad had roamed free and been viewed with respect, while in our own day they were confined to asylums and treated as sick, in a triumph of "misguided philanthropy." What seemed like an enlightened and humane application of scientific knowledge turned out, in Foucault's view, to be a subtle and insidious new form of social control. The broader implications of this argument only became clear to the general public several years later, when Foucault's book emerged as a key text for a group of "anti-psychiatrists" that included R. D. Laing, David Cooper, and Thomas Szasz. Yet even in 1961, a number of prominent French critics and scholars—among them Fernand Braudel, Roland Barthes, and the philosopher Gaston Bachelard—expressed their admiration for the boldness of Foucault's thesis, the quality of his research, and the beauty of his language. His reputation began to grow in France. And with the appearance of *Madness and Civilization* in English in 1965, that reputation began to grow abroad as well.[3]

The following year, in 1966, *The Order of Things,* Foucault's second major book, became a surprise bestseller in France. In this work, he undertook an audacious comparative study of the development of economics, the natural sciences, and linguistics in the eighteenth and nineteenth centuries. Though often difficult, the writing sparkled with flashy neologisms and striking formulations. Of these, none was more famous than the book's last sentence, wagering that "man" will soon disappear, "like a face drawn in sand at the edge of the sea." It was the controversy over this passage, heralding the death of man as Nietzsche a century before had trumpeted the death of God, that made Foucault, for the first time, a figure to be reckoned with.[4]

But it was only after the events of May '68 that Foucault's ascendancy was complete. In the wake of the global student revolt of that year, he developed an abiding passion for politics. For the rest of his life, he routinely commented on current affairs, signed petitions, and participated in demonstrations, always ready to protest the plight of the wretched and powerless: French prisoners, Algerian immigrants, Polish trade unionists, Vietnamese refugees. At the same time, he rose to a new pinnacle of academic prestige: following in the footsteps of Henri Bergson, Maurice Merleau-Ponty, and his own mentor, Jean Hyppolite, he was elected in 1970 to the Collège de France, the nation's most eminent institution of research and learning.

In these later years, perhaps the most widely remarked aspect of Foucault's work was his idea of "power." Like Nietzsche, his avowed model and precursor, he understood power not as a fixed quantity of physical force, but rather as a stream of energy flowing through every living organism and every human society, its formless flux harnessed in various patterns of behavior, habits of introspection, and systems of knowledge, in addition to different types of political, social, and military organization.

In *Discipline and Punish,* perhaps the most influential of his works, published in France in 1975, he applied this notion of power in recounting the rise of the modern prison. Though his reading of the historical evidence was, as always, richly textured, his overarching thesis was once again startling. The effort to introduce "more kindness, more respect, more 'humanity' " into the prison system was a trap: through its very success in softening the often harsh edges of corporal punishment, the modern prison epitomized an unobtrusive, essentially painless type of coercion typical of the modern world generally. From schools and the professions to the army and the prison, the central institutions of our society, charged Foucault, strove with sinister efficiency to supervise the individual, "to neutralize his dangerous states," and to alter his conduct by inculcating numbing codes of discipline. The inevitable result was "docile bodies" and obedient souls, drained of creative energy.[5]

Though Foucault first explicitly addressed the issue of power in this book, it had always been one of his preoccupations. All of his work, from *Madness and Civilization* on, pivots around asymmetrical relationships in which power is exercised, sometimes thoughtfully, often wantonly. The figures haunting his pages enact an allegory of endless domination, from the hangman torturing the murderer to the doctor locking up the deviant.

Could society, as socialists from Marx to Sartre had dreamed, ever be freed from the cruel grip of power? It is hard to see how, if we take at all seriously Foucault's sweeping (and unfinished) History of Sexuality. In the controversial first volume of this work, published in 1976, Foucault disputed the common view that modern culture is sexually repressive, only to replace it with an even more disquieting view: the pleasure in exercising power, driven out of "docile bodies," must inevitably reappear, transmogrified, in sexual fantasies, erupting in *"perpetual spirals* of power and pleasure," fueling an uncontrollable growth of new, polymorphous perversions, sometimes vitalizing, sometimes virulent. [6]

No wonder Foucault regarded death as the only form of grace vouchsafed to a human being. Indeed, to die from "diseases of love," he declared in 1963, in a typically gnomic aside, was to experience "the Passion." It was to give to a cursedly singular life "a face that cannot be exchanged." In an implicit inversion of the apotheosis of Christ on the cross, the man martyred for his erotic practices reveals not the eternal glory of God in heaven, but the "lyrical core of man, his invisible truth, his visible secret." [7]

That the philosopher, like some improbable character in a Borges story, should have thus offered a commentary in advance on the possible implications of his own death exemplifies the uncanniness that marks all of Foucault's writing.

Here was a style of thought—learned, unmistakably original, with an air of mystery and a whiff of danger—that postwar France turned into a major export industry. For many readers, Foucault will doubtless always be linked with the other Parisian savants who first came to international prominence in the sixties. This generation included many of his mentors, friends, and rivals: Louis Althusser, the doyen of a rigorously scientific Marxism; Jacques Lacan, the daunting Freudian gnostic; Roland Barthes, theorist of signs, connoisseur of contemporary myth, champion of the "new novel"; and Jacques Derrida, anti-philosopher and enemy of metaphysics.

As a group, these men first achieved fame as critics of humanism. Skeptical of rationalist and personalist philosophies, critical of teleological treatments of history as a story with a happy ending, they were wary of liberalism and (with the exception of Althusser) impatient with Marxism. And though Foucault, for one, would eventually aim to be a new kind of intellectual, modest and without mystifying pretense, he, like the others, was universally regarded as *un maître à penser*—a master of thought, the affectionate phrase the French use for the handful of Olympian figures they invest with sovereign authority.

And like the others, Foucault had gone out of his way to make a sharp break with his immediate precursors. The experience of fascism and total war had driven Sartre and his generation back to the truisms of the Enlightenment: for many of them, Marxism and the idea of a universal history seemed to offer a necessary moral compass. Foucault's generation, by contrast, felt no such need for morality, for compasses, for fixed roadmaps of reality: the recourse to a universal history and the nostalgia, cloaked in Marxist rhetoric, for Hegel's vision of a harmonious synthesis of reason and freedom, seemed to them little short of a failure of philosophical nerve. Foucault himself frankly rejected the old "theme of solidarity," and urged readers to admit that we "can and must make of man a negative experience, lived in the form of hate and aggression."[8] And just as the twilight of French colonialism in Algeria became a testing ground for Sartre's generation of existentialists, the unexpected vehemence of the student revolt of May '68, and the various liberation movements that followed—above all, women's liberation and gay liberation—made Foucault's work seem of historical moment.

In this charged context it began to reach a global audience. Around the world after 1968, in Italy and Spain, in Germany and Great Britain, in Japan and Brazil, but above all in the United States, countless academics, cloistered on campuses but hungry for the tang of combat, if only in the vicarious form of championing ideas that clashed with prevailing orthodoxies, took up Foucault's philosophy as their own. As inevitably happens when enthusiastic disciples imitate "a founder of discursivity"—Foucault's neologism for powerfully original thinkers like himself—what was most startling and singular about his work was soon travestied through thoughtless repetition.[9] Still, as his influence grew, the most uncanny ideas of this most uncanny of thinkers could not help seeping into the mainstream of received opinion, insensibly shaping the tenor and tone of our own *fin-de-siècle* culture.

Since his death, Foucault's academic stock has only risen. In the words of one expert, he now holds an "almost unparalleled position of intellectual dominance over the interpretation of many key aspects of the evolution of Western civilization since the seventeenth century." Historians studying psychiatry and medicine, crime and punishment, sexuality and the family, can scarcely proceed without reference to him, even if only to correct or dismiss his findings. He has similarly set new agendas for research in sociology and political theory. By suggesting that society need not punish the criminal or segregate the mad, he has affected, both directly and indirectly, movements for prison reform and the practice of psychiatry: at least one prominent doctor in the United States, observing the increase in homeless schizophrenics, has deplored the influence of Foucault's ideas. [10] His hypothesis about the constitutive impact of social beliefs and practices on the human body and its desires has played a key role in stimulating debates over gender identity, and has also given a sense of direction to a great many gay activists in the United States and Europe. Analyzing the interplay of knowledge and power, he has raised fresh doubts about the meaning of truth, the scope of reason, and the proper regulation of human conduct, inspiring some of the world's foremost philosophers—Gilles Deleuze in France, Jürgen Habermas in Germany, Charles Taylor in Canada, Alasdair MacIntyre, Richard Rorty, and Hilary Putnam in the United States—to use his work (each in quite different ways) as a springboard for their own critical thinking. An incisive connoisseur of poetry and music, literature and painting, Foucault has left his mark on more than one generation of artists and literary critics.

Yet in almost every one of these fields, Foucault's accomplishment is hotly contested. Hailed by Paul Veyne and others as one of the century's preeminent geniuses, he has also been bitterly attacked as "the founding father of our *Kathedernihilismus*," a new-wave sophist who bewitched his public with deceptive rhetoric and evaded the responsibilities of rigorous scholarship. More than one reader has been left baffled. Moral theorists have demanded "normative criteria" for his reiterated protests against the powers that be. Historians have wondered what, if any, principles govern his selection of evidence. Unrepentant liberals have expressed alarm over the political implications of his theories, while philosophers continue to debate the coherence of Foucault's views, from his claims about truth to his concept of power. It is symptomatic that one astute critic, after finishing *The Order of Things,* perhaps Foucault's most fiendishly intricate text, was reminded of nothing so much as Felix the Cat, the cartoon character, striding briskly alongside a cliff, only to notice, "at the same time as the viewer, that the ground has gone out from under him." [11]

Yet despite the appearance in 1989 of a major biography that for the first time established the central facts about his life and career, the man himself remains as elusive and enigmatic as ever. To the naive question, "Who is the real author?" Foucault responded characteristically, quoting Samuel Beckett: "What matters who's speaking?" Friends describe a man of daunting complexity, of diplomatic charm and icy reserve, of awkward silences and explosive mirth—his laugh, sometimes caustic, often ironic, was legendary. To different people in private he presented different—and often contradictory—faces. But in public, he virtually never spoke, or wrote, about himself—at least not straightforwardly. A virtuoso of self-effacement, he loved donning masks in his own theater of ideas. "Do not ask who I am and do not ask me to remain the same," he wrote in one of the passages most frequently cited in the posthumous tributes: "More than one person, doubtless like me, writes in order to have no face."[12]

Still, as he came to admit at the end of his life, Foucault was the kind of thinker who enacts his ideas through his own personal odyssey, in his writing, of course, but also in his life. Hostile to the encyclopedic ideal in the human sciences and to transcendental claims in philosophy, Foucault left behind no synoptic critique of society, no system of ethics, no comprehensive theory of power, not even (current impressions to the contrary) a generally useful historical method. What value, then, does his work really have? What can it mean for us? How should it be used? As Foucault well knew, a fresh answer to these kinds of questions could not help but reinforce the "enigmatic stitching" that ties together "the work and the author." The key to understanding a philosopher's work, as he conceded near the end of his life, was to study that philosopher's "ethos." And to illuminate the character of this ethos, and to conjure up the imaginative universe of "the one who says 'I,' " Foucault agreed, it was necessary to examine a broad range of evidence: not just a writer's books and essays, but also his lectures and interviews, his drafts and scattered notes, his diaries and private journals, as well as his public acts, political speeches, and manifestos, the impression he left on students, the memories he shared with friends—even information about his sexual preferences.[13]

"I believe that . . . someone who is a writer is not simply doing his work in his books," he remarked in 1983, "but that his major work is, in the end, himself in the process of writing his books. The private life of an individual, his sexual preference, and his work are interrelated, not because his work translates his sexual life, but because *the work includes the whole life as well as the text.*"[14]

Given the spirit of such comments, it is worth taking seriously, as well, what at first glance must seem among the most startling and farfetched of Foucault's apparent convictions: that a man's manner of dying, as the capstone of his "whole life," may reveal, in a flash, as it were, the "lyrical core" of his life—*the* key to a writer's "personal poetic attitude." This was not idle rhetoric. In the one book he devoted to another author, the poet and novelist Raymond Roussel, Foucault himself began at the end, by pondering the possible significance of a purely biographical fact: namely, Roussel's apparent suicide in 1933, after weeks spent drugged, in a state of intense euphoria. [15]

Death, and its significance, was one of Foucault's lifelong obsessions. "In the depths of his dream," he declared in 1954, "what man encounters in his death"—and quite possibly a welcome "fulfillment of his existence." Thirty years later, already in the grip of his own mortal illness, taking solace from the "desire for death" articulated by the ancient Stoics, he fondly cited Seneca: "Let us hasten to grow old, let us hasten to the appointed time which permits us to rejoin our selves." Inspired by Bichat, the father of pathological anatomy, Foucault perceived death as the constant companion of life, its "white brightness" always lurking in "the black coffer of the body." And like the Heidegger of *Being and Time,* he believed that only death, in its culminating conquest, could define the unmistakable singularity—the authenticity—of a human life: "It is in death," Foucault wrote in 1963, "that the individual becomes at one with himself, escaping from monotonous lives and their levelling effect; in the slow, half-subterranean, but already visible approach of death, the dull, common life at last becomes an individuality; a black border isolates it, and gives it the style of its truth." [16]

It was with passages like these in mind, no doubt, that Gilles Deleuze—Foucault's philosophical alter ego and the thinker who perhaps understood him better than any other—laconically remarked that "few men have died like Foucault, in a way commensurate with their conception of death." Deleuze even ventured a discreet bit of speculation: "perhaps he chose death, like Roussel. . . ." [17]

But how, in fact, did Foucault die? For months, the "black border" around his own life remained as shrouded in mystery as the "lyrical core" of his individuality. To explain the origins of this morbid mystery and its ultimate resolution requires the telling of a tangled tale. But if Foucault was right—if "the *morbid,*" as he once put it, indeed "permits a subtle perception of the way in which life finds in death its most differentiated figure"—then the facts about his death, and how they came to be known, must form, paradoxically, the proper starting point for any serious effort to examine the unique "style" of his life: as if by unveiling a dead man's "visible secret," we might illuminate, as well, the still vital heart of an otherwise "invisible truth." [18]

❧

On June 27, 1984, *Le Monde* reprinted the medical bulletin issued by his doctors and cleared by his family: "Michel Foucault entered the clinic for diseases of the nervous system at the Hôpital de la Salpêtrière on June 9, 1984, in order to allow complementary investigation of neurological symptoms complicated by septicemia," an infection of the blood. "These examinations revealed the existence of several areas of cerebral suppuration. Antibiotic treatment at first had a favorable effect: a remission allowed Michel Foucault in the last week to take notice of the initial reactions to the appearance of his last books," *The Use of Pleasure* and *The Care of the Self*, the second and third volumes of the History of Sexuality he left incomplete at his death. "An acute deterioration removed all hope of effective treatment, and the death occurred on June 25 at 1:15 P.M."[19]

On June 26, a slightly different account had appeared in *Libération,* a newspaper much more tightly linked to Foucault and his closest associates. Along with this account had appeared an extremely odd commentary: "Since his death, rumors have flourished. Foucault might have died from AIDS. As if an exceptional intellectual, because he was also homosexual— very discreetly, it is true—would appear to be an ideal target for this stylish disease." Since, according to *Libération,* nothing about Foucault's case suggested AIDS, "the viciousness of the rumor remains astounding. As if Foucault must have died shamefully."[20]

In the days that followed, the left-wing daily was besieged by letters, many wondering why, in a newspaper called "liberation," of all places, a disease like AIDS would be described as "shameful." Foucault's French biographer reports that the journalist who wrote this piece had been a friend of the philosopher, and wished to preclude any campaign to discredit him.[21]

If nothing else, the journalist's effort is symptomatic of the panic provoked by AIDS. The disease had been named only two years before, in 1982; and the first cases of it reported only two years before that, in 1980. As one expert put it, "the first surprise grew from the discovery of a category of diseases scarcely foreseen by medical theory"—and worse was to follow. "Mass hysteria greeted the disclosure that this disease was linked to sex, blood, and drugs. The disease was felt to be not only 'strange,' because of its singular clinical and epidemiologic characteristics, but also 'foreign,' coming from 'strangers.' It seemed to have burst into one's orderly world from another world entirely, a world that was underdeveloped and peopled by marginal and morally reprehensible classes. As the title of one of the first books on AIDS neatly stated, its cause could only be '[a] strange virus from beyond.' "[22]

The first cases to be analyzed in the developed world had all come from gay communities in California and New York, leading to speculation about a kind of "gay cancer." The speculation was misguided. As more cases emerged, first among hemophiliacs, and then among intravenous drug users, the pieces of the puzzle began to fall into place: body fluids, whether semen or blood, had to pass from one person to another under circumstances that permitted entry into the bloodstream. By the spring of 1984, a new virus had been identified, and in 1986, an international commission on virological nomenclature officially named it: henceforth, it would be called HIV, for Human Immunodeficiency Virus.[23]

This was no "gay cancer." It was, rather, a retrovirus carried in the drops of blood on needles passed from one addict to the next, in the bottles of blood and blood products in hospitals and blood banks, in the vaginal fluids of women, and in the semen of men. The circumstances of transmission became increasingly clear. Anal intercourse, for example, allowed the virus to enter the bloodstream. Intravenous needles, surgical instruments, sex toys that pierced the skin, all could carry droplets of blood containing the virus. And, of course, the odds of becoming infected increased with the frequency of exposure to the virus.

In June of 1984, though, much scientific work remained to be done; coverage of AIDS in the media, particularly in France, was often ill-informed; for years to come, the first crude impressions of the disease—as a kind of biological curse, visited upon sinners—would linger in the popular imagination, fueling anxiety about the "virus from beyond." Fact and science fiction became grotesquely intertwined, forcing all too many carriers of the virus to wage war on two fronts: against a lethal malady which modern medicine had yet to master; and against an *a priori* attribution of moral blame. For many conservatives—and even, evidently, for the journalist at *Libération*—AIDS amounted to a sign of guilt, if not divine retribution for crimes against nature; even though, as one critic has commented, "it is a very strange God who chooses to punish male homosexuals and not female, and who is angry with drug-takers who inject intravenously but not with those who sniff."[24]

Under these circumstances, it is scarcely surprising that no well-known figures dared to admit publicly that they were dying of the disorder until Rock Hudson did in August 1984, two months after Foucault's death. The subject remains charged. To speak openly of Foucault's manner of dying may tempt some, bewitched by the moralizing power of AIDS as a metaphor, and confident of their own grasp of good and evil, simply to dismiss his entire lifework; and tempt still others, justifiably angry at the same moralizing power, and confident of their own command of the cultural battlefield, to dismiss any extended discussion of the questions as a figment of "pathologizing discourse" that reinforces the worst sort of stereotyping.

The qualms of the political activists are understandable; the dangers are real. But as Foucault himself insisted at the end of his life, it is *worth* trying to tell the truth—even when doing so is dangerous.[25]

In any case, the circumstances of Foucault's death are still not entirely clear. According to one source, the original death certificate gave AIDS as the cause of death. This piece of information supposedly came as a rude shock to Foucault's mother, sister, and brother—and also to Daniel Defert, the philosopher's longtime companion. The family, according to this source, demanded that the cause of death be suppressed, fearful that some prying biographer might learn the truth.[26]

Exactly when the doctors made their diagnosis is unknown; Foucault's death came relatively early in the epidemic, before a blood test for the presence of antibodies to the virus was widely available. Foucault had been feeling unwell for some time: according to several sources, by the fall of 1983, if not earlier, he had begun to worry that he might have AIDS. Still, it seems that a definite diagnosis was made only belatedly, probably at the end of 1983 or the beginning of 1984. Hospitalized at that time, he responded well enough to treatment with antibiotics that he proved able to deliver a final set of lectures at the Collège de France.[27]

Whether his doctors ever explicitly revealed their diagnosis to their patient also remains uncertain. French doctors are renowned for their reticence; and there is some evidence that Foucault himself, like many patients with a terminal disease, was not particularly eager to know all the facts. According to one source, he waved away the doctor who came to talk to him about the diagnosis, asking only, 'How long?'[28]

Foucault's death put Daniel Defert in a difficult position. For nearly a quarter century, he had shared Foucault's life; in the last days, he had shared as well in the agony of his death. But now, he realized, no one— neither the doctor, nor Foucault, if he knew—had told him the truth.

In private, one friend of his has confided, Defert was furious. After all, his longtime lover had perhaps deceived him. He was upset as well that Foucault had not turned his death from AIDS into a public, political issue. Defert, a seasoned activist, must have known that a rare opportunity to educate the public had been squandered.[29]

Shortly after Foucault's death, Defert set to work establishing the first national French AIDS organization, Association AIDES. (The name is a bilingual pun, combining the French word *"aide,"* which means "help," with the English acronym "AIDS"—in France, the disease is known as SIDA, for *Syndrome d'Immuno-Déficience Acquise.*) It was a fitting tribute: Association AIDES has played a leading role in France in mobilizing those at risk to fight the spread of the virus, and in offering practical and emotional support to people with AIDS. But its existence could scarcely combat the rumors about how Foucault had actually died, which now, in part because the facts were still denied, took on a lurid life of their own. [30]

The ironies surrounding Foucault's death began to multiply. First, he had died in the Hôpital de la Salpêtrière—the very institution that he had studied in *Madness and Civilization*, a place that served in the seventeenth and eighteenth centuries as a de facto prison for beggars, prostitutes, criminals, and the mad, the same place humanitarian reformers after the Revolution had turned into an asylum for the insane. Then, immediately after his death, he had become ensnared, not in one of the "games of truth" he had devoted his life to studying, but rather in a web of deceit. In the months that followed, the onetime student of "infamous men" came to be surreptitiously portrayed in intellectual gossip as just such an "infamous man" himself. Worst of all, he had in fact perished from a kind of modern plague, producing modern lepers and provoking just the kind of response that he had caustically described ten years before, in his account of the plague mentality in *Discipline and Punish*: "a whole set of techniques and institutions for measuring, supervising and correcting the abnormal" in order to isolate those putatively "guilty" and to exorcise the imagined threat "of 'contagions,' . . . of rebellions, crimes, vagabondage, desertions, people who appear and disappear, live and die in disorder." [31]

As the second anniversary of Foucault's death approached, Defert and one of his colleagues in Association AIDES, Jean Le Bitoux, decided it was time to clear the air. Their agent was a young American graduate student and journalist who was planning to file a "Letter from Paris" for the American gay weekly, *The Advocate*, fittingly enough published in California, Foucault's favorite destination for the last decade of his life. [32]

Halfway through this article—the journalist had deliberately buried the news in order to muffle its impact—Le Bitoux, acting with Defert's blessings, for the first time publicly revealed the truth: "Association AIDES . . . was started by Foucault's friends, Le Bitoux said, 'who in his memory wanted to confront this disease, which he had caught.' Foucault's death was attributed publicly to a 'neurological disorder,' but Le Bitoux speaks frankly: 'The way he died was a frightening sign, a last message in that he faced death with great courage and modesty, and in that it recalled [the gay community] to something we had lost: an awareness of concerning ourselves with our own affairs, and our own health.' "[33]

This declaration came too late. By then, Foucault's reputation, particularly among some gay activists, had already been damaged. A year later, when Jean-Paul Aron, a French historian who was Foucault's onetime friend and latter-day nemesis, announced publicly that *he* was dying of AIDS, he used the occasion to impugn the dead man's integrity. Conceding that his attack was motivated in part by sheer jealousy, Aron accused Foucault of being "ashamed" of his homosexuality, "even though he sometimes lived it in an insane fashion." The philosopher's refusal to admit publicly that he had AIDS was "the silence of shame, not the silence of an intellectual."[34]

Replying to Aron in the pages of *Libération*, Defert struggled loyally to defend Foucault's memory: "I shared twenty-three years of life and moral choices with Foucault, and if we had been ashamed homosexuals as Aron says, I would never have created Association AIDES. In his work, Michel Foucault inserted the practice of confession within a problematic of power. He never valued confession as such, he always showed the policing process at work in it. For the rest, as the president of AIDES, it is not for me to judge a man who, because of AIDS, avails himself of confessions and a sense of shame."[35]

At stake in this testy exchange is exactly what Foucault had foreseen twenty years before: the philosopher's "invisible truth, his visible secret." And just as he predicted (and perhaps feared), he was inexorably acquiring through the peculiar circumstances of his own death what he had for so long avoided through the labyrinthine style of his writing: "a face that cannot be exchanged."

"He refused for a long time to appear as a gay person," Jean Le Bitoux has recalled: "It was difficult for him, but he explained that if he had been labeled a 'gay intellectual,' he wouldn't have had the audience that was his here and in the United States." For these reasons alone, Foucault was deeply ambivalent about "coming out." But he ultimately did "come out" in his own discreet way, granting frequent interviews in the final years of his life about gay sexuality and the fight for gay rights and quietly defending, as Le Bitoux points out, "any number of gay men and boy lovers in the course of difficult legal proceedings."[36]

But perhaps there was a still deeper and much darker reason for Foucault's silence, not about homosexuality (which, after all, he did eventually discuss openly)—but about AIDS.

Over the summer of 1983, the philosopher had developed a scratchy dry cough, doubtless raising fears that he might have contracted the disorder. "Everybody in the [United] States was talking about AIDS," recalls Daniel Defert, "and our American friends who used to come here would all speak of it. So even if he was not certain about his own situation, the fact [of AIDS] was on his mind." Indeed, Defert thinks that "it is quite possible" Foucault in these months "had a real knowledge" that he was "near death."[37]

Though the virus was still not well understood, public awareness of its apparent dangers was growing rapidly, particularly within the North American gay community, where grass-roots efforts were underway to change sexual behaviors. In the previous months, some of Foucault's closest friends—doctors, lovers, gay friends already committed to practicing "safe sex"—had urged him to take better care of himself, to watch what he was doing. But Foucault had ignored their entreaties. Keeping a check on himself—particularly when he was in San Francisco—was not his style.[38]

Ever since his first visit to the Bay Area in 1975, he had been enthralled by the gay community that flourished there. He had originally come to the West Coast to teach at the University of California at Berkeley. But gay colleagues soon enough drove him over the Bay Bridge to San Francisco, to Castro Street and to the area around Folsom Street. In these neighborhoods, an unprecedented number of clubs, bars, and bathhouses, catering to a wide variety of sexual tastes, supported a defiantly public and exuberantly experimental array of different gay subcultures—a spectacular result of the gay liberation movement that had first gathered steam in the late 1960s. As never before, Foucault felt free in San Francisco to explore his abiding interest in "forbidden pleasures."[39]

He returned to the Bay Area in 1979, in 1980, and in the spring of 1983, usually spending his days in Berkeley and his nights in San Francisco. And even as friends in Paris worried about his deteriorating health, he was looking forward to yet another trip to the West Coast in the fall of 1983. "It's a simple pulmonary infection," he reassured one of them: "As soon as I am in California, I will be better."[40]

By then, the gay community of San Francisco had become for him a kind of magical "heterotopia," a place of dumbfounding excess that left him happily speechless. Promising a welcome "limbo of nonidentity," the city's countless bathhouses enabled Foucault as never before to grapple with his lifelong fascination with "the overwhelming, the unspeakable, the creepy, the stupefying, the ecstatic," embracing "a pure violence, a wordless gesture." And in the interviews that he had granted in the last years of his life to the gay press, Foucault made no secret of his special interest in "S/M," the consensual form of sado-masochistic eroticism that flourished in a number of San Francisco bathhouses. "I don't think that this movement of sexual practices has anything to do with the disclosure or the uncovering of S/M tendencies deep within our unconscious," he said in 1982: "I think S/M is much more than that; it's the real creation of new possibilities of pleasure, which people had no idea about previously."[41]

"I think that the kind of pleasure I would consider as *the* real pleasure would be so deep, so intense, so overwhelming that I couldn't survive it," Foucault explained in another interview that year: "Complete total pleasure . . . for me, it's related to death."[42]

This sentiment—that pleasure, for him, was somehow "related to death"—had haunted Foucault throughout his life, as we shall see. It raised, both in his writing and in his conduct, "overwhelming" and "unspeakable" possibilities, which became even more overwhelming and unspeakable in San Francisco in the fall of 1983.

These were bleak months in the city's gay community. The number of AIDS cases was continuing to grow at rates that alarmed public health officials—and terrified a growing number of gay men. Everybody's worst fears about the disease were in the process of being confirmed. More and more people were dying while their doctors stood by helplessly, still uncertain about exactly what the new disorder was, still unclear about precisely how it was spread, still unable to slow its deadly course. Anxious men crowded into public lectures on AIDS and talked among themselves about what to do. By the summer of 1983, a few of the more community-oriented private sex clubs had begun to distribute "safe sex" information. But since other gay bathhouses, fearful of scaring away patrons, were reluctant to distribute AIDS pamphlets or promote new kinds of sexual practices, a growing number of doctors and gay community activists were beginning to argue that such establishments needed to be strictly regulated, or shut down entirely. This would eventually happen—but only a year later, starting in October 1984.[43]

In the meantime, many sexually adventurous gay men, unsure about who to believe and how to respond, wondered if they were doomed to die no matter how they behaved. The list of fatalities from the S/M community was already long, and seemed likely to grow inexorably longer. Many, like Foucault, felt that S/M had been one of the most positive and constructive forces in their life—a way of consensually expressing, and gaining a sense of mastery over, a host of otherwise taboo impulses. But due to the monstrous coincidence of AIDS, these vibrant forms of eroticism had become fraught with potentially lethal consequences. Under these morbid circumstances, some resolved to change their sexual practices, embracing either a terrified celibacy or a new moderation, cutting down on sexual contacts and avoiding the exchange of bodily fluids. But others, feeling confused or resigned—or both—expressed a defiant abandon, partying on, as one censorious eyewitness would later remark, "like the revellers in Edgar Allan Poe's 'Masque of the Red Death.' "[44]

The conditions were chilling. Still, in some bathhouses in San Francisco in the fall of 1983, in the eyes of someone disposed to see matters in this light, the scene on some nights may have strangely recalled that conjured up by Foucault ten years before, in his account of plagues and the macabre carnivals of death that medieval writers imagined to accompany them: "Laws suspended, prohibitions lifted, the frenzy of time that is passing away, bodies mingling together without respect, individuals unmasked, abandoning their statutory identity and the figure under which they were recognized, allowing an entirely different truth to appear."[45]

As the lyrical intensity of this passage suggests, the possibility of what Foucault elsewhere called a "suicide-orgy" exerted an unusual fascination over him. Given the anxiety that AIDS continues to provoke, the singularity of Foucault's preoccupations must be stressed: most members of the gay and S/M communities would *never* have seen the situation in such terms. Foucault, by contrast, had long placed death—and the preparation for suicide—at the heart of his concerns: summoning what he once called "that courage of clandestine knowledge that endures malediction," he was evidently serious about his implicit lifelong conviction that "to comprehend life is given only to a cruel, reductive and already infernal knowledge that only wishes it dead."[46]

That fall, he later told friends, he returned to the bathhouses of San Francisco. Accepting the new level of risk, he joined again in the orgies of torture, trembling with "the most exquisite agonies," voluntarily effacing himself, exploding the limits of consciousness, letting real, corporeal pain insensibly melt into pleasure through the alchemy of eroticism.[47]

Years later, in his *roman à clef* about AIDS, *To the Friend Who Did Not Save My Life*, the French novelist Hervé Guibert, at the time one of the people closest to Foucault, recounted how the philosopher in his tale had returned from a fall visit to California "eager to report on his latest escapades in the baths of San Francisco. 'Those places must be completely deserted now because of AIDS.' 'Don't be silly,' " the philosopher replies, " 'it's just the opposite: the baths have never been so popular, and now they're amazing.' " The menace in the air had created new complicities, a new tenderness, a new sense of solidarity: " 'Before, no one ever said a word; now, everyone talks. Each of us knows exactly why he is there.' "[48]

But why was Michel Foucault there? If he already had the virus, as he perhaps suspected, then he might be endangering one of his partners. And if any of his partners, as was likely, had the virus, then he might be wagering his own life.

Was this perhaps his own deliberately chosen apotheosis, his own singular experience of "The Passion"? Does his conceivable embrace of a death-dealing "disease of love" reveal, as he implied that it would, the "lyrical core" of his life—*the* key to his "personal poetic attitude"?

What exactly Foucault did in San Francisco in the fall of 1983—and why—may never be known. The evidence currently available is incomplete and sometimes contested. Daniel Defert, for one, sharply disputes the general impression left by Hervé Guibert, dismissing his novel as a vicious fantasy. Still, there seems little doubt that Foucault on his last visit to San Francisco was preoccupied by AIDS, and by his own possible death from it—as Defert himself stresses. "He took AIDS very seriously," says Defert: "When he went to San Francisco for the last time, he took it as a *limit-experience*."[49]

An ambiguous word, "experience"—but also crucial for understanding the "enigmatic stitching" that ties together Foucault's death, life, and work. Near the end of his life, he briefly defined "experience" in this way: it was, he explained, a form of being "that can and must be thought," a form "historically constituted" through "games of truth."[50]

In the spirit of Kant, Foucault sometimes analyzed these "games" in their "positivity." By "positivity," he seems to have had in mind how certain ways of thinking, by embodying a certain style of reasoning, ordered some aspect of existence or defined some field of knowledge. A system of thought acquires "positivity" in this sense when its propositions become open to scrutiny in terms of their truth or falsity. In *The Birth of the Clinic* (1963) and *The Order of Things*, Foucault showed, for example, how in the nineteenth century, clinical anatomy, economics, zoology, botany, and linguistics each crystallized as internally coherent "discourses," thereby constituting new disciplines of understanding, and regulating the conduct of inquiry in each of these branches of "positive" (or "scientific") knowledge. And at the end of his life, in *The Use of Pleasure* and *The Care of the Self*, Foucault investigated how classical thinkers from Socrates to Seneca had elaborated their own, more personal regimens of "truth," trying to bring a measure of reason and just proportion to their existence, regulating the conduct of life in an effort to shape oneself into something "positive" (or "good").[51]

As a connoisseur of literature and art, by contrast, Foucault, in the spirit of Nietzsche and the French *philosophe maudit* Georges Bataille, was also interested in exploring experience in what he sometimes called its "negativity," probing into aspects of human existence that seemed to defy rational understanding. In *Madness and Civilization*, for example, he took away from his encounter with the tormented vision of Goya, the cruel erotic fantasies of Sade, and the insane glossolalia of Artaud, "something that can and must be thought," something that startles and disconcerts— a mystical kind of experience that "you come out of changed."[52]

Heartened by the possibility of changing himself, Foucault sought out potentially transformative "limit-experiences" on his own, deliberately pushing his mind and body to the breaking point, hazarding "a sacrifice, an actual sacrifice of life," as he put it in 1969, "a voluntary obliteration that does not have to be represented in books because it takes place in the very existence of the writer."[53]

In an unusually revealing 1981 interview, he described in some detail the appeal to him of certain extreme forms of Passion, implicitly linking a shattering type of "suffering-pleasure," the lifelong preparation for suicide—and the ability, thanks to potentially self-destructive yet mysteriously revealing states of intense dissociation, to see the world "completely differently." Through intoxication, reverie, the Dionysian abandon of the artist, the most punishing of ascetic practices, and an uninhibited exploration of sado-masochistic eroticism, it seemed possible to breach, however briefly, the boundaries separating the conscious and unconscious, reason and unreason, pleasure and pain—and, at the ultimate limit, life and death—thus starkly revealing how distinctions central to the play of true and false are pliable, uncertain, contingent.[54]

At this breaking point, "experience" becomes a zone full of turbulence, unformed energy, chaos—*l'espace d'une extériorité sauvage*," he called it in *L'ordre du discours* ("The Order of Discourse," 1971), "the space of an untamed exteriority." Like few thinkers before him, Foucault was at home in this no-man's-land. Sometimes he seems to have considered himself an exemplary seeker of "clandestine knowledge," a hero of truly Nietzschean stature, precariously balanced on a high wire, heralding "the dim light of dawn," fearlessly pointing the way to "a future thought."[55]

But perhaps, as Foucault himself at other times implies, he was simply a figure of quixotic folly—a philosophical Felix the Cat, forced to learn the laws of gravity the hard way.

"The individual driven, in spite of himself, by the somber madness of sex" would then, as he wrote in 1976, be "something like a nature gone awry." His own death, though revealing, might then be seen merely as "the supernatural return of the insult, a retribution thwarting the flight into counter-nature."[56]

Despite his understandable misgivings about the philosophical value of his own interest in experimenting with unusual bodily sensations and altered states of consciousness, Foucault on more than one occasion in the final decade of his life discreetly implied that *all* of his work, for better or worse, had grown out of his personal fascination with experience.

In 1981, for example, he had slipped a revealing comment into an otherwise pedestrian interview with Didier Eribon, the journalist who would become his first biographer. "Each time I have attempted to do theoretical work," wrote Foucault, "it has been on the basis of elements from my experience." He said much the same thing in the last interview he gave, on his deathbed in the Hôpital de la Salpêtrière. There he confessed that in previous books he had used "somewhat rhetorical methods of avoiding one of the fundamental domains of experience"—namely, the domain of the subject, of the self, of the individual and his conduct. But in fact each of his books, as "a kind of fragment of an autobiography," could be approached as a "field of experience to be studied, mapped out and organized," precisely by reinserting the previously occluded dimension—of the author putting his "nature," and his knowledge, to the test in his "very existence."[57]

In a 1978 interview with the Italian journalist Duccio Trombadori, Foucault enumerated three crucial implications of his lifelong preoccupation with "experience." The first was that there was "no continuous and systematic theoretical 'background,'" or rule of method, to his work. The second implication, he said, was that "there is not a book I have written that does not grow, at least in part, out of a direct, personal experience," with "madness, with psychiatric hospitals, with sickness"—and "also with death." The third implication, as Foucault explained it, was more complex.

Even when starting from some personally transformative "limit-experience," "it is necessary," he admitted, "to open the way for a transformation, a metamorphosis, that is not simply individual but has a character accessible to others." For this reason, he always labored to connect the full range of his own experience, in a "certain fashion, to a collective practice, to a manner of thinking." At different times in his life, he had thus played the language games of structuralism, of Maoism, of the most superficially impersonal sort of classical philology. Yet even at this public level, he stressed, much of what readers might find puzzling about "the relationship between 'limit-experience' and 'the history of truth'" could be clarified only by picking up "the threads of certain episodes in my life."[58]

"What I say does not have objective value," he concluded with disarming candor: but viewed through the lens of "limit-experience," what he had said, and written, could nevertheless "perhaps help to clarify the problems that I have tried to bring to light, and their consequences."[59]

Foucault's lifelong preoccupation with "experience" and its limits thus represents more than a dramatic and sometimes disturbing aspect of one philosopher's quest for truth: it also suggests a new way of looking at his major texts and assessing their significance; and of reexamining how a profound modern skeptic, avowedly "beyond good and evil," handled the vocation of philosophy, the making of political commitments, and the shaping of a public "self." At the same time, a look at Foucault's lifework in terms of "experience" may provide a fresh insight into a host of contemporary debates—over the meaning of human "rights," including "the right to be different"; over the range of human conduct that ought to be left unregulated by society; and, more generally, over the scope of reason, language, and human nature.

For even during the most apparently insane moments of his life, Foucault never stopped thinking, never stopped trying to decipher the significance of his own positive *and* negative experience, in its genealogy, in its historically constituted preconditions and limits, always circling back to the four questions Kant had posed: What can I know? What ought I to do? What may I hope? What is man?

In his own books, as he suggested in a text he completed in the spring of 1984, he had in effect pursued a series of questions parallel to those posed by Kant: "Through what games of truth does man devote himself to thinking about his being when he perceives himself as mad, when he regards himself as sick, when he reflects on himself as a living, speaking, laboring being, when he judges himself and punishes himself as a criminal case?"[60]

These questions may arise from the peculiarities of his own unusual experience, but, as Foucault once said of Raymond Roussel, "the anguish" of this individual, as well as the implications of his personal discoveries about the possible limits of reason, language, and human nature "makes the illness of this man our problem."[61]

Foucault's book on Roussel in many ways helps to illuminate his own evident "anguish," and also, perhaps, the hermetic impulse behind his own lifelong interest in forms of experience often called "mad," "sick," or "criminal." In pondering the ambiguity of Foucault's possible "limit-experience" with AIDS in San Francisco, for example, one is reminded of how Foucault himself lingered over the similar ambiguity of Roussel's last act. Roussel died of a drug overdose—whether by accident or by design has never been resolved. His corpse was discovered near the threshold of a door, normally open, that had been locked from the inside. Had this door "been shut carefully" by Roussel himself "on an inescapable death"? Or was there not, wondered Foucault, something, perhaps somewhere in the work of the artist himself, a formula, a key that would have unlocked the door, for him and for us, revealing a figure still reeling from childhood experiences, searching throughout his life "to rediscover their clarity," taking drugs to find something he had lost, trying through these states of intense euphoria to grasp his truth and his secret, "always in vain, except perhaps for that last night?"[62]

Maybe Roussel in a fit of madness had deliberately locked himself in. Or maybe, enlightened and transformed at last, precisely by his own potentially suicidal act, he had died quite by accident, struggling in vain to turn the key that would finally have set him free—the same key he had tried to grasp, equally in vain, in every word that he had ever written.

"One writes to become someone other than who one is," remarked Foucault in that fall of 1983, in an interview explaining his fascination with Roussel. "You know, for him writing was that! There's a beautiful passage in which he said that after his first book he expected that the next morning there would be rays of light streaming from his person and that everyone on the street would be able to see that he had written a book. That's the obscure desire of a person who writes. It is true that the first text one writes is neither written for others, nor for who one is . . . There is an attempt at modifying one's way of being through the act of writing.

It is this transformation of his way of being that [Roussel] observed, he believed in, he sought after, and for which he suffered horribly"—and not just in his writing.[63]

In Foucault's last two books, he, too, was evidently writing in order "to become someone other than who one is." These texts are largely about classical theories of self-control and moderation, of harmony and beauty. He had written these books, he explained, in an effort to "get free of oneself," to let go of oneself, or, more idiomatically still (the French phrase is "*se déprendre de soi-même*"), to lose one's fondness for one's self.[64]

The prose style of these final works, sharply different from almost everything else he had written, mirrors their subject matter: it is limpid, sober, and serene, as if Foucault, as one old friend observed, "were seeking a new, desexualized austerity in the very act of writing."[65]

Foucault's work was drawing to an end; and his life, like Roussel's, was ending in an ambiguous gesture, as if he had finally grasped the full significance, too late, of the fatal temptation he had first identified nearly ten years earlier, long before AIDS had become a tangible threat: "The Faustian pact, whose temptation has been instilled in us by the deployment of sexuality, is now as follows: to exchange life in its entirety for sex itself, for the truth and the sovereignty of sex. Sex is worth dying for."[66]

While charting the yawning emptiness of this historically delimited space of "untamed exteriority," what could possibly snatch the mind away from the void, pull it back from death?[67] This is a question raised, of course, not only by Foucault's own erotic experience. It is a question raised more generally, as he well knew, by our own century of death camps and total war. It is the question that led Foucault in his final books to contemplate the answers given by Socrates and Seneca. It is the kind of question that sent Foucault's precursors scrambling for a moral compass. Perhaps Sartre's quest had ended in failure. But what about Foucault's?

Daniel Defert recalls one of his last visits with Foucault in the Hôpital de la Salpêtrière. The final two volumes of the History of Sexuality had just been published. "You know," Defert recalls, "at the very end, a few days before he died, I said, 'If it turns out to be AIDS, your last books are just like *Les fleurs du mal*,' because, you know, Baudelaire wrote *Les fleurs du mal* about his own sexual life and syphilis."[68]

Foucault, he recalls, laughed and said: Why not?

On the morning of June 29, 1984, four days after Foucault's death, friends and admirers of the dead philosopher gathered in a small courtyard at the rear of the Hôpital de la Salpêtrière. They had come to witness the ceremony, traditional in France, of "*la levée du corps*," literally, "the raising of the body"—the moment when the coffin leaves the morgue. The ceremony is often the occasion for the exchange of greetings and banter, but on that sunny morning, silence gripped the courtyard.[69]

At least one prominent mourner later confessed to feeling "obscurely embarrassed, not to be there, but not to be there secretly."[70] In the cramped confines, that was scarcely possible. Word of the ceremony had initially been passed only to friends, but then the event was announced in *Le Monde*. The courtyard was too small to hold comfortably the crowd of several hundred that gathered. Uncertain of how the event would be marked, old friends slowly threaded their way through the packed throng in search of familiar faces. Jacques Derrida was there, and so were some of Foucault's distinguished colleagues from the Collège de France: Paul Veyne, Pierre Bourdieu, and Georges Dumézil, the historian of ancient religion, who had done as much as any single person to advance Foucault's career. Pierre Boulez, the composer and another old friend, came to pay his last respects; and so did Robert Badinter, the French minister of justice. Lapsed militant leftists mingled with old lovers, intimate friends, famous publishers, movie stars. Yves Montand and Simone Signoret, longtime activists who had frequently marched alongside Foucault, were both there, Signoret visibly shaken—the suddenness of Foucault's death had caught many unprepared.

As the wait for the coffin continued, the silence, already oppressive, only deepened.

In the corner of the courtyard next to the morgue, Gilles Deleuze mounted a small box. In a trembling voice that was barely audible, he began to read.

The words had been chosen by Defert. They came from the searing preface to the last two volumes of Foucault's History of Sexuality, one of the last texts he composed. These words come as close as any to summarizing what is most admirable—and also most harrowing—about this great thinker's plunge into "the Passion" of limit-experience:

"As for the motive that compelled me, it was very simple. In the eyes of some, I hope that it will suffice by itself. It was curiosity—the only kind of curiosity, in any case, that merits the pain of being practiced with a little obstinancy: not the kind that searches out in order to digest whatever is agreeable to know, but rather the kind that permits one to get free of oneself. What would be the value of the stubborn determination to know if it merely insured the acquisition of understanding, rather than the aberration, in a certain fashion and to the extent possible, of he who understands?

"There are times in life when the question of knowing if one can think differently than one thinks and perceive differently than one sees is absolutely necessary if one is to go on looking and reflecting at all.

"People will say, perhaps, that these games with oneself need only go on behind the scenes; that they are, at best, part of those labors of preparation that efface themselves when they have had their effects. But what, then, is philosophy today—philosophical activity, I mean—if not the critical labor of thought upon itself? And if it does not consist, in place of legitimating what one already knows, in undertaking to know how, and up to what limit, it would be possible to think differently?"[71]

The ceremony ended. The crowd waited for a moment, and then began to disperse. Beginning its long journey back to the province of Poitou, the philosopher's birthplace and final destination, the coach bearing the corpse drove up the street, turned the corner, and disappeared.

— 2 —

WAITING

for

GODOT

ON THE AFTERNOON OF April 19, 1980, the streets of the Latin Quarter were teeming with life. Some fifty thousand people had turned up to say good-bye, marching in a long column toward Montparnasse cemetery, following the casket of Jean-Paul Sartre. The sky was gray, the mood strangely festive. No one had expected a demonstration: yet there was one, prompted by sentiments of sorrow and gratitude. As the crowd snaked along past Sartre's old haunts, past the Café de Flore, past Le Coupole, past his old flat, bystanders stopped in silence, waiters bowed, parents hoisted children on shoulders to watch. In the four decades since he had first won fame as the oracle of existentialism, Sartre had become an international emblem of courage, critical independence, and stubborn optimism. Parisians had cause to mark the moment, for they were witnessing not only the end of a life, but the passing of an era—a time when philosophers had been beacons of hope.[1]

In France, that era had actually ended years before, thanks to the ascendancy of thinkers like Michel Foucault. Sartre's indomitable style of humanism—his unrelenting emphasis on freedom, his stern stress on responsibility—had been under attack since the mid-sixties, with Foucault among the most vocal of the critics.

Still, in his own peculiar way, Foucault, as much as any man alive, had been inspired by Sartre's example. Throughout the seventies, the two men had marched side by side countless times: to protest the plight of factory workers, to agitate for better conditions in prisons, to demand that the French government pay more attention to refugees from Vietnam. What-ever their philosophical disagreements, which were many—and however much Foucault tried to pretend, which he strenuously did, that they were different kinds of intellectuals—they were cut from the same cloth.[2]

And so when one of Foucault's former students called him to see if he would be attending the funeral, he did not hesitate: Why, of course he was going! On that dreary spring afternoon, lost in the vast crowd coursing through the boulevards of the Left Bank, Michel Foucault thus found his path crossing that of Jean-Paul Sartre one last time, his very presence bespeaking his recognition, however reluctant, of Sartre's greatness.

But to his former student, who was alongside him in the cortege, Foucault expressed neither respect nor affection. As a young man, he explained as they followed the coffin, "it was him, and all that he represented . . . that I wished to renounce." Sartre's impact he summed up in a word: "terrorism."[3]

The Sartrean era that came to a formal end that day had begun thirty-five years before, in the immediate aftermath of World War II. It was in the fall of 1945 that Sartre underwent his public apotheosis as France's first bona fide philosophical celebrity since Henri Bergson. And it was in that same fall that the young Paul-Michel Foucault, eighteen years old but already an aspiring philosopher, first arrived in Paris, and began his youthful quest to find a voice of his own, free of Sartre's overwhelming influence.

The French capital had been liberated by the Allied armies scarcely twelve months before. And though the city had been spared serious damage, the aftershocks of the war were evident everywhere. Food and fuel were scarce. And for many, the psychological scars had yet to begin to heal. Families had lost sons, wives had lost husbands—but perhaps more important, the nation as a whole had lost, in some measure, its self-respect. Having all but capitulated in 1940 to the German onslaught, France could not easily dodge questions of complicity and guilt, particularly after the full extent of the Nazi horror became known. The public revelation of the death camps for the first time made plain the evil that had nearly engulfed Western civilization.

It was in this context that Sartre's stern call to uphold freedom and accept responsibility, even in a world bereft of redeeming significance, hit home. As Foucault later remarked, "Given the absurdity of wars, slaughters and despotism, it seemed to be up to the individual subject to give meaning to his existential choices."[4]

As a teenager growing up in Poitiers, an old Roman town to the southwest of Paris, Foucault, like the rest of his generation, had experienced most of the war at one remove. Too young to fight (and for the French, there had been little fighting after 1940), he was old enough to know fear. Allied planes from time to time flew sorties over the town, targeting the railroad station. Located twenty kilometers inside the frontier of Vichy France, Poitiers itself was throughout the war under the control of German officials, who periodically rounded up Jewish refugees and spirited them off to concentration camps. Foucault thus came of age in a world where the threat of death was ubiquitous yet largely invisible, more a nightmarish rumor than a tangible reality. "I have very early memories of an absolutely threatening world, which could crush us," Foucault recalled in 1981. "To have lived as an adolescent in a situation that had to end, that had to lead to another world, for better or worse, was to have the impression of spending one's entire childhood in the night, waiting for dawn. That prospect of another world marked the people of my generation, and we have carried with us, perhaps to excess, a dream of Apocalypse."[5]

Poitiers till 1945 had been the scene of his entire life. Born there on October 15, 1926, he had been christened Paul-Michel Foucault, named after his father, Dr. Paul Foucault, a surgeon of great local prestige. He had grown up in *haute bourgeoise* comfort, the firstborn son and second of three children. The family honored the conventions. A nurse cared for the children, a cook for the house; schooling was conservative, attending mass on Sundays was a family ritual. Yet the Foucaults were not especially religious; and the political atmosphere at home, as Daniel Defert later recalled, was solidly anti-Vichy.[6]

In later years, Foucault rarely spoke of his childhood. He had been a "juvenile delinquent," he would sometimes say. His father, he told friends, had been a "bully." He had "disciplined and punished him," and, unhappy with his son's academic progress, enrolled him in 1940 in "the most regimented Catholic school he could find," the collège Saint-Stanislas. The father tried, unsuccessfully, to force the boy to follow in his footsteps and become a surgeon.[7]

Foucault's father died in 1959. His older sister and his younger brother, who did become a surgeon, he would later seldom see. His mother, however, he remained close to, often putting the finishing touches on a manuscript while visiting her at the family's rural estate outside of Poitiers.[8]

His French biographer paints a picture of an enigmatic and withdrawn adolescent. As one critic has summed up the evidence, which remains sketchy, the young Paul-Michel seems to have "suffered, like Zarathustra, in fierce if lofty isolation." A striking picture shows him with his classmates from Poitiers: "The students pose against a rock face in two comradely ranks, above which, his body twisted as if recoiling from the camera, his gaze inquisitorially querulous beneath pent brows, utterly alone and utterly strange, stands the future author of *Folie et déraison*."[9]

Aloof he may have been—but gifted as well. At the collège Saint-Stanislas, Paul-Michel blossomed into a highly promising young student of philosophy, history, and literature. Defying his father's wishes, he came to Paris with his sights set on winning admission to France's elite École Normale Supérieure. The first step was to attend special classes at the lycée Henri-IV, one of the most prestigious schools in France.

Henri-IV was located behind the Panthéon, a short walk away from the unofficial world headquarters of existentialism at the Café de Flore on the boulevard Saint-Germain. It was a lycée already storied in French intellectual history, the very place where Jean-Paul Sartre had begun his own philosophical odyssey a generation before.

Here Foucault set to work. Of his teachers, the most important was Jean Hyppolite, a renowned Hegel scholar. A member of Sartre's generation, Hyppolite was highly sympathetic to existentialism. Since Sartre had borrowed the key terms in *Being and Nothingness* from Hegel's *Logic* as well as from Heidegger's *Being and Time,* Hyppolite's admiration is not surprising. Along with Maurice Merleau-Ponty, perhaps the most gifted pure philosopher of this generation, Hyppolite gladly participated with Sartre in the elaboration of a new kind of syncretic humanism, a credo patched together during the 1940s with elements from Hegel and the young Marx, Husserl and Heidegger—all thinkers Foucault, too, would be forced to grapple with.[10]

Sartre's own work, of course, was impossible to avoid. His first novel, *Nausea,* had appeared in 1938, and his most important philosophical treatise, *Being and Nothingness,* in 1943. The novelist Michel Tournier—two years Foucault's senior and a close friend of Foucault's future philosophical alter ego, Gilles Deleuze—has recalled how *Being and Nothingness* fell like "a meteor" onto students' desks in 1943: "After a moment's stupor there was a long mulling over. Weighty and hairy, the book exuded irresistible power; it was full of exquisite subtleties; encyclopedic, proudly technical, with an intuition of diamondlike simplicity running through it from start to finish. . . . And the final sentence on the final page filled our heads with dreams: 'We shall devote a future work,' it said, 'to the questions left unanswered by this one.' "[11]

With the appearance of *Being and Nothingness,* it was clear that a comprehensive new philosophy was poised to change the way the world thought. Joining Sartre, Jean Hyppolite applied his erudition to integrating Hegel and Marx into the new way of thinking. As Hyppolite once summed up the existentialism he had helped elaborate, "it is the theme of alienation and the conquest of alienation which is now at the center of our attention." Like Sartre, Hyppolite throughout his life expressed a confidence in the value of progress. History was, just as Hegel and Marx had claimed, the story of human freedom. The plot of the story, however, hinged, far more radically than either Hegel or Marx had understood, on the courage and conviction of real individuals, imbued with a heightened sense of historical responsibility—and unafraid to exercise their free wills. What existentialism supplied was, precisely, a new account of moral motivation, a dimension missing in Marx. "There is a universal value for us in reflection upon the relationship between Hegel and Marx," Hyppolite reaffirmed near the end of his life. "It is not just a historical legacy. It involves a problem which can always be reexamined and which can acquire fresh meaning at any given time in history."[12]

After Hyppolite's death in 1968, Foucault expressed unstinting admiration for his mentor's work, praising his insistence, in the spirit of Hegel and Marx, that history was the true medium of philosophy, and also praising his scholarly mien, which had led to "the systematic effacement of his own subjectivity." Hyppolite, he recalled, "loved to cite Hegel's maxim about the modesty of the philosopher who loses all singularity."[13]

The "systematic effacement of his own subjectivity," and the conviction that the work of philosophy must proceed through a study of history, were certainly the most lasting lessons Foucault learned from his teacher. For the heart of Hyppolite's credo—particularly his conviction that alienation can and ought to be conquered—Foucault would later reject in no uncertain terms.

At the time, however, his attitude was sharply different. In his first published works, which would not appear until 1954, Foucault upheld Marx's "revolutionary promise"—and something like Hyppolite's brand of humanism. Like Hyppolite, he evidently looked forward in these years to reversing "History as it has developed up to the present," endorsing the "goal of ending alienation." At the same time, the young Foucault spoke optimistically of grasping the "truth of the human essence" through a new "science of man." Following in the footsteps of Hyppolite and Merleau-Ponty, he defended "an anthropological understanding of concrete man" that would combine a Marxist view of history with an existential outlook on the free human being and its "ethical task."[14]

In the fall of 1945, however, the clarification of such emerging personal convictions doubtless had to wait, as Foucault and his young classmates struggled simply to keep up with Hyppolite's recondite lectures, readying themselves to vie for a slot at the École Normale Supérieure.

To this day, entrance to the École Normale is determined by a series of highly competitive examinations. Perhaps the grandest and most demanding of France's famous "*grandes écoles*," the school accepts but a tiny fraction of those competing nationwide for admission—in 1946, only thirty-eight students in the humanities. Students who have already demonstrated unusual promise attend a special preparatory class, or "*Khâgne*," at schools such as Henri-IV. A distinctively French institution, these classes uproot precocious adolescents from their normal lives and plunge them instead into a hothouse of ideas. Day and night the chosen few pore over the canonic works of Western civilization, from Plato to Kant. As one student of the system has quipped, the typical candidate "undergoes an experience comparable to that of Perigord geese."[15]

A few weeks after Foucault had entered Henri-IV and begun its gruelling diet of books, Jean-Paul Sartre (École Normale, class of 1924) presided over the intellectual event of 1945: a public lecture with the title "Existentialism is a Humanism." Innocuous though it seems a half century later, this title was meant to strike a note of defiance, tacitly declaring war on Sartre's critics. Existentialism was then under sharp attack, from Catholics for its immoralism, and from Communists for its nihilism. That the Frenchman, then forty, should admittedly have taken heart from the work of the German philosopher Martin Heidegger, notorious for his Nazi sympathies, alarmed the left as much as his own outspoken atheism irritated the right.[16]

When Sartre arrived at the theater on the Right Bank where the lecture was scheduled, he discovered a mob. At first, he feared the Communist Party had organized a demonstration. It turned out instead that the throng had assembled to praise, not to bury him. After an hour's delay, while some semblance of decorum was restored in the theater, the shambling little professor was hoisted bodily over the waiting crowd and passed up to the podium. As he began to speak, he seemed like some hero in an improbable Hollywood movie—cool, calm, preternaturally lucid. Addressing his critics, he explained that existentialism, properly understood, "cannot be regarded as a philosophy of quietism since it defines man by his action; nor as a pessimistic description of man, for no doctrine is more optimistic, the destiny of man is placed within himself." The principles of the new philosophy, he said, were relatively simple. Like Descartes, he had found a foundation for "absolute truth" in "one's immediate sense of one's self"; and like Kant, he had formulated his own version of the Golden Rule: "Everything happens to every man as though the whole human race had its eyes fixed upon what he is doing and regulated its conduct accordingly." In an early example of the kind of trademark slogan that would become the stock in trade of the postwar *maîtres à penser*, Sartre boiled his basic idea down to a sentence: "Man is condemned to be free." Even his most apparently blind passions the individual had to answer for: "From the moment he is thrown into this world he is responsible for everything he does"—*everything*. This, admittedly, was a heavy burden. Still, there was no escaping it: it was the moral duty of every individual at every moment to ask of himself, " 'Am I really a man who has the right to act in such a manner that humanity regulates itself by what I do?' "[17]

The night was warm and air scarce: as women fainted, they were piled on a convenient grand piano. The drama of the occasion captured the imagination of the press: TOO MANY ATTEND SARTRE LECTURE was the headline to one story: FAINTING SPELLS, POLICE. LAWRENCE OF ARABIA AN EXISTENTIALIST.[18]

Had philosophy ever sounded so sexy? Maybe in ancient Athens; but in an era when deep thinkers were expected to communicate in the most rebarbative and forbidding kind of prose, a style Sartre himself had mastered in *Being and Nothingness,* the simple formulas in this lecture struck a chord with the public at large, first in France, and, soon enough, around the world. In effect, Sartre's performance launched existentialism as an international fad—and set the agenda for every aspiring philosopher of Foucault's generation.

Among young students girding themselves for the academic jousting that might carry them to intellectual glory, the reaction was paradoxical. Even though they had exulted in *Being and Nothingness,* Michel Tournier and Gilles Deleuze were both stunned by Sartre's speech. Oblivious to their idol's efforts to defend himself against his critics, they were left aghast at his invocation of Descartes and the Golden Rule: "Our master had gone and fished up that worn-out old duffer Humanism." The poor man had gone soft, they speculated derisively: perhaps he had lost his nerve while a prisoner of war; at this rate, he would soon enough come out in favor of some new-fangled version of old-fashioned socialism.[19]

Which would duly happen. Still, as Tournier adds, "This reaction should be taken for what it was: a liquidation of the father by overgrown adolescents afflicted with the awareness that they owed him everything."[20]

Superficial appearances to the contrary, Foucault too owed Sartre, if not everything, then a great deal. In later years, he would struggle with Sartre's example in ways that suggest an intense, unresolved ambivalence. Tape-recording an interview in 1968 for French radio, he vehemently dissociated himself from Sartre and his era, decrying the way "in which a philosophical text, a theoretical text, finally had to tell you what life, death, and sexuality were, if God existed or not, what freedom consisted of, what one had to do in political life, how to behave in regard to others and so forth." Foucault later asked that these comments be edited out of the program before it was broadcast. When an unedited transcript of the interview was nevertheless published subsequently by mistake, he blew up. Addressing an angry letter to the offending magazine, Foucault was humility incarnate: "I think that the vast oeuvre of Sartre, as well as his political action, will mark an epoch. It is true that many today are working in another direction. I would not allow anyone to compare—particularly in order to oppose them—the minor historical and methodological spade work that I have undertaken with an oeuvre like his."[21]

False modesty was one of Foucault's most salient characteristics—but there can be no doubt about his anguish over how to approach the older thinker's example. In one of his earliest essays, on the significance of dreams, he went out of his way to criticize Sartre's views on imagination. Seven years later, in 1961, trying to publish his first major book, *Madness and Civilization*, he submitted the manuscript (unsuccessfully) to Gallimard because, as he told friends, it had published the great philosophical works of the previous generation, notably *Being and Nothingness*. When Plon eventually published *Madness and Civilization*, the book quickly won the esteem of Foucault's peers. Still, he was not satisfied—for he wished, like Sartre, to speak not merely to historians and philosophers, but to the general public. In his next major book, *The Order of Things*, he therefore took aim directly at Sartre himself, explicitly criticizing his 1960 *Critique of Dialectical Reason*. Yet—in another symptom of Foucault's ambivalence—these passages, which appeared in the book's galleys, were removed from the final, printed text. No matter: French reviewers (and Sartre himself) understood perfectly well that Sartre's humanism, his view of history—and, implicitly, his intellectual leadership—were all under attack.[22]

Sartre's challenge, in short, Foucault found irresistible—and inescapable. His fame was unprecedented. And his "oeuvre," as Foucault called it, had set a daunting new standard for what the philosophical life could mean: not just the creation of an original way of thought, but its public enactment, not merely in a university classroom, but on a stage that, thanks to the steady spread of mass media, was now global.

For any aspiring philosopher with serious ambitions—and the lycée student from Poitiers was nothing if not ambitious—Sartre had raised a whole new set of hurdles. Still, on a purely academic level, the young Foucault so far gave every indication of being able to clear them. An "elite student," commented one of his teachers at Henri-IV. Among the candidates admitted to the École Normale in the fall of 1946, he was ranked fourth.

So Foucault entered the École Normale, a kind of monastery for boy geniuses. There he was again immersed in ideas, in a potentially claustrophobic social setting—like most students, Foucault for the next few years lived in the dormitory attached to the classrooms at rue d'Ulm.

As his classmates and teachers soon discovered, he was a very odd young man. Though the culture of the school welcomed, indeed demanded, dazzling eccentricity, the violence of his idiosyncrasies quickly set him apart. His dorm room was decorated in the most disquieting fashion, with Goya's etchings of the victims of war, tortured and tormented, twisted in agony. His behavior was sometimes just as disquieting: one night he was spotted chasing a classmate with a dagger. Even in intellectual debate he was unpredictably aggressive: normally reserved and introverted, the boy from Poitiers, given the occasion, could be bitterly sarcastic and mocking. In a milieu where ideas were routinely wielded like swords in courtly games of combat, Foucault went for the jugular. Honing a rare in-depth knowledge of the Marquis de Sade, he was contemptuous of those who were not adepts. Most of his classmates couldn't stand him. Others thought he was just crazy.[23]

Everyone, though, agreed that he was brilliant. He read voraciously. And when he was not lost in a book or quarrelling over ideas, he attended seminars and lectures. Already students were preparing for the next big competitive exam, roughly four years hence, the *agrégation* that would be their passport to teaching in the French school system. And thanks to

Sartre's unprecedented popularity, philosophy displaced literature as the field in which the best and the brightest *normaliens* competed to demonstrate their intellectual prowess.

Foucault, for his part, concentrated on philosophy. With Jean Beaufret, he studied Kant. With Merleau-Ponty, Sartre's colleague, he studied different approaches to the mind-body problem, doubtless learning about Merleau-Ponty's view that the true subject was not consciousness per se, but "existence, or being in the world through a body." On his own, Foucault, like everyone else, steeped himself in Hegel, Marx, and Husserl.[24]

But it was Heidegger alone, he later admitted, who became for him "the essential philosopher. . . . My entire philosophical development was determined by my reading of Heidegger."[25]

The impact of Martin Heidegger on two generations of French philosophers is one of the most important—and peculiar—episodes in modern intellectual history. In many ways, the story begins with Sartre; not because he was the first Frenchman to discover Heidegger (he was not); but rather because he was the first to put Heidegger on the French cultural map—to make his thought *the* touchstone for philosophy in our time.

By the late 1930s, when Sartre first read him seriously, Heidegger was already one of the most influential philosophers in Germany. As Hannah Arendt, one of Heidegger's earliest students, later recalled, "the rumor of the hidden king" had spread since 1919, when he became an instructor and assistant to the great philosopher and phenomenologist Edmund Husserl. "The rumor about Heidegger put it quite simply," Arendt wrote. "Thinking has come to life again; the cultural treasures of the past, believed to be dead, are being made to speak, in the course of which it turns out that they propose things altogether different from the familiar, worn-out trivialities they had been presumed to say. There exists a teacher; one can perhaps learn to think."[26]

Neither Sartre, nor Foucault, ever studied with Heidegger. But both men read his work, and for both, the decisive text was Heidegger's masterpiece, *Being and Time,* first published in 1927. Reading this book twelve years later, in quest of a philosophy that somehow might embody "a wisdom, a heroism, a holiness," Sartre, certain that he had found what he was looking for, exulted in "the apparition in the world of a free consciousness."[27]

It was a paradoxical meeting of two minds, based on a monumental misunderstanding perhaps, but one fateful for both parties. Sartre was in many ways everything Heidegger was not: classically French, stubbornly Cartesian, a rationalist at heart, an old-fashioned moralist, too. And odder still, Sartre, at the moment he was reading Heidegger, and noting in his diary entry for February 1, 1940 the apparition of a "free consciousness," was himself a prisoner in a German camp. Heidegger, meanwhile, was ensconced at the University of Freiburg, having pledged his allegiance to the "inner truth and greatness" of the Nazi regime, which in September of 1939 had plunged the world into total war. [28]

That the Frenchman should have thus discovered, and embraced, a German philosophy of *Untergang* in the midst of World War II was an irony that Sartre himself wryly noted. As he pointed out, *Being and Time* was, on one level, a kind of daunting philosophical codicil to Oswald Spengler's *Decline of the West*. Still, in Sartre's view, *Being and Time* expressed "a free surpassing toward philosophy of this pathetic profile of history. . . . So I can rediscover Heidegger's assumption of his destiny as a German, in that wretched Germany of the postwar years, in order to help me assume my destiny as a Frenchman in the France of '40." [29]

If nothing else, Sartre's enthusiasm helped change the course of Heidegger's career: after Germany's defeat, just as he was being stripped of his chair in philosophy, and exiled to his home in the Black Forest, he became, thanks to the global uproar over Sartre and existentialism, a prophet with honor, and not just in France. But the story is stranger still. For Heidegger, far from being pleased with the claims made on his behalf, took pains to disavow them. After reading the text of Sartre's "Existentialism is a Humanism," he was moved to explain that he himself was neither a humanist nor, for that matter, an "existentialist." In response to a series of questions posed by his most prominent French disciple—the École Normale's own Jean Beaufret—Heidegger composed an open "Letter on Humanism," first published in 1947. Like some demigod glowering atop a philosophical Mt. Olympus, the disgraced German sage hurled thunderbolts. Sartre, he declared with a withering scorn hard for the uninitiated to savor fully, "stays with metaphysics in oblivion of the truth of Being." [30]

With one fell stroke, Heidegger made his own work a central influence on Foucault's generation of French philosophers—the very generation anxious to escape from Sartre's shadow.

In strictly philosophical terms, Heidegger was obviously right to disavow Sartre's lecture. His own thinking, he insisted, had never been designed "for the sake of man so that civilization and culture through man's doings might be vindicated." For him, as for Nietzsche and Spengler, modern history was nothing less than a calamity—not the happy emergence of the harmonious human freedom anticipated by Kant, Hegel, and Marx. In these circumstances, to reproduce without modification or serious criticism the formulas of modern humanism, as Sartre seemed to, amounted to an evasion: it was as if the French philosopher had flinched when faced with the full implications of the essence of being human. This essence Heidegger throughout his life described not in terms of "consciousness," but of "transcendence": "Being is the *transcendens* pure and simple."[31]

Whether "transcendence" was understood properly or not—and with an esoteric writer like Heidegger it is always hard to know—this idea was implicitly the starting point for all of the dominant French philosophers of the postwar period, from Sartre and Merleau-Ponty to Foucault and Jacques Derrida. A distinctively human capacity (though most human beings, Heidegger thought, failed to grasp its significance), "transcendence" gave to every single person the power to start over, to begin anew—to take up, reshape, and transform the world. Like modern philosophers from Kant to Sartre, Heidegger sometimes called this power "freedom"; that it was a *power* he had learned from Nietzsche, who spoke of the same capacity as "will to power." Call it freedom or call it transcendence, Heidegger in his letter to Beaufret reiterated his own view that this mysterious capacity was intrinsically without rule, norm, reason, or conscious purpose; indeed, like Nietzsche, he argued that all of these had no basis other than the power of transcendence. To pretend, as Sartre did in his lecture, that something approximating Kant's moral philosophy was logically entailed by something like Heidegger's view of "existence" was therefore to betray a profound misunderstanding of both "Being" and "transcendence."[32]

But this was not the end of Heidegger's letter to Beaufret. It also marked a crucial turning point in Heidegger's own thought—and, as a consequence of Heidegger's renewed influence in France, a turning point in the central philosophical preoccupations of Foucault and his generation.

In the first phase of Heidegger's work, epitomized by *Being and Time*, the German thinker had primarily been interested in "the being of man" ("*das Sein der Menschen*," or "*Dasein*" for short). In the 1930s and 1940s, it had seemed feasible to a number of French readers of *Being and Time*, including Hyppolite and Merleau-Ponty, to amalgamate this stress on *Dasein* with Hegel's teleological philosophy of history and with Karl Marx's famous dictum, in his "Theses on Feuerbach," that "all the mysteries which lead theory towards mysticism find their rational solution in human practice." Heidegger himself in *Being and Time* had dwelled on transcendence as "the very possibility of taking action"—an emphasis that climaxed in the book's highly abstract and deeply enigmatic summons to *Dasein* to rise up resolutely in "*the moment of vision*," to meet its historical fate, and "to choose its hero."[33]

But the coming of World War II, and the catastrophic defeat of the "hero" Heidegger himself had chosen in 1933—namely, Adolf Hitler—led the German philosopher to what he himself called a "reversal," or turning back. In Heidegger's new understanding (as Hannah Arendt once helpfully struggled to sum it up in plain English), "the very possibility of taking action," presented now as "the will to rule and to dominate," looms as "a kind of original sin, of which he found himself guilty when he tried to come to terms with his . . . past in the Nazi movement."[34]

In "The Letter on Humanism," Heidegger in effect tried to purge transcendence of its conventional ties, not simply to logic, morality, and metaphysics (already challenged in *Being and Time*), but also to the "very possibility of taking action." He marked this shift largely through the words he chose to emphasize. Instead of *Dasein*, he now stressed *Sein*, or "Being" as such. To illuminate Being as such, he now thought required not action, but rather a silent waiting, an essentially reverent contemplativeness that might keep open the (slight) possibility of a new, neo-pagan religion of man arising from the ashes of Hitler's aborted revolution. As one of Heidegger's shrewdest French readers, Jacques Derrida, would later point out, the "Letter on Humanism" abounds in images of light and metaphors that evoke "the values of neighboring, shelter, house, service, guard, voice, and listening." "Man," Heidegger declares, "does not decide whether and how beings appear," as many readers of *Being and Time* had concluded. Rather "man" is merely "the shepherd of Being."[35]

At first glance, the vocation of the "shepherd" sounds idyllic. But a darker, more disquieting note was also sounded repeatedly in Heidegger's letter—and it was this note that would resonate most deeply with Foucault, who already knew from Sade and Goya something about dark and disquieting visions of the world. For a human being committed neither to reason nor to purposive action must, as it were, be prepared to let itself go. To surrender one's customary inhibitions and descend into what Heidegger called the "unthought," the thinker had first to "learn to exist in the nameless." To accomplish this paradoxical task, it was not philosophy but poetry and art that might light the way. "Language," as Heidegger famously asserts, "is the house of Being"; but the metaphor is deceptive. For to inhabit, however contemplatively, the world revealed by the language of Sade, for example, was as likely to disturb as it was to comfort. "Concealed in the step back," away from logic and conscious action, is "a thinking that is shattered." Probing beyond the limits of reason, thinking sooner or later finds itself without statute or rule, structure or order, and face-to-face with *nothing*. To thus discover, as Heidegger puts it, that "Being" and "the nothing" are "the Same" is to "risk discord." Heidegger's new way of thinking might bring about a healing "ascent into grace," but by the same token it might also unleash "evil," "the malice of rage," and the "compulsion to malignancy" with uncertain and potentially fatal consequences. As the title of one of Goya's most famous etchings summed up the risks, "The sleep of reason brings forth monsters."[36]

The consequences of "a thinking that is shattered" may thus be tragic: in the "Letter on Humanism," Heidegger refers more than once to the poet Hölderlin, who, like Nietzsche, spent the last years of his life insane. (The blood sacrifice of the recent war also weighs silently, and ambiguously, on the philosopher's words.) Still, "if such thinking were to go fortunately for a man," Heidegger adds in a typically portentous tautology, "no misfortune would befall him." He would then enjoy "the only gift that can come to thinking from Being." Emerging from his "adventure" into "the unthought," the thinker would find the world, as before, untouched and unaltered, but with its aura of primordial mystery (and possible horror) restored. The vocation of the thinker was now to evoke that aura, as a poet would, by laying "inconspicuous furrows in language." Perhaps the seeds scattered there would bear fruit; the time to reap what had been sown might yet come; but in the meantime, the thinker would be a living example of how to "let Being—be."[37]

Foucault would later say that he did "not know Heidegger well enough." This is probably true—his knowledge of Heidegger certainly cannot compare with his subsequent command of Nietzsche. But that he took heart from Heidegger's approach to philosophy can scarcely be doubted.

In his first published writing, in 1954, he would refer with erudition and warm sympathy to the work of the great Heideggerian psychiatrist Ludwig Binswanger. And years later, he would speak in even warmer terms about the philosophical outlook Heidegger had expressed in "The Letter on Humanism." Writing in *The Order of Things* in 1966, Foucault welcomed a "form of reflection far removed from both Cartesianism and Kantian analysis" that, "for the first time," reveals "the being of man in that dimension where thought addresses the unthought and articulates itself upon it." Thanks to Heidegger (who Foucault clearly alludes to without explicitly naming), there appears "an ontology of the unthought" that "short-circuits the primacy of the 'I think,'" facilitating the exploration of "somber mechanisms, faceless determinations, a whole landscape of shadow." Traversing this dim, nocturnal terrain—in Foucault as in Sade and Goya, it is images of darkness that prevail—"modern thought is advancing toward that region where the Other of man must become the Same as him."[38]

As Foucault confided on his deathbed, of all the notes that he took in these years, none outweighed those on the imposing sphinx of twentieth-century German thought: "I still have . . . the notes that I took when I was reading Heidegger. I've got tons of them! And they are much more extensive than the ones I took on Hegel or Marx."[39]

Still, Foucault *did* take notes on Hegel and Marx, just as he doubtless took notes on Hyppolite and Merleau-Ponty. As he stressed in a later interview, "we should not forget that throughout the period from 1945 to 1955 in France, the entire French university—the young French university, as opposed to what had been the traditional university—was very much preoccupied with the task of building something which was . . . Husserlian-Marxist: the phenomenology-Marxist relation."[40]

In the late 1940s, the relationship between Marxism and phenomenology was in the midst of being vigorously elaborated by Foucault's most prominent teacher at the École Normale, Merleau-Ponty. A good Hegelian Marxist, he (like Hyppolite) talked a lot in these years about the *meaning* of history—as if it were obvious that history should have a singular meaning. At the same time, Merleau-Ponty hoped to anchor his global account of the human condition in minutely detailed descriptions of corporeal experience. Extending an approach to philosophy he had learned from Husserl and the Heidegger of *Being and Time*, Merleau-Ponty in his masterpiece, *Phenomenology of Perception*, first published in 1945, tried to unravel the origins of what Kant had considered the "transcendental unity" of the sentient individual by describing the perceptual and behavioral dispositions through which a human being unreflectively conferred order and meaning on the world.

The importance given to this "phenomenological" method in France after the war doubtless owed something to the institutional context, as Foucault himself once suggested: "for the French university, since philosophy began with Descartes, could only advance in a Cartesian manner." But while Jean-Paul Sartre was indeed a professed Cartesian, depicting consciousness as strangely disembodied, it would be misleading to assume that Merleau-Ponty (or Hyppolite) shared Sartre's views on this matter. On the contrary, Merleau-Ponty was sharply critical of Sartre's Cartesian dualism; he consistently asserted the embodied character of the knowing subject, and (like Hyppolite) he just as consistently emphasized its historical situation. These differences were not trivial: Merleau-Ponty felt that the freedom of the human being was far more stringently limited than Sartre had suggested in *Being and Nothingness*.[41]

Still, Merleau-Ponty and Sartre were at one in their esteem for the introspective methods of Husserl. Both took seriously the existential analysis of Heidegger in *Being and Time*. And for all their philosophical disagreements, both tended to emphasize the purposiveness, or "operative intentionality," of the human being's singular power of "transcendence"—an emphasis that was in some ways problematic.

It was not clear, for example, how "intentionality" could account for the significance of certain impersonal factors in history, such as climate, nutrition, or demographic trends. Nor was it obvious how an existential style of analysis could illuminate the phenomenon of language—a subject of growing importance, particularly since Heidegger had called it "the house of Being."

The French phenomenologists were scarcely oblivious to such problems; but their struggle to engage questions of history and language had a paradoxical impact. "I remember clearly," Foucault recalled years later, "some lectures in which Merleau-Ponty began speaking of Saussure," the Swiss father of structural linguistics, at the time virtually unknown to the general public: "So the problem of language appeared and it was clear that phenomenology was no match for structural analysis in accounting for the effects of meaning that could be produced by a structure of the linguistic type, in which the subject (in the phenomenological sense) did not intervene to confer meaning. And quite naturally, with the phenomenological spouse finding herself disqualified by her inability to address language, structuralism became the new bride."[42]

So far as it goes, Foucault's retrospective explanation of his later antipathy to the Husserlian-Marxist strand in French philosophy makes a good deal of sense. But it does not go far enough. Something is missing. After all, by the late 1940s French phenomenology was a mansion with many rooms.[43] Furthermore, given the easy availability of perfectly respectable alternatives—from the linguistics of Saussure to the later thought of Heidegger—why should Sartre's philosophy, in particular, have struck Foucault as a kind of "terrorism?" The word itself conjures up not only involuntary subjugation, but also fear. Why fear?

To suggest a possible answer to this question, it is helpful to recall the moral aim of Sartre's philosophy. This he once summed up, in a word, as "authenticity." This meant "having a true and lucid consciousness of [a] situation . . . [and] assuming the responsibilities and risks that it involves." That these criteria will not be met by most people, most of the time, Sartre makes plain. It was our fate, in effect, to be constantly guilty. Hence the pregnancy of Sartre's slogan: man is *condemned* to be free.[44]

One of the most famous passages in *Being and Nothingness* illustrates some of the implications of this way of looking at the world. Sartre imagines himself crouching at a door, peeping through its keyhole. Moved by jealousy, he is straining to see what is happening on the other side of the door. At this moment, comments Sartre, "there is no self to inhabit my consciousness, nothing therefore to which I can refer my acts. . . . They are in no way *known*." At this moment, "I *am my acts* . . . [in] a pure mode of losing myself in the world, of causing myself to be drunk in by things as ink is by a blotter." Yet even at this very instant, pleasurably feeling one's self dissolve, the ensemble of elements—the door, the keyhole, the man peeping through it—"exists only in relation to a free project of my possibilities. Jealousy, as the possibility which I *am*, organizes this instrumental complex. . . ."[45]

But suddenly, Sartre continues, "I hear footsteps in the hall. Someone is looking at me!"[46]

The whole situation is suddenly transformed. "I now exist as *myself* . . . : I see myself because suddenly somebody sees me." In a flash, he recognizes his freedom and responsibility—but only in the form of *shame*. "Shame . . . is shame of self; it is the *recognition* of the fact that I *am* indeed that object which the Other is looking at and judging." In fact, and inescapably, Sartre *is* the jealous peeping tom at the keyhole.[47]

One night while Foucault was at the École Normale, a somewhat similar incident occurred to him. By chance, a teacher at the school rounded a corner and came upon the young student in a hall. Paul-Michel was lying on the ground. He had just slashed his chest with a razor.[48]

To imagine oneself frozen under the scowl of Sartre's moralizing philosophy at such a moment cannot have been an inviting prospect. "Masochism," Sartre had flatly declared in *Being and Nothingness*, "is on principle a failure," a blameworthy "vice," a deplorable and doomed effort "to *annihilate* the subject's subjectivity."[49] From Sartre's perspective, what could Foucault possibly have felt but shame?

"Visibility," Foucault would remark years later, "is a trap"—and so, from his point of view, was Sartre's philosophy. As Sartre's remarks on masochism suggest, and as his lecture on humanism confirms, the older existentialist was inclined to uphold some surprisingly conventional moral judgments. At the same time, his unrelenting stress on freedom and responsibility made the weight of these judgments all the harder to bear: after all, according to Sartre, it was the duty of each of us to behave "as though the whole human race had its eyes fixed upon" every single act. This punishing standard of "authenticity" Foucault vehemently rejected: "I think that from the theoretical point of view," he remarked in an interview in 1983, "Sartre avoids the idea of the self as something which is given to us, but through the moral notion of authenticity, he turns back to the idea that we have to be ourselves—to be truly our true self." To be burdened not merely by what one person at one time might see, but by what the "whole human race," no less, might think, if only *it* could see, was to imprison oneself "in an infinitely self-referring gaze," as Foucault once put it. Particularly for anyone who experienced moments of madness, "it was finally to be chained to the humiliation of being an object for himself. Awareness was now linked to the shame of being identical to this other, of being compromised in him, and"—this was perhaps the crucial point—"of already despising oneself before being able to recognize or to know oneself."[50]

No wonder the young Foucault evidently preferred Heidegger's philosophy to that of Sartre. From Heidegger's perspective, after all, even a moment of self-lacerating madness might be regarded as a fruitful encounter with the "unthought." Instead of casting moral aspersions on such a discordant experience, Heidegger seemed to welcome it. A "compulsion to malignancy," like a "thinking that is shattered," far from being shameful, might somehow provoke an "ascent into grace."

A little "grace" was something Paul-Michel Foucault could have used: for his gesture of self-mutilation was no isolated incident. In 1948, he attempted to commit suicide. Over the next few years, more suicide attempts followed—how many is unclear. He tried slashing his wrists. He joked about hanging himself. The idea obsessed him. His father, alarmed, arranged for him to be evaluated in the Hôpital Sainte-Anne by one of the leading lights of modern French psychiatry, Jean Delay. When, to the surprise of everyone, Foucault failed to pass the *agrégation* on his first attempt in 1950, one of his teachers, worried that the distraught student might commit yet another "blunder," asked a classmate to keep a check on him.[51]

To the end of his life, Foucault defended "everyone's right to kill himself," as he cheerfully told a startled interviewer in 1983. Suicide, he wrote in another essay, published in 1979, was "the simplest of pleasures." One ought to prepare for the act of suicide "bit by bit, decorate it, arrange the details, find the ingredients, imagine it, choose it, get advice on it, shape it into a work without spectators, one which exists only for oneself, just for that shortest little moment of life." Admittedly, it "often leaves discouraging traces. . . . Do you think it's pleasant to have to hang yourself in the kitchen and to leave a blue tongue dangling? Or to close yourself in the garage and turn on the gas? Or to leave a tiny bit of brain lying on the pavement for the dogs to sniff?" It would be better, of course, if society properly valued suicide: "If I won a few billion francs in the national lottery," he said in the 1983 interview, "I'd set up an institute where people who wanted to die could come and spend a weekend, a week or a month, enjoying themselves as far as possible, perhaps with the help of drugs, and then disappear. . . ." In his 1979 essay, he imagines "suicide-festivals" and "suicide-orgies" and also a kind of special retreat where those planning to commit suicide could look "for partners without names, for occasions to die liberated from every identity." That dying is sensuous (just as Sade, for one, had said) Foucault insists: to die, he writes, is to experience the "formless form of an absolutely simple pleasure," a "limitless pleasure whose patient preparation, with neither rest nor predetermination, will illuminate the entirety of your life."[52]

This, it is tempting to say, is just a joke.

Or is it? Given the trajectory of Foucault's life, from his first suicide attempt in 1948 to the specter of death he evidently embraced in San Francisco in 1983, one has to wonder.

The École Normale's doctor chalked up the young Foucault's suicidal behavior to one simple thing: distress over his homosexuality. Didier Eribon, his French biographer, tacitly agrees, depicting the young philosopher as paralyzed with guilt after his frequent nocturnal forays into the gay demimonde of postwar Paris.[53]

In his 1979 essay on suicide, oddly enough, Foucault draws the same connection, in order overtly to ridicule it; though, again, given the biographical subtext, one has to wonder: "We might imagine tall, slender, pallid creatures unable to cross over the threshold to the other sex, in a faceoff with death all through life, only to end it finally by slamming the door with a loud bang (which never fails to annoy the neighbors). Instead of marrying the opposite sex, [homosexuals] marry death. But they are just as incapable of dying as they are of really living. In this risible game, homosexuals and suicide discredit each other."[54]

Certainly, to be young and gay was no simple matter in the Paris of the late forties. "Up until 1970," Foucault later recalled, "one knew very well that the patrons of bars and of baths were harassed by the police and that there was a complex, efficient, and burdensome spiral of police repression." But Foucault also later claimed that he loved the games that had to be played in those dark times before gay liberation: belonging to an underground fraternity was exciting as well as dangerous.[55]

His sexuality was not, in any case, something that Foucault was just discovering. He told friends that his first crushes on other boys had occurred years before in Poitiers. At the École Normale, he neither flaunted nor hid his sexuality. France has long been a relatively sophisticated country sexually, with its own distinct code of discretion and de facto tolerance. *Normaliens*, moreover, are traditionally given a very wide berth; ample allowances are made for unusual behavior. It would be naive to assume that either officials or students at the school would have found Foucault's sexual pursuits, in themselves, either offensive or particularly shocking.[56]

In later life, if Foucault harbored any lingering anxiety about his sexual desires, certainly none of his gay friends noticed it. He normally made light of the whole matter. When the American novelist Edmund White once asked him how he got to be so smart, Foucault characteristically joked that it was all due to his lust for boys: " 'I wasn't always smart, I was actually very stupid in school,' " White recalls Foucault saying, " 'so I was sent off to a new school' " (which in fact happened). In this new school, Foucault continued, " 'there was a boy who was very attractive who was even stupider than I was. And in order to ingratiate myself with this boy who was very beautiful, I began to do his homework for him—and that's how I became smart, I had to do all this work to just keep ahead of him a little bit, in order to help him.

" 'In a sense,' " Foucault concluded with a flourish, " 'all the rest of my life I've been trying to do intellectual things that would attract beautiful boys.' "[57]

Daniel Defert, who in later years knew Foucault better than anyone else, thinks that his longtime companion suffered in these years not from homosexuality, but from some other, more enigmatic kind of distress. One factor, suggests Defert, was the anxiety Foucault felt about "not being handsome." Still another factor, Defert speculates, was perhaps Foucault's early experimentation with drugs, a fascination as deep and abiding as his lifelong interest in suicide. "I don't know if he injected," says Defert, but the drugs Foucault used at that time were, he asserts, certainly stronger than mere alcohol or hashish. Still, as Defert concedes, it is "a very mysterious period." It is also our earliest glimpse at the peculiarly death-haunted form of "experience" that Foucault would spend a lifetime trying to fathom.[58]

In 1948, just as the young Foucault began to struggle in earnest with his own suicidal impulses, a flashy new figure arrived at the École Normale. His name was Louis Althusser, and in the years that followed, he managed to open up new doors for the unhappy student from Poitiers, suggesting new ways to apply philosophy to the study of history and the understanding of psychology—and also new ways to work on changing a world that in certain respects Foucault evidently found intolerable.

Althusser was the school's new philosophy tutor—or, in the argot of *normaliens*, the new "caïman" (the animal, akin to the crocodile, that the Cayman Islands are named after). A fiery spirit of fierce discipline and Jesuitical craftiness, Althusser was on his way out of the Catholic church and into the Communist Party. Already afflicted with the recurrent manic-depressive episodes that would lead to his permanent commitment to a mental hospital after strangling his wife in 1981, the young tutor often missed his classes. He nevertheless proved to be a spellbinding teacher, a quality that helped him recruit an unprecedented number of *normaliens*, including Foucault, into the Communist Party.[59]

"In the immediate postwar period," as Foucault later recalled, the Communist Party "exercised . . . a triple legitimacy: historical, political and theoretical." Capitalizing on the leading role it had played in the Resistance, the party set the agenda for postwar French socialists: "Over anyone who pretended to be on the left, it 'laid down the law.' One was either for, or against; an ally, or an adversary."[60]

Foucault was an ally. Already in open rebellion against the bourgeois primness of his family, and searching for some practical way to transcend his sense of personal alienation, he was also opposed, more concretely, to the growing French war in Indochina. Thanks to Althusser's influence, the Communists had replaced the Socialists as the party of protest and social change at the École Normale. As Foucault would later recall of his generation, "we were in quest of other intellectual ways to reach that point at which it seemed that something was taking shape or already existed that was totally 'other'—namely, Communism." Sometime in 1950, he joined the *Parti communiste français* (or PCF).[61]

If nothing else, his experience during the roughly three years he spent in the party taught him something about the pliability of the truth—and also about the ability of the trained mind to believe, and find reasons for believing, almost anything. Learning to toe the party's line on everything from international affairs to reflex psychology, Foucault learned how to lend credence to the incredible: "Being obliged to stand behind a fact that was totally beyond credibility," he later explained, "was part of that exercise of the 'dissolution of the self,' of the quest for a way to be 'other.'" Still, as Foucault discovered, being a Communist was not quite the "other" way of life he was looking for. Far from being a liberation, life inside the Party soon enough felt like another kind of strait-jacket. "I was never really integrated into the Communist Party because I was homosexual," he later said. "It was an institution that reinforced all the values of the most traditional bourgeois life"—all the values he now wanted to jettison.[62]

Although it is impossible to establish precisely the dates of Foucault's active involvement in the French Communist Party, it seems he left by the summer of 1953. The last straw, he would recall, had been the so-called "Doctors' Plot." This putative plot was first "unmasked" by Soviet newspapers in January, 1953. In a series of inflammatory articles, Party journalists charged that a cabal of traitorous doctors, most with ties to an international Jewish organization, had conspired to murder prominent Bolsheviks and to poison Stalin himself, who was then in the throes of his final illness. The slanderous accusation pandered to anti-Semitic sentiments and provoked a government sponsored campaign to purge Jews from positions of public responsibility in the Soviet Union. Throughout his life, Foucault was intensely hostile to any hint of anti-Semitism. The blatant racism of this propaganda initiative, combined with the evident mendacity of the charges, left him aghast: "The fact is, from that moment on I moved away from the PCF."[63]

In the years that followed, Foucault expressed scant sympathy for communist parties, movements, or regimes. Even during his alliance with the French ultra-left after May '68, as Daniel Defert recalls, he scorned the widespread infatuation with Communist China, and refused to accompany Defert when he journeyed to Peking for a firsthand look at Mao Tse-tung's "cultural revolution."[64]

Despite the later staunchness of his own anti-communist convictions, Foucault's break with Marxism as a mode of thought was neither sudden nor, for several years at least, clear-cut. His first two published works, which appeared shortly after he had left the PCF, both still bear the stamp of a Marxist style of reasoning, particularly in the optimism they express about the prospects for conquering alienation. Indeed, for the rest of Foucault's life, long after he had explicitly repudiated this and most of the other salient features of Marxism, an amorphous aura of revolutionary hope—an implicit conviction that confining social forms may yet be totally transfigured—would temper his otherwise discomfiting approach to philosophy, imbuing it with a diffuse mood of eschatological expectation.

Foucault also remained friendly in later years with Althusser, who in the 1960s emerged as the French Communist Party's leading theoretician. Even at the end of the 1970s, once it had become fashionable in France to dismiss both Althusser and Marxism out of hand, Foucault stood loyally by his old mentor and privately rebuked those who criticized him.[65]

But as events would show, Althusser's most lasting influence on Foucault was not political at all: it was purely intellectual. For Althusser, besides being a Marxist-Leninist mandarin of the most sublimely scholastic cunning, was also a serious student of the French philosophy of science, an interest he passed on to his pupil.

As Foucault himself once explained, French philosophy in the 1930s and '40s can be divided into "a philosophy of experience, of sense and subject," on the one hand, and "a philosophy of knowledge, of rationality and of concept," on the other. "One network is that of Sartre and Merleau-Ponty; and then another is that of Cavaillès, Bachelard, and Canguilhem."[66]

The roots of this distinctively French alternative to existentialism Foucault would later trace to Kant's *Critique of Pure Reason*: "For the first time," as Foucault explained, "rational thought was put in question not only as to its nature, its foundation, its powers and its rights, but also as to its history and its geography; as to its immediate past and its present reality; as to its time and its place."[67]

It was this critical project that the French historians of science, along with such German counterparts as Ernst Cassirer (whom Foucault also admired), took up and elaborated in the years after World War I. Jean Cavaillès (1903–1944), as Foucault once summed him up, was "a historian of mathematics who was interested in the development of its internal structures." A partisan in the French Resistance, he died at the hands of the Nazis—a fact of no small significance to Foucault. Since neither Sartre nor Merleau-Ponty had come close to making such a sacrifice in the Resistance, the life and death of Cavaillès showed up the hollowness of existentialism's political pretensions.[68]

Georges Canguilhem, born in 1904, would become, after 1961, one of Foucault's closest intellectual friends and allies. Primarily interested in biology and medicine, Canguilhem was in many ways an heir to Bergson's vitalism. Life, he thought, was an unstanchable force of transcendence, a turbulent stream of vital energy, marked by instability, irregularity, abnormality, and (as Bichat before him had pointed out) morbidity. "It is the abnormal which arouses theoretical interest in the normal," Canguilhem declared in his most important work, an *Essay on Some Problems Concerning the Normal and the Pathological*, first published in 1943. "Norms are recognized as such only through infractions. Functions are revealed only by their breakdown. Life rises to the consciousness and science of itself only through maladaptation, failure and pain"—sentiments that Foucault would later implicitly echo in his understanding of the epistemological significance of "limit-experiences."[69]

At the same time, as Foucault pointed out, Canguilhem "brought the history of science down from the heights (mathematics, astronomy, Galilean mechanics, Newtonian physics, relativity theory) toward the middle regions"—his own later area of interest, as well. By focusing on biology and medicine, Canguilhem, in Foucault's admiring words, shed fresh light on those domains "where knowledge is much less deductive, much more dependent on external processes (economic stimulations or institutional supports) and where it has remained tied much longer to the marvels of the imagination."[70]

Of all the French historians of science, however, it was surely Gaston Bachelard (1884–1962) who was the most eccentric and, for Foucault in his formative years, the most important. "I was never directly his student," Foucault later recalled, "but I had read his books. And, to be honest, of all the contemporary philosophers alive when I was a student, Bachelard was the one I read the most," absorbing "an enormous number of things that I have elaborated."[71]

Bachelard was that rarity in French higher education—a bona fide outsider. An autodidact, he had taught himself chemistry while working as a postman. Turning his attention to the history of science, he had slowly scaled all the rungs in the French academic ladder, ending up as a professor of philosophy at the Sorbonne in the 1940s. He devoted studies to mathematics and the physics of Einstein—and also to the role played by illusion, error, and seductive imagery in blocking the progress of science.

The more Bachelard studied the perverse power of the imagination, the more fascinated by it he became. In 1938, he began what turned into a sequence of studies on the role played in the imagination by the four primal elements—earth, air, fire and water. In each book, he classified the chimeras of poets with the rigor of a chemist. Some of Foucault's most beautiful pages in *Madness and Civilization*, on the aquatic world plied by the medieval "Ship of Fools," owe a very large debt to the way Bachelard analyzed the reverie of water. "No one," Foucault would declare in 1954, "has better understood the dynamic work of the imagination."[72]

But Bachelard's impact on Foucault did not stop there. For out of his unusual and sustained encounter with both poetry and modern physics, Bachelard wrested a world view that stressed ruptures, breaks, cleavages; instead of a dialectical harmony, he saw a human condition broken in two, with reason on one side and reverie on the other: "between concept and image there is no possible synthesis." And though the rigorous application of reasoning in science might disclose the truth of what really is, only fluid images of poetry and the dreamworld could make reality sing. The imagination that could produce obstacles to scientific progress became for Bachelard a harbinger of a person's "secret being" and "inner destiny," pointing a way "beyond thought," perhaps transgressing "the most certain of laws and human values"—yet also provoking "a leap toward a new life." By thus stressing the revelatory power of poetry and art, Bachelard's later work curiously converged with that of Heidegger.[73]

All of the French philosophers of science, from Cavaillès to Bachelard, rejected the idea that scientific discovery involved an accumulation of immutable truths that merely needed to be fitted together like some cosmic jigsaw puzzle. Instead, they stressed the creative role played by the scientist: far from being a gradual evolution, the history of science had been rocked by a series of conceptual revolutions, producing demonstrable "breaks," marking fault lines in the way that scientists thought about the world. Our modern conception of the "true" was, in part, a historical product of these changing scientific theories, theories that were liable to change again in the future. If this general view of science recalls, for American readers, Thomas Kuhn's widely-influential *The Structure of Scientific Revolutions*, first published in 1962, it is for a very good reason: Kuhn knew and admired the French historians of science—and, like Foucault, had his doubts about the creative potential of "normal science."[74]

In 1951, Foucault finally passed the *agrégation* in philosophy on his second try. Over the next four years, aided by the École Normale's powerful patronage network, he supported himself at a series of odd jobs, doing research and teaching, all the while pursuing his deepening interest in the philosophy of science. It was in these years that he began to study systematically the history of psychology and psychiatry, making a habit of going each day to the Bibliothèque Nationale, mastering different theories of mental illness, reading everyone from Pavlov and Piaget to Jaspers and

Freud. At Althusser's invitation, one of his jobs was at the École Normale, where, as an instructor in psychology between 1951 and 1955, his reputation began to grow.[75]

At the same time, he returned to the Hôpital Sainte-Anne, one of the biggest and most modern psychiatric facilities in France, this time to do research. An unofficial intern, he helped conduct experiments in an electroencephalographic laboratory, learning how to analyze abnormalities in the electrical activity of the brain in order to diagnose brain injuries, epilepsy, and various neurological disorders. He also routinely visited the hospital with his students from the École Normale in order to watch the public examination of patients by young doctors practicing their clinical technique. "I had a very strange status there," Foucault later recalled. "Nobody worried about what I should be doing; I was free to do anything. I was actually in a position between the staff and the patients." The ambiguity of his position, one imagines, was also heightened by his own recent brushes with madness. "I had been mad enough to study reason," he later quipped: "I was reasonable enough to study madness." Maintaining "a distance from the staff," he began to experience a "kind of malaise." He spent a lot of time simply watching: "I felt very close to and not very different from the inmates." He observed the patients, and he observed how the doctors treated them. But "it was only years later when I started writing a book on the history of psychiatry that this malaise, this personal experience, took the form of a historicial criticism."[76]

He approached psychoanalysis in these years with curiosity as well as ambivalence. He worked with one of Sartre's old classmates at the École Normale, Daniel Lagache, and also audited some of the seminars, later famous, that Jacques Lacan conducted at Sainte-Anne starting in 1953. He even briefly entered into analysis himself, only to terminate in a fit of pique when his therapist went on vacation.[77]

Key Freudian ideas stayed with him, though, throughout his life. The unconscious, for example, which Sartre had glibly tried to refute in one of the weakest passages in *Being and Nothingness*, Foucault was always keen to explore: it was, as he put it in *The Order of Things*, "the blind stain by which it is possible to know" the being of man, the shadowy empire of what Heidegger had called the "unthought." He rejected the death instinct as an invariant biological component of human behavior, but accepted it as a historical reality, further evidence, independent of his own preoccupation with suicide, that modern man, haunted by death, "can and must" experience "hate and aggression."[78]

The interpretation of dreams, finally, was a practice that never lost its fascination for him. At the end of his life, he was writing about the pioneering "dream book" of the Greek philosopher Artemidorus, while in the beginning he was naturally curious about his own dreams. "In order to show me the validity of Freudian ideas," a friend from these years has recalled, "he cited a dream that he had during [his analysis] of a floating surgeon's knife: his analyst had no trouble in making him recognize a fantasy of castration." And the historian, remembering that the young Paul-Michel once attacked himself with a razor, cannot help but recall, too, that Foucault's father was a surgeon.[79]

In fact, Foucault had grown to detest his father. "He was a violent man," recalls Daniel Defert, who knew of him only through the son's bitter recollections. "He would quarrel a lot, speaking loudly. He was a brilliant man, but very strong, very commanding."[80]

Foucault as a young man made one small but telling gesture of revenge: in an act of self-assertion—and nominal self-mutilation—aimed directly at the bullying patriarch, Paul-Michel chopped off his *nom du père*, becoming simply "Michel Foucault."[81]

That was the name that would appear on his first book, a brief but encyclopedic survey, *Mental Illness and Personality*, published in 1954. This work reflects the variety and heterogeneous character of Foucault's formative interests, and also the ambiguity (if not confusion) of his own emerging convictions. Formulations of a bleakly Heideggerian temper nestle uneasily beside sunny Marxist formulas. Part of the book's problem is simply the amount of ground it tries to cover: in 110 pages of densely packed prose, Foucault offers a sweeping historical survey of the early organic psychological theories of Kraepelin and Bleuler, the classical psychoanalysis of Freud, the existential psychoanalysis of Binswanger, and the reflex psychology of Pavlov, ending on an upbeat note of hope for a Marxist "science of man" aimed at ameliorating mental illness by ending social alienation. But despite the book's erudition and evident intelligence, Foucault's survey lacks the kind of fire and flair readers would later come to expect from him.[82]

At the age of twenty-eight, after his years of studying Heidegger, Marx, and the history of modern scientific approaches to mental illness, he had yet to find his own voice.

The story goes that Jean-Paul Sartre discovered his *daimon* in a mug of beer. The miracle occurred one day in 1933, when Raymond Aron, just back from Germany, grandly informed his old classmate that *this* glass, *this* table—these simple things, for phenomenologists like Husserl, were the very stuff of philosophy.[83]

Foucault's own youthful epiphany was not nearly so sudden. It all began, as he later recalled, in a darkened theater one night in the winter of 1953.[84]

The curtain went up, and revealed a barren set. Just the skeleton of a tree. On stage appeared two tramps. "Nothing to be done," says one. "I'm beginning to come round to that opinion," says the other.[85]

Of no discernible age or calling, the tramps chatter idly.

"What about hanging ourselves," says one.

"Hmmm. It'd give us an erection," says the other.

"An erection! . . . Let's hang ourselves immediately."[86]

But this exchange, like every other, comes to nothing.

Off stage, a whip cracks. A man appears, leading a slave tethered to a rope tied around his neck. "I present myself," the master says with pompous grandiloquence: "Pozzo."[87]

A play-within-the-play unfolds. The slave will perform. Pozzo jerks the rope: "Think, pig!" The otherwise mute man abruptly lurches into a shouted soliloquy: "Given the existence as uttered forth in the public works of Puncher and Wattmann of a personal God quaquaquaqua with white beard quaquaquaqua outside time without extension who from the heights of divine apathia divine athambia divine aphasia loves us dearly with some exceptions for reasons unknown but time will tell. . . ."[88]

This explosion of words is doubtless the most exciting single moment in a nearly three-hour performance. For the rest, it is a matter of endless waiting—waiting for someone called Godot.

Samuel Beckett's play was the intellectual event of that season in Paris. It rocked the intelligentsia, much as Sartre's lecture on existentialism had eight years before. Night after night, audiences sat solemnly, as if watching a dramatization of Heidegger's philosophy—which is precisely what the young novelist Alain Robbe-Grillet declared the play to be. A farce with the air of tragedy, its vagrant heroes had nothing to do and little to say, their hypnotically boring patter broken only by the slave's mad parody of scholasticism. Offered as a kind of philosophical parable, the play seduced Parisian audiences with its irresistible hints of a deep and important mystery just waiting to be unraveled.[89]

It is obvious, Robbe-Grillet declared in his influential review, that Godot is God: "After all, why not? Godot—why not, just as well?—is the earthly ideal of a better social order. Do we not aspire to a better life, better food, better clothes, as well as to the possibility of no longer being beaten? And this Pozzo, who is precisely *not* Godot—is he not the man who keeps

thought enslaved? Or else Godot is death: tomorrow we will hang ourselves, if it does not come all by itself. Godot is silence; we must speak
while waiting for it: in order to have the right, ultimately, to keep still.
Godot is that inaccessible *self* Beckett pursues through his entire oeuvre,
with this constant hope, 'This time, perhaps, it will be me, at last.' "[90]

Shortly before his death, Foucault summed up his intellectual odyssey
in these years. "I belong to that generation who, as students, had before
their eyes, and were limited by, a horizon consisting of Marxism, phenomenology, and existentialism," he said. "For me the break was first Beckett's *Waiting for Godot*, a breathtaking performance."[91]

That this drama of futility, folly, and aborted metaphysics should have
suggested the best way yet to escape from Sartre's "terrorism" is not accidental. The world of *Godot* is a world where the very ideas of freedom
and responsibility have been dramatically emptied of any lingering moral
significance. "Moral values are not accessible," Beckett would later declare.
"It is not even possible to talk about truth, that's part of the anguish.
Paradoxically, through form, by giving form to what is formless, the artist
can find a possible way out."[92]

In the winter of 1953, Foucault had yet to invent his own "possible
way out." But that would come soon enough. For this time, perhaps, it
was himself, at last, that he was finding.

3

THE HEART

LAID BARE

IN AUGUST OF 1953, Michel Foucault left Paris for a vacation in Italy. The preceding months had been full of ferment. Inspired by *Waiting for Godot,* he had returned to his work with renewed zeal. He had embarked on a detailed study of the Swiss psychiatrist Ludwig Binswanger, a Freudian and follower of Martin Heidegger. He was in the midst of a love affair with the composer Jean Barraqué. As never before, he was immersed in the world of the Parisian avant-garde.

It was the era of "the new novel," the heyday of the "theater of the absurd," a time of exuberant experimentation in music. But it was not a novel or a play or a piece of new music that captured Foucault's imagination: it was rather an eighty-year old collection of essays—Friedrich Nietzsche's *Untimely Meditations.*

Years later, Maurice Pinguet, a friend and fellow *normalien* who visited Italy with Foucault that summer, recalled watching him "reading in the sun, on the beach of Civitavecchia," lost in the pages of Nietzsche's book. The avidity of Foucault's interest shocked Pinguet: "I would have found it more in line with my idea of a philosopher if he had been deciphering Hegel or Husserl: without barbed concepts, no philosophy." In the minds of many, Nietzsche was still tainted by the way the Nazis had exploited ideas like the "will to power" and the "overman." Foucault, though, was fascinated by Nietzsche's work. "We scarcely had time to read," recalls Pinguet, "engrossed as we were by everything there was to see every step of the way. But from time to time, during a half hour of rest, on the beach, or on the terrace of a café, I would see him open this book, a bilingual edition, and continue his reading."[1]

Pinguet dates the end of his friend's intellectual apprenticeship from this encounter with Nietzsche, and so, in more than one interview, did

Foucault. Of course, like any good *normalien* he had in fact read Nietzsche years before. But that summer, familiar ideas suddenly looked and felt new, and reading Nietzsche *this* time produced, Foucault recalled, a "philosophical shock." "Nietzsche was a revelation," he explained in a 1982 interview. "I read him with a great passion and broke with my life. . . . I had the feeling I had been trapped. Through Nietzsche, I had become a stranger to all that."[2]

In the preface he published to *Madness and Civilization* in 1961, Foucault summarized his projected lifework in terms that suggest the profundity of Nietzsche's impact on him in these formative years. His goal, he declared elliptically, would be "to confront the dialectics of history with the unchanging structure of the tragic." This would require a multifaceted "inquiry," into madness of course, but also, in future books, into dreams and into "sexual prohibitions" and "the happy world of desire." But he would conduct *all* of these inquiries, he stressed, *"sous le soleil de la grande recherche nietzschéene"*—under the sun of the great Nietzschean quest.[3]

A cryptic phrase, an enigmatic epiphany. For what did Foucault mean by "the great Nietzschean quest"? And why did Nietzsche, and specifically the Nietzsche of the *Untimely Meditations,* suddenly speak to him so powerfully under the sun of Civitavecchia in that August of 1953?

The book that captured Foucault's imagination was in many ways a direct by-product of Nietzsche's own desperate struggle to understand who he was, and what he might yet become. The four essays collected in the *Untimely Meditations* were composed between 1873 and 1876, after the frosty reception accorded to Nietzsche's first book, *The Birth of Tragedy.* In this work, originally published in 1872, the precocious German classicist, already a professor at the University of Basel at the age of twenty-seven, had propounded a bold new theory of tragedy. "The unchanging structure of the tragic," according to Nietzsche, pitted two timeless drives against each other: the Apollonian propensity to shape the world with forms of just and pleasing proportion; and the Dionysian tendency to shatter such forms and violently transgress the boundaries between the conscious and unconscious, reason and unreason. *The Birth of Tragedy* had some famous admirers—Richard Wagner was one—but they were all from outside the academy. When the book appeared, Nietzsche's fellow classicists impugned its scholarship, ridiculed its historical thesis, and altogether ignored its challenging new view of the world. The following winter, the young professor's seminar at Basel collapsed. Plagued by an endless series of somatic problems—stomach ailments, acute myopia, nervous disorders—Nietzsche felt increasingly isolated, uncertain as never before about where he was going, and what he would make of himself. "It is the *free man's* task to live for himself, without regard to others," he wrote in one of his notebooks from this period. "Most men are obviously in the world *by accident:* no higher necessity is visible in them." By trying to conform to the expectations of others, "men reveal a pathetic *modesty.* . . . When each man finds his own goal in someone else, then *nobody has any purpose of his own in existing.*"[4]

The essays in the *Untimely Meditations* all express in various ways Nietzsche's effort to find his own purpose, his own "higher necessity." The *Untimely Meditations,* he later explained, offer "a vision of my future, . . . my innermost history, my *becoming.*" Above all, it was the essay that he called "Schopenhauer as Educator" that illuminated the inner logic of what became Nietzsche's own lifelong quest—to understand, as the famous subtitle of *Ecce Homo* puts it, "how one becomes what one is."[5]

That Foucault was struck by this paradoxical task is clear from the marked copy of the *Untimely Meditations* that he kept in his personal library. In "Schopenhauer as Educator," Foucault singled out one of Nietzsche's key formulations: "The riddle which man must solve, he can only solve in being, in being what he is and not something else, in the immutable."[6]

A strange and baffling doctrine is summed up by this sentence—a sentence worth struggling to understand, both because Foucault thought it important while reading the text, and also because it leads to the heart of his own "great Nietzschean quest."

The first sentences of "Schopenhauer as Educator" lay out Nietzsche's central theme with compact eloquence: "A traveler who had visited many countries and peoples and several continents, was asked what trait he had discovered to be common to all men, and replied: a tendency to laziness. Some will think that he might have answered more accurately and truthfully: They are all afraid. They hide behind custom and opinions. Basically, every man knows quite well that, being unique, he is on this earth only once, and that no accident, however unusual, could ever again combine this wonderful diversity into the unity he is. He knows this, but hides it like a bad conscience."[7]

Hence the importance to a person's proper education of communing with a truly original spirit. It is only the great thinkers and artists, contends Nietzsche, who can teach a student to "despise this aimless drifting about in borrowed manners," unveiling "the secret, everyone's bad conscience, the principle that every man is a unique miracle." Shaken up by such a principle, the student may finally learn to stop hiding and to "follow his conscience, which cries out to him: 'Be yourself! You are none of the things you now do, think, desire.' "[8]

Such was Schopenhauer's impact on Nietzsche. And such, it seems, was Nietzsche's impact on Foucault. At first glance, however, it is hard to see how either Nietzsche or Foucault could consistently embrace anything like these sentiments. Throughout most of his life, Nietzsche, like Foucault, rejected the idea that the self is something merely given. In the eyes of both men, "truth," including the "truth" about one's self, "is not something there, that might be found or discovered—but something that must be created." "Our body is but a social structure," as Nietzsche once put it— and our self is but the contingent and changing product of a shifting deployment of cultural and corporeal forces.[9]

If the self, like truth, is, at least in part, constructed rather than simply discovered, one implication seems obvious: human beings as such lack any unchangeable rule, statute, or norm. But both Nietzsche and Foucault at the same time depict the human being as formed by a host of historically contingent rules, statutes, and norms, defined by the customs, practices, and institutions every human being must grow up within. A creature of history, every human being embodies a compound of nature and culture, chaos and order, instinct and reason—two heterogeneous dimensions of being human symbolized, as Nietzsche saw it, by Dionysus and Apollo.

These two dimensions, Nietzsche thought, had somehow to be combined and balanced if a human being would forge "a purpose of his own in existing." But Christianity, he feared, had taught Europeans to hate the body and its untamed animal energy. And with the growing ability of the modern state to regulate every area of life, the Dionysian dimension of being human was in danger of disappearing, a victim of the effort to make men conform to the most numbing and uniform of cultural codes: "Once we possess that common economic management of the earth that will soon be inevitable," he wrote in one of his notebooks from 1887, "mankind will be able to find its best meaning as a machine in the service of this economy—as a tremendous clockwork, composed of ever smaller, ever more subtly 'adapted' gears."[10]

"To become what one is," particularly under these circumstances, was thus no simple task. For a start, one had to rediscover the chaos hidden within—a reservoir of unformed corporeal energy that might yet, as Nietzsche put it in *Thus Spoke Zarathustra,* enable even us creatures of modern civilization to "give birth to a dancing star."[11] To tap the primal essence of our own animal nature was, for Nietzsche, to grasp anew the mysterious capacity of "transcendence," and to exercise what he called the "will to power." As important and as liberating as this capacity was, however, it touched only the Dionysian element of the human compound.

The Apollonian element, by contrast, lay in part beyond the power of the will. Having inculcated patterns of behavior, a culture has roots sunk in the past, and "the will," as Nietzsche put it, "cannot will backwards." Born and raised in a tradition, a human being at first may experience its cultural inheritance as a cozy haven of custom and habit. But each person's cozy routines turn out, on closer inspection, to be a singularly haphazard concatenation of "fragment and riddle and dreadful accident," hidden beneath a comforting veneer of "borrowed manners and received opinion." Sorting through the manners and opinions, and the desires and appetites, that any culture implants in every soul—and trying to imagine transforming them—is, in effect, the challenge every truly creative human being must resolve.[12]

"Nobody can build you the bridge over which you must cross the river of life, nobody but you alone," Nietzsche writes in "Schopenhauer as Educator". "True, there are countless paths and bridges and demigods that would like to carry you across the river, but only at the price of your self; you would pledge your self, and lose it. In this world there is one unique path which no one but you may walk. Where does it lead? Do not ask; take it."[13]

This is poetically put. But what does it mean? How can Nietzsche assert that there exists, for each individual, "one unique path"? Standing at a crossroads, how will we know which path is truly ours?

In 1875 and after, Nietzsche's search for "one unique path" implicitly invokes the archaic—and, to the modern mind, bizarre—idea that every human being is haunted by a singular *daimon*. For the ancient Greeks, the word "*daimon*" defined the otherwise unknowable power that drove an individual more or less blindly forward. If it helped carry the individual to great glory, then he was honored in death as a *daimon* himself—as if he had come to embody his own "higher necessity" by freely merging with a ghostly double. For the ordinary Greek, however, the idea of the *daimonic* described whatever the individual experienced as unpredictable, out of control, and not of his own doing; it was, in short, a word for the power of a singular fate.[14]

A number of Greek philosophers supposed that the *daimonic* aspects of one's existence might be divined by a human being. The Pythagoreans, for example, speculated that *daimons* were intermediate beings, superhuman guardians assigned to specific human beings: Hovering in the air, the *daimons* dispatched dreams and portents to those they watched over, and these signs, properly deciphered, could yield to a person some premonition of his or her fate. Heraclitus rejected such views, remarking in one of his paradoxical aphorisms that "character is for man his *daimon*." Socrates, on the other hand, regarded his *daimon* as an indwelling and audible divinity, a being other than himself who sometimes spoke to him, leading him to stop, say no, turn about, change his mind, and modify his behavior. Socrates' professed intimacy with his *daimon* fueled popular suspicion that he was inventing a new (and literally self-serving) god—one of the charges that cost the philosopher his life. [15]

Whether knowable or not—and whether a contingent by-product of human character, or a lot drawn at birth and held in trust by a divine, or quasi-divine, spirit—the nature of one's *daimon* defined the course of one's life. Blessed was the soul with a good *daimon*: swimming with the tide, it became *eudaimon,* or happy. But there was another, more disquieting possibility, dramatized in Greek tragedy: sometimes a person, even a heroic and great person had to bear the brunt of a bad *daimon*. It was this possibility that the theologians of early Christianity evoked by using the word *daimon* to mean a diabolical fiend, or "demon"—an emissary of the devil, haunting one's heart, lurking in one's dreams, presiding over carnal desires, posing a constant temptation to do wrong, resistible only at the price of mortification and self-renunciation. [16]

Nietzsche (like Goethe before him) rejected this Christian stigmatization of the demonic aspect of the human being. If becoming "what one is" unleashes a compulsion to malignancy, so be it: "Man needs what is most evil in him for what is best in him." If acting in harmony with a particularly cursed demon brings disaster, so be it: "The secret for harvesting from existence the greatest fruitfulness and the greatest enjoyment is—to *live dangerously!*" For better or worse, the human being who would find (and not renounce) itself had no choice. "There is no drearier and more repulsive creature," comments Nietzsche, "than the man who has evaded his genius." [17] Call it genius or consider it one's unique *daimon*—here is Nietzsche's own key for unlocking "the riddle which man must solve," the riddle "he can only solve in being, in being what he is and not something else."

❧

It was a key that Foucault grasped. "The Demon is not the Other," he once declared in terms that characteristically combine the gist of Nietzsche's thinking with the hermetic abstractness of Heidegger's style of writing. Far from being an atavism from a remote era of dark superstition, the "Demon," Foucault suggests, is "something strange and unsettling that leaves one baffled and motionless: the Same, the perfect Likeness"—the very image of our being, if only we would recognize it. In this context, Foucault goes on to point out the crucial role played by "the Demon" in one of Nietzsche's most famous aphorisms: "What if some day or night a demon were to steal after you into your loneliest loneliness and say to you: 'This life as you now live it, and have lived it, you will have to live once more and innumerable times more. . . .' "[18]

Nietzsche's Demon is, like the Greek *daimon*, a figure of fate. He poses a difficult challenge: to become what one is, one must welcome not only chaos and transcendence and the power to start anew, but also embrace every unchangeable aspect of the past, every uncontrollable aspect of the present, every unintended result in the future. " 'The eternal hourglass of existence is turned upside down again and again, and you with it, speck of dust.' " To be able truly to *love* this fate—even if it seems at first glance a "dreadful accident"—would then amount, in Foucault's terms, to recognizing that the Demon represents the perfect Likeness of "*I myself*" and saying, with joy: " 'You are a *god* and never have I heard anything more divine.' "[19]

"What returns," writes Nietzsche, "what finally comes home to me, is my own self."[20]

But that is just the start of "the great Nietzschean quest." For however one awakens to the existence of one's *daimon*—in a mug of beer, in a darkened theater, in an ecstasy or trance, or perhaps simply while reading a book by a philosopher like Schopenhauer or Nietzsche (or Foucault)— this uncanny sense of suddenly finding one's "higher necessity" wrenches anybody who experiences it out of the routines and habits of everyday life. It leaves a person "baffled and motionless," as if paralyzed by "a frightful decision." For now the person concerned about measuring up to his or her own fate "must descend," as Nietzsche puts it, "into the depths of existence with a string of curious questions on his lips: Why am I alive? What lesson am I to learn from life? How did I become what I am and why do I suffer from being what I am?" The man who seriously pursues such questions "tortures himself," writes Nietzsche, and "observes that nobody else tortures himself in the same way."[21]

Foucault's effort to address Nietzsche's questions began in earnest with his inquiry into the work of Ludwig Binswanger. In 1953, Binswanger was in the twilight of his career. He had been born in 1881 into an eminent family line of Swiss physicians and psychiatrists—his uncle, Otto Binswanger, had treated Nietzsche during the philosopher's final years of madness. Educated at the University of Zurich, the younger Binswanger came to know C. G. Jung, who introduced him to Freud. Through every subsequent twist and turn in the psychoanalytic movement he remained loyal to Freud. Not that Binswanger toed the party line: in 1927, yearning to integrate "something like a basic religious category" of spirit into Freud's understanding of the human being, he found the words for what he was trying to say in the pages of Heidegger's *Being and Time,* which appeared that year. In his subsequent work, Freud's notion of eros, like Heidegger's idea of authenticity, becomes suffused with Binswanger's own implicitly religious preoccupation with "love": only the redemptive power of the union of "I and Thou" can offer the human being a healing sense of spiritual wholeness. "If Nietzsche and psychoanalysis have shown that instinctuality, especially in the form of sexuality, extends its reach up to the highest pinnacles of human spirituality," Binswanger wrote in 1932, "then we have attempted to show the degree to which spirituality extends its reach down to the deepest valleys of 'vitality.'"[22]

Foucault had come to Binswanger's work through the interest of Jacqueline Verdeaux, a young protégé of Jacques Lacan who was then studying at the Hôpital Sainte-Anne. In 1952, she had embarked on the first translation of Binswanger's work into French. Since Foucault, as a serious reader of Heidegger, could explain Binswanger's philosophical terminology, she requested his help on the translation. In the following months, the two of them had gone together not only to talk with Binswanger directly about his work, but also to consult with Gaston Bachelard, whose studies of reverie had been an important influence on the Swiss psychiatrist.[23]

Foucault approached Binswanger's work with characteristic thoroughness. Daniel Defert reports finding after Foucault's death carefully marked copies of all of Binswanger's major articles and books, from *Changes in Understanding and Interpretation of the Dream From the Greeks to the Present* (1928) to *The Basic Forms and Knowledge of Human 'Dasein'* (1942).[24]

And Foucault could not help pondering the psychiatrist's most famous clinical paper, "The Case of Ellen West." First published in 1944, this study offers a stunning account of a suicidal patient, one whose agonizing fate—much like Foucault's own—was to struggle with the wish to die.

At the time of her referral to Binswanger's sanatorium, Ellen West was thirty-three. A bright, well-educated, and uncommonly articulate middle-class woman, she suffered from anorexia and depression. Since the age of twenty-one, she had been consumed by uncontrollable fantasies of dying: "Death is the greatest happiness in life," she declares in one of the diaries that Binswanger quotes—it is Ellen's own voice, indeed, that gives Binswanger's paper much of its emotional force. [25]

Though her moods subsequently ebbed and flowed, the possibility of dying remained Ellen West's only certain consolation. She submerged herself in academic work and became enmeshed in a romantic triangle, meanwhile growing ever more emaciated. At the age of twenty-eight, she finally married one of her suitors; but her weight continued to fall, finally reaching a point where her health was in jeopardy.

At the age of thirty-three, having spent most of the previous decade trying to starve herself to death, she attempted to commit suicide four times. She overdosed twice on pills, threw herself in front of a car, and tried to jump out of her analyst's window. After the last attempt, she was committed to an asylum, and shortly afterward transferred to the care of Dr. Binswanger.

In her diary from these days, Ellen West complains that "I don't understand myself at all. It is terrible not to understand yourself. *I confront myself as a strange person.* I am afraid of myself, I am afraid of the feelings to which I am defenselessly delivered over every minute. This is the horrible part of my life: It is filled with dread. . . . Existence is only torture. . . . Life has become a prison camp. . . . I long to be violated—*and indeed I do violence to myself every hour.*" [26]

"The murderer who constantly sees in his mind's eye the picture of the victim," she continues, "must feel somewhat as I do. He can work, even slave, from early until late, can go out, can talk, can attempt to divert himself: all in vain. Always and always again he will see the picture of the victim before him. He feels an overpowering pull toward the place of the murder. He knows that this makes him suspect. Even worse—he has a horror of that place, but still he must go there. Something that is stronger than his reason and his will controls him and makes of his life a frightful scene of devastation." [27]

In her sessions with Binswanger, Ellen West is alert, amiable, and apparently consumed by the desire to die: "I can find no redemption—except in death." [28]

On the basis of his interviews, her diaries, and material gathered from her husband, Binswanger diagnoses a "progressive schizophrenic psychosis." He consults with two other psychiatrists, who agree that her case is hopeless. They decide that Ellen West should be released from the asylum, even though she will almost certainly kill herself. When Binswanger tells her husband of this plan, he concurs. Ellen West returns home. Three days later, she is in a strangely festive mood. That night she takes a lethal dose of poison, and dies. [29]

"Desperately not wanting to be oneself but 'different,' " Binswanger comments, and at the same time "desperately wanting to be oneself—such desperation clearly has a special relationship to death. When the torture of despair consists precisely in this, that one cannot die, that even the last hope, death, does not come, that one cannot get rid of oneself, then suicide, as in our case, and with it the Nothingness, takes on a 'desperately' positive meaning." Thus Ellen West's final embrace of death is paradoxically festive, "not only because death comes as a friend, . . . but also for the much deeper reason that in the voluntary-necessary resolve for death the existence is no longer 'desperately itself' but has authentically and totally become itself! [30]

"Only in her decision for death did she find herself and choose herself. The festival of death was the festival of the birth of her existence. But where the existence can exist only by relinquishing life, there the existence is a tragic existence." [31]

Foucault found "The Case of Ellen West" fascinating. West, he wrote in one of his two comments on the case, was "caught between the wish to fly, to float in an ethereal jubilation, and the obsessive fear of being trapped in a muddy earth that oppressed and paralyzed her." To fly toward death, "that distant and lofty space of light," was to end life. But by committing suicide, "a totally free existence could arise"—if only for a moment—"one that would no longer know the weight of living but only that transparency where love is totalized in the eternity of an instant." [32]

That Foucault found in Binswanger an unusually sympathetic guide to understanding a preoccupation with dying is obvious enough. But that was not the sole reason Binswanger was important to Foucault in these months. For Binswanger's work not only described suicide with unusual forbearance, as the last, best hope of some human beings; it also suggested a constructive means of recognizing, and unriddling, in Nietzsche's terms, "what one is."

Foucault had been helping Jacqueline Verdeaux translate a paper, "Dream and Existence," which Binswanger had originally published in 1930. When the translation was finished, Verdeaux asked her collaborator if he might like to write an introduction. Foucault said yes. And a few months later, around Easter 1954, Foucault sent her his text. At first, Verdeaux was stunned: Foucault's piece was more than twice as long as Binswanger's original essay. But when she sat down to read it, she became more and more excited.[33]

Foucault had found his voice at last.

At first glance, Foucault's introduction looks utterly conventional. Ostensibly an exegesis of Binswanger's work, it offers the kind of "commentary" that Foucault himself would later take pains to reject. Like his only other published work from this period, the book *Mental Illness and Personality*, the essay concludes on an old-fashioned, quasi-Marxist note of optimism about "objective history" and the "ethical task" of "real man."[34]

But these first impressions are misleading. For a closer examination of Foucault's essay reveals that it has only the most tenuous of ties to Binswanger's thought—or to Foucault's own professed faith in the historical calling of "real man," which in this context sounds like a hopelessly wan prayer for deliverance. Indeed, like Nietzsche's "Schopenhauer as Educator," Foucault's essay on Binswanger really offers a vision, under the pretext of speaking about something else, of the author's *own* "innermost history" and inescapable destiny, a destiny that is now to be deciphered not through a social or class analysis, as a Marxist might assume—but rather through a proper understanding of "the dream."

Binswanger's original essay, of course, was also about dreams. Following Freud, Binswanger regarded dreams as "the royal road to the unconscious." But in this seminal essay, Binswanger reinterpreted dreams in the light of Heidegger's *Being and Time*. Freud, he implies, was wrong to explain dreams as the repository only of repressed wishes and their (unreal) fulfillment, representing the vicissitudes of animal instincts; for the dream, Binswanger asserts, is also a repository of intelligible fantasies arising from everyday experience, fantasies that might yet become useful in conscious existence. Thus one of the tasks of psychoanalysis, in Binswanger's view, is to help the dreamer wake up and start translating his or her fantasies into reality. In Heideggerian terms, the dream itself is "inauthentic," almost by definition, for it is the product, according to Binswanger, of a "self-forgetting" existence. In order to become authentic, the human being must "*make* something" of itself, in the shared sphere of history; only then does the human being (or *Dasein*) emerge, healed and whole, to "participate in the life of the universal"—a vision of the ultimate goal that Binswanger borrows from Hegel as much as from Heidegger.[35] Yet for all the philosophical window-dressing, the clinical point of dream-analysis for Binswanger remains broadly what it was for Freud: a means of helping patients to recover a sense of mastery over their lives that restores them to effective functioning in the real world.

Foucault in his introduction, by contrast, turns both Binswanger and Freud upside down. "Psychoanalysis," he bluntly asserts, "has never succeeded in making images speak." And after some preliminary praise for Binswanger, Foucault makes it perfectly clear that he will go his own way, even if the result seems to be "a problematic that Binswanger never formulated."[36]

Foucault's main thesis is shockingly simple: the dream "is the birth of the world," "the origin of existence itself." The dream must therefore be approached, not as a psychological symptom to be analysed, but rather as a key for solving the riddle of being—just as André Breton and the surrealists had been arguing since the 1920s.[37]

"In the darkest night," writes Foucault, "the glow of the dream is more luminous than the light of day, and the intuition borne with it the most elevated form of knowledge." Far from being "inauthentic," as Binswanger supposes, the dream can "throw into bright light the secret and hidden power at work in the most manifest forms of presence." For Foucault, the dream is a privileged domain for thinking through what Heidegger called the unthought—a shadowy clearing where, in a moment of vision, a human being can, as it were, recognize itself and grasp its fate.[38]

The "inauthenticity" of Ellen West's existence, from Foucault's perspective, lay in the fact that she tried, up till the last moment of her life, to evade her fate, running away from the fascination with dying that her dreams disclosed, fleeing through starvation from "the imminence of this death attached to her flesh," unable and unwilling to "take up her past in the authentic form of repetition."[39]

What must be "repeated"—the fate one needs to embrace, according to Nietzsche's parable of eternal recurrence—is precisely what the dream reveals. While dreaming, a human being "is an existence carving itself out in barren space, shattering in chaos, exploding in pandemonium, netting itself, a scarcely breathing animal, in the webs of death." Out of this chaotic vortex are spun certain themes, motifs that recur over and over again, entangling "an existence fallen of its own motion into a definite determination," pointing toward an inescapable fate. "Man has known, since antiquity, that in dreams he encounters what he is and what he will be, what he has done and what he is going to do, discovering there the knot that ties his freedom to the necessity of the world."[40]

Here Foucault joins with Binswanger against Freud, insisting that the fate revealed in the dream cannot be reduced to "the biological equipment of the libidinal instinct." The ancient Greeks and romantic poets were closer to the mark: "In the dream, the soul, freed of its body, plunges into the *kosmos,* becomes immersed in it, and mingles with its motions in a sort of aquatic union." Encapsulated in the dream is "the whole Odyssey of human freedom," illuminating "what is most individual in the individual," the "ethical content" of a singular life. As Nietzsche once put it, "nothing is *more* your own than your dreams."[41]

Foucault agrees. In the dream, he writes, we find "the heart laid bare."[42]

But what if "the heart laid bare" reveals only the most disquieting of oracles? "One must desire to dream and know how to dream," Baudelaire had declared in the famous journal he entitled "My Heart Laid Bare": "A magic art. To sit down at once and write." But to what purpose? For what Baudelaire's dreams revealed when he wrote them down was a "delight in bloodshed," "the intoxication of the tortured (Damiens)," a "natural delight in crime," a "natural pleasure in destruction," an inescapable feeling that "cruelty and sensual pleasure are identical, like extreme heat and extreme cold."[43]

Foucault's dreams also seethe with cruelty and destruction. When he consults "the law of my heart," in order to "read my destiny there," he discovers not only that "I am not my own master," but that he is possessed by a "determination to ruin the simplest things."[44]

Passing over fantasies of crime, torture, and bloodshed, Foucault dreams an even darker dream. Like Ellen West, he dreams a dream of death, and of death alone, "of violent death, of savage death, of horrified death."[45]

"In the depth of his dream," writes Foucault, "what man encounters is his death, a death which in its most inauthentic form is but the brutal and bloody interruption of life, yet in its authentic form, is the fulfillment of his very existence."[46]

"Suicide is the ultimate myth," he goes on to explain: "the 'Last Judgment' of the imagination, as the dream is its genesis, its absolute origin. . . . Every suicidal desire is filled by that world in which I would no longer be present here, or there, but everywhere, in every sector: a world transparent to me and signifying its indebtedness to my absolute presence.

Suicide is not a way of cancelling the world or myself, or the two together, but a way of rediscovering the original moment in which I make myself world. . . . To commit suicide is the ultimate mode of imagining." To dream one's death as "the fulfillment of existence" is to imagine, over and over again, "the moment in which life reaches its fullness in a world about to close in."[47]

This, then, is Foucault's "heart laid bare." He has met his *daimon*—and it is his hangman.

But what could he do with this revelation? West embraced her "higher necessity" by killing herself. Was there some other, equally "authentic form of repetition" by which one might "say yes," in the spirit of Nietzsche—even to a recurrent fantasy of death?[48]

Such questions preoccupied not only Foucault but also the circle of young artists and musicians he was part of, which included the brilliant young composer Jean Barraqué, Foucault's friend and lover during the time he was grappling with his dream essay. "I owe my first great cultural jolt," Foucault remarked in a 1967 interview, "to the French serialists and deodecaphonic musicians—such as Boulez and Barraqué—to whom I was linked by relations of friendship." Along with Beckett, these composers represented for Foucault "the first 'tear' in the dialectical universe in which I had lived."[49]

In 1948, at the age of twenty, Barraqué had joined the celebrated seminar in musical analysis conducted by Olivier Messiaen. Open only to students of remarkable promise, this seminar attracted some of the most gifted young composers of the postwar period, Pierre Boulez and Karlheinz Stockhausen among them. Messiaen himself was a composer of profoundly religious feeling, but the methods he used, and taught, were anything but pious. In his own music, he employed Gregorian melodies, bird calls, Asiatic rhythms—and in his advanced analysis seminar, he demanded that students master the language of serialism. Introduced by Arnold Schoenberg in the 1920s and later refined by Alban Berg and Anton Webern, serialism is a method of composition in which one or more musical elements are ordered in a fixed series that is then used to organize themes and variations. Schoenberg applied the technique to create "tone rows" from the twelve pitch-classes of the well-tempered scale; Messiaen and his young disciples expanded the technique to organize virtually every element of a composition, from the dynamics and duration of sounds to their timbre and pitch.[50]

When Foucault first met Barraqué, in 1952, the composer was part of a band of crusading young rebels, uncompromising serialists all, which included Pierre Boulez. It was, in fact, Boulez, three years Barraqué's elder, whom Foucault had first met. By 1952, Boulez had already produced a number of important works: two piano sonatas, a string quartet, and also two remarkable cantatas based on the poetry of René Char. Inspired by Char's hermetic language and the possibilities for a similar form of expression opened up by serialism, Boulez's early compositions aimed to convey the most high-strung of emotions through the most austere of formal structures. The verbal instructions for the final chord of his First Sonata aptly summed up his youthful style: "very brutal and very dry." Inspired by the renegade surrealist Antonin Artaud and his ideas about a "theater of cruelty," Boulez in the late 1940s declared that "music should be collective hysteria and spells." Indeed, one of his cantatas based on Char's poetry, *Le visage nuptial*, grew out of an episode of personal hysteria in Boulez's life, a tormented love affair that had climaxed with an abortive joint-suicide pact.[51]

Jean Barraqué shared Boulez's violent expressivism—if anything, he wished to raise it to an even higher pitch of apocalyptic fervor. "For me music is everything," Barraqué explained in an interview four years before his death in 1973. "Music is drama, it is pathos, it is death. It is an utter gamble, trembling on the verge of suicide. If music is not that, if it is not the exceeding of limits, it is nothing."[52]

A self-styled "*musicien maudit,*" the young man whom Foucault fell in love with had dedicated his life to a lonely and difficult quest for the absolute. He was physically unimposing, with a sallow, puffy face framed by thick glasses that, in some photographs, magnified a gaze of driven intensity. Like Baudelaire and the surrealists, Barraqué wished to live life on the edge. "Creativity in its aesthetic necessity," he declared in 1952, "remains incomprehensible," unless one "starts with the moment where 'it explodes' "—that moment when "a man involuntarily leaves the rational in order to enter the irrational, becoming mad." In the spirit of Rimbaud, another of his heroes, Barraqué worked at making himself "a *seer* by a long, gigantic and rational *derangement of the senses,*" exploring "all forms of love, suffering, and madness," exhausting "all poisons in himself," extracting "only their quintessences" through the systematic use of intoxicants—alcohol was his favorite—and concentrating the force of his personal revelations in the intricate forms of his music. His musical idol was the Beethoven of the final sonatas and late quartets; and like Richard Wagner, he dreamed of creating a "total artwork," a composition bold enough to take the measure of a century he considered calamitous: for Barraqué, as for Foucault, a world of death camps and total war demanded a work of epic ambition and dithyrambic fury.[53]

A perfectionist even more fanatical than Boulez, Barraqué by 1952 had produced only one composition he deemed suitable for performance: a piano sonata. Demanding, intense, sustained, it instantly earned the composer a reputation in new music circles as one of the great geniuses of his generation. As the critic André Hodeir, a friend and champion of Barraqué's music, once described it, the sonata "is the Orphean work par excellence, inviting the listener on a journey to the Underworld from which there is no return. . . . Here, for the first time in history, perhaps, Music comes face to face with her arch-enemy, Silence," crystallizing a "despair in which the Dionysian spirit reveals its most secret visage"—the face of death. "The finale attains a summit of agonizing grandeur; the relentless process is coming to an end now, and Music cracks under the inhuman strain, disintegrates and is sucked into the void. Whole slabs of sound crumble and vanish beneath the all-engulfing ocean of silence, until only the twelve notes of the [serial tone] row remain, and even these are plucked off, one by one."[54]

For both Barraqué and Foucault, the problem was this: if, probing beyond the limits of reason, the mind sooner or later—in dreaming, in drinking, in moments of shared erotic rapture—discovers that "Being" and "the nothing," life and death, are "the Same," what, then, is the point of "the great Nietzschean quest"—or of any quest at all?

Samuel Beckett, burdened with a similar experience of the world, had spoken of how "paradoxically, through form, by giving form to what is formless, the artist can find a possible way out." Formalism—embraced with a vengeance—was certainly the way out for Barraqué and Boulez. In a 1983 interview, Foucault in fact suggested that formalism was a more important influence on his own work than so-called "structuralism." "I'm not sure how interesting it would be to attempt a redefinition of . . . structuralism," Foucault remarked. "It would be interesting, though, to study formal thought and the different kinds of formalism that ran through Western culture during the twentieth century. When we consider the extraordinary destiny of formalism in painting or formal research in music, or the importance of formalism in the analysis of folklore and legend"—the fields of interest to Georges Dumézil, who in 1955 would become one of Foucault's closest scholarly friends—"it is clear that formalism in general has probably been one of the strongest and at the same time one of the most varied currents in twentieth-century Europe."[55]

Music and the analysis of folklore were not the only areas of formalist ferment that interested Foucault in these years. Between 1953 and 1956, he also followed closely the book reviews published each month in the *Nouvelle Revue Française* by Maurice Blanchot—a critic preoccupied, like both Barraqué and Foucault, with the relationship between the formal unities of an artwork and the anguish of the artist haunted by death.[56]

In the 1950s, Maurice Blanchot was one of France's most famous invisible men. A working critic whose stature in his own country warrants comparison with Edmund Wilson's in America, Blanchot eschewed any direct contact with his public. Like J. D. Salinger, he generated a mystique and sustained a kind of cult following by making a fetish of anonymity. He permitted no photographs of himself to circulate. He never lectured or read his work in public. He granted no interviews, though he did make a habit of "interviewing" himself.[57]

Foucault found Blanchot's mystique irresistible. "At that time, I dreamt of being Blanchot," he confided to one friend years later. A close student of Blanchot's critical theories, he also studied his rhetoric, using the device of "interviewing" himself in his book *Raymond Roussel* and also at the end of *The Archeology of Knowledge*. In a touching homage to the faceless author, he even turned down an invitation to meet Blanchot over dinner, remarking to Daniel Defert that he knew the writing—and had no need to know the writer.[58]

Literary scholars have been less reverent. In spite of Blanchot's painstaking gestures of self-effacement, they have managed to cobble together the outlines of a portrait. A member of Sartre's generation, Blanchot admits to having been born in 1907. He has also confessed that it was through his friendship with Emmanuel Levinas, a Lithuanian Jewish emigré who became one of the earliest French students of phenomenology and existentialism, that he discovered Heidegger's *Being and Time* shortly after it appeared in 1927.[59]

Like Heidegger, Blanchot in these years was alarmed by the Decline of the West. In the 1930s, he supported France's most important fascist political party, Action Française, and published essays in the right-wing journal *Combat* castigating the cowardice of France's political elite.[60]

Germany's invasion of France changed all this. A fervent patriot above all, Blanchot joined the Resistance. The experience left him chastened: and after the war, he disavowed activism and, like the Heidegger of the "Letter on Humanism," embraced instead "a passivity beyond all passivity."[61]

In the decade after the war, Blanchot transcribed into a plain yet fittingly opaque French many of Heidegger's most enigmatic and characteristic concerns—with death and "the nothing," with the "nameless" and "unthought." He explored these ideas as well in a series of increasingly austere and actionless *récits* that helped clear the way for the "new novel" of Alain Robbe-Grillet and others. Composed in style both "graceful and maddening," as an exasperated American reviewer once summed it up, Blanchot's fiction offered "a cascade of mystification bejewelled with melodramatic glances and gothic gewgaws."[62]

"It is extremely hard to find a language faithful to this thought," Foucault conceded in the essay he published in 1966 about Blanchot's work. When a writer like Blanchot (or Heidegger, for that matter) takes language to its limits, "what it finds," Foucault writes, "is not a positivity that contradicts it, but the void that will obliterate it." To confront, through writing, this void, Foucault nevertheless felt to be the authentic if elusive task of the author. Only such a confrontation, he asserts (agreeing with Blanchot and Heidegger) can free the author "for a new beginning—a beginning that is a pure origin because its only principles are itself and the void."[63]

According to Blanchot, every truly powerful work of art is a singular compound of form and chaos: "The work is the pure circle where, even as he writes the work, the author dangerously exposes himself to, but also protects himself against, the pressure that demands that he write." Like André Breton and the surrealists, Blanchot regarded works wrested from delirium, dreaming, and the terrible beauty of uncontrollable passion as communicating a special kind of wisdom. The dream, he once declared, amounts to a "dangerous call," a "premonition of the other," a "double that is still somebody." Exploring the unconscious and the unthought, what an author discovers is "a part of himself, and, more than that, his truth, his solitary truth," swirling in "a cold immobility from which he cannot turn away, but near which he cannot linger"—for the repetitions and recurrences are (just as Freud had divined in his analysis of *thanatos,* Blanchot noted) the siren song "of death itself."[64]

The writer in Blanchot's view thus becomes a figure strangely like Ellen West: someone who cannot help being fascinated by death, "attracted by an ordeal in which everything is risked, by an essential risk where being is at stake, where nothingness slips away, where, that is, the right, the power to die is wagered."[65]

Yet if the work that grows out of such an ordeal is successful, the author will not only survive, he will (just as Heidegger promised) experience a miraculous kind of ascent into grace: "Through an inexplicable maneuver, through some distraction or through the sheer excessiveness of his patience," the author will find himself "suddenly inside the circle," folded back upon himself, the void now contained by the work, which "forms a part of himself from which he feels he is free and from which the work has contributed to freeing him."[66]

The forms in which a work could accomplish this magical feat of transforming (and so "saving") its author were as protean and varied as the creative genius of each truly creative individual. As a matter of taste, Blanchot was a connoisseur of modernism: in the late 1940s and 1950s, he devoted incisive essays to the poets Baudelaire, Rimbaud, Mallarmé, Rilke, and René Char; and to the novelists and short-story writers Kafka, Beckett, Borges, and Robbe-Grillet. He was the only prominent French critic of the time to take the Marquis de Sade as seriously as Foucault did. And he was a dedicated reader of modern philosophy: besides Heidegger, he admired Nietzsche, and also the pioneering French Nietzschean, Georges Bataille.[67]

But the most important gift that Blanchot gave to Foucault and, through him, to Jean Barraqué in these years, may well have been an appreciation for Hermann Broch's great novel *The Death of Virgil*—one of the most sustained and lyrical treatments of death ever written.

Broch's book, wrote Blanchot in his review of the French translation that appeared in 1955, was nothing less than "the answer. . . . Not that his book tells us what unity is—rather, it is the picture of unity itself." For Foucault and Barraqué, Broch's book became the model of everything a *work*, in Blanchot's strong sense, could be.[68]

Broch, too, knew that he had accomplished something extraordinary with his book. When it first appeared in German in 1945, the experimental form of the work invited comparison with James Joyce's *Ulysses*. On one level, the novel, which describes the last day in the life of the Roman poet Virgil, was designed as an allegory of a civilization in its death-throes; on still another, deeper level, the book drew upon Broch's own inward preparation to face death when he was thrown into prison in Austria (his crime was being Jewish). Above all, Broch himself wished the book to be nothing less than "a *lyrical commentary on the self*"—a demonstration of the fragile unity that a man may make of his life when, like Broch's Virgil (and Nietzsche's Zarathustra) he comes to realize that "in my beginning is my end, in my end is my beginning."[69]

An epic interior monologue, the book again and again pressed language to the limits of intelligibility, unfurling words in endless sentences, using repetition and incantation to generate a stream of percussive sounds that rocked gently back and forth like the waves lapping at the bark on which the poet floated helplessly toward his death. And at the center of this odyssey, both literally and figuratively, stood five elegies on fate, evoking the "million-faceted transparency of dreaming" with its inexhaustible tidings of "myself," "Creation" and death. By combining images born of fate and the freedom to order the world anew, the dream, according to the cosmogony of Broch's book, revealed the mysterious unity of being, bridging past and future, memory and prophecy, life and the "homecoming" of death.[70]

For Jean Barraqué, Broch's book became an unrelenting obsession. After reading it, he decided to set the text to music, and create an epic opera that would be longer than *Parsifal* and *The Saint Matthew Passion* combined, a piece of music that would confirm, he hoped, his genius as the greatest composer of his era (for such and nothing less it was his ambition to become).[71]

Foucault's interest in the book, though less consuming, was equally profound. If the "Case of Ellen West" expressed, as few pieces of writing do, the inner experience of a human being haunted by the wish to die, *The Death of Virgil* for nearly five hundred pages evoked the experience of dying itself—not as a frightening fate but as a unique affirmation of life, language, and spirit, in "the word beyond speech."[72]

Perhaps to dream of death was mad. Perhaps the experience of the void eluded every effort to communicate it. Perhaps the nihilism palpable in the death camps could find in a work that embraced the void no adequate response. Perhaps the very ideas of the void, the Nothing and the "unthought" were solecisms as pointless and sterile as the archaic belief in demons.

But Broch's novel, like Blanchot's theory of literature, suggested otherwise. And so did the work of Georges Bataille, the tutelary spirit whose example, more than any other in these decisive years, suggested to Foucault how to expand further and radically deepen "the great Nietzschean quest" he was now embarked upon by making his sexuality and bodily desires yet another field of philosophical inquiry—and yet another possible arena for grappling with the Demon of death.

Years later, Foucault would introduce the first volume of Gallimard's handsome edition of Bataille's *Complete Works* by calling him "one of the most important writers of our century."[73] But in the mid-fifties, Bataille, unlike Blanchot, scarcely had an audience. His early essays were scattered in obscure scholarly journals and avant-garde reviews. Most French readers, if they knew his name at all, knew of him only as the editor of *Critique*, the journal that Bataille founded in 1946.

Born in 1897, Bataille was trained as a medievalist; he also had studied with the celebrated French anthropologist Marcel Mauss. In the 1920s, he began what became a lifelong, though stormy, relationship with the surrealist movement and its leader, André Breton. By then, Bataille was an avid Nietzschean as well, thanks to a reading of *Beyond Good and Evil* that had shattered, once and for all, his youthful faith in God.[74]

Supporting himself between 1922 and 1942 by working as a librarian at the Bibliothèque Nationale, Bataille wrote prolifically. He produced scholarly monographs, violent polemics, speculative anthropological treatises, pornographic novels of an exquisitely sado-masochistic temper, and, perhaps most impressive of all, a three-volume collection of highly personal and sometimes oracular aphorisms, immodestly presented to the world as the *Summa Atheologica*—Bataille's deliberately perverse response to the systematic theology of St. Thomas Aquinas.

Like Nietzsche, Bataille throughout his life sang the praises of Dionysian moments of communal effervescence, of reverie and madness, of intoxication and ecstasy—all "moments of excess that stir us to the roots of our being and give us strength enough to allow free rein to our elemental nature." And like the Marquis de Sade, his other great intellectual hero, he thought that impulses commonly called cruel were central to our elemental nature: the pursuit of an uninhibited eroticism laid bare a deep-seated drive "to destroy," "to annihilate," to spoil even the simplest things, and (at the limit) to embrace death in a "torment of orgies," in a sensuous lust for blood so sanguinary that it welcomed even "the agony of war."[75]

On one level, this was sheer bluster: like the mousy protagonist in one of his favorite books, Dostoyevsky's *Notes From Underground*, Bataille took malicious delight in being "impossible," in making outrageous statements and stubbornly standing by them. But on another level, Bataille was a deeply serious man. An habitué of the demimonde, he acted out a great many of the erotic fantasies he described. And some of his most alarming political ideas he earnestly tried to put into practice.[76]

In the 1930s for example, he entertained the possibility of creating a neo-pagan society, organized around sacred rituals of death and human sacrifice. In these same years, Bataille and a few friends, hoping to recapture the sanguinary élan of the ancient Aztecs, laid plans to stage an actual "sacrifice" of their own. Evoking nothing so much as a French version of Leopold and Loeb, Bataille's group even targeted a specific victim. But then World War II broke out, spoiling the point of the gesture.[77]

As Bataille would later concede, some of his writing in this period brought him uncomfortably close to fascism. But Bataille also embraced a bizarre kind of Marxism, believing (with apparent fervor in the 1930s) that the only way to unleash the alienated elemental nature of the human being was through "a fiery and bloody revolution" that would smash the suffocating values Bataille associated not just with bourgeois legality and capitalism, but also with nationalism and organized militarism.[78]

For Foucault in these years, however, the heart of Bataille's achievement was not his theory of revolution, but rather his understanding of erotic transgression. "Perhaps one day," Foucault speculated in an essay written shortly after Bataille's death in 1962, the idea of transgression "will seem as decisive for our culture, as much a part of its soil, as the experience of contradiction was at an earlier time for dialectical thought."[79]

"Transgression," as Foucault defines Bataille's idea, "is an act which involves the limit," violently breaching the customary restraints on sexual behavior and putting into play the sort of " 'denaturalized' " eroticism so vividly imagined by the Marquis de Sade. The very violence of Sade's erotic fantasies testifies to the force of those elemental impulses that most modern societies have tried to brand as abnormal. Yet even the most civilized creatures of modern cultures, as Foucault had remarked in 1954, "can and must make of man a negative experience, lived in the form of hate and aggression." It was Bataille's peculiar genius to suggest that eroticism, taken to its most extreme limits in sado-masochistic practices, was a uniquely creative way to grapple with otherwise unconscious and unthinkable aspects of this "negative experience," turning it into something positive, enabling a person to "say yes" in the spirit of Nietzsche—even to a recurrent fantasy of death.[80]

Foucault, like Bataille, had more than a theoretical interest in transgression. In these years, he evidently began to explore for himself a "shattering of the philosophical subject," not just through intoxication and dreaming—but also through an erotic kind of "suffering" that *breaks apart.* In his 1962 essay on transgression, he quoted one of Bataille's most lyrical descriptions of the experience, which evokes a moment of "divine agony" when "I instantly reenter the night of a lost child, and enter the anguish, in order to prolong a rapture with no end other than exhaustion and no exit other than fainting. It is the joy of torture."[81]

This most excruciating (and mysterious) of pleasures was not an end in itself for either Bataille or Foucault. For Bataille, it was one basis for a kind of philosophical critique, laying bare the "nonsense of the will to know"—and the purely negative freedom of the human being. By illuminating the enigma of transcendence, sado-masochistic eroticism offered an esoteric but potentially fruitful means of self-analysis, a way to pursue a "psychological quest." And at the ultimate limit, where torture turned into ecstasy, a voluptuously painful eroticism made possible as well a "negative theology founded on mystical experience," permitting a person (in Bataille's words) "to look death in the face and to perceive in death the pathway into unknowable and incomprehensible continuity."[82]

Foucault agreed. "Nothing is negative in transgression," he declared in his 1962 essay on Bataille, explaining (and implicitly defending) a form of extreme erotic experience that is simultaneously "pure" and "confused." By letting its most agonizing impulses run wild in an erotic theater of cruelty, a human being might "recognize itself for the first time"—and simultaneously feel the transformative force of "the *transcendens* pure and simple." "Transgression," Foucault writes, thus "affirms the limited being"—namely, the human being—"and it affirms this limitlessness into which it leaps," opening a space of possible transfiguration and offering us moderns our "*sole* manner of discovering the sacred in its unmediated content." Because this was the occult prospect conjured up by Bataille's books, Foucault was only exaggerating slightly when he described them as a kind of "consecration undone: a transubstantiation ritualized in reverse"—an unholy communion with uncanny *daimonic* forces, "where real presence becomes again a recumbent body."[83]

That Bataille's claim to originality rests, in part, on his approach to eroticism seems clear enough. Nietzsche, for all of his talk about bodies and power, was a man mortified by his own sexuality; it is in this area that Bataille most dramatically extends his master's thought. That the uninhibited pursuit of eroticism might enable a person to "say yes" to life, even "up to the point of death," also seems plausible. Through the imaginative dramas that give to erotic rituals a pattern and unity, human beings can act out freely, and so gain a sense of mastery over, impulses and memories otherwise experienced as involuntary and perhaps intolerable. In fact, much that seems farfetched about Bataille's way of thinking—his stress on the hateful and morbid aspects of sexual excitement, and his belief that cruel and unusual forms of eroticism can help carry a human being "to the farthest bound of possibility"—has been corroborated, albeit in more modest terms, by other students of sexual excitement, and by other aficionados of consensual sado-masochism. According to their testimony, it is indeed possible to heal old wounds and to experience a kind of mystical rapture through forms of erotic behavior that transform guilt into joy, pain into pleasure, torture into ecstasy, and (most miraculously of all) the wish to die into an overwhelming and unspeakable feeling of love: sometimes for another human being; sometimes for the world in its "unknowable and incomprehensible continuity;" and sometimes simply for "what one is."[84]

As Foucault expressed this possibility in typically oblique terms, a human being who in the paroxysm of the erotic moment embraces the "pure violence" of forbidden pleasures might feel paradoxically "fulfilled," momentarily satisfied "by this alien plenitude which invades it to the core of its being," revealing "its positive truth in its downward fall."[85]

Or, as one of Bataille's besotted erotic heroes describes the experience in *Story of the Eye*, the greatest of his novels: "It struck me that death was the sole outcome of my erection" and that "the goal of my sexual licentiousness" was "a geometric incandescence (among other things, the coinciding point of life and death, being and nothingness), perfectly fulgurating."[86]

These preoccupations can be found, beautifully sublimated, in Jean Barraqué's most important composition from this period, *Séquence*, a concerto for soprano, percussion and "diverse instruments," which he completed in 1955. Barraqué had begun work on *Séquence* before meeting Foucault, planning at first to use poems by Rimbaud and the surrealist Paul Eluard as texts. Foucault, however, persuaded his lover to drop these texts and to use, instead, four poems by Nietzsche. The work is carefully shaped to climax with the most important of the poems, "Ariadne's Lament."[87]

Nietzsche's poem appears in both *Thus Spoke Zarathustra* and, in slightly expanded form, in the *Dithyrambs of Dionysus*, the small volume of poetry Nietzsche published in 1888, shortly before he collapsed on a street in Turin and went mad. At the heart of "Ariadne's Lament" is one of the key intuitions that Nietzsche in fact shares with Sade: that pleasure and pain are permeable, and that experiencing the transmutation of pain into pleasure, of hate into love, in Dionysian ecstasy, is the beginning of wisdom. As Gilles Deleuze would later gloss the philosophical subtext of the poem, "what we in fact know of the will to power is suffering and torture, but the will to power is still the unknown joy, the unknown happiness, the unknown God."[88]

In the poem, Ariadne bewails her fate. For her, love is an unremitting ordeal. Why, she cries, must "I lie, bend myself, twist myself, tortured by every eternal torment, smitten by you. . . . Why do you look down, unwearied of human pain, with malicious divine flashing eyes? Will you not kill, only torment, torment? Why—torment *me*, you malicious, unknown god?"[89]

"Be wise, Ariadne!" Dionysus admonishes her at the end of the last version of the poem, the one that Barraqué uses: "Must we not first hate ourselves if we are to love ourselves? . . . *I am your labyrinth.*"[90]

Barraqué rearranged the standard French translation of this text, breaking the syllables into phonetic raw material to create a fractured and feverish sense of mounting discord. As André Hodeir has pointed out, the piece "quivers with an intense life of its own from start to finish," wasting no time on thematic repetition—with one important exception. Near the end, Barraqué reiterates a dramatic pattern used once before in the piece—"a long silence tinged with dread," followed by "a shriek of despair"—to direct the listener's attention to what becomes the key word in the key passage of "Ariadne's Lament": "Shameless! Unknown thief!" Ariadne wails, "What do you get by stealing? What do you get by listening? What do you get by extorting? You who. . . ."—the musicians fall briefly silent. And then the soprano cries: "*torture!* You—the hangman god!"[91]

Barraqué and Foucault balanced their shared moments of Dionysian abandon through alcohol and sado-masochistic eroticism with their shared interest in unity and form. Both wished to forge out of their delirium works that might simultaneously express *and* contain what Foucault once called "an infinite void that opens beneath the feet of the person it attracts." In these circumstances, the ideal of a carefully crafted "work" became as central to the conduct of one's life as it was to the artifacts one produced. As Baudelaire had pointed out a century before, the person who would probe the limits of experience had a special need for "a system of gymnastics designed to fortify the will and discipline the soul." Only a strict *ethos*, a singular "cult of the self," could create a form of life both sturdy enough and flexible enough to survive the pursuit of pleasure and beauty.[92]

Nietzsche, too, had emphasized the need "to 'give style' to one's character." A person's sense of his or her own being, like the Dionysian element in tragedy, could become powerful only when given shape and form, the stamp and style of a unique and fully Apollonian *character*. This "great and rare" art could only be practiced by "those who survey all the strengths and weaknesses of their nature and then fit them into an artistic plan until every one of them appears as art and reason, and even weaknesses delight the eye. Here a large mass of second nature has been added; there a piece of original nature has been removed—both times through long practice and daily work at it. Here the ugliness that could not be removed is concealed; there it has been reinterpreted and made sublime. . . . In the end, when the work is finished, it becomes evident how the constraint of a single taste governed and formed everything large and small." By freely applying the power of the will to sculpting and "styling" a self, one might cast into bold relief one's "higher necessity," and thereby turn even the most "dreadful accident" of fate into a thing of beauty. To become master of what one was, "to compel one's chaos to become form"—that, as Nietzsche put it, "is the grand ambition here."[93]

But maintaining the right balance between form and chaos was fiendishly difficult, in life even more than in art. Barraqué's friends warned him that Foucault's obsessions were potentially destructive. And according to Foucault's French biographer, Didier Eribon, Barraqué's unpublished correspondence confirms that the composer was increasingly distressed by Foucault's behavior. The basic problem was simple (though Eribon felt obliged in his own book to refer to it only in the most discreet of terms): it was Barraqué's unease with playing any part in Foucault's erotic theater of cruelty. In the spring of 1956, he finally withdrew from the relationship. "I do not wish to be the actor or the spectator of this debasement," he wrote to Foucault: "I have come out of that vertigo of madness."[94]

For his part, Foucault in his later years rarely touched a glass of alcohol. He had come to realize that Barraqué's *own* personal obsession, with drink, might well kill him—as indeed it did. The composer died in 1973, his epic opera of death largely unfinished, his ambition to become the Beethoven of his era pathetically unfulfilled.[95]

By the time that Barraqué ended their affair, Foucault had voluntarily exiled himself to Sweden, far from the Parisian avant-garde. For the next five years, he worked at a variety of jobs, first in Uppsala, then Warsaw, and finally Frankfurt. For large stretches of time, he later told one friend, he was largely celibate. He disappeared into his work, though he scarcely lived the life of a monk. One photograph taken in Sweden shows the young exile in a sober suit, his hair thinning, his smile cocky, his outward demeanor the very image of the confident young academic. Another photograph shows him standing beside his proudest possession, a flashy white

Jaguar. "The prudence of Epicurus, moderation, a measured satisfaction, were not his style," Maurice Pinguet has recalled: the Jaguar "allowed him, en route from Uppsala to Paris, to set new speed records. Frivolity only made him laugh. But risk, always, attracted him."[96]

It was the seedtime of *Madness and Civilization*.

He wished, one suspects, to create a work that would rival Barraqué's projected opera about death, a work that would be the sum of everything he had learned, a book that would establish him as the paramount thinker of his age.

But behind this vaulting ambition, giving it purpose and making it problematic, one also imagines Foucault's Nietzschean Demon posing again the curious question: "How did I become what I am and why do I suffer so from being what I am?"

Like a pearl growing around an abrasive grain of sand, his lifelong project had begun to take shape.

Jettisoning the last vestiges of his youthful attachment to a Marxist brand of humanism and its philosophical anthropology, Foucault decided to investigate "the very historicity of forms of experience" directly, starting with the experience of madness.[97]

According to his emerging philosophical convictions, his inquiry would have to proceed simultaneously on different fronts. On the one hand, the historian and scholar, using methods he had learned from Bachelard, would meticulously reconstruct, through a history of thought, the changing beliefs and practices that defined the world in its "positivity," describing how different researchers working within different institutional settings differently put into play categories like the true and the false, reason and unreason, right and wrong, the normal and the pathological, in different times and different places differently constituting the knowable objects of experience and "the human being as a subject of knowledge."[98]

On the other hand, Foucault, in the spirit of Nietzsche and Bataille, would also hazard a personal exploration, through "transgression" and eroticism, of experience in its "negativity." As Foucault put it near the end of his life, "the historical-critical attitude must also be an experimental one."[99]

In a revealing 1957 essay on "Scientific Research and Psychology," Foucault for the first time formulated his new approach, summing up the connection between the two aspects of "experience" in this way: "Its positivity psychology borrows from the negative experience that man makes of himself."[100]

"It is only starting from death that a science of life is possible," Foucault explained. "In the same way, it is from the perspective of the unconscious that a psychology of the conscious can be found that is not a pure transcendental reflection; from the perspective of perversion that a psychology of love becomes possible without turning into an ethic; from the perspective of folly that a psychology of intelligence can be constituted without at least implicit recourse to a theory of knowledge; it is from the perspective of sleep, of automatism and the involuntary that one can create a psychology of the waking and sentient man that avoids being locked into a pure phenomenological description."[101]

To approach the "positive" phenomena of "psychology" in such "negative" terms, as Foucault points out, means abandoning the methods of conventional research—and also his own previous hopes for a Marxist science of "man." "Science is no longer a means of access to the enigma of the world." But the investigator of "negative experience" had other resources. After all, "to put into question the signifying subject," as Foucault remarked years later, "is to try out a practice"—a practice "that ends in the veritable destruction of this subject, in its dissociation, in its upheaval into something radically 'other.' "[102]

In one of those peculiar turns of phrase that give his writing its aura of unsettling strangeness, Foucault in his 1957 essay thus concluded that one might still illuminate "the enigma of the world" and the riddle of being human—but only by undertaking "*recherches de sac et de corde,*" inquiries with sack and cord: "a hangman's quest."[103]

To plumb "negative experience" in this way of course was risky. One had to break one's fall at just the right moment. "If the language of philosophy is one in which the philosopher's torments are tirelessly repeated," Foucault conceded in his essay on Bataille, then a disquieting possibility "inevitably arises," the "possibility of the mad philosopher."[104]

Still, a human being might come to know its "positive truth" in its "downward fall." And in 1957, Foucault embraced the hazards with the kind of eschatological brio that would become another one of his stylistic trademarks: "Psychology," he concluded, "can only be saved by a return to the Inferno."[105]

Nietzsche once put it this way: "The path to one's own heaven always leads through the voluptuousness of one's own hell."[106]

4

THE CASTLE

of

MURDERS

THE FIGURE ON STAGE looked old, gaunt, possessed. Stiffly seated before the manuscript he was reading, he raked the air restlessly, his hands churning frantically—the gestures of a drowning man, thought one observer. His words poured out chaotically, in a hoarse whisper that was scarcely audible, his speech punctuated by stuttering, sobs, and agonizingly long pauses.[1]

It had been advertised as a "Tête-à-tête with Antonin Artaud," and the overflow audience packed into the small Paris theater on January 24, 1947, gaped in wonder. On stage was one of the most storied figures of the prewar Parisian avant-garde. A decade before, the actor and artist had announced his plans to create a new kind of drama, a new type of theatrical performance—a display of delirium designed to "stir up shadows" and to spark, as if by contagion, "a spasm in which life is continually lacerated," convulsing the spectator "with the truthful precipitates of dreams, in which his taste for crime, his erotic obsessions, his savagery, his chimeras, his utopian sense of life and matter, even his cannibalism pour out, on a level not counterfeit and illusory, but interior."[2]

That night in 1947, something like Artaud's improbable plans for a "theater of cruelty" came strangely, disturbingly to life. Only a few months before, he had been a patient in a psychiatric hospital in Rodez; for most of the previous decade, he had been continuously confined in various mental institutions. He had not performed in public since 1935. Nobody knew what to expect.

The actor read poems. Even his closest friends could understand little of what Artaud was saying: hermetic, strange, his incantations boiled with visceral rage. "The anchored mind," he declaimed, "screwed into me by the psycho-lubricious thrust of heaven is the one that thinks every temptation, every desire, every inhibition."[3]

He chanted:

> o dedi
> o dada orzoura
> o dou zoura
> a dada skizi.[4]

At first, the audience tittered nervously. But this was no joke. A stunned silence slowly settled over the theater. Words exploded like bombs. "Saliva." "Syphilis." "Piss." "Electroshock."[5]

The man on stage would not let his audience ignore his pain, his suffering, his nine years of psychiatric confinement, the more than sixty convulsive shock treatments he had been forced to undergo.[6]

"If there had been no doctors there would never have been any sick people," he raved on. "Death too must live; and there's nothing like an insane asylum to tenderly incubate death." "War will replace the father-mother." "There rises again the old warrior of the insurgent cruelty, the unspeakable cruelty of living and having no being that can justify you."[7]

Repeatedly, he fell silent. He seemed lost. Repeatedly, he started over.

And so it went for almost three hours, hands flying, words tumbling, silent pauses creating a mounting sense of apprehension.

Then, an accident: in a sweeping gesture, Artaud knocked over the papers he was reading. Stopping, he bent down to retrieve the manuscript. His glasses fell off. He dropped to his knees. Groping blindly, he searched for his poetry.

"We were all in extreme anguish," one old friend later recalled. "He told us afterward that the void in the room made him afraid."[8]

"Partial panic convulsed the audience," another spectator remembered.[9]

Sitting in the front row was André Gide, at seventy-eight the dean of French letters. From his seat, he tried to show Artaud where his manuscript had fallen.

It was no use. Slowly, unsteadily, the actor, as if suddenly a broken man, lifted himself up and sank back into his seat. "I put myself in your place," he said, "and I can see that what I tell you isn't at all interesting. It's still theater. What can one do to be truly sincere?"[10]

The show was over. With the help of a neighbor, Gide rose to his feet, walked on stage, embraced Artaud, and guided him to the wings. It was Artaud's last public appearance; fourteen months later, he was dead.

The questions raised by Artaud's "tête-à-tête" are the questions at the heart of Foucault's first great book—*Folie et déraison* ("Madness and Unreason," retitled in English as *Madness and Civilization*).

Was the great actor simply out of his mind? Or—bizarre idea—was he, as Foucault would imply, a modern prophet like Nietzsche's Zarathustra?

As André Gide later recalled, the audience leaving the theater that night "remained silent. What could they say? They had just seen an unhappy man, fearfully shaken by a god."[11]

André Breton lamented the exploitation of a pathetically sick artist. Another writer deplored "the atrocious bad taste in the exhibition of such misery."[12]

Gide, however, concluded that it was Artaud's finest hour: "Never before had he seemed so admirable to me."[13]

He certainly seemed admirable in retrospect to Michel Foucault. As he suggested in countless allusions and references throughout *Madness and Civilization*, Artaud was a figure of *daimonic* heroism, an artist who embodied a new way of knowing. He had conveyed his uncanny genius through the modern alchemy of poetry and drama, convulsively expressing his apparent madness in a singular *work*, precisely in Blanchot's strong sense—and particularly on that night in 1947. Improvising a unified performance that breached the boundaries between acting and being, artifice and uncontrollable impulse, Artaud had put his mind to the test, unforgettably evoking for his audience, as Foucault later put it, "that space of physical suffering and terror which surrounds or rather coincides with the void."[14]

A dithyramb in praise of folly, in its own way as impassioned and shocking as anything Artaud ever said or did, *Madness and Civilization*, Foucault's own "work of madness," is boldly conceived, lyrically executed—and cunningly disguised. At first glance, it does not look like a dithyramb at all. It looks like "the most rational kind of history possible," just as Foucault once described the book.[15]

First published in France in 1961, the book had been completed in draft form by 1958, when Foucault left Sweden for a job as cultural attaché in Warsaw, Poland. Foucault had done his primary research while living in Uppsala. In the two years of exile that followed, first in Poland and then in Germany, he continued to work on the text, refining its style and argument. [16]

As the deceptively modest subtitle puts it, the text offers a "History of Madness in the Classical Age." (As if to emphasize the sober historiographic aspirations of his work, Foucault in the second French edition replaced the original title with this subtitle.) Large stretches of the book recount developments in the treatment of the mentally ill between 1650 and 1789, the classical "Age of Reason." According to Foucault, the movement to segregate the mentally ill by placing them in special institutions first took hold in these decades. To support his interpretation, he carefully marshalled different kinds of evidence, scrupulously noting his sources.

When Foucault arrived in Sweden in 1955, he had discovered that the library at the University of Uppsala, where he was teaching, contained a trove of documents about the history of psychiatry. He had developed a routine: every day between ten in the morning and three or four in the afternoon he disappeared into the archives, trolling for inspiration. [17]

What stirred his imagination was varied and often unusual: in the opening pages alone, his footnotes refer readers to a nineteenth-century biography of a saint; an eighteenth-century history of Paris; German, English, and French accounts of leprosariums, most published in the nineteenth century; a sixteenth-century manuscript about hospitals for venereal disease; a 1527 book on penitence and purgatory; the medieval archives of the hospital of Melun; a variety of twentieth-century studies of the sixteenth-century Lowlands painter Hieronymus Bosch; Erasmus's *Praise of Folly*; Montaigne's *Essays*; Cervantes' *Don Quixote*; Shakespeare's *Macbeth*; Calvin's *Christian Institutes*; and (last but not least) Antonin Artaud's strange posthumous work, *The Life and Death of Satan the Fool*. [18]

The text itself sprawls over nearly 600 printed pages. Flamboyantly learned, it is also deeply personal. Every one of Foucault's intellectual areas of interest—art, literature, philosophy, science, history—is engaged. Every one of his great themes—death, prison, sexuality, the truth value of fantasy, the "terrorism" of modern doctrines of moral responsibility—is somewhere broached.

A reader's first impression is of a work of magisterial authority, full of subtle distinctions and meticulous analyses. It is often hard to follow: bold generalizations are hazarded, only to be hedged, qualified, carefully circumscribed; the author's own convictions are insinuated more than argued, with a handful of memorable images leaving an impression that outweighs page after page of detailed, often intricate historical documentation.

Foucault needed to choose his words carefully, for they would serve several functions simultaneously. A tacit monument to his own effort to "become what one is," the book also had to serve as Foucault's *thèse principale*, roughly the French equivalent of a doctoral dissertation, though the standards in France are substantially more exacting than those in the United States. At the same time, the work was to be Foucault's opening bid for intellectual glory, a youthful summa to rival a work like *Being and Nothingness*.

In length and complexity alone, *Madness and Civilization* certainly bears comparison with Sartre's magnum opus. And like the older philosopher's book, Foucault's text is also organized around an intuition of diamondlike simplicity.

"Madness only exists in society," Foucault declared in 1961 to a reporter from *Le Monde*, usefully summing up what he took to be his book's central argument. "It does not exist outside of the forms of sensibility that isolate it, and the forms of repulsion that expel it or capture it. Thus one can say that from the Middle Ages up to the Renaissance, madness was present within the social horizon as an aesthetic and mundane fact; then in the seventeenth century—starting with the confinement [of the mad]—madness underwent a period of silence, of exclusion. It lost the function of manifestation, of revelation, that it had had in the age of Shakespeare and Cervantes (for example, Lady Macbeth begins to speak the truth when she becomes mad), it becomes laughable, delusory. Finally the twentieth century collars madness, reduces it to a natural phenomenon, linked to the truth of the world. From this positivist expropriation derive both the misguided philanthropy that all psychiatry exhibits towards the mad, and the lyrical protest that one finds in poetry from Nerval to Artaud, and which is an effort to restore to the experience of madness the profundity and power of revelation that was extinguished by confinement."[19]

Foucault's own genius—and the hermetic complexity of the work it animates—is evident from the outset of *Madness and Civilization*. Setting the tone for the rest of the book is the stunning first chapter. A bravura feat of symbolic historiography, it weaves together archival research and mythic images in a rich and multifaceted allegory of madness vindicated.

"At the end of the Middle Ages," the narrative begins, "leprosy disappeared from the Western world."[20]

Already, a reader feels surprise: for what is ostensibly a history of madness in the Age of Reason starts by talking about something else entirely. In what follows, Foucault will treat the "cursed cities" built to house the lepers of the Middle Ages as an archetype for every subsequent effort to quarantine and confine those deemed dangerous or different, from the sick to the insane. But in these opening sentences, after alluding to perhaps the most morally charged of historical diseases, Foucault evokes not a figure of confinement but rather a landscape left desolate and empty: "On the margins of the community, at the gates of cities, there stretched great zones that evil had ceased to haunt but had left sterile and long uninhabitable. For centuries, these reaches would belong to the nonhuman. From the fourteenth to the seventeenth century, they would wait, soliciting with strange incantations a new incarnation of evil," as if beckoning some new victim of disease to roam again this inhuman habitat, beyond the reach of custom and morality, like the heath upon which Shakespeare's Lear stumbles helplessly.[21]

In the sixteenth century, according to Foucault, such figures appeared, and not only in Shakespeare's tragedies. Taking up the lepers' old social role of the outcast, those deemed mad by Renaissance society renewed the old magical rites, becoming "hieratic witnesses of evil," their deranged existence testifying anew to the nearness of death.[22]

Foucault goes out of his way to stress the link between madness and death. Here, as elsewhere in the work, a connection that seems forced historically, and arbitrary philosophically, makes sense as an esoteric, essentially autobiographical allegory. According to Foucault, the madman takes the "absolute limit of death" and turns it inward "in a continuous irony," disarming its mortal sting, "making it an object of derision by giving it an everyday, tamed form." It is as if the person who is mad must repeat incessantly the drama of dying—in fantasy, in delirium, in the absence of reason. "The head that will become a skull is already empty. Madness is the *déjà-là* of death."[23]

This death-haunted delirium, which later ages would punish or seek to cure, the Renaissance mind invested with a certain prestige, Foucault contends. In farces and tragic dramas, in paintings and etchings and fictional narratives, the madman appears as "the guardian of truth." In a "simpleton's language, which makes no show of reason," he reveals "the nothingness of existence," as this is "experienced from within."[24]

Implicity recognizing the peculiar domain of truth limned by the mad-man, towns in the Renaissance drove the insane "outside their limits." There they were left free to wander "in the open countryside," the death-haunted landscape left vacant by leprosy, the symbolic space of what Foucault elsewhere calls "an untamed exteriority."[25]

Foucault tacitly acknowledges that he is painting a mythic picture. In these very years, he concedes in passing, "certain madmen," far from roaming the countryside, were "admitted to hospitals and cared for as such." Indeed, "in the majority of the cities of Europe there existed through-out the Middle Ages and Renaissance a place of detention reserved for the insane."[26]

It is easy to miss such scholarly qualifications, however, since Foucault directs the reader's attention elsewhere, above all to what becomes the book's guiding image: the Ship of Fools. This is, "of course," as Foucault stresses, a "literary composition"—a fanciful emblem, the subject of one of Bosch's most famous paintings, a "*bateau ivre*" or "drunken boat" more redolent, in Foucault's hands, of Rimbaud's poetry than of any real Ren-aissance practice. And yet, as Foucault emphasizes, "they did exist, these boats that conveyed their insane cargo from one city to another." "The simplest of pictures," the Ship of Fools is "the most symbolic as well," straddling the line between dream and reality.[27]

"The custom," Foucault writes, "was especially frequent in Germany. . . . In Frankfurt in 1399, seamen were instructed to rid the city of a madman who walked about the streets naked; in the first years of the fifteenth century, a criminal madman was expelled in the same manner from Mainz."[28]

Using as a factual pretext these two minor recorded incidents, and intertwining an interpretation of Bosch's imagery, Foucault constructs an intricate aquatic reverie, linking madness with water "and the dark mass of its own values." Water "carries off," but it also "purifies." If solid ground has conventionally been associated with reason, water has for centuries been the symbolic element of unreason: "Madness is the liquid and stream-ing exterior of rocky reason," and water an "infinite, uncertain space," the oceanic element of "dark disorder" and "a moving chaos."[29]

That is why the image of the ship setting sail is so well suited to evoke the *daimonic* forces at play in every person's life: "Navigation delivers man to the uncertainty of fate; on water, each of us is in the hands of his own destiny." Particularly for the madman who has ironically "tamed" death, "every embarkation is, potentially, the last." While the madman preoc-cupied with death has "his truth," he can discover it only in "that fruitless expanse" beyond "the solid land, with its solid cities," casting himself adrift like "a skiff, abandoned on the infinite sea of desires." Once underway on this quest, "there is no escape": the madman is "delivered to that great uncertainty external to everything. He is a prisoner in the most free of domains, the openest of routes: bound fast at the infinite crossroads."[30]

The image of this emblematic "dream fleet" filled with "highly symbolic cargoes of madmen in search of their reason," Foucault argues, arises at a singular moment in Western history: a transitional era when the symbolism of medieval paintings and sculpture had become so complex that "the picture no longer speaks for itself." The canvases of Bosch, with their fantastic monsters and demented forms, were meant in part to convey a theology; but to the Renaissance imagination (or is Foucault perhaps again surreptitiously referring to himself?) they communicate instead, "by an astonishing reversal," the "phantasms of madness."[31]

A bestiality formerly domesticated "by human symbols and values" stands revealed as "the secret nature of man," exposing "the dark rage, the sterile madness that lie in men's hearts." In Bosch's "pure vision," especially once that vision has been cut off from its symbolic association with faith, madness reveals all of its glory, and "deploys its powers. Phantasms and menaces, pure appearances of the dream and secret destiny of the world— madness here retains the primitive force of revelation: revelation that the dream is real," and that "the entire reality of the world will one day be reabsorbed in a fantastic Image," in an apocalyptic commingling of "being and nothingness that is the delirium of pure destruction."[32]

We must now imagine the Ship of Fools sailing toward one of Bosch's fiery and infernal landscapes—a paradoxical paradise "where all is offered to desire," yet torture, death, and the End of Time still loom, ever present. For "when man deploys the arbitrary nature of his madness," Foucault contends, he discovers no Rousseauian domain of innocent freedom, but rather "the dark necessity of the world; the animal that haunts his nightmares and his nights of privation is his own nature, which will lay bare the pitiless truth of Hell."[33]

The Ship of Fools thus becomes, as it were, the central panel in a triptych, flanked by a picture of a desolate void on one side—and a scene of the Last Judgment, teeming with the agonized grimaces of the damned, on the other.[34]

A complication arises. That Renaissance thinkers regarded madness with unwonted sympathy Foucault easily shows through an interpretation of Erasmus and Montaigne. But in the humanist treatments of madness— above all, in Erasmus's *Praise of Folly*—Foucault finds the roots of what he regards as the modern era's condescension toward the mad: "Whereas Bosch, Brueghel, and Dürer were fearfully terrestrial spectators, implicated in that madness they saw surging around them, Erasmus observes it from far enough away to be out of danger."[35]

Foucault detects a subtle fault-line. Two divergent approaches to madness are in the process of forming: the "tragic experience" communicated by Bosch, and a "critical consciousness," first formulated by Erasmus. "On the one hand, there will be a Ship of Fools, filled with wild faces, that little by little sinks into the night of the world, traversing a landscape that speaks of the strange alchemy of knowledge, the pressing menace of bestiality, and the end of time. On the other, there will be a Ship of Fools that forms for the wise the exemplary, and didactic, Odyssey of human faults."[36]

The "humanist" praise of folly, in Foucault's view, thus inaugurates a long tradition that will seek to define, control, and ultimately "confiscate" the experience of madness. This tradition—culminating in psychoanalysis four centuries later—tries to make of madness an experience in which the human being is constantly confronted with "his moral truth," revealing "the rules proper to his nature," turning "what was formerly a visible fortress of order" into "the castle of our conscience." The result is "not a radical destruction"—madness and unreason persist—"but only an occultation." The "tragic figures" of madness painted by Bosch, and brought back to life on stage by Artaud that night in January, 1947, are cast "into the shade."[37]

Foucault quotes Artaud directly: "The Humanism of the Renaissance was not an enlargement, but rather a diminution of man."[38]

The story that Foucault will tell in the body of this book is nuanced, complex, intricate. But the allegory of the first chapter conveys its essence. For what ultimately is at stake in *Madness and Civilization* is as subtle as the difference between Bosch and Erasmus—and as vivid (and problematic) as Artaud's last public outburst.

Will figures of "tragic experience" like Artaud continue to be confined to the dungeons of modern society, held prisoner in the castles built by moral conscience?

Or will a new Ship of Fools, like that painted by Bosch before the dawn of the Age of Reason, set sail again, ferrying its cargo of contemporary outcasts ("the debauched, the dissipated, the homosexual, the magician, the suicide, the libertine") over the boundaries of custom and morality, destination unknown?[39]

Among the first readers of *Madness and Civilization* were the professors assigned by the Sorbonne to evaluate the learning and scholarship of Foucault's doctoral thesis. Everyone was dazzled by the author's erudition and command of hitherto untapped archival sources. Despite reservations that only multiplied the longer they pondered the text, they all appreciated as well its exceptional intelligence. But the book's central argument—and, even more, its intricate literary form—they found puzzling, even vaguely disturbing.[40]

The first scholar to review the massive 943-page typescript was Georges Canguilhem, who had been appointed by the Sorbonne to clear the text for publication—in those days, a prerequisite for a successful thesis defense. The older historian immediately grasped the originality of Foucault's work: on page after page, it provoked "surprise," as Canguilhem remarked in his official report.[41]

For the veteran student of science, perhaps nothing was more surprising than Foucault's central intuition: that madness was an "*invention*," a product of social relations—and not an independent biological reality. The implications were dizzying. For if Foucault was right, Canguilhem observed, then "every previous history of the origins of modern psychiatry was vitiated by the anachronistic illusion that madness was already *given*—however unnoticed—in human nature."[42]

That Foucault's hypothesis was historically fruitful, Canguilhem could not deny: the arguments and documentation in Foucault's manuscript had persuaded him that the development of the scientific concept of madness could not be separated from a history of "social ethics." But that Canguilhem was uneasy about the role left for science and modern medicine in Foucault's account is equally clear: "Mister Foucault," he remarks, "cannot ignore that madness has always been, to some degree, an object of medical concern."[43]

Foucault's views in *Madness and Civilization* about the medical and biological aspects of madness as a type of physical disease are in fact surprisingly elusive. As Canguilhem sensed, the book is not really about mental illness at all—it is, rather, about the philosophical value accorded to the lives, utterances, and works of artists and thinkers conventionally deemed "mad."

In a 1964 essay, subsequently republished as an appendix to the French edition of 1972, Foucault went out of his way to make this point clearly.

He sharply distinguishes "mental illness" from "madness," calling them "two different configurations, which met and were confounded with each other from the seventeenth century on." He concedes that mental illness "will undoubtedly enter an increasingly well-controlled technical field;" in modern hospitals like Sainte Anne, "pharmacology has already transformed violent wards into huge and lukewarm fish tanks." The philosophical problem of madness—and of unreason—will nevertheless persist: though modern medicine may rob insanity of its terrifying edge, madness, "that lyrical halo around the illness," has already, thanks to the surrealists and their fellow-travellers, from Raymond Roussel to Antonin Artaud, entered into a new kinship with literature, "far away from pathology."[44]

That Foucault's own treatment of madness had an unusual—and enigmatic—kinship with literature was obvious to both Canguilhem and Henri Gouhier, the Sorbonne historian who presided over Foucault's oral defense of his thesis. Canguilhem, for one, had urged Foucault to tone down his rhetoric and to drop certain passages that seemed to him too sweeping and peremptory, but the younger man had refused. Foucault was wed to the form of his work and would not change a word.[45]

The peculiar and highly literary *style* of the work was, in fact, its single most disquieting feature. During Foucault's public thesis defense, Gouhier expressed his reservations, noting that the author "thinks in allegories." Foucault's thesis, he complained, repeatedly evoked the experience of madness "through mythological concepts" and fictional characters, from Macbeth to Rameau's nephew, Diderot's figure of enlightened folly. "It is these personifications," Gouhier acutely remarked, "that allow a sort of metaphysical incursion into history, and which in a fashion transform the narrative into epic, and history into an allegorical drama, bringing to life a philosophy."[46]

"Mister Foucault is certainly a writer," the jury conceded in its official written report on the oral thesis defense, but the author's indisputable talent left his interlocutors feeling uneasy. Again and again, Foucault seemed "to go spontaneously beyond the facts." Again and again, his style seemed to express "a certain 'valorization' of the experience of madness in the light of cases like that of Antonin Artaud."[47]

The jury's report was a preview of the ambivalent scholarly response that would greet this and all of Foucault's subsequent books. As few works of history do, *Madness and Civilization* opened up a new perspective on the past. It provoked an outpouring of new research on the changing treatment of the insane. But the longer professional historians worked with the archival materials, the more doubts and reservations they registered about the accuracy of Foucault's own account.[48]

As Gouhier and Canguilhem both understood, something other than scholarship was at stake in the pages of *Madness and Civilization*. But if the book was not, appearances to the contrary, a conventional work of history—what, then, was it?

In his original preface to *Madness and Civilization*, Foucault attempted, very obliquely, to address this question. The first in a projected series of historical inquiries into "limit-experience," to be conducted "under the sun of the great Nietzschean quest," the book, he explained, in a passage of almost impenetrable abstraction, was an effort to rescue from oblivion an "undifferentiated experience," an "experience, not yet divided, of division itself." His book "is not a question of a history of knowledge," he insists, but rather a history of "the rudimentary movements of an experience."[49]

The idea of "experience," as Foucault used it here, owed more to Bataille than Kant. In the first volume of his *Summa Atheologica*, Bataille had defined the raptures of oneirism, madness, and eroticism as so many forms of "inner experience," coining an incongruously bland term of art to describe a dimension of being human he envisioned in terms of violence and discord, dissociation and anguish, cruelty and chaos. Bataille treated such "inner experience" as a kind of atheist ecstasy, an unholy revelation of the human being in its unformed, Dionysian essence.[50]

A society could of course seek to wall off and condemn the Dionysian aspects of being human. "The old master of drunkenness, of anarchy, of death forever revived," as Foucault once described Dionysus, posed a genuine threat to civilized order. Still, no matter how strenuously a culture tried to outlaw the Dionysian impulse, it could only be fettered, never transcended: after all, Dionysus, in the Nietzschean view, symbolized the power of transcendence itself. As Foucault puts it in his preface, this power remained eternally accessible, just outside "the gates of time."[51]

A variety of different paths could lead to these gates. In dreams, writes Foucault, a man "could not be stopped from examining his own truth" in all of its raw *daimonic* purity; in eroticism, he could glimpse the "happy world of desire," prior to its "tragic division" into normal and abnormal acts; and in moments of madness, he could confront, as we have seen, "the nothingness of existence" as the "*déjà-là* of death."[52]

Madness, as Foucault defines it in his preface, is "*the absence of work,*" using "work" in Blanchot's sense. Madness shatters the singular compound of form and chaos that permits the "work" to exist: words fail, silence descends; the human being experiences the void. About this pure experience of madness, nothing, by definition, can be said.[53]

But at the *limit* of madness—astride the line separating reason from unreason, balanced between the Dionysian and Apollonian—the "rudimentary" experience of madness is not entirely inaccessible. By paying heed to "a very original and crude language, much more primordial than that of science," the historian of madness might yet represent "those stammered, imperfect words without fixed syntax" in which an "exchange between madness and reason" sometimes occurs.[54]

At such moments—and Foucault thought they were preserved in some of the Western world's greatest works of art—something like "an original division" become visible. To restore the value of such an "inner experience" within the confines of a reasoned history of mental illness would be to demonstrate anew how "the man of madness and the man of reason," though "moving apart, are not yet disjunct."[55]

That his task is difficult, Foucault concedes: "The perception that tries to seize" madness and unreason "in their unfettered state belongs necessarily to a world that has already captured them. The freedom of madness is only audible from high in the fortress where it has been taken prisoner."[56]

Still, Foucault insists, groans and shrieks from the dungeon *are* dimly audible. Guided by these distant voices—and as Bataille reminds us, they are inner voices, as well as voices from the past—the historian can survey not just the plays, poems, and paintings of the past, but also "notions, institutions, juridical and police measures, scientific concepts," listening for murmurs, looking for clues to what has been buried deep in the castle keep, searching for firsthand witnesses, however tortured, to an "experience, not yet divided, of division itself."[57]

This evidence, as we have seen, Foucault finds: he discovers it, not in the lucid arguments of thinkers like Erasmus and Montaigne, but rather in the grotesque imagery of Bosch and in the insane outbursts of Artaud. "Thus reappears the lightning decision, heterogeneous to the time of history, but inconceivable outside of it, that separates the language of reason and the promises of time from the somber murmur of insects." A typical touch, this passing reference to murmuring insects: one thinks of the rebel angels Bosch depicted as a fearful plague of locusts raining down from heaven and infesting paradise with their diabolical promise of sin.[58]

To interrogate a culture from the perspective of such a demonic fall is "to question it from the margins of history." And to *express* this experience requires, not scholarship, and certainly not rational argument (which would rob limit-experience of its tragic power) but rather *artistry*—the fury of a poet like Artaud, the monstrous imagination of a painter like Bosch: "It is necessary to strain one's ears, bending down toward this muttering of the world, trying to perceive the many images that have never turned into poetry, so many phantasms that have never reached the colors of wakefulness."[59]

In the decade to come, Foucault would take a certain malicious glee in hiding his artistry behind a barrage of methodological pronouncements that endowed his work with a dazzling and deceptive air of scholarly authority. These ex post facto declarations doubtless served a strategic purpose, particularly in France, where an intellectual without a rule of method would seem about as trustworthy as a sailor without a compass; but isolated from the experience expressed and evoked by the idiosyncratic *style* of Foucault's work itself, they will lead—and have led—the unwary astray.

Writing in his original preface to *Madness and Civilization*, by contrast, Foucault, though customarily oblique, is relatively honest. His approach, he admits, entails "a kind of relativism without recourse," a "language without support." And for "a rule of method," he confides, "I have retained only one, that which is contained in a text of Char, where can be read as well a definition of the most urgent and reserved truth: 'I removed from things the illusion they produce to protect us, and left them the part that they grant us.' "[60]

This and the other references to René Char in the preface remind us of Foucault's original "rule of method." For at the outset of his Nietzschean quest, in 1953, he had discovered his *daimon* in the dream—that form of "inner experience" which throws "into bright light the secret and hidden power at work in the most manifest forms of presence."[61]

Char, too, had sought to unriddle his *daimon* in the dream, which is not surprising: like so many of the other crucial influences on Foucault's thought, from Bataille to Artaud, Char had begun his career as a member of the surrealist movement. During the 1930s, he had drifted away from Breton and his circle, becoming friends with Maurice Blanchot, who championed his poetry, as did Martin Heidegger. During World War II, Char served as a captain in the Resistance; his evocation of the experience, in the "clenched serenity" of the poems and aphoristic fragments he published together in 1948 as *Fureur et mystère* ("Fury and Mystery") earned him the accolades of Albert Camus, who called him "our greatest living poet."[62]

Elliptical, hermetic, intensely personal, Char's prose and poetry Foucault committed to memory. Along with Nietzsche and Sade, Char seems to have been the writer he knew best. It is therefore worth pondering the prose poem by Char that Foucault chose as the epigraph for both his essay on Binswanger and for *Madness and Civilization*.

"When I reached manhood," Char writes, "I saw rising and growing upon the wall shared by life and death a ladder ever more bare, invested with a power of unique evulsion: the dream." That the dream could extract the truth of the world was, of course, a surrealist bromide, and also one of the central points of Foucault's Binswanger essay. "Now see darkness draw away," Char continued, "and LIVING become, in the form of a harsh allegorical asceticism, the conquest of extraordinary powers. . . ." Char's reference to "allegorical asceticism" here evokes his own rigorous attention to form, his own sustained effort to express, through the craft of poetry, the enigmatic truths revealed in sleep. His demand for a kind of self-abnegating artistic discipline put Char at odds with the surrealist emphasis on "automatic writing," but brought him into close harmony with his friend Blanchot's views about the need for formal unity in the *work*—a need that Foucault also felt.[63]

This part of Char's prose poem Foucault used as the epigraph for his Binswanger essay. But it was the climax of the same brief work that he cited at the end of the original preface to *Madness and Civilization*—as if to underline the connection between his first major book and the "great Nietzschean quest," to "become what one is," launched in his earlier essay on the dream.

"Pathetic companions who scarcely murmur," Char's prose poem concludes, "go to the extinguished lamp and give back the jewels. A new mystery sings in your bones. Develop your legitimate strangeness."[64]

"Strangeness," legitimate or not, one supposes might be more easily developed in poetry, or in aphorisms such as Nietzsche wrote, or even in the kind of philosophical pornography that Bataille crafted—almost anything, in fact, but the kind of painstakingly documented histories that Foucault actually offered to the world. Daniel Defert recalls that in the years immediately after the publication of *Madness and Civilization*, Foucault periodically discussed the possibility of writing a novel. That it never happened is a testimony to Foucault's love of historical research: he found a special pleasure in anchoring his work in the dense, complex realities of the past revealed in archives and documents.[65]

"Reality is frighteningly superior to all fiction," as Artaud once put it. "All you need is the genius to know how to interpret it."[66]

Genius Foucault had in abundance, and all of the historical evidence in *Madness and Civilization* he implicitly organized around the nagging question posed by his singular *daimon*: "How did I become what I am and why do I suffer from being what I am?" Searching for the roots of his own mad fascination with death, he was creating a "work" *of* madness, as well as *about* madness, giving form to (as Blanchot put it) "a part of himself from which he feels he is free and from which the work has contributed to freeing him."[67]

He proceeded, one supposes, by letting his mind wander in the archives: for the modern library, as he once put it, had created a new and historically unprecedented "imaginative space." While turning page after page of a dusty old manuscript, a scholar might meet his *daimon* as surely and unmistakably as when he fell asleep. "The imaginary now resides between the book and the lamp," Foucault asserted in an essay written in 1964: "We no longer bear the fantastic in our heart" alone. "To dream it is no longer necessary to close our eyes—only to read. The true image springs from knowledge: that of words spoken in the past, of exact recensions, of masses of detailed information, of infinitesimal fragments of monuments, of reproductions of reproductions." All these "phenomena of the library," Foucault concludes, provoke an "experience," putting one in touch with "the power of the impossible"—and also revealing the documentary basis for elaborating a distinctively modern kind of surrealist historiography that is, simultaneously, a throwback to a premodern era when myth and magic still shaped the stories people told about the past.[68]

The historian at grips with his *daimon* through the heterogeneous media of archival documents and his own "inner experience" becomes, in effect, a visionary—"the individual who *sees* and who recounts from the starting point of his sight." Pronouncing "afresh so many words that had been muffled," he may even resurrect the *experience* of the limit, and enunciate anew the normally mute Dionysian dimension of being human, evoking it through images, in the parade of figures that fills the pages of his own book. He thus makes of his text a kind of vessel, offering free passage, through its cargo of words, to "the truthful precipitate of dreams," conveying "the very essence of man."[69]

But what exactly is this "essence"? What does the "experience" of madness in our own day reveal about the human being?

It is time to follow the sounds still audible from "high inside the fortress," and descend to the dungeon where "madness has been taken prisoner."

An image: Hands strapped to the ceiling, the victim watches helplessly as bands are wrapped around each arm and tightened. A man with a surgeon's knife quickly lances a vein in each arm. Geysers of blood erupt. Transfixed by the sight of the crimson fountains, the assailant drops to his knees. An aide fondles his cock. While the victim, bled white, hovers on the threshold of death, the torturer enjoys a convulsive orgasm.[70]

Another fantasy: You have been kidnapped. Bound and tied, you are slipped into a noose. "The torture is sweeter than you may imagine. You will approach death only by way of unspeakably pleasurable sensations; the pressure this noose will bring to bear upon your nervous system will set fire to the organs of voluptuousness; the effect is certain; were all the people who are condemned to this torture to know in what an intoxication of joy it makes one die, less terrified by this retribution for their crimes they would commit them more often. . . ."[71]

Final scene: Ten corpses—a man, a wife, their eight children—lie in the smoldering ruins of a burned house. The libertine who torched it surveys her handiwork: "I examine the charred bodies one by one, recognize each: these people were alive this morning, I muse, and now, but a few hours later, here they are, dead; killed by me. And why did I do it? Out of fun. To spill my fuck. So this is what murder is!"[72]

Three vignettes from *Justine* and *Juliette*, three illustrations of a central thesis of *Madness and Civilization*: In the nineteenth and twentieth centuries, the sustained effort, in the name of enlightened psychiatry, to quarantine, cast out, and "confiscate" insanity has helped create a monstrous new "system of the transgressive." Isolated and confined, the impulses called "mad" now boil and seethe as "the strange contradiction of human appetites: the complicity of desire and murder, of cruelty and the longing to suffer, of sovereignty and slavery, of insult and humiliation." As it has done eternally, "unreason continues to watch by night; but in this vigil it joins with fresh powers. The nonbeing it once was now becomes the power to annihilate." The shadowy truth and tragic promise of madness is now expressed in "the insane dialogue of love and death"—a dialogue inaugurated by the Marquis de Sade.[73]

"One could say, in an approximate manner," explains Foucault, "that up until the Renaissance, the ethical world"—and particularly those figures of madness who existed "beyond the division between Good and Evil"—

experienced a kind of "equilibrium" or "tragic unity, which was that of destiny or providence and the divine predilection." But in the eighteenth century, this unity was shattered, almost beyond recall, "dissociated by the decisive division between reason and unreason. A crisis of the ethical world begins, which doubles the great conflict between Good and Evil by the irreconcilable conflict between reason and unreason." Excommunicated, unreason comes to comprise "a field of experience doubtless too secret to be formulated in clear terms, too reproved as well, from the Renaissance to our own modern epoch, to have been permitted the right of expression." No longer treated as a revelation of the world and its shadowy powers, linked instead to immorality on the one hand and the scientific understanding of mental illness on the other, madness becomes a "human fact," associated with such specific social types as the pervert and the homosexual.[74]

In this account, Sade becomes a pivotal figure, embodying simultaneously the close of the Age of Reason and the dawn of our own modern era. Sade after all was a victim of the classical practice of confining the mad indiscriminately with criminals, prostitutes, delinquents, the poor. For much of his life, he was in prison, at first for raping and allegedly poisoning several young women, later for the crime of writing *Justine* and *Juliette*, works that gave evidence, officials declared, of "licentious insanity." "It is no accident," writes Foucault, "that sadism, as an individual phenomenon bearing the name of a man, was born of confinement and, within confinement, that Sade's entire work is dominated by the images of the Fortress, the Cell, the Cellar, the Convent, the inaccessible Island, which thus form, as it were, the natural habitat of unreason."[75] That this habitat is, in fact, unnatural and historically contingent Foucault has already demonstrated: the image of the Ship of Fools, sailing the empty expanse of an untamed exteriority, offers the starkest possible contrast.

At the same time, Sade, for Foucault, expresses a distinctively modern idea of "tragic experience," thus blazing a path later followed by Friedrich Hölderlin, Gérard de Nerval, Friedrich Nietzsche, Vincent Van Gogh, Raymond Roussel, and Antonin Artaud—a philosopher, a painter, and four poets; three of whom committed suicide; all of whom, like Sade, were at some time in their lives officially declared "mad."[76]

"After Sade," contends Foucault, "unreason belongs to whatever is decisive, for the modern world, in every work; that is, in every work that admits of the murderous and coercive." In contact with such works, "man communicates with what is deepest in himself, and most solitary," rediscovering "the most internal, and at the same time the most savagely free of forces." It is this enigmatic power that apparently erupts in the "limitless application of the right of death" in Sade. It figures as well in "the bold joy of life" Hölderlin found in the death of his tragic hero Empedocles, who, fleeing "to Nature's heart," "flung himself down into the glorious flames" of Mount Etna. It is perhaps the same dark force that surfaces in the suicidal delirium of Nerval's last night, in the black crows swirling in Van Gogh's last painting, in the murmuring "repetition of death" in Roussel's writing, in the shrieks and tortured sobs of Artaud's final appearance on stage in 1947.[77]

As this litany suggests, madness, in its modern apotheosis, contains all "the ambiguity of chaos and apocalypse." For the fascination with cruelty, torture, and death is "a sign that Nature is lacerating herself, that she has reached the extreme point of her dissension." Dreaming of the charred corpses littering Sade's premonition of Auschwitz—or enjoying the "unspeakably pleasurable sensations" of dangling from a noose and watching life slip away—Nature as it were reveals "a sovereignty which is both herself and something quite outside herself: the sovereignty of a mad heart that has attained, in its solitude, the limits of the world that wounds it, that turns it against itself and abolishes it at the moment when to have mastered it so well gives it the right to identify itself with that world."[78]

This dizzyingly abstract paean to the profane rapture of dying, with its eerie echoes of the suicidal dreams of Ellen West, will doubtless strike some readers as crazy. It is precisely in order to disarm this reflexive response that Foucault has composed his entire book. And that is not all. For in the "insane dialogue between life and death," Foucault discovers an untamed power of "*total* contestation," a mad form of being that calls into question the very roots of modern culture: "Everything that morality, everything that a botched society, has stifled in man, revives in the castle of murders."[79]

An amazing claim—so strange that few readers of *Madness and Civilization* have lingered over it, or tried to fathom its implications. Perhaps it is fortunate that the hermetic style leaves shrouded in mystery just what Foucault has in mind. As a figment of autobiographical allegory, on the other hand, Foucault's proposition could not be more richly suggestive. For Sade of course speaks directly to the substance of Foucault's own singular "madness"—his unrelenting fascination with death.

In an interview years later with the Italian journalist Duccio Trombadori, Foucault spoke with rare candor about the origins and personal significance of *Madness and Civilization*. Like all of his books, it was, he confided, a means of "realizing direct, personal experiences." "I had had a personal, complex, and direct relationship with madness," he explained to Trombadori in 1978, "and also with death."[80]

But the *work*, he goes on, referring explicitly to Blanchot, is *itself* meant to *provoke*, in the reader as it did in the writer, an "experience" in its own right, an experience that upsets our preconceptions, forcing us to see the world in a new light: "The book constituted for me—and for those who read or used it—a transformation in the relationship that we have with madness (as this is marked historically, theoretically, and also from an ethical point of view)."[81]

The book's message to historians is clear enough: after reading *Madness and Civilization*, it is impossible, as Canguilhem immediately grasped, to write a history of mental illness that assumes madness is a biological *given*. The book's theoretical impact is equally obvious: it calls into question the scientific status not only of classical but also of modern psychiatry. But what, one may well wonder, *is* the book's "ethical point of view"?

To understand this crucial but obscure aspect of *Madness and Civilization*, it is helpful to look at Foucault's critique of the psychiatrists who rang down the curtain on the classical age, William Tuke (1732–1822) and Philippe Pinel (1745–1826). As historians have subsequently suggested, this is one of the most tendentious and least persuasive parts of the book from a scholarly point of view; not coincidentally, it is also one of the richest parts of the book from what implicitly is Foucault's *personal* point of view.[82]

In traditional accounts, Tuke and Pinel are portrayed as pioneers in the humane and enlightened treatment of the mentally ill. Tuke established an asylum in York, England, that was renowned for its bucolic setting and lack of physical restraints; Pinel at the height of the French Revolution liberated the inmates at Bicêtre, declaring, according to the legend, that "these madmen are so intractable only because they have been deprived of air and freedom."[83]

In a radical reevaluation that would become characteristic of his work, Foucault cast a jaundiced eye on the reforms of both Tuke and Pinel, charging that what looks like progress is really an insidious new form of social control: thanks to their innovations, madness was "imprisoned in a moral world," up to "our own day at least."[84]

Stressing Tuke's Quaker background, Foucault documents his efforts to effect a moral reformation among his patients, in part by trying to teach

religious principles, in part by placing the inmates under perpetual surveillance: "For the free terror of madness," he charges, Tuke substituted
"the enclosed anguish of responsibility."[85]

Pinel, he contends, achieved a similar end with different means. In
Pinel's asylum, too, the absence of visible constraints signifies "not unreason liberated, but madness long since mastered," through a disciplined
regimen designed to inculcate a sense of repentance and remorse.[86]

The result, charges Foucault, was all the more devastating for being
largely invisible and unobtrusive: stripped of the aura of supernatural mystery, "the madman found himself purified of his animality, or at least that
part of his animality that was violence, predation, rage, savagery." Trying
to make coercion and physical constraints needless, Tuke and Pinel aimed
to produce "a docile animality." The patients in Pinel's asylum were ushered
into "the calm world of the traditional virtues." What under the ancien
régime had been "a visible fortress of order" with tangible chains and
spectacular punishments was turned into "the castle of our conscience."[87]

Our conscience—hence, Foucault's as well.

From this perspective, Pinel's "liberation" has, as Foucault stresses in
a passage of the most profound personal resonance, "a paradoxical meaning. The dungeon, the chains, the continual spectacle, the sarcasms were,
to the sufferer in his delirium, the very element of his freedom." In chains,
the madman "could not be dislodged from his immediate truth." But once
the chains were taken away, and the madman inserted into a system of
virtue, internalized in his conscience, he found himself confined anew,
"in the limited use of an empty freedom. . . . Henceforth more genuinely
confined than he could have been in a dungeon and chains, a prisoner of
nothing but himself, the sufferer was caught in a relation to himself that
was of the order of transgression, and in a nonrelation to others that was
of the order of shame." Society in this way is made to seem innocent: "The
guilt is shifted inside."[88]

Unless the man called "mad" could somehow shift back the burden of
guilt, there was no escape from this joyless, eternally repeated cycle of
transgression and shame: "He feels himself punished, and he sees the sign
of his innocence in that fact; free from all physical punishment, he must
prove himself guilty." Caught in just this cycle of transgression, Pinel's
symbolic "other," Sade, also cannot escape: the Castle of Murders, like the
Castle of Conscience, is a figure of confinement. The violence of Sade's
transgression promises pain as much as pleasure: resurrecting the "glory"
of torture and physical punishment in a mad effort to recover the innocent

freedom of Nature, the libertine is caught in "the endlessly repeated non-existence of gratification."[89]

The theoretical assumptions behind this account, which yokes together morality and cruel impulses, guilt and a murderous kind of transgression, Foucault most clearly elaborated in an essay published in 1962. "In every culture there exists a coherent series of gestures of division," Foucault writes, reiterating a central theme of *Madness and Civilization*. But "gestures of division" like "the delimitation of madness" and "the prohibition of incest" are inherently ambiguous: "the moment they mark a limit, they create the space of a possible transgression." This is a timeless possibility: there is no limit that cannot be breached, no law that cannot be broken. Yet the field of possible transgression is always historically specific: every epoch "forms what one can call a 'system of the transgressive.' Properly speaking, this space coincides neither with the illegal nor the criminal, neither with the revolutionary, the monstrous nor the abnormal, not even with the sum total of all these deviant forms; but each of these terms designates at least an angle."[90]

Acts of "transgression" may put a human being in touch with the chaotic power that Nietzsche called Dionysian; but no act of transgression can escape its origins in a historical field that, in crucial part, motivates, defines—and insofar as the object of transgression is to tap the untamed energy of transcendence—(de)forms it. "Transgression, then, is not related to the limit as black to white, the prohibited to the lawful, the outside to the inside, or as the open area of a building to its enclosed spaces. Rather, their relationship takes the form of a spiral which no simple infraction can exhaust."[91]

The individual with mad impulses will thus discover that his or her struggle to express the self disclosed in the unreason of dreams and delirium is implicated, like it or not, in a specific, typically modern "system of the transgressive," a kind of negative mirror image of the positive system of humanist virtue introduced by social reformers like Pinel.

To become what one is now requires, in Foucault's view, casting one's fate with those tragic figures, from Sade to Nietzsche and Artaud, who have resisted the "gigantic moral imprisonment" symbolized, in *Madness and Civilization*, by Tuke and Pinel. To escape from the Castle of Conscience, we must first enter into a Castle of Murders: against the alleged virtues inculcated by the psychiatrists, transgression will unleash vice; against philanthropic kindness, vengeful cruelty; against a docile animality, a seething lust for corporeal sensation, no matter how painful or self-destructive.

This descent into the Inferno is obviously no upbeat "liberation." Entering Sade's dungeon of dreams, the human being becomes, both figuratively and literally, a "prisoner of the passage," "a slave of desires and the servant of the heart." For the madman, whether confined in a castle or free to set sail, is "bound fast at the infinite crossroads"—specifically, the "infinite crossroads" of history.[92]

"Captive in the human heart, hammered into it, madness can formulate that which was at the outset true of man," but it can never return "to the native land," it cannot recapture the liberty of an untrammeled transcendence, the *ding-an-sich* of Kant's pure freedom. Indeed, the experience of madness, like that of dreams, reveals "the knot that ties freedom to the necessity of the world."[93]

But there is more. By exhaustively documenting how the powers of transcendence called mad are tethered by cultural forms beyond the human being's control, Foucault's account suggests that the notions of guilt and responsibility formulated by modern philosophers from Kant to Sartre are radically mistaken: "Everything that has been formulated as the truth of man passes over to the side of irresponsibility." The kind of "experience" explored by Bataille and Blanchot, Foucault will later assert in *The Order of Things*, discloses through "repetition" an "original innocence"—a mark of the human being's "finitude (trapped in the opening and bondage of that finitude)."[94]

Nietzsche, too, in *Human, All Too Human* (first published in 1878), had hypothesized that every human being was a "necessary consequence" of an almost unintelligibly complex web of factors "assembled from the elements and influence of things past and present." A human being's character was not unalterable, according to Nietzsche: the capacity of transcendence he called "will to power" meant that a person could always, to some extent, start anew. Still, "during the brief lifetime of a man" Nietzsche supposed that "the effective motives are unable to scratch deeply enough to erase the imprinted script of many millennia." Much about "what one was" could simply not be changed, try as one might. "Trapped in the opening and bondage" of a history, the will was never entirely free. Viewed without the blinkers of traditional moral philosophy, the individual, Nietzsche thought, could therefore "be made accountable for nothing, not for his nature, nor for his motives, nor for his actions, nor for the effects he produces." The man who deviated from the norm, Nietzsche stressed, was particularly blameless: for in such cases, "our tame, mediocre, emasculated society" often took "the strong human being and made him sick." Feelings of shame were unwarranted. Guilt was a figment of the Judeo-Christian tradition, a crippling fiction, buried deep in the body, coded in "the imprinted script of many millenia."[95]

The "ethical point of view" expressed in *Madness and Civilization* may now be summarized briefly:

—It is not immoral to be convulsed by singular fantasies and wild impulses: such limit-experiences are to be valued as a way of winning back access to the occluded, Dionsyian dimension of being human.

—It is not a human being's fault if these impulses, confined and regimented, have been driven inward and transmogrified, creating potentially murderous new impulses. The insane and volatile configuration of these impulses today is a legacy of the history of confinement and moral reproach recounted in the pages of *Madness and Civilization*.

The man called "mad" is innocent.

It is *society* that is guilty.

And, Foucault adds, it is the peculiar burden of every modern "work" forged from an engagement with the *daimonic* and delirious to hold society accountable for its crimes.

Lonely, strange, and alien, desperately trying to rescue from oblivion the animal energies of being human, the works of Sade, Hölderlin, Nerval, Nietzsche, Van Gogh, Roussel, and Artaud *of necessity* issue in a frenzy of cruel and morbid fantasies, before lapsing into the silence of madness— or the suicidal embrace of death. That is the tragedy of these works, but also their harrowing power: "by the madness which interrupts it," such liminal works keep alive the possibility, for all those who come thoughtfully into contact with them, of a liminal experience, laying open for shared inspection, Foucault asserts, "a void, a moment of silence, a question without answer, . . . a breach without reconciliation," where "the world is made aware of its guilt."[96]

"Ruse and new triumph of madness," Foucault concludes with a flourish: for "the world that thought to measure and justify madness through psychiatry must [now] justify itself before madness." And "nothing" in our own placidly civilized world of humane virtues—especially "not what it can know of madness" through the lives and works of its tortured votaries—"assures the world that it is justified by such works of madness."[97]

Foucault's own work of madness, ferrying its strange cargo of tragic heroes, first sailed into public view in May of 1961. It was originally published not by Gallimard, as Foucault had hoped, but rather by Plon, the publisher of works by the anthropologist Claude Lévi-Strauss.

That Foucault wanted his work to escape from the ghetto of academic publishing is clear: he turned down an offer from the Presses Universitaires de France, preferring to try to follow in the footsteps of Lévi-Strauss—a man of learning who, like Sartre, had reached out to the general public. (In the same spirit, Foucault in 1964 radically abridged his work, to permit its publication as a mass-market paperback; it was this condensed version that was translated into English one year later.)[98]

In many ways, Foucault's text met with enviable success. Shortly after it was published, Maurice Blanchot praised the book in the pages of the *Nouvelle Revue Française*: recognizing a kindred spirit, Blanchot paid Foucault the highest possible compliment, comparing his approach to "limit-experience" with that of his old friend Georges Bataille. In another admiring review, the young philosopher Michel Serres pointed out the work's similarities with Nietzsche's *Birth of Tragedy*. And Roland Barthes, already an important critic, applauded Foucault's "structural" approach to history (though Barthes had to concede that a "more formalistic mind might have exploited more intensely" some of Foucault's discoveries). The philosopher Gaston Bachelard and the historian Fernand Braudel also conveyed their admiration.[99]

Still, the praise of his peers did not suffice, for Foucault harbored other ambitions. His book at first failed to reach the larger audience that *Being and Nothingness* had tapped. The authority of Sartre remained unrivaled, the grip of his moralizing humanism unbroken.

Meanwhile younger thinkers were already beginning to take aim at Foucault himself—one sure sign that his reputation was already growing, however slowly. On March 4, 1963, a conference was held at the Sorbonne featuring an up-and-coming philosopher named Jacques Derrida. His talk, entitled "The Cogito and the History of Madness," was a stinging critique of *Madness and Civilization*.[100]

Four years younger than Foucault, Derrida had been a student in his course on psychology at the École Normale in the early 1950s. Like Foucault, he was steeped in the thought of the later Heidegger and interested in plumbing the "unthought"; like his old teacher, he also knew intimately the work of Artaud, Bataille, and, above all, Blanchot, who offered Derrida a model of how to approach literature. Despite such similarities, Derrida had pursued a more traditional path of study, mastering the canonic philosophers, refining a rare genius for reading, closely, the most difficult and rebarbative of theoretical arguments, paying unusual attention to the literary as well as logical aspects of each work. Unlike many, he had no difficulty following every twist and turn in Foucault's allusive text. [101]

At the time of his encounter with *Madness and Civilization*, Derrida was in the midst of refining his own unique voice. Elevating the search for paradox and contradiction into the stuff of high literary drama, he treated the art of philosophical commentary much as Foucault had treated the history of madness—as an apocalyptic and breathtakingly radical rupture "with constituted normality." Whether reading Plato or Rousseau, Derrida probed for inconsistencies, trying to unmask hypocrisies that were symptomatic of the ambiguities inherent in language and thought. In thinkers ostensibly liberated from metaphysics, such as Heidegger, he looked for the unavowed persistence of metaphysical ideas; in classical rationalists, by contrast, he looked for references, damning because disavowed, to imagination and metaphor. [102]

His approach to Foucault was characteristic. He attacked along two different fronts. In what became a trademark tactic, he homed in on a passage that at first glance seemed marginal to the argument, namely Foucault's brief discussion, in passing, of a short passage from the *Meditations* of Descartes. With an intimidating—indeed, condescending—display of exegetical finesse, Derrida contested the interpretation of this passage, calling Foucault's reading of it "naive." [103]

Derrida's second line of attack was broader and more interesting. Pointing out (as Michel Serres had) the resemblance between Foucault's account of the Renaissance regard for unreason and Nietzsche's account of the ancient Greek fascination with the Dionysian, Derrida questioned "the historico-philosophical motivations" behind these transparently mythic approaches to history: "The attempt to write the history of the decision, division, difference," suggests Derrida, "runs the risk of construing the division as an event or a structure subsequent to the unity of an original presence, thereby confirming metaphysics in its fundamental operation." [104]

These were fighting words. To accuse an avant-garde French philosopher of "metaphysics" in these years was a little like accusing a communist intellectual of "revisionism"—it was a humiliatingly rote gesture of disdain.

But Derrida goes on to pose a still more needling set of questions: for if Foucault is unable to escape from metaphysics, Derrida contends, then he will be unable to praise folly without emasculating it—the same charge Foucault levelled against Erasmus. "I would be tempted," writes Derrida with the scarcely concealed glee of a professional debater going for the jugular, "to consider Foucault's book a powerful gesture of protection and internment"—perhaps, he adds triumphantly, a gesture written "in the *confessed* terror of going mad."[105]

Foucault, who heard Derrida deliver his paper at the Sorbonne, was no stranger to such ceremonial tilting: ritualized jousts were a part of every *normalien*'s education. As he must have known, it was a dazzling and damaging performance. Again and again, his old student drew blood. The skirmishing over Descartes may have been essentially empty, but Derrida's remark about the "terror of going mad" was anything but. Years later, Gilles Deleuze, who probably knew Foucault as well as anyone, said much the same thing, remarking that Foucault used the study of history "as a means of not becoming mad."[106]

Derrida's critique was not trivial, then: it was, in fact, perspicacious, profound—and brutally personal. How could Foucault respond?

At the Sorbonne, he in fact said nothing. Listening silently, he kept his own counsel, which was probably just as well—the violence of Foucault's temper, when provoked, was legendary.[107]

Derrida subsequently published his paper, first in an issue of the *Revue de métaphysique et de morale* and then in *Writing and Difference*, a collection of essays published in 1967, the same year that Derrida's first important book, *Of Grammatology*, appeared. By then, Foucault had become a major intellectual figure, thanks to the popular success in France of *The Order of Things*, published in 1966. But when Derrida's books were greeted with similar acclaim—when the younger man had to be taken seriously as a potential rival—Foucault finally decided to break his long silence.

His response was characteristically complex. Striking a tactical retreat, he suppressed his preface to the first edition of *Madness and Civilization*. He even issued a kind of methodological *mea culpa*, declaring in 1969 that "*Madness and Civilization* accorded far too great a place, and a very enigmatic one too, to what is called an 'experience.' " He realized in retrospect, he said, that he could not really "reconstitute what madness itself might be, in the form in which it first presented itself in some primitive, fundamental, deaf, scarcely articulated experience."[108]

Though it is not at all obvious that *Madness and Civilization* really succumbs to such a naive view of the possibility of grasping madness as a thing-in-itself, Foucault was not about to let himself be accused of committing an elementary philosophical blunder.

His next step was to compose a furious response to Derrida, a polemic as vicious as anything he ever wrote. Ignoring the most telling, and personal, of Derrida's charges, Foucault focused instead on their disagreement over Descartes. Taking a page from his adversary's book, he tried to meet Derrida on his own philosophical ground, showing how a close reading of Descartes' text undermined Derrida's own assumptions about interpretation. "The stakes of the debate are clearly indicated," Foucault asserts: "Could there be anything anterior or exterior to philosophical discourse?" As if to answer his own rhetorical question, Foucault stresses Descartes' use of the Latin terms *demens* and *amens*: "terms that are in the first place juridical, before being medical, and which designate a whole category of people incapable of certain religious, civil, and judicial acts." By narrowly focusing on "signs" and "the truth of ideas," Derrida, he charges, in effect misses the wider historical context that informs Descartes' use of a term like *demens*.[109]

"I will not say that it is metaphysics," Foucault concludes, sneering at Derrida's Heideggerian term of abuse. "I'll go much further than that: I shall say that what can be seen here so visibly is a historically well-determined little pedagogy. . . . A pedagogy which gives . . . to the master's voice the limitless sovereignty which allows it to restate the text indefinitely."[110]

After this tiff, Derrida and Foucault did not talk for years. But they did eventually reconcile, in 1981, after Foucault had gone out of his way to defend Derrida when the younger man was arrested in Prague on a charge, apparently trumped up, of possessing marijuana.[111]

But that is not quite the end of the story. Foucault's criticism of *Madness and Civilization* is not nearly as clear-cut as it seems. As Gilles Deleuze has suggested, it is, in fact, largely "feigned."[112]

For Foucault in these years also explicitly reasserts, *sotto voce*, that "I have no wish . . . to exclude any effort to uncover and free . . . 'prediscursive' experiences," the very type of "experience" at issue in the work of Bataille, Blanchot, and Foucault himself. He never gives up the dream of crafting a "work," in Blanchot's strong sense, leaving traces of a preoccupation with death on page after page, silently trying to fathom, and to change, both himself and the world he shares with his readers.[113]

Thus Foucault in the second edition of *Madness and Civilization* (1972) placed in an appendix not only his critique of Derrida, but also an essay, titled "Madness, the Absence of Work." In this essay he reiterated, in slightly more cautious language, the central contentions of his original preface. He also offered a very rare glimpse into his own "utopian sense of life and matter," as Artaud once put it.

"Some day perhaps man will no longer know what madness was," Foucault declares. And on that day, "Artaud will belong to the soil of our language and no longer to its breaking point."[114]

If Artaud's kind of delirious creativity were to become a key to the enigma of being human, rather than a threat that must be somehow confined, "everything that we today feel shaped by the limit, or by the uncanny, or by the intolerable"—from the most untamed of impulses to the wildest of fantasies—might somehow, Foucault speculates, be "transferred to the serenity of positive things." If that were to happen, what now seems "exterior"—dreaming, intoxication, the uninhibited pursuit of pleasure—might "indicate our very selves."[115]

A hidden fantasy is lurking here. In a different kind of world, one free of the infernal recurrence of transgression and guilt, perhaps the poet on stage that night in 1947 would not have acted like a drowning man. Perhaps he would not have experienced his own most inescapable impulses as cruel, violent, insanely self-destructive. Perhaps he would no longer have suffered for being what he was.

What would it feel like to inhabit such a world?

Michel Foucault, like Antonin Artaud, did not live long enough to find out.

5

IN THE

LABYRINTH

IN THE DECADE AFTER *Madness and Civilization*, Michel Foucault set out deliberately to efface himself—to erase the signs of his own singular existence from the texts that he composed. "Do not ask me who I am, and do not tell me to remain the same," he wrote in 1969, in a celebrated declaration that sums up one of the most difficult riddles of his work in this period: "More than one person, like me no doubt, writes in order to have no face."[1]

To accomplish this task—a paradoxical one, since as Foucault well knew, to write was also, perforce, to express and reveal—he refined an austere new language in his larger works of history. With a "relentless erudition" that grew ever more "gray, meticulous, and patiently documentary," he constructed what Nietzsche once called "cyclopean structures." Composing studies of the past out of "discreet and apparently insignificant truths," he scrutinized "all that has given color to existence," surveying everything from the bland "manners of scholars" to the shadowy domain of "violence, life and death, desire and sexuality." His curiosity was as insatiable as the one-eyed monsters once thought to haunt the frontiers of the ancient Greek world.[2]

Setting aside his announced intention to write a series of histories of "limit-experience," he turned instead to a painstaking analysis of the "fundamental codes" of Western culture. Language became his obsession. It seemed to him to be "everywhere," he explained in an unusually revealing interview in 1967: it "hangs over us, leading us forward in our blindness." Yet the logic of its sense escapes us: the meaning we wish to decipher is perpetually melting away, "its face inclined toward a night of which we know nothing." In a rare moment of personal revelation, he confided in his interviewer: "A nightmare has pursued me since childhood. I have under my eyes a text that I am not able to read, of which only a minuscule part can be deciphered by me; I pretend to read it, but I know that I am making it up; then the text suddenly blurs completely, I am no longer able to read anything or even make it up; my throat tightens, and I wake up."[3]

As if to prove his mastery over a domain that he experienced in the recurrent form of anguish and enigma, Foucault in these years demonstrated his ability to read the specialized texts of medicine, botany, and economics with apparently cool objectivity. The propositions and phrases of scientific discourse he carved up into "events and functional segments," ostensibly in an effort to reveal the "system" of understanding, yet also drawing from the dismembered fragments strange and improbable new narratives, evoking a sort of "negative entropy of knowledge," as he once put it.[4]

In *The Birth of the Clinic* (1963), he explored, through a history of medicine in the eighteenth and early nineteenth centuries, the changing ways in which Western society has conceptualized disease and death. And in *The Order of Things* (1966)—his most demanding book, and certainly his most intricate essay in effacement—he attempted to demonstrate, through a comparative history of the sciences of life, language, and economic exchange from the Renaissance to our own day, how "knowledge and theory became possible," and how the apparently solid foundation of knowledge in the modern human sciences "is once more stirring under our feet."[5]

Refining what his friend Gilles Deleuze once called a "rarified positivism, which is itself poetic," Foucault's style in these works reached a new pitch of hermetic abstractness. He deployed a bewildering array of new terms— "*épistémè*," "discursive formations," "enunciative modalities"—all redolent of rigor, analytic precision, scholastic exactness. Yet his thought in these years keeps circling back, as Deleuze noted at the time, to "the subject," to the human being, even (quietly) to the idea of the self, evoking the imaginative universe revealed by Foucault's own nightmare—a world where the logic of things, from the language we speak to the stories that we were told in childhood, forever eludes us, inviting us to explain, but also to invent, fantasize, elaborate, in an endless effort to ward off silence and a fate that looms as a kind of suffocation.[6]

In a series of interviews and in the treatise on method that he called *The Archeology of Knowledge* (1969), Foucault labored to explain the peculiarities of his new approach, suggesting that in his historiography, at least, he was following reasonable rules of method. At the same time, in a series of essays on literature, he implicitly suggested still another way to approach his work—as an unusual new species of fiction. Like Theseus lost in a maze of forking paths, the reader was often left guessing, uncertain which way to turn.

The more baffling his work became, the more people wanted to read it. Foucault had long harbored the ambition to craft a work that might reach beyond the academy, to touch Sartre's larger public. And when *The Order of Things* was first published in France in the spring of 1966, it became a bestseller.

Though unanticipated, his popular triumph was not entirely surprising. The very complexity of his prose proved to be a central ingredient in his success. As Foucault himself later admitted, his style in these years was, in part, an elaborate "game," an illustration and embodiment of the larger philosophical claim of *The Order of Things*, that "truth" itself was a kind of "*jeu.*" To puzzle out the meaning of Foucault's own peculiar claims about "truth" became a popular parlor sport. Prominently displayed next to the art books in the private libraries of educated Parisians, *The Order of Things* served as the literary equivalent of those carefully pruned labyrinths the aristocracy had once taken pride in placing in formal gardens. (Two decades later, Umberto Eco's *The Name of the Rose* would serve a somewhat similar function in the United States.)[7]

At the same time, more deeply buried than before, there still lurked in his language the promise of Luciferian revolt. Despite the protean and perplexing character of his work in these years, *all* of Foucault's writings, from the most literary of the essays to the most recondite of his histories, sounded certain themes with revealing frequency. Intimations of evil, madness, and death appear on page after page, a mute echo of the kind of "limit-experience" apotheosized in *Madness and Civilization*—and a reminder of the personal stakes in Foucault's own "great Nietzschean quest."

In the fall of 1960, Foucault returned to France to become a professor of psychology at the University of Clermont-Ferrand. Old friends who had not seen him in the six years he had been away in Sweden, Poland, and Germany were struck by how much he had changed. Confident and animated, he generally seemed at ease in the world—a far cry from the tortured young man who had disconcerted his classmates at the École Normale.[8]

His academic reputation assured by the success of *Madness and Civilization* in 1961, he now embarked on what outwardly seemed like a more or less orthodox university career. For the next six years, Foucault spent one day a week in Clermont-Ferrand, the provincial capital of the Auvergne, some six hours by train from Paris, where he chose to live. During these years, he published articles in scholarly journals, kept in contact with old mentors like Jean Beaufret and Jean Hyppolite, and made new friends like Georges Canguilhem. Despite his growing academic respectability and his newfound flair for the flamboyant gesture—instead of a suit and tie, he preferred white turtleneck sweaters, black corduroy jackets, and sometimes he sported as well a green wool cape—he remained in many respects a prickly character, quick to anger, often hard to read; gossip about his past and his homosexuality continued to dog him, complicating his efforts to move up the academic ladder. By 1965, he was nevertheless regarded as an authority of suffcent stature to appear on French television, discussing the problem of "truth" with Hyppolite, Canguilhem, and the phenomenologist Paul Ricoeur.[9]

At the same time, Foucault established new links with the Parisian literary world. In 1962, he joined the editorial board of Bataille's old journal, *Critique*; he became friendly with the editors of a new literary quarterly called *Tel quel*; and he published a dazzling sequence of essays on some of his favorite writers: Bataille, Blanchot, Hölderlin, Roussel, the scholastic pornographer Pierre Klossowski, and, last but not least, the leading apostle of the "new novel," Alain Robbe-Grillet—one of the touchstones of Foucault's thinking in these years.[10]

"Man, a stranger to the world, is a stranger to himself," Robbe-Grillet once explained, in words that ring true for Foucault as well. "Literature is not for entertainment. It is a quest," an imaginative odyssey of self-invention and self-discovery.[11]

Inspired by the stark language of Beckett, the actionless *récits* of Blanchot and the later philosophy of Heidegger, Robbe-Grillet had launched his own creative quest in the early 1950s. In *The Erasers* (1953), *The Voyeur* (1955), *Jealousy* (1957), and *In the Labyrinth* (1959), he had refined a blank new style of writing—the "new novel," he called it. In his screenplay for *Last Year at Marienbad* (1961), he brought a similar vision to international film audiences. And in a series of polemical essays, he explained and defended his techniques.[12]

As much as any Frenchman of his generation, it is Robbe-Grillet who deserves the credit, or blame, for delegitimating humanism and the old "myths" of subjectivity and psychological depth. In an essay published in 1957, he argued that the modern world had fallen under the sway of bureaucracy and "administrative number," and that the novelist, if he would grapple with his times, had better jettison a number of obsolete ideas: for example, that the character of any one person made a difference; that telling stories about such characters was a useful and edifying enterprise; that one's own political and moral attitude mattered in the way that Sartre, for one, supposed. A "genuine writer," in Robbe-Grillet's view, might well have "nothing to say." No matter. He could still say whatever he had to say as well as he could say it, in a voice that was unmistakably his own, by elaborating a "way of speaking, starting from nothing, from the dust. . . ."[13]

Practicing what he preached, Robbe-Grillet composed his novels in a singular style of studied apathy, flouting the consolations of narrative drama and ignoring naturalistic conventions of psychological portraiture, developing instead an uninflected voice that seemed empty of all subjective reference, even though the people he wrote about were, just as he said, "*always* engaged . . . in an emotional adventure of the most obsessive kind, to the point of often distorting . . . vision and of producing imaginings close to delirium."[14]

To a certain extent, Robbe-Grillet did empty his novels of "interiority," just as his early admirers supposed. But impersonal though his writing seemed, *all* of it, as he confessed years later, had in fact grown out of the torment and turmoil of his own "emotional adventure": "I have never spoken of anything but myself. From within, and so it has hardly been noticed." As he explained in his memoir *Ghosts in the Mirror* (1984), his parents, virulent anti-Semites, had avidly collaborated with the Nazis after 1940. A teenager when Germany conquered France, Robbe-Grillet was haunted, like Foucault in the same years, by a dream of apocalypse. From the early 1940s on, as Robbe-Grillet later recalled, he was obsessed by the fantasy of being "sucked reluctantly into the heart of an unknown, unstable, irrational liquid universe ready to engulf me, its ineffable face at once the face of death and of desire." The revelation of the concentration camps left Robbe-Grillet stunned. The fascist demand for order, personified by his parents, had led to genocide; his own fantasies of death, he could now see, represented still another kind of "fatal temptation." Looking for some way to grapple with these demons, "I was quite naturally drawn to problematic experimentation with fiction and its contradictions (I stress once more that this is how I see my adventure today) as the most promising arena in which to act out this permanent imbalance: the fight to the death between order and freedom, the insoluble conflict between rational classification and subversion, otherwise known as disorder."[15]

"Writing novels to exorcise the ghosts I couldn't come to terms with," Robbe-Grillet approached each book as a "battlefield and stake. Instead of advancing like some blind justice obeying a divine law," he wrote in 1984, a text should "on the contrary expose publicly and stage accurately the multiple impossibilities with which it is contending. . . . Hence the complicated sequences, digressions, cuts and repetitions, aporias, blind alleys, shifts in perspective, various permutations, dislocations, or inversions." Evoking the human being as an "empty center," the writer could draw up meticulous inventories of the objects that flashed before the eyes of his fevered protagonists. "Measuring, locating, limiting, defining," his narrators approached the world like detectives trying to solve a murder case. The universe he conjured up in this fashion was one of the most sinister sort of factuality—icy, unyielding, disquieting.[16]

It was a style that Foucault loved: "The importance of Robbe-Grillet," he declared in 1963, "can be measured by the question his work poses to every work that is contemporary with it." This "question," Foucault thought, involved nothing less than the inner structure and expressive "possibilities of language." In "the sovereign and obsessive language" of Robbe-Grillet, he concluded, "more than one"—and he surely includes himself—"has found his labyrinth."[17]

Many others shared Foucault's fascination with Robbe-Grillet. In 1960, *Tel quel* was launched, buoyed by the promise of the "new novel." Its editor was Philippe Sollers, an aspiring writer and dedicated libertine, still in his early twenties; its resident theoretician was Roland Barthes, the critic and essayist, who had also been one of Robbe-Grillet's staunchest advocates in the 1950s. Like Robbe-Grillet, the critics and writers affiliated with *Tel quel* wished, in Barthes's phrase, "to achieve a *Dasein* of literary language, a sort of blankness of writing (but not an innocence)." Like Bataille, another one of their heroes, they were fascinated by eroticism and "limit-experience" as sources of creative energy. And like Nietzsche, they embraced the enigmatic idea of "eternal recurrence," taking the journal's name and epigraph from one of his aphorisms: "I want the world and want it AS IS [*tel quel*], want it again, want it eternally."[18]

Recognizing the convergence of their interests, Foucault and Sollers struck up a brief collaboration. The young editor, as one witness has recalled, was "superbly intelligent, lavish in his expenditures, sensitive to every form of femininity"—and an operator *par excellence*, unswervingly dedicated to his own "cult of success." Sollers's alliance with Foucault would not last long: Sollers was too facile and fashion-conscious, Foucault too prickly and difficult. Given the rather weightless conflation of texts and pleasures promoted by Sollers and his circle, the unrelenting character of Foucault's preoccupations must have been unsettling. In a roman à clef published years later, Julia Kristeva, one of the most prominent members of the *Tel quel* group (she would eventually marry Sollers), portrayed the philosopher in the most disturbing terms, as the high priest of a blasphemous new cult, built around "the adoration of death." This was too much for Sollers and his friends. For all their talk about forging a convulsive new style of art, the *Tel quel* ideal in literature, as in life, was aristocratic—an epitome of powerful appetites satisfied with "taste and tolerance." It was in this spirit that Roland Barthes would reassure the journal's readers that "the sole Sadian universe is the universe of his discourse." The divine Marquis must therefore be read "*according to a principle of tact.*"[19]

Foucault obviously had somewhat different views about the nature of the "Sadian universe," and much else besides. It took a few years, however, for such differences to harden into open disagreement. And in 1963, fascinated by the "universe of discourse" opened up by *Madness and Civilization*, Sollers invited Foucault to lead a "Debate on the Novel" with members of the *Tel quel* group.

In his introductory comments to this exchange, Foucault offered a suggestive sketch of how he saw the concerns of art and philosophy converging in the work of writers like Robbe-Grillet, Sollers—and, implicitly, himself. "I am struck by one thing," Foucault remarked. "In the novels that I have read [by Robbe-Grillet and the writers linked with *Tel quel*] there is an endless reference to a certain number of experiences—if you will, I would call these, in quotes, 'spiritual experiences' (though of course the word 'spiritual' is not good)—like the dream, like madness, like unreason, like repetition, the double, the flight of time, the return, etc. These experiences form a constellation that is probably very coherent. I am struck by the fact that one finds this constellation sketched in nearly the same fashion by the surrealists."[20]

Given the obvious affinities of the "new novel" with surrealism, what, Foucault asks, are the differences? There are two major ones, he suggests. First, the notion of "experience" (for Sollers and, implicitly, for Foucault himself) has been separated from the domain of psychology, where André Breton, under the influence of Freud, had left it. Experience has become instead a matter for "thinking." The credit for showing the way to this new, properly *philosophical* appreciation of "experience" Foucault gives to Bataille, Blanchot, and Robbe-Grillet.[21]

The second major difference, according to Foucault, is that for the surrealists language had merely been an instrument, a means of representing experience. For the writers grouped around *Tel quel*, by contrast (and, again, implicitly for himself), language is an end in itself: "the book" becomes an "experience" in its own right. Literature now conveys a "thought that speaks:" it is a "thinking word."[22]

As these remarks suggest, it would be a mistake to isolate, as is often done, the literary and philosophical dimensions of Foucault's work in these years. "Fiction does not exist because language is at a distance from things," he explained in another essay published in 1963, carefully defining the scope of "fiction": "Language *is* the distance." It is as if words produced a kind of diffuse and artificially generated "light," revealing that things exist while simultaneously reminding us of the "inaccessibility" of these things apart from language, "the simulacra that gives them their sole presence; and all language that instead of forgetting this distance is maintained in it, and maintains it in itself, *all* language that speaks of this distance by moving into it is a language of fiction." As Foucault emphasizes, this "fictive" language, as he has defined it, can be put into play in "*all* prose and all poetry," in "all novels and *all* reflection, without discrimination."[23]

That Foucault took seriously a convergence of fiction and "reflection" is suggested by the simultaneous publication, on exactly the same day in 1963, of *The Birth of the Clinic*, Foucault's monograph on modern medicine, and *Raymond Roussel*, his study of the poet and novelist.[24]

At first glance, the two works seem completely different. One is a work of history, the other a piece of literary criticism; one is empirical, the other transparently imaginative. Yet both works are "about space, about language, and about death." And by analyzing different "games" in which "things and words are designated and withdrawn, betrayed and masked," both works illuminate "the inexhaustible configurations of the domain common to language and being."[25]

In *The Birth of the Clinic*, the language-game at issue involves the constitution, through the new doctrines and practices of modern pathological anatomy, of the human body as "the space of the origin and distribution of disease." The chief architect of this new understanding, in Foucault's account, was Marie François Xavier Bichat (1771–1802). By defining "a system of *analytic classes* for disease," in part by classifying twenty-one different types of tissue, from arteries to the epidermis, Bichat enunciated a new "principle of deciphering corporal space," one that cast both the body and disease in a new light. Looking at the body in Bichat's terms, disease ceases to be an alien "pathology that inserts itself in the body wherever possible; it is the body itself, become diseased." Foucault calls this view a breakthrough to "a more genuinely scientific empiricism." But he refuses to regard Bichat's theory as an act of "epistemological purification," describing it instead as a total "syntactical reorganization." As Foucault writes, it is "not a matter of the same game, somewhat improved, but of a quite different game," with quite different rules. And it is only thanks to these new rules that "the abyss beneath illness [*le mal*]"—the constant presence of "death in life"—can emerge "into the light of language."[26]

Roussel's language-game, as Foucault describes it, eerily mirrors that of Bichat. Like the scientist, the artist articulates a language in which death becomes a positive phenomenon, taking "positive," as Foucault once put it, "in the strong sense": in the writing of both men, "disease [*la maladie*] breaks away from the metaphysic of evil [*du mal*], to which it had been related for centuries; and it finds in the visibility of death the full form in which its content appears in positive terms." Like Bichat, Roussel affirms the constant presence of "death in life." This presence, however, Roussel experienced not as an objective fact to be grasped through orderly inquiry, but rather as an insane fascination: on one occasion, after slitting his wrists in a bathtub, Roussel was pleased and surprised to find "how easy it was to die." It was in a similar spirit of rapturous abandon that he apparently overdosed in 1933 on his drug of choice, barbiturates.[27]

In Foucault's view, it is, paradoxically enough, the artist and not the scientist who most clearly reveals "the general law of the Game of Signs, in which is pursued our reasonable history." The use of the word "game" here underlines the claim—familiar from Wittgenstein, whose work Foucault knew in at least broad outline—that language is part of a human activity, a "form of life"; its rules are accordingly not something fixed, given once for all; new types of language-games—scientific, literary, moral—come into existence, while others become obsolete, and, falling into disuse, are forgotten.[28]

The invention of new language-games was something of a mania with Roussel, who elaborated his extraordinary and often sinister fantasies with the deadpan humor, and mock-scientific attention to detail, of a Rube Goldberg. A flamboyantly eccentric playwright, poet, and novelist—and also a former patient of the well-known French psychiatrist Pierre Janet—Roussel submitted himself to a variety of arbitrary but rigorous rules for composing his poems and novels. Obsessed with puns, he liked to build narratives around homophonic structures: words and entire sentences that sounded identical, yet had completely different meanings. In the *New Impressions of Africa*, his most widely read poem, "each canto starts off innocently," as one critic has written, "but the narrative is constantly interrupted by a parenthetical thought. New words suggest new parentheses; sometimes as many as five pairs of parentheses ((((()))) isolate one idea buried in the surrounding verbiage like the central sphere in a Chinese puzzle. In order to finish the first sentence, one must turn ahead to the last line of the canto, and by working backward and forward one can at last piece the poem together."[29]

Despite the apparently impersonal rigor of Roussel's different methods, all of his writing teems with imagery that reveals the work as a whole to be a kind of involuntary and phantasmagorical autobiography. As his lifelong friend Michel Leiris pointed out, every one of his works contained "deep layers of emotion, as is attested by the striking frequency of certain themes in his work as a whole: control over the universe or the fusion of the microcosm with the macrocosm, ecstasy, paradise, hidden treasure, the obsession with death, enigma, fetishistic or sado-masochistic sorts of themes, etc." Beneath "the systematically fabricated chance" that regulated the facade of Roussel's work, Foucault, too, pointed out "the anguish of the signified"—above all, in the "interminably recounted repetition of death."[30]

At first glance, it is hard to see how the suicidal "anguish" of this mad artist could remotely approach the general significance of Bichat's scientific discoveries about disease, anatomy, and the structure of human tissues. But Foucault argues that "quite unique forms of experience (quite 'deviant,' that is to say, disorienting)" are necessary "to expose this bare linguistic fact": the vertiginous power of language "to say things—all things," and in this way to "make appear," as if by magic, "things never before said, nor heard, nor seen." Exploring these "bare linguistic facts" without the inhibitions of the scientist, the artist is able to reveal, and positively affirm, a previously "blind and negative side of an experience that surfaces in our time"—the other side, as it were, of the human morbidity that modern medicine has turned into an object of scientific inquiry, through the language-game first devised by Bichat.[31]

In effect, Roussel, through the work of art he made out of his death-haunted life, and Bichat, through the object of knowledge he made out of the human corpse, *both* illustrate, *conjointly*, three crucial aspects of Foucault's own understanding of language and the order of things:

—Language alone makes possible order and reasoned knowledge of the world.

—At the same time, language makes thinkable the unreal and unreasonable.

—Language therefore calls into question the world and ultimately itself in a dizzying spiral of possibilities and impossibilities, realities and unrealities, that may well climax, as it did for Roussel, in a mad and lyrical embrace of the void, oblivion and death—"that formless, silent, unsignifying region where language can free itself."[32]

In his focus on language, Foucault was exploring an area of growing concern, not just in France, but in Europe and North America as well. The sources of this international interest were varied, from Wittgenstein and the logical positivists to the later Heidegger, who declared that language was the "house of being." In the late forties, Merleau-Ponty had begun to speak about the philosophical implications of the theories of Ferdinand de Saussure, the Swiss father of structural linguistics. By 1963, when *Birth of the Clinic* and *Raymond Roussel* appeared, Saussure was sufficiently well known in France that Foucault was able to signal his own interest in language with a handful of rhetorical gestures: in both books, he spoke of "signifier" and "signified," borrowing Saussure's terms for the "sound-image" of a word, and what the "sound-image" was used to indicate. And in *The Birth of the Clinic*, Foucault placed himself squarely within the intellectual movement, founded on Saussure's linguistics, then gathering steam in Paris: for his historiography, he declared, offers "a structural analysis."[33]

These were giddy years in Paris. Dazzled by Saussure's dictum that "*the linguistic sign is arbitrary*," a new generation of writers and thinkers had thrown off the old existentialist stress on the commitments and responsibilities of the individual. Language was a game! In the minds of some, it was as if the discoveries of modern science had vindicated the nihilist slogan: Nothing is true, anything is permitted! The study of language, as one astute observer summed up the Parisian scene in the sixties, became "an aesthetic activity, a release, so to speak, from the tyranny of time and history."[34]

The oracle of the hour became Roland Barthes, a central figure in the *Tel quel* group, and also Foucault's colleague on the editorial board of

Critique. (Though their relations were normally cordial, they seem never to have been close friends.) As one connoisseur of French intellectual life put it, Barthes conjured up the image of "a spirit floating on every breeze, quivering at every touch, able to absorb every impression and to retransmit it in turn, but needing to be set in motion by a neighboring spirit, always eager to borrow a watchword, which so many others would then come to seek from him." Barthes's watchword in the fifties had been the "new novel." For much of the sixties it would be "semiology." Lured by the idea that the world is one vast text, he was swept away, not simply by his own exquisitely refined powers of interpretation, but also by the prospect of creating a rigorous new science of signs. *Tel quel* quickly followed his lead. By the end of the sixties, it had become all but impossible to publish an article in the journal without accompanying diagrams and equations, giving its pages the slightly forbidding (and utterly misleading) look of a mathematics journal.[35]

The basic idea behind Barthes's enthusiasm in the sixties was nothing new: that a science of signs might have applications beyond the narrow field of linguistics had already been demonstrated by Claude Lévi-Strauss, an anthropologist of Sartre's generation. Trained in the French sociological tradition of Émile Durkheim and Marcel Mauss, but inspired as well by the theories of Saussure, Lévi-Strauss regarded anthropology as the study of "the life of signs at the heart of social life." Whether analyzing myth and ritual, or marriage rules and kinship systems, his aim, as he once put it, was "to classify types, to analyze their constituent parts, and to establish correlations between them," bringing to light a cognitive structure that remained as unconscious as the system of phonetic differences any given individual put into play in speaking a language.[36]

It seems clear in retrospect that Foucault watched the growing surge of interest in structuralism with sympathy, detachment—and a strategist's shrewd sense of the forces at play. Here was a language-game he was perfectly equipped to play. By training and temperament, he was a formalist. The idea of a "structure" of thought, underlying even the apparently random flow of images in reverie, he had long ago learned from such French historians of science as Bachelard and Canguilhem. The jargon of these historians—their emphasis on "*coupures*," or breaks between scientific paradigms, their stress on revolutionary discontinuities rather than incremental evolution—Foucault had learned from another master of formalist theory, his old teacher Louis Althusser, who had burst on the Parisian scene in 1965 as an avatar of a rigorously "structuralist" Marxism. Foucault had also become acquainted, years before, with the work of

Jacques Lacan, the proponent of a rigorously "structural" reading of Freud, and also the object of intense debate after the publication of his *Écrits* in 1966—though Foucault on at least one occasion blithely declared that Lacan's impenetrable prose left him baffled.[37]

Perhaps more important than any of these estimable figures, though, was the example of Foucault's most powerful academic patron, Georges Dumézil (1898–1988), who in 1970 would lead a successful campaign to have his protégé elected to the Collège de France. A student of comparative mythology trained in philology and the history of religion, Dumézil was a man jealous of his independence, and averse to passing fads and schools of thought. Trained in the old-fashioned evolutionist approach to folklore that the English anthropologist James Frazer had used in *The Golden Bough*, Dumézil in the 1920s transformed his method after studying Durkheim and Mauss. Like Lévi-Strauss, he came to embrace one of Durkheim's key propositions: that the concepts and supernatural beings of myth "collectively represent" important social and cultural realities. Unlike Lévi-Strauss, however, Dumézil never claimed to have discovered universal forms that inhered in the human mind; instead, he emphasized the temporal and spatial limitations of the different structures that he studied. "For me the word 'structure' evokes the image of a spider web often used by Marcel Mauss," he once explained. "In a system of thought, when one draws on a concept everything comes with it, since between all the parts run threads."[38]

Foucault, too, linked the idea of structure to the image of a "dark, but firm net." Dumézil's example and influence he directly acknowledged on more than one occasion, from the original preface of *Madness and Civilization* to his final lectures at the Collège de France in 1984. At the height of Foucault's early fame, when he was widely regarded as France's resident structuralist philosopher, he would often cite examples culled from Dumézil to explain his understanding of what the ideas of system and structure entailed. Rebutting critics who charged that structuralism and the study of history were incompatible, he found it useful to point out that "a structural analysis like that of Dumézil can be linked up with a historical analysis." After all, Dumézil had tried to show—as Foucault once summed the argument up—how specific transformations of archaic Indo-European myths in Horace's poetry illuminated the concurrent "transformation of the old Roman society into a society controlled by the state." By treating such work as exemplary, Foucault could say, and did, that "an analysis is structural when it studies a transformable system and the conditions under which its transformations come to pass."[39]

It was, in short, in the spirit of Dumézil that Foucault joined—briefly but unmistakably—the structuralist chorus of the sixties. From his perspective, indeed, a kind of tactical alliance made a great deal of sense. For as different as Dumézil, Barthes, Lévi-Strauss, Althusser, and Lacan obviously were, each from the other, and Foucault from each of them in turn, they all had at least one thing in common: a wish to destroy the intellectual hegemony of Jean-Paul Sartre.

Foucault's return to France in the fall of 1960 had coincided with the most spectacular transformation of Sartre's public stature since his lecture on existentialism fifteen years before. The occasion was the civil war in Algeria, still a French colony at the time; the cause was "the Manifesto of the 121," a defiant proclamation issued in September, 1960. Signed by a diverse group of well-known intellectuals, the manifesto defended "the right to insubordination in the Algerian war."[40]

Though Foucault himself was opposed to the war, he felt no need to voice his own views publicly. His days of outspoken activism were still to come, as were his days of public notoriety. Unknown at the time (*Madness and Civilization* had not yet been published), he was never approached to sign the manifesto.[41]

Those who did sign it were soon swept up in an explosive controversy. French authorities treated the manifesto as an act of treason. No journal dared to publish it; charges were brought in court against several of those who had signed it; and France's network of police was mobilized to track down the perpetrators. The manifesto had in fact been drafted largely by Maurice Blanchot, in conjunction with old comrades from the surrealist movement. But in this charged context, public attention was increasingly focused on the one signatory who became the symbol of the whole affair: Jean-Paul Sartre.[42]

As he had in 1945, Sartre rose to the occasion. The right-wing clamored for his arrest. With stubborn courage, Sartre reiterated his personal support, not only for the right of insubordination, but also for the worldwide movement against colonialism. It was perhaps his finest hour. The protests of the right-wing grew louder and louder. Finally, French President Charles de Gaulle, no less, made it plain that Sartre was untouchable: "You do not imprison Voltaire."[43]

Sartre's prestige had never been greater—a more vivid demonstration of his sovereign authority would be hard to imagine. His intervention had helped defuse a volatile situation: the charges brought against the signatories of the manifesto were quietly dropped. But that was not all. For Sartre in 1960 did not simply emerge as the anointed intellectual conscience of his country. For the first time in over a decade, he was also at the center of philosophical debate, thanks to the publication earlier in the year of his long-awaited sequel to *Being and Nothingness*, the *Critique of Dialectical Reason*.[44]

In this interminable text, Sartre undertook a synthesis of existentialism and Marxism, which he declared to be the unsurpassable "philosophy of our time." Even longer than *Being and Nothingness* (and far murkier, due, perhaps, to its slapdash composition under the influence of amphetamines), the *Critique* attempted to lay bare the manifold ways in which the freedom of the human being could be actively alienated, fettered by social forces of the human being's own making and maintenance. By describing in detail the "dialectic" through which conscious individuals, acting in concert, could produce collective social structures at first glance utterly foreign to their conscious intentions, Sartre claimed to have put on a secure new footing "the *Truth of history*." "We are attempting," he solemnly declared, "to lay the basis for a 'Prolegomena to any Future Anthropology.'"[45]

These were large and sweeping claims, which doubtless attracted the attention of Foucault. For as it happens, the younger man had just finished a first draft of his own "Prolegomena to any Future Anthropology." This was his unpublished *thèse complémentaire* on Kant's *Anthropology*—the seed from which ultimately grew *The Order of Things*.

In Foucault's day, a doctorate required the submission of two theses, one of publishable quality, the other—the *thèse complémentaire*—a smaller piece of work on a different topic, indicating the range of the candidate's scholarship. To meet the requirement, Foucault in 1960 had submitted to the Sorbonne jury, in addition to *Madness and Civilization*, a translation of Kant's *Anthropology From a Pragmatic Point of View*, which Foucault had rendered into French for the first time, along with a commentary that, in typescript, is 128 pages long.[46]

By "anthropology," Kant meant not ethnography, in the narrow sense of modern cultural anthropology, but rather the empirical study of the human being in every conceivable aspect. In a famous passage from his *Logic*, Kant himself suggested that anthropology might even be regarded as the fundamental issue of his philosophy, since all of the other questions he had tried to answer—What can I know? What ought I to do? What may I hope?—could be incorporated into the general question, What is Man?[47]

Kant himself made a serious and sustained effort to illuminate this last question. Throughout his teaching career, he regularly lectured on anthropology. But with the conspicuous exception of Heidegger (whose book on *Kant and the Problem of Metaphysics* implicitly informs Foucault's argument), subsequent philosophers have rarely taken Kant's comments about anthropology seriously. In part, this is due to the eccentricity of the one book Kant devoted to the subject. Instead of offering a conventionally philosophical answer to the question—What is Man?—the book *Anthropology*, published near the end of his life in 1798, offers a variety of comments and maxims about a bewildering array of different topics, from the most abstract issues of cognition to the most concrete matters of everyday behavior. No matter what the subject, Kant invariably strove "to deduce from these phenomena" pragmatic "rules of conduct." The result is a mélange of the most subtle distinctions, banal platitudes, and groundless prejudices, a sort of metaphysician's "Dear Abby": "A young, intelligent wife will have better luck in marriage with a healthy, but nevertheless, noticeably older man"; "that people allow themselves to be engaged in treasure seeking, alchemy, and trading in lotteries, is not to be attributed to their stupidity, but to their evil intent in wanting to get rich at the expense of others without a proportionate effort of their own"; "the greatest sensuous pleasure, which is not accompanied by any loathing at all, is found under healthy conditions in resting after work"; and so forth, for several hundred pages.[48]

Though the temptation must have been great, Foucault does not have sport with Kant's strange text. He takes Kant's comment in the *Logic* seriously—indeed, he takes Kant's entire oeuvre seriously.

For Foucault never ceased to regard himself as a kind of Kantian. Kant's critical method, he declares in his *thèse*, shows philosophy "the authentic form of its self-realization." In *The Order of Things*, he affirms that "Kantian critique" still forms an essential part of "the immediate space of our reflection. We think on this premise." And in an essay completed shortly before his death, a self-portrait for a French *Dictionary of Philosophers*, Foucault again explicitly situated his own work within "the *critical* tradition of Kant." This tradition, as Foucault sums it up, entails "an analysis of the conditions under which certain relations of subject to object are formed or modified," and a demonstration of how these conditions "are constitutive of a possible knowledge."[49]

As every student of philosophy is taught, Kant maintained that our experience of the world could arise only on the basis of certain *a priori* categories: "Though all our knowledge begins with experience," declared Kant, "it does not follow that it all arises out of experience." The *a priori* categories he considered most essential to the ordering of experience— cause and substance among them—Kant took to be a product of the understanding, exercised in conjunction with the two other main human faculties, the imagination and sensibility (seeing, hearing, etc.). By thus focusing philosophy on the capacities of the human being, Kant abandoned the view, shared by thinkers as different as Plato and Locke, that our concepts and categories for understanding the world, in order to be "true," must conform to some independently existing reality; it was part of Kant's "Copernican revolution" in philosophy to argue instead that a number of the most essential categories of thought conform to a specific "lawfulness of cognition" (as Ernst Cassirer once put it), "to which a determinate form of objectivity (be it theoretical, ethical, or aesthetic in kind) is to be traced back."⁵⁰

Kant had developed his new approach in an effort to secure the foundations of knowledge against skeptical attack. In trying to establish the limits of trustworthy knowledge, he felt compelled to draw a sharp line between the empirical knowledge that arose in the course of experience, and transcendental ideas, formed by speculative reason alone, of what lay beyond all possible experience. Of these "Ideas of Reason," perhaps the most unsettling was that of free will. For the will, Kant supposed, though enigmatic, unprovable, and, strictly speaking, unknowable, nevertheless seemed to him able to put the transcendental into practice, turning certain "Ideas" into objects of possible experience, and thus apparently bridging the chasm between the empirical and transcendental: "How great a gulf may still have to be left between the idea [of reason] and its realization [in practice]," he wrote in the *Critique of Pure Reason*, "are questions which no one can, or ought to, answer. For the issue depends on freedom; and it is in the power of freedom to pass beyond any and every specified limit."⁵¹

Hence the second aspect of Kant's "Copernican revolution" in philosophy: his suggestion that human beings are both able and obliged to *construct* a moral and political world for themselves, using Ideas of Reason. And though Kant believed that such a construction, if carried out within the bounds of reason, would vindicate traditional Christian ideas of God, moral responsibility, and the soul's immortality, an inescapable consequence of Kant's "transcendental" critique was to grant to the human being a creative power of intrinsically uncertain scope. After Kant's critical revolution, Foucault comments, "the world appears as a city to be built, rather than as a cosmos already given."[52]

Kant's *Anthropology* stands in a complex relationship to the larger edifice of his philosophy. On one level, as Foucault points out in his thesis, the bizarre assortment of *idées reçues* and maxims in the *Anthropology* exists independently of the philosopher's critical system of thought, even though Kant organizes his material using categories borrowed from this system. But on another level, Foucault suggests, Kant's *Anthropology* lays bare the "truly temporal dimension" of the *a priori* concepts analyzed in Kant's three Critiques: for the *idées reçues* inventoried in the *Anthropology* repeat "in the same order and in the same language the *a priori* of the understanding and the imperative of the morality"; what is "given" in such precepts "mimics" the reasoning in the Critiques, and "seems to be able to function as an *a priori*."[53]

Thus, Kant's *Anthropology*, far from being a piece of crackpot pseudo-science, opens up an important new philosophical horizon. Despite its apparent eccentricity, Kant's book underlines for Foucault the manifold ways in which "the self, by becoming an object" of regulated social practices, "takes its place in the field of experience and finds there a concrete system of belonging." This system is "immediate and imperative"; no human being may escape it; it is transmitted in "the regulated element of language," organized "without the intervention of a force or authority," activated within each subject "purely and simply because he speaks."[54]

At first glance, the evident power of social practices to construct, regulate, and limit the significance accorded experience underlines the extent to which the human being must grow up within a world not of its own making. Yet on another level, comments Foucault, "the secret of Power" is revealed in the sheer disorderly proliferation of the phenomena investigated by Kant in his anthropology: "egoism, the effective consciousness of respresentation; or, in addition, the imagination as a power of creative 'invention,' the imagination in the shipwreck of the dream, the imagination in the poetry linked to the sign; or, in addition: the power of desire with its emotions; the false truth of passion. . . ."[55]

For Kant, the explanation for the sheer diversity of human practices lay in freedom. What was "practical," as he defined the term in *The Critique of Pure Reason*, was "everything that is possible through freedom." The uncertain status of the *Anthropology*, in Kant's work, derives from the uncertain limits of its "practical" precepts. As Foucault puts it, the practices that Kant describes exhibit "the ambiguity of Play (game = plaything)" and "the uncertainty of Art (skill = trick)."[56]

Call them "play" or call them a type of "artifice," what attitude should we take toward these practices? If transcendental ideas might become practical through the exercise of the mysterious and, strictly speaking, unknowable power of free will, by what right or rule could Kant (or society) limit the scope of this power?

Heidegger, for one, thought that Kant had tried to evade the implications of his philosophical breakthrough. In the *Critique of Pure Reason*, Kant had laid bare the synthetic powers of freedom and imagination, only to draw back, wrote Heidegger, "before this abyss. He saw the unknown; he had to draw back." Instead of taking the full measure of his discoveries, Kant tried to justify "the notions of the composition and characterization of the subjectivity of the subject provided by traditional anthropology." Because "anthropology in general does not raise the question of transcendence," Kant's turn to anthropology amounted to a failure of nerve.[57]

Foucault shared Heidegger's view. Though Kant had opened, "in a manner which is still enigmatic, metaphysical discourse and a reflection on the limits of reason," he ended by "closing this opening when he ultimately referred all critical interrogation to the anthropological question." Instead of exercising the power of free will and imagining "a city to be built," Kant in his *Anthropology* tried to vindicate a "normative understanding," not only by codifying the kind of savoir faire acquired in the course of everyday life, but also by accusing of "high treason" anyone who regarded such know-how as counterfeit and illusory. As Foucault sums up the argument of his thesis in *The Order of Things*, Kant's philosophy produces, "surreptitiously and in advance, the confusion of the empirical and the transcendental, even though Kant had demonstrated the division between them."[58]

It is precisely this confusion that Foucault thinks vitiates the phenomenology of Husserl and his existentialist successors. They revert to "a precritical analysis" in their celebration of the "life-world"—a domain of passive rather than active synthesis.[59]

Foucault, by contrast, wishes, at least provisionally, to uphold Kant's sharp division between the empirical and the transcendental. Like Heidegger, he believes that Kant has laid bare the transcendental power of the human being, even if he has recoiled from the implications of our ability to transcend every limit; in addition, he supposes that Kant's *Anthropology* has revealed, even if inadvertently, the "truly temporal dimension" of the *a priori*: our essential categories and judgments grow out of customs, habits, and inclinations, transmitted through language and regulated by social institutions.

The task of philosophy in the wake of Kant is thus twofold: first, it must examine the "historical *a prioris*" of possible experience through an empirical investigation of their tangled and often buried de facto roots in customs, habits, social institutions, scientific disciplines, and the specific language-games and styles of reasoning that informed each of these different domains. Spurning the composition of conventional philosophical treatises and commentaries, Foucault would devote his life to investigating many of the same topics treated in *Anthropology from a Pragmatic Point of View*—notably dreams, mental illness, and "the marvelous play of the human imagination"; the relative value of visual images, symbols, and abstract ideas as means of communication; the structure of cognition and its limits; the faculty of desire and "the character of the sexes"—showing how institutions and practices traverse all of these facets of the human being, enclosing and cultivating the field of possible experience, long before the active understanding of the individual comes into play. This endeavor he will come to call "the analytics of truth."[60]

The second part of the twofold task of philosophy is to explore, without Kant's inhibitions, the frontiers of possible experience. By exercising the transcendental freedom that Kant himself established as one basis of critique, one might also obtain a critical perspective on the "dark, firm net" of custom and habit, and elaborate what Foucault later called an "ontology of ourselves." And one might do this most forcefully, as Foucault cryptically writes in his thesis, by moving from "an interrogation of the limit and of transgression" toward "an interrogation of the return of the self."[61]

Only one thinker, Foucault concludes in 1960, has so far grasped the full implications of this twofold task—Friedrich Nietzsche: "The trajectory of the question, What is Man?, in the field of philosophy, culminates in the challenging and disarming response: the Overman."[62]

In the years after completing his thesis, Foucault pursued the implications of Kant's philosophy along two parallel paths. On the level of empirical inquiry, he investigated, using the techniques of Bachelard and Canguilhem, the prehistory of the human sciences, one of the most important sources for the material in Kant's original *Anthropology*.

"I was above all trying to order and compare three different scientific practices," he later recalled. "By 'scientific practice,' I mean a certain way of regulating and constructing discourses that define, in turn, a particular domain of objects while simultaneously determining an ideal subject destined to know them. I had found it striking that three distinct domains—natural history, grammar, and political economy—had been constituted, in regard to their rules, more or less in the same period, during the seventeenth century, and had undergone, one hundred years later, analogous transformations."[63]

Perhaps by isolating, through a comparative empirical analysis, a certain "style" of reasoning informing the play of true and false in such apparently disparate disciplines, it would be possible to reveal the "truly temporal dimension" of the *a priori* categories in terms of which any living, speaking, and laboring being in the seventeenth, eighteenth, and nineteenth centuries might order, and so come to know, the world, and itself, as objects of rational understanding.

On the level of transcendental inquiry, on the other hand, Foucault remained fascinated by "an interrogation of the limit and of transgression," directed toward "the return of the self"—the Dionysian project of Nietzsche, and also of Roussel, Bataille, and Blanchot: "Ought we not to remind ourselves," he asked in the *The Order of Things*, "that we are bound to the back of a tiger?"[64]

Interrogating the limit, a thinker might yet recapture the "experience, not yet divided, of division itself," thereby illuminating simultaneously the empirical and transcendental dimensions of the human being. "Perhaps the experience of transgression," Foucault speculated, "in the movement which carries it toward utter night, brings to light the relation of finitude to being, the moment of the limit which anthropological thought, since Kant, could only designate from afar." To the extent that it makes possible a revelation of the limits of reason and of the human being, transgression accomplishes a kind of post-Kantian "critique" in "a three-fold sense": "it brings to light the conceptual and historical *a priori*; it discerns the conditions in which [philosophical thought] can find or transcend its forms of stability; it ultimately passes judgment and makes a decision about its possibilities of existence."[65]

By taking thought to its breaking point, transgression thus paradoxically renews "the project for a general critique of reason." Transcendental reflection is transformed, almost beyond recognition: it breaks free of the analytic understanding, where Kant had anchored it, and sails forth into madness, the dream, and erotic delirium. In the process, Kant's original anthropological question—What is man?—is transformed implicitly into Nietzsche's question: How did I become what I am, and why do I suffer so from being what I am? "This is why transcendental reflection in its modern form does not, as in Kant, find its fundamental necessity in the existence of a science of nature . . . but in the existence—mute, yet ready to speak, and secretly impregnated with a potential discourse—of that not-known from which man is endlessly called toward knowledge of the self."[66]

To express this obscure "potential discourse" requires a language that can "speak of this distance by moving into it." Philosophy "regains its speech and gets a grip on itself again only on its borders and limits." What restores to thought "its sovereign power is not knowledge (which is ever more predictable) or fable (which has its conventions), but, between the two and as if in an invisible no-man's-land, the shining play of fiction."[67]

That such an "interrogation" of the limit through "transgression," in writing, but also in everyday existence, is dangerous, Foucault not only concedes, but insists: to think through and act out the enigmatic ability of the human being to pass beyond any and every specified limit is to risk a fatal vertigo ("a relativism without recourse," as Foucault put it in 1961). The thinker flirts with self-destruction. For when the void around language "emerges in all its nakedness," when "Desire reigns in an untamed state, as if the rigor of its rule had levelled all opposition, when Death dominates every psychological function and stands above it as its unique and devastating norm; then we recognize madness in its present form, madness as it is posited in the modern experience, as its *truth*"—a strong word, here—"and its alterity."[68]

Putting himself to the test, the philosopher does not hesitate. In order to know the truth, and perhaps also to find himself, he will risk losing himself: "and it is at the center of this disappearance of the philosophizing subject that philosophical language proceeds, as if through a labyrinth."[69]

The labyrinth is the central emblem of Foucault's great Nietzschean quest in these years. In his book on Roussel and in his 1962 essay, "Such a Cruel Knowledge," he elaborated his own, highly personal myth of death and rebirth, by giving a number of new twists to the original Greek story of the labyrinth.[70]

Traditionally the labyrinth was considered to be the handiwork of paganism's greatest inventor, Daedalus. Foucault, however, sees the labyrinth not simply as a testimony to the genius of its designer, but also as the disquieting symbol of a deeply mysterious sort of transcendence, indicating "the simultaneous presence and absence of Daedalus in the incomprehensible and dead sovereignty of his knowledge."[71]

To enter the gates of the maze is to enter a theater of "Dionysian castration"; it is to undergo a "paradoxical initiation, not to a lost secret, but to all of the suffering of which man has never lost the memory," the "oldest cruelties of the world." Once caught in its winding corridors, "flight is not conceivable; there is no exit apart from this somber point that indicates the center, the infernal fire, the law of the image."[72]

The symbol of this "law" (a figure, therefore, of the synthetic power of freedom at play in imagination) is the Minotaur—half man, half beast, the monster that Theseus slays in the Greek myth.

In Foucault's retelling, however, Theseus does nothing of the sort: bewitched by the mystery of the Minotaur, the would-be conquering hero falls captive, captivated.[73]

Even Ariadne, a figure of reason and prudence who keeps a grip on the thread that might allow Theseus to escape, proves powerless: "one can miss Ariadne, one cannot miss the Minotaur. She is the uncertain, the improbable, the distant." (Foucault in another context pictures Ariadne lost and dying—strangled by her own thread.)[74]

The Minotaur alone "is the certain, the very near," and yet also the "absolutely alien"—an emblem of "the limits of the human and inhuman."[75]

Two great mythic spaces crisscross in Foucault's retelling of the old story. The first space, of the labyrinth proper, is "rigid, forbidden, enveloping." The second space, of the personal metamorphosis Foucault's labyrinth makes possible, is "communicating, polymorphous, continuous, and irreversible."[76]

The two spaces intersect where the Minotaur hides. By "his very being," Foucault writes, the Minotaur "opens a second labyrinth: the entrapment of man, of the beast, and of the gods, knot of appetites, mute thought. The winding of corridors begins again, unless perhaps it is the same one; and the mixed being refers to the inextricable geometry that leads to him; the labyrinth would then be simultaneously the truth and nature of the Minotaur, that which confines him externally, and that which brings him to light on the inside."[77]

Exploring the enigma of the new maze opened up by the nature of the monster within, fascinated by a rigorous yet elusive plan that seems to point toward an inescapable fusion of divine freedom with inhuman bestiality, the human being traverses time as well as space, as if spiralling back toward a "rediscovered origin." "Chronos is the time of becoming and beginning anew," Foucault writes: "Chronos devours bit by bit that to which it gives birth and that which it causes to be reborn in its time. This monstrous and lawless becoming—the great destruction of each instant, the gobbling up of all life, the scattering of its limbs—is linked to the exactitude of a beginning anew: Becoming leads into this great, interior labyrinth"—a labyrinth "no different in nature from the monster it contains."[78]

Moving towards the core of this "great interior labyrinth," trying to understand the monster that one has become, the captive pilgrim helplessly watches the "destiny of man . . . being spun before [his] very eyes, but being spun in reverse"; the threads of destiny lead into the past, taking the human being "back, by those strange bobbins, to the forms of its birth, to the homeland that made it possible." To proceed, however, the prisoner of the passage must submit to the harshest and most agonizing of punishments, "a pure and simple duplication of the labyrinth constructed out of cruelty" to hide the innocence of being at birth. (The maze here becomes a figure of the human being's inescapable fate—as if perhaps it was not Daedalus, but rather Time, congealed in the form of History, that has designed the inner labyrinth as this singular ordeal.)[79]

His innocence painfully resurrected by the tortures suffered en route, the pilgrim finally arrives at the heart of the second maze, finding the "radiant light" of the "rediscovered origin." At last he unriddles his *daimon*, learning that the "star" on his forehead is "an image of metamorphosis where chance and repetition are united; the accident of the sign, thrown before every thing, initiates a time and a space in which each figure will echo itself."[80]

For all of its "teeming adventures, life will never be anything but the double of its star"—the unique sign of a "higher necessity."[81]

At this "most enigmatic moment," when "all paths break off and when one feels at a loss, or at the absolute origin, when one is on the threshold of something else, the labyrinth suddenly offers the *Same*: its last puzzle, the ruse hidden in the center—the mirror behind which one finds the identical."[82]

Situated at the core of the maze within the maze, this "mirror, which reflects the unriddled birth, is reflected in the mirror where death sees itself, which in turn is reflected in it. . . ." The labyrinth here reveals its deepest secret—"the passage from life to death, and the maintenance of life in death."[83]

Moreover, the existence of this mysterious "inner labyrinth," as Foucault imagines in another context, also suggests that behind the "deceptive surfaces" of modern society lurks a human "nature metamorphosized in depth by the powers of a counter-nature." Containing, as it does, "the passage from life to death," the "great interior labyrinth," like Sade's Castle of Murders, organizes a space proper to "modern perversity." "A cage," the labyrinth "makes of man a beast of desire"; "a tomb," it "weaves beneath states a counter-city"; a diabolically clever invention, it is designed to unleash "all the volcanoes of madness,"—threatening to "destroy the oldest laws and pacts."[84]

As Foucault well knew, labyrinths are not just figures of imagination. Producing perplexity by design, they are also tools of potential utility in the everyday world of human affairs. In the Middle Ages, mazes supplemented moats as a line of defense around castles. In the Age of Reason, hedge mazes became an aristocratic diversion. And in every epoch, writers have grasped the possibility of forming out of words a labyrinth in which to hide. That a maze of language could also hold the reader "captive," because "captivated," was a possibility Foucault had learned from Robbe-Grillet, Roussel, and also from Jorge Luis Borges, the Argentine writer and tutelary spirit whom Foucault would credit as the inspiration for *The Order of Things*.[85]

The appeal of the labyrinth to the writer's imagination was therefore doubtless manifold: a structure in which to hide, a line of defense, a machine of war, a source of amusement, a space of *daimonic* revelation, a place where a person might come to "think differently," it facilitated, as a literary device, self-effacement and self-expression simultaneously.

It was in this spirit, Foucault speculated, that Roussel had taken such care to encipher the secret of his singular destiny in the books that he wrote, turning his prose into a highly personal maze that simultaneously concealed and revealed. The possibility of being "caught," as Roussel once explained to his psychiatrist, was a part of the pleasure: "Practicing forbidden acts in private knowing that they are prohibited, risking punishment or at least the contempt of respectable people, that is perfection."[86]

At the same time, by carefully hiding the traces of a personal destiny, even the man who feared himself mad might join "the community of rational men," as Foucault himself once pointed out. "Writing in order to have no face," he could forge "an alliance without language between an anonymous desire and a knowledge of which the rule hides the empty face of the Master." Through his books, he might then express his deepest sense of himself while remaining "the perfect stranger"—a "man whose strangeness does not reveal itself."[87]

In 1966, an odd and unanticipated metamorphosis abruptly overtook Michel Foucault. Years later, not without envy, Jean-Paul Aron remembered how Foucault, joining "the community of rational men" with *éclat*, had become not only "the perfect stranger," but also, paradoxically, the most famous French philosopher since Sartre. The pivotal event, Aron recalled, was the appearance in *L'Express* of a review of *Les mots et les choses*— "Words and Things," translated into English in 1970 as *The Order of Things*. A French version of *Time* magazine, *L'Express* is a newsweekly aimed at educated professionals; as a rule, it features in its book section reviews of new novels and likely bestsellers. But the issue dated May 29, 1966, announced something new.[88]

"THE GREATEST REVOLUTION SINCE EXISTENTIALISM," screamed the headline. Above it stretched a three-quarter page photograph: in a trench coat, beneath an *art nouveau* Metro sign stood the author—eyes gazing out from behind thick glasses, a faint smile playing on his lips, his balding dome gleaming in the light. "MICHEL FOUCAULT," explained the caption: "Man is a recent invention."[89]

The time was ripe. The war in Algeria had ended four years before. With the passing of the old colonial order, the political atmosphere in France had calmed down as well. The economy was booming. Change was in the air. With each passing month, the existentialist world view, born of defeat and war, seemed part of a bygone era. It was the heyday of Godard, Truffaut, and the "new wave" in French cinema. The work of Lévi-Strauss, Barthes, and Althusser had already begun to transform the Parisian intellectual landscape. And news of the ferment was quickly spreading: one of Lévi-Strauss's most important works, *The Savage Mind*, had appeared in English that year, and so had one of the first translations of Lacan, in a special issue of *Yale French Studies* devoted to structuralism. A global marketplace of ideas was emerging—and thanks to the success of existentialism, Paris was widely regarded as its fashion center.[90]

The reviewer in *L'Express* never used the magic word "structuralism" because she did not need to; readers already knew which way the wind was blowing. In the cramped columns of the newsweekly, the nuances and complexities of Foucault's own analysis naturally went unexplained and unanalyzed, his structuralist sympathies telegraphed by a mention of "system" and a reference to Lévi-Strauss.[91]

"We are in a pivotal sequence," Aron sourly commented years later, "where the barrage of publicity," heralding the significance of phenomena that have been emptied of meaning, begins to assault the domain of high culture: "Exquisite and singular moment, where the real and the simulacrum seem, as in a baroque scroll, to embrace, envelop, and intertwine, the one imparting its factitiousness to the other, which in return supplies its plausibility."[92]

Certainly, no reader of the review in *L'Express* could fathom what really was at stake in *The Order of Things*—given the deviousness and complexity of Foucault's thought in these years, how could it be otherwise? Madeleine Chapsal, the reviewer, could only assure her readers that the author had already "astonished his peers," and that even novices "scarcely familiar with philosophy" would relish the book's dazzling "insights about the world in which we live."[93]

For example, the idea of "Man," according to Foucault, was about to disappear, go pffft . . . just like a "crease" being ironed out of a wrinkled shirt![94]

This is the kind of claim no journalist can resist. It is big; it is bold; it is startling. What it might possibly mean, of course, is impossible to explain, at least in 500 words or less. No matter. "A young man has come on the intellectual scene," the review concludes, "in order to announce the excellent news: the death of Man and, at the same time, the renewal of the one who invented him, then destroyed him, the *Philosopher*. This demands notice."[95]

Notice France did. A first printing of 3000 copies sold out within a week; a second, larger printing in June quickly sold out, too. By August, the book was on the bestseller list; each passing month brought more sales, more debate, more sales, in a self-perpetuating spiral.[96]

The work, though long and difficult, quickly came to number among those signs of outward culture that every *bien-pensant* Parisian needed to acquire: "Have *you* read it?" In 1966, one's social and intellectual status in France depended on the response.[97]

In the interviews he gave in these pivotal months, Foucault emphasized the fit between his own work and the structuralist *zeitgeist*—even while he quietly drew attention to some of the peculiarities of his own approach. He presents *The Order of Things* as a sequel and companion to *Madness*

and Civilization, as a "history of resemblance, sameness, and identity" that supplements the earlier work's history of difference, otherness, and dissociation.[98]

His new book thus offers a kind of post-Kantian "Critique of Impure Reason" that (like Kant's *Anthropology*) deals "with practices, institutions, and theories on the same plane" by looking for the "isomorphisms," or similarities in form, that organize (into a kind of historical *a priori*) the field of experience in any epoch. In conducting his research, Foucault acknowledges, he had in mind such precursors as Lévi-Strauss, Lacan, Althusser, and Dumézil—all thinkers who showed, beneath the level of conscious meaning explored by Sartre and the phenomenologists, another level, unconscious and unthought, anonymous and impersonal, that regulated the play of meaning in advance. The human being is therefore not absolutely free (or absolutely responsible), as Sartre supposed, but always restrained, pinioned, snared in a web of language and practices beyond its control. In order to make plain the novelty of the domain he wishes to analyze, Foucault even coins a new term for it, "*épistémè*," borrowing from ancient Greek the word for knowledge (and the archaic linguistic root of the modern French and English words for theories of knowledge, "*épistémologie*" and "epistemology"). An "episteme," as Foucault defines it, is "an epistemological space specific to a particular period," a general form of thinking and theorizing that establishes "what ideas can appear, what sciences can be constituted, what experiences can be reflected in philosophies, what rationalities can be formed, only, perhaps, to dissolve and vanish soon afterwards."[99]

From the perspective of the new form of theorizing that Foucault's latest work exemplifies, it seems evident that Sartre's brand of existentialism belongs to a bygone era. A new generation, "not yet twenty during the war," has supplanted, as Foucault explains, "the generation of *Temps modernes* that had been our law for thinking and our model for existing." To this younger generation, Sartre's *Critique of Dialectical Reason* seems "pathetic," a doomed "effort of a nineteenth-century man to think through our twentieth century." The syncretic humanism of the postwar era—a moralistic fusion, he explains, of Sartre, Camus, and Teilhard de Chardin—pretended to resolve problems it had not even understood: for example, "all those obsessions that absolutely do not merit being theoretical problems." Forming a "monstrous alliance," Sartre and Chardin spoke "in whose name? Man's! Who dares to speak of the evil in man!"[100]

Far from being "evil" (or "mad"), something like an obsesssion with death was a logical outgrowth of the most advanced thought of our time:

"Man would die from the signs that were born in him—that's what Nietzsche, the first one to see this, meant." And though the analysis of the field of signs through the search for isomorphisms might seem hopelessly abstract, Foucault suggests that the outcome of this quest is something quite different: "The writers that please us the most," he tells Madeleine Chapsal in 1966, "we 'cold' systematizers, are Sade and Nietzsche—those who, in effect, speak 'of the evil in man.' Are they not, also, the most passionate of writers?"[101]

Foucault's own text has never ceased to puzzle and provoke. *The Order of Things* is ostensibly a specimen of modern historiography, like *Madness and Civilization*. As before, five centuries are surveyed: once more, the erudition and learning are daunting. Yet as before, historians have subsequently called into question the accuracy of a host of various details, and also the overall thesis—raising again the suspicion that this book, like its predecessor, is not what it seems.[102]

Following "the same articulations in time" as the study of madness, *The Order of Things* traces the same general pattern. In the Renaissance, thinking retained a certain "mobility": "no path has been determined in advance, no distance laid down, no enchainment prescribed"; even hate, the ferocity of appetite, madness, and the disorders of disease were all assigned a certain value; the world presented itself as a "vast open book" to be deciphered through an inherently unstable combination of erudition and "magic."[103]

In the classical Age of Reason, by contrast the "mobility" of thought was restricted: the field of experience was surveyed, measured, defined, enclosed; "raw being" was tamed, colonized by a host of new disciplines, from medicine and botany to the study of general grammar; these disciplines classified, sorted, and separated, carving up "the confused monotony of space."[104]

Yet this apparently firm organization of experience dissolved with surprising suddenness in the years around 1800, when "knowledge closed in upon itself." With the world now a complex product of the empirical necessities grasped by science and the enigmatic powers revealed by transcendental freedom, knowledge became "mixed in its levels." A great and ambiguous fault-line divides Western thought—the very line brought to light by Kant. On one side of the line stands the positive understanding of the human being, codified in disciplines like economics, zoology, and linguistics—inheritors of the classical legacy of analysis through division;

on the other side survive "the most obscure and most real powers of language," resurrected in the form of modern "literature"—a vestige of the lost world of the Renaissance, "when words glittered in the universal resemblance of things."[105]

According to the book's subtitle, Foucault offers an "archeology of the human sciences." Yet from the standpoint of the human sciences, as Gilles Deleuze once remarked, *The Order of Things* is a "malicious gift." For Foucault's approach once again has the curious effect of causing the object under investigation to crumble before our eyes: just as "madness" was stripped of its self-evident reference to an underlying medical reality, Foucault's study of the human sciences reveals, as Deleuze remarked, "a poisoned foundation." His is "an archeology that smashes its idols." The sciences of man are not sciences at all; in the pages of his book, nineteenth-century linguistics, economics, and zoology are systematically treated as a type of fiction, parochial, transient, confining. Even Marxism, which Sartre just six years before had declared to be unsurpassable, Foucault gleefully dismisses as a kind of useless antique. "Marxism exists in nineteenth-century thought like a fish in water," he taunts: its critique of " 'bourgeois' theories of economics" may have created "a few waves," but these "are no more than storms in a children's paddling pool." To speak (as Foucault himself once had) of the historical tasks of "real man" is therefore to fall prey to an illusion: for the Marxist idea of "man" no more refers to an underlying reality than does the idea of "madness."[106]

This much seems clear. Clear, too, is the general novelty of the book's approach to the past—one of its most widely remarked features. Instead of surveying the history of thought in the spirit of Hegel and Marx, as a kind of collective and cumulative learning process, Foucault, as the historian Paul Veyne once put it, approached the past as if it were a kaleidoscope containing a number of discrete fragments. It reveals a pattern, but one shaped by chance; to move from one "episteme" to another was, as it were, to twist the kaleidoscope, and create a new pattern; the sequence of patterns obeyed no inner logic, conformed to no universal norm of reason, and evinced no higher purpose; it could therefore not be regarded as a form of "progress," for the latest pattern is "neither more true nor more false than those that preceded it."[107]

Though Foucault's book grew out of his study of Kant, and his argument bristles with philosophical allusions (to Heidegger, Sartre, and Merleau-Ponty, among others), philosophers as such figure only in the margins of the text. Instead, a large stretch of the book discusses the work of Georges Cuvier (1769–1832), Franz Bopp (1791–1867), and David Ricardo

(1772–1823)—thinkers sufficiently obscure to the general public that *Le Nouvel Observateur* included with its review of *The Order of Things* a sidebar, explaining just who the three main characters were. (Cuvier was a pioneer in the science of comparative anatomy; Bopp was the father of modern linguistics; and Ricardo was an important early political economist.)[108]

Still, even with a simplified synopsis—and by now there are several good ones to choose from—the book sooner or later leaves a reader feeling baffled. After finishing it, even Foucault's philosophical ally Georges Canguilhem had to wonder whether it was really possible, as Foucault asserts, to compose a history of different forms of knowledge without recourse to any criterion whatsoever for evaluating their relative "rational value," without ever assessing the success or failure of a single putatively scientific theory. The longer one ponders the book's argument, the stranger it seems. As the French historian Michel de Certeau remarked in perhaps the single most acute essay on the book, "the dazzle and, at times, preciosity of the style combine with the minute dexterity of the analysis to produce an obscurity in which both author and reader fade from view."[109]

What logic, if any, governs the book's intricate design? If changes in the way that scientists and philosophers think are not, strictly speaking, "rational," how does such change occur? Why does the "kaleidoscope" of a culture suddenly twist? What can possibly account for such an abrupt transformation? For that matter, where does the author himself stand? How is it that *he*, of all people, has managed to elude what "contains thought" and to describe, as if from the outside, our modern "episteme" as a whole?

These are apparently intractable questions. But Foucault himself offered one key to approaching them in an essay entitled, suggestively enough, "The Thought from Outside." Published in 1966 in an issue of *Critique* that appeared shortly after *The Order of Things* had arrived in the bookstores, the essay implicitly illuminates the elusive *style* of the larger work.

The topic of Foucault's essay is Blanchot's work and "the breakthrough to a language from which the subject is excluded." This breakthrough, Foucault concedes, is strange, mysterious, fraught with paradox; it reveals "an abyss that had long been invisible." Yet it also renews an archaic "form of thought whose still vague possibility was sketched by Western culture on its margins." This long-forgotten form—"the thought from outside," he calls it—stands "outside subjectivity." A kind of "thinking that is shattered," it lets thought "loom up suddenly as the exterior of limits, articulating its own end, making its dissipation scintillate"; at the same time, it lets the thinker behold "the threshold of *all* positivity," rediscovering the space where thought unfolds, "the void that serves as its site."[110]

As these formulations suggest, "the thought from outside" is a kind of rapture or ecstasy, "born of that tradition of mystical thinking which, from the time of Pseudo-Dionysus, has prowled the borderlands of Christianity: perhaps it survived for a millennium or so in the various forms of negative theology," only to go into eclipse at the dawn of the classical age.[111]

But not for long. In our own age, a kind of mystical thinking again haunts the frontiers of philosophy, resurrected, "paradoxically," in "the long-drawn monologue of the Marquis de Sade," who "in the age of Kant and Hegel" gives voice "to the nakedness of desire as the lawless law of the world."[112]

"Sade constitutes a perfect example," Foucault explained in a 1967 interview, "whether it is a question of renouncing the subject in eroticism, or of deploying structures in their most arithmetical positivity." An insane yet rigorous expression of the confinement of unreason by reason, the work of "Sade is nothing but the development, up to the most extreme consequences, of every erotic combination, from that which evinces the most logic to that which is a kind of exaltation (at least in the case of juliette) of the subject itself—an exaltation that leads to its complete explosion."[113]

It is not surprising, given sentiments like this, to find Sade's thought standing in *The Order of Things* just where it stood in *Madness and Civilization*—at the threshold to a new way of thinking: "After him, violence, life and death, desire and sexuality will extend, below the level of representation, an immense expanse of shade which we are now attempting to recover, as far as we can, in our discourse, in our freedom"—a rare appearance of Kant's transcendental idea in Foucault's work in these years—"in our thought."[114]

The erotic "experience" first articulated by Sade has remained "not exactly hidden" (since anyone can now read Sade) "but afloat, foreign, exterior to our interiority," to the type of "subjectivity" and conscience that the modern human sciences define. The locus of this way of thinking in our own day therefore becomes not science (and certainly not politics, where it is taboo), but "literature": in "The Thought from Outside" alone, Foucault mentions Hölderlin, Nietzsche, Mallarmé, Heidegger, Artaud, Bataille, Klossowski, and, of course, Blanchot himself.[115]

Such writers, as Foucault hints in *The Order of Things*, may illuminate the mysterious origins of change, innovation, and the ability of the human being "to begin anew." "Discontinuity—the fact that within the space of a few years a culture sometimes ceases to think as it had been thinking up till then and begins to think other things in a new way—probably begins with an erosion *from outside*."[116]

The singular value of Blanchot's work, however, lies neither in his appreciation of ecstasy nor in his understanding of "the outside"—it lies, rather, in his use of *language*. Outwardly flat, affectless, even (as Sade had counseled) "apathetic," his prose is invariably precise. It is geometric. It is rigorous. Like the language of Robbe-Grillet after him, it communicates "in the gray tones of everyday life and the anonymous." When it provokes "wonderment," it is not by directing attention to the author, or even to specific words, "but rather to the void that surrounds them, to the space where they are set, rootless and baseless."[117]

The virtual invisibility of Blanchot's artistic touch makes him "perhaps more than just another witness" to a long tradition of ecstatic thinking, Foucault concludes: "So far has he withdrawn into the manifestation of his work, so completely is he, not hidden by his texts, but absent from their existence and absent by virtue of the marvelous force of their existence, that for us *he is that thought itself*"—the thought from outside—"its real, absolutely distant, shimmering, invisible presence, its inevitable law, its calm, infinite measured strength."[118]

To evoke, not through a novel, but rather through the prose of the world, "the thought from outside"—as Foucault tries to do in *The Order of Things*—would be, in effect, just as he promises, to restore "to our silent and apparently immobile soil its rifts, its instability, its flaws." It would be to remind ourselves "that we are bound to the back of a tiger." It would finally be to conjure up, from every angle, an "essential void"—that formless vortex of animal energies that Nietzsche called Dionysian.[119]

"Those thinkers in whom all stars move in cyclic orbits are not the most profound," Nietzsche once wrote, casting aspersions on the dream of a *mathesis universalis* characteristic of Plato and those modern rationalists who have tried to follow in his footsteps: "Whoever looks into himself as into vast space, and carries galaxies in himself, also knows how irregular all galaxies are; they lead into the chaos and labyrinth of existence."[120]

To the extent that the human being still had access to this chaos within, Nietzsche supposed that a man might "give birth to a star"—something singular, unique, unmistakably creative, the sign, in Foucault's own myth of the labyrinth, of an individual's "higher necessity."

But "the time of the most despicable man" was coming, Nietzsche warned: "Behold, I show you the *last man*." Docile and oblivious, this "man" was a stranger to animal energy, unable to take flight, unwilling to be different: " 'What is love? What is creation? What is longing? What is a star?' thus asks the last man, and he blinks."[121]

By recounting "the wandering of the last man," Foucault remarks in *The Order of Things*, Nietzsche "took up anthropological finitude once more," examining again those hybrid historical *a prioris* already laid bare by Kant in his *Anthropology*. Nietzsche did this, however, not in an effort to demonstrate the normative limits of the idea of "man." Instead he fashioned a critique of morality—and an attack on the "last man"—as "a basis for the prodigious leap of the overman," sending "all these stable forms up in flames."[122]

"We must be prepared to state our choice," Nietzsche declared, in an aphorism Foucault cites elsewhere: "Do we wish humanity to end in fire and light or to end in the sands?"[123]

"Are we not," wondered Nietzsche, "with this tremendous objective of obliterating all the sharp edges of life, well on the way to turning mankind into *sand*?"[124]

From this Nietzschean perspective, it is no wonder that Foucault, in his famous conclusion to *The Order of Things*, eagerly wagers that the normative ideal of "man" will soon be "effaced, like a face drawn in sand at the edge of the sea." Wiped clean by the waves, pulverized by the ocean, Kant's anthropological ideal ("less cruelty, less pain, more kindness, more respect, more 'humanity' ") will be washed away by the sea: Nietzsche's symbol of the overman—Foucault's old emblem of unreason, a formless and uncertain element that, according to the aquatic allegory of *Madness and Civilization*, purifies and carries off.[125]

To traverse this "bottomless sea" would be to navigate in new ways the chaos of existence. It would be to brave the hazards of an uncertain voyage to an uncertain destination. It would be to explore the shadowy expanse first plumbed by Sade.

As Foucault elliptically explains in the final pages of *The Order of Things*, an analysis of the human being only truly " 'recognizes itself' when it is confronted with those very psychoses that nevertheless (or rather for that very reason) it has scarcely any means of reaching; as if psychosis were displaying in a savage illumination, and offering in a mode not too distant but precisely too close, that toward which analysis must slowly make its way." Following in the footsteps of Sade and Nietzsche as well as Kant and Freud, the analyst must take up "a practice in which it is not only the understanding one has of man that is involved, but man himself— man together with this Death that is at work in his suffering, this Desire that has lost its object, and this language by means of which, and through which, his Law is silently articulated. *All analytic knowledge is thus invincibly linked to a practice*, to a *strangulation* produced by the relationship between two individuals, one of whom is listening to the other's language, thus freeing his desire from the object it has lost (making him understand he has lost it), liberating him from the ever-repeated proximity to death (making him understand that one day he will die)."[126]

Suspended over an "infinite void that opens beneath the feet of the person it attracts," rising in rapture above "the Death that is at work in his suffering," the human being might then (having at last arrived at the heart of the great interior labyrinth of *The Order of Things*) discover what Nietzsche's thought, in Foucault's view, portends: not only "the death of man," but also the appearance of "new gods, the same gods," that "are already swelling the future Ocean." Far from simply announcing "the death of God," explains Foucault—"or, rather in the wake of that death and in a profound correlation with it"—what Nietzsche's thought heralds is the "Perfect Likeness," the *daimon*, the "Identical": "the Return of the Same" through "the absolute dissipation of man."[127]

"What returns," as Nietzsche himself put it, "what finally comes home to me, is my own self."[128]

The reception of *The Order of Things* left Foucault both pleased and dissatisfied. He was glad to have met Sartre on his own level, and thrilled to be at the center of intellectual and scholarly discussion—throughout his life, even long after he had become famous, he craved the respect and serious consideration of fellow historians and philosophers. According to those who knew him in these years, he had never been happier.[129]

Yet the book itself he soon came to consider deeply flawed—with good reason. *Madness and Civilization* may have sprawled, but it was also tied together by a handful of recurrent themes and images. *The Order of Things* by contrast is awkward, disjointed, elliptical to a fault. In its eccentricity, it calls to mind its original pretext, Kant's *Anthropology*; yet Foucault's pivotal conclusions about Kant, apart from a few scattered passages, are conveyed largely through the needlessly mystifying idea that the human being is an "empirico-transcendental doublet." The text's strategically placed praise for psychoanalysis and ethnology, which leapt out at every French reader in 1966, rings false: it also blunts the impact of Foucault's climactic exercise in gnostic self-cancellation. His opening analysis, of the Velázquez painting *Las Meninas*, which he presents as an emblem of the paradoxical play of identity and difference in reflection—and also as an image of the absence of "man" from the premodern "episteme"—is one of his most elegant pieces of writing. The body of the book, by contrast, is methodologically self-conscious, drab, faintly labored: as if Foucault, by donning the mask of a structuralist historian, felt obliged (as he once put it) "to blur his own perspective and replace it with the fiction of a universal geometry." As a result, the vertiginous final chapters amount to a free-floating Book of Revelation that exists in an all but unfathomable relationship to the improbably monolithic sequence of historical snapshots that have preceded it. As one chagrined reader summed it up, the overall effect suggests "a Spengler toying with the style of Spinoza."[130]

Foucault grew unhappy enough with *The Order of Things* that he seriously considered withdrawing the book. At one point, he asked Gallimard to stop printing it, only to realize the futility of such a request. Daniel Defert recalls that Foucault privately expressed his dislike of the book on more than one occasion—a sentiment he sometimes voiced as well in public: "It is the most difficult, the most tiresome book I ever wrote," he declared with exasperation in a 1978 interview: it "was seriously intended to be read only by about two thousand academics." The book, he confided in another interview that year, addressed "problems that do not impassion me the most. . . . Madness, death, sexuality, crime—these are the subjects that attract most of my attention. By contrast, I have always considered *The Order of Things* to be a kind of formal exercise."[131]

As the months went by, and his book's reputation grew, Foucault became increasingly irritated by the uncomprehending enthusiasm of his large new public, and by the equally uncomprehending animosity of a growing number of critics.

Scholars coming to Foucault's work from quite different angles were arriving at equally negative conclusions. The psychologist Jean Piaget, a student of Kant and Freud who also fancied himself a kind of structuralist, was appalled by the arbitrary arabesques of Foucault's analysis, which seemed to him tricked up, a thing of smoke and mirrors: *The Order of Things*, he wrote, offered "a structuralism without structures." Others simply dismissed the book as a symptom of cultural rot, an "ideology of the irrational," "very close," as one alarmed psychiatrist wrote, to Hitler's *Mein Kampf*. [132]

Before 1966 was over, Jean-Paul Sartre had reacted in the most withering terms possible. In an interview published in the journal *L'Arc*, in a special issue called, simply, "Sartre Responds," the older philosopher complained that Foucault "had replaced movies with a magic lantern, movement with a sequence of immobile images." The very success of the book, declared Sartre, "proves that it was to be expected"—a truly original work would never garner such applause. (Never mind the success of *Being and Nothingness* or the *Critique of Dialectical Reason*—Sartre was not one to worry over inconsistency.) Foucault, he charged, a little more plausibly, "gives people what they want: an eclectic synthesis where Robbe-Grillet, structuralism, linguistics, Lacan, and *Tel quel* are used in turn to demonstrate the impossibility of a historical reflection." This pastiche was, in Sartre's view, a distraction, a figment of ideology—"the last barricade the bourgeoisie can still erect against Marx." [133]

"Poor bourgeoisie," Foucault quipped years later: "If they needed me as a 'barricade,' then they had already lost power!" [134]

At the height of the uproar, Foucault disappeared—this time, literally. In the fall of 1966, he moved from Paris to Tunisia, where he would spend the next two years teaching at the University of Tunis. There he would begin to work on the lectures and essays that he would eventually transform into *The Archeology of Knowledge*, the explanation and defense of his method that he published in 1969. [135]

This turned out to be perhaps his most curious book of all: a loving, minutely detailed account of many of the categories and techniques that Foucault had used in *The Order of Things* to analyze the "discursive productions" of the human sciences, in order to lay bare their "internal rules" and "conditions of appearance." In this domain—constituted by the kinds of authoritative language used by scholars (and bureaucrats) to define, circumscribe, and regulate—few things can be said; the criterion of "originality" is no longer relevant; what counts is the "regularity" of a statement. An essentially anonymous domain, stripped of personal pronouns, it is the place where most of the time "one" speaks (what Heidegger, in *Being and Time*, called "*das Man*"—"the One," or "the They"). Occasionally, though, as sometimes happens on the most featureless of plains, a volcano erupts: and these mysteriously "sudden eruptions" naturally change the landscape of language-games the historian must map out. He is simply an innocent observer: "a happy positivist," he calls himself. [136]

In this cheerful spirit, Foucault issues a number of potentially misleading statements, offering an overt "discourse on method" interlaced with a more softly enunciated, almost imperceptible "poem of his previous works," as Gilles Deleuze once put it. [137]

His research, Foucault insists, is "nothing more than a rewriting" (as if it belied no trace of novelty, as if it did not mark the emergence, or "eruption," of a certain kind of discontinuity, or "difference"—which of course it did, just as he says in his essay's conclusion). Criticizing his own previous preoccupation with "what I called an 'experience,' " he now maintains that it would be "vain to seek, beyond structural, formal, or interpretative analyses of language, a domain that is at last liberated from all positivity, in which the freedom of the subject, the labor of the human being, or the unfurling of the transcendental purpose could be displayed" (as if the question of the human being and its possible freedom had no meaning for Foucault, which is not quite accurate: as he admits in his conclusion, he has deliberately "ignored" the phenomenon of "transcendence"—but only, so he says, in an effort to shed fresh light on how certain human beings, caught like everyone else in their culture's web of "discursive practices," may nevertheless come "to speak of different objects, to have contrary opinions, and to make contradictory choices"). Since the very categories of "subject," "author," and "oeuvre" are demonstrably the product of certain "synthesizing operations of a purely psychological kind," it would be a mistake, Foucault finally—and famously—argues, to use such terms in order to analyze "the intention of the author, the form of his mind, the rigor of his thought, the themes that obsess him, the project that traverses his existence and gives it meaning" (as if Foucault himself could not possibly have intentions, or obsessions, or an overarching project—which again is not quite accurate: as he discreetly admits here, his "diagnosis" in *The Order of Things*, like that in *Madness and Civilization*, was meant to illuminate, "if only in an oblique way," a shadowy domain that "deprives us of our continuities," "breaks the thread of transcendental teleology," and "dissipates the temporal identity in which we are pleased to gaze at ourselves," dissolving consciousness in a way that "bursts open the other," exploding "all interiority in an outside that is so indifferent to my life, and so *neutral*, that it makes no distinction between my life and my death"). [138]

Doubtless looking over his shoulder at critics like Sartre and Piaget, Foucault in effect was methodically describing how he had built his labyrinth of language, without explaining straightforwardly why, or what it might contain.

The book takes swipes at various critics. Sartre is scored for his apparent ignorance of the practices of real historians. Even a passing acquaintance with the work of Braudel and the other *Annales* historians would discredit Sartre's teleological pipe dream of a history with a happy ending. It would also call into question Sartre's old-fashioned emphasis on political events such as the storming of the Bastille and his concomitant lack of interest in less spectacular but arguably more important events, like the appearance of a new virus, or a change in the foods people commonly eat. As Foucault remarked in one of the lectures he delivered during these months, "the sudden increase in the quantity of protein eaten by a population is, in a way, much more serious than a change in the constitution or the passage from a monarchy to a republic."[139]

At the same time, *The Archeology of Knowledge* also carefully removed Foucault from the structuralist camp. "The opposition of structure and becoming" he now declared to be irrelevant to "the definition of the historical field." In his preface to the English translation of *Les mots et les choses* that appeared one year later, in 1970, Foucault was even more emphatic: "In France, certain half-witted 'commentators' persist in labelling me a 'structuralist.' I have been unable to get it into their tiny minds that I have used none of the methods, concepts, or key terms that characterize structural analysis."[140]

His own enterprise, by contrast, he defends in the most modest of terms. "It is an attempt to define a particular site," he says. "Rather than trying to reduce others to silence, by claiming what they say is worthless," he writes, "I have tried to define this blank space from which I speak, and which is slowly taking shape in a discourse that I still feel to be so precarious and so unsure."[141]

This seems a little too meek, coming from the man who imagined modern humanism being wiped out, like a face drawn in sand at the edge of the sea.

Two years before, in 1967, Foucault had explained himself with considerably less coyness. The occasion was an interview that he had arranged with his friend Raymond Bellour, one year after the appearance of *The*

Order of Things. "He had not liked how most people had read *The Order of Things*," Bellour recalls, "and he wanted to talk about his own sense of the book, and explain its style of analysis."[142]

"My book is a pure and simple 'fiction,' " Foucault told Bellour. "It's a novel, but it's not me who invented it."[143]

A subject speaks in its pages, he explains, but it is not his own "I." After Blanchot, "we know that the work does not belong to the author's project"; it is not, as Sartre supposes, purely a product of conscious intentions. The work wells up from the unthought and the unthinkable: it exists vis-à-vis the writer in a relationship "of negation and destruction." For as Blanchot has shown, the language of "fiction" opens the writer up to "the flowing of an eternal outside": the words merely converge on the man named Michel Foucault, who functions as a kind of spiritual medium. [144]

"Personally I am rather haunted by the existence of discourse," Foucault explains, going on to recall his nightmare: staring at a text that he cannot decipher, feeling his throat tighten. [145]

The book that grew out of this terrifying dream, as he describes it to Bellour, combines the will to know with a wish to disappear. As a "formal exercise," *The Order of Things* was an effort not only to hollow out "the whole mass of discourse that has accumulated under our feet," but also "to conquer the anonymous, to justify for ourselves the enormous presumption of one day finally becoming anonymous. . . . The problem in the past for the one who wrote was to tear himself out of the anonymity of everything; nowadays, it's to succeed in effacing one's own name and of coming to lodge one's voice in this great anonymous murmur of discourses held today."[146]

Foucault's words here, like his lifelong quest for a due measure of academic recognition, suggest a profound ambivalence: an unstable oscillation between the wish to become a conventional (hence anonymous) scholar, and the desire to let blossom in secrecy a singular kind of genius.

Disappearing into the inner core of a rigorously designed labyrinth of language, Michel Foucault might as it were become "Michel Foucault"— modest man of learning, "happy positivist," contributing his share to the growth of knowledge.

Or, perhaps, beneath this mask, surrendering to his fantasies, he is quietly elaborating a kind of "counter-nature," mapping out "a counter-city that promises to destroy the oldest laws and pacts."

How is one to evaluate this strange and profoundly ambiguous "rage to apply the eraser"?

On one level, surely, Foucault's experiment in anonymity was, if not a hypocritical farce, then at least a comic failure. Unlike Blanchot, Foucault never prohibited photographs, never shied away from interviews or even television appearances—all tools of growing importance in postwar France for securing intellectual power and prestige. The man who "wrote in order to have no face" succeeded most spectacularly, not in evoking "the thought from outside" in most of his readers, but rather in confusing some, dazzling others, outraging still more, becoming a world-famous intellectual in the process.

As Foucault himself well knew from his study of literature, his labyrinthine language, quite apart from the celebrity it ironically facilitated, had a deeply paradoxical result even in the composed texts themselves. A mad rapture that unleashed "the thought from outside" could be expressed only by establishing, as he once put it, "a subterranean relationship in which the work and what it is not formulate their exteriority within the language of a dark interiority." A prose forged from the obliteration of consciousness could not help betraying, at every turn, like a smudged fingerprint, a cluster of recurring motifs and images, the "trace" of inescapable and involuntary impulses, a kind of negative image of everything that an individual writer, try as one might, could not transform, or change, or erase. [147]

"The eraser marks intended to attain the anonymous," Foucault tells Bellour, "indicate more surely the signature of a name than the ostentatious penholder." [148]

On still another level, however, Foucault's experiment in effacement obviously succeeded, probably far beyond his wildest dreams. Welcomed into "the community of rational men," he became, for a surprisingly large number of readers around the world, "a man whose strangeness does not reveal itself." In the wake of *The Order of Things*, Foucault became, as it were, "normalized." The volcanic "eruption" of his own singular prose produced a kind of soft black ash, easy to use for drawing new faces in the sand. Quoted, imitated, travestied, the "enunciative" peculiarites of his "discourse" became "regularities." As his trademark neologisms circulated ever more widely, flashed at academic conferences as a kind of off-the-rack fashion statement, Foucault's work became at last truly, and deeply, "anonymous," lost in the great "murmur of discourses held today." [149]

Yet on perhaps the most important level, it is difficult to know, finally, just how to take the measure of Foucault's unusual effort to efface the signs of his own singular existence in these years.

In his preface to *The Archeology of Knowledge*, evoking "this blank space from which I speak," Foucault himself silently alludes to what is at stake in his own "great Nietzschean quest." Singing the praises of a certain anonymity, Nietzsche, too, had once referred with admiration to the thinker who "tunnels and mines and undermines," going forward "slowly, cautiously," as though (as Nietzsche put it) "he perhaps desires this prolonged obscurity, desires to be incomprehensible, concealed, enigmatic, because he knows what he will thereby also acquire: his own morning, his own redemption, his own *daybreak*."[150]

"He will return," promises Nietzsche, "that is certain: do not ask him what he is looking for down there, he will tell you himself of his own accord, this seeming Trophonius and subterranean, as soon as he has 'become a man.' "[151]

Had Foucault yet "become a man," in Nietzsche's sense?

"Do not ask who I am and do not ask me to remain the same," Foucault replied in 1969, sounding very much like Nietzsche's Trophonius. "Do you imagine that I would take so much pain and so much pleasure in writing, do you think that I would be so stubborn, so reckless, if I were not preparing—with a rather feverish hand—a labyrinth into which I can venture, shifting my purpose, opening for it underground passages, pushing it far from itself, finding for it overhangs that epitomize and deform its journey, where I can lose myself and appear at last to eyes I will never have to meet again."[152]

One is reminded of the great unspoken aim of Foucault's lifework—the *daimonic* effort to become what one is.

One is reminded as well of the oracle and fate of Trophonius, according to Greek myth: "Live merrily and indulge yourself in every pleasure for six days; on the seventh, your heart's desire shall be granted"—and on the seventh day he died.[153]

One is reminded, finally, of the appearance, at the end of Nietzsche's poem "Ariadne's Lament," of Dionysus: "I am your labyrinth."[154]

And so Foucault now appears before us as well: a baffling figure of self-creation, self-destruction, and self-discovery, "withdrawn into the manifestation of his work." A creature of heterogeneous dimensions, he evokes Daedalus and the Minotaur, Ariadne and Dionysus—Kant and Sade—somehow combined into one. Balanced between reason and unreason, his words conjure up an "invisible presence"—the traces of an underground man, still tunnelling, doubtless still suffering, destination still unknown.

— 6 —

BE CRUEL!

THE NIGHT OF MAY 10, 1968 began tensely in Paris. In the preceding days, schools throughout France had been rocked by demonstrations. Confrontations between students and police had erupted at Nanterre, at the Sorbonne, and then, it seemed, at virtually every university and lycée in the country. Since the beginning of May, news of the disturbances had filled more and more pages of *Le Monde*. The mounting vehemence of the protests had left government officials stunned and student leaders astonished. By the night of May 10, nobody knew what to expect.[1]

The big political event that evening was a rally of lycée students at the place Denfert-Rochereau. As dusk gathered, a crowd of some twenty thousand young people flocked into the Parisian crossroads. Their immediate goals were clear enough: they were expressing outrage at the government, which had shut down the Sorbonne on May 2, after a student demonstration; they were protesting the brutality of the police, who had beaten a number of innocent bystanders; and they were demanding freedom for four jailed comrades.

Their larger goals were no mystery either: critical of the authoritarianism of French education, they talked in terms of radical democracy; schooled in the various catechisms of the left, they also spoke of class struggle, workers' control—and permanent revolution.

But on another level, their objectives were anything but clear, even to the demonstrators themselves. Some were silently bewildered. "The fact was that to anyone who asked rationally enough 'What do you want?' I had no answer," a professed Maoist recalled years later. "I couldn't say that I didn't even know who these comrades were, couldn't say that I was demonstrating for the sake of demonstrating."[2]

After the rally was over, police watched nervously while the students milled aimlessly.

Spontaneously, without plan or discussion, the crowd began to move, streaming first toward the prison where their comrades were being held, and then, with the bridges over the Seine blocked by police, back toward the heart of the Latin Quarter.

Stopping on the boulevard Saint-Michel after they had marched past police guarding the Sorbonne, the nominal leaders huddled together and tried to improvise their next step.

An assault on the Sorbonne was out of the question: it would provoke a bloodbath. But retreat had become unthinkable: defiance was in the air.

The leaders hastily resolved to take control of the unprotected streets of the Latin Quarter in front of them.

The students fanned out. Some moved south, down rue Gay Lussac and rue Saint Jacques; others went east, toward rue Mouffetard.

But if the police attacked, how could they defend themselves?

With cobblestones, someone suggested.

In the rue le Goff, at around 9:15, they started digging. A hole in the road appeared, revealing a fine, yellowish sand. With a can of spray paint, a bystander put the image into words on a blank wall: BENEATH THE PAVEMENT, THE BEACH. Near the wall, a pile of stones quickly mounted. Without plan or discussion, a barricade had appeared.[3]

A barricade!

It made little sense tactically. It made perfect sense symbolically. For a barricade, in the mind of every educated French citizen, was *the* mythic emblem of revolt, a living image of the revolutionary tradition begun in 1789 and renewed in 1830, 1848, 1871, 1936—and now, improbably, in May, 1968.

The barricades grew. Ten appeared on rue Gay Lussac, two on rue d'Ulm, two more on rue Tournefort; before the night was over, there were sixty barricades in all.[4]

The disorder was intoxicating. Billboards were ripped apart, sign posts uprooted, scaffolding and barbed wire pulled down, parked cars tipped over. Piles of debris mounted in the middle of the boulevards. The mood was giddy, the atmosphere festive. "Everyone instantly recognized the reality of their desires," one participant wrote shortly afterward, summing up the prevailing spirit. "Never had the passion for destruction been shown to be more creative."[5]

Radio reporters roamed the streets. Dramatic but futile negotiations between the rebels and government officials were beamed live across

France. Lured by the promise of adventure, reinforcements began to pour into the Latin Quarter. On the barricades, the transistor radios carried the news, and the protesters took heart: they were making history!

Drunk on the idea, thousands steeled themselves to meet their destiny.

Shortly after 2:00 A.M., the police donned gas masks. At 2:15, the attack began.

The forces of order lobbed incendiary grenades and tear gas. The forces of disorder responded with cobblestones and Molotov cocktails. The cries of attacking police, the groans of wounded students, and the muffled roar of distant explosions filled the air throughout France, as an audience of millions listened, riveted to their radios.[6]

Three hours later, "The Night of the Barricades" would be over. But for a generation of young activists—and for Michel Foucault as well—a new world had suddenly appeared.

Dawn revealed a devastated landscape. In the Latin Quarter, the skeletons of almost two hundred automobiles, torched during the night, littered the elegant boulevards where the barricades had briefly stood. No one had died—the battle, though bloody, had been a kind of game, played with a tacit understanding of its limits by both police and protesters. But witnesses were still in shock over the savage efficiency of the police assault, which had left more than 350 wounded, some seriously. To protest the government crackdown, the country's largest trade unions, including the powerful CGT, controlled by the French Communist Party, called for a general strike on Monday, May 13.[7]

That Monday, more than one million people filled the streets of Paris. The student revolt had turned into a general protest against the authoritarianism of the Gaullist state—and, less clearly but more explosively, against the very order of things in the modern world generally.

Belatedly recognizing the gravity of events, the government on Monday night announced it was making concessions: the police had been withdrawn from the Sorbonne, and the four students still in jail had been set free.

It was too little, too late: the regime of Charles de Gaulle suddenly seemed vulnerable. Instantly the Sorbonne was occupied by young radicals. Graffiti—perhaps the most revealing expression of the movement's true novelty—began to appear everywhere, defacing the walls, defying reason, apparently aiming to provoke passion, puzzlement, and furious energy all at once:

BE CRUEL!

IT IS FORBIDDEN TO FORBID

WE WILL CLAIM RESPONSIBILITY FOR NOTHING, WE WILL DE-
MAND NOTHING, WE WILL SEIZE, WE WILL OCCUPY

ACTIONS, NO! WORDS, YES!

I TAKE MY DESIRES FOR REALITY, BECAUSE I BELIEVE IN THE
REALITY OF MY DESIRES

RUN, COMRADE, THE OLD WORLD IS BEHIND YOU!

QUICK[8]

Throwing open the doors to the Sorbonne, students declared it to be
a "free university." Into the old temple of learning poured thousands of
unruly young people. Together, they began to debate what form the new
world might take. "May everybody be carried away by his enthusiasm
without feeling guilty," suggested one widely distributed manifesto. "All
artistic creation is violence, all political action is violence," another declared. "Violence is the only way for subjectivity to express itself."[9]

Yearnings long silenced suddenly found expression. In offices throughout France, staffers met and debated how to reorganize the division of
labor. In factories, workers rose up in contagious anger, staging one wildcat
strike after another. At the Sorbonne, a "Revolutionary Pederasty Action
Committee" met, talked, disbanded, leaving no organizational trace, yet
forming one inspiration for the French gay liberation movement that would
crystallize in the months that followed.[10]

As a young philosopher named André Glucksmann summed up the
May movement shortly afterwards, the uprising had united "all society's
semi-pariahs—youth, immigrant labour, etc."; it had obliterated "ghettos"
and traditional limits, ending "social and racial segregation, sexual repression, etc."; it had turned the Sorbonne into "a new 'ship of fools' "—and
in this ship, promised Glucksmann, the ruling class would rediscover "all
the perversions that haunt them."[11]

Michel Foucault had cause to take note: for the Night of the Barricades,
it seemed, had unleashed *his* kind of revolution.

But unlike Jean-Paul Sartre, who once again emerged as a cynosure of
protest, Michel Foucault was nowhere to be seen.

He was over a thousand miles away—in Tunisia.

Foucault had moved there in the fall of 1966, fleeing the provincial
stuffiness of the University of Clermont-Ferrand. For nearly two years, he
had lived in a modest little house perched on a hill overlooking the

Mediterranean outside of Tunis, in the small village of Sidi-Bou-Saïd. He had taught philosophy at the University of Tunis, and devoted long hours to thinking, and to writing the essay on method that became *The Archeology of Knowledge*. But work was not his only passion in these months. He also revelled in Tunisia's abundance of sunny beaches and good cheap hashish, indulging his appetite for pleasure and enjoying the company of Daniel Defert, his companion since 1960. A photograph hanging in Foucault's old Paris apartment, where Defert still lived in 1990, showed the two of them together in Tunisia, sharing a small pipe. [12]

Jean Daniel, who first met Foucault in these years, later recalled that the philosopher cut a curious figure: he seemed "a kind of frail samurai, gnarled, dry, hieratic, with bleached eyebrows, a slightly sulphurous charm, and an avid and affable curiosity intriguing to everyone." Observing him at work and at play, Daniel perceived "an inner struggle, between a sharp temptation to sink into voluptuous delights and an apparent will to contain this temptation by converting it into a method of ascesis, or a conceptual exercise." [13]

The character and stakes of this inner struggle were to be transformed, irrevocably, by the events of May 10, 1968.

As it happens, Defert was in Paris at the time. That night, he watched as the barricades went up on rue Gay Lussac, and then returned to the apartment where he was staying. With the promise of disorder hanging in the air like a hologram of bliss, Defert called Foucault in Tunis, told him what was happening—and then placed the telephone next to a radio. Like much of the French nation, Foucault thus followed the pitched battle over the airwaves. [14]

The Night of the Barricades proved pivotal: for the first time in years, Foucault could imagine that a new kind of politics might yet change French society.

"It's a fact," he remarked in an interview in 1982, "that people's everyday lives have changed from the early sixties to now, and certainly within my own life." A number of the issues that preoccupied him—from lifting the burden of guilt to exploring the frontiers of experience—had entered the public domain. After May '68, his earlier books, especially *Madness and Civilization*, would reach an entirely new audience, attuned to their practical implications. "And surely," as Foucault put it in 1982, "that is not due to political parties, but is the result of many *movements*. These social movements have really changed our whole lives, our mentality, our attitudes, *and* the attitudes and mentality of other people—people who do not belong to these movements. And that is something very important and positive." [15]

A good many of these changes came about because of May '68 and its aftermath in France. But Foucault's own first steps as an *engagé* intellectual in 1968 were taken, not in reaction to events in Paris, but rather in response to a student uprising that had broken out two months before—this time, in Tunisia itself.

The source of the trouble was the institution where Foucault was working: the University of Tunis. In the twelve years since France had granted Tunisia independence, the state's president and self-appointed moral censor, Habib Bourguiba, had attempted to make of Tunisia a "monument without cracks." A fervent nationalist, influenced by revolutionary French traditions and deeply committed to modernization, Bourguiba fancied himself a kind of modern-day Robespierre, purging his nation of religious superstition, forging from an archaic society an enlightened people, the uncorrupted unity of its will expressed through the country's one legal party. The focus of Bourguiba's secular vision became the university system. As part of the expansion of higher education, the University of Tunis created a program in philosophy in 1963; it was to this faculty that Foucault brought his gifts and reputation, quite formidable after the publication of *The Order of Things*. [16]

By the time that Foucault arrived, however, the educational system was lurching toward crisis. In alarming numbers, Tunisia's best and brightest young people were finding enlightenment, not in the civic religion of national unity sanctioned by the state, but rather in the vision of progress-through-conflict offered by Marx, Trotsky, and Foucault's old friend and teacher, Louis Althusser, then at the height of his prestige among francophone radicals. An education intended to bolster the ranks of the state's modernizing elite was generating, instead, chronic criticism, threatening to crack apart Bourguiba's civic "monument."

In December of 1966, shortly after Foucault arrived at the University of Tunis, an unprecedented number of students staged a daring demonstration, protesting the paternalism of the government and also its pro-American, staunchly anti-Communist foreign policy. The dissent spread to the faculty, and the campus remained tense—until the explosion of March 1968.

"I witnessed student riots, very strong, very intense," Foucault recalled in an interview several years later. "This was in March 1968, and the agitation lasted the whole year: strikes, suspension of courses with arrests in March, a general strike of students. The police entered the university and beat students, badly wounding many and taking them to jail. There was a trial, during which some students received sentences of eight, ten, fourteen years in jail."[17]

Up until then, Foucault had stood apart from the mounting turmoil. At first, the doctrinaire Marxism of the student's rhetoric repelled him. Even more troubling to him was their occasionally virulent hostility toward Israel. When the six-day Arab-Israeli war erupted in 1967, a series of vehemently anti-Semitic student riots, orchestrated in part by the government, broke out in Tunis, leaving Foucault shaken and deeply saddened. As Daniel Defert puts it, "Michel was profoundly philo-Semitic." Throughout his life, he was haunted by the memory of Hitler's total war and the Nazi death camps: in his view, the legitimacy of the Zionist state was simply not open to debate.[18]

But the student riots of March 1968, struck him quite differently. The more he saw—and as one of the most famous foreign teachers at the University, he was allowed to see a great deal—the more he became convinced that the Tunisian student movement embodied "an utterly remarkable act of existence." As he came to realize, Marxism in this setting functioned as a kind of *myth*, in Georges Sorel's sense—a body of images capable of inspiring "a kind of moral energy," exciting "a violence, an intensity, an utterly remarkable passion," enabling students to accept "formidable risks, publishing a manifesto, distributing it, calling for a strike: taking risks that might deprive them of their freedom. This impressed me incredibly."[19]

In the aftermath of the Tunisian student uprising, Foucault had a decision to make. He could speak out in public on behalf of the students, and face expulsion from the country. Or he could help the students surreptitiously, trying to exploit his own prominent position for their benefit. At the students' behest, he chose the latter course. At some risk to himself, he helped students who had escaped arrest, hiding them in his apartment. He also hid a mimeograph machine, which the students used to print manifestos. On more than one occasion, he tried, without success, to intervene on behalf of those in prison. And he began to read, again, Marx, Rosa Luxemburg, and the great *History of the Russian Revolution* by Leon Trotsky. On a trip back to Paris that spring, he astonished Defert by blithely declaring, tongue only partially in cheek, that he was a Trotskyist![20]

"It was a formative experience for me," Foucault later recalled.[21]

It was, in fact, his first inkling that politics, like art and eroticism, could occasion a kind of "limit-experience."

It would be misleading, however, to leave the impression that Foucault had, somehow, been politicized overnight by the events of 1968. This, after all, was a man who had been a member of the Communist Party for three years; a thinker who had welcomed, in the pages of his most important book, a "total contestation" of Western culture; a writer fascinated by the fantasy that "volcanos of madness" might, somehow, "destroy the oldest laws and pacts"; a philosopher who had tried to demonstrate the constructive relation of his ideas to "a progressive political intervention" in an essay that would be published, by coincidence, in May 1968. To regard such a person as apolitical scarcely does justice to the evidence.[22]

At the same time, it is not surprising that colleagues like Georges Dumézil and left-wing intellectuals like Sartre took Foucault to be a rather conventional, even conservative academic mandarin. As Foucault remarked in a 1978 interview, his days in the Communist Party and his subsequent travels in Soviet Eastern Europe had produced "a certain bitterness, a certain very contemplative skepticism, I do not hide it." After his return to France in 1960, he would later recall, the mainstream parties left him indifferent, while the debates that raged among intellectuals struck him as "very academic, very cold." This was the heyday, on the independent left, of socialist humanism and Sartrean existentialism. In response, he had drifted into a kind of inner exile, disappearing into his own labyrinth of language. Readers only superficially acquainted with his work began to suspect him of being some weird new kind of Gaullist, spouting heartless structuralist jargon.[23]

During these years, Foucault also seems to have played the academic game with genuine relish and a certain cunning. Without qualms—indeed, with apparent zeal—he served between 1965 and 1966 on a commission established by de Gaulle's minister of education, Christian Fouchet, in order to reform higher education in France. Like Clark Kerr at the same time in the United States, Fouchet wished to streamline and modernize the university—goals that Foucault himself endorsed in principle. "If an honest man, today, has the impression of a barbarous culture," Foucault remarked in an interview in 1966, "this impression is due to a single fact: our system of education dates from the nineteenth century and there still reigns there the most insipid pyschology, the most antiquated humanism."[24]

Foucault's outspoken hostility toward any form of "humanism" was the final straw for a number of leftists. For what program of political change could possibly grow out of such convictions?

In an interview in 1967, Foucault himself not only conceded the problem, but went out of his way to stress one of the most disquieting political implications of his perspective. "We are apparently in the midst of discussing the problem of humanism," he remarked to his interlocutor, "but I wonder if in reality we are not in the midst of referring to a much more simple problem, that of happiness. I believe that humanism, at least on the level of politics, might be defined as every attitude that considers the aim of politics to be the production of happiness. Now, I do not think that the notion of happiness is truly thinkable. *Happiness does not exist— and the happiness of men exists still less.*"[25]

Happiness might not be "truly thinkable" according to Foucault's Sado-Nietzschean view of the world. But the raptures of an unleashed creative energy most certainly were. And no matter what Dumézil or Sartre might think—or Foucault himself might have supposed before 1968—such raptures were by no means of purely personal or strictly literary moment.

The Night of the Barricades, coming on the heels of the student revolt in Tunisia, had shown that something like a *shared* rapture, shattering customary inhibitions, was possible, at least at certain extraordinary instants. Perhaps even in our own day such an explosion of untamed collective energy might rekindle, as Foucault put it in 1978, "the craving, the taste, the capacity, the possibility of an absolute sacrifice"—a sacrifice of liberty, even of life, "without any profit whatsoever, without any ambition."[26]

At the end of May, Foucault returned to Paris for a brief visit. Ever since Defert's telephone call on May 10, he had followed events in France as closely as those in Tunisia, reading *Le Monde*, listening to the radio, his perceptions shaped (and perhaps distorted) by his experience in Tunis. When he finally arrived to see for himself what was going on, the Sorbonne was still occupied, the regime still in trouble, the youthful *enragés* still drunk on fantasies of permanent revolution.

While he was in Paris, he attended a meeting at the Sorbonne. It was on this occasion, apparently, that he exchanged a few words, for the only time in his life, with his favorite literary theorist, Maurice Blanchot—

though Foucault, fittingly enough, had no idea of whom he was talking to. "Whatever the detractors of May might say," Blanchot later commented, "it was a beautiful moment, when each could speak to the other, anonymously, impersonally, as a man among men, welcomed with no other justification than that of being another man."[27]

During his brief stay, Foucault also took a stroll with Jean Daniel, whose job, as the editor of *Le Nouvel Observateur*, had kept him in close contact with the course of events. Catching sight of a procession of students, Foucault turned to Daniel.

"They are not making the revolution," said the philosopher, "they *are* the revolution."[28]

But what kind of revolution did these young men and women embody? Foucault had reason to wonder: for the revolutionary idea of creating an entirely "new man," an ideal common to both Marx and Nietzsche, pointed in two contradictory directions.

Marx's new man was to be a creature of joyful harmony, beyond the cruel conflicts between master and slave, boss and worker—a figure of Promethean freedom and universal understanding, embodying in thought, labor, and love the beatific essence of the entire species. For a "humanism of the Marxist type," as Foucault remarked in a 1978 interview, the problem was "to recover our 'lost' identity, to liberate our imprisoned nature, our truth at bottom." With the end of alienation—and triumph of communism—what Marx called "the real individual" would stand forth, whole at last.[29]

Nietzsche's new man, by contrast, was to be a creature of destructive creativity, beyond good and evil—a figure of blinding power and *daimonic* fury, uninhibited by the yearning of ordinary mortals for happiness, justice, or pity. "For me," Foucault explained in 1978, "what must be produced is not," as in Marx, "the man identical with himself, such as nature has designated him, or according to his essence. . . . It is a question, rather, of the destruction of what we are, and of the creation of something totally other—a total innovation."[30]

In those heady days in May 1968, students in Paris, like those in Berkeley and Berlin, hesitated between love and hate, harmony and strife, peace and war. Looking for guidance, some turned to Marx, others to Nietzsche. What kind of world did they want? What sort of new men—and new women—would they become?

On May 30, 1968, President de Gaulle, after a moment of hesitation of his own—he seriously considered resigning—told the French nation that he would not step down; that he would dissolve Parliament and call for new elections; that he was mobilizing the armed forces to crush any further resistance; in short, that he was going to fight. The great man's authority thus reaffirmed, thousands poured into the streets of Paris—this time, to demonstrate on behalf of law and order.[31]

The Communist Party urged its millions of members to return to work. The government moved swiftly to outlaw the most militant of the student groups. And in the third week of June, the Gaullist regime won an overwhelming victory at the polls, cutting in half the number of Communist and Socialist deputies in parliament.

For the *enragés*, the party was over—and the struggle about to begin in earnest.

That summer, Foucault received an offer that flowed from the events of May: he had been invited to become the chairman of a new philosophy department, to be located at a new, experimental campus in Vincennes, near Paris. De Gaulle's new minister of education, Edgar Faure, had launched a bold series of reforms, aimed to streamline the educational system—and also to defuse the student movement. Vincennes was to be Faure's showcase. A model institution, it was to be democratic, interdisciplinary, on the cutting edge of current research. At the same time, it was to be a magnet for dissidents: by drawing radical students out of the Latin Quarter, to a campus located outside of the city limits, the disruptive impact of the militants could be isolated—this, at least, was the gambit.[32]

The faculty drawn to this ambiguous endeavor included idealists, liberals, and the most intolerant ultra-leftists, insuring a clash of divergent interests. The students drawn to Vincennes, on the other hand, included, just as the planners had hoped, the cream of the militant crop, many of them veterans of the street-fighting in May.[33]

The first hint of the jousting to come occurred on November 6, 1968, at an assembly of faculty and students. Seizing the initiative, an implacable cadre of militants, led by André Glucksmann, staged a noisy demonstration, urging students to ignore idle debates over empty reforms. One of their targets was Foucault: hiring the controversial philosopher was a ploy, they charged; the government was trying "to distract opinion with academic quarrels."[34]

The message was blunt: forget structuralism. For that matter: forget the university. The revolution was in the streets!

The militants had misjudged their man. Inspired by his experience in Tunisia, Foucault moved quickly to build a highly unconventional philosophy department. He offered senior slots to Michel Serres, a polymath trained in mathematics yet fascinated by literature; and to François Chatelet, a slightly older scholar who also combined to an unusual degree erudition and imagination. Both were thinkers of deep scholarship and genuine originality, just like Foucault himself.[35]

The junior faculty members he hired, though perforce less accomplished, were almost as unusual: all of them were veterans of the May uprising. Indeed he even offered a job to André Glucksmann! Though Glucksmann declined the offer, Foucault's junior colleagues were cut from the same cloth: the department included a Trotskyist, a Communist, and—more fatefully still—a critical mass of self-styled Maoists, affiliated with the *Gauche Prolétarienne*.[36]

Of all the ultra-left groups that rose to prominence in France after May '68, none would prove more important for the development of the French student left—or for Michel Foucault—than the *Gauche Prolétarienne* (or "GP"). Founded at the end of 1968 by a young militant named Benny Lévy (who in these years operated under the alias "Pierre Victor"), the GP united veterans from the anarchistic *Mouvement du 22 mars*, which had sparked the May student revolt, and a cadre from the outlawed *Union des jeunesses communistes [marxiste-léniniste]* (or "UJC[m-1]"), an ultra-Marxist sect. Always quite small, the GP at its height only claimed some two thousand full-fledged members. Tiny though it was, its prestige was great: embodying the most stringent standards of ardor and commitment, the group managed to combine the delight in disorder evinced by a Bakunin with the ruthless genius for tactical maneuver displayed by a Lenin. As no other French group could, the GP promised to carry forward the movement started in May, prolonging the moment by mastering its chaotic energies.[37]

Through its Marxist cadre, the GP inherited the classic Bolshevik repertoire of agitation and clandestine action: it exercised much of its influence through satellite institutions (such as the newspaper *La Cause du Peuple*), affiliated popular front organizations (such as *Les Amis de la Cause du Peuple*), and covert paramilitary groups. Schooled in the political haiku of Chairman Mao, the group took to heart his famous maxim that "political power grows out of the barrel of a gun"; they also took at face value the anti-hierarchical and anti-bureaucratic slogans of the Cultural Revolution. (Naturally, most members of the GP, preoccupied as they were with fantasies of revolt, at the time betrayed scant interest in the brutal realities of Chinese political life.)[38]

At the same time, the GP had inherited from the May '68 student uprising a suspicion of political parties and an emphasis on direct action as a means of sparking insurrection. In this spirit, the group in 1970 distributed free subway rides to workers to protest a price increase. In the same year, a "commando" unit affiliated with the group staged a spectacular Robin Hood raid on Fauchon, one of Paris's most luxurious grocery stores, stealing the pâté of the rich in order to give it to poor immigrant workers.[39]

At first glance, it is hard to see how a sectarian group like the *Gauche Prolétarienne*, with its ascetic zeal and fanatic Marxism, could ever appeal to Foucault. "The eruption of theories, of political discussions, of anathemas, of exclusions, of sectarianism," he admitted in 1978, "scarcely interested and completely frustrated me."[40]

Still, his experience in Tunisia had also taught him that some varieties of superficially doctrinaire Marxism, in some circumstances, might retain some value as a kind of Sorelian myth. He also recognized that most of the militants in the GP, like most student rebels around the world, were at heart "much closer to Rosa Luxemburg than Lenin," as Foucault explained in 1970. "They have put more trust in the spontaneity of the masses than in a theoretical analysis"—or in the edicts of a revolutionary elite. Above all, the GP's defiant style of direct action fit well with his own newfound interest, kindled in Tunis, in forms of rebellion that might provoke "the craving, the taste, the capacity, the possibility of an absolute sacrifice."[41]

As 1968 drew to a close and his new job at Vincennes was about to begin, Foucault wished, as he later explained, to experiment with types of political action that would require "a personal, physical commitment, that would be real and would pose a problem in concrete, precise, definite terms. . . . What I was trying to do from that moment on was to constitute for myself a certain manner of recapturing both what had preoccupied me in my work on madness . . . and also what I had just seen in Tunisia: one rediscovered, then, *experience*."[42]

Pursuing a similar interest in "experience" in the 1930s, Georges Bataille (whose work, back in print, was suddenly in vogue among French students) had welcomed "the sudden explosion of limitless riots," "the explosive tumult of peoples," the sanguinary excesses of "catastrophic change." In an analogous vein, André Glucksmann in 1968 had hailed "the madness of renewed revolution." And in the months ahead, other leaders of the *Gauche Prolétarienne* would call for "executions of despots, all sorts of reprisals for all the extortions suffered over the centuries."[43]

But just where did Foucault stand on these matters? In his thirst for "experience," would he, too, now welcome "limitless riots," "all sorts of reprisals"—"the madness of renewed revolution"?

One answer came on January 23, 1969. That afternoon at Vincennes, Foucault joined a handful of other professors and some five hundred students and militants in occupying the administration building and amphitheater of the new campus, which had been opened for classes just days before. The seizure was ostensibly a show of solidarity with students who had occupied the rector's office at the Sorbonne earlier that day, in response to the appearance of police on the Paris campus. But to paraphrase a good slogan from the American student movement in those days, the issue was not the issue. The main point, one suspects, was to explore, again, the creative potential of disorder—the Night of the Barricades, revisited.[44]

In the days before the seizure, the militants at Vincennes had staged a series of increasingly vociferous demonstrations, aimed to "expose the myth of Vincennes, the miraculous faculty." They had denounced the experimental student-teacher assemblies—during the assemblies, naturally—as a "vast hoax," offering only a simulacrum of participation. "Professorial power," they declared, was "null and void."[45]

"Down with the University!" chimed in the GP, which also resurrected Voltaire's anti-clerical slogan: "Crush infamy!"[46]

The occupation of Vincennes lasted less than a day. Police began their assault on the administration building in the predawn hours of January 24. Those still inside, including Foucault, fought back furiously. They clogged the building's stairways with tables, cabinets, and chairs. The police in response shot tear gas through the windows.

Some surrendered. Others, including Foucault, fled to the roof. There, they set about hurling bricks at the police gathered below.

Witnesses recall that Foucault exulted in the moment, gleefully lobbing stones—although he was careful not to dirty his beautiful black velour suit.[47]

"He was very courageous, physically very courageous," recalls André Glucksmann, who fought alongside the philosopher that night: "When the police came at night, he wanted to be in the front ranks, to fight. . . . I admired that."[48]

The battle of Vincennes marked the emergence of a new and highly visible Michel Foucault: an underground man no more, he became an oracle of the ultra-left.

He had changed his physical appearance as well: while living in Tunisia, he had Daniel Defert shave off all of his hair, which left him with a skull that gleamed like a spearhead. With his wire-rimmed glasses and smile of ivory and gold, he now looked faintly sadistic, like a bullying field marshal: for years, the *London Review of Books* would use his familiar image in advertisements ordering its readers to subscribe.[49]

His rhetoric had changed apace. Meeting the Maoists on their own discursive ground, as he had joined in the language-game of structuralism a decade before, Foucault for the next several years exploited the rhetoric of class struggle and even the iconic authority of Chairman Mao.

At the same time, paradoxically, by fulfilling the hallowed French role of the *engagé* intellectual, he began to command the respectful attention of the larger French public.

Glucksmann, for one, was not the least bit surprised by Foucault's latest metamorphosis. "It's normal in France," he says. "You are first an intellectual; and then you are a militant. It was the same for Sartre."[50]

Sartre! Wherever Foucault turned, it seemed that he could not escape the existentialist's shadow. Though Sartre was nearly sixty-five years old, he remained the quintessential French intellectual—quick to condemn, determined to expose abuses of power, unafraid to echo Émile Zola's old battle cry, "*J'accuse!*" He had confirmed this status during May '68, if only by his storied appearance at the Sorbonne at the height of the student uprising.

This status, though, Foucault now began to challenge directly—not simply on matters of philosophy, as before, but on issues of political strategy and tactics. Sartre might give speeches. But as Foucault demonstrated at Vincennes, he was ready to go further: he would take action.

In the meantime, Foucault, like Dr. Frankenstein, had to cope with the monster he had created in the form of the Vincennes philosophy department.

Offering countless courses with titles like "Cultural Revolutions" and "Ideological Struggle," Foucault's department naturally attracted dissidents of every conceivable type. Many of his militant colleagues were swept up in the enthusiasm of the moment: in 1970, Judith Miller, a professed Maoist (and Jacques Lacan's daughter), handed out certifications of course credit in philosophy to total strangers on a bus, explaining afterward in the pages of *L'Express* that "the university is a figment of capitalist society."[51]

The president of the Republic was not amused. The minister of education fired Miller, and moved quickly to decertify the department as a whole, announcing that the degree in philosophy granted by Vincennes no longer qualified the holder to teach in the French educational system.

In public, Foucault staunchly defended his program, and also the continuing rebellion in the universities. "We have tried to produce the experience of freedom," he explained in the pages of *Le Nouvel Observateur*. "I will not say total freedom, but as complete as possible in a university like that at Vincennes." The teaching of philosophy in France, he argued, had long functioned as an insidious kind of indoctrination, creating a "politico-moral consciousness. A national guard of consciences." To preserve the traditional curriculum in philosophy, as the government wanted, "would be to fall into a trap." Besides, added Foucault, "I am not sure, you know, if philosophy really exists. What exists are 'philosophers,' a certain category of men whose discourse and activities have varied a great deal from age to age."[52]

"It seems to me that what students are trying to do, in what at first glance may appear merely folkloric, and what I myself am trying to accomplish in the dust of my books, is basically the same thing," Foucault explained in still another interview in these months. "We must free ourselves from . . . cultural conservativism, as well as from political conservativism. We must see our rituals for what they are: completely arbitrary things, tied to our bourgeois way of life; it is good—and that is the real theater—to transcend them in the manner of play, by means of games and irony; it is good to be dirty and bearded, to have long hair, to look like a girl when one is a boy (and vice versa); one must put 'in play,' show up, transform, and reverse the systems which quietly order us about. As far as I am concerned, that is what I try to do in my work."[53]

In these years, Foucault, like other professors sympathetic to the student revolt, modified some aspects of his own approach to teaching. As never before, he struggled to moderate, if not suppress altogether, the harsh judgments he was inclined to pass on the work of others. At the same time, he continued to lecture *ex cathedra*, making no effort (as many radical professors did in these years) to conceal or soften the power and authority of his own intellect. "When I lecture dogmatically," he explained, "I tell myself: I am paid to bring to my students a certain form and content of knowledge; I must fashion my lecture or my course a little as one might make a shoe, no more and no less. I design an object, I try to make it as well as possible. I make a lot of trouble for myself (not always, perhaps, but often), I bring this object to the desk, I show it, and then I leave it up to the audience to do with it what they want. I consider myself more like an artisan doing a certain piece of work and offering it for consumption than a master making his slaves work." In practice, Foucault did not object to displays of deference: pupils were apprentices, and he was the master craftsman. Yet his modest image of himself as an artisan was by no means entirely false: for the rest of his life, he consistently spurned the role of the academic guru surrounded by fawning disciples (a role that Lacan, for one, played to perfection). If his students had a question, Foucault would try to answer it; if they needed help, he would try to provide it. Otherwise, he preferred simply to let them go their own way, offering himself as an example, rather than trying to impose doctrinal conformity.[54]

Setting an example, though, was becoming harder and harder to do at Vincennes. The campus was constantly in an uproar, roiled by strikes, marches, and classroom demonstrations. Following the time-honored radical precept that "my closest friend is my most dangerous enemy," militant students targeted Foucault's lectures for disruption.[55]

His patience wore thin. It was one thing to express solidarity with the left in interviews, or by pitching stones from roof tops—that was fun! But it was quite another thing to have to put up, day in and day out, with the insane harangues of the various ultra-left sects that stormed through his classroom.

Foucault had begun to feel, as he once suggested, like Sade at Charenton: staging subversive plays in the asylum, and then having the inmates rise in rebellion against the master himself.[56]

Foucault's solution was simple. He spent as little time as possible on campus, concentrating instead on his research and reading in the Bibliothèque Nationale.[57]

His thinking was taking a new turn. Moving away from the method-ological issues he had addressed in *The Archeology of Knowledge*, he devoted a series of lectures at Vincennes to "The Discourse of Sexuality," returning to one of the domains of "limit-experience" he had promised to investigate in the original preface to *Madness and Civilization*. Picking up the guiding thread of his "great Nietzschean quest," he also devoted a course at Vin-cennes to Nietzsche, subsequently composing his only major essay on his favorite philosopher, "Nietzsche, Genealogy, History."[58]

"The body," he now asserted, "is the locus of *Herkunft*," Nietzsche's term for origins—the place where willing, and feeling, and thinking all take root. But as Foucault described it, this place of origins was also a place of obscure wounds, baffling torments, and uncertain instincts. The body comprised an unfamiliar kind of map, inscribed in the flesh, of past events. Unreadable through reason alone, the traces of these events were palpable in a welter of contradictory inclinations and aversions, strengths and weaknesses, pleasures and pains. Yet even here, the body presented a confusing picture, like a battlefield cloaked in smoke. The task of the Nietzschean historian was, in effect, to survey this battlefield carefully, and discern *all* of the corporeal forces in play, even those on "the margins." This survey, Foucault supposed, could in fact be performed—but only by employing "a kind of dissociating gaze able to dissociate itself." Such a gaze would show "the body totally imprinted by history, and history ruining the body."[59]

It was as if, in the changed climate after May '68—having seen the violent "sacrifices" of the student movement in Tunisia, and having fought courageously at Vincennes—Foucault felt able as never before to explore directly the place of the body in politics and history, trying to understand its scars, trying to transform its configuration of warring wants and weak-nesses.

"The essence of being radical," as he once put it, "is *physical*; the essence of being radical is the radicalness of existence itself."[60]

At the same time, despite his deepening involvement in the political and social movements around him, his research remained almost entirely focused on the past. "History has a more important task than to be hand-maiden to philosophy," he wrote in his essay on Nietzsche. "It has to be a differential knowledge of energies and weaknesses, of heights and break-downs, of poisons and antidotes. It has to be a science of remedies"—if only for the historian himself.[61]

Or, as Nietzsche himself once explained in an aphorism Foucault cites, "to live in the present, within a single culture, does not suffice as a universal prescription: too many people of utility who cannot breathe properly in it would die out. With the aid of history one can give them *air*."[62]

After 1970, it became much easier for Foucault himself to "breathe properly." Starting in December, he was able to pursue the historiographic aspects of his "great Nietzschean quest" from a more elevated platform than Vincennes—as a professor at the Collège de France.

For years, Foucault had yearned for an academic post worthy of his talents—if not at the Sorbonne, then at the Collège; for years, he had pulled all the strings that he could to win the post he wanted, getting crucial support from friends like Georges Dumézil, who had himself entered the Collège in 1968.[63]

A uniquely French institution, the Collège de France traces its origins back to the sixteenth century. Unlike other institutions of higher learning, it requires no diploma of its members, and grants no degree to its students. Its native chairholders (some fifty in all) are elected by the professors themselves to reward the most distinguished French practitioners in the arts and sciences, from music to mathematics. Those chosen are expected to give an annual course of lectures in which they discuss original work in progress; these courses are open to the public, without any requirement for registration.[64]

On December 2, 1970, famous peers, old friends, and a delegation of young admirers crowded into the Collège de France to hear Foucault deliver his inaugural lecture. Before an audience "waiting to be enchanted," as Jean Lacouture described the scene for *Le Monde*, there appeared "a hairless personage, of ivory tint, Buddhist in demeanor, Mephistophelean in his gaze, undeterred by the gravity of the occasion from expressing an irrepressible irony."[65]

His lecture was a high-wire act, delicately balanced between the demands of the ceremony, and the articulation of his own thought. As one might expect, he responded with perhaps his most artfully veiled piece of writing. "In typical fashion," as one discerning critic summed up the text, "he addressed his audience across the centuries, as it were, outlining projects on nothing less than truth, rationality, and normality in a voice that was simultaneously Beckettian in its gnomic ellipses and Renanian in its portentous sonority."[66]

Among the "gnomic ellipses" were fleeting references to his own "transitory existence, doubtless confessed in order to be effaced." He evoked, deftly, the "disquiet" that certain kinds of "discourse" might arouse, particularly when one finds "the truth within the space of an untamed exteriority"; for however "mundane and grey" it might appear, even modern scholarship sometimes expressed "powers and dangers that one imagines evil."[67]

As he explained to his audience, various protocols governing discourse might neutralize such "powers and dangers" in a variety of ways: by imposing rules of logic and grammar; by censoring certain words and topics; by stipulating the kinds of research and propositions acceptable within a discipline; by crediting only certain styles of commentary on certain chosen texts; by postulating the author as the conscious (and hence accountable) creative source of texts. All of these disparate strategems, argued Foucault, could be used to "exorcise the powers and dangers" of discourse, much as priests once attempted to exorcise Demons. The complex web of conventions regulating language had to be understood therefore as "a violence we do to things," a "practice we impose upon them"— a kind of unconscious "discursive 'policing' that one must reactivate in every utterance."[68]

Foucault here sketched out his increasingly explicit interest in power, linking it with his previous interest in the limits of reason and the "thought from outside." He also implied that he, for one, had nevertheless broken the mold by going beyond scholarly discourse and resurrecting, in its place, a long-forgotten kind of "true" discourse, one filled with untamed power. Such a discourse, if one were unafraid of the dangers it carried with it, might provoke, as the works of the ancient Greek poets had, "respect and terror." By inspiring human beings to think and to act differently, it might even change the world, "weaving itself into the fabric of fate."[69]

Yet at the same time, Foucault eloquently expressed a wish to be, among other things, a scholar among scholars. In the conclusion to his speech, he rendered an elaborate homage to the man whose chair he had inherited, Jean Hyppolite, his former teacher and mentor.

His lecture (in this respect like *The Order of Things*) embodied a paradox. It was radically subversive in its declared intentions, yet reassuringly classical in its display of eloquence and learning. The traditional form of the discourse was, in effect, a "violence," done by Foucault himself, in order to contain—and communicate—his own unruly "thought from outside."[70]

Elevated into a consecrated institution, Foucault on one level played by the rules. He performed his collegial duties at the Collège de France;

taking the institution's charter seriously, he painstakingly crafted lectures of profound originality and erudition. But that was the extent of his investment. Unlike many other professors there, Foucault made no effort to establish an independent base in one of Paris's research centers; he continued to evince no interest whatsoever in recruiting disciples. As his colleague Pierre Bourdieu has observed, Foucault throughout his career was "almost entirely bereft of specifically academic and even scientific powers, and therefore of the clientele which these powers afford, even if because of his fame he wielded considerable power over the press and, through it, over the whole field of cultural production."[71]

This last power, on the other hand—over "the whole field of cultural production"—Foucault after 1970 embraced with a vengeance. He tried to exploit his fame for his own political purposes, treating the mass media as a megaphone. He joined an elite circle of glamorous dissidents—a circle that included Sartre (of course), writers like Genet, and outspoken movie stars like Yves Montand and Simone Signoret. And in February 1971, just two months after giving his inaugural lecture at the Collège de France, he announced with some fanfare that he was launching a political initiative of his own, the "Groupe d'information sur les prisons."

The idea for this initiative had been worked out by Foucault in conjunction with Daniel Defert, who now emerged as his key political collaborator.[72]

"I had met Michel in September 1960," recalls Defert, who was then a philosophy student, just finished with *Khâgne*, and more than ten years younger than Foucault. While pursuing his studies in Paris, Defert plunged into left-wing politics, becoming an active member of UNEF (*l'Union Nationale des Étudiants de France*), an outspoken student federation that had taken the lead in opposing France's war in Algeria.[73]

Though Foucault shared Defert's opposition to the Algerian war, he did not agree with the French left's analysis of the Gaullist state in the early 1960s, conveyed by their slogan, "fascism will not prevail." As Defert recalls, Foucault "never accepted this conflation. *This is essential.*" To imply that Gaullism was a phenomenon analogous to Nazism struck Foucault as grotesque, as would similar formulas fashionable on the French left after May '68.[74]

Foucault's new young friend was dashing and handsome—but it was the style of his political life, intense and committed, that perhaps most fascinated him, as Defert recalls: "I think that Michel became attached to me during this period because of the militant life I was leading." Taking him under his wing, Foucault secured a post for Defert at Clermont-Ferrand. When the younger man left for Tunisia in 1964 to fulfill his volunteer service obligations, Foucault followed him, finding a job for himself at the University of Tunis. And after 1968, the two were united yet again, this time at Vincennes, where Defert became a professor of sociology, and battled the police alongside Foucault on the night of January 24, 1969.[75]

Like any intimate relationship, this one had its ups and downs. But through it all, Defert remained loyal to Foucault: "I think Daniel really loved him," says one friend who knew them both.[76]

At the same time, Foucault felt deeply attached to Defert. "I have lived for eighteen years in a state of passion towards someone," Foucault remarked in a 1981 interview. "At some moments, this passion has taken the form of love. But in truth, it is a matter of a state of passion between the two of us." A "state of passion," as Foucault described it in this interview, was a state beyond love, beyond reason, beyond even a focused desire for another person; it was rather an oceanic and dissociative state, destroying "the sense of being oneself," creating instead an intense, fused feeling of "suffering-pleasure," enabling one to "see things entirely differently." "Completely invested" as he was in exploring this "state of passion between the two of us," Foucault confided that "I think that there is nothing in the world—nothing at all—that could stop me when it comes to finding him, and speaking to him."[77]

Speak to Defert, Foucault frequently did—particularly, after 1968, about their newest shared interest, politics. Defert's longstanding taste for activism had been rekindled by the new student left, and particularly by the emergence, at the end of 1968, of the *Gauche Prolétarienne*. Shortly after the group was officially outlawed in 1970, Defert himself became a clandestine member: "I entered," as he recalls, "because it had been banned and outlawed, because it was dangerous."[78]

Like Defert, Foucault was also now keen to explore for himself new forms of political action; and he, too, had been drawn, for this reason, to the *Gauche Prolétarienne*.

But it was by no means clear how someone of Foucault's stature and talents might most fruitfully become allied with an outlawed revolutionary movement. Together, Foucault and Defert searched for some way to link the philosopher's preoccupations with the Maoists' program. For the *Gauche Prolétarienne*, as Defert recalls, the object was simply to forge "an alliance with the Collège de France," and form, in Marxist jargon, a kind of "popular front" with bourgeois intellectuals. For Foucault, as Defert recalls, the aim was slightly different: he wanted to find some way "to extend the project announced in *Madness and Civilization*" by exploring politics as a field of "limit-experience."[79]

The solution that Foucault and Defert came up with was elegant in its simplicity. Defert proposed to his Maoist comrades that Foucault head a commission of inquiry into the conditions inside French prisons, where a number of Maoist militants were then serving jail sentences. The commission would direct the public's attention to the deplorable state of the French prison system—and also provide a pretext for the Maoists in jail to organize their fellow prisoners. Though some members of the *Gauche Prolétarienne* were opposed to Defert's idea, on the grounds that common criminals and the "lumpen-proletariat" were (just as Marx had argued) unfit agents of social change, Defert carried the day.[80]

The political venture he thus devised would prove to be the most consequential, by far, of Foucault's practical experiments in the new revolutionary politics.

On February 8, 1971, Foucault stepped before cameras and microphones in the chapelle Saint-Bernard, in the Montparnasse train station, to announce the formation of the Groupe d'Information sur les Prisons"— the "Prison Information Group," or GIP. The time and place of this announcement were not without significance: in the preceding two weeks, the chapelle Saint-Bernard had been occupied by Maoists staging a hunger strike, to protest the conditions in which their comrades were being held in French jails. ("Maoist" by then had become a catchall phrase in France for any militant more-or-less closely linked to veterans of the *Gauche Prolétarienne*; since the GP itself had been outlawed, the amorphous nomenclature proved useful to the militants themselves.)[81]

On that morning, Maoists had organized a large public demonstration to protest the plight of their jailed comrades. While the demonstration was going on, the government had announced that it was making certain concessions: it was establishing a commission to study the conditions inside French prisons; and it was also reclassifying the jailed militants as "political prisoners," who under French law were entitled to more lenient treatment. The press conference at the chapelle Saint-Bernard had begun with an announcement that the Maoist hunger strike, having accomplished its chief objectives, was ending. When Foucault's polished skull hoved into view, then, it was in an atmosphere of *gauchiste* jubilation.[82]

The professor from the Collège de France was there, however, not to celebrate a victory, but rather to announce the formation of his new organization. While the cameras rolled, Foucault read a brief statement summarizing the aims of the group he had formed with the support of Pierre Vidal-Naquet, the eminent classicist, and Jean-Marie Domenach, the editor of the Catholic review *Esprit*. Their goal, as Foucault explained it, was concrete and modest: he and his colleagues wished to gather information about the deplorable conditions inside French prisons. They were particularly interested in soliciting accounts from anyone with a firsthand experience of prison. To facilitate the exchange of such information, the GIP urged those in prison to contact the group. The group also announced that a questionnaire was available on demand, and that the answers given would be made public at a future date. [83]

The statement that Foucault read at this press conference was in many ways misleading. Despite the support of prominent figures like Vidal-Naquet and Domenach, the GIP was, in fact, not a conventional "organization" at all—it was rather a free-floating focus for agitation, largely improvised by Defert and Foucault. It was never intended to be a simple exercise in information gathering or philanthropic reformism. As the Maoist context implies, it was also, from the start, meant to be a machine of war, a new kind of cultural weapon. [84]

Above all, the GIP was meant to be a testing ground for a new type of intellectual—self-effacing yet subversive, modest yet cunning.

The target, as always, was Jean-Paul Sartre—the world's most famous living intellectual, and the very embodiment of France's venerable tradition of moral dissent. Within this tradition, as Foucault once summed it up, "the intellectual spoke the truth to those who had yet to see it, in the name of those who were forbidden to speak the truth: he was conscience, consciousness, and eloquence." It was in this Olympian spirit that the postwar existentialists had told people, as Foucault sarcastically put it, "what freedom consisted of, what one had to do in political life, how to behave in regard to others, and so forth." These were just the sort of overweening claims to moral authority that Foucault was determined to renounce for himself, and to undermine in society as a whole. The GIP's strategy in this respect was straightforward: it would create a forum in which those who had defied moral authority could describe directly, in their own voice, the cruel ways in which an ostensibly "humane" society had punished them. [85]

"I dream of the intellectual who destroys evidence and generalities," Foucault declared in a 1977 interview. Here as elsewhere in these years, he imagined the new intellectual as a kind of elusive guerrilla warrior, hard to pin down, always on the prowl. Sniping from the margins (as he had once imagined his underground man stoking volcanos of madness), the intellectual "locates and marks the weak points, the openings, the lines of force" in "the inertias and constraints of the present time." Refusing to issue blueprints for the future, he is "incessantly on the move," and "doesn't know exactly where he is heading nor what he will think tomorrow." No longer tunnelling, though his destination was still unknown, Foucault now welcomed public combat—an engagement of forces that, he hoped, would help clarify "whether the revolution is worth the punishment, and what kind (I mean, what kind of revolution and what kind of punishment), it being understood that the question can be answered only by those who are willing to risk their lives to bring it about."[86]

Ironically, Sartre in these months had pledged allegiance, in principle, to a similar program of guerrilla warfare, declaring "the old concept of the intellectual" to be obsolete. Sartre, too, had become aligned with the Maoists: in 1970, he had assumed the titular editorship of *La Cause du Peuple* in order to prevent it from being banned. Afterwards, he drifted under the influence of Pierre Victor (a.k.a. Benny Lévy), who would eventually become his personal secretary.[87]

All the more reason, then, to launch the GIP as an independent experiment, and put to the test Foucault's alternative vision. "It is not up to us to suggest a reform," the founding statement of the GIP concluded, alluding to this vision. "We wish only to make known the reality. And to make it known instantly, nearly day by day: for the issue is pressing. We must alert opinion, and keep it alert."[88]

The GIP proceeded on several fronts. Defert and Foucault devised a questionnaire; Defert handed it out to families visiting relatives in prison; as responses to the questionnaires came back, the two men sifted through them, selecting excerpts to publish in a series of broadsides. Working with prisoners' families, the GIP also led an effort to allow daily newspapers, previously banned, to be circulated freely inside the prisons; it convened committees of sympathetic professionals—doctors, laywers, and social workers—in order to publicize the conditions inside specific prisons; and it organized rallies in support of prison hunger strikes as they occurred.[89]

"Prison is the only place where power is manifested in its naked state, and where it is justified as moral force," Foucault explained in 1972. "What is fascinating about prisons is that, for once, power doesn't hide or mask itself; it reveals itself as tyranny pursued down to the smallest details; it is cynical and at the same time pure and entirely 'justified' because its practice can be totally formulated within the framework of morality. Its brutal tyranny consequently appears as the serene domination of Good over Evil, of order over disorder."[90]

But sometimes, unpredictably, spontaneously, as if by chance (this was one lesson both Foucault and the Maoists had drawn from May '68), the forces of disorder might boil over and erupt, storming the Castle of Conscience, tearing down the facade of "morality." In the spirit of the Maoist left, such moments of spontaneous revolt were to be cultivated, their occurrence made a focus of agitation.

"Michel," as Gilles Deleuze recalled years later, "had a political intuition: the feeling that something [was] going to happen at a particular point, and nowhere else." Deleuze was one of Defert and Foucault's most important allies in the GIP—a kindred spirit who had become a philosophical comrade-in-arms. Accomplished though Deleuze himself was, he nevertheless regarded Foucault with a certain awe. "He was in some fashion a seer," Deleuze later explained. "He saw things, and like all people who know how to see, who see something and see it deeply, he found what he saw to be intolerable."[91]

As events would show—and the documents collected by the GIP would demonstrate—the conditions inside French prisons were often truly intolerable: the prison was a beautiful symbol of how savage "justice" could be. Even better, the French prisons in the early 1970s offered an unusually promising *practical* target for reform. Filled with jailed Maoists, they were places where activists on the inside could fan the flames of revolt—while the GIP, on the outside, spread the news across France.[92]

"Michel sensed that there was some movement and unrest in the prisons," Deleuze recalled, "and that these were not just small problems."[93]

And so the GIP went to work. Deleuze helped Defert and Foucault gather information. They distributed pamphlets. They watched with keen interest as convicts at Attica, a prison in upstate New York, staged a bloody rebellion, widely covered in the French press.[94]

And they waited.

On December 9, 1971, the prison at Toul erupted in violence. One group of prisoners sacked the prison's carpentry shop; another group set fire to the prison library; individual prisoners smashed the bars on their cell windows and hurled out beds, chairs, dishes. Seizing one of the prison's three buildings, the rebels chanted "Down with dictatorship!" and sang the *Marseillaise*. The prison's priest relayed their principal demands: warm baths, better dental care. (The apparent triviality of such demands, repeated at other French prison revolts in these years, Foucault welcomed as a sign of *"déculpabilisation,"* demonstrating how shameless and "un-guilty" modern convicts had become.)[95]

Hearing news of the insurrection on the radio, Maoists in Paris set to work planning special newspaper coverage and organizing a fact-finding mission.

Meanwhile, the prison erupted in a second rebellion. This time, police struck back quickly, seizing control of the prison and wounding scores of inmates in the process.

Shortly afterward, Foucault arrived in Toul with Gilles Deleuze to hold a press conference. One of the prison's doctors, a psychiatrist named Edith Rose, had come forward with an affidavit describing, in harrowing detail, the conditions inside Toul. It was her account that Foucault and Deleuze presented to the press—both as a document in its own right, and as an object lesson in how an authorized expert might dare to break the code of professional silence by revealing, in the plainest possible terms, just what she had witnessed.[96]

Her tone was in fact disarming: "The thing that most disheartened and pained me," wrote Dr. Rose, "was to see men chained for a week and longer. I swear under oath that they did not detach them even in order to let them eat. From my office in the infirmary, I heard them calling a guard to feed them with a fork. . . . Certain witnesses tell me that they were left in their excrement, though I have not seen this myself." She had certainly seen enough, however, to report that the conditions at Toul made even dying seem pleasant by comparison. "I affirm that I have been struck, since my arrival at Toul, by the extreme frequency of suicide attempts," she declared: "hangings, the slashing of wrists, the ingesting of spoons, forks, neon tubes, etc."[97]

This was precisely the sort of documentation that always impassioned Foucault, whether he discovered it in the Bibliothèque Nationale, or had it handed to him by someone like Dr. Rose. "Instead of *criticizing*" the prison as an institution, Dr. Rose, as Foucault noted with evident approval, had simply *"exposed* what had happened, on such a day, in such a place, in such circumstances." In an affectless voice that curiously recalled one of Robbe-Grillet's blank narrators, the prison psychiatrist coolly rehearsed the grisliest of details.[98]

In an introduction to the doctor's report published in *Le Nouvel Observateur*, Foucault himself summarized the most shocking details: "men for days chained in place by their feet and fists . . . the routine alternation between punishments and sedatives, detention/injection, dungeon/valium (oh, tranquilizing morality); car thieves that one transforms at the age of twenty into delinquents for life" (a claim that would become central to *Discipline and Punish*); and—how could Foucault not pause over the fact?—"suicide attempts nearly every night."[99]

In fact, the GIP devoted its fourth and final pamphlet to this topic. Published by Gallimard in 1973, *Suicides in Prison*, like its predecessors, was intended to be a documentary broadside, collating facts and firsthand memoirs that were presented to the reader with a minimum of commentary. The pamphlet began by tabulating the known facts about the shockingly high number of self-inflicted deaths—thirty-two—that had occurred in French prisons in 1972. Listing all the deaths in chronological order, the editors offered details on the cause of each one: hanging, drug overdose, poisoning, swallowing a fork, even one case of self-immolation on a burning mattress.[100]

But the primary document consisted of a series of letters from a prisoner identified only as "H.M." The product of a broken family (his father was an alcoholic), H.M. was a thirty-two year old homosexual addicted to opium. First convicted of a crime at the age of seventeen, he had served time in over a dozen different prisons for a variety of offenses: theft, assault, drug-trafficking. His most recent arrest, he claimed in several letters, was a set-up: undercover agents lured him into purchasing opium. Back in prison, he made no secret of his lust for men—and after an argument, a guard reported his sexual activities. Condemned, as a result, to solitary confinement, H.M. hanged himself.[101]

It is not hard to see why Foucault found his correspondence fascinating. H.M.'s prose is smart and vivid, laced with references to the writers he admires (Baudelaire, R. D. Laing), to the music he loves (the Doors)—and to his seething rage at his lot in life. He experiences his existence as a kind of "trap," constructed by the various prison experts assigned to treat him: "Perhaps it is the good men who have done me the most harm." But articulate though H.M. is, he is also remarkably unselfconscious: as Foucault pointed out in a brief unsigned commentary, the letters "keep turning over all manner of things that form an obsession," thereby offering readers an uncommonly revealing glimpse *"at what a prisoner thinks."*[102]

If H.M.'s letters are any guide, what "a prisoner thinks" is perfectly simple: he yearns (not unlike Foucault himself) "to flee," to disappear, to vanish.

At different times in his correspondence, H.M. dreams of running away to India, of melting into the Hare Krishna movement, of evading reality like one of Laing's schizophrenics, of travelling "outside time and space" on drugs, of breaking out of prison like Black Panther George Jackson. (Gunned down during a 1971 jailbreak in California, Jackson was the subject of the GIP's previous pamphlet.) [103]

Above all, on the threshold of his death—fearing that there is, in fact, no other means of escape—H.M. dreams the ultimate dream, the essential dream, according to Foucault's essay on Binswanger: he dreams of killing himself.

"It is something that I consider every day," he writes in a passage Foucault cites. "It is as difficult to live as it is to die." [104]

Perhaps the most startling aspect of Foucault's commentary is the significance he imputes to this wish to die. H.M.'s letters, though "born in solitude" and ending with his death, must be regarded, according to Foucault, as a properly *political* document expressing "a new genre of political reflection that tends to efface the traditional distinctions between public and private, the sexual and the social, collective demands and a style of personal life." And though some might consider a style of personal life that issues in suicide to be a rather poor candidate for furthering a revolution, Foucault emphatically disagrees. [105]

"The border," he declares, "is often narrow between a permanent temptation to commit suicide and the birth of a certain form of political consciousness." [106]

To the heroic image of the Tunisian students fearlessly facing "the possibility of an absolute sacrifice," Foucault thus added a much stranger and much darker image of political struggle—a mortal combat, driven inward. It was as if the act of suicide, in certain desperate circumstances, if properly understood, might in some way expose, dramatically, as Foucault had put it in his essay on Nietzsche, a "body totally imprinted by history"—and, through the violence of the act itself, "history ruining the body." [107]

"The GIP was a kind of experiment in thinking," Gilles Deleuze recalled in an interview after Foucault's death. "Michel always considered the process of thinking to be an experiment; this was his Nietzschean heritage.

In this case, the point was not to experiment with prisons, but to comprehend the prison as a place where a certain experience is lived by prisoners, an experience that intellectuals—or at least intellectuals as conceived by Foucault—should also think about."[108]

That Deleuze in these years should have become Foucault's closest philosophical companion seems only fitting: for if any French thinker of his generation grasped the implications of Foucault's singular genius—including his unrelenting preoccupation with suicide and death—it was surely Gilles Deleuze.

Born in 1925, Deleuze studied philosophy at the Sorbonne, passing his *agrégation* in philosophy in 1948. Like Foucault, he developed a youthful passion for Artaud, and a lifelong aversion to the Sartre of "Existentialism is a Humanism." Unlike Foucault (and most other students of his generation), he never joined the Communist Party; and he exhibited only a passing interest in Heidegger, though he absorbed a good many of his key ideas indirectly, through Maurice Blanchot. [109]

Spurning the conventional French focus on German thought in these years, Deleuze developed instead an idiosyncratic expertise in Anglo-American literature and philosophy. His first book, *Empiricism and Subjectivity*, was about David Hume, whose skeptical critique of the reality of the self and unity of consciousness became one premise of Deleuze's thought. "The mind is a kind of theater," Hume had written, developing an image that Deleuze would take to heart. "There is properly no *simplicity* in it at one time, nor *identity* in different," only "a perpetual flux and movement," a constant variation, in which "several perceptions successively make their appearance; pass, re-pass, glide away, and mingle in an infinite variety of postures and situations."[110]

This picture of perpetual flux Deleuze reiterated and elaborated in the early sixties in a series of brilliantly original historical studies on Kant, Spinoza, and the vitalist philosopher Henri Bergson; on the erotic author Leopold von Sacher-Masoch; on Marcel Proust; and, above all, on Friedrich Nietzsche—the writer who changed his life. [111]

"I for a long time 'did' the history of philosophy," Deleuze once explained. "It was Nietzsche, whom I had read late, who pulled me out of all this. . . . He gives you a perverse inclination (which neither Marx nor Freud has ever given anyone . . .): the inclination to say simple things in your own proper name, to speak through affects, intensities, experiences, experiments. To say something in one's own name is very curious; for it is not at all when one takes one's self as an 'I,' a person or a subject, that one speaks in one's name. On the contrary, an individual acquires a real proper name only through the most severe exercise in depersonalization, when he opens himself to the multiplicities that traverse him from head to toe, to the intensities that flow through him," letting himself explore without inhibition an "infinite variety of postures and situations."[112]

When Foucault read Deleuze's *Nietzsche and Philosophy*, he was naturally struck by the similarity of their philosophical interests. Shortly afterward, he tried to hire Deleuze at Clermont-Ferrand. Though he failed in this effort (as he would six years later, when he tried again to hire Deleuze, this time at Vincennes), the two met, and became fast friends. "It was not simply a question of [mutual] understanding or intellectual accord," Deleuze later recalled, "but of intensity, of resonance, of a *musical* accord."[113]

Together, they probed the limits of reason in their writing, expressing pleasure in "amorphous fluidity," seeking the right words to evoke "an irreality that communicates itself," like a cognitive virus, "to understanding and people through language." After 1962, each closely followed the other's work, reading each new book carefully, commenting on it, finding in it a challenge and inspiration to dig deeper and go further, making a concerted effort to destroy "common sense as the assignation of fixed identities," as Deleuze put it.[114]

After the events of May '68, the philosophical and political alliance between the two deepened. "May '68 was the manifestation, the eruption of becoming in its pure state," Deleuze would later say. "It was exactly what Nietzsche called the Untimely."[115]

Swept up in the student movement, Deleuze, like Foucault, welcomed the host of new groups committed to experimenting with "amorphous fluidity." He commenced a long and fruitful collaboration with the psychoanalyst Félix Guattari, a neo-Marxist and militant critic of orthodox Freudianism; together with Guattari and Foucault, he participated in a *gauchiste* research center studying urbanism; he joined in the work of the GIP, and supported the more direct action of the Maoist militants; he also defended the new lifestyles springing up in the counter-culture, from the use of drugs in communes to the first stirrings of the French gay liberation movement.[116]

When Foucault entered the Collège de France, Deleuze took over his job at Vincennes—and his old role as the oracle of the ultra-left. "Like a tightrope walker with an intense gaze," one veteran of those heady days has recalled, "Deleuze each week faced an audience so compact that the little room where he spoke seemed drowned in the vapors of some Turkish bath," choked with cigarette smoke. "Febrile, exalted, and always tolerant, he formulated his thoughts in the manner of some singing madman."

Ranging over topics "from Spinoza to modern music, from Chinese metallurgy to bird-song, from linguistics to gang warfare," he aimed, as he once told his seminar, at "the manufacture of materials to harness forces, to think the unthinkable."[117]

Ironically, Deleuze himself—in this respect, as different from Foucault as one could imagine—betrayed little visible interest in actually *doing* many of the daring and risky things he so vividly conjured up in his lectures and writing. Married, with two children, he outwardly lived the life of a conventional French professor. His most conspicuous eccentricity was his fingernails: these he kept long and untrimmed because, as he once explained, he lacked "normal protective finger prints," and therefore could not "touch an object, particularly a piece of cloth, with the pads of my fingers without sharp pain." Despite his fascination with wandering tribes (he fancied himself a "nomad" thinker), he rarely travelled. As had happened with Hume, the apparent discrepancy between the boldness of his beliefs and the mild equanimity of his personal existence aroused hostile criticism. "If I don't move, if I don't travel, I have had, like everyone, trips sitting still," Deleuze once replied. "What difference is my relationship with homosexuals, alcoholics, or drug addicts if I obtain for myself similar effects with different means?"[118]

Perhaps the most important of these "different means" was his increasingly unbuttoned approach to writing: after 1968, Deleuze's style grew ever more delirious, reaching a new pitch of incandescent "irrealism" in *The Logic of Sense*, published in 1969. This is arguably Deleuze's greatest single work, a summum of everything he had learned so far, and the beginning of his adventures in "wonderland." Despite its sober title, *The Logic of Sense* is no conventional treatise: inspired by Lewis Carroll's "Alice" books, it is rather a sequence of thought-experiments, in which philosophy disappears down a rabbit hole, growing (like Alice) simultaneously bigger and smaller. Abandoning its old territorial claims to logical rigor and the orderly demonstration of reasonable propositions, philosophy is transformed, as if by magic, into a mobile army of metaphors. By following in Alice's footsteps, Deleuze hoped to give fresh voice to "rebel becomings," showing how the production of "sense" was a function, paradoxically, of "nonsense"—and how new ideas grew out of "phantasms" and corporeal dissipation. Though carefully defining all of his key terms, Deleuze plunged the reader into perplexity, making the mind reel and the skin crawl, tracing an intricate and bewildering zigzag line of creative discovery—the image of a "great, interior labyrinth," as Foucault enthusiastically summed up Deleuze's book.[119]

But a Nietzschean passion for labyrinths was by no means the only thing Foucault shared with Deleuze. For at the inner core of the labyrinth of language, both philosophers (like Blanchot before them) discovered death—the "event of events," as Foucault glossed Deleuze's conception. [120]

The reiterated "will to nothingness"—what Freud had called "the death instinct"—"is not only a will to power, a quality of the will to power," Deleuze declared at the climax of *Nietzsche and Philosophy*, "but the *ratio cognoscendi of the will to power in general*"—the only way in which we moderns may come to know the will to power as such. Under the impact of civilization, the will to power has been driven inward and turned against itself—creating within the human being "a new inclination: to destroy himself." It was precisely this inclination, formed by Western asceticism and issuing in modern nihilism, that led to "the focal point"—and central puzzle—of Deleuze's "Dionysian philosophy." For how could the will to. power, by Nietzsche's account an impulse *to live*, possibly surmount its own historically constituted inclination to self-destruction? [121]

The solution, according to Deleuze, was both simple and fraught with paradox. To recover his health, the Dionysian must exploit his will to nothingness. *Exercising* his power to destroy, he would destroy himself *actively*, obliterating whatever shackled his power, rediscovering a host of unfamiliar impulses. Deleuze himself was particularly interested in the shattering transmutation of pain into pleasure produced by masochistic eroticism; in the hallucinations set loose by drugs and alcohol (in this regard he discussed the English novelist Malcolm Lowry); in the disorder wrought by guerrilla warfare; in the psychological disintegration of schizophrenia; and—at the ultimate limit—in the deliberate embrace of death in suicide. [122]

Yet stopping short of madness, murder, and suicide, von Sacher-Masoch and Lowry, like the students in May '68, and like Artaud (another of Deleuze's heroes), had each shown how the will to nothingness, when seized actively and applied creatively, might be transformed into its opposite—an energetic (re)affirmation of the will to power in its (uncivilized) vital essence. "Each one risked something," noted Deleuze, be it health, sanity, or life; yet "each one drew from it an imprescriptible right," passing beyond fixed limits, blasting open a "hole": BENEATH THE PAVEMENT, THE BEACH. Through such cracks in the social and psychological monuments erected by civilization, one might glimpse "a pure becoming without measure" (a "monstrous and lawless becoming," as Foucault commented). Emboldened by such glimpses, one might then be able to go "farther than one would have believed possible," elaborating new images, new ideas, "new forms of life," beyond good, beyond evil, beyond "the will to nothingness" as well. Only then, taught Deleuze, could "the 'great politics' begin."[123]

Deleuze nevertheless had to admit that grave dangers lurked down this particular rabbit hole. While convulsively unburdening oneself—of pain, of guilt, of pity; of reason, of logic, of laws—one might lose all sense of order, plummeting uncontrollably into a void. "This is the 'black hole' phenomenon," Deleuze once explained: an individual "rushes into a black hole from which it will not be able to extricate itself." Deleuze took seriously the likelihood of a "crack-up," quoting F. Scott Fitzgerald's rueful observation: "Of course, all life is a process of breaking down." Those who fell into the catatonia of madness, or became addicted to drugs, or surrendered to the "micro-fascism" of political violence and terrorism, provoked "a slight horror," Deleuze once confided: "in any case, they scare me."[124]

Still, Deleuze managed to conquer his fears and all-too-sensible misgivings. "Anything that is good and great in humanity," he declared with icy resolve in *The Logic of Sense*, can arise only "in people ready to destroy themselves—better death than the health which we are given."[125]

Or, as Nietzsche's Zarathustra put it, in a passage that Deleuze knew well: "I love all those who are heavy drops, falling one by one out of the dark cloud that hangs over men: they herald the advent of lightning, and, as heralds, they perish."[126]

Foucault of course agreed. Besides, as he said in a 1971 interview, referring to May '68 and its aftermath, "the system is being shattered"—and there was a world to win.[127]

Apart from his agitation with the Groupe d'Information sur les Prisons, Foucault elaborated his own political views in these years in a series of public appearances and interviews, repeatedly expressing his own interest in what Nietzsche called the "joy in destroying."[128]

In the middle of 1971, for example, Foucault sat down with a group of militant young lycée students, to discuss the movement and its direction. The tape-recorded conversation appeared in *Actuel*, the most freewheeling magazine of the French alternative press after 1968, a monthly larded with the cartoons of R. Crumb and full of news about every facet of the international counter-culture, from Maoism to LSD.[129]

The conversation began with Foucault turning the tables. He asked the students about "the most intolerable forms of repression" they suffered.

But soon enough, the questions circled back to the philosopher himself, who responded by offering a primer on his political views.[130]

"The communication of knowledge," he agreed with one student, "is always positive"—even when the knowledge communicated is "biased," as another student complained. "As the events of May showed convincingly," knowledge always entailed "a double repression" in terms of what it excluded, and in terms of the order it imposed. For example, in French history texts, "popular movements . . . are said to arise from famines, taxes, or unemployment; and they never appear as the result of a struggle for power, as if the masses could dream of a full stomach but never of exercising power." Power was simply disregarded. At the same time, by employing a host of reassuring categories—"truth, man, culture, writing, etc."—the books tried "to dispel the shock of daily occurrences," to dissolve "the radical break introduced by events," to smooth out and cover up the Deleuzian "holes" blown open by such eruptions as the Night of the Barricades.[131]

The crux of the problem, Foucault suggested, was quite simple: it was "humanism." And the problem with humanism, it turned out, was also quite simple: at least, it was more baldly stated here than anywhere else in Foucault's work:

"Humanism is everything in Western civilization that restricts *the desire for power*."[132]

Nietzsche's central concept—*power*—here, finally, claimed its rightful place as a central term in Foucault's own vocabulary: his political goal, as he now explained it, was "a 'desubjectification' of the will to power."[133]

To reach this goal required "revolutionary action"—a "simultaneous agitation of consciousness and institutions."[134]

The institutional objective, as he stressed, was sweeping: it was, indeed, nothing less than the demolition of modern society as a cohesive, integrated totality. " 'The unity of society' is precisely that which should not be considered except as something to be destroyed. And then, it must be hoped that there will no longer be anything resembling the unity of society." In waging such an unconditional war against the oldest laws and pacts, it might well happen (as it usually did in wartime) that traditional moral beliefs restraining the will to power melted away. From a Nietzschean point of view, this was good. But short of a bloody civil war, these beliefs might also be usefully weakened by the more pacific and local agitation of groups like Foucault's own GIP: "The ultimate goal of its interventions," as the philosopher told the students, "was not to extend the visiting rights of prisoners to thirty minutes or to procure flush toilets for the cells, but to question the social and moral distinction between the innocent and the guilty." If successful, the GIP would destroy "a simple, basic ideology"—the "ideology of good and evil." Hence the title of this conversation: "Beyond Good and Evil."[135]

At the same time, insofar as the crux of the political problem was "subjectification," a human being could always engage the enemy at close quarters—and approach "consciousness" itself as a field of combat in which to overthrow "the subject as a pseudosovereign."[136]

At times, his young interlocutors had a hard time following Foucault's logic. "Does this mean," asked one, "that your primary objective is to modify consciousness and that you can neglect for the moment the struggle against political and economic institutions?"[137]

No, responded Foucault, "you have badly misunderstood me." It was a question, after all, not simply of changing consciousness, but of transforming institutions as well.[138]

Both goals might be approached simultaneously, Foucault suggested, through a kind of " 'cultural' attack" that would threaten old institutions by experimenting with new practices: "the suppression of sexual taboos, limitations, and divisions; the exploration of communal existence; the loosening of inhibitions with regard to drugs; the breaking of all the prohibitions that form and guide the development of the normal individual." (In endorsing such acts of transgression, Foucault was taking anything but an orthodox Maoist line: committed militants were expected to swear off drugs, which were regarded as a "petty-bourgeois" vice.)[139]

"I am referring to all those experiences that have been rejected by our civilization," Foucault explained, "or which it accepts only within literature." But times had changed: since May '68, "limit-experiences" were no longer simply the province of the writer and private person—they were at the very heart of the new politics being forged "beyond good and evil."[140]

And "it is possible," Foucault concluded optimistically, "that the rough outline of future society is supplied by the recent experiences with drugs, sex, communes, other forms of consciousness, and other forms of individuality. If scientific socialism emerged from the *utopias* of the nineteenth century, it is possible that a genuine socialization will emerge, in the twentieth century, from *experiences*."[141]

If Foucault's way of thinking was fundamentally alien, even to militant young lycée students versed in French philosophy, it was even more unfathomable to a great many political activists and intellectuals, both inside and outside France.

The most vivid (and amusing) example of the sort of reaction Foucault could provoke may be his debate with the American linguist Noam Chomsky. Staged for Dutch television, the meeting took place in November, 1971—and Chomsky still remembers it well. "He struck me as completely amoral," says Chomsky. "I'd never met anyone who was so totally amoral."[142]

On one level, pairing off Chomsky and Foucault for a discussion made a certain amount of sense. By 1971, both were internationally famous intellectuals; both had devoted works to the structure of language, though Chomsky's training was in linguistics, not philosophy; above all, both had become renowned for their combative political views—Chomsky, in 1967, had published in *The New York Review of Books* one of the single most influential articles attacking the war in Vietnam.

As Chomsky recalls, they met and spent several hours together before the program was taped, establishing some common ground despite the language barriers (Chomsky spoke little French, and Foucault was not yet as proficient in English as he would become). They exchanged political small talk, and discussed the Port-Royal grammarians, one of their shared scholarly interests.[143]

But there were already signs that this was not going to be any ordinary debate. Hoping to puncture the prim sobriety of the Dutch audience, the program's host, Fons Elders, a professed anarchist, had obtained a bright red wig, which he tried, unsuccessfully, to convince Foucault to wear. Meanwhile, unbeknownst to Chomsky, Foucault had received, in partial payment for his appearance, a large chunk of hashish, which for months afterwards, Foucault and his Parisian friends would jokingly refer to as the "Chomsky hash."[144]

The television program itself began placidly enough: Chomsky defended the idea of "a biologically given, unchangeable" foundation to human nature, and Foucault raised some doubts. Chomsky summarized his ideas about generative grammar, and Foucault briefly explained why historiography for him required "effacing the dilemma of the knowing subject."[145]

As the conversation continued in this vein, Elders kept poking Foucault under the table, pointing to the red wig on his lap, and whispering, "put it on, put it on." Foucault tried to ignore him, but as Elders' questions became more and more needling, he began to bristle.[146]

Why was he so interested in politics? Elders wanted to know. Why shouldn't he be? Foucault retorted. "What blindness, what deafness, what density of ideology would have to weigh me down to prevent me from being interested in what is probably the most crucial subject to our existence? . . . The essence of our life consists, after all, of the political functioning of the society in which we find ourselves."[147]

With the conversation now focused on politics, sparks started to fly.

Chomsky laid out his own anarchist utopia "of a federated, decentralised system of free associations." Foucault, by contrast, refused, as he consistently did, to elaborate any "ideal social model."[148]

Chomsky then spoke of the need for "some firm and humane concept of the human essence or human nature." Foucault, again, disagreed: "Isn't there a risk that we will be led into error? Mao Tse-tung spoke of bourgeois human nature and proletarian human nature, and he considers that they are not the same thing."[149]

Foucault now challenged Chomsky directly: "When, in the United States, you commit an illegal act, do you justify it in terms of justice or of a superior legality, or do you justify it by the necessity of the class struggle, which is at the present time essential for the proletariat in their struggle against the ruling class?"[150]

Chomsky was stunned by this line of questioning. He had read *The Order of Things*, and knew Foucault's work on eighteenth-century linguistics. But here Foucault was, invoking Mao Tse-tung and denying the need for even the most rudimentary principles of justice! Perhaps he had misunderstood.

Maintaining his composure, Chomsky answered earnestly: yes, he, too, as a conscientious objector sometimes regarded the state as criminal, and its laws as null and void; but that certainly did not mean that the *principle* of justice ought to be abandoned; on the contrary. His own resistance to laws he perceived as unjust in fact *required* some principle of justice. Concluded Chomsky: "We must act as sensitive and responsible human beings."[151]

That might seem a banal sentiment; in this context, it was anything but.

Foucault in fact would have none of it: responsibility, sensitivity, justice, law—these were all empty ideas, tokens of ideology, repressive, misleading, pernicious. "The proletariat doesn't wage war against the ruling class because it considers such a war to be just," he declared. "The proletariat makes war with the ruling class because, for the first time in history, it wants to take power."[152]

Chomsky was taken aback: "I don't agree," he stammered.

Foucault: "One makes war to win, not because it's just."

Chomsky: "I don't, personally, agree with that. . . ."

Foucault: "When the proletariat takes power, it may be quite possible that the proletariat will exert toward the classes over which it has triumphed, a violent, dictatorial, and even bloody power. I can't see what objection one could make to this."[153]

"Usually, when you talk to someone, you take for granted that you share some moral territory," Chomsky says, looking back. "Usually, what you find is self-justification in terms of shared moral criteria; in that case, you can have an argument, you can pursue it, you can find out what's right and what's wrong about the position. With him, though, I felt like I was talking to someone who didn't inhabit the same moral universe.

"I mean, I liked him personally. It's just that I couldn't make sense of him. It's as if he was from a different species, or something."[154]

The nonchalant savagery of Foucault's political views in these years startled not only radical humanists like Chomsky, it also dumbfounded some of the philosopher's young Maoist allies, who were then in the midst of debating the scope and meaning of "popular justice."

In these months, Pierre Victor (a.k.a. Benny Lévy) had become an ardent proponent of creating "popular tribunals." These were public forums in which people organized by the Maoist left would form a kind of "court," passing judgment on crimes and misdemeanors otherwise ignored or covered up by the state's courts. In December of 1970, Sartre had presided over the first such "popular tribunal" in the northern mining town of Lens, where sixteen workers had died in a mine explosion. At Lens, the tribunal had served as both a forum for publicizing certain facts, and a theatrical device for dramatizing the role played by corporate negligence in the accident that had occurred. As was true of many Maoist actions in these years, this tribunal had a number of merits: it focused attention on a real problem; it stimulated public debate; and it also forced normally isolated intellectuals to establish some rapport with ordinary people (always difficult to do, always a useful exercise).[155]

Buoyed by their experience at Lens, the Maoists created still another "popular tribunal," this one designed to judge, *in absentia*, police who had been accused of brutality. But as the months went by, and rank-and-file enthusiasm for the idea of popular justice began to grow, the slogans grew increasingly ominous: "A boss can be imprisoned." "The struggle for freedom should be waged in anger." "A deputy can be lynched." Such slogans had a certain logic—and they pointed toward the kind of terrorist "popular justice" practiced by ultra-leftists like the Baader-Meinhof gang in Germany and the Red Brigades in Italy.[156]

"It was a very hard question," recalls André Glucksmann, who had by this time gravitated into the inner core of the Maoist movement. "We were very close, in fact, technically, to the Baader-Meinhof gang and the Red Brigades. We had the means of terrorism, we had a secret organization with weapons. We could do what Baader-Meinhof did"—kidnap, torture, murder. "Some of us were on the way to that kind of action. And you must know that when Foucault was speaking, he was speaking to people who were in the mood of terrorism."[157]

On February 5, 1972, Foucault sat down with Pierre Victor to debate the meaning of "popular justice" for a special issue of Sartre's magazine, *Les temps modernes*. By then, Victor's sanguinary zeal had begun to alarm a growing number of his allies and intellectual fellow-travellers, who, as Glucksmann recalls, hoped to clip his wings by subjecting his position to sustained criticism.[158]

In their debate, Foucault in fact cast a jaundiced eye on Victor's enthusiasm for popular tribunals. Rejecting the very "form of the court," Foucault criticized any attempt, whether in the name of the state or in the name of the people, to seize an individual who might otherwise go unpunished, bring him before a court, persuade a jury to judge him "by reference to certain forms of equity," and then force the individual judged guilty to undergo punishment.[159]

Instead, Foucault proposed starting, not with the form of the court, but with "acts of justice by the people. . . . Now my hypothesis is not so much that the court is the natural expression of popular justice, but rather that its historical function is to ensnare it, to master it and to repress it, by reinscribing it within institutions that are typical of the machinery of the state."[160]

For "the natural expression of popular justice," Foucault suggested, we must look not to the courts, but to the streets—for example, to the September Massacres of 1792!

Bloody minded though Victor was, he was obviously taken aback by the implications of the example. At the height of the French Revolution, crowds of Parisian militants, inflamed by rumors of a royalist plot, had stormed the prisons and set upon suspected traitors. Those believed guilty—among them, a number of prostitutes and ordinary criminals—were forced to run a gauntlet of clubs, pikes, axes, knives, sabers, even, in one instance, a carpenter's saw. After the victims had been bludgeoned to death and hacked to pieces, the lucky ones were thrown onto a bloody heap; the others had their body parts—decapitated heads, mutilated gen-italia—mounted on pikes and triumphantly paraded through the streets of Paris. Before the orgy of killing was over, more than one thousand men and women had died.[161]

Baffled to discover himself outflanked on the left but quickly recovering his wits, Victor hastened to agree with Foucault: of course, the masses at the start of any revolution would rise up and slaughter their enemies. Yes, "executions of despots, all sorts of reprisals for all the extortions suffered over the centuries" will naturally take place, Victor said. "All this is fine." *Still*, he added defensively, before such bloodletting became routine, *surely* it was essential to reestablish the rule of law; surely it was crucial to create new courts—precisely in order to decide whether or not "this particular execution or that particular act of vengeance is not simply a matter of an individual settling of accounts, that is, purely and simply an egotistical revenge."[162]

Foucault disagreed.

Popular justice would best be served, he countered, by throwing open every prison and shutting down every court. Instead of instituting a process of "normalization," and rendering judgment according to laws, it would be better simply to relay fresh information to the masses (as had happened at the tribunal at Lens)—and then let the popular "need for retaliation" run its course. Exercising their power without inhibitions, the masses might resurrect "a certain number of ancient rites which were features of 'pre-judicial' justice."[163]

In this context, Foucault mentions the "old German custom" of putting "the head of an enemy on a stake, for public viewing, when he had been killed." Thus, after storming the Bastille prison on July 14, 1789, the mob paraded through the streets of Paris with the severed head of its commanding officer. Comments Foucault, with evident approval: "Around the symbol of the repressive apparatus," the Bastille, "revolves, with its ancient ancestral rights, a popular practice which does not recognize itself in any judicial proceedings."[164]

In the course of this astonishing conversation, Foucault did qualify some of these views. Under the repeated questioning of Victor, he conceded that "acts of justice by which one responds to the class enemy cannot be entrusted to a kind of instantaneous, unreflective spontaneity." He even conceded that a "revolutionary state apparatus" might have a constructive role to play—not through the creation of new courts, but rather through the "political formation" of the masses:

"So is it the job of this state apparatus here to determine sentences?

Not at all—it is to educate the masses and the will of the masses in such a way that it is the masses themselves who come to say, 'In fact we cannot kill this man,' or, 'In fact we must kill him.' "[165]

The issues broached in this interview were by no means academic.

On February 25, 1972, three weeks after the debate between Foucault and Victor had been taped, a Maoist worker named Pierre Overney, fired from his job at a Renault plant along with a number of his politically active comrades, was shot to death by a Renault security guard during a demonstration outside the factory gates.[166]

That night, Foucault joined his Maoist friends in a demonstration at the Renault plant that erupted into a mêlée with the police.

Once again, Foucault was engaging in an act of physical resistance against the forces of order. And at the height of the battle, witnesses glimpsed the gleaming skull of the great professor at the Collège de France absorbing blow after blow from the truncheon of a police officer.[167]

On March 8, the "need for retaliation" was slaked when a clandestine Maoist commando group calling itself the *Groupe Pierre-Overney de la Nouvelle Résistance* seized and held in an undisclosed location the chief personnel officer of the Renault plant.[168]

The kidnapping created an uproar, not just among conservatives and liberals, but also among fellow militants on the French student left.

In return for releasing the Renault officer, the commando group demanded an amnesty for all the Renault protestors who had been arrested, and a job for every fired worker.

The government refused to negotiate.

Buckling under the criticism of erstwhile allies on the French left, the Maoist commandos relented. Two days later, the Renault officer was released, unharmed. Unlike their friends in Germany and Italy, the French Maoists had drawn the line at political murder.[169]

But why this line, and not some other?[170]

For Foucault, who was in the midst of writing a book on crime and punishment, this had to be a difficult, and perhaps intractable question. Nearly two decades before, in 1953, he had declared that "man can and must experience himself negatively, through hate and aggression." Emboldened by his own "limit-experience" of politics fifteen years later, first in Tunisia, then in France, he had participated in pitched battles with the police; he had helped foment discontent in French prisons; and, contemplating with evident equanimity the bloodshed in popular revolts, he had called for destroying "the unity of society."

It is not surprising then, that issues of "hate and aggression" should play a critical and tortuously complex role in the next phase of Foucault's life, and, above all, in the most influential of his works—the "genealogy of modern morals" he would call *Discipline and Punish*.

7

A N   A R T
of
UNBEARABLE
SENSATIONS

THE BOOK'S OPENING LINES are uninflected, matter-of-fact—and, in the words of an early reviewer, "unbearable":

> [The regicide Damiens] had been condemned, on March 2, 1757, "to make honorable amends before the main door of the Church of Paris," where he was to be "brought on a cart, naked but for a shirt, holding a torch of burning wax weighing two pounds"; then, "in said cart taken to the place de Grève, where, on a scaffold that will be erected there, the flesh will be torn from his breasts, arms, thighs, and calves with red-hot pincers, his right hand, holding the knife with which he committed the said [regicide], burned with sulphur, and, on those places where the flesh will be torn away, poured molten lead, boiling oil, burning resin, wax, and sulphur melted together, and then his body drawn and quartered by four horses and his limbs and body consumed by fire, reduced to ashes and his ashes thrown to the wind."[1]

In the event—and the text spares nothing in the documents it is citing—the torture was botched. Four horses tethered to each limb proved unable to dismember Damiens. Next, six horses tried—and failed. " 'After two or three attempts,' " the executioner drew a knife " 'and cut the body at the thighs instead of severing the legs at the joints; the . . . horses gave a tug and carried off the two thighs after them, namely, that of the right side first, the other following; then the same was done to the arms, the shoulders, the armpits, and the four limbs; the flesh had to be cut almost to the bone. . . .' "[2]

Thus begins *Surveiller et punir*. Published in France early in 1975, the book was translated into English two years later as *Discipline and Punish*. Conceived during the most militant period of Foucault's activism with the

French Maoists and the Groupe d'Information sur les Prisons, it was composed between 1972 and 1974, at a time when the French ultra-left found itself in retreat and disarray. Foucault's most important essay in political theory, the text stages "multiple impossibilities," condemning humanism, implicitly justifying popular violence—and forcing the reader to grapple with the problematic role of hate and aggression in modern society, and in the modern psyche.

In the author's own eyes, it was the capstone of his career. "My first book," Foucault called it—and one can see why. Never before had his writing displayed such confidence and command. Never again would it radiate such concentrated—and disconcerting—power.[3]

The opening pages are a perfect example. Anonymous yet uncanny, they amount to a commentary "à la Borges," as Foucault once called it— a commentary that represents nothing but "the reappearance, word for word (but this time solemn and considered), of that which it comments upon."[4] As he explained, the "novelty" (and philosophical burden) of such a commentary lies "not in what is said, but in the occasion for its return," its curious repetition, its loving reiteration—in this case, as the new beginning of a new book by Michel Foucault:

> The sulphur was lit, but the flame was so poor that only the top skin of the hand was burnt, and that only slightly. Then the executioner, his sleeves rolled up, took the steel pincers, which had been especially made for the occasion, and which were about a foot and a half long, and pulled first at the calf of the right leg, then at the thigh, and from there at the two fleshy parts of the right arm, then at the breasts. Though a strong and sturdy fellow, this executioner found it so difficult to tear away the pieces of flesh that he set about the same spot two or three times, twisting the pincers as he did so, and what he took away formed at each part a wound about the size of a six-pound crown piece. . . .
>
> At each torment, [Damiens] screamed as one imagines the damned screaming, saying nothing but "Forgive me, my God! Forgive me, Lord!"[5]

Damiens' agonizing ordeal does not stand alone. It is followed immediately in Foucault's text by another commentary "à la Borges," a long quotation from a book published in 1838 by the French prison reformer Leon Faucher. The excerpt outlines an ideal daily regimen for young convicts:

At the first drumroll, the prisoners must rise and dress in silence, as the supervisor opens the cell door. At the second drumroll, they must be dressed and make their beds. At the third, they must line up and proceed to the chapel for morning prayer. There is a five-minute interval between each drum roll. . . .

At a quarter to six in the summer, a quarter to seven in the winter, the prisoners go down into the courtyard where they must wash their hands and face, and receive their first ration of bread. Immediately afterwards, they form into work teams and go off to work, which must begin at six in summer and seven in winter. . . .

At half-past seven [in the evening] in summer, half-past eight in winter, the prisoners must be back in their cells after the washing of hands and the inspection of clothes in the courtyard; at the first drumroll, they must undress, and at the second get into bed. The cell doors are closed and the supervisors go the rounds in the corridors, to ensure order and silence.[6]

Two different documents, two different images: one of a public execution, the other of a model prison. Each illustrates two starkly different approaches to punishment, two different ways to enforce the rules of a society. The first way, expressing the sovereign will of a king, has as its target the flesh: it is savage, spectacular, revolting. The second way, expressing the modern rule of law, evinces "a certain discretion." It is methodical, austere, numbing: "The age of sobriety in punishment has begun."[7]

The book that follows is elegant, intricate—and, as always with Foucault's major works, deeply perplexing. An estimably erudite study, its aim on one level is clear enough: to describe in detail how the "style" of punishment changed in Europe between the torture of Damiens in 1757, and the birth of the modern prison around 1840. Like the account of the asylum in *Madness and Civilization* before it, Foucault's history of the changing technology of punishment opened up a startling new perspective on the past, stimulating a fresh approach to a previously neglected area of history.

Once again, however, subsequent research by scholars has suggested how peculiar Foucault's own history is. His text offers a characteristic blend of nuanced analyses, authoritative references, and abundant documentation—combined with fabulous images, bald assertions, and wild generalizations.[8]

At the heart of the work, moreover, stands a disarmingly simple philosophical fable: for the "prison" at issue in Foucault's account is not only the kind patrolled by wardens and built out of bricks and steel; it is also the "prison" within—the kind patrolled by conscience and built out of aptitudes and inclinations. On this level, Foucault's work was, just as he said it was, an allegory about "the soul, effect and instrument of political anatomy; the soul, prison of the body."[9]

On more than one occasion, Foucault in interviews and public debates conceded the peculiarity of *Discipline and Punish*, and tried, not always with much success, to explain to others what he was up to, and why.

In the most general terms, he explained, this historical study, like all those that had come before, broached, admittedly with great difficulty, the "problem of truth." The difficulty lay in knowing what history was, given that his studies had all demonstrated, among other things, how the distinctions and categories essential to "knowing" as such, above all the distinction between what was true and what was false, were themselves transient and changing products of transient and changing institutions and practices: "What historical knowledge is possible of a history that itself produces the true/false distinction on which such knowledge depends?"[10]

Once again, then, the reader is faced with a strange, almost surreal sort of historiography. On the one hand, as Foucault explained in a 1978 interview, "I use methods drawn from the classical repertoire: demonstration, proof of historical documentation, reference to texts, recourse to authorized commentaries, [interpretation of] relations between ideas and facts, proposition of explanatory schemes, etc." This part of his work, certified as factual by the footnotes and references, may of course be rejected, revised, or confirmed according to the most rigorous standards of historiographic inquiry.[11]

On the other hand, Foucault still was committed to importing "fiction," as he called the element of transcendence in language, into the play of his otherwise fastidiously "factual" prose. "It seems to me," he remarked in a 1977 interview, "that the possibility exists for fiction to work within truth, for a fictive discourse to induce effects of truth, and for bringing it about that a true discourse engenders, or 'fabricates' something that does not yet exist, that is, 'fictions' it."[12]

Thus *Discipline and Punish*, as he once put it, "makes use of 'true' documents, but in such a way that through them it is possible to effect not only a certification of the truth, but also an *experience* that authorizes an alteration, a transformation in the relationship that we have with ourselves and with our cultural universe: in a word, with our 'knowledge.'"

The "fictive" part of his book is, in effect, designed to evoke a kind of "limit-experience" in the reader, triggering a change in our selves, in our "souls," and in our understanding of "truth," all together.[13]

But what might this change involve?

In *Discipline and Punish*, Foucault deliberately multiplies themes and vignettes, opening up new "analytical 'salients,' " as he once put it, producing an "increasing polymorphism" of imagery, detailing a dizzying and "dazzling array of perverse inventions, cynical discourses and meticulous horrors" (as Gilles Deleuze once summed up his general impression of the book). The cumulative effect, however, is both simple and clear: it is to *sharpen* the tension established at the outset, by the first two images in the book.[14]

Damiens' death by torture is spectacular, grotesque—and unforgettable. Faucher's prison timetable pales by comparison: it is drab, precise, rational to a fault.

Within the larger context of Foucault's argument, the second image illustrates the rigid structure of the modern prison, while the first displays the cruel and unusual type of punishment the modern prison was designed to replace. In the hands of almost any other storyteller, this outcome might even offer a kind of consolation. Most historians, after all, have welcomed the disappearance of torture as part of a salutary process of "humanization" that has softened the often savage violence of premodern societies.

Foucault famously does nothing of the sort. Far from welcoming the disappearance of torture, he raises ever more pressing doubts about the hidden costs of a "penal style" that would avoid visible coercion and act instead "in depth" by seeking to transform "the heart, the thoughts, the will, the inclinations." Efforts to institute "less cruelty, less suffering, more gentleness, more respect, more 'humanity,' " have, according to Foucault, had the perverse effect of reinventing the entirety of modern society on the model of a prison, imposing ever more subtle, and insidiously punishing kinds of "discipline," not just on convicts, but also on soldiers, on workers, on students, even on the various professionals trained to supervise various "disciplinary" institutions, in the process refining new "corrective technologies of the individual"—and producing a "double effect: a 'soul' to be known and a subjection to be maintained."[15]

The scenes that open the book therefore turn out to be doubly disturbing. For if Foucault's text arouses the most profound skepticism about reforms intended to lessen pain, it simultaneously invites the reader to contemplate with unwonted sympathy the cruel power at play in what Foucault calls "*l'éclat des supplices*"—the splendor and explosive glory of death-by-torture.[16]

This strange double transvaluation goes a long way toward explaining the disquiet one may feel on finishing Foucault's remarkable book. Thinking through the issues raised in *Discipline and Punish* is like walking into a fiendishly clever philosophical fun house. While negotiating its labyrinthine twists and turns, trying to avoid dead ends and patiently exploring detours in pursuit of answers to the many riddles it poses—about chronology, about method, about genealogy—it is easy to let slip from view the troubling substantive issues to which the text nevertheless keeps circling back.

What, for example, are we to make of Foucault's apparent fascination with death-by-torture?

Or, to pose the question more abstractly, in terms of the ethical issue raised as well by Foucault's own political "limit-experiences" after May '68: what role ought cruelty and violence to play in the organization of body, soul, and society?

Foucault was, of course, not the first modern thinker to raise these questions. Sade, Bataille, and Artaud had raised questions about cruelty and violence as well—and so, too, had Gilles Deleuze. So, above all, had Friedrich Nietzsche. In the works that Foucault had written before, many of these authors had been invoked in a kind of gnostic mantra, as if to summon the shattering raptures of "the thought from outside." But one of the most striking stylistic breakthroughs in *Discipline and Punish* was the omission of this familiar litany of names, its absence marked, as it were, by the book's uninflected literary frontispiece. Apathetically rendered though it is, the death-by-torture of Damiens peculiarly colors everything that follows—as does the silent presence, presiding over this uncanny theater of cruelty, of Nietzsche, whose influence looms larger than ever before.[17]

It was Nietzsche, after all, who had first linked the technology of punishment to the production of the human "soul," thereby placing questions of cruelty and violence at the center of modern thought. And Foucault on more than one occasion acknowledged his philosophical debt to Nietzsche and his line of argument: "If I wanted to be pretentious," he remarked in an interview shortly after *Discipline and Punish* had been published, alluding to the work in which Nietzsche drew these connections, "I would use 'the genealogy of morals' as the general title of what I am doing."[18]

In the early 1970s, Foucault had returned to Nietzsche's thought with fresh interest. In 1970, he had devoted one of his courses at Vincennes to Nietzsche; and in 1971, in his first series of lectures at the Collège de France, he had undertaken a comparative analysis of Aristotle's *Metaphysics* and Nietzsche's *The Gay Science* in a course with the Nietzschean title "*La volonté de savoir*"—"The Will to Know."[19]

Summarizing Nietzsche's convictions about "knowledge" in a short précis of these lectures, Foucault enumerated, as well, some of his *own* central convictions—themes and theses that informed the approach of *Discipline and Punish*:

> —Knowledge is an "invention" behind which lies something completely different from itself: a play of instincts, impulses, desires, fear, a will to appropriate. It is on the stage where these elements battle one another that knowledge is produced.
>
> —It is produced not as a result of the harmony or happy equilibrium of these elements, but rather as the result of their antagonism, of their dubious and provisional compromise, of a fragile truce that they are always prepared to betray. Knowledge is not a permanent faculty, it is an event, or perhaps a series of events.
>
> —It is always enslaved, dependent, and enthralled (not to itself but to whatever can enthrall an instinct, or the instincts that dominate it).
>
> —And if it presents itself as knowledge of the truth, it is because it produces the truth, through the play of a primary and always reconstituted falsification, which establishes the distinction between the true and the false.[20]

At first glance, these four propositions about the status of "knowledge" and the origin of "truth" may seem quite remote from the problem of punishment and the origin of the modern prison. But for Foucault, as for Nietzsche, "knowledge" was a by-product of corporeal powers, and intimately intertwined with an attempt to regulate these powers; the attempt to regulate power was, for both, tied to the prohibition of violent, cruel, and aggressive impulses, a prohibition enforced through punishment; both men hypothesized that such violent, cruel, and aggressive impulses, once blocked from external discharge, rather than vanishing, were merely driven inward—explaining, "no doubt," as Foucault glossed this quintessentially

Nietzschean idea in *Discipline and Punish*, how "the man of modern humanism was born"—and how the soul became a "prison" of the body.[21]

❧

Nietzsche had analyzed the character of this process in the famous second essay of the *Genealogy of Morals*, on the birth of " 'Guilt,' 'Bad Conscience' and the Like." As a review of Nietzsche's argument makes plain, Foucault in *Discipline and Punish* builds on its assumptions and recapitulates its major themes with remarkable fidelity.

Once upon a time, according to Nietzsche's fable about *homo natura* (which Freud would repeat from a different angle), human beings were the hapless "slaves of momentary affect and desire." No matter the consequences, they acted on every passing whim. In this imagined state of nature, the strong enjoyed "the highest gratification of the feeling of power" through the practice of "cruelty," inflicting and suffering pain at will; capricious "beasts of prey," they could emerge "from a disgusting procession of murder, arson, rape, and torture, exhilarated and undisturbed of soul, as if it were no more than a students' prank, convinced they have provided the poets with a lot more material for song and praise." Such beasts of prey understandably provoked fear and distrust in their neighbors; for most people in the Nietzschean state of nature, life was nasty, brutish, and short; thus many felt a need to regulate and control an otherwise "constant state of war."[22]

Such regulation occurred through the imposition of what Nietzsche calls "the social straitjacket"—the elaboration of customs and mores and laws designed to make human beings "calculable, regular, necessary," in short, *tame*. But how, he asks, can this transformation occur? How can one impress something on a murderous beast of prey, "attuned only to the passing moment, in such a way that it will stay there?"[23]

The answer, thought Nietzsche, was a terrible kind of "*mnemotechnics*," as he called it, designed to forge "a real *memory of the will*"; for memory alone might enable a human being to act with constancy and to forbear acting with perdurance. " 'If something is to stay in the memory' "—this was the crux of his "mnemotechnic" hypothesis—" 'it must be burned in: only that which never ceases to *hurt* stays in the memory.' "[24]

For centuries, states, many governed by barely civilized "beasts of prey," therefore employed the most "fearful means" of molding their human material, forcing subjects to renounce violence, building law on "the promise of blood" (as Foucault puts it). "Consider the old German punishments," wrote Nietzsche, gleefully listing the most gruesome, "for example, stoning . . . , breaking on the wheel . . . , piercing with stakes, tearing apart or trampling by horses . . . , boiling of the criminal in oil or wine . . . , the popular flaying alive . . . , cutting flesh from the chest, and also the practice of smearing the wrongdoer with honey and leaving him in the blazing sun for the flies."[25]

As the very gaiety of Nietzsche's tone suggests, the spectacle of such punishments long offered human beings pleasure as well as pain—an assertion confirmed and amplified by Foucault in his own discussion of "*l'éclat des supplices*" ("the glory of torture"). The word *éclat* here evokes a Nietzschean notion underlined throughout *Discipline and Punish*: torture, far from being the disgusting act of blind savagery modern humanists often assume it to be, was rather a carefully calibrated instrument of culture, a regulated practice with its own splendors and glory. An "art of unbearable sensations," a "theater of hell," "the poetry of Dante put into laws," the public ritual of death-by-torture offered an occasion for experiencing, if only vicariously, pleasures otherwise routinely forbidden. "If the crowd gathered round the scaffold, it was not simply to witness the sufferings of a condemned man or to excite the anger of the executioner: it was also to hear someone who had nothing left to lose curse the judges, laws, power, religion. Death-by-torture allowed the condemned man this momentary saturnalia, where nothing was prohibited or punishable."[26]

As Nietzsche explained in the *Genealogy of Morals*, the harshest penal practices paradoxically honored and preserved some of the human being's most elemental impulses: "In punishment there is so much that is *festive!*" To "see others suffer does one good." Witnessing the most cruel of punishments, the spectator must sense that "the type" of the criminal's actions "*as such*" cannot be completely reprehensible, since one sees "exactly the same kind of actions practiced in the service of justice and approved of with a good conscience: . . . violence, defamation, imprisonment, torture, murder, practiced as a matter of principle and without even emotion to excuse them."[27]

Summing up the argument of his second essay in the *Genealogy of Morals*, Nietzsche stressed one essential point: "*cruelty* is here exposed for the first time as one of the most ancient and basic substrata of culture that simply cannot be imagined away."[28]

With the passage of time, however, the human being's most cruel impulses had nevertheless been slowly but surely subdued. Producing "an increase of fear, a heightening of prudence, mastery of the desires," the very success of the harshest methods of punishment had made them less and less necessary. Not that punishment had succeeded in making men any "better." On the contrary. As Foucault once summed up the gist of Nietzsche's theory, the renunciation of natural impulses testified not to "a great moral conversion"—but rather, "properly speaking, to a *perversion*."[29]

It was properly speaking a "*perversion*" because, for both Nietzsche and Foucault, taming threatened to hobble the *transcendens* that Nietzsche called will to power. In its unmutilated essence, as Nietzsche described it, this power was "spontaneous, aggressive, expansive, form-giving"—and naturally cruel. "To practice cruelty is to enjoy the *highest* gratification of the feeling of power," Nietzsche had written in 1880. To exercise power without inhibition was, in effect, to *be* cruel: that was his hard teaching.[30]

Still, the renunciation of violence and cruelty among the subjects of civilized society was not simply a privation. According to both Foucault and Nietzsche, it also produced an entirely new deployment of impulses and powers within the human animal: "All instincts that do not discharge themselves outwardly *turn inward*," suggested Nietzsche. "Thus it was that man first developed what was later called his 'soul'."[31]

The elaboration of a soul divided the human animal. "Its instinct for freedom pushed back and repressed, incarcerated within, and finally able to discharge and vent itself only on itself," as Nietzsche put it, the organism in effect entered into a state of permanent war with itself—the conflict of instincts, impulses, and desires that Foucault had described in his first course at the Collège de France.[32]

Suing for peace, most human beings in time came to swear fealty to various sorts of psychological "oligarchies," with "regulation, foresight, and premeditation" keeping at bay "our underworld of utility organs working with and against one another." With the "aid of the morality of mores," the organism's oligarchy was kept in power; as time passed, the human being learned "to be ashamed of all his instincts." Stifling its cruel and murderous impulses, the human being became a subject of civilized reason and morality.[33]

But the organism's cruel impulses did not, for all that, disappear altogether. What otherwise might be inexplicable—namely, the pleasure human beings have clearly learned to feel in taking pains to rule themselves—Nietzsche explained through the survival of *internalized* cruelty, and the paradoxical convergence of pleasure and pain that characterizes it. The idea of "self-chosen torture"—*prima facie*, a monstrous oxymoron—becomes the key in the *Genealogy of Morals* to interpreting a host of intertwined phenomena: guilt, the bad conscience, and, as the historical foundation of both, the triumph of asceticism in Christianity.[34]

The internalization of cruel impulses represented by the triumph of asceticism ramified in unpredictable ways. Guilt hobbled the human being's animal energies; shared taboos made exercising the will difficult and sometimes dangerous. Yet in some rare souls, the masochistic pleasures of self-rule paradoxically strengthened the will to power in all of its cruel splendor; the old animal impulses, cultivated with foresight and transmogrified through the use of memory, imagination, and reason, erupted in new forms of mastery. "This secret self-ravishment, this artist's cruelty, this delight in imposing a form upon oneself as a hard, recalcitrant, suffering material, and in burning a will, a critique, a contradiction, a contempt, a No into it, this uncanny, dreadfully joyous labor of a soul voluntarily at odds with itself that makes itself suffer out of joy in making suffer—eventually this entire *active* bad conscience—you will have guessed it—as the womb of all ideal and imaginative phenomena, also brought to life an abundance of strange new beauty and affirmation, and perhaps beauty itself."[35]

In *Beyond Good and Evil*, Nietzsche summarized this history by using the metaphor of a ladder. The "great ladder of religious cruelty," as he called it, had three rungs. The first step leads to the sacrifice of human beings for the sake of one's god. Next, "one sacrificed to one's god one's own strongest instincts, one's 'nature': *this* festive joy lights up the cruel eyes of the ascetic." Finally comes the "paradoxical mystery of the final cruelty," the sacrifice of God.[36]

This is the form of cruelty proper to the philosopher. Driven by the will to know—a will nurtured and preserved by the practice of asceticism—thinkers finally appear who, recognizing that the idea of truth is itself a kind of fiction, spare nothing to tell those who will listen that everything we hold as solid and certain about the world is, upon closer examination, demonstrably accidental, contingent, or false: laws, ideas, philosophies, religions, moralities, everything. Such honesty risks ending in nihilism—the catastrophic conviction that nothing is true, everything is permitted. Subverting, as it does, rules, assumptions, and convictions that enable societies to function and most people to feel at home in the world, the philosopher's will to truth is "a kind of sublime wickedness." There is in the Nietzschean will to know, as Foucault described it in 1971, "something of the murderous," something at odds with "the happiness of mankind"; for this terrible will to know "sweeps along with an ever more furious determination; instinctive violence accelarates in it and increases."[37]

But the violence of the Dionysian philosopher is no longer driven inward; it is rather aimed outward, taking joy in destroying whatever mutilates life, and a malicious delight in translating "man back into nature"—an animal "nature" characterized, among other things, by cruelty: the primordial pleasure to be found in inflicting, and suffering, pain.[38]

Discipline and Punish recapitulated Nietzsche's argument, but it also extended it, showing how the modern human sciences had taken over the role of Christianity in disciplining the body, substituting for the Christian soul, "born in sin and subject to punishment," an even meeker modern soul, born under supervision and subject to an indefinite discipline, "an interrogation without limits."[39]

Unlike Nietzsche, Foucault had the training and temperament of a modern historian: *Discipline and Punish* was festooned with footnotes, promising verifiable evidence of just how the "mnemotechnics" of modern European societies had changed during the eighteenth and nineteenth centuries.

Sometime around the French Revolution, this evidence suggested, punishment as a grisly spectacle of torture fell into disfavor, to be replaced by new and more discreet approaches to burning the rules of society into the soul. The aim, in Foucault's words, was "not to punish less, but to punish better; to punish with an attenuated severity perhaps, but in order to punish with more universality and necessity; to insert the power to punish more deeply into the social body."[40]

What was responsible for this shift, as he described it, was not so much a change in thinking about what constituted a sin or a crime, though a number of such changes did in fact occur, but rather a more fundamental change in the technology of government. For the first time, it became possible to supervise, in detail, "the plebeian, popular, proletarian and peasant population," as Foucault put it in a 1973 interview, "a general, continuous submission to supervision through new forms of political power. . . . I would say, if you will, that what had been invented at the end of the eighteenth century and beginning of the nineteenth was *panopticism*."[41]

The analysis of "panopticism" was the heart of *Discipline and Punish*. The neologism itself, which designated the modern "physics of power" that replaced the crude "mnemotechnics" of torture, was inspired by Jeremy Bentham and his book *Panopticon*. In this work, first published in 1791, the English jurist and reformer proposed building a circular prison in which the prisoners could be continuously supervised—hence the book's title, from the Greek word *"panoptes,"* for "all-seeing."

Most people today, if they know Bentham at all, know him only as the founding father of "utilitarianism." By reformulating ethics in terms of an intricate calculus designed to maximize pleasures and minimize pains, Bentham hoped to secure "the greatest happiness of the greatest number"— an aim that might, without too much exaggeration, be said to define the modern welfare state.

Yet Bentham, despite being admired by fellow thinkers like James Mill, was for many years scarcely appreciated as a legal scholar or political philosopher. On the contrary, the larger British public long regarded him only as a crank, a philanthropic fanatic with one idea—the Panopticon. Bentham was convinced that this "simple idea in Architecture" could solve one of the most vexing problems of Enlightenment social thought. By applying the principle of perpetual "inspection" in a wide variety of different settings, from prisons and hospitals to factories and schools, one might harmoniously coordinate (self) interest and (social) duty, enforcing as painlessly as possible a sense of conscientiousness. "The fundamental advantage of the Panopticon," as Bentham put it, "is so evident that one is in danger of obscuring it in the desire to prove it. To be incessantly under the eyes of the inspector is to lose in effect the power to do evil and almost the thought of wanting to do it."[42]

For several decades, Bentham lavished much of his time and family fortune on implementing the Panopticon. In 1791, hoping that a regime of revolutionaries might consider without prejudice his radical plan, he even offered his services to the French National Assembly. To no avail. For his efforts, the French made him an honorary citizen. In England, however, perhaps the most tangible impact of his scheme was on the language: thanks to the popular derision of his panacea, "panopticon" entered nineteenth-century English usage not only as a term for "a place where everything is visible," but also as "a showroom for novelties."[43]

By the time Foucault started his research, Bentham's book had become a historical curio. Nobody read it. Yet Foucault could not help noticing that the book was routinely referred to in the nineteenth-century literature on prison reform: "There was scarcely a text or a proposal about the prisons that didn't mention Bentham's 'device,' " he later recalled.[44]

One can well imagine his excitement when he finally got hold of Bentham's book. He could not have invented a more striking emblem of everything he detested about modern society.

Bentham's Panopticon was undeniably elegant—and also undeniably sinister. "We know the principle," Foucault writes, conjuring up the image with caustic precision: "at the periphery, an annular building; at the center, a tower; this tower is pierced with wide windows that open onto the inner side of the ring; the peripheric building is divided into cells, each of which extends the whole width of the building; they have two windows, one on the inside, corresponding to the windows of the tower; the other, on the outside, allows the light to cross the cell from one end to the other. All that is needed, then, is to place a supervisor in a central tower and to confine in each cell a madman, someone sick, someone condemned, a worker, or a schoolboy. By the effect of backlighting, one can observe from the tower, standing out precisely against the light, the small captive silhouettes in the cells of the periphery. They are like so many cages, so many small theatres, in which each actor is alone, perfectly individualized and constantly visible."[45]

Bentham himself had conceded that his "high-wrought contrivance" might seem perversely self-defeating, exchanging the "liberal spirit and energy of a free citizen" for the "mechanical discipline of a soldier," producing "a set of *machines* under the similitude of *men*." But the great reformer was convinced that his "new mode of obtaining power of mind over mind" was an unrivalled means for securing the greatest happiness of the greatest number. "Call them soldiers," wrote Bentham, "call them machines: so they were but *happy* ones, I should not care."[46]

In effect, the utilitarian thinker had imagined a perfect way to produce, and then patrol, the kind of world Nietzsche had feared most: a world on the model of a "tremendous clockwork, composed of ever smaller, ever more subtly 'adapted' gears," in which there is "an ever-growing superfluity of all dominating and commanding elements," in which individuals represent "*minimal forces, minimal values*." Such individuals, deprived of the spectacle of punishment and tired of the war within, craved peace, tranquility, an end to chaos and suffering. With "*nothing any more to be afraid of*," the human being was "no longer able to despise himself," no longer able even to find pleasure in pain. At the end of this path lay Nietzsche's "last man": " 'We have invented happiness,' say the last men, and they blink."[47]

On one level, of course, Bentham and Nietzsche were both dealing in hypothetical futures: the Panopticon was no more real than Nietzsche's nightmare of the "last man." Yet Foucault insisted that the Panopticon was more than just an idle fantasy. Bentham's "simple idea in Architecture" offered, he wrote, "the diagram of a mechanism of power reduced to its ideal form"; it mapped out the specific anatomy of modern power that Foucault called "discipline."[48]

Unlike the power of sovereignty, which was spectacularly violent (as the painful death of Damiens demonstrated), the power of discipline was mild, humane—and insidious, precisely because it was exercised invisibly, through discreet surveillance rather than overt coercion. Such supervision, as Foucault described it, "dissociates power from the body," leaving it compliant, "normalized" (another one of Foucault's influential neologisms), ready to take orders from above, like a soldier in a modern army. The result, in principle, was an "automatic functioning of power"—a "perfection of power" that tended, paradoxically, "to render its actual exercise useless" (not a praiseworthy trait in the eyes of a Nietzschean).[49]

In Foucault's view, the abstract idea of "panopticism" illuminated a host of real institutions that were in the process of transforming modern life. "In my book on the birth of the prison," as he explained in a 1978 interview, "I tried to show precisely how the idea of a technology of individuals, a certain type of power, was exercised over individuals in order to tame them, shape them, and guide their conduct," as a kind of "strict correlative" to "the birth of a type of liberal regime." Beyond the prison itself, a "carceral" style of reasoning, focused on punishable deviations from the norm, thus came to inform a wide variety of modern institutions. In schools, factories, and army barracks, authorities carefully regulated the use of time (punishing tardiness, slowness, the interruption of tasks); activity (punishing inattention, negligence, a lack of zeal); speech (punishing idle chatter, insolence, profanity); the body (punishing poor posture, dirtiness, lapses in stipulated reflexes); and, finally, sexuality (punishing impurity, indecency, abnormal behavior). In "a natural extension," the principles first enunciated by Bentham now authorized, Foucault suggested in the apocalyptic final chapter of *Discipline and Punish*, an "indefinite discipline," geared to produce "docile bodies" through an "interrogation without end," not simply of convicts but of every modern soul, "an investigation that would be extended without limit to a meticulous and ever more analytical observation, a judgment that would at the same time be the constitution of a file that was never closed, the calculated leniency of a penalty that would be interlaced with the ruthless curiosity of an examination"—in short, Nietzsche's nightmare come true.[50]

As Foucault summed up this bleak vision, in a "system of surveillance there is no need for arms, physical violence, material constraints. Just a gaze. An inspecting gaze, a gaze which each individual under its weight will end by internalizing to the point that he is his own supervisor, each individual thus exercising this surveillance over, and against, himself. A superb formula: power exercised continuously and for what turns out to be a minimal cost"—at least from the point of view of society.[51]

From the other side, however, things looked different. With the human being set ever more sharply at odds with its animal impulses, the potential for a renewed war within perforce intensified. In a world ruled by "last men," warned Nietzsche, "everybody wants the same, everybody is the same," and "whoever feels different goes into a madhouse." "Oh this insane, pathetic beast," he wrote in the *Genealogy of Morals*: "What ideas he has, what unnaturalness, what paroxysms of nonsense, what *bestiality of thought* erupts as soon as he is prevented just a little from being a *beast in deed!*"[52]

Outwardly in modern society, to the gaze of its supervisors, bodies might seem to be docile. But inwardly bodies and souls boiled and seethed, their secret dreams of a mastery without mercy "isolated, intensified, incorporated." Driven inward, cut off from its old links to the punishing Christian conscience that externalized itself in the great atrocities of the Inquisition, cruelty, to borrow one of Foucault's phrases, turns from "jousts to phantasms."[53]

The reference to phantasms is worth pursuing a little further, since fantasy, dream, and imagination together play a central role in Foucault's way of thinking about cruelty. "Phantasms," he once remarked (glossing one of Deleuze's theories), "topologize the materiality of the body"—they map out the otherwise invisible deployment of impulses and drives in any particular human being. The capacity to fantasize gives every human being "disturbing and nocturnal powers," driving it more or less blindly forward, as if haunted by a singular *daimon*. Given any "healthy, normal, and law-abiding adult," it is always possible to illuminate the singular form of these "nocturnal powers" by asking, as Foucault puts it in *Discipline and Punish*, "how much of the child he has in him, what secret madness dwells within him, what fundamental crime he has wished to commit." However disturbing certain recurrent dreams may seem, "phantasms," as Foucault puts it, "are the welcome of appearance in the light of origin"—the sign of each person's unique "higher necessity," the granite from which each of us must carve the statue we will call our "self." Like Deleuze, Foucault thus urged that phantasms "should be freed from the restrictions we impose upon them, freed from the dilemmas of truth and falsehood and of being and non-being . . . they must be allowed to conduct their dance," even though the dance of fantasy may produce results that are, in Foucault's words, "simultaneously topological"—that is, mapped back onto the materiality of the body as carnal desires—"and cruel."[54]

There is more. Insofar as the dreamworld becomes the last, irrepressible redoubt of the primordial pleasure to be felt in inflicting and suffering pain, fantasy undergoes an epochal transformation. "Sadism," as Foucault had put it in *Madness and Civilization*, "constitutes one of the greatest conversions of the Western imagination: unreason transformed into delirium of the heart, madness of desire, the insane dialogue of love and death."[55]

The effects of this "conversion" marked the modern body politic. For no matter how vigilantly policed a society was, its ramparts were sometimes violently breached. A "fatal return and revolt of what is repressed," crime for just this reason "bears within itself a figure and a future," as the most radical followers of the French utopian socialist Fourier had argued in the 1830s—and as Foucault had suggested in some of his remarks about the Groupe d'Information sur les Prisons in the early 1970s. Simply by describing their own experience, convicted criminals could launch a productive "counter-discourse" intended to disrupt the "serene domination of Good over Evil." For as Foucault remarked in *Discipline and Punish*, "the existence of crime happily manifests 'an irrepressibility of human nature'; it is necessary to see in it, not a weakness or a disease, but rather an energy that is straightening itself out, a 'striking protestation of human individuality,' which no doubt gives it, in the eyes of all, its strange power of fascination."[56]

Foucault, of course, was talking about himself. Through his research for *Discipline and Punish*, as well as his work with the GIP, he had grown ever more bewitched by "the lives of infamous men," as he once put it. Insatiable in his curiosity, he had combed through the responses to the GIP questionnaires, and spent hours in the archives examining old police dossiers and court records, pausing over documents that struck a nerve. Sometimes as he read through the file of some obscure convict—one of "those lowly lives reduced to ashes," as he put it—he would feel a strange "vibration": one imagines him in the Bibliothèque Nationale, quivering like a diviner in a desert, standing over a hidden spring.[57]

As a trained historian of science, he wanted "to know," as he later put it, "why in a society like our own it had suddenly become so important to 'suppress' (as one stifles a cry, smothers a fire, or suffocates an animal) a scandalous monk or a fantastic and inconsequential usurer." As a student of Bataille and Blanchot, on the other hand, he had to concede that "the primary intensities that had motivated me remained on the outside," unable to enter fully into "the order of reasons."[58]

Still, however shadowy the causes for his own particular fascination, the kind of "infamous lives" that most impassioned Foucault were no mystery at all. He was transfixed by those punished with the most hideous torture, such as Damiens (whose agony had haunted the imagination of Baudelaire a century before). He was fascinated by the fate of modern-day convicts like H.M., their "crimes" petty, their lot in life appallingly unjust—men longing to escape, with no visible exit, apart from suicide and death.

Above all, perhaps, he was drawn to those truly "dangerous individuals," whose motives were unfathomable and whose deeds seemed unforgivable—men like Pierre Rivière, whose life he exhumed and analyzed with loving care, with the help of his students in a two-year long seminar at the Collège de France.

As Foucault himself explained in his 1972 *"résumé des cours"* for the Collège de France, Pierre Rivière was "a little-known murderer of the nineteenth century; at the age of twenty, he had slaughtered his mother, brother, and sister; after his arrest, he had prepared an explanatory memoir that was submitted to the judges, and to the doctors who had been asked to give a psychiatric evaluation."[59]

Foucault organized his seminar to help him reconstruct the larger cultural context of the murder and subsequent trial. The case was not without historiographic interest: Rivière had first come to trial in 1835, at a time when French experts were just beginning to debate the use of psychiatric concepts in criminal justice. Initially, Rivière had been condemned to death. But after the intervention of psychiatric experts, including the redoubtable Esquirol, one of the most storied names in early French psychiatry, his sentence was commuted to life in prison. Rivière's case thus offered a unique opportunity to study the changing criteria of criminal insanity.[60]

But as Foucault himself conceded, this was not the real reason he had spent two years studying the short life of Pierre Rivière: "It all began with our own stupefaction. . . . We were captivated by the parricide with reddish-brown eyes."[61]

What a character to be captivated by!

Pierre was a paragon of primitive sadism. According to the documents meticulously collated by Foucault and his team of researchers, the young boy from the small village of la Faucterie had taken delight in torturing small animals: crucifying birds, flaying frogs, inventing clever new instruments of his own design for heightening pain while inflicting death. And animals were not the only creatures he took pleasure in terrorizing: he was notorious for chasing after children with a scythe. He once tied his younger brother to a pothook and lit a fire beneath him.

Neighbors naturally thought his behavior bizarre, and tried to formulate reasons for it: "His aversion to women was constantly noted." He had frequently passed nights, it was said, at a local stone quarry where, some darkly speculated, he had dealings with the devil. [62]

Rivière, however, fancied himself a kind of philosopher; in his spare time, he read works of theology and speculative thought; in his own mind, he was an unusually enlightened character, unrestrained by the petty norms that bound others: "I knew the laws of man and the laws of the police," he later wrote in his memoir, "but I deemed myself wiser than they." [63]

As the regional prosecutor summed him up, Pierre was naturally gifted, with a taste for philosophy and an aptitude for learning—all spoiled by "an ardent, cruel, and violent imagination." [64]

On the morning of June 3, 1835, local officials discovered that "a dreadful murder had just been committed" at the Rivière home in la Faucterie. Three corpses were found. The head of Pierre's mother, who was pregnant, had been slashed and nearly severed; the skull of his brother had been scored, stabbed, and crushed; and the face of his dead sister had been carved up and mutilated as well. [65]

This was, to borrow a phrase from Foucault, a "great criminal event of the most violent and rarest sort." More than a routine murder, it was a crime "against nature, against those laws which are perceived to be inscribed directly on the human heart, and which link families and generations." At stake, in short, was precisely the sort of gratuitously cruel act Sade had only dreamed about—an act of such unfathomable hatred and aggressiveness that it amounted to a "total contestation" of the kind of modern society analyzed in *Discipline and Punish*. [66]

Shortly after slaughtering his mother, sister, and brother, Pierre fled from the house with a bloody pruning hook. "I have just delivered my father from all his troubles," he declared to one passerby: "I know that they will put me to death, but no matter." [67]

Then he disappeared.

For nearly a month, he lived in the woods on plants and roots. He was finally apprehended on July 2, 1835.

"He claims that he committed the crime by command of heaven," a newspaper reported shortly afterward: "that God the father appeared to him amid his angels; that he was ablaze with light"—all evidence, the report concluded, that the poor boy suffered from "religious mania or madness."[68]

In his memoir, Rivière laid the story out with cool logic and apparently unselfconscious candor. He hated his mother, he explained; she had tormented his father, driving him from home; he wished to rid the family of this terrible shrew and also "make some noise in the world"; for as the self-taught young philosopher explained, it "has always been the stronger in body who have laid down the law among themselves."[69]

"Now that I have made known my monstrosity," Rivière's memoir concludes, "I await the fate that is destined for me." He welcomed the pain and the torment and the coming of death—because his sins merited such punishment; and because death alone could "put an end to all my resentments."[70]

Composed though it apparently was "to summon death," Rivière's memoir had the opposite effect. Unlike Damiens a century before, Pierre Rivière would not be allowed the "momentary saturnalia" of death-by-torture.[71]

Instead, he became a "case" to be analyzed, classified, and confined. News of his butchery aroused the interest of psychiatrists. In their estimation, his memoir, lucid though it might seem, revealed that Pierre in fact was insane. As one judge summed up the evidence, the young man had succumbed to a "chain of false reasonings" that revealed "the greatest possible aberration of judgment." After consulting some of the nation's most eminent doctors, France's minister of justice agreed. Concluding that Pierre was mad, he commuted his death sentence to life in prison.[72]

Robbed of his rendezvous with death and confined instead to a cell, the murderer (as Foucault stresses in his brief commentary) believed himself "already dead." He refused to take care of his body; he said that he wanted to cut off his head; and in 1840, more than five years after slaughtering his family, the newspapers reported that Pierre Rivière had at last succeeded in killing himself, by hanging.[73]

In the dossier that Foucault and his seminar students prepared for publication, the documents were reprinted in chronological order, in another commentary "à la Borges." As Foucault explained, this allowed "the power of derangement proper to a discourse like that of Rivière" to speak for itself (just as H.M. had been allowed to speak for himself in the GIP broadside *Suicides in Prison*). At the same time, the republication, also without comment, of the coldly clinical reports of judges and doctors might display the "ensemble of tactics" nineteenth-century experts used "to reconstitute" the life of monstrous figures like Rivière, by labelling them either as "madmen" or as "criminals."[74]

In Foucault's view, the application of such categories was a way to "defuse the terror" of a life such as Rivière's—and so to rob it of its true "power." He thought that Rivière's acts merited neither therapy nor confinement. Rather—in his words—they warranted "a sort of reverence." "The most intense point of lives, that which concentrates their energy," he wrote, "is precisely where they clash with power, struggle with it, and attempt to use its forces or escape its traps." Through this struggle, and through "sacrificial and glorious murders," a man like Rivière became a "lightning-existence," illuminating the "ambiguity of the justifiable and the outlawed," revealing "the relation between power and the people, stripped down to essentials: the order to kill, the prohibition against killing; to make oneself kill, to be executed; voluntary sacrifice, ordained punishment; memory, oblivion."[75]

Rivière, in short, was a "tragic" hero—just like Sade, or Artaud. His murders, like his memoirs, were an admirable work of art. Foucault himself compared his dossier on Rivière with his book on Raymond Roussel. "In both works," he explained, "there was the same interrogation: what is the threshold at which a discourse (be it that of a sick person, or that of a criminal) starts to function in a field where it qualifies as literature?"[76]

Rivière's memoir, he declared in yet another interview, was "so strong and so strange that the crime ends up not existing anymore."[77]

The crime ends up not existing anymore?

It is as if the most murderous of acts, if properly commemorated in a work of art, could somehow be redeemed, transfigured in depth, thereby producing from the most heinous of lives, as Foucault had put it in *Madness and Civilization*, "a void, a moment of silence, a question without answer. . . a breach without reconciliation," where "the world is made aware of its guilt."[78]

In 1973, shortly after he published his book of documents about the Rivière case, Foucault sat down with the editors of the radical Belgian law review *Pro Justitia* to discuss the other book that he was still working on at the time, about the birth of the modern prison. This interview, in which Foucault specified the links between his research and his contemporary work with the Groupe d'Information sur les Prisons, offers a reminder that *Discipline and Punish* had been inspired not simply by Nietzsche and the "reverence" the author felt for "infamous men" like Pierre Rivière— but also by Foucault's personal involvement with a movement of outlawed revolutionaries. [79]

"In any regime," Foucault explained to the editors of *Pro Justitia*, "different social groups, different classes, different castes, each have their illegalities," which are "integral to the very exercise of power." In every epoch the range and character of these tacitly tolerated illegalities varied widely. Under the ancien régime, for example, peasants and artisans struggled to evade taxes; merchants routinely broke the rules governing commercial practices; and monstrous criminals like Pierre Rivière were customarily transformed in flysheets and popular songs into plebeian heroes who demonstrated "the beauty and greatness of crime," showing "how men have been able to rise against power, traverse the law, and expose themselves to death through death."[80]

Before 1789, a relatively wide range of illegalities went unpunished in France: the power of the sovereign, though absolute in theory, was limited in practice. What punishment did occur was spectacularly cruel—a visible reminder of what sovereign power meant in theory, and where it lay. When the French Revolution broke out, new forms of *popular* power were therefore able to blossom rapidly, without inhibition, through spectacularly cruel acts meted out as a kind of spontaneous counter-justice: for example, on July 14, 1789, when a mob stormed the Bastille, captured and then beheaded the prison's commanding officer—and so abruptly changed the course of history.

The Revolution, as Foucault put it, embodied "a new form of political illegality, of political struggle against the existing system." Benefitting from the new forms of "political struggle," the bourgeoisie at first permitted, and even encouraged the surge of popular violence. But as time went by, and the potential dangers of the unchecked revolutionary impulse became ever more clear, thanks to such bloody outbreaks as the September Massacres of 1792, the new leaders of the new French regime became eager "to muzzle" (as Foucault put it) the new political illegality, by introducing a new legal code, a new kind of penal system—and, eventually, the new form of political power that Foucault in 1973 was already calling "panopticism."[81]

From a revolutionary point of view, the effects of reform were therefore *prima facie* pernicious—a point that Foucault would drive home in *Discipline and Punish* by stressing the popular turmoil that could erupt during the ritual of death-by-torture. As he described the practice, *supplice* had always been an uncertain and volatile public ritual "in which violence was instantaneously reversible." "In these executions, which ought to have shown only the terrifying power of the prince, there was a whole aspect of carnival, in which the roles were inverted, the powerful mocked, and criminals transformed into heroes." Invigorated by the shared pleasure of witnessing spectacular acts of cruelty, the crowd under the ancien régime had its own latent power, as an "army of disorder," silently reinforced. It was this cruel power that had erupted on the great *journées* of the French Revolution, in a "sort of constantly recommenced liturgy" of "combat and sacrifice."[82]

With the coming of the modern prison system, by contrast, "the people was robbed of its old pride in its crimes." No longer was transgressing the law permitted to be a source of public pleasure. It became increasingly difficult for characters like Pierre Rivière to be cast as heroic outlaws, fitting adversaries of sovereign power; as the story of Rivière suggested, such men were increasingly regarded as "deviant," aberrations from the norms of a universal humanity, and therefore "cases" to be analyzed, rehabilitated, and, if possible, cured. Those deemed incurable, on the other hand, could be classified as hopeless "delinquents" who set a "negative example," as Foucault put it, to workers: "if you don't go to the factory, this is where you'll end up." As he explained to the editors of *Pro Justitia*, delinquents also made splendid informers, scabs, and strikebreakers; and if nothing else, hardened convicts could always be shipped overseas and exploited as a labor force, as they were in the nineteenth century in European colonies like Australia and Algeria.[83]

As Foucault summed up the political implications in 1973, "I think that the penal system, and above all the general system of surveillance erected at the end of the eighteenth century and the beginning of the nineteenth, in all of the countries of Europe, is the sanction of the new situation: that the old popular illegality, which had been in certain forms tolerated under the ancien régime, has become, literally, impossible."[84]

As so often, he was exaggerating.

Surveillance may have become "generalized" during the nineteenth century, but the possibilities for both personal and collective revolt had by no means been snuffed out, as he himself stressed at the close of his conversation with the editors of *Pro Justitia*. "Cracks" kept unpredictably opening up: in the soul, through the indomitable power of "an ardent, cruel, and violent imagination;" and in society, through such modern-day "liturgies" of "combat and sacrifice" as the Night of the Barricades. Even in the bowels of closely supervised modern prisons, the convicts themselves sometimes rose up in concert, as witness the riots at Attica and at Toul in 1971.

"It is interesting," as Foucault put it in his 1973 interview, "to see that it is indeed something like the same movement that currently leads to the revolt of patients in pyschiatric hospitals, students in lycées, prisoners in their penitentiaries. They are involved, in a sense, in the same revolt, since it is indeed directed against the same type of power," namely "panopticism." And, as Foucault added, "the problem therefore becomes politically very interesting and also very difficult. Starting from such different economic and social bases, how is one going to lead a struggle against one and the same type of power? That is the essential question."[85]

Ironically, by 1975, when *Discipline and Punish* itself was belatedly published, the global revolt that had provoked Foucault's "essential question" had already begun to fade from view.

The GIP itself had quietly dissolved in December 1972, many of its old functions assumed by a new organization, the Comité d'Action des Prisonniers, a group staffed entirely by prisoners and former convicts. In retrospect, Daniel Defert reckoned that the GIP's agitation in the early 1970s had played a role in sparking the more than two dozen prison revolts that occurred in France between 1971 and 1973. Foucault, for his part, vacillated in later years between dismissing the GIP as a total failure, and dwelling on the group's most tangible (and uncontroversial) accomplishments: forcing prison authorities to let inmates read newspapers; enabling convicts to speak in their own voices; and breaking the media's silence about the conditions inside French prisons.[86]

The French Maoist movement had begun to disintegrate in these months, too, torn apart by bickering over strategy, and mounting discord over the lynch-mob logic of the group's commitment to "popular justice." In May of 1972, three months after a Maoist commando unit had kidnapped a Renault official, the debate over violence in the movement flared up again, this time over events in the small mining town of Bruay-en-Artois. In April, a sixteen-year-old girl from a working-class family had been found brutally murdered in a vacant lot; shortly afterward, a local judge charged a prominent lawyer with the crime and imprisoned him without bail; the case was promptly appealed and taken to a higher court, which eventually dropped the charges. In the meantime, Maoist militants mobilized the populace of Bruay, demanding that the accused man be kept in jail, and brought to justice. The kind of "popular justice" demanded in the pages of *La Cause du peuple*, the Maoist newpaper, grew ever more sadistic: "He must be made to suffer by degrees." "Give him to us, we will carve him up with a razor bit by bit." "I'll tie him up and drag him behind my car at sixty miles an hour." The Maoist leader Pierre Victor (a.k.a. Benny Lévy) chimed in with a sweeping defense of vigilante violence. "To overthrow the authority of the bourgeois class," declared Victor, "the humiliated population has reason to institute a brief period of terror and to assault bodily a handful of contemptible, hateful individuals. It is difficult to attack the authority of a class without a few heads belonging to members of this class being paraded on the end of a stake."[87]

This sounded like Foucault's brand of "popular justice." Like a number of other intellectuals, Foucault travelled to the small mining town. Investigating the scene of the crime for himself, he concluded that the accused lawyer was guilty. More than one witness suggests that he was fascinated by Victor's rhetoric, and intrigued by the prospect of a plebeian revolt against the French system of justice.

But despite Foucault's ringing endorsement of the September Massacres as a model of justice just a few weeks before, he did not become directly involved in the agitation at Bruay. Instead, after his visit, he kept his distance. He also kept his own counsel, saying nothing about the Bruay affair in public—and saying different things to different people in private. Sometimes he was strongly critical, suggesting that the Maoist newspaper articles about Bruay had been dishonest and manipulative; while at still other times, he insisted that the agitation in Bruay was useful and justified.[88]

As the months went by, Foucault's apparent ambivalence only deepened—as did the debate over violence within the Maoist movement itself. Coming on the heels of the Renault kidnapping, the Bruay affair starkly revealed the escalating stakes of the struggle: "a libidinal Marxism, a joyous immoralism" (as Lévy later characterized it) had led the French ultra-left into a murderous game of political poker. The time had come to call the bet—or fold.[89]

One by one, prominent militants, wearied as well as alarmed by the continuing threat of violence, began to bail out. André Glucksmann still remembers the sobering impact of the Arab attack on the Munich Olympics during the summer of 1972, an attack that left eleven Israeli athletes dead. Like a number of other French Maoists, Glucksmann was Jewish; he had come to the brink of committing acts of terrorism by imagining that he was part of a new Resistance to a new French form of fascism; but as the implications of the Arab terrorist raid sank in, he began to sense a connection between his *own* fascination with political violence, and the willingness of Arabs to murder Jews. "The Munich affair was a great problem for us," he recalled years later. "So we took the problem of terrorism seriously, more seriously than [the ultra-left] in Germany or in Italy at that time."[90]

Michel Foucault, too, had been flirting since May '68 with the most savage kinds of political violence. But as the larger Maoist movement disintegrated in 1972 and 1973, he, like Glucksmann, pulled back, and quietly began to rethink his position.

Years later, Foucault would admit, at least in private, that he had been wrong to assume that the lawyer in Bruay had been guilty. As we shall see, he would eventually express open skepticism about the "very desirability of the revolution." And he would sometimes even ruefully concede that his great experiment in the politics of Dionysian revolt had perhaps ended in abject failure.[91]

"In the beginning of the seventies, I thought that it was possible to put in light, the real, the concrete, the actual problem," Foucault remarked in one public discussion, "and then that a political movement could come and take this problem and, from the data of the problem, elaborate something else. But I think I was wrong. . . . The political, spontaneous movement in which, with a great effort, I put my experience, my hopes—well, that didn't happen."[92]

What *did* happen is that Foucault, at the height of his political ardor, conceived his most powerful piece of writing yet. Indeed, by far the most important—and profoundly ambiguous—result of Foucault's political experimentation after May '68 was surely *Discipline and Punish* itself: a byproduct of his personal commitment to a revolutionary movement, refined, polished, and completed only after that movement had collapsed.

His first major book in almost a decade, it was published in February 1975—and rapidly translated into a host of different languages: Italian, Spanish, and German in 1976; English and Danish in 1977; more than a dozen different languages in all.[93]

In France, the book was an event. *Le Monde* devoted two pages to a review and commentary. The venerable journal *Critique* ran no less than three separate essays about the book. And the monthly *Magazine Littéraire* put Foucault on its cover, and published an elaborate twenty-eight-page "dossier" that included a review, essays, an interview, an annotated bibliography, even a brief answer to a question inevitable by 1975, "What was the GIP?"[94]

For a large number of readers, in France and elsewhere, no matter how ignorant they might be of the particulars surrounding the rise and fall of Foucault's activism since May '68, the sheer *fact* of that activism was enough to transform their perceptions of the author and his new book. From the start, *Discipline and Punish* was treated as a seminal work of radical social criticism. In countries like the United States, it was avidly consumed by politically committed readers only faintly aware of *The Order of Things*, let alone *Madness and Civilization*. Many of these new readers had already begun, like Foucault and his Maoist comrades, to reassess, critically, the nature and goals of the social movements of the sixties. Coming on the heels of the sectarian ultra-Marxism that had engulfed a great many of these movements around the world, Foucault's approach seemed strikingly fresh and original. It also seemed to fit well with one of the central ambitions of this generation of leftists: to elaborate a critique of modern culture and society that avoided both the crude materialism of orthodox Marxism and the conservative empiricism of most mainstream social science.

From this perspective, perhaps the most important passages in *Discipline and Punish* were the most abstract: namely, the few paragraphs in the first chapter in which Foucault laconically spelled out some of the implications of his concept of "power." If—as he now asserted—power was "exercised rather than possessed"; if in practice it was diffuse, rather than concentrated in the hands of a small ruling class; if it could be understood only through "the correlative constitution of a field of knowledge"; if the effects of such knowledge might be discerned in the aptitudes and inclinations of every single individual; then a number of the old Marxist formulas no longer made sense. To change the world required changing our selves, our bodies, our souls, and all of our old ways of "knowing," in addition to changing the economy and society. To "seize" and exercise a dictatorial kind of power might thus simply reproduce the old patterns of subjectification under a new name—as had obviously happened in actually existing socialist societies, where homosexuals and drug addicts, for example, were often as harshly treated as ever.[95]

"It is as if, finally, something new were emerging in the wake of Marx," Gilles Deleuze remarked in his review of *Discipline and Punish*, voicing sentiments widely shared in the 1970s by readers still committed, on paper at least, to the revolutionary experiment begun in May '68. "Foucault is not content to say that we must rethink certain notions; he does not even say it, he does it, and thus suggests new coordinates for practice."[96]

What electrified Deleuze and countless avant-garde academics around the world left a good many other readers frankly baffled. The reviewer for *L'Express* felt the book's argument was exaggerated. Others, including a number of professionals active in prison-reform movements, were confused by what they took to be the book's lack of practical application. "Often," as Foucault recalled in a 1978 interview, "people, even those who loved the book, have said: this book completely paralyzes us." The effect, Foucault claimed on more than one occasion, was intentional: "It's true that certain people, such as those who work in the institutional setting of the prison . . . are not likely to find advice or instructions in my books to tell them 'what is to be done.' But my project is precisely to bring it about that they 'no longer know what to do,' so that the acts, gestures, discourses that up until then had seemed to go without saying become problematic, difficult, dangerous."[97]

If such readers were immobilized by doubt, so much the better. As Daniel Defert recalls, the popular reaction to *Discipline and Punish* on the whole left Foucault almost entirely satisfied—a far cry from the unhappiness he felt after *The Order of Things* became a bestseller.[98]

There was one exception. Perhaps predictably, a great many professional historians reacted coolly to *Discipline and Punish*. Somewhat less predictably, Foucault was still wounded by their criticism, in one instance pleading, almost plaintively, for "the probity" of his own "scientific work."[99]

No accumulation of footnotes and documentation, however, could quite hide the fact that *Discipline and Punish* was a most unusual piece of modern historiography. Unlike *Madness and Civilization*, it made few concessions to the new social history, and for the most part ignored the broader context of "the birth of the prison." Despite the apparent erudition of the work, it was based on a relatively small number of archival sources. As always, Foucault hazarded the kind of bold generalizations that make most professional historians deeply nervous. The book contained nothing like a traditional narrative, and offered little in the way of conventional explanations. And to top it all off, there was the disturbing character of Foucault's critical perspective—hard to pin down, easy to feel.

As the Princeton historian Lawrence Stone acutely noted, a strange kind of argument ran through *all* of his books. Whether the subject was prisons, hospitals, or asylums, remarked Stone, "we find a denial of the Enlightenment as an advance in human understanding and sensibility, and a causal linkage of it to the sexual fantasies of domination, violation, and torture which obsessed the mind of Sade." The "central issue," Stone concluded, was moral and political: it was Foucault's "recurrent emphasis on control, domination, and punishment as the only mediating qualities possible in personal and social relationships."[100]

In May '68, the "central issue" had in fact been reduced to a slogan: *SOYON CRUELS!*—"BE CRUEL!" Perhaps the militant who sprayed this graffiti on the walls of the Sorbonne had read Foucault, though probably not: sentiments like this were in the air. Still, the slogan, in its terse economy, perfectly sums up the Nietzschean convictions at the heart of *Discipline and Punish*—and also at the root, one suspects, of a great many people's reservations about the value of Foucault's oeuvre.[101]

Indeed, a strong dose of skepticism, even a sense of humor, often seems in order when trying to assess this oeuvre. Reading Foucault at his most insouciantly provocative, expressing "reverence" for a character like Pierre Rivière, one is reminded of Georges Bataille's exuberant early essay on "The Use Value of D.A.F. de Sade." After slashing away at André Breton and the surrealists for expressing their admiration for the Marquis de Sade without showing the slightest inclination to put sadism into practice, Bataille solemnly declares that "it is time to choose between the conduct of cowards afraid of their own joyful excesses," and brave, truly serious sadists, presumably like Bataille himself, who calls for the creation, after a "fiery and bloody Revolution," of "organizations that have ecstasy and frenzy as their goal (the spectacular deaths of animals, partial tortures, orgiastic dances, etc.)."[102]

This is silly. And twenty-five years later, in the great magnum opus of his maturity, *Erotism: Death and Sensuality*, Bataille admitted as much. "Such a strange doctrine" as Sade's, Bataille wrote in 1955, "could obviously not be generally accepted, nor even generally propounded, unless it were glossed over, deprived of significance, and reduced to a trivial piece of pyrotechnics. Obviously, if it were taken seriously, no society could accept it for a single instant."[103]

So what *could* a society accept? What can the injunction to BE CRUEL! mean?

Here are some of the possibilities suggested by Foucault:

—BE CRUEL in your quest for the truth, ruthless in your honesty, savage in your irreverence. This we may call the cruelty proper to the Nietzschean philosopher, a cruelty certainly practiced by Foucault, one of whose great and not-so-secret crimes was to butcher gleefully the concept of "man," as this had been understood by modern humanists from Kant to Sartre.

—BE CRUEL in your resoluteness, welcome the harsh renunciations and sometimes brutal costs of relentlessly pursuing any vaulting ideal, be it truth, godliness, or revolutionary purity. This we may call the cruelty proper to the ascetic, an eagerness to suffer the pains entailed by unswerving commitment to any burning faith or transcendent ambition, a cruelty willingly accepted by both Foucault and Nietzsche.

—BE CRUEL in the works of imagination that you create: spare nothing in painting the demons in the desert who tempt Saint Anthony: a horseman with a head made of thistle, a mermaid riding on a rat, a tonsured devil with a pig's snout; etch two beatifically radiant whores holding captive a dignified libertine with the body of a chicken, and jabbing the quill of a plucked feather up his ass; give us the death of Damiens in unbearable detail, make us queasy, tell us exactly how red-hot pincers singed his flesh, how his thighs were carved up and pulled apart. This we may call the cruelty proper to the artist, a cruelty to be found in both Nietzsche and Foucault, and also in the canvases of Bosch, the *Caprichos* and *Disparates* of Goya, the theater of Artaud, the pornography of Bataille.[104]

—BE CRUEL in your erotic play: snap on handcuffs, neck-collars, and chains, lock pins and clips on nipples, administer meticulous floggings; or, be a slave for a night and, with your master's help, mimic the ancient "art of unbearable sensations," tremble with "the most exquisite agonies," savor the disintegration and humiliation of the self in the *jouissance* of exploded limits. This we may call the cruelty proper to Sade and Sacher-Masoch, a kind of make-believe cruelty never directly mentioned in Nietzsche but one soon to be endorsed explicitly by Foucault, who in the years to come would publicly praise sado-masochistic sexual practices for "inventing new possibilities of pleasure" through the "eroticization of power."[105]

—BE CRUEL in the license you give to individual acts and political practices that issue in suffering and death: sing the praise of murderers, unrestrained sovereigns, and bloody movements of popular revolt. This is akin to the cruelty embraced by Sade's heroes, Machiavelli's prince, and the French ultra-left's would-be guerrilla warriors. It is a form of real cruelty explicitly entertained by both Nietzsche and Foucault who certainly did not rule it out—on the contrary, both men in different contexts enthusiastically commended it. [106]

To sum up crudely the gist of these different possibilities, Foucault, like Nietzsche, seems to be saying: better externalized than internalized cruelty; it is healthier, more "active," rather than weak and "reactive." Better internalized cruelty than no cruelty at all: both the ruthless resoluteness of the ascetic and the brutal fantasies of the artist and solitary onanist at least bear witness to the continuing chaos of instinctive violence—the kind of chaos needed to give birth to "a dancing star." [107]

But as the disintegration of the Maoist movement had demonstrated, there was a danger here—the danger of disappearing into a "black hole," as Deleuze had put it. What if the human being, allowing its normally tabooed cruel impulses free play, were to slip insensibly from philosophical to ascetic to aesthetic to erotic to political acts of cruelty, finally embracing murder and death?

The links—and differences—between the different forms of cruelty are by no means clear. Perhaps externalizing cruelty, if only in art and erotic play, offers a useful outlet for aggressive impulses, giving shape to energies that might otherwise break society apart. Or perhaps expressing aggressive impulses, even if only in art and erotic play, merely stimulates the appetite for them, increasing the likelihood that murderous energies will in fact succeed in breaking society apart. As the interminability of current debates over the censorship of pornography and representations of violence may suggest, we still know very little about the complex differences and similarities between the various possible forms of cruelty.

There was nevertheless a certain logic to the move from philosophical to political cruelty. It was the kind of logic that had apparently led Foucault, in his 1972 debate with the Maoist leader Pierre Victor, to endorse the most sanguinary acts of "popular justice."

And it was an ominously similar kind of logic that had led a number of fascist and Nazi philosophers, many also intoxicated by fantasies of Dionysian revolt, to condone savage displays of violence, in some cases calling for "total war," in other cases welcoming a cataclysmic "disaster" that, no matter how "tragic," might nevertheless offer a rare opportunity to will "the unprecedented," hurling the human being through a "breach" in which "suddenly the unbound powers of being come forth and are accomplished as history"—thus Martin Heidegger in 1935.[108]

In 1939, a "breach" in fact had opened. "Unbound powers" came forth. The "unprecedented" happened. On a scale that still beggars belief, the injunction to BE CRUEL was "accomplished as history." And in the Nazi death camps, the world rediscovered what acts of depravity—what monstrous "crimes against nature"—the human animal was still all too capable of.

These complex and highly ambiguous connections—between the Nietzschean wager, a kind of Faustian pact with the death-instinct and the hecatombs of the fascist adventure—were not lost on Foucault, or on his *compagnons de voyage*. Worried by the growing fascination of the French Maoists with terrorism in the mid-1970s, Gilles Deleuze had begun to warn against the dangers of a "micro-fascism" on the ultra-left. In these same years, André Glucksmann, much more emphatically, began to write about the links that he now saw between the guerrilla violence of the French Maoists and the state terrorism that had enabled Stalin as well as Hitler to slaughter millions without remorse in the 1930s. Foucault too, fell silent about the festive violence of "popular justice"—and, after 1975, began to address "the fascism in us all."[109]

The drift of the ultra-left toward terrorism, like the drift of a Nietzschean politics toward an affirmation of power "without statute and limit, without structure and order," made urgent, paradoxically, precisely a reaffirmation, somehow, of statute and limit, structure and order. "Power without limitation," as Foucault remarked in 1983, "is directly related to madness." (For the author of *Madness and Civilization*, of course, this statement cuts two ways.)[110]

But how could an affirmation of limits be made effective? What kind of structure—and what kind of order—could be affirmed? For a Nietzschean, such questions admitted of no easy answer. As Nietzsche himself had insisted, a thin line separated the "superhuman" from the "inhuman," above all in those commanding souls strong enough to practice a "great" politics. "One does not reckon with such natures," Nietzsche warned. "They come like fate, without reason, consideration, or pretext; they appear as lightning appears, too terrible, too sudden, too convincing, too 'different' even to be hated. Their work is an instinctive creation and imposition of forms; they are the most involuntary, unconscious artists there are."[111]

Yet once one had surrendered to the unconscious in practice, no one could know where the injunction to BE CRUEL might actually lead. No one could predict what "unthinkable" acts a modern soul, boiling with bestial phantasms, might commit. "Doubtless there are astonishing oscillations of the unconscious, from one pole of delirium to the other," wrote Deleuze and Guattari in 1972, describing "the ways in which an unexpected revolutionary force breaks free"—and "inversely, the way in which everything turns fascist or envelops itself in fascism." Swept up in the vortex of a political "limit-experience," it was all but impossible to sort out what was genuinely creative (hence, in Deleuze's terms, truly "revolutionary") and what was merely a blind reiteration of the most viciously destructive impulses (and thus, in Deleuze's view, a deadly reinforcement of the most rigid power relations, hence potentially "fascist"). [112]

For anyone committed to exploring the "unbound powers" of the human being, the effort to identify and uproot the "fascism in us all" had therefore to be ruthless and unrelenting:

"How," wondered Foucault, "does one keep from being fascist, even (especially) when one believes oneself to be a revolutionary militant? How do we rid our speech and our acts, our hearts and our pleasures of fascism? How do we ferret out the fascism that is ingrained in our behavior?"[113]

How indeed?

"I do not say things because I think them," Foucault explained to an understandably mystified interlocutor in 1971, summing up the anguish and doubt lurking behind the Dionysian abandon of his work in these years:

"I say them rather with the aim of self-destruction, so that I will not have to think [them] anymore, so that I can be certain that from now on, they will live a life outside me, or die the death in which I will not have to recognize myself."[114]

On the very day that Foucault completed the last draft of *Discipline and Punish* he began writing his next book, the first volume of his History of Sexuality.

Daniel Defert remembers being startled. They were two "very different books," he recalls, "and on the same day he finishes one, he starts the other, that was very surprising."[115]

The books are not as different as they seem. As Foucault himself had stressed, *Discipline and Punish* was an effort to "produce a genealogy of modern morals through a political history of bodies." In its pages, he had argued that "the human body was entering a machinery of power that digs into it, breaks it down and rearranges it"—transforming, inevitably, the experience of sexuality as well. [116]

As Defert recalls, Foucault started his new book by writing about what he called, enigmatically, the "Right of Death and Power over Life." These dense and difficult pages would eventually appear in 1976 as the last chapter of the first volume of the History of Sexuality. Foucault himself considered them to be "the fundamental part of the book," perhaps because they marked his first effort to grapple with the romance of violence—and the "fascism" within. [117]

In these pages, in swift and often dizzyingly elliptical strokes, he tried to illuminate one of the most striking paradoxes of modern European history—namely, the coincidence of a general softening of social life with an eruption of ever more lethal forms of mass violence.

"Those who died on the scaffold became fewer and fewer," he writes, alluding to the book he had just completed, "in contrast to those who died in wars." [118]

Why this discrepancy? Foucault offers no direct answer, but rather a surprising series of loosely linked and highly speculative hypotheses, climaxed by a puzzling call for a radically new kind of approach to the body.

He begins by evoking, again, the shift from a sovereign monarch "who evidenced his power over life only through the death he was capable of requiring," to a liberal society "bent on generating forces, making them grow, and ordering them," thus evincing its power, no longer through the menace of death, but rather through the management of life. [119]

As the modern state refined its control over the behavior of individuals, it also extended its reach over the entire population, through new mechanisms designed to regulate the conditions of life: Foucault mentions the enforcement of national standards of public hygiene, medical assistance, workplace safety, and support for the elderly.

As never before, the grip of death on human affairs began to loosen. The dangers of epidemic and famine receded. A society still prey to random violence gradually gave way to one uniformly policed by a centralized state that claimed a monopoly on the legitimate use of force. Death-by-torture vanished as well, and with it one of the chief public rituals that had integrated death into everyday life and made it "acceptable," giving some "meaning to its permanent aggression." In the normal organization of modern society, the phenomenon of death was "carefully evaded," deliberately bundled off the stage of history—as if death were something shameful and threatening. [120]

And in one way, death *was* something threatening: "In the passage from this world to the other," remarks Foucault, "death was the manner in which a terrestrial sovereignty was relieved by another, singularly more powerful sovereignty." The mounting power of the modern state was circumscribed by a higher necessity: "Death is power's limit, the moment that escapes it." An end "beyond all endings, a limit beyond all limits" (as Heidegger once put it), it offered an uncanny reminder that to be human was, ultimately, to be exiled from all worldly structure and order in the "issuelessness of death." [121]

Thus one facet of the continuing and paradoxical allure of death in modern society: "the most secret aspect of existence," it was also the most indomitable. When every other means of protest failed, suicide always remained: and "this determination to die, strange and yet so persistent and constant in its manifestations . . . was one of the first astonishments of a society in which political power had assigned itself the task of administering life." [122]

Suicide, however, was only the most morbid symptom of "a very real process of struggle" that had erupted within modern society from its inception. Taking at face value the new political emphasis on life as a supreme good, groups organized to demand the satisfaction of basic needs. They fought for decent work, better wages, and an end to all oppression, in the process elaborating a new and unprecedented kind of "right"—"to rediscover what one is and all that one can be." [123]

It was in this context, Foucault remarks, that sex emerged as a political issue: "Through the themes of health, progeny, race, the future of the species, the vitality of the social body, power spoke *of* sexuality and *to* sexuality." While families tried to enforce taboos against incest and masturbation, eugenicists dreamed of administering the sex life of society as a whole, through an exacting regulation of marriages, of fertility, of the health and safety of children. [124]

But from the outset, the status of sex was as essentially contested as the meaning of death. In the analyses of Sade and those who would follow in his footsteps (including, of course, Foucault), "sex is without any norm or intrinsic rule that might be formulated from its own nature." At the same time, by glorifying torture, cruelty, and death, the work of Sade and his followers suggested that the effort to evade death and regulate sex had created, through a kind of reflux motion, a strange and disturbing new alliance between eros and thanatos. "The Faustian pact, whose temptation has been instilled in us by the deployment of sexuality, is now as follows: to exchange life in its entirety for sex itself, for the truth and the sovereignty of sex. Sex is worth dying for. It is in this (strictly historical) sense that sex is indeed imbued with the death instinct."[125]

This part of Foucault's thesis, though it recurs in every one of his major works, has rarely been noticed, much less taken seriously. Perhaps, apart from its obvious autobiographical resonance, it seems too farfetched: that is certainly how Lawrence Stone seems to have regarded it. Yet interestingly enough, a similar thesis appears in *Man Before Death*, the magisterial study of death in Western civilization, published in 1977 by the great French historian Philippe Ariès. The "omnipotence of nature asserts itself in two areas: sex and death," comments Ariès, writing of developments in the nineteenth century. "The order of reason, work, and discipline gave way before the assault of love and death, agony and orgasm, corruption and fertility. The first breaches were made in the realm of the imaginary, which in turn opened the passage to the real. Through these two gates, in the nineteenth century, the savagery of nature invaded the city of man just as the latter was preparing to colonize nature by expanding the frontiers of technological advancement and rational organization. It is almost as if society, in its effort to conquer nature and the environment, abandoned the old defense system that had surrounded sex and death, and nature, which had apparently been conquered, surged back *inside* man, crept in through the abandoned fortifications and made him savage again."[126]

This renascent savagery was perhaps one of the reasons, Foucault implies, for the otherwise puzzling virulence of the wars waged by modern states. Once, he observes, armed conflicts had been relatively limited in aim, fought on behalf of a sovereign whose commands required execution. No longer. Now, as he puts it, "wars are waged on behalf of the existence of all; entire populations are trained to kill each other. Massacres have become vital"—and never more lethally so than in Nazi Germany.[127]

And so we come to the only passage in all of his major works where Foucault addresses, however briefly, the "problems" posed by the Nazi experience.

On one level, he argues, Hitler's regime merely refined and perfected nineteenth-century techniques of social discipline. But on yet another level, Hitler's regime was a deliberate throwback to an archaic "society of blood," one centered on a revived public cult of death. "An absolutely suicidal state," Germany after 1932 became an "absolutely murderous state," in which the sovereignty of the national will was demonstrated through a free embrace of death. Unleashing an "oneiric exaltation" of savagery,

Nazism issued in "the systematic genocide of others, and the risk to oneself of a total sacrifice."[128]

It is in this charged context that Foucault—also for the only time in all of his major works—ventures a criticism of the Marquis de Sade.

Sade too, after all, expressed an "oneiric exaltation" of savagery. Celebrating the convergence of eros and thanatos in his endless fantasies of unrestricted slaughter, he asserted the "unlimited right of an all-powerful monstrosity."[129]

This fantasy, of "an all-powerful monstrosity," had once seemed to Foucault to offer a usefully "total contestation" of Western culture.

No more. For Foucault's remarks about Sade here struck a sharply different note—of sobriety and caution. The libertine's nostalgia for a "society of blood," he warned, was "in the last analysis a 'retro-version.' "[130]

Foucault still wishes to counter the sway of modern society over the body; he is committed to the struggle "to rediscover what one is and all that one can be."

But he now suggests that the "rallying point" in this struggle can no longer be an unqualified glorification of "transgression."[131]

"We must not think that by saying yes to sex, one says no to power." For modern society has, as it were, reinvented the body, putting sex and death into an uncanny and potentially catastrophic new alliance, expressed in a historically unique constellation of murderous and insane fantasies.[132]

What, then, is to be done?

In this situation, the intellectual, as Foucault put it, was no longer "the rhapsodist of the eternal, but the strategist of life and death."[133]

The objective remained to rout the hostile forces pinning down the powers of the individual, somehow redeploying these powers without surrendering to the archaic phantasms that had infiltrated our speech and our acts, our hearts and our deepest, most unconscious desires, functioning as the most sinister kind of fifth column.

Struggling to defeat "the fascism in us all"—the lust for domination, the yearning for a rebirth of "a violent, dictatorial and even bloody power"—the human being must, in effect, open up a new front, create a new point of attack, beyond transgression, beyond the lust for death, beyond, somehow, "sex-desire" itself.[134]

And where might the forces for such a counter-attack be found?

In what Foucault enigmatically calls "bodies and pleasures"—the occult focus of the next stage of his "great Nietzschean quest."[135]

8

THE WILL

TO KNOW

NIGHT HAD FALLEN on Death Valley. Next to a car parked in the lot at Zabriskie Point, a portable tape recorder was playing a piece of electronic music, Karlheinz Stockhausen's *Kontakte*. Near the recorder sat Michel Foucault, alongside two young Americans, Simeon Wade, a professor of history, and his lover Michael, a pianist and aspiring composer. As synthetic blips and bleeps filled the cool desert air, the three men stared silently into space. Two hours before, all three had taken LSD.[1]

Foucault was about to enjoy what he would later call the greatest experience in his life—an epiphany that climaxed a series of similarly intense "limit-experiences" in the gay community of San Francisco. As a result of these experiences, Foucault's thought would take a dramatic new turn, transforming, in paradoxical and surprising ways, his continuing effort to illuminate what Nietzsche had called "the riddle which man must solve"—the riddle of his own singular being.

Foucault had long rejected the traditional ways of approaching this riddle. To discover "what one is," a human being had to "open himself up to the multiplicities that traverse him from head to toe," undergoing "the most severe exercise in depersonalization," as Gilles Deleuze once put it. It was in this spirit of rigorous self-effacement and deliberate self-destruction that Foucault for years had been trying to resolve Nietzsche's strange question: "How did I become what I am and why do I suffer from being what I am?" The most visible fruit of his efforts was, of course, his ongoing historical inquiry into the different "games of truth" through which a human being was brought to think of itself as mad, as sick, as a criminal case. But as Foucault had remarked in his 1969 essay, "What is an Author?," these texts did not stand alone; for "writing is now linked to sacrifice, to the sacrifice even of life: it is a voluntary obliteration of the self that does not need to be represented in books because it is accomplished in the very existence of the writer."[2]

And so it was that Michel Foucault, "militant and professor at the Collège de France," found himself, improbably enough, perched on the edge of a cliff in the middle of a desert in the spring of 1975, stoned on LSD.[3]

Once more, in quest of himself he was obliterating himself—disorganizing his mind, surrendering his body, opening himself to the otherwise unthinkable, trying to unriddle the singular constellation of impulses and fantasies that had produced (at least according to his Nietzschean theory of "knowledge") the works of fictive genealogy that the institutions of higher culture had already consecrated as evidence of a rare and sublime sort of genius.

Like a number of other pivotal events in his life, Foucault's Death Valley trip happened largely by chance.

It had all begun with a letter from Simeon Wade, an assistant professor at the Claremont Graduate School, a small institution affiliated with a cluster of prestigious colleges located in Claremont, California, just outside of Los Angeles. Wade had written to Foucault in the fall of 1974, soon after learning that the philosopher, like a growing number of Parisian gurus, was coming to America. Foucault had agreed to spend the spring of 1975 teaching at the University of California at Berkeley, under the auspices of the French department.

Foucault was not widely known in the United States. He had only spent time in the country twice before, in 1970 and in 1972, both times as a professor in the French department at the State University of New York at Buffalo. But he had already become a cult figure among some American academics.

The Order of Things had swept Wade away. Convinced that Foucault was nothing less than the greatest thinker of the twentieth century, Wade devoted himself to mastering his work, tracking down every arcane allusion and reference. A Harvard-trained historian politicized by the rebellions of the sixties, he had previously schooled himself in Marxist-Hegelian approaches to history while exploring various alternatives to mainstream historiography. He was also, perhaps more pertinently, an unabashed hedonist, ardently committed to gay liberation.

In his first letter to Foucault, Wade politely invited the philosopher to give a public lecture in Claremont. Foucault demurred, pleading ignorance of his American schedule; but he invited Wade to write him again, after he had arrived in Berkeley.

Wade did. In his second letter, he proposed a detailed schedule of seminars, lectures, and parties. He also audaciously proposed an excursion to Death Valley, suggesting that this was a special place where Foucault might feel "suspended among the forms hoping for nothing but the wind"—Wade here was quoting a line from Artaud's *A Voyage to the Land of the Tarahumara,* an account of the playwright's Mexican peyote experiments in 1936.

Although Wade did not say so explicitly in his letter, a similar experiment in Death Valley was just what he had in mind. After all, he reasoned, "had not Artaud received his tongue of fire after taking peyote trips with the Tarahumara Indians in the Grand Canyon of Mexico? And couldn't we expect more, much more from Michel Foucault?"[4]

The great man did not respond. Wade was crestfallen. Still, he persevered.

Several weeks later, Foucault flew south to deliver a public address at the University of California at Irvine, a short drive from Claremont. Wade, along with his lover Michael, went to Irvine to see the philosopher in person—and to try giving him one last pitch. After the lecture, Wade and his companion fought through the throng of well-wishers who had engulfed Foucault; they introduced themselves, and Wade extended yet another invitation to visit Claremont.

Foucault begged off. " 'I fear I have been rude,' " Wade recalls him saying, " 'but I have so many engagements while I am in California that I do not think I will have time to visit Claremont on this trip.' "

Wade and his friend would not give up. They suggested a one-day visit.

Foucault, perhaps remembering Wade's second letter, fell silent. He sized up the unyielding disciples in front of him. Their gaze was piercing. He could not mistake their seriousness. Foucault finally flashed his ivory smile: " 'But how can I see the Valley of Death if I only spend one day with you?' "

The philosopher told Wade to call him at his office in Berkeley.

When Wade phoned the following week, Foucault's response was firm. " 'I have decided to visit you in Claremont,' " Wade recalls him saying. " 'I hope we will have time to visit the Valley of Death.' "[5]

Several weeks later, on a Sunday morning at the end of May 1975, Foucault found himself in a car with Wade and Michael, headed for Death

Valley. The night before, Foucault had eaten dinner with his American hosts, listened to some music, and smoked some marijuana. So far, nobody had said anything about LSD.

" 'We have prepared something special for you to take in the desert,' " Wade remarked as they drove out of Los Angeles.

" 'What's that?' " Wade recalls Foucault responding.

" 'We brought along some acid,' " the young professor explained. " 'We thought you might enjoy a visionary quest in Death Valley.' "

" 'I would like that,' " said Foucault without hesitation. " 'I can hardly wait to get started.' "[6]

His eagerness is not surprising. As Wade well knew, Foucault had long been fascinated with the power of drugs to give rise to "thought as intensive irregularity—disintegration of the self." In a 1967 interview, he had defended the value of certain drugs as a means to breach cultural limits, allowing a person to enter into "a state of 'nonreason' in which the experience of madness is outside the distinction between the normal and the pathological." Since drugs generally dissolved fixed categories of thought, they "have nothing at all to do with the true and the false," Foucault wrote in 1970. "But perhaps, if thought has to look mute animality in the face, the drug that mobilizes it, that colors, agitates, furrows, and dissipates it, that populates it with differences and substitutes for the rare flash a continuous phosphorescence, perhaps this drug occasions a quasi-thought. Perhaps."[7]

In a 1970 essay (on the work of Gilles Deleuze, who wondered out loud, in a published footnote to this passage, "What will they think of us?"), Foucault evoked the specific effects of opium (which "ensures a weightless immobility, the stupor of a butterfly")—and also of LSD: "It no sooner sets aside the suzerainty of categories than it uproots the basis for its indifference and nullifies the gloomy grimace of mute animality, and it presents this univocal and acategorical mass not only as variegated, mobile, asymmetrical, decentered, spiraloid, and reverberating, but causes it to rise, at each instant, as a swarming of phantasm-events."[8]

This mischievous passage is deliriously contrived—and slightly misleading. For until his trip to Death Valley—and despite his lifelong experimentation with a variety of other drugs, from hashish to opium—Foucault had never actually tried LSD.

" 'I have had the opportunity, but have never taken it,' " Wade recalls Foucault saying during their car ride to Death Valley. It was hard to find pure drugs in Paris, he later explained to Wade—but the crux of his hesitation, he said, was personal. Whenever he had been offered LSD in

Paris, Daniel Defert had refused for the two of them. " 'Perhaps he resists hallucinogens because he has a certain relationship to his body,' " Wade recalls Foucault musing. " 'After all, we are our bodies' "—and, added the philosopher, after a pause—" 'something else' " besides.[9]

That was a problem. For how might LSD affect this elusive "something else"? French philosophers often talked in the most daring of terms about experimentation and cultural revolt—but like intellectuals everywhere, most of them preferred to keep a tight rein on their minds. Sartre once took some mescaline under the supervision of the psychiatrist Jean Lagache in the Hôpital Sainte-Anne, but the experience of losing control was disagreeable, and he swore never to touch the stuff again.[10]

Artaud, of course, had gone all the way—but he had also spent much of the following decade in an insane asylum.

Foucault (and Daniel Defert, too) thus had every reason to weigh carefully the possible consequences of taking any drug as powerful as LSD.

And so did Simeon Wade. "I knew we were taking a risk," Wade later recalled. "Ingesting the philosopher's stone might blow the fuses of the master thinker of our era." Or—perhaps even more disappointing!—"it might have no effect at all."

His wager, as Wade recalls, was simple: by taking Foucault to Death Valley for an LSD trip, he might produce "an intellectual power approaching the wonders of science fiction, something on the order of Dr. Morbius in [the 1956 film] *Forbidden Planet,* or the Galaxy Being from the first episode of [the 1963 television series] *The Outer Limits.*"[11]

What really happened in Death Valley would fall short of such bizarre fantasies. But it was remarkable enough.

After spending most of the day traversing the arid, empty expanse of the Mojave Desert, the three men arrived at Furnace Creek Ranch, a resort situated in an oasis just outside of Death Valley. They checked into their room, and Foucault took a brief nap.

Refreshed, they drove into Death Valley itself. Parking at an observation point, they surveyed the desert floor, its rainbow hues blazing at sunset. After a short walk along an empty path, Michael stopped to begin the ceremony of ingestion.

He produced three tablets of LSD.

Looking worried, Foucault abruptly walked away.

When he returned, Foucault announced that he wished to take only a half dose, since this would be his first experience with a drug so powerful.

Wade took the philosopher by the hand. They went for a walk. The young professor patiently explained why, to enjoy the magical effects of the chemical elixir, it was necessary to take a full dose.

Foucault thought it over. When they returned, he asked Michael how he should ingest the drug.

He then swallowed the tablet offered to him.[12]

Two hours later, listening to Stockhausen and staring into space from his perch on Zabriskie Point, Foucault smiled, and as Wade later recalled, gestured toward the stars: " 'The sky has exploded,' " he said, " 'and the stars are raining down upon me. I know this is not true, but it is the Truth.' "

Foucault fell silent.

Wade, doubtless relieved that the master thinker's mind had not yet melted like one of Salvador Dali's clocks, babbled on about the use of psychedelic potions among the ancient Sumerians. Finally, he, too, fell silent again.

The three men gazed at the black void overhead, the electronic music cascading in the background.

" 'At last I understand the meaning of Malcolm Lowry's *Under the Volcano,*' " said Foucault.

Lowry was one of his favorite novelists, and *Under the Volcano,* with its lyrical evocation of the alcoholic trances of the main character, the Consul, had long served the philosopher as a window into the otherwise inaccessible world of Jean Barraqué, who had died two years before, in 1973, of complications arising from alcoholism.

" 'The Consul's mescal,' " said Foucault, " 'served as a drug which filtered his perception in a manner similar to a hallucinogen.' "[13]

For Lowry's character, for Barraqué—and for Foucault as well—drugs were a tool of thought. "Night, and once again, the nightly grapple with death," Lowry had written, describing the Consul's stream of consciousness under the influence of the Mexican liquor. "I think I know a great deal about physical suffering, but this is worst of all, to feel your soul dying. I wonder if it is because tonight my soul has really died that I feel at the moment something like peace. Or is it because right through hell there is a path, as Blake well knew, and though I may not take it, sometimes lately in dreams I have been able to see it? . . . I seem to see now, between mescals, this path, and beyond it strange vistas, like visions of a new life. . . ."[14]

The LSD continued to grow in potency—and Foucault, too, began to sense "strange vistas, like visions of a new life."

Trying to take the measure of his feelings, Foucault conjured up the image of another kind of "limit-experience," one that had become routine for him in the previous weeks in San Francisco:

" 'The only thing I can compare this experience to in my life is sex with a stranger,' " he said. " 'Contact with a strange body affords an experience of the truth similar to what I am experiencing now.' "[15]

Questions raced through Wade's mind. This was the moment he had waited for. What else was the great man thinking?

Wade, however, curbed his tongue: it would be inappropriate to pry.

Time passed.

The three men huddled closer together as a strong and chilly wind buffeted the promontory where they were sitting.

At last, Foucault spoke. " 'I am very happy,' " Wade recalls him saying. Tears were streaming down his cheeks.

" 'Tonight I have achieved a fresh perspective on myself,' " he said.

" 'I now understand my sexuality. . . .'[16]

" 'We *must* go home again.' "

He paused.

" 'We must go home again.' "[17]

He fell silent.

Foucault's visit to California changed his life.

It also changed the way he had been thinking about sex and sexuality.

When he arrived at Berkeley in the spring of 1975, he was deeply involved in writing his History of Sexuality—a project that he had first announced fourteen years before, in his original preface to *Madness and Civilization*. "In fact," he later explained, "I had this idea," of a History of Sexuality, "from the moment I began writing the 'History of Madness.' They were twin projects. Even then, I wanted to see how the normal and the pathological are divided in the case of sex as well."[18]

For years, Foucault had quietly pursued his research, reading books, combing archives, compiling material; in the previous months, since finishing *Discipline and Punish*, he had been immersed in this material, mulling it over, classifying it, analyzing it. By the time of his visit to California in the spring of 1975, his research was nearly finished. He knew what he wanted to say; and he had already started to say it, composing rough drafts, summing up his reading of the documents. Only the last step—taking the results of his historiographic research, and turning them, through a "fictive" style of writing, into a work of art—remained to be done.[19]

This last step, however, was critical: for Foucault had long dreamed that his History of Sexuality would not be just another book, but, in Mallarmé's words "The Book"—a work of "ecstasy in which we become immortal for a brief hour, free of all reality, and raise our obsessions to the level of creation."[20]

This dream Foucault would never fulfill—not least, it seems, because of the disconcerting implications of his epiphany in Death Valley.

When he returned to Paris in June, he set aside the voluminous rough drafts for his History of Sexuality—hundreds of pages, on masturbation, on incest, on hysteria, on perversion, on eugenics.[21]

Ignoring the mountain of manuscripts he had already completed, he threw himself into writing a small essay on method, enunciating a few general principles—a kind of anti-Kantian "Prolegomena to Any Future Physics," further elaborating his Nietzschean concept of power, and describing, in highly abstract language, some of its implications for thinking about the body.

By then, as Daniel Defert recalls, he had already given up his original plan for a monumental seven-volume work. He wrote to Simeon Wade in similar terms, reporting that his Death Valley trip had led him to shelve almost everything that he had previously written about sexuality.[22]

Though he would pretend for several years to come that he was going forward as originally planned, he in fact was starting over.

The stage for his metamorphosis had been set in San Francisco. There the historian of sexuality had discovered—to his consternation and delight—one of the most uninhibited sexual communities in history. And there, in the days leading up to his Death Valley epiphany, Michel Foucault's California odyssey had taken the first, and most fateful, of its unexpected twists.

San Francisco in these years had become a mecca for gay men: between 1969 and 1973, some nine thousand flocked to the city, followed by twenty thousand more by 1978. The origins of this mass migration lay in the so-called "Summer of Love," in 1967. That was the year that *Time* magazine advertised the city's Haight-Ashbury neighborhood as "the vibrant epicenter of the hippie movement," turning San Francisco into an international magnet for daredevil dropouts in quest of free sex, good acid, and altered states of consciousness. Most of the young tourists of the counter-culture came and went quickly; but those who stayed transformed the temper and tone of the city's social—and sexual—mores. Group sex was in; promiscuity was hip; and so was an uninhibited openness to the polymorphously perverse. The city's small but growing number of gay nightclubs and bathhouses reflected the new mood: for the first time, "orgy rooms" began to appear. And the city's policies were adjusted to reflect the change in public opinion: after 1966, police raids had diminished; a decade later, all sexual acts between consenting adults were officially decriminalized in California. By then, the gay migration to San Francisco was in full swing. New gay neighborhoods were flourishing in the areas around Castro Street, Polk Street, and Folsom Street. The city's growing profusion of gay bars, gay clubs, and gay bathhouses facilitated an exuberant outpouring of experimentation with new forms of self-expression, new styles of libertinism, new blends of drugs and sex, new—and sometimes prodigiously imaginative—combinations of "bodies and pleasures."[23]

"San Francisco is where gay fantasies come true," Edmund White wrote in 1980, at a time when the only restraints on the city's erotic adventurers seemed to be boredom and fatigue. "The problem the city presents is whether, after all, we wanted these particular dreams to be fulfilled—or would we have preferred others? Did we know what price these dreams would exact? Did we anticipate the ways in which, vivid and continuous, they would unsuit us for the business of daily life? Or should our notion of daily life itself be transformed?"[24]

Eager, as always, to transform the texture of his own daily life, Foucault plunged passionately into San Francisco's gay community. As Daniel Defert recalls, he loved the unabashed conviviality and openness of the city's gay lifestyle. "In America," says Defert, "he had the possibility of different experiences that [were] organized socially. . . . When he was living in Sweden, a country of 'sexual liberation,' . . . people referred to all of their experiences in terms of psychology. . . . What Foucault appreciated, I think, in the California culture was that these experiences were experiences of [a] community," rather than a "psychological drama for individuals."[25]

But if Foucault appreciated the sense of community he first discovered in San Francisco, he was considerably more ambivalent about the political tactics favored by the most outspoken members of this community. The day after he had taken LSD in Death Valley, he was approached at a party by a young gay militant. The man expressed thanks to Foucault, whose way of thinking, he said (as Simeon Wade recalls the exchange), had " 'made things like gay liberation possible.' "[26]

Foucault politely refused the compliment. " 'This is a nice thing to say to me,' " Wade recalls him remarking, " 'but really my work has had nothing to do with gay liberation.' "

" 'What was it like for you before gay liberation?' " the young man continued, undeterred by the lukewarm response.

" 'You might not believe this,' " Foucault replied, " 'but I actually liked the scene before gay liberation, when everything was more covert. It was like an underground fraternity, exciting and a bit dangerous. Friendship meant a lot, it meant a lot of trust, we protected each other, we related to each other by secret codes.' "

" 'What do you think of gay liberation now?' " wondered the young man.

" 'I believe the term "gay" has become obsolete,' " Wade recalls Foucault responding. " 'The reason for this is the transformation of our understanding of sexuality. We see the extent to which our pursuit of pleasure has been limited in large part by a vocabulary foisted upon us. People are neither this nor that, gay nor straight. There is an infinite range of what we call sexual behavior. . . .' "[27]

Despite Foucault's evident misgivings about a militant social movement organized around the public assertion of a putative sexual identity, "gay liberation" as it had developed in North America would become perhaps the single most important political influence on Foucault's thinking after the collapse of the *Gauche Prolétarienne*.[28]

Like French Maoism, the American movement for gay rights had its origins in the revolts of the late sixties. It had begun with a riot. On June 27, 1969, police in New York City raided and shut down a gay bar in Greenwich Village called the Stonewall Inn. Such harassment was routine—but the response of New York City's gay community on this day was anything but. Some patrons resisted arrest; bystanders grew angry; bricks and bottles began to fly; before it was all over, the bar had been burned down, and crowds of angry homosexuals had battled police far into the night.

The next day, graffiti proclaiming GAY POWER—emulating the BLACK POWER asserted by African-American militants—had been sprayed on walls and sidewalks throughout Greenwich Village. Within weeks, gay activists had formed a new organization, the "Gay Liberation Front" (or GLF).

"We are a revolutionary homosexual group of men and women formed with the realization that complete liberation of all people cannot come about unless existing social institutions are abolished," the GLF declared in its founding manifesto. "We reject society's attempt to impose sexual roles and definitions of our nature."[29]

News of the Stonewall riots was not long in crossing the Atlantic. In March of 1971, a small group of French ultra-leftists announced the formation of the "Front Homosexual d'Action Révolutionnaire" (or FHAR), a group explicitly modelled on the American Gay Liberation Front. On June 27 of that year, FHAR, paying homage to its North American inspiration, celebrated a French "Gay Pride Day" on the second anniversary of the Stonewall riots. Although FHAR was a small and relatively short-lived organization, it did manage to politicize the question of homosexuality in France—no small accomplishment in a country that to this day places a premium on *pudeur,* or "decency," particularly when it comes to talking about intimate matters.[30]

Like its American counterpart, FHAR viewed itself as a revolutionary organization, inspired by a global critique of social oppression. The group's chief theoretician was a gifted young philosopher named Guy Hocquenghem, a veteran of May '68, and an avowed Nietzschean in the mold of Foucault and Deleuze. In his book *Homosexual Desire,* published in 1972, Hocquenghem, borrowing much of his theoretical framework from Deleuze and Guattari's *Anti-Oedipus,* argued that although desire, as such, was amorphous and without gender, "homosexual desire," as it had developed under modern conditions of oppression, paradoxically preserved a greater degree of freedom and fluidity than "heterosexual desire." Homosexuals, once they were liberated from guilt, were free, as heterosexuals were not, to experiment (in Hocqueghem's Deleuzian argot) with "the plugging in of organs subject to no rule or law." Such experimentation could provoke a radical contestation of the roles and sexual identities that modern society had imposed on all of its members.[31]

These sentiments, so far as they went, were consonant with Foucault's convictions and temperament. Much harder for him to accept, however, was perhaps the single most important tactic of the gay liberation movement—what activists called "coming out."

Originally, the phrase referred only to a frank acknowledgment to oneself, and to one's gay peers, that one was a homosexual. But the gay liberation movement turned what had been a discreet and highly informal process into a politicized ritual of public avowal. To proclaim, defiantly, that one was gay was to reject, dramatically, the idea that one's sexuality ought to be regarded as shameful or sick; it was to flout social taboos and to prove the courage of one's convictions at the risk of losing friends, the support of one's family, and even one's job; it was to cross a critical line, and to wager on the success of a public movement of protest. In the process, gay activists hoped to demonstrate their own freedom from self-hatred—and their resistance to the institutions of an oppressive society. As a Gay Liberation Front slogan exhorted, "COME OUT FOR FREEDOM! COME OUT NOW! . . . COME OUT OF THE CLOSET BEFORE THE DOOR IS SHUT!"[32]

The problem with this tactic, from Foucault's point of view, was simple: it assumed that one had a more or less fixed sexual identity that was *worth* avowing in public. This assumption he had long rejected. "The relationships we have to have with ourselves," as he put it in a 1982 interview with gay activists, "are not ones of identity, rather they must be relationships of differentiation, of creation, of innovation. To be the same is really boring."[33]

At the same time, Foucault was understandably wary about becoming too closely linked in the popular mind with the gay subculture he was part of. As Leo Bersani, perhaps his closest friend at Berkeley, puts it, Foucault did not want his work "taken as talk about a potentially sequesterable minority."[34]

"It affected Foucault very much," Bersani recalls. "I remember a young student at one of his lectures at Berkeley, who had obviously come to ask just one question: Why hadn't he talked more about gay liberation? That affected him, because the kid was very sincere, he was obviously someone who admired Foucault, and at the same time he was very angry."[35]

"Between the affirmation, 'I am a homosexual,' and the refusal to say this, there lies a highly ambiguous dialectic," Foucault remarked in a 1982 interview, scarcely veiling his exasperation over the unrelenting pressure to take a stand. "It is a necessary affirmation of a right, but at the same time a cage, a trap. One day the question, 'Are you homosexual?' will seem as natural as the question, 'Are you celibate?'"[36]

Since the question would not go away, Foucault improvised a characteristically complex strategy for dealing with gay issues in public. In France, he discreetly but firmly supported the activists in FHAR. And he also began to speak out with growing boldness about the legal status of homosexuals, and about the penal code more generally.

In 1978, shortly after the French government's Commission for the Reform of Penal Law had solicited his advice, Foucault joined Guy Hocquenghem in sharply criticizing the articles in the French penal code that concerned homosexual behavior. Like Hocquenghem, Foucault publicly urged the government to establish a uniform age of sexual consent (since 1942, the age of consent in France for homosexuals had been 21, while that for heterosexuals was 16). Foucault and Hocquenghem also favored substantially liberalizing the laws regulating sex between adults and children. Indeed, both men argued in principle against the imposition by law of *any* age of consent. "No one signs a contract before making love," quipped Hocquenghem during a joint radio appearance in 1978. "Yes," agreed Foucault, "it is quite difficult to lay down barriers," particularly since "it could be that the child, with his own sexuality, may have desired that adult."[37]

In another public conversation in these months, Foucault went even further, suggesting that it might make sense to abolish altogether the criminal sanctions regulating sexual conduct—even those punishing rape. "I think one can say in principle," he explained, "that in no circumstances should sexuality be subject to any kind of legislation whatsoever. . . . And when one punishes rape one should be punishing physical violence and nothing but that. And to say that it is nothing more than an act of aggression: that there is no difference, in principle, between sticking one's fist into someone's face or one's penis into their genitalia [*sexe*]."[38]

Though Foucault's specific proposals are highly questionable—some will doubtless think them either obscene, or absurd, or both—his courage is beyond dispute. Plainly stating some of the conceivable implications of some of his own deepest convictions, he was willing to broach normally taboo topics, exploring possibilities that have made more than one of his admirers deeply uncomfortable. At the same time, he was outspoken in his public support of "movements for the liberation of women, and for the liberation of homosexual men and women."[39]

Still, it was only after 1978 that Foucault, pressed by activists in North America as well as in France, began—usually in interviews for gay publications with limited circulations—to comment on the culture and politics of the gay community directly. By speaking out on such matters, he was, in effect, "coming out"—belatedly, perhaps, but also decisively.

Foucault's first interviews devoted exclusively to gay issues were initiated by a young activist and editor named Jean Le Bitoux, who in 1979 had started a new gay journal in France called *Gai Pied*. The year before, Le Bitoux, impressed by Foucault's willingness to criticize publicly the sanctions against pederasty in the French legal code, had approached the philosopher for advice and help. A veteran of May '68, and also of FHAR,

Le Bitoux had stood as an avowedly "gay" candidate in the 1977 legislative elections with Guy Hocquenghem (both were defeated); like Hocquenghem, he was committed to creating a gay liberation movement in France on the American model.[40]

"Foucault and I often discussed his reservations about the problematic necessity of 'coming out,' " Le Bitoux has recalled. "These personal reservations never stopped Foucault from fighting for gay rights"—or for helping Le Bitoux launch *Gai Pied*. The magazine's name, in fact, was one of Foucault's contributions. (*"Gai pied,"* literally "gay foot," is a pun on *"guepiers,"* or "wasp's nest"; and also on the slang expression *"pendre son pied"*— "to have an orgasm.")[41]

In its first issue, *Gai Pied* featured a short essay by Foucault. And in 1981, the magazine published a longer interview, billed as "A Conversation with a Fifty-year-old Reader," who is otherwise unnamed—though, at the end, his interlocutors discreetly say, "Thank you, Michel Foucault."[42]

In this interview, the philosopher—for virtually the first time in his life—spoke openly and at length about his hopes for elaborating what he had begun to call "a homosexual style of life." Rejecting, as he consistently did in public, any attempt to trace "the question of homosexuality to the problem, 'Who am I? What is the secret of my desire?' " Foucault asserted that it would be better to ask, " 'What relations, through homosexuality, can be established, invented, multiplied, modulated?' " Homosexuality, as he put it, "is not a form of desire but something desirable. We have therefore to insist on *becoming* homosexual."[43]

For Foucault, the "quest for a style of life" proper to "becoming what one is" (in Nietzsche's sense) entailed an unusual kind of "homosexual ascesis." "Asceticism as a renunciation of pleasure has a bad reputation," he explained. "But ascesis is something else: it is the labor that one undertakes by oneself on oneself in order to be transformed, or in order to have this *self* appear, which happily never happens."[44]

Expanding on this quintessentially convoluted and self-cancelling formulation—which simultaneously affirms the possibility, and denies the likelihood, of an indentifiable "self" emerging as a sort of existential "work" achieved somehow through an exploration of "bodies and pleasures"— Foucault remarked that he was interested in having "the homosexual culture" forge "instruments for polymorphic, varied, individually modulated relations. But the idea of a program and of propositions is dangerous." The differences between different individuals and different national cultures had to be respected: "It is necessary to have an inventiveness appropriate to our own [French] situation and to this craving that the

Americans call 'coming out' "—the phrase is in English—"that is to say, being open and demonstrative."[45]

"It is necessary to dig deeply," he concluded, alluding to his own "archeological" inquiry into the history of sexuality, "in order to show how things are historically contingent, for such and such an intelligible but not necessary reason." But an awareness of history, though invaluable, was not sufficient: "To think of what exists is far from exploring all the possible spaces. Let us make a truly incontrovertible challenge out of the question: 'At what can we play, and how can we invent a game?' "[46]

This interview, like others that followed, is notable, among other things, for its extraordinary abstractness. As Leo Bersani would point out in an essay written after Foucault's death, the rhetoric of the philosopher's public statements on gay issues was "challenging, provoking, and yet, in spite of his radical intentions, somewhat appeasing," above all in its evasion of the corporeal practices at issue. The very abstractness of the language had the "perverse" effect, as Bersani put it, of turning "our attention away from the body—from the acts in which it engages, from the pain it inflicts and begs for." From Bersani's perspective, Foucault's most utopian language— his repeated gestures toward the idea of reinventing the body and its pleasures—amounted to a kind of denial of his own unrelenting erotic preoccupations, obfuscating what Bersani in his essay called "the terrifying appeal of a loss of the ego, of a self-debasement."[47]

Indeed, as Bersani's comments imply, perhaps the most difficult subject for Foucault to speak about directly was neither homosexuality as such, nor the body as such—but rather his ongoing preoccupation with sado-masochistic eroticism.

In practice, he was now able to explore this preoccupation more openly than ever before. Thanks to the gay liberation movement, previously stigmatized varieties of erotic behavior had become the focus of defiantly public subcultures in the gay neighborhoods of New York City, Chicago, Los Angeles, and San Francisco. And ever since his first visit to California in 1975, Foucault had made no secret of his fascination with the unusual array of pleasures to be found on Folsom Street—the hub of San Francisco's flourishing "leather" scene.[48]

By 1975, "leather" had become a sartorial as well as linguistic shorthand within the American gay community for men into sado-masochistic eroticism, or "S/M." Like the sexuality it symbolized, the subculture's public style was rough, brawny, and flamboyant. When the sun set on San Francisco, the dimly lit warehouse district that Folsom traversed filled up with men, many on motorcycles, wearing blue jeans and black leather jackets, trying to look like the hoodlums in the 1954 Marlon Brando movie *The Wild One*. Many stuffed carefully color-coded handkerchiefs into a rear pant pocket to indicate their erotic preferences—a hankie in the left pocket signaled a "sadist," or "top"; a hankie in the right, a "masochist," or "bottom"; blue was for old fashioned fucking; black was for really serious S/M; and that was just the beginning. Thus flagging their inclinations, the men crowded into bars and bathhouses with names like "The Barracks," "The Brig," and "The Boot Camp." Each place offered a somewhat different atmosphere, evoking various "fantasy environments"—many simulating settings that, historically, had been dangerous for gay men. "Glory holes" recreated toilet stalls. Mazes allowed players safely to reenact furtive as-signations in dark places. Welcoming dungeons filled with whips, chains, and cells conjured up an image of prison as the cozy habitat of the sexual outlaw and his punishing "master." The menu of masochistic possibilities ran the gamut, from solitary confinement in a coffin to public humiliation on a cross. Depending on the club, one could savor the illusion of bon-dage—or experience the most directly physical sorts of self-chosen "torture."[49]

"I visited the area many times," Edmund White wrote of the Folsom neighborhood in *States of Desire,* his insouciant account of travels in the new gay America. "At the Black and Blue the customers are so butch they swill Perrier water right out of the bottle (the bartenders jam the lime down into it). In the largest room a motorcycle rampant is suspended above the pool table under a heaven of twinkling electric stars. A bootblack plies his brushes and snaps his cloth below an old-fashioned stand from which a capped and goggled sadist can survey his minions. Two fenced-in yards open off this room; one is a corral for bikes, the other contains an al fresco bath tub in which a naked undinist can sit and gambol about in water jetting from human fountains."[50]

Other places were darker and harder. Instead of communal warmth, or a circus atmosphere of friendly revels, they offered dim rooms for group sex, flanked by labyrinthine hallways lined with small cubicles, their doors left ajar, their nameless occupants silently waiting for "contact with a strange body."

Foucault was no virgin. But he'd never seen anything like Folsom Street.

At the beginning of his stay in California in 1975, he had sublet a student apartment in Berkeley. Shortly afterwards, however, he moved across the Bay to a room not far from Folsom Street. With the help of a

Berkeley colleague who was also into the S/M scene, he went shopping, stocking up on the tools of the leatherman's trade. (A black leather jacket, black leather chaps, and black leather cap with visor; and, for play, a variety of "toys": cockrings, tit clamps, and handcuffs; hoods, gags, and blindfolds; whips, paddles, and riding crops; and so forth.)

Much of the S/M world in France had long been furtive, somber, professionalized, the province of an old-fashioned "rough trade"—take a trip to the docks at Le Havre, and get beaten black and blue. Nothing could be further from the wide-open, almost giddy social whirl of the leather scene in San Francisco.[51]

During their car ride to Death Valley, Simeon Wade asked Foucault if he had been to Folsom Street yet. " 'Of course,' " Wade recalls Foucault answering, flashing a big grin. Even the kinkiest of the leather pleasure palaces, the notorious Barracks? " 'Yes,' " said Foucault: " 'What a tough place! Never have I seen such an open display of sexuality in a public bar.' " Other places left him even more astonished: " 'One night at the baths I met an attractive young man who told me that he and many others go to the baths a few times a week, frequently under the influence of uppers and amyl.' " ("Uppers," or amphetamines, stimulate the nervous system, thereby producing a sense of heightened bodily energy and mental acuity. "Amyl" is amyl nitrite, or "poppers," in those days one of the most commonly used drugs on the gay scene: "Immediately after inhaling," as one expert describes the sensation, "the user can tolerate more pain than normal, and the induced dizziness after a number of 'hits' over perhaps an hour's time creates a pleasant, glowing inner warmth.")[52]

" 'Such a way of life,' " Foucault exclaimed to Wade, " 'is extraordinary to me, unbelievable. These men live for casual sex and drugs. Incredible! There are no such places in France.' "[53]

Foucault found the scene irresistible.

"There was something explosive about his fascination," recalls Leo Bersani. "I mean, the scene was fun—but it wasn't *that* much fun!"[54]

Bersani, like others, was taken aback by the gusto with which Foucault plunged into every aspect of the leather scene, as if galvanized by the spectacle of excess. "I felt there was some sort of European version of glamorizing certain things, or of aestheticizing them," says Bersani. "I think he thought that I was too rationalistically skeptical about some of these things, which I was—I've never had any interest in drugs. So we didn't talk about some of this.

"At the same time, he was one of the only French intellectuals who, when he came to America, seemed able to open his eyes. And what he opened his eyes to was the whole California and San Francisco gay scene, and drugs. And all this meant something to his mind. It was not simply a matter of having a good time. You know, a lot of the French come over, go out, they're a bad boy, they go home—and it doesn't mean anything. But that wasn't true of Foucault. These were all important experiences: The life of his body was important to the life of his mind."[55]

It would be several years before Foucault himself would talk openly about S/M. His reticence is scarcely surprising. Along with incest and boy love, S/M is still one of the most widely stigmatized of sexual practices. Although it is not illegal as such in the United States, other laws, such as those regulating prostitution and "indecent behavior," and those prohibiting assault, still are sometimes used to persecute members of the S/M community. (A person cannot legally consent to an "assault.")[56]

That Foucault ultimately *did* discuss S/M in public is further testimony to his own considerable courage. He addressed the subject in passing in several conversations published after 1979, and also discussed S/M at length in two major interviews with gay activists. The first of these interviews occurred in 1978, in a conversation arranged by Jean Le Bitoux in Paris; the second in 1982, in a conversation with Bob Gallagher and Andrew Wilson in Toronto, Canada.[57]

The Le Bitoux interview was a by-product of Foucault's efforts to help the younger man launch *Gai Pied*. Hoping to forestall government censorship, Foucault had agreed to make a prominent contribution to the first issue. The two of them decided that an interview would be appropriate. But once it had been conducted, Foucault, betraying the extent of his own ambivalence about the value of openly discussing such matters, withdrew the interview, and contributed instead an ostensibly tongue-in-cheek essay on homosexuality and suicide. The 1978 interview with Le Bitoux never appeared in *Gai Pied*. With Foucault's blessing, it did, however, appear four years later—but in Holland, published in Dutch. (After Foucault's death, Le Bitoux published the original French transcript in a short-lived gay journal called *Mec*.)[58]

The Gallagher and Wilson interview came about because of Foucault's friendship with Gallagher, whom he had met in 1982 while residing in Toronto and serving on the faculty of a summer semiotics institute affiliated with the University of Toronto. A graduate student who was writing his dissertation on Foucault's theory of power, Gallagher was enrolled in the philosopher's seminar that summer. An activist with close ties to a number of important figures in the Anglo-American gay intelligentsia, he was also a connoisseur of S/M. At the philosopher's behest, he introduced Foucault to Toronto's leather scene. (It was not hard for Foucault to figure out that Gallagher was a part of the subculture, since he wore his leathers in public.) Shortly after Foucault had joined Gallagher in marching in Toronto's Gay Pride Day parade on June 27, he agreed to be interviewed, in English, about various gay issues by Gallagher and Andrew Wilson, who was connected, like Gallagher, to the gay journal *Body Politic*. Foucault, as was his practice, carefully edited the interview, deleting some material on S/M that he found "too polemical." After being rejected by the American radical quarterly *Social Review* as "uninteresting," the interview eventually ran in the North American gay weekly, the *Advocate*.[59]

"I don't think that this movement of sexual practices has anything to do with the disclosure or the understanding of S/M tendencies deep within our unconscious," Foucault told Gallagher and Wilson. "I think that S/M is much more than that: it's the real creation of new possibilities of pleasure." Through S/M, people "are inventing new possibilities of pleasure with strange parts of their body—through the eroticization of the body. I think it's a kind of creation, a creative enterprise, which has as one of its main features what I call the desexualization of pleasure. The idea that bodily pleasure should always come from sexual pleasure, and the idea that sexual pleasure is the root of *all* our possible pleasure—I think *that's* something quite wrong."[60]

In this context, Foucault had words of praise for drugs "which can produce very intense pleasure"; for the theatricality of S/M, which permitted players to act out a variety of roles in a variety of different scenes and settings; and also for the bathhouse as an institution that facilitated making "contact with a strange body."[61]

"The S/M game is very interesting," Foucault said to Gallagher and Wilson, "because it is a strategic relation, but it is always fluid. Of course, there are roles, but everybody knows very well that those roles can be reversed. Sometimes the scene begins with the master and slave, and at the end the slave has become the master. Or, even when the roles are stabilized, you know very well that it is always a game: either the rules are transgressed, or there is an agreement, either explicit or tacit, that makes them aware of certain boundaries." In such a game, to borrow one of Foucault's hermetic formulations in the History of Sexuality, "pleasure and power do not cancel or turn back against one another; they seek out, overlap, and reinforce one another. They are linked together by complex mechanisms and devices of excitation and incitement."[62]

The bathhouse, by contrast, allowed a quite different kind of "game" to unfold, one that was unpredictable, anonymous, random. "I think that it is politically important," Foucault said to Le Bitoux, "that sexuality is able to function as it functions in the bathhouses. You meet men there who are to you as you are to them: nothing but a body with which combinations and productions of pleasure are possible. You cease to be imprisoned in your own face, in your own past, in your own identity.

"It is regrettable that such places for erotic experience"—for limitless anonymous encounters—"do not yet exist for heterosexuals," continued Foucault. "For would it not, in effect, be marvelous to have the power, at any hour of day or night, to enter a place equipped with all the comforts and all the possibilities that one might imagine, and to meet there a body at once tangible and fugitive? There is an exceptional possibility in this context to desubjectify oneself, to desubjugate oneself," to "desexualize oneself" by affirming a "non-identity" through "a kind of plunge beneath the water sufficiently prolonged that one returns from it with none of this appetite, with none of this torment one sometimes still feels even after satisfying sexual relationships."[63]

But the key, as Foucault explained to Le Bitoux and also to Gallagher and Wilson, was the unfathomable alchemy of S/M, and the ways in which, by using its tools and techniques, one might work on the body, and transmute pain into pleasure.

Foucault himself said little in his public conversations about the specific erotic practices that interested him. But these practices are helpfully explained in apologias for the subculture like *Urban Aboriginals* by Geoff Mains, in saucy travelogues like Edmund White's *States of Desire,* and, above all, in *The Leatherman's Handbook* by Larry Townshend, the most widely read gay S/M manual.[64]

S/M, as Townshend defined it in his pioneering 1972 primer, involves: "1) A dominant-submissive relationship. 2) A giving and receiving of pain that is pleasurable to both parites. 3) Fantasy and/or role playing on the part of one or both partners. 4) A conscious humbling of one partner by the other (humiliation). 5) Some form of fetish involvement. 6) The acting out of one or more ritualized interactions (bondage, flagellation, etc.)."[65]

Though the most widely used S/M techniques, such as bondage and flagellation, are relatively mild, the "etc." in Townshend's list of "ritualized interactions" covers a wide range of possibilities: gagging, piercing, cutting, hanging, electric-shocking, stretching on racks, imprisoning, branding, blindfolding, mummifying, pissing on, shitting on, shaving, burning, crucifying, suspending, clamping, suffocating, fist-fucking.[66]

Four points are worth keeping in mind.

The first is that S/M, despite the almost exclusively gay male clientele of Folsom Street in the mid-seventies, is *not* an exclusively gay or exclusively male preoccupation. Although the first S/M bars and baths in the 1950s largely catered to homosexuals, there was already then, as there is today, a relatively large and flourishing *heterosexual* S/M underground, organized primarily through informal networks and private liaisons. One expert, Gayle Rubin, reckons there are far more straight than gay practitioners of S/M. This should come as no surprise. After all, S/M on one level merely makes explicit the sadistic and masochistic fantasies implicitly at play in most, perhaps all, human relationships. "Just as somewhere in most of us not brain dead is depression and paranoia," remarks the American psychoanalyst Robert J. Stoller, "so there are sado-masochistic mental states. But sado-masochism is only a noun, not a molecule."[67]

The second point to bear in mind is that S/M as an organized subculture is built upon *trust*. As Edmund White puts it, "the freedom to start and stop a sex scene is part of almost every S&M contract." The very existence of such a contract must be stressed: as it was usually practiced on Folsom Street in the mid-seventies, S/M was *consensual*. These sado-masochists appreciated partners sophisticated enough to play the game within limits— which meant, paradoxically, knowing just when to stretch the limits of pleasure-in-pain, and by just how much.[68]

The third point to stress is that aficionados of S/M are not the neo-Nazi thugs outsiders often imagine. On the whole, they are as nonviolent and well-adjusted as any other segment of the population. As White remarks (and as the best psychiatric research confirms), "their sex lives, one might say, so thoroughly drain off the normal human reservoir of nastiness that they emerge as relatively benign beings."[69]

The fourth point is that the Grand Guignol props of many S/M scenes— the handcuffs and whips—are just that: *props*. The vast majority of S/M scenes do not involve any real cruelty or physical violence. "Consensual sado-masochists do not brutalize, humiliate, or torture each other," writes Robert Stoller, one of the few psychiatrists who has actually taken the trouble to conduct empirical research on the organized S/M subculture: "they tantalize and then satisfy." Playing with the props of torture in a variety of humiliating and degrading scripts, the actors get to savor the *illusion* of cruelty, of helplessness, of living on the edge. "The art of sado-masochism," as Stoller puts it, "is its theater: its delicious simulation of harm, of high risk."[70]

This "simulation of harm," under controlled conditions, voluntarily entered into, seems to account, in part, for the appeal of S/M. Through the imaginative scripts that give to many S/M scenes a certain pattern and unity, the "top" and "bottom" are both able to reenact, deliberately, fantasies of domination and debasement otherwise experienced as involuntary. "The reenactment lowers anxiety whether one is playing the master or the slave," White comments. "Relief is afforded not by the particular role that is assumed but because the drama is something one has initiated and can end at any moment."[71]

Not that S/M is pure theater. It is not. For some of its techniques, in the hands of its most daring practitioners, can be used to produce shattering states of intense "suffering-pleasure."

The "most common, almost universal component" of S/M scenes, according to Townshend, is "bondage": the partner playing the role of "masochist" (or bottom) is bound, tied down, handcuffed, blindfolded, perhaps given a "light whipping" as a kind of appetizer.[72]

From there, players can move on to more specialized techniques, using the tools of the leatherman's trade. For the dedicated masochist "who likes to be reminded of his status," there are "leather cockrings with pinpricks inside"—as the penis becomes erect, the prongs cut into its flesh. A similar device, also attached to the cock, is the "very popular English Cage Harness," a toy made of leather with metal rings, which can be used "as a modest genital torture device" by hanging weights from the rings, thus pulling on the testicles.[73]

In "tit torture," the players use clamps, stretchers, and harnesses, "sometimes with weights attached," sometimes with the nipple clamps attached to genital clamps. Fitted with adjustable screws, the clamps could be tightened gradually, delivering just the right dose of pain. "There comes a point in tit play when anything goes," explains Geoff Mains in *Urban Aboriginals*. "Pain of any form becomes sheer ecstasy. Needles through the flesh. Hot candle wax dribbled over alligator clips. The most extraordinary pressure on muscles or connective tissue. The frontier between pain and pleasure has been crossed."[74]

Similarly with fist-fucking—the gentle insertion of one person's hand and forearm up another person's ass. It is an act of corporeal acrobatics that, in the words of one expert, requires "seducing one of the jumpiest and tightest muscles in the body." A long and elaborate ritual is necessary to perform the act at all, beginning with a douche and manicure, continuing with the slow, gradual introduction of first fingers, then the hand, and eventually the arm, lubricated by vast quantities of Crisco. "Once penetration has been achieved," writes Mains, "internal massage coupled with in and out motions generates paroxysms of intense euphoria."[75]

First popularized in the heyday of the gay subculture of the seventies, fist-fucking was something new—a practice that neither Sade nor Sacher-Masoch had ever dreamed of. It was also, like a number of other S/M techniques, a practice that was, for many, all foreplay and no climax: its pleasures stopped short of orgasm. "The physical feelings are so intense as to be almost asexual," Larry Townshend explains, "in that most scenes are carried out with neither partner having an erection." Writes Mains: "Many participants aren't interested in coming. It's much more of a mind space between two people."[76]

Similarly evocative psychologically—and similarly asexual and anorgasmic in outcome—were a variety of far more unusual and voluptuously "painful" scenes. (As Stoller has remarked, in writing about S/M one senses "a vocabulary weakness; there are not enough words for the colors of pain.")[77]

In a "suspension" scene, for example, the masochist was hung from a leather harness, blindfolded, and flogged, producing in the "bottom," as Townshend puts it, "a sensation of complete helplessness, while at the same time he seems almost to be flying."[78]

A variation was a "crucifixion" scene, in which the partner electing "martyrdom" had his wrists and ankles lashed to a wooden cross, "for some extensive tit work and/or cock and ball torture."[79]

In medical scenes, by contrast, a "doctor" might set his "patient" on an operating table and use a lancet to pierce "the nipple, the skin of the penis," or the scrotum. "There is certainly pain," comments Townshend, "and sometimes a small amount of blood, but the real trip is mental."[80]

Townshend even claims to have witnessed a "castration" scene in which the victim's testicles were cut off and placed in his mouth for a short period of time. This, one suspects, is sheer fantasy—it certainly has nothing to do with the mainstream of S/M practices. And as Townshend himself hastens to add, those few men excited by the idea of castration generally prefer to act out their castration fantasies in safer ways: by piercing the cock; by "torturing" the testicles through the use of clamps and weights; or, more boldly, by driving a nail through the loose skin of the penis into a board.[81]

In the heyday of the San Francisco S/M scene in the 1970s, such "heavy pain trips" were sometimes enhanced by the use of drugs; among the most common were amyl nitrite, LSD, and MDA. Amyl, or "poppers," took the edge off the pain; LSD intensified the dissociative effects of the psychological melodrama and the physiological suffering; while MDA, an amphetamine-related substance, had a more mellow psychedelic effect, producing "a sense of tenderness and empathy, even joy."[82]

At the outer limits of this subculture, where the most fearless players experimented with shifting scripts, changing "scenes," and new combinations of bondage, drugs, and the infliction of intense physical suffering, altered states of consciousness appeared.

"In bondage," as Geoff Mains evokes the sensations, "a man comes to better understand the map of his own body"—and the structure of his mind. "In immobilization, the mind of dreams, memories, and aspirations takes on new balance against that world we record at any moment through the senses." In "torture" scenes, by contrast, the body was plunged into pleasure-pain, its "map" obliterated and redrawn, through techniques and tools that took the organism, as Mains puts it, "to its known boundaries and beyond."[83]

At these boundaries, as Robert Stoller has wisely remarked, received knowledge fails us: "There are questions we do not even know enough to ask." As Stoller points out, the kind of ecstatic experiences described by Mains and other adepts of S/M recall the kinds of raptures reported by "philosophers of the drug culture"; by theorists of "other societies and religions who use drugs, physical pain, starvation, or other means of altering consciousness"; and by "some people with near-death surgical and other physical illness experiences, people who were drowning, and some who only by chance survive certain types of suicide attempts." Perhaps, as Geoff Mains has speculated, the intense pain produced in certain S/M scenes, like the pain produced by other forms of physical suffering, triggers an individual's endogenous opioids, inhibiting pain transmission, in effect turning pain into a kind of pleasure, plunging a person into a self-administered narcotic trance. Whatever the combination of physiological, psychological, and cultural factors put into play, one can only agree with Stoller when he concludes that "the experience of extreme suffering points us to frontiers of human behavior far beyond the exotica of perverse sado-masochism."[84]

Foucault did not say much in public about the specific instruments and practices of S/M. But what he did say suggests that this variety of "limit-experience" had a profound philosophical significance for him.

"Physical practices like fist-fucking," he explained to Jean Le Bitoux in 1978, "are practices that one can call devirilizing, or desexualizing. They are in fact *extraordinary falsifications of pleasure*, which one achieves with the aid of a certain number of instruments, of signs, of symbols, or of drugs such as poppers and MDA." With the help of the right "instruments" (tit clamps, cockrings, whips, chains, lancets) and "symbols" (cells, operating tables, dungeons, crucifixes), one might be able, as Foucault explained to Le Bitoux, "to invent oneself"—to make a new "self" appear— and also "to make of one's body a place for the production of extraordinarily polymorphic pleasures, while simultaneously detaching it from a valorization of the genitalia" (the French word is *sexe*), "and particularly of the male genitalia."[85]

In these remarks, perhaps the most startling single word is "falsification." It is an unusual term in Foucault's vocabulary. But it does appear in one other important context—namely in his discussion, in his first series of lectures at the Collège de France, of Nietzsche's theory of knowledge, of "truth" as a product of "a primary and always reconstituted falsification, which establishes the distinction between the true and the false."[86]

It is as if Foucault wished to suggest that S/M was itself, in some way, a kind of Nietzschean "game of truth"—a game played with the body itself.

To regard S/M as an occasion for the production of a singular kind of "truth" seems at first glance farfetched. Yet Foucault himself in these years spoke of an "erotics of truth." He talked of a "relentless search for a certain truth of pleasure"—a "truth" approached through "experience, analyzed according to its quality, pursued throughout its reverberations in the body and the soul." A "quintessential knowledge," as Foucault called it, this "erotics of truth" was "transmitted by magisterial initiation, with the stamp of secrecy, to those who have shown themselves to be worthy of it, and who would make use of it at the very level of their pleasure, to intensify it, and to make it more acute and fulfilling."[87]

This description certainly fits the subculture of S/M. Still, as Foucault well knew, most people—and certainly most of his colleagues—could scarcely imagine approaching either "truth" or "pleasure" through "initiation" into an esoteric erotic practice. Indeed, what kind of "truth" could such a practice express?

In a series of lectures delivered in 1973 and 1974, and subsequently incorporated into several of his texts, Foucault indirectly addressed this question, by distinguishing between two divergent approaches to "truth," one emphasizing a family of practices that Foucault defined by their common use of "*l'enquête*," the other emphasizing a group of esoteric rituals that he defined by their recourse to "*l'épreuve*." *Enquête* can be rendered into English as "inquiry," "survey," or "inquest"; *épreuve* can be translated as "ordeal," "test", or "trial."[88]

The idea of a "truth" that could be approached through an inquiry was, according to Foucault, distinctly modern, and one of the methodological foundations of contemporary science. In an inquiry, one gathered evidence on the assumption that "truth" was objective, the sort of thing that could be confirmed by anyone with the appropriate training and type of knowledge. Such a model of inquiry became central to the judicial process in the modern state—and also to scientific procedures for gathering information about the natural world. Once this model was assimilated to the techniques and tools of controlled laboratory experimentation, in the final decades of the eighteenth century, as Foucault dates the transformation, the kind of "truth" verified by scientific inquiry was taken to be universal, and independent of time and place, since different researchers in different laboratories could confirm the validity of observations made by others elsewhere.[89]

This scientific conception of "truth" has proven its power in practice. Still, as Foucault pointed out in an essay contrasting *l'enquête* and *l'épreuve*, "we also find profoundly rooted in our civilization another idea [of truth], repugnant to both science and philosophy." Within this shadowy counter-tradition, "truth" appears as the singular product of "propitious moments" and "privileged places" where a ritualized "ordeal" can unfold.[90]

The "privileged places" that Foucault mentions include Delphi, where Socrates received the oracle that triggered his own lifelong quest to know the truth. He also evokes the caves in the desert where the early Christian ascetics, such as Saint Anthony, retreated to joust with the Devil, testing the mettle of their faith.[91]

And the "propitious moments" that Foucault discusses include the "crisis" in premodern medicine; the ancient art of torture; and the martial pageantry of the tournament, in which a turbulent spirit of aggression was made manifest, and honored, through the organized bloodshed of public war games.

The idea of a ritual form of combat to determine virtue and valor, innocence or guilt, became for Foucault a paradigm of sorts: "The ordeal that submits the accused to a test [*épreuve*], or the duel that confronts the accused with the accuser (or each one's representatives) was not some crude and irrational way to 'detect' the truth and to know 'what had really happened' in the affair under dispute; it was rather a way of deciding on which side God *at that moment* had weighed the scales of chance or force that led to the success of one or the other of the adversaries. . . . Truth was an effect produced by the ritual determination of a victor."[92]

Torture, as Foucault described it, belonged to this tradition of determining the "truth." "Suffering, confrontation, and truth" were linked, as he wrote in *Discipline and Punish*, in a kind of "joust," or "battle," or "duel"; and it was only the "victory of one adversary over another, that 'produced' truth according to a ritual." Most of the time, of course, it was the will of the sovereign that emerged triumphant, since he could use the hangman's "art of unbearable sensations" to extract a confession. Still, in the course of this agonizing ordeal, chance factors and strange forces sometimes intervened. And if the suspect "held out," his innocence was assumed proven; the magistrate had to drop charges. By braving the most intense pain— and by facing the possibility of death—the tortured man might win back his life.[93]

A similarly paradoxical drama unfolded in the medical "crisis," as Foucault described it. Here, too, a kind of ritual "combat" occurred—in this case with a deadly disease. The course of the illness was an "autonomous movement," yet one in which the doctor could participate by helping the sick person prepare for his or her "moment of truth." At the height of the crisis, "the pathological process, through its own force, escaped from its shackles." Those at the bedside watched helplessly as the fever ran its course. Life hung in the balance; the patient might die; yet letting the sick person plunge into a febrile delirium often seemed to offer the last, best hope for the recovery of health.[94]

"One may then suppose in our civilization," as Foucault summed up his hypothesis, "a whole technology of truth that scientific practice has step-by-step discredited, covered up, and driven out. The truth here does not belong to the order of that which is, but rather of that which happens: it is an event. It is not recorded, but aroused: a production in the place of apophantics" (a technical term of philosophy, used to describe propositions that refer to something real).[95]

The "truth," in this archaic and discredited sense, Foucault continues, "is not given by the mediation of instruments," such as those found in modern laboratories; it is rather produced directly, inscribed in the body and soul of a single person. Far from being regulated by rigorous rules of method, "truth" as the outcome of an "ordeal" is "provoked by rituals; it is attained by tricks, one seizes it only by chance: through strategy and not method. The happening [of 'truth'] thus produced in the individual who lies in wait for it, and is struck by it, creates a relationship, not of an object to a knowing subject, but rather a relationship that is ambiguous, reversible, bellicose in its mastery, its domination, its triumph—a relationship of power."[96]

Did S/M belong to this occult and discredited way of producing a singular—and potentially transformative—kind of "truth"?

Foucault's friend Gilles Deleuze apparently thought so. "Masochism," he wrote in his 1967 study of Sacher-Masoch, "in its material aspects is a phenomenon of the senses (i.e., a certain combination of pain and pleasure); in its moral aspects it is a function of feeling or sentiment. But beyond all sensation or feeling there is a third aspect, a super-personal element" that, as in Nietzsche's dream of the *übermensch*, leads—so Deleuze asserted—to the "birth of the new Man."[97]

Foucault was characteristically more circumspect in his own writing. Still, as he argued in the first volume of his History of Sexuality—the methodological prolegomenon that he would publish in December 1976, under the Nietzschean title *La volonté de savoir* ("The Will to Know")— we moderns, like it or not, are condemned to unriddle our sense of *personal* "truth" through sexuality and sex: "All of the world's enigmas appear frivolous to us compared to this secret, minuscule in each of us, but of a density that makes it more serious than any other." No matter how "imaginary" and historically contingent our own culturally constituted experience of genital sex might yet prove to be, it was now "through sex . . . that each person must pass in order to have access to his own intelligibility (since it is simultaneously the hidden element and the productive principle of sense), to the totality of his body (since it is a real and menaced part of it, and symbolically constitutes the whole), to his identity (since it joins to the force of an impulse the singularity of a history)."[98]

Equally striking in this book was Foucault's enigmatic suggestion that the only way *beyond* a crippling identification of ourselves with our "sex-desire" (or "genital-desire") lay in a return to "bodies and pleasures."[99]

In his view such a return was possible, as rarely before in history. The preconditions for its occurrence had been laid down, paradoxically enough, by the accelerating spread of "perversions" produced by modern culture. "Regular sexuality" was being challenged "through a reflux movement, originating in these peripheral sexualities," which were swept up in "*perpetual spirals of power and pleasure*," inciting new and polymorphous relationships. Writing about such "heretical sexualities" in 1976, after his return from California, Foucault sounded warmly optimistic: "Never have there existed more centers of power; never more manifest and prolix thoughtfulness; never more circular contacts and linkages; never more hotbeds for kindling, in order to disseminate still further, the strength of pleasures and the stubborn waywardness of powers."[100]

All of Foucault's "limit-experiences" in California, first on Folsom Street, and then in Death Valley, had dramatically confirmed his thesis that the body, like the soul, was in some sense socially constructed—and therefore, in principle at least, open to being changed. Even "sex" itself—the cluster of psychological desires and physiological drives we associate with the reproductive organs—was, as he wrote in the first volume of the History of Sexuality, only "an imaginary point," the historically contingent product of "power in its grip on bodies and their materiality, their forces, energies, sensations, and pleasures." (Here, as elsewhere, when Foucault uses the French word "*sexe*," the term strongly connotes the genitalia in a way that its English cognate does not.)[101]

The radicalism of this view has perhaps too rarely been stressed. For Foucault here implies that the human organism is an intrinsically formless flux of impulses and energies, impossible though it may be to articulate this intuition within the "games of truth" played by modern science. A great many physiological drives that seemed at first glance to function like fixed instincts, including the preoccupation with (genital) sex itself, were figments of the collective imagination, open to collective play—open, even, to a great cultural experiment in "desexualization."[102]

As he summed up one of the central political points of the book in a 1977 interview, "one should aim," in the new feminist and gay social movements, not at a "liberation" of "sex-desire," but rather "at a general economy of pleasure not based on sexual norms."[103]

Moreover, as Foucault suggested in one of the first interviews he gave after returning from California, one might put the "truth" of this vision to the test—and verify for oneself, through a certain kind of "*épreuve*," the formless flux of the (desexualized) body. This one might do by deliberately exploring "the slow motions of pleasure-pain," as the philosopher discreetly put it. Rocked to and fro, drifting from feelings of pain to feelings of pleasure and back again, buffeted by wave after wave of unfamiliar sensations, the habitual dispositions of the body seemed to break down, its instincts and drives turning into a teeming mass of "formless pseudo-pods"—as if every zone of the body, like an amoeba through its pseu-dopodia, was now able to change constantly its shape. "It is a matter of a multiplication and burgeoning of bodies," producing "an exaltation of a kind of autonomy of its smallest parts, of the smallest possibilities of a part of the body," Foucault remarked, trying to evoke the experience. "There is a creation of anarchy within the body, where its hierarchies, its localizations and designations, its organicity, if you will, is in the process of disintegrating. . . . This is something 'unnameable,' 'useless,' outside of all the programs of desire. It is the body made totally plastic by pleasure: something that opens itself, that tightens, that throbs, that beats, that gapes." [104]

Foucault well knew how odd—and how open to "ridicule"—was any such vision of an "other body, utterly new, utterly beautiful." In the first volume of his History of Sexuality, he even imagines, with evident equa-nimity, the objections that will be raised: "Someone will say to me: this is to indulge in a historicism more hasty than radical; it is to evade the biologically solid existence of sexual functions, for the sake of phenomena that, though perhaps variable, are fragile, secondary, and, above all, su-perficial; it is to speak of sexuality as if the genitals [*le sexe*] did not exist. . . . 'For you there remain only groundless effects, ramifications with-out roots, a sexuality without genitalia [*sexe*]. Castration, all over again.' " [105]

Confronted with this imaginary objection, Foucault does not flinch. He reiterates his conviction that society transforms in depth the body, shaping even its "physiological functions." *And* he reiterates, in the strongest pos-sible terms, his view that the genitalia ("*sexe*"), far from being a "biologically solid" basis for writing a history of sexuality, are rather "the most ideal, the most speculative element" in such a history. [106]

Moreover, if the desires associated with the genitalia are in some im-portant sense only "an imaginary point," a kind of seductive mirage, par-adoxically generated by the contingent atmospheric conditions of our own arid cultural climate and marvelously dissolved by "the great pleasure of the body in explosion," then the incredulity currently elicited by the prospect of a life lived free of a preoccupation with penises, vaginas, and orgasms, may one day come to seem as myopic, and historically curious, as the Victorian dread of masturbation. [107]

On this score, Foucault's critique of "the austere monarchy of sex [*sexe*]" recalls that which was elaborated in the third century by the Christian philosopher Origen, who is said to have castrated himself in an unusually zealous effort to live a life of ecstatic purity. Like Foucault, Origen supposed that the body, under the impact of a certain kind of "limit-experience"— for the theologian, it was a yearning to receive God's wisdom—could become less "thick," less "coagulated," less "hardened," fluid and free at last. As the historian Peter Brown has summed up the implications of such a conviction, "human life, lived in a body endowed with sexual charac-teristics, was but the last dark hour of a long night that would vanish with the dawn. The body was poised on the edge of a transformation so enor-mous as to make all present notions of identity tied to sexual differences, and all social roles based upon marriage, procreation, and childbirth, seem as fragile as dust dancing in a sunbeam."[108]

But Foucault, who developed a lively interest in the views of ascetics like Origen, did not need to go so far afield to find support for his own, equally unconventional hopes for reinventing the body. After all, Artaud had voiced a similar hope; trying to get beyond a corporeality he expe-rienced as a "perpetual crucifixion," he had experimented with halluci-nogenic drugs and deliberately flirted with madness in a desperate effort to transform and somehow transfigure "this ill-assembled heap of organs which I was and which I had the impression of witnessing like a vast landscape on the point of breaking up."[109]

"So it is man whom we must now make up our minds to emasculate," Artaud had declared at the climax of his 1947 radio play, *To Be Done with the Judgment of God*, proposing a sort of "Dionysian castration" (to borrow one of Foucault's most haunting turns of phrase):

> —By placing him again, for the last time, on the autopsy
>   table to remake his anatomy.
> I say, to remake his anatomy.
> Man is sick because he is badly constructed.
> We must make up our minds to strip him bare in order to
>   scrape off that animalcule that itches him mortally,
>   god,
>   and with god
>   his organs.
> For you can tie me up if you wish,
> but there is nothing more useless than an organ.
> When you will have made him a body without organs,
> then you will have delivered him from all his automatic
>   reactions and restored him to his true freedom.

Then you will teach him again to dance wrong side out
as in the frenzy of dance halls
and this wrong side out will be his real place. [110]

Artaud's idea of creating an atheist "body without organs," like Origen's equally extreme but antithetical notion of turning the body into a "temple of God," may seem absurd, if not insane. But in *Anti-Oedipus*, a work that Foucault knew and admired, Gilles Deleuze and Félix Guattari systematically elaborated Artaud's idea. And in an essay they published in 1974, Deleuze and Guattari went even further, proposing a number of concrete ways to produce a "body without organs." Of these, none was more striking—or more pertinent to Foucault's own erotic concerns—than what Deleuze and Guattari called "the *masochist body*." [111]
Here is their recipe:

1) You may tie me down on the table, ropes drawn tight, for ten to fifteen minutes, time enough to prepare the instruments; 2) One hundred lashes at least, a pause of several minutes; 3) You begin sewing, you sew up the hole in the glans; you sew the skin around the glans to the glans itself, preventing the top from tearing; you sew the scrotum to the skin of the thighs. You sew the breasts, securely attaching a button with four holes to each nipple. You may connect them with an elastic band with buttonholes—*Now you go on to the second phase*: 4) You can choose either to turn me over on the table so I am tied lying on my stomach, but with my legs together, or to bind me to the post with my wrists together, and my legs also, my whole body tightly bound; 5) You whip my back buttocks and thighs a hundred lashes at least; 6) You sew my buttocks together, all the way up and down the crack of my ass. Tightly, with a double thread, each stitch knotted. If I am on the table, now tie me to the post; 7) You give me fifty thrashes on the buttocks; 8) If you wish to intensify the torture and carry out your threat from last time, stick the pins all the way into my buttocks as far as they go; 9) Then you may tie me to the chair; you give me thirty lashes on the breasts and stick in the smaller pins; if you wish, you may heat them red-hot beforehand, all or some. I should be tightly bound to the chair, hands behind my back so my chest sticks out. I haven't mentioned burns, only because I have a medical exam coming up in a while, and they take a long time to heal.

Comment Deleuze and Guattari: "This is not a fantasy, it is a program."[112]

This, of course, was a "program" that a person, if he or she wished, could actively pursue in the S/M subculture, by using all of the "heretical" techniques and tools of S/M, as Foucault himself had described them.

Through an ordeal of self-chosen "torture," a human being might get beyond conventional ways of thinking, and also beyond a reified "valorization" of the genitalia. Mobilizing old impulses and fantasies, one might be able to give a new twist to the singular configuration of compulsions and *idées fixes* that the modern "mnemotechnics" of morality and guilt had burned into the body and soul. Surrendering to a "kind of dissociative gaze able to dissociate itself," one might then be able to see—at a glance, as it were—"the body totally imprinted by history, and history ruining the body."[113]

Armed with this quintessentially Nietzschean kind of "knowledge," the genealogist of "suffering-pleasure" might even be able to imagine *new* combinations of impulses and phantasms, *new* relationships of power, a *new* "style" of life—perhaps even a new "game" of truth.[114]

But did a practice like S/M really enable Foucault (or anyone else, for that matter) to "think differently"?

Could an erotic "ordeal," as he implied, really enable a human being to grasp creatively, in a "moment of truth," its singular *daimon*—and thus transfigure its historical fate, facilitating "the birth of the new Man"?

Or did S/M (as some feminists have charged) merely allow a person to act out the crudest and cruelest sorts of (masculine) fantasies of violent domination and abject submission, in the process reinforcing, through what a Freudian might call a "repetition compulsion," the morbid convergence of sex and death that Foucault had warned about at the end of *The Will to Know?*[115]

That there were risks, Foucault well knew: the kind of "truth" obtained through an "ordeal," he had stressed, was always "ambiguous" and "reversible." He had made a similar point in his 1971 lectures on Nietzsche's theory of knowledge. From a Nietzschean perspective, "knowledge" (including perforce Foucault's own expressed "will to know") was always "dubious," a "provisional compromise" between antagonistic instincts, impulses and desires. "Knowledge" itself, so Foucault said, "was always enslaved, dependent and enthralled (not to itself, but to whatever can enthrall an instinct . . .)."[116]

Or, as Foucault more simply put it in a 1977 interview, "*there is always within each of us something that fights something else.*"[117]

Now, among the things that he explicitly wished to combat was "the fascism in us all." As he had conceded in the last chapter of *The Will to Know*, an "oneiric exaltation" of "the unlimited right of an all-powerful monstrosity" linked the death-haunted lusts of the Marquis de Sade to the death camps of the Nazis.[118]

A delicate balance had to be struck. For on the one hand, "Sade's great experiment," as Foucault put it in a 1973 interview, was "to introduce the disorder of desire into a world dominated by order and classification." One philosophical consequence of this "great experiment," in Foucault's view, was "the dissociation of the ego, at least in the form in which that term is understood from Descartes onward." It is "exactly this orgiastic quality of contemporary sexuality," first broached in Sade, "that has raised the question of the subject's position." This aspect of Sade's work Foucault never disavowed.[119]

But Sade had not gone far enough. He was a transitional figure, shaped by the classical Age of Reason even as he inaugurated (in Foucault's idiosyncratic view) our own modern counter-culture premised on "fiction" and "limit-experience."

As Foucault explained in a 1975 interview, Sade remained trapped within a conventional view of the body as an organic hierarchy. "The body as Sade sees it," he remarked, "is still strongly organic, anchored in this hierarchy, the difference being that the hierarchy is not organized, as in the old fable, starting from the head, but starting from the genitalia [*sexe*]." Because he remained fixated on genital sex, Sade had formulated an "eroticism appropriate to a disciplinary society: a regulated society, anatomical, hierarchicalized, with its carefully allotted times, its controlled spaces, its duties, and surveillances."[120]

"It is a question of escaping from all that," said Foucault in 1975, after his return from California. "It is necessary to invent with the body, with its elements, its surfaces, its volumes, its depths, a nondisciplinary eroticism: that of the body plunged into a volatile and diffused state through chance encounters and incalculable pleasures."[121]

This "body dis-organizing itself," would be "the *opposite* of sadism." The sensation of "suffering-pleasure is very different from what one finds in [conventional sexual] desire or in what one calls sadism or masochism." "The idea that S/M is related to a deep violence, that S/M practice is a way of liberating this violence, this aggression, is stupid."[122]

Far from simply realizing Sade's own cruel fantasies, the "slow motions of pleasure-pain" might liberate a human being *from* these cruel fantasies by illuminating a historically contingent erotic obsession with violence and aggression, while dissolving in practice the morbid reification of "sex-desire" that Freud had called the "death instinct."

This, in effect, is one of the occult possibilities alluded to at the end of *The Will to Know*.

But in this shadowy ordeal, putting body and soul to the test, and letting all of its warring impulses and phantasms run wild in a kind of erotic "duel" or "joust," the outcome was always in doubt. "What is this power that dumbfounds those who have looked it straight in the face, and which condemns to *madness* all those who have hazarded the ordeal [*épreuve*] of Unreason?" Foucault asked rhetorically in 1961, evoking the risks that had been run by such oracles of the "thought from outside" as Sade and Artaud.[123]

"The critical ontology of ourselves," as Foucault had more soberly summed up the uncertain character of his own approach to "thinking differently" in 1983, "has to be considered not, certainly, as a theory, a doctrine, nor even a permanent body of knowledge that is accumulating; it has to be conceived as an attitude, an ethos, a philosophical life in which the critique of what we are is at one and the same time the historical analysis of the limits that are imposed on us and the ordeal [*épreuve*] of their possible transcendence."[124]

An "ordeal," then (borrowing an image from Sade):

Your hands will be strapped to the ceiling. Bands will be wrapped around each of your arms and tightened. A man with a lancet will approach you, and pierce a vein in each arm. Helplessly you will watch the blood begin to drain from your body.[125]

The ordeal is structured like the "crisis" in medieval medicine. It is a "game," a carefully regulated ritual, a spectacle of "immobile contemplation, of death mimed." Its aim: to *express* passionately and actively an agonizing lust for blood and for death; to turn this lust outward "in a continuous irony"—and so, through a kind of "perverse mysticism," to purge it, to drain it, to "disarm it in advance."[126]

Surrendering to a kind of hallucinatory fever, as the spectacle of your own blood plunges you into delirium, you are going to face your "moment of truth."

You are going to experience directly, in a way that scientific inquiry has never been able to illuminate, "the silent world of the entrails, the whole dark underside of the body lined with endless unseeing dreams."[127]

And through this experience—which will safely whisk you to the threshold of your own imagined death—you are going to feel the pathological process, through its own force, snap the soul's shackles.

Will the ordeal work?

"We talked a lot about Sade," Bob Gallagher recalls of the month he spent with Foucault in the summer of 1982, exploring Toronto's S/M subculture. "Many of our discussions were around S/M. And actually around sexual practices, which to some degree he intellectualized. And so we would talk about Sade—even though it was well past the time when, if you read his books, he should have been concerned about Sade. But in his personal life, in his sexual life, he was still very concerned with Sade.

"Our conversations almost always occurred around sexual scenes. It would have to do with tastes, with techniques, and he would often give a kind of survey of Sade, and the use of excess, he would talk about Sade in an almost sermon-like way: in terms of one's search for ecstasy; in terms of the sensuality of surrender, the sensuality of agony, the sensuality of pain, the sensuality of death.

"My sense is that his obsession with death—and there is no doubt but that he was obsessed with it—had something to do with death as a kind of presentation of self, death as an indication of self, death as a distancing of self.

"Sade was very much on his mind during this period. At the time, I took it at face value. But looking back, I've always wondered why he was so obsessed with Sade."[128]

One of Foucault's closest intellectual companions in Paris, the philosopher, translator, and pornographic novelist Pierre Klossowski, had a peculiar but perhaps relevant theory.

In Klossowski's view, which he first enunciated in a lecture delivered in 1939, the Marquis de Sade, far from being an Anti-Christ, was a kindred spirit of his contemporary, Joseph de Maistre, perhaps the darkest of the conservative Christian critics of the French Revolution. According to Klossowski's reading of *Justine* and *Juliette*, Sade had cleverly smuggled into these pages a kind of gnostic theology of original sin, as bleakly Manichean in temper as de Maistre's philosophy, but deceptively esoteric in method, "disguising itself as atheism in order to combat atheism," speaking "the language of moral skepticism in order to combat moral skepticism."[129]

Sade in effect revealed evil to be a natural upshot of free will: in the modern democratic state, avowedly founded on free will, the possibility of evil erupting constituted "a constant threat"; the democratic state, while publicly honoring freedom of will, hence simultaneously tried to control its outward expression; as a result, the culture of democracy drove "the germs of evil deep within," perversely increasing the danger that evil might erupt in an even more virulent form. It was this danger—made palpable by the terrorism of the French Revolution, which Sade famously deplored—that obsessed the divine Marquis. "It was necessary somewhere to strip bare the secret impulse of the revolutionary mass," Klossowski explained. "And this was not done in its political demonstrations since even when they beat to death, drowned, hanged, pillaged, burned, and raped, it was never other than in the name of the sovereign people." What superficially seems in the work of Sade to be an outpouring of the most vile and revolting fantasies Klossowski regarded as a hermetic exorcism of incalculable political consequence: "*This evil must, therefore, erupt once and for all; the bad seed has to flourish so the mind can tear it out and consume it.*"[130]

It is as if an "art of unbearable sensations"—an erotic theater of cruelty—might, as Foucault had put it in his 1978 interview with Le Bitoux, provoke "a kind of plunge beneath the water sufficiently prolonged that one returns from it with none of this appetite, with none of this torment one sometimes still feels, even after satisfying sexual relationships."[131]

"Michel Foucault was a man deeply attracted to power in its most totalitarian forms, politically and sexually," Edmund White remarked after his death. "Throughout his life, he struggled against this attraction. That is what I most admired about him."[132]

At the end of May in 1975, two days after Foucault experienced his epiphany in Death Valley, Simeon Wade took the philosopher to visit a self-styled "Taoist" commune, where a number of young men lived in cabins nestled on the slopes of Mount Baldy in Southern California. Foucault had asked to take the trip after meeting one of the residents of the commune, a beautiful young man, at a party the night before. And so, on a cool May morning in 1975, Wade and Foucault hiked up a trail that snaked past Ponderosa pines and large cedar trees. The air, as Wade recalls, was filled with the musky fragrance of chaparral. Both men were still savoring the afterglow of their LSD trip.[133]

When they arrived at the cabin, they found the young man who had caught Foucault's eye, a graduate student named David. He invited Foucault and Wade to come in and warm themselves by the fireplace while he made a pot of coffee. Learning of the distinguished visitor, the young men of the commune began to drift over to join the conversation. Moving on to the cabin's porch, where he could look out over the tops of pines and cedar trees further down the mountainside, Foucault entertained questions from the students surrounding him, enjoying, as he always did, the chance to play the role of a modern-day Socrates.

One of the young men plaintively remarked that he felt completely lost.

" 'You have to be lost as a young man,' " Wade recalls Foucault replying: " 'You are not really trying unless you are lost. That is a good sign. I was lost as a young man too.' "

" 'Should I take chances with my life?' " the student asked earnestly.

" 'By all means! Take risks, go out on a limb!'

" 'But I yearn for solutions.'

" 'There are no solutions,' " said the French philosopher firmly.

" 'Then at least some answers.'

" 'There are no answers!,' " exclaimed Foucault.[134]

The fire was dying, so Foucault volunteered to go chop some more wood. After selecting some pieces from a woodpile outside the cabin, he wielded the ax with such force that Wade, for one, was left dumbfounded. He snapped a photograph—an image long cherished by Foucault himself, who had the picture framed for display in the living room of his Paris apartment.[135]

After the group had gathered round the fireplace again, another one of the young men said that he felt he needed psychotherapy, and asked Foucault what kind he would recommend. " 'Freudian will be fine,' " said the philosopher.

Wade, who was steeped in the theories of Foucault's friend Deleuze, was surprised: "I would have thought 'schizoanalysis' would be more in order," said Wade, alluding to the mind-boggling vision of psychology that Deleuze and Guattari had elaborated in *Anti-Oedipus*.

Foucault roared with laughter.

Finally composing himself, he said, as Wade recalls, " 'There cannot be a general theory of psychoanalysis—*everyone must do it for themselves.*' "[136]

The group decided to hike up to a nearby pool in the rocks. While a few of the young men took a midday swim, the others gathered round the philosopher, who sat on a large rock beside a waterfall.

David resumed the conversation: " 'Michel, are you happy?' "

Foucault, as Wade recalls, perked up: " 'I am happy with my life,' " he said—but " '*not so much with my self.*' "

David was puzzled: " 'In other words,' " he asked, " 'you don't feel proud of yourself, but you are happy with the way your life has taken shape and is unfolding?' "

" 'Yes,' " said the philosopher.

" 'But it seems to me,' " said David, " 'that it is hard to make such a distinction. If you like the way your life has developed and you feel some sort of responsibility for it, then it seems you probably would feel good about yourself too.' "

" 'Well,' " Wade recalls Foucault responding, " 'I don't feel reponsible for what's happened to me in my life.' "

David was still puzzled: " 'But don't you think that Nietzsche believed that it is important to try to feel *the will* that you have within yourself as a person?' "

" 'No,' " said Foucault, " 'I don't think Nietzsche was saying that. . . . Nietzsche was saying how little a man is responsible for his nature, especially in terms of what he considered to be his morality. Morality has been constitutive of the individual's being. The individual is contingent, formed by the weight of moral tradition, not really autonomous.' "[137]

"No one is accountable for his deeds, no one for his nature; to judge is the same thing as to be unjust," Nietzsche had written in 1878.[138]

And so it had seemed to Foucault throughout his life.

The ability to transcend every fixed form—the capacity that Nietzsche called will to power—was, as Foucault reiterated in 1983, always "limited and determined." As Nietzsche had lamented a century before, "during the brief lifetime of a man, the effective motives are unable to scratch deeply enough to erase the imprinted script of many millennia."[139]

Still, as Foucault himself had also argued throughout his life, a human being, though trapped in "general structures," possessed certain resources with which it might escape their oppressive power, if only for a moment— and perhaps even "scratch" deeply enough to obliterate, however temporarily, "the imprinted script of many millennia."[140]

As he put it in a 1971 essay on Deleuze, a "perverse and theatrical exercise," by putting into play our "wicked will," might paradoxically produce a "sudden shift of the kaleidoscope, signs that light up for an instant, the results of the thrown dice, the outcome of another game."

Foucault's "kaleidoscope" had dramatically shifted in California in the spring of 1975.

Though it would take him years to collect his thoughts about what had happened, and to express his sentiments openly, he seems to have felt that his "ordeals of truth" on Folsom Street and in Death Valley, in concert with his experience of gay liberation in San Francisco, had imbued him not only with a new understanding of his sexuality, but also with a new feeling of power—and a new, and utterly unexpected, sense of freedom.

As a result of this "work done at the limit of ourselves," he was in "the position of beginning again."[141]

But where to start? And how to proceed?

9

THE DISTANT

R O A R

of

B A T T L E

THE GREAT HALL WHERE Henri Bergson once lectured was packed. Auditors crowded the aisles and spilled onto the floor in front of the dais. Students had erected a small forest of tape recorders around the table where Michel Foucault was to speak. A murmur greeted his appearance. Without ceremony, he cleared a path to his chair and sat down with his manuscript— he rarely spoke extemporaneously in these courses at the Collège de France. His papers illuminated by a small desk lamp, his gaze focused intensely, he started to read.[1]

He began by lamenting the inadequacy of his work to date. Such laments had become a ritualized feature of Foucault's rhetoric; still, on this occasion, inaugurating a new series of lectures on January 7, 1976 (and also facing his French public for the first time since his return from California), he sounded unusually vehement. His previous lectures, he complained, had been "diffuse and at the same time repetitive." Despite the ostensible variety of the topics discussed—truth, the penal code, psychiatric concepts—they had "continually re-trod the same ground, invoked the same themes, the same concepts, etc." "Repetitive and disconnected," his work perhaps "advances nowhere. Since indeed it never ceases to say the same thing, it perhaps says nothing." It was "tangled up," "indecipherable," "inconclusive," "disorganized," a "muddle."[2]

Of course, perhaps the appearance of disorganization was misleading: "I could claim," Foucault continued, "that these were only trails to be followed, no matter where they led." There is an echo here of Nietzsche's *Schopenhauer as Educator:* "In this world there is one unique path which no one but you may walk. Where does it lead? Do not ask; take it."[3]

"For my part," remarked Foucault, discreetly alluding to the peculiar character of his own "great Nietzschean quest," "it has struck me that I might have seemed a bit like a whale that leaps to the surface of the water disturbing it momentarily with a tiny jet of spray and lets it be believed, or pretends to believe, or wants to believe"—to "believe," in this matter, apparently involving dissimulation and the risk of self-deception—"that down in the depths where nobody sees him anymore, where he is no longer witnessed nor controlled by anyone, he follows a more profound, coherent, and reasoned trajectory."[4]

With his own sense of his otherwise submerged "self" having thus briefly surfaced in the improbable image of a sea monster, Foucault moved on to evoke one of the experiences that he had in common with a great many people in the room: their involvement in the political struggles symbolized by May '68.

"It seems to me," said Foucault, "that the work we have done could be justified by the claim that it is adequate to a restricted period, that of the last ten, fifteen, at most twenty years." This, in his view, was a period notable primarily for an "insurrection of subjugated knowledges." It had been an era of new social movements, to deinstitutionalize the insane, to shift the burden of guilt in crime, to express without shame impulses previously labeled "sick." But a new set of questions had been raised, precisely by the growing power of such movements: "Is the relation of forces today still such as to allow these disinterred knowledges some kind of autonomous life? Can they be isolated by these means from every subjugating relationship? What force do they have in themselves?"[5]

For the last few years, Foucault had approached such questions by exploring what he here called "Nietzsche's hypothesis"—namely, that "power is war, a war continued by other means." History staged but a single drama, an endlessly repeated play of conquest and revolt. In any society, the rulers exploited their power to regulate and to punish, engraving codes of logic and tables of law "on things and even within bodies," giving rise to a "universe of rules, which is by no means designed to soften violence, but rather to satisfy it." Even when a society seemed at peace, it was only the "promise of blood," however veiled, that quelled the constant danger of disorder, creating a pattern of latent combat in "social institutions, in economic inequalities, in language," and—last but not least—"in the bodies themselves of each and every one of us." Foucault's aim had long been to document "the fact of domination, to expose both its latent nature and its brutality," by amplifying the "distant roar of battle" behind the docile surfaces of modern life. The potential for renewed open combat was, after all, endless: depending on one's perspective, this was the most hopeful—or fearful—part of "Nietzsche's hypothesis." "Humanity does not gradually progress from combat to combat until it arrives at a universal reciprocity," Foucault wrote in 1971, summing up one of the most disquieting implications of his Nietzschean way of thought. "Humanity settles each one of its violences within a system of rules, and thus goes from domination to domination."[6]

It was this way of thinking that Foucault now wished to reconsider, "both because it is still insufficiently elaborated at a whole number of points," he said, "and because I believe that these two notions, of repression and war, must themselves be considerably modified if not ultimately abandoned." Social movements like gay liberation seemed on the verge of some kind of victory. But if these "liberation" movements were to be truly liberating—if they were to preserve "some kind of autonomous life"— they would need to elaborate some "new form of right," freed "from every subjugating relationship." And to *imagine* what form this new kind of "right" might take, it was critical to challenge—and, if possible, move beyond—"Nietzsche's hypothesis."[7]

Struggling with these unwonted political and ethical dilemmas, Foucault was plunged into a period of prolonged intellectual and personal crisis. Between 1968 and 1975, he had known what he wanted to say; politically, he had known where he wanted to go. This, for him, had been a time "of strength and jubilation, of creative gaiety," as Gilles Deleuze later recalled. In the years that followed, by contrast, Foucault struck Deleuze as "very different, more inward, perhaps more depressive, more secret." In ways that Deleuze sometimes found disagreeable, Foucault began to modify the character of his political commitments; he changed the direction of his research; as never before, he seemed uncertain about his "one unique path."[8]

The style of his lectures was symptomatic: no longer explosive and scintillating, Foucault's prose grew sober, cautious, occasionally even grim. His most important political statement in this period, his introduction to the History of Sexuality, left him dissatisfied. He turned restlessly from Nietzsche to Machiavelli to Ludwig von Mises. Hurling himself into new areas of inquiry, he tried to transform his theory of power, his understanding of politics—and, eventually, his approach to writing about that most elusive of subjects, the self.

None of this research unfolded smoothly; much of it was "tangled up" and "inconclusive," just as Foucault feared. Grappling with Nietzsche's hypothesis, he was, after all, grappling with himself, trying to unriddle a part of who he was—and of what he might yet become. It was not a straightforward process. Detours led to dead ends; lost and discouraged, he kept starting over again; at times, as one friend later recalled, he seemed "struck with boredom, or some awful doubt."[9] Still, he kept going. And to evoke this tortuous phase of his lifelong quest, it is wise to adhere to the surface of events, and to describe, in sequence, some of the ideas that he explored in public, and some of the actions that he took—looking for a new way to think.

In his lectures at the Collège de France in the winter of 1976, Foucault resorted to an old-fashioned technique he would use with growing frequency for the rest of his life. Turning himself into a philologist, he lived among texts. Despite the contemporary issues raised in his first two lectures—about how to elaborate some positive political foundation for the new social movements—he focused his subsequent inquiry quite narrowly, asking a specific historiographic question: "How and when did the belief arise that it is war that functions in power relations, that an uninterrupted combat is at work in peace, and that civil order is fundamentally a battle order?"[10]

Or, more pointedly still: "Who has sought in the noise and confusion of war, in the grime of battle, the principle of intelligibility, of order, of institutions, of history?"[11]

This question he illuminated with learned indirection, by examining at length the works of three early modern political theorists: Sir Edward Coke (1552–1634), the English parliamentary jurist who asserted the rule of law against the absolute right of kings; John Lilburne (1614–1657), the leader of the Levellers, a radically egalitarian Puritan political group that flourished briefly during the English Civil War of the 1640s; and Henri de Boulainvilliers (1658–1722), an influential critic of the theory of absolute monarchy so pithily summed up by Louis XIV: "*L'ètat, c'est moi.*"[12]

Despite a number of evident differences between these pioneering critics of monarchy, Foucault detected in all three a "new type of discourse," and a distinct new "form of analysis," which he defined in terms of three principal criteria:

First, the "subject who speaks in this discourse" does not—and cannot—"occupy the position of the jurist or the philosopher, namely the position of a universal subject," a disinterested umpire above the social fray. Unlike Solon, the legendary Greek lawgiver, or Kant (to borrow Foucault's own examples), the modern adversary of absolute power does not stand on the political sidelines: he is rather "in the battle; he has enemies; he is fighting for victory. No doubt he seeks to assert a right; but it is his own right that is at issue—a singular right, marked by a relation to conquest."[13]

Second, Coke, Lilburne, and Boulainvilliers all had recourse to historical arguments, based on bravura but deliberately misleading interpretations of archaic documents such as the Magna Carta. "This type of discourse develops entirely in the historical dimension," Foucault noted. "It does not undertake to gauge history, unjust governments, or abuses and violence by the ideal principle of a reason or law; on the contrary, it seeks to revive beneath the form of institutions and legislations the forgotten past of real struggles, of masked victories or defeats, the blood that has dried on the codes of law." A discourse that is "capable of bearing equally well the nostalgia of declining aristocracies and the ardor of popular vengeance," it does not shrink from using "traditional mythic forms," in order to compose essentially fictive histories to further the strategic aims of the author.[14]

Third, the recourse to history "turns the traditional values of intelligibility inside out." Though Coke, Lilburne, and Boulainvilliers go in quest of right and truth, they each regard "universal truth and general right" as "illusions or traps." They seek "the principle of decipherment" elsewhere, in "the confusion of violence, of passions, of hatred and revenge. . . . It is only above this entanglement that a growing rationality will be sketched out—a rationality which becomes more fragile, treacherous, and tied to illusions, to fantasies and mystifications, the higher we go and the more it develops. . . . The elliptical and somber God of battles must enlighten the long days of order, labor, and peace. Fury must explain the harmonies."[15]

If nothing else, this analysis amounts to an astonishing feat of intellectual ventriloquy: for at every turn, it is impossible not to hear, in Foucault's description of Coke, Lilburne, and Boulainvilliers, an even more vivid description of the author of *Discipline and Punish*.

The sense of veiled self-analysis became even stronger in the final lecture in this 1976 series, when Foucault surveyed some of the results of this "strategic" style of thought in the nineteenth century.

He began by reminding his listeners that Coke, Lilburne, and Boulainvilliers had all viewed the historical battle as primarily waged "between two hostile races who differ in their institutions and interests." For the

English theorists, the relevant conflict was between Saxon common law and the "Norman yoke" imposed by William the Conqueror; while for Boulainvilliers a century later, the crucial struggle was between an aristocracy claiming Germanic descent, and a degenerate monarchy willing to collude with "a bourgeoisie of Gallo-Romanic origin." In the nineteenth century, embattled aristocrats in France and Germany could seize on the element of racism in this way of thinking, and portray history as a "biological confrontation"; while liberals and socialists inspired by the "ardor of popular vengeance" in the same period could exploit this way of thinking in order to present history as a "class struggle." Foucault here referred to Augustin Thierry (1795–1856), a crusading liberal who was fascinated by the role of violence in securing rights—and the man Marx once called "*le père* of the 'class struggle' in French historiography."[16]

In this last lecture, however, Foucault did not linger over the texts of either Thierry or Marx. He rather proceeded to describe the emergence of a new kind of "bio-politics" in which the modern state tried to regulate the life of the populace as a whole, by policing health, hygiene, and public safety. These were all topics that Foucault would discuss again in the first volume of his History of Sexuality. But though he mentions sexuality in passing, his main emphasis in this last lecture falls, not on the Marquis de Sade and the morbid intertwining of sex and death (as it does in the book), but rather on the similarly morbid way in which modern *politics* has, in our day, become intertwined with the romance of a battle to the death. A way of thinking exemplified by Thierry thus issued, at the end of the century, in a variety of recipes for civil war, some concocted by reactionary nationalists—and others cooked up by revolutionary socialists.[17]

The new warriors of the far left and far right alike were fascinated by "the blood that has dried on the codes of law"—and disgusted by the efforts of the modern state to renounce its origins in violence. Despite profound ideological disagreements, both proto-fascists and militant socialists welcomed the prospect of naked violence: " 'in order to flourish,' " both implied, " 'it is necessary that you massacre your enemies.' " In his lecture, Foucault defined this fascination with civil war as a kind of "racism"; in *The Will to Know,* by contrast, he will speak, more simply, of "a preoccupation with blood."[18]

"Every time that socialism has been obliged to insist on the problem of struggle," he asserted, a preoccupation with blood has intensified; or, as Foucault put it in his lecture, using his own idiosyncratic language, "*racism has revived.*" The blood spilled in class warfare has been glorified as a means for forging a new kind of man; and in the struggle to eliminate "the adversary at the very heart of capitalist society," certain groups have been targeted for extinction. Foucault may seem to be exaggerating—until one recalls Stalin's forced starvation of Ukrainian "kulaks" in 1932–1933; or Stalin's similarly vicious effort in 1953 to purge Jews from positions of influence within the Soviet Union (the event that had provoked Foucault into leaving the French Communist Party); or, to to take a contemporary example, Pol Pot's liquidation of the urban population of Cambodia in 1975–1978.[19]

"As a result," Foucault concluded, "every time that you have socialisms, or forms of socialism, or moments of socialism that accent the problem of struggle, you have racism. Therefore the most racist forms of socialism have been, of course, Blanquism, the Commune, and anarchism. . . ."[20]

This list is astonishing. It singles out for criticism not only the conspiratorial tradition inaugurated by Auguste Blanqui (1805–1881), who pioneered clandestine and paramilitary techniques of revolt; but also the Paris Commune of 1871, perhaps the most important spontaneous popular uprising of the nineteenth century (famously celebrated by Karl Marx in his book *The Civil War in France*); and, in addition, the anti-authoritarian anarchists of the same period, relentless critics of the modern state— though they too, like Blanqui and the Paris Communards, did not shrink from acts of exemplary violence.

That all three of these examples come from the nineteenth century is slightly misleading. After all, Blanqui, the Communards, and the anarchists each defined enduring styles of violent revolt, emulated with some frequency in the twentieth century, not least by the international New Left of the 1960s. And though Foucault does not explicitly mention the renewal in France of these styles of militant revolt after May '68, no veteran of the *Gauche Prolétarienne* could mistake the contemporary resonance of his critique—a surprising climax to a surprising series of lectures.

But of what practical consequence was this veiled self-criticism?

"If one wants to look for a nondisciplinary form of power," Foucault had remarked at the beginning of his 1976 course at the Collège de France, "it is not toward the ancient right of sovereignty that one should turn" (as had Sade and Georges Bataille), "but toward the possibility of a new form of right," no longer haunted by the distant roar of battle. This possibility he never returned to in his lectures: just what this "new form of right" might look like remained a mystery.[21]

But it was a mystery he thought he could illuminate, as is clear from his next major piece of work—the first volume in his History of Sexuality.[22]

Foucault's new book appeared in December of 1976. Called *La volonté de savoir* (or "The Will to Know"), it was quickly rendered into the major European languages, appearing in English in 1978 under the somewhat misleading main title *The History of Sexuality*.

It is a very odd piece of work. An essay in methodology cast in the form of a polemic, it was aimed against a view then widespread on the international left: namely, that sexuality had been repressed in modern society. On the contrary, Foucault argues, sexuality is an *invention* of modern society—a new way of thinking, built around an idea first formulated in the nineteenth century, that each of us can be known, and defined, by our sexual instincts and desires.

The text is a tricky and complex performance, full of irony, packed with arresting ideas tossed out in passing, with no concern for documentation, and little effort at sustained argument. Assertive in style, passionate in tone, it is composed at such an elegantly high pitch of abstraction that concrete issues become difficult to keep in focus.

Puzzling as parts of the book were, its main polemical thrust was hard to miss in 1976. The common picture of repression, especially as it appears in the work of a Marxist Freudian like Wilhelm Reich, is much too simple. For all the taboos and prohibitions that still restrict our sexual freedom, we live in a world saturated with sex, and not just with talk about it. (Foucault, after all, had recently corroborated this point firsthand, in the gay subculture of San Francisco.) By placing under unprecedented scrutiny "the sexuality of children, madmen, and criminals," and detailing the sexual aspect of "reveries, obsessions, petty manias, and great transports of rage," modern science had paradoxically facilitated the spread of "polymorphous" sexual behavior, since the more attention was focused on sex, and the more information about unusual sexual acts was gathered and circulated, the easier it became to imagine committing such acts. ("Modern society is perverse," writes Foucault with understandable emphasis. "Not in spite of its puritanism, or as a consequence of its hypocrisy; it is truly and directly perverse.") The effort to outlaw certain sexual acts as "unnatural" has similarly backfired, producing still odder new forms of bodily delight. (As the rituals of S/M illustrate, even the most viciously repressive practices can be turned into erotically charged games, opening up unforeseen new possibilities of pleasure.) For all these reasons, the focus of the Marxist Freudians on the lifting of taboos and prohibitions can yield but a callow concept of "liberation." If sexuality and sex, like the body generally, are both shaped in depth through a kind of "bio-power," determining our corporeal sense of being in the world, then a simple declaration of sexual freedom will not, and cannot, by itself usher in a "New City" of erotic happiness. Merely removing the various legal and social sanctions that regulate and restrict outward sexual behavior would (among other things) leave intact the iron cage of guilt, its foundations laid deep in the unconscious, its cruel mnemotechnics silently (de)forming our somatic universe of impulses and desires, driving us, like it or not, into paroxysms of interminable self-analysis revolving around sexuality. (The apparent ineluctability of this obsession Foucault of course had experienced with special force during his LSD epiphany in Death Valley in May of 1975.)[23]

In an interview about the book, Foucault summed up the main problem as he saw it: "How is it that in a society like ours, sexuality is not simply a means of reproducing the species, the family, and the individual? Not simply a means to obtain pleasure and enjoyment? How has sexuality come to be considered the privileged place where our deepest 'truth' is read and expressed?"[24]

Grappling with this problem, it is worth pointing out, scarcely entails abandoning the repressive hypothesis *tout court*. Foucault's text rather invites us to transform our concept of how power functions, introducing nuance, complexity—and a feeling for radical paradox. Despite the alarming and sometimes apocalyptic tenor of his most startling assertions in these months—"power has made man into a sexual monster," he cheerfully declared in one interview—he consistently voiced a cockeyed, if cryptic sort of optimism about the future.[25]

"I am for the decentralization, the regionalization, the privatization of all pleasures," he exclaimed to a reporter from *L'Express* shortly after his book appeared. "We are inventing new pleasures! Beyond sex!" He went on to recount, with a wink, an inside joke: "A young man, just returned from a visit to the progressive milieu of California, had run straight to him to announce, rapturously, the glad news: 'Erections are out!'"[26]

But the possibilities that Foucault here alluded to were so remote from the lives of most readers that the book left a good many of them either puzzled or confused. Despite a raft of glowing reviews, the author was disappointed. He had wanted to shake people up, to make them think in new ways, to provoke a fresh discussion, particularly on the left. But a great many readers, particularly on the left, seemed to mistake the signs of his perplexity—his critique of the idea of repression, his recommenced inquiry into the possible forms of power, his summons to transcend "sex-desire"—as authorizing a new set of dogmas. And nobody, he lamented, was willing (or perhaps able) to discuss the book's crucial but enigmatic closing chapter, about the "Right of Death and Power over Life."[27]

On one level, of course, he had only himself to blame. A large part of the problem lay in the hermetic style of his prose, particularly in the final pages of the book. The arcana of his own peculiar "erotics of truth" he had chosen to transmit only under a "stamp of secrecy."[28]

But this was not the sole source of misunderstanding. As Foucault came to recognize, the reception of *The Will to Know* was symptomatic, as well, of larger social forces that were in the midst of transforming the means of intellectual production in these years. In 1945, Sartre had become a global celebrity thanks to a public lecture, "Existentialism is a Humanism"; in 1966, Foucault would accomplish the same feat, thanks largely to a prominent review of *The Order of Things* in a mass-circulation newsmagazine; ten years later, the chief medium shaping the Parisian market for new ideas had become, not the public lecture or the prominent book review, but rather the repartee broadcast weekly on *Apostrophes,* a television show about books launched in 1974 by a literary impresario named Bernard Pivot. The extraordinary popularity of Pivot's roundtable discussions— some three million viewers stayed home to watch *Apostrophes* every Friday night—dramatically widened the intellectual's potential audience, while reinforcing the tendency, already strong in Paris, to treat philosophical treatises as fashion statements, emblems of status to be displayed on coffee tables.[29]

"What happens," Foucault explained to a German interviewer in 1983, "is that a fairly evolved discourse, instead of being relayed by additional work which perfects it (either with criticism or amplification), rendering it more difficult and even finer, nowadays undergoes a process of amplification from the bottom up. Little by little, from the book to the review, to the newspaper article, and from the newspaper article to television, we come to summarize a work, or a problem, in terms of slogans. . . . It took fifteen years to convert my book about madness into a slogan: in the eighteenth century, all mad people were confined. But it did not take even fifteen months—it only took three weeks—to convert my book on the will to know into the slogan 'sexuality has never been repressed.' "[30]

Foucault himself appeared only once on *Apostrophes*—but it was a memorable show. Invited to speak about *The Will to Know* in December of 1976, Foucault insisted in talking instead about another book entirely, about the trial of a Soviet dissident. Bernard Pivot was incredulous: "So you really don't want to talk about your book?" Foucault was adamant: "Finishing a book," he said, "is not wanting to see it anymore." He found it impossible to keep a straight face. Years later, on the night that he died, a clip from the *Apostrophes* appearance—his last on French television—was broadcast again. It showed the philosopher, dressed stiffly in a three-piece suit, exploding in laughter, "literally cracking up," as one old friend marvelled, "at a moment when everyone expected him to be as serious as the pope and to pontificate about some declaration in his subversive history of behavior. . . ."[31]

Foucault's latest provocation was soon enough forgotten, as the intelligentsia of Paris plunged headlong into a burlesque re-run of debates from the first years of the Cold War. Shortly after *The Will to Know* appeared, a new philosophical vogue swept through Paris, propelled by the appearance on *Apostrophes* of two dashing younger writers, Bernard-Henri Lévy and—in a startling about-face—André Glucksmann, the veteran of May '68 and the *Gauche Prolétarienne*. Suddenly their pictures seemed to be everywhere: on magazines, on television spots, on posters, on t-shirts. Promoted like rock stars, they were immodestly christened, by Lévy himself, "the new philosophers." And in a matter of days, the crux of their "philosophy" (if that is the right word) had been reduced to a jingle: "Marxism is dead."[32]

Since Marxism had been criticized and rejected some thirty years before by a great many intellectuals in North America and Europe—and since the level of the French debate was often shockingly low—the controversy over "the new philosophers" is easy to ridicule. As one observer acidly quipped, a great many French intellectuals reacted "as if the liberty of individuals were a new idea"—and the tyranny of communism a fresh discovery. Still, as Foucault had reason to recognize, serious issues were at stake—particularly in Glucksmann's *Les maîtres penseurs* (translated into English in 1980 as *The Master Thinkers*).[33]

The culmination of a theoretical odyssey that had begun some five years before, when he stepped away from the French Maoist movement, Glucksmann's book was baroque, convoluted—and, beneath the florid rhetorical trimmings, an unmistakable *cri du coeur*. How had he—and his genera-

tion—fallen prey to murderous political fantasies? One answer, Glucksmann argued, lay in the sacred texts they had been reared on. Hegel, Marx,
and Nietzsche had offered dogmatic certainties and final solutions, raising
"to the level of the speakable," as Glucksmann put it, "that will to power
which inspires, more pettily, more covertly, the bosses and under-bosses
of disciplinary societies." One logical result of such philosophical *hubris,*
in his view, was Auschwitz; another was the Gulag. The right wing had
no monopoly on evil.[34]

Whatever its other merits, Glucksmann's book was a trenchant piece
of self-criticism. The totalitarian impulse, as he stressed, was not something
external, to be smugly denounced as it appeared in others: rather, this
impulse affected *"everyone."* Each of us was "dual," caught in the snares
of power, and prey to the temptation to abuse it. And "if one takes account
of this internal division," he concluded, "it becomes impossible to imagine
a single, ultimate revolution, wherein good and bad face each other in a
decisive battle."[35]

For some veterans of May '68, these were fighting words. Many of
Glucksmann's old allies—Gilles Deleuze, for one—were sufficiently
provoked by *The Master Thinkers* to respond, often in tones of bitter
derision.[36]

Foucault, however, took a sharply different tack. In a prominent review,
printed in *Le Nouvel Observateur,* he emphatically praised Glucksmann's
account. "In the Gulag," wrote Foucault, elaborating a theme he had
broached the year before in his lectures on war and class struggle, "one
sees not the consequences of any unhappy mistake, but the effects of the
'truest' of theories in the political order." The fact that Stalin's atrocities
had occurred in the name of a revolutionary ideal called into question the
ideal itself—and not simply Stalin's understanding of it. "What is the
Revolution?" Foucault now asked, posing even more radically one of the
implications of *The Will to Know:* "Can it, should it, begin anew? If it is
incomplete, is it necessary to finish it? If it is finished, what other history
now begins? What henceforth is to be done to make the Revolution, or
to avert it?"[37]

"Glucksmann does not invoke a new Dionysus beneath Apollo," Foucault concluded. "In the heart of the most lofty philosophical discourse,
he conjures up its fugitives, its victims, its implacable enemies, its constantly redressed dissidents—in short, its '*blood-soaked heads*'." Coming
from the Nietzschean philosopher who, five years before, had commended
"the old German custom" of parading the heads of slaughtered enemies
on stakes, this was a telling turnabout. In so many words, Foucault was

ratifying Glucksmann's political metamorphosis—and joining in his gesture of political self-renunciation.[38]

Gilles Deleuze could not mistake the shift in his old friend's attitude. For more than a decade, he and Foucault had searched together for "Dionysus beneath Apollo." But now their alliance was at an end.

On the level of philosophy, it was possible to read Foucault's critique of "sex-desire" in *The Will to Know* as a veiled critique, as well, of Deleuze and Guattari's *Anti-Oedipus*—a book, after all, profoundly influenced by Wilhelm Reich. Deleuze in fact privately reacted, writing Foucault a detailed response.[39]

Shortly afterward, Foucault abruptly decided that he would see no more of Deleuze. "This was a crazy side of Foucault," says one friend, "a personal difficulty of his at this time." In the years that followed, the two philosophers would occasionally exchange ideas by mail. But they would never again meet face-to-face.[40]

Their political differences began to multiply. Their views now diverged on the value of Marxism and on the legacy of May '68. In matters of Middle-Eastern politics, Deleuze was staunchly pro-Palestinian, while Foucault was just as staunchly pro-Israeli.[41]

And then there was the question of left-wing terrorism, which arose again in France late in 1977. The occasion this time was not an act of violence by French ultra-leftists, since the Maoist movement had by now largely disappeared. It was, rather, a legal *cause célèbre* involving Klaus Croissant, the principal German lawyer representing the Baader-Meinhof gang. Facing a sentence in Germany for illegally passing matériel to members of the terrorist group in prison, Croissant had been smuggled into France, where he requested political asylum. Germany asked that the lawyer be extradited; and as the French government moved to comply with this request, protest erupted on the French left, sparking the usual round of manifestos, denunciations, demonstrations, and, at the prison in Paris where Croissant was being held, a violent confrontation with the police.[42]

Foucault and Deleuze both fought against Croissant's extradition—but by invoking sharply different criteria. Deleuze not only wished to protest Croissant's plight, but also to protest what he regarded as Germany's "state terrorism," implicitly endorsing the image of the government held by the Baader-Meinhof gang itself. Foucault, on the other hand, couched his own position in terms of *right*. "There exists a right, to have a lawyer who speaks for you, with you, who allows you to be heard and to preserve your life, your identity and the force of your refusal," Foucault wrote in *Le Nouvel Observateur*. "This right is not a juridical abstraction, nor is it some dreamy ideal; this right forms part of our historical reality and must not be erased from it." By defending a client's right to have a lawyer, Foucault in effect was upholding a political agenda not only at odds with that of the Baader-Meinhof gang—but also at odds with his own previous convictions about "popular justice."[43]

Years later, Deleuze would make three points about the rupture in what had been one of the most important intellectual associations in his life—and, certainly, one of the most important in Foucault's life, as well.

"First of all," Deleuze explained, "it is evident that there is not a single answer" to the simple question, "What happened?" "One of us might give one answer one day, and another answer another day. Not out of fickleness. But this is a domain where reasons are multiple, no one being 'essential.' Precisely because no one of these reasons is essential, there are always several simultaneously involved. The only important thing is that for a long time I had followed [Foucault] politically; and at a certain moment, I no longer totally shared his evaluation of many issues.

"Second, this did not entail an 'alienation' between us, nor does it require a 'commentary.' We saw each other less often by force of circumstance, and therefore it became for us more and more difficult to see each other again. Oddly, it was not out of disagreement that we stopped seeing each other, but on the contrary, it was because we no longer saw each other that a kind of incomprehension, or distance, settled in.

"Third, I can tell you to what extent I have constantly and increasingly regretted not seeing him. What kept me from calling him on the telephone? It is here that there arises a reason more profound and more essential than all the others. Rightly or wrongly, I believed that he desired a deeper solitude, for his life, for his thought, and that he had need of this solitude, maintaining relationships only with his closest friends. I now think that I should have tried to see him again, but I did not think to try, out of respect.

"I suffer still for not having seen him again, all the more so because I do not believe that there was any apparent reason."[44]

For the academic year 1977–1978, Foucault was slated to present a series of lectures at the Collège de France entitled "Security, Territory and Population." (He had given no lectures the year before, because he was on sabbatical.) The title, with its reference to "population," suggested that the philosopher would pick up where he had left off in 1976, discussing racism, class struggle, and the virulence of "vital massacres" in recent history, deepening the analysis of "bio-politics" sketched in the last chapter of *The Will to Know*.

As one of Foucault's closest associates at the Collège would later recall, the course did not go as planned.

"For a long time," says this witness, "Foucault didn't know where he was going. To me, this period seemed very difficult for him. I remember it well, it was the Christmas holidays, and I spoke with Foucault about his upcoming lectures. They were to be about issues from the last chapter of *The Will to Know*. But Foucault told me it was too difficult; and he did not know what he could speak about. Foucault was secretive, so we can't know his feelings. But it is clear that it was a time of crisis for him. When the series of lectures began," on January 11, 1978, "nobody could have foreseen that the subject would be absolutely different."[45]

Every week, Foucault's associate at the Collège watched as Foucault struggled with his material. "When you heard each lecture," he says, "you heard the suffering, the *pain*. It was absolutely clear."[46]

Foucault began predictably, by talking about security and bio-politics. But then, abruptly—shortly after the course had started, his associate recalls—"he stopped. He could not go on. And it was clear that this problematic, of bio-politics, was over for him—it was *finished*.

"His approach changed. But he still didn't know where he was going."[47]

In his 1978 lectures, Foucault turned abruptly to a new topic—what he came to call "governmentality." The unwieldy neologism indicated his interest not only in the political aspects of government, but also in its pedagogical, spiritual, and religious dimensions. Still trying to understand "how we have been trapped in our own history," he now began to analyze how we had been brought to think about a series of interrelated questions: "How to govern oneself, how to be governed, how to govern others, how to accept the one who is to govern us, how to become the best possible governor, etc."[48]

He speculated that the modern approach to such questions had first crystallized in the sixteenth century, in response to two intersecting processes: the rise of "the great territorial, administrative, and colonial states," which made it necessary to manage large and varied populations; and the religious warfare between Protestants and Catholics, which made urgent "the manner in which one is to be spiritually ruled and led on this earth in order to achieve eternal salvation."[49]

In these circumstances, Foucault argued, early modern theorists of government began to combine two previously disparate ways of thinking. On the one hand, secular philosophers had long approached the art of government in worldly terms alone: it was the goal of the statesman to manage conflict and protect the territory of the city, insuring harmony and peace. Theologians, by contrast, had approached the art of government in terms that were explicitly *other*worldly: the goal of the "pastoral" leader was spiritual; seeing to the salvation of souls, he would watch over the conscience of each individual like a shepherd guarding his sheep. In the sixteenth and seventeenth centuries, Foucault hypothesized, these two ways of thinking came together in practice for the first time. The result was a hybrid new art of government, concerned as never before with regulating and monitoring the outward *and* inward life of each and every citizen.[50]

As he had in 1976, Foucault explored his hypothesis largely through a close reading of various texts, primarily classical treatises about the art of government and "*raison d'État.*" For example, in the fourth lecture in the series, the only one published in his lifetime, he analyzed the influence of Machiavelli, and also offered an interpretation of *The Mirror of Policy,* a relatively obscure work, published in 1555 by Guillaume de La Perrière, who enunciated an ideal of the political commonwealth as a harmoniously ordered whole in conjunction with an apology for unlimited royal sovereignty.[51]

The rise of "the great forms and economies of power in the West" Foucault now divided schematically into three stages. First came a "State of justice," consolidated in the Middle Ages, and organized through customs and laws that aimed to integrate each citizen into the life of the community. Next, in the sixteenth century, appeared an "administrative," or "police State," organized through new techniques of pedagogy and political science that sought a "concrete, precise, and measured knowledge as to the state's strength" in order to rule the lives of individuals "in such a way that their development also fosters that of the strength of the state." Finally came what Foucault called the "governmental State," refined in the eighteenth and nineteenth centuries, that wielded an unprecedented kind of power to determine the fate of individuals and the destiny of peoples.[52]

The cumulative result of this long development, as Foucault summed it up in a 1979 interview, was that political power "now reaches the very grain of the individual, touches his body, intrudes into his gestures, his attitudes, his discourse, his apprenticeship, his daily life."[53]

Foucault's lectures on "governmentality" are erudite, incisive, and often provocative—a tribute to his own unflagging (and all too rare) ability to rethink and reconceptualize fundamental issues in social and political thought. There is nevertheless a certain irony about his work in these months. Despite the deployment of fresh historical evidence and the marshalling of a new battery of concepts, the disposition of forces described at the end of his research into "governmentality" is essentially the same as that described in the pages of *Discipline and Punish*. On one side stands an all but omnipotent machine of government, meticulously designed to etch the Law into "the very grain of the individual"; while on the other side stands the solitary human being, its instinct for freedom pushed back, incarcerated, and "finally able to vent itself only on itself"—just as the *Genealogy of Morals* had suggested.[54]

Try as he might, Foucault, it seems, could not get beyond Nietzsche's hypothesis; and in the distance we must still hear "the roar of battle."

In these months, as one of his closest associates at the Collège de France recalls, Foucault had begun to read the early church fathers: Augustine, Ambrose, Jerome, Benedict. Analyzing in one context early modern political thought, he was concentrating in another on the earliest Christian thinking about the soul and its proper care, still in doubt about how to reorganize his History of Sexuality—still uncertain about where to start over.[55]

On May 27, 1978, Foucault addressed the *Société française de philosophie*. Speaking before the same society of philosophers nine years before, he had pondered a question that the vogue for semiotics had made pressing, asking "What is an author?" On this occasion, as if to mark a certain symmetry, Foucault broached a question that his own political itinerary had made pressing, asking "What is critique?"[56]

The word itself had been given fresh currency in the 1970s, when a renewed enthusiasm for "critique" spawned a variety of "minor polemical-professional activities," as Foucault rather archly refers to the outpouring of left-wing social criticism in this period. Though Kantian in its modern provenance, as Foucault duly notes, "critique" was a term that Marx had made his own, fashioning "A Contribution to the Critique of Political Economy." For both Marx and Kant, the purpose of critique was to render explicit what otherwise would remain implicit, bringing to light buried assumptions that regulated the way we think, and submitting these assumptions to public examination. In Kant's work, critique revealed the limits of reason, as well as the indomitable urge of the human spirit to pass beyond those limits; in Marx's work, on the other hand, critique revealed how the categories of modern economics corresponded to "the conditions and relations of a definite, historically determined mode of production."[57]

Foucault's own concept of "critique" was remarkable on a number of counts, not the least being the idiosyncratic way in which he interpreted this historical tradition. He approached "critique" not as an instrument used by certain German theorists, but rather as an "attitude," or "a virtue in general." Hence his preliminary definition of "critique" as "the art of not being governed, or, better still"—since this art always arose in a specific historical context—"the art of not being governed in a certain way and at a certain price."[58]

This "art," Foucault hypothesized, had first taken shape not in the work of Kant or Marx, but rather in the heretical practices of dissenting religious sects during the Reformation, when Protestants challenged the authority of the Catholic church. From the world of religion, the new art passed into the world of secular political thought, as parliamentary and republican critics of absolutism (one thinks of Coke and Lilburne) began to assert "universal and imprescriptible rights." Finally, in the seventeenth and eighteenth centuries, the critical attitude assumed a philosophical significance, as a variety of thinkers undertook a fresh examination of the character of knowledge in general by attacking prejudice and superstition, and raising anew the "problem of certainty in the face of authority." As Foucault summed up this long historical development, "I would say that critique is the movement by which the subject is given the right to discover the truth" by exercising "an art of voluntary insubordination, of thoughtful disobedience."[59]

The first surprise in this account is the stress it places on the refusal of a subject to be "subjected." The second surprise comes when Foucault immediately links this idiosyncratic account with Immanuel Kant's famous definition of "enlightenment."

Kant had offered his definition in an essay that addressed the question "What is enlightenment?" It was first published in 1784, three years after the first edition of his *Critique of Pure Reason* had appeared. "Enlightenment is man's exit from his self-incurred tutelage," Kant had written. "Tutelage is man's inability to make use of his understanding without direction from another. Self-incurred is this tutelage when its cause lies not in lack of reason but in lack of resolution and courage to use it without direction from another. *Sapere aude!* [Dare to know!] 'Have courage to use your own reason!'—that is the motto of enlightenment."[60]

As Foucault reads this definition—which he tacitly endorses as a fitting description of his lifework—the emphasis falls on *courage,* as the specific virtue of the "will to know"; and, above all, on the admonition "to use your *own* reason," a stress that, in effect, transforms Kant's injunction into a precursor of Nietzsche's injunction, to discover "the meaning of your *own* life."

After Kant, it is indeed Nietzsche who perhaps came closest to describing "the problem of enlightenment" as Foucault himself understood it. Philosophers, Nietzsche had written some one hundred years after Kant's essay, "must no longer accept concepts as a gift, nor merely purify and polish them, but first *make* and *create* them, present them and make them convincing. Hitherto one has generally trusted one's concepts as if they were a wonderful dowry from some sort of wonderland." But this trust must be replaced by mistrust: "What is needed above all"—and this is where the Nietzschean "will to know" finds its true vocation—"is an absolute skepticism toward all concepts." Hence "critique."[61]

Posed in such terms, Foucault considers "the problem of enlightenment" to be, after all, *the* central problem of modern philosophy. For how can one evaluate inherited concepts? How might one acquire the "attitude"— and summon the "courage"—necessary to think for oneself? Through what styles of reasoning—and through what art of living—might one escape from one's "self-incurred tutelage?"

Questions like these had been taken up in a variety of different ways by a variety of different modern philosophers, from Hegel to Marx to Schopenhauer and Wittgenstein, from Nietzsche and Heidegger to Karl Popper and Gaston Bachelard.

Foucault's own approach, as he described it on this occasion, had been to decipher "the relationship between power, truth, and the subject," through "a certain practice that one could call historical-philosophical." By design, his practice was, literally, inimitable: "It is a question, in fact," says Foucault, "of making oneself one's *own* history" by carefully sorting through the unique "dowry" of concepts one has inherited, while trying simultaneously to forge *new* concepts, "fabricated as in a fiction."[62]

That a fictive kind of conceptual history should claim the mantle of

Kantian critique is strange enough; but that is not the end of the peculiarities with Foucault's approach to "the problem of enlightenment." For unlike Kant (and Marx, too), Foucault had made no effort, so he said, to establish "what is true and false, founded or unfounded, real or illusory, scientific or ideological, legitimate or abusive." By studying the different ways human beings at different times have thought about madness, crime, and disease, he was simply trying "to know what links and connections can be discovered between mechanisms of coercion and elements of understanding," thus calling into question what previously had seemed unquestionable. "It wasn't as a matter of course that mad people came to be regarded as mentally ill; it wasn't self-evident that the only thing to be done with a criminal was to lock him up, it wasn't self-evident that the causes of illness were to be sought through the individual examination of bodies; and so on."[63]

Merely "to describe the nexus of knowledge and power" in this fashion, he asserted, is to make that nexus intolerable—for what the historical-philosophical critique reveals is the "arbitrariness" of understanding, and the "violence" of power.[64]

But why should a simple description of arbitrariness and violence provoke any reaction at all?

Because, responds Foucault, games of truth are by their nature "always variable and uncertain" thanks to "the logic of interactions" among human beings. The order of things to some extent always depends on "subjects, on types of behavior, on decisions, on choices." Instead of bending before the arbitrariness and violence of what had previously seemed to be self-evidently true, the human being can always summon the courage to resist and think differently.[65]

It was on this note that Foucault concluded his talk. "If it is necessary to pose the question of the understanding in its relation to domination"—and by 1978, he evidently thought that it was—then "it must above all be by starting from *a certain decisive will not to be governed.*"[66]

The philosophers in his audience were struck by the strangeness of this conclusion, particularly coming from Michel Foucault.

The talk finished, Foucault fielded questions. One interlocutor wondered whether his approach did not depend on an "occult foundation." Beneath the discursive practices he had so meticulously described in his books on madness and punishment, there seemed to be a "kind of common essence of knowledge and power"—an essence, the questioner commented, that "I am obliged to call the will to power."[67]

"Absolutely," Foucault responded. "There, precisely, I have been insufficiently clear." For outside of "the braided network" of power and knowledge there did indeed, in his view, exist something else—something evidently like "the *transcendens* pure and simple," the unconditioned capacity to pass spontaneously beyond any and every specified limit that Kant had called "freedom," and Nietzsche "will to power." Just what this "something" was, however, Foucault had trouble specifying: one is reminded of Kant, who once remarked that "*the inscrutability of the idea of freedom* precludes all positive presentation." Still, he agrees with his interlocutor that it is just this occult "essence" that "I have been trying to make appear," as a "kind of glimmering," at the limits of his "historical-philosophical practice."[68]

"You have spoken . . . of 'the decisive will not to be governed,'" remarked another member of the audience. "Shouldn't this last proposition itself be made the object of an interrogation, of a questioning?" If the critical attitude in Foucault's account rested in an act of will, what more could be said about this act?[69]

"If one wishes to carry on an exploration of this dimension of critique," Foucault responded, one must turn away from philosophy in the narrow sense, and think about the ways in which freedom has appeared in history, through the "practice of revolt." Surveying the period since the Renaissance, "what forcibly strikes me," volunteered Foucault—"though I am perhaps haunted because these are things that preoccupy me a great deal right now"—is an "astonishing" convergence between the "spiritual" struggle of the individual to escape from the grip of power, and the "political struggle" of a collectivity to change the outward institutions of government. Comparing Marxism in our own day to Protestantism in the sixteenth century, Foucault remarked that they seemed similar to him in their "manner of being" and in the kind of ineffable "hope" both had aroused—for an abrupt transfiguration of both consciousness and society.[70]

In this regard, he concluded, perhaps it was necessary to reexamine the whole problem of the will in relation to "*mysticism.*" After all, individual mystics had appeared historically, in the Reformation, not as the foes of enlightened "critique," but rather as unwitting partisans, defining "one of the first great forms of revolt in the West"—and helping to make manifest, and then defend in principle, the otherwise hidden experience of freedom.[71]

A few weeks later, Foucault enjoyed one of the most important mystical experiences of his life. It was July, and the philosopher, in quest of "those incredibly intense joys that I am looking for and that I am not able to experience, to afford by myself," had been smoking opium.[72]

Leaving his apartment, he started to walk across the rue de Vaugirard. That was where the car hit him.

He was thrown to the ground. Time seemed to stop. He saw himself leaving his body.[73]

Entering an orphic dimension that had long ago captured his imagination, he felt enraptured.[74]

Foucault survived. But the accident confirmed one of his oldest convictions: Death was nothing to fear. On the contrary. Approaching the "limit beyond all limits," he had experienced a rare sort of bliss: dying seemed to be just as "unspeakably pleasurable" as Sade had promised it would be.

"I think that pleasure is a very difficult behavior," Foucault explained to an interviewer in 1982. "It's not as simple as that"—he laughed—"to enjoy one's self. And I must say that's my dream. I would like and I hope I'll die of an overdose"—he laughed again—"of pleasure of any kind. Because I think it's really difficult and I always have the feeling that I do not feel *the* pleasure, the complete total pleasure and, for me, it's related to death."[75]

His interviewer was startled: "Why would you say that?"

"Because I think that the kind of pleasure I would consider as *the* real pleasure," responded the philosopher, "would be so deep, so intense, so overwhelming that I couldn't survive it. I would die. I'll give you a clearer and simpler example. Once I was struck by a car in the street. I was walking. And for maybe two seconds I had the impression that I was dying and it was really a very, very intense pleasure. The weather was wonderful. It was seven o'clock during the summer. The sun was descending. The sky was very wonderful and blue and so on. It was, it still is now, one of my best memories."[76]

He laughed again.

Every forty days, the crowds would appear, to mourn the dead; every forty days, the police would attack, producing more martyrs. A country with one of the most lethal armies in the world was sinking into chaos, faced with a population suddenly eager to die. All the tanks, bombs, and machine guns in the nation's arsenal were helpless to stem the tide of suicidal revolt. In every town, in every quarter of every large city, disem-bodied voices preached mystical sermons from cassette recorders. Burning with religious zeal, preoccupied more with spiritual immortality than with victory in a looming civil war, their message was harsh and unflinching, as if tapping into some elemental and long-forgotten yearning, conjuring up the unquiet spirits of Savonarola in Florence, John of Leyden in Münster, the Levellers in the time of Cromwell.[77]

Such was the uncanny character of events in Iran in the fall of 1978— at least as Michel Foucault understood them. Perhaps the spirit of revo-lution was not dead after all; perhaps a revolt against entrenched power was still possible; perhaps an "art of not being governed" might be forged without techniques of discipline, and without recourse to an armed class struggle, through a kind of tragic liturgy of suffering and death, unleashing, through ritualized demonstrations of defiance, the latent counter-power of a people, both to topple a regime—and to transfigure itself spiritually.[78]

About one crucial thing Foucault was not mistaken: the revolt in Iran really was, in the words of one soberly academic expert, "one of the greatest populist explosions in human history."[79]

The roots of the unrest ran deep: a long history of opposition to the secularizing policies of the Iranian monarchy on the part of the country's independent Shi'ite religious leadership; a growing popular resentment of the regime's subservience to Western and specifically American interests; the corruption and growing brutality of the Shah's increasingly megalo-maniacal rule, enforced by his feared secret police force SAVAK, notorious for its cruelty and use of torture.[80]

The latest cycle of unrest in Iran had begun on January 8, 1978, when police had fired into a crowd of seminarians in the shrine city of Qom, a center of traditional Shiah learning. The crowd had been calling for the return of the Shiah religious leader, the Ayatollah Khomeini, a longtime critic of the government of the Shah of Iran. When the guns fell silent, some twenty seminarians were dead—martyrs to the cause of revolt.

Forty days after a death, Shiah Muslims gather to mourn the dead. Every forty days for the next fourteen months, Shiah mourners poured into the streets of major cities around Iran, honoring the martyrs, defying the regime, provoking violent retaliation from the Shah's police, producing still more martyrs. Slowly, inexorably, as more and more people experi-enced the death of a friend or relative, Iranians were drawn into a com-munity of grief, in which the days of mourning became occasions for an outpouring of vehement protest, bolstered by the growing willingness of a growing number of people to die.[81]

Some months before, Foucault had been invited by the editors of the Italian daily newspaper *Corriere della Sera* to contribute a column. His curiosity piqued by the events in Iran, Foucault suggested that he be dispatched there to gather information for a series of essays. Becoming a journalist was a longstanding fantasy of Foucault's; but he also viewed the possibility of a visit to Iran as a part of his ongoing effort to redefine the vocation of the intellectual. "I was thinking that it was a role that the intellectual ought to play," Foucault remarked in the fall of 1978, explaining his interest in Iran: "to go see what was happening, rather than referring to what was taking place abroad without being informed in a way that was precise, meticulous and, to the extent possible, generous."[82]

The editors of *Corriere della Sera* agreed to dispatch Foucault to Iran (it is not unusual for European newspapers to solicit reports from famous intellectuals). And so Foucault found himself on an airplane headed for Tehran in September of 1978, hoping to learn more about a revolt that had already astonished most outside observers in its duration, scope, and growing strength.

He landed shortly after the revolt had reached a new pitch of passion, provoked by the massacre, on "Black Friday," September 8, of scores of protesters in Tehran—an event that, more than any other single episode, transformed the majority of Iranians from passive spectators into revolutionary actors.

"When I arrived in Iran, immediately after the September massacres," Foucault later recalled, "I said to myself that I was going to find a terrorized city, because there had been four thousand dead. Now I can't say that I found happy people, but there was an absence of fear and an intensity of courage, or rather, the intensity that people were capable of when danger, though still not removed, had already been transcended."[83]

As in Tunisia a decade before, Foucault was transfixed by the spectacle of a people united by "the craving, the taste, the capacity, the possibility of an absolute sacrifice." At first, though, he aimed for some degree of journalistic objectivity in the dispatches he filed from Tehran. Working with a research assistant and seeking out the company of other foreign journalists, the neophyte reporter interviewed a variety of sources, talking to representatives of the Shah's army, to American advisers, to political opposition leaders like Mehdi Bazargan and Abol Hassan Bani-Sadr, and also to the Ayatollah Shari'atmadari, at the time widely regarded as the most influential of Iran's mainstream religious leaders.[84]

In his first articles, Foucault duly noted the growing xenophobia of the anti-government demonstrations, and also the currency of anti-Semitic sentiments. More clearly than many foreign reporters, he also grasped the religious dimensions of the revolt. As he wrote in his third dispatch for *Corriere della Sera*, published on October 8, " 'Shi'ism,' confronted with an established power, arms its faithful with an unrelenting impatience. It inspires in them an ardor that is simultaneously political and religious."[85]

Again and again, he went out of his way to stress that the religious opponents of the Shah were *not*, as they were often glibly portrayed in the Western media, "fanatics." The mullahs struck him as creditable megaphones for the popular will, amplifying "the anger and aspirations of the community." He believed that the professed goal of establishing a new "Islamic government" held out the promise of a welcome new form of "*political spirituality*," unknown in the West "since the Renaissance and the great crises of Christianity." With good reason, Foucault viewed the commanding but distant figure of the Ayatollah Khomeini, who was still in exile, as a kind of mythic "saint," engaged in a larger-than-life struggle against an equally mythic "king." Khomeini's own agenda, however, he scarcely paused to examine, perhaps because he took him to be a figurehead—a mistake made by more than one leader of Iran's secular opposition in these months.[86]

As the weeks passed and the revolt continued to gather strength, Foucault's enthusiasm only grew. In November, he returned to Iran; and reporting on this visit, his prose reached a new pitch of chiliastic fervor. Writing in the issue of *Corriere della Sera* published on November 26, he wondered if Iran might not be "the first great insurrection against the planetary system, the most mad and most modern form of revolt." The Iranians were struggling not simply against the Shah, but also against "global hegemony." They were trying to change not only the form of government but the shape of their everyday lives, casting off "the weight of the order of the entire world." Inspirited by a "religion of combat and sacrifice," they had forged an authentically "collective will," producing that rarest of historical phenomena—the possibility of a total "transfiguration of this world."[87]

The generosity—and folly—of Foucault's response to the Iranian revolution brings to mind one of Immanuel Kant's most famous remarks about the French Revolution. "The revolution of a gifted people," Kant had written in a work published in 1798, "may succeed or miscarry; it may be filled with misery and atrocities to the point that a sensible man, were he boldly to hope to execute it successfully the second time, would never resolve to make the experiment at such cost—this revolution, I say, nonetheless finds in the hearts of all spectators (who are not engaged in this game themselves) a wishful participation that borders closely on enthusiasm, the very expression of which is fraught with danger; this sympathy, therefore, can have no other cause than a moral predisposition in the human race."[88]

For Kant, one name for this "moral predisposition" was freedom; for Foucault, perhaps it was "the will not to be governed."[89]

On January 10, 1979, Foucault began his annual series of lectures at the Collège de France. Ignoring current events, as he normally did, he took up again the theme of "governmentality." But once more, his political reflections veered off in a surprising direction.

Despite his own "wishful participation" in the revolution in Iran, he advised his students to look elsewhere for ways to think about "the will not to be governed." He asked them to read with special care the collected works of Ludwig von Mises and Frederick Hayek—distinguished Austrian economists, strident yet prescient critics of Marxism, apostles of a libertarian strand of modern social thought rooted in a defense of the free market as a citadel of individual liberty and a bulwark against the power of the state.[90]

In his public lectures, Foucault at the same time turned his own attention to modern liberalism, analyzing its character with unprecedented sympathy. As he afterwards summed up the gist of these lectures, liberalism had to be understood as a novel "principle and method for rationalizing the exercise of government." Its novelty, according to Foucault, lay in its break with the rival modern principle of "*raison d'État*," which he had analyzed the previous year. According to the Machiavellian principle of "*raison d'État*," the state constituted an end in itself, regulated only by its internal structure, and enjoying its own justification in terms of its success in increasing the scope and power of its rule. A reader of *Discipline and Punish* might well suppose that *every* modern state, in Foucault's view, adhered to the Machiavellian maxim that "one governs too little"—and so sought to extend the force of the State into an ever more detailed administration of individual conduct.[91]

But in these 1979 lectures, Foucault introduces an entirely new—and complicating—dimension into his historical view of the nineteenth century. For liberalism, in stark contrast to Machiavellianism, is defined, as Foucault puts it, by the maxim, " 'one always governs too much'—or at least, it is necessary to suspect that one governs too much." As a consequence of this liberal principle, "governmentality cannot be exercised without a 'critique.' " Every form of government must be examined, not merely in terms of the goods and well-being it manages to secure for its subjects, but, even more, in terms of the legitimacy of its claim to rule. Why is it necessary for the state to govern any given aspect of life at all?[92]

In his summary of the course, Foucault stressed the "polymorphism" of nineteenth-century European liberalism. He pointed out "the evolution and ambiguities of Bentham and the Benthamites," who moved from a trust in rational administration to a defense of representative democracy. And he recalled the disagreements among German and French liberals, some of whom relied on a market economy as the chief means "to repair the effects of an excess of governmentality," while others placed greater stress on " '*L'État de droit*,' the *Rechsstaat*, and the Rule of Law."[93]

Despite his newfound appreciation for the diversity of the liberal persuasion as it emerged in the nineteenth century, Foucault conspicuously omitted any mention of the republican strand of French liberal thought that runs from Rousseau to Durkheim and beyond. This was no oversight. As he remarked in an interview, it was Rousseau's reverie—of a republic of virtue, to be instituted through an untrammeled exercise of popular sovereignty—that had inspired some of the most intolerable aspects of modern "governmentality." "It was the dream of a transparent society, visible and legible in each of its parts, the dream of there no longer existing any zones of darkness, zones established by the privileges of royal power or the prerogatives of some corporation, zones of disorder. It was the dream that each individual, whatever position he occupied, might be able to see the whole of society, that men's hearts should communicate, their vision be unobstructed by obstacles, and that opinion of all reign over each."[94]

Rousseau's reverie was Foucault's nightmare. He dreaded situations in which others "enveloped him on all sides," making him constantly aware "that he is watched, judged, and condemned." The totalitarian implications of institutions that aimed to routinize such situations he had conjured up in the pages of both *Madness and Civilization* and *Discipline and Punish*, by detailing the horrors of Pinel's model asylum and Bentham's model prison. The utopian effort to forge communities of "ethical uniformity," as Foucault put it, trapped any human being who didn't conform into "a relation to himself that was of the order of transgression, and in a nonrelation to others that was of the order of shame."[95]

In contrast with the putatively "positive" freedom secured by such institutions, it was now evidently an alternative idea, of a purely "negative" freedom, expressed in the demand "*not* to be governed," that aroused Foucault's belated interest in liberalism. To be free, in this strictly negative sense, meant, as Isaiah Berlin once put it, "not being interfered with by others." "The wider the area of noninterference," suggested Berlin, "the wider my freedom." Or, to use Foucault's terms, the less discipline and "bio-power" imposed from above, the larger the scope left open for the individual's enigmatic but "decisive" will.[96]

On May 11, 1979, shortly after finishing his lectures on liberalism at the Collège de France, Foucault published in *Le Monde* perhaps his single most passionate piece of political writing. In it, he offered his answer to the question posed by the front-page headline: IS IT USELESS TO REVOLT?[97]

The question had been raised by the results of the revolution in Iran. On January 11, 1979, a central goal of the revolt had been accomplished: the Shah, fearing for his life, had fled the country. On February 1, the Ayatollah Khomeini had returned to Iran. Ten days later, the caretaker government appointed by the Shah had collapsed, and Khomeini, seated in a courtyard in a high school in Tehran, was left free to review column after column of troops demonstrating their fealty to a new sovereign.[98]

The furies that now gripped Iran went far beyond anything that Foucault, or almost any other observer, had dreamed possible. Thousands of Iranians associated with the old regime were rounded up and tortured, or summarily executed, or both. A new and draconian code of justice, inspired by Khomeini's understanding of "Islamic government," fell upon the land. Everyday injuries were avenged by a wound of the width, length, and depth of the original wound. Homosexuals were dispatched to firing squads. Adulterers were stoned to death. The chimera of a "political spirituality" was dispelled by the reality of a ruthless theocracy.[99]

In this context, Foucault could, in principle, have expressed his newfound sympathy for a certain style of liberal reasoning, perhaps even applying the maxim that "one always governs too much" to a critique of Khomeini's new Islamic regime. In practice, he did nothing of the sort. Unrepentant, he stood by his enthusiasm for the revolution in Iran—and justified it in no uncertain terms.

"Last summer the Iranians said, 'We are ready to die by the thousands in order to get the Shah to go,'" he began his piece in *Le Monde*. "Today it is the Ayatollah who says, 'Let Iran bleed so that the revolution may be strong.' There is a strange echo between these phrases which link them to one another. Does the horror of the second condemn the rapture (*ivresse*)of the first?"[100]

As if to underline the Nietzschean sense, in this last sentence, of the French word *ivresse* (which can be rendered into English as "rapture" or "intoxication" or "ecstasy" or, more literally, "drunkenness": hence a word redolent of "Dionysus beneath Apollo"), Foucault went on to link the abandon of revolt with an uncanny eruption of the Untimely. "While revolts take place in history, they also escape it in a certain manner. Some movements are irreducible: those in which a single man, a group, a minority, or a whole people asserts that it will no longer obey and risks its life before a power that is considered unjust. *There is no power that is capable of making such a movement impossible.*"[101]

The cost of the Shiah great awakening provoked horror: between ten and twelve thousand Iranians died during the uprising of 1978 alone—and thousands more in its aftermath. Perhaps every revolt was doomed to end in a bloodbath; perhaps every society was fated to function as an engine of almost unthinkable suffering; perhaps power normally *was* war, "a war continued by other means."

Still, the only chance for change was revolt—whatever its human costs, however tragic the outcome. Whoever died in a revolution achieved a kind of immortality, as if crossing "the frontiers of heaven and earth, in a dream of history that was as much religious as political." And whoever could appreciate the "rapture" of such an ordeal would cherish the memory of its martyrs and victims, whose example might rekindle, yet again, "the revolutionary experience"—"literally a light," as Foucault evoked its appearance among the Iranians, "that lit up in all of them, that bathed all of them at the same time."[102]

At such moments, a nation, and all those watching, might catch a glimpse of the only ground for hope that Foucault could discern. "All the forms of freedom, acquired or claimed," he wrote, "doubtless find in revolt a last point on which to anchor themselves, one that is more solid and near than 'natural rights.' If there are societies which hold firm and live, that is to say, if there are powers that are not 'absolutely absolute,' it is due to the fact that behind all the submissions and coercions, and beyond the menace, the violence, the persuasion, there is the possibility of the moment when life will no longer barter itself, when the powers can no longer do anything, and when, before the gallows and the machine guns, men revolt."[103]

It was the end of an era for Foucault.

Never again would he find the occasion to express enthusiasm for a revolt against the order of things in the modern world generally. Never again would he articulate openly his essentially mystical vision of politics as a "limit-experience."

For the French left as well, an era was ending. Since World War II, virtually every major intellectual on the left, from Sartre to Foucault, had flirted with the apocalyptic fantasies of either the communists, or, after May '68, of the French Maoist ultra-left; in word as well as deed, they had repeatedly expressed their hostility to the authoritarian liberalism of de Gaulle, and then to the technocratic liberalism of his successors, Georges Pompidou and Valéry Giscard d'Estaing.

Yet by 1979, the communist idea had fallen into intellectual disrepute, and the French Communist Party had entered a long period of apparently irreversible decline; while those few votaries of May '68 still drunk on the idea of violent confrontation were left with little to do except circle their wagons in defense of the terrorist cells of the Baader-Meinhof gang and the Red Brigades. By default, much of the French left—including Foucault, despite his momentary enthusiasm for the Iranian revolution—found itself embracing a kind of liberal (and chastened) vision of what politics might achieve, a vision given its most dramatic expression in the "human rights" movement that was then still gathering momentum in the Soviet Union and Eastern Europe.

On June 26, 1979, Foucault joined his old nemesis, Jean-Paul Sartre, for what proved to be their last joint appearance in public. They had come together for a press conference at the Collège de France after a delegation of intellectuals led by Sartre had gone to the Elysée to see the President of the Republic, Valéry Giscard d'Estaing, in order to urge that the French government offer more support for Vietnamese refugees, who were then emigrating by the thousand, setting sail in makeshift seacraft, fleeing from their war-ravaged country and its communist dictatorship. Joining Sartre and Foucault at the press conference afterwards were André Glucksmann, an organizer of the event; Yves Montand and Simone Signoret, two of the dissenting left's most glamorous members; and—most surprising of all—Raymond Aron, the long-isolated dean of French liberalism. This improbable political rapprochement between Sartre and Aron the French press, not without reason, treated as evidence of a new climacteric in French intellectual life. Less than a year later, Sartre was dead. [104]

Foucault's growing involvement in efforts to ameliorate the plight of refugees and to safeguard the rights of dissidents around the world, like his public support for the "*nouveaux philosophes,*" and his lectures on liberalism in 1979, left their mark on a generation of French intellectuals. In a eulogy composed shortly after Foucault's death, André Glucksmann praised the philosopher for breaking with "the terrorist radicalism of theoretical avant-gardes since Dada." In the last years of his life, as Glucksmann says, Foucault exemplified a new style of political conduct, evincing "acuteness in the analysis of evils, and restraint in the matter of commitment." As much as any figure of his generation, he helped inspire a resurgent neo-liberalism in France in the 1980s. [105]

He had in some ways successfully transformed his way of thinking about politics. He no longer viewed every legal code, as he once had, merely "in terms of the method of subjugation that it institutes." He no longer treated the "model of war" as a paradigm for the analysis of society: "Taking that route leads directly to oppression," he now argued, adding that the social critic must always proceed with caution and humility. Asserting the rights of the individual against the power of government now seemed to him a useful and worthy enterprise. [106]

Still, Foucault did not—indeed could not—commit himself wholeheartedly to any conventional understanding of liberalism. Dangerous and potentially lethal forms of disorder still sometimes held out the possibility of a total transfiguration of human existence—such, in Foucault's view, was the great promise, tragically betrayed, of the revolution in Iran in 1978. Given his continuing fascination with the creative prospects opened up by such moments of rapturous rebellion, he could not rest content, as liberal theorists are often wont to do, with the assertion of various rights. Indeed, he could not regard rights as anything other than a partisan invention, won through struggle and ultimately maintained only by the readiness of vigilant individuals and groups to challenge abuses of power. Unable, in effect, to get beyond "Nietzsche's hypothesis," he was unable to imagine himself in the shoes of the liberal jurist or the Kantian moral philosopher, struggling to see things impartially, from the perspective of a "universal subject." The idea of "right" he could not help but regard as a kind of political "fiction," however useful that fiction now seemed to him (as it had seemed to Coke and Lilburne before him). As he freely admitted, his defense of human rights was therefore basically "tactical." It ultimately involved an act of will rather than a reasoned argument. For even if, as he asserted, "all the forms of freedom, acquired or claimed, all the rights that one values" found in revolt "a last point on which to anchor themselves"—a point, he wrote, that "is more solid and near than 'natural rights' "—it was also Foucault's conviction that the phenomenon of revolt was itself inherently mysterious and inscrutable. "There is no explanation for the man who revolts," he wrote. "His action is necessarily a tearing that breaks the thread of history and its long chain of reasons."[107]

Furthermore, even in societies where human rights and a certain measure of personal freedom were both guaranteed by law, the work of the philosopher, as Foucault understood it, had scarcely begun. As he put it in a 1982 interview: "If what we want to do is create a new way of life"— and this was his lifelong goal—"then the question of individual rights is not pertinent."[108]

What *was* pertinent was the unrelenting practice of "critique," as Foucault now understood it. Faced with any form of government, be it liberal or totalitarian, it was the vocation of the intellectual to exercise a "decisive will not to be governed," voicing concerns in public about whatever appeared to be intolerable. By withholding consent, the intellectual could remind others of their "self-incurred tutelage"—and also of their ability to escape from this tutelage. That techniques for exacting a thoughtless conformity had, as a matter of historical fact, played a central role in securing the triumph of liberalism in our time (according to Tocqueville and John Stuart Mill, and not just to Michel Foucault) opened liberalism itself to criticism. Perhaps certain rights and laws, when enforced universally, also tended toward the miscarriage of justice in particular cases— this, too, was an issue fit for criticism.[109]

"We must refuse the division of labor that is often proposed to us: between individuals who become indignant and speak out; and governments which reflect and act," Foucault declared in 1981, summing up his own final view of his political role. "The will of individuals must be joined," in an ongoing effort to challenge, in theory as well as in practice, "every abuse of power, whoever the author, whoever the victims. After all, we are all governed—and, as such, we are in solidarity."[110]

The philosopher had arrived at a crossroads. For the first time since May '68, he was above the fray of political combat, disengaged from a life of militant activism. And for the first time in his career as a public thinker, he had conceded the need to address what he was now calling "the problem of the will."

This was an issue that Western philosophy had always approached gingerly, with great "precaution and difficulty," as Foucault had remarked to the *Société française de philosophie* in 1978. For years, he confessed to the same audience, he had been inclined to "avoid" the problem altogether, ignoring the will "insofar as possible," despite the appearance of the word, at least, in the title of his last book (*The Will to Know*).[111]

But his evasiveness was ending. Since his limit-experiences in California in 1975, "the problem of individual conduct" had forced itself into the foreground of his thinking. His efforts to find a new way to think about politics had led him to a new appreciation for human rights—and a new sense of how frail the limits imposed by any external code really were. So he now began to explore some of the possible ways in which the human being might exercise its free will, in order to govern—and set limits—for itself.

In these months, he drafted several short programmatic notes, indicating the direction he was now headed in. The title he chose for his notes, when he published them, was "The Subject and Power." In these notes, he once again linked his own approach to Kant's ideal of "enlightenment." And more explicitly than ever before, he declared his "general theme" to be "not power, but the *subject*."[112]

"At the very heart of the power relationship," he wrote, "are the re-calcitrance of the will and the intransigence of freedom. Rather than speaking of an essential freedom, it would be better to speak of an 'agonism'." Through this neologism, he evoked a kind of organized contest—what the Greeks called an "agon"—in which the will and power constantly collided, the one mysteriously summoning the other in a "permanent provocation." And at the center of this "agon," pulled now this way and now that, one imagines Foucault himself—perplexed, as always, about the limits of power, testing anew the extent of his free-dom.[113]

"Who are we?" wondered Foucault in this programmatic note, echoing the question he had raised in 1976. "Who seeks in the noise and the confusion of war, in the grime of battle, the principle for the intelligiblity of order?"[114]

As a new decade began, he was perhaps no closer to answering these gnomic questions than he had been four years before. His battle with himself raged on, unabated. But through his ongoing exploration of "bodies and pleasures"—and through a disciplined effort to understand how the thinkers of late antiquity had supposed that a man might come to know, and perhaps master, his demons, dreams, and lusts—Foucault's work was about to take its final, long-deferred turn: from "an interrogation of the limit and transgression," as he had put it in 1960, to "an interrogation of the return of the self." [115]

10

THE SCRIPTING

of

THE SELF

AT LONG LAST, Michel Foucault began to talk openly about the origins and character of his own hermetic quest—to understand who he was, and what he might yet become. Not that he had suddenly decided to reveal himself. Though he in fact did speak about many aspects of his own life with unwonted frequency and often surprising candor, particularly in the growing number of interviews he granted to the gay press, his whole approach in these years suggested a deepening perplexity about what this thing called the "self" actually was.

This perplexity he began to explore systematically, mainly in a long series of lectures and essays on different approaches to the self in ancient Greece and Rome. Erudite and austere, his work at first glance seems more impersonal and serenely detached than ever. But as so often with Foucault, this impression is slightly misleading. For he was in fact tunnelling his way deeper and deeper into his own labyrinth, spiraling back toward "the rediscovered origin," struggling more fiercely than ever before with his unrelenting fascination with death, trying to unriddle, in part through his writing, and in part through his ongoing pursuit of erotic ecstasy, the great Nietzschean questions: "Why am I alive? What lesson am I to learn from life? How did I become what I am, and why do I suffer from being what I am?"[1]

Foucault's new scholarly interest in the self had grown out of his study of sexuality. Before his LSD epiphany in Death Valley in 1975, he had intended to devote the different volumes of his monumental History of Sexuality to a detailed account of topics like hysteria, incest, masturbation, and perversion, analyzing developments in nineteenth-century biology, medicine, and psychopathology. But in the course of reformulating his thoughts about sexuality in the late 1970s, his focus changed dramatically.

Instead of trying to untangle the ways in which our modern sense of our selves had come to be tied up with a putatively scientific interpretation of a more or less fixed bundle of sexual drives and desires, Foucault leapt backward in time, embarking on a painstaking inventory of some of the quite different ways in which Western philosophers and theologians from Socrates to Augustine had thought about the self.

Justifying this radical shift, Foucault explained that he had come to fear that still another examination of nineteenth-century modes of thought might merely reproduce, "with regard to sexuality," the same patterns of "control and coercion" familiar from his previous books on madness and criminality, and from his lectures on "governmentality." By studying the texts of antiquity, Foucault in effect transported himself to another world. "Rather than placing myself at the threshold of the formation of the experience of sexuality, I tried to analyze the formation of a certain mode of relation to the self in the experience of the flesh."[2]

This surprising new direction of Foucault's thought, recondite though it may seem, was widely remarked and eagerly discussed, since he was now at the height of his fame. By 1980, almost all of his major books had been translated into all of the world's major languages, sparking a large, and growing, scholarly literature on the master's canonic texts, from *Madness and Civilization* to *Discipline and Punish*. In the eyes of many, he had become the cynosure of a new style of intellectual life—militant, subversive, elusive.

Ironically, the more attention was focused on him, the stronger became Foucault's old urge to vanish from view. He vehemently renounced the philosophical throne left vacant by Sartre's death in 1980, chiding those who "hanker," in "the world of ideas, for a little monarchy." He kept trying to break the Parisian rules. Interviewed by *Le Monde* in April of 1980, he insisted on remaining anonymous. "I shall propose a game," he declared with mock solemnity: "that of the 'year without a name.' For a year books would be published without their author's names." Critics would have to be honest; readers would have to think for themselves—and, best of all, writers would become invisible![3]

But Foucault's old fantasy had become harder and harder to fulfill. In Paris, he could not venture out at night without being mobbed by fans. And even in America, he had become a star of sorts, particularly on many college campuses. Students weaned on the Talking Heads and David Lynch flocked to his public appearances, cherishing the bald savant as a kind of postmodernist sphinx, a metaphysical Eraserhead whose demeanor was weird, whose utterances were cryptic—and whose philosophy, *mirabile dictu*, could nevertheless be summed in a simple mantra, consisting of two words: "power" and "knowledge."[4]

So it was that Michel Foucault, on the night of October 20, 1980, found himself facing a mob at the University of California at Berkeley.

That evening he was slated to deliver the first of his two Howison lectures on the campus; in these lectures, he would be offering the most succinct overview yet of where his research was headed—namely, back to the founding fathers of Western thought. His American public, however, knew nothing about this program. Students were still stuck on the grisly opening of *Discipline and Punish*—and the mysterious ending of *The Will to Know*. Bodies! Pleasures! Torture! Had philosophy ever sounded so sexy?

They began arriving an hour in advance, filling every seat in the large hall. And still they kept coming. Soon several hundred more people had gathered outside the hall, clamoring to get in. Police rushed to the scene. The doors to the hall were locked shut. Enraged, the crowd outside began to push and shout, pounding on the doors.[5]

Foucault was nonplussed. Advised of the baying throng, he turned to Hubert Dreyfus, the Berkeley professor who was to introduce him, and begged him to do something, *anything*, to make these people *go away*.

Halfheartedly, Dreyfus addressed the crowd—and complied with Foucault's wishes: "Michel Foucault says this is a very technical lecture, and difficult, and, I think, he wants to imply, boring; and he suggests that it would be better for everyone to leave *now*."[6]

Nobody budged.

If the great man's talk was to be obscure and difficult—so much the bettter! The promise of esoteric revelations was by now a part of his appeal.

The topic of Foucault's Howison lectures was, as he explained in his carefully enunciated English, "the genealogy of the modern subject." Confessing that this had been "my obsession for years," he proceeded to offer a lucid survey of his new interest in the self. He began with an autobiographical sketch. In his previous research, he explained (as the crowd outside continued to thrum in the distance), he had been primarily interested "in those institutions like hospitals, asylums, and prisons where certain subjects," classified as mad, sick, or criminal, "became objects of knowledge and at the same time objects of domination." In these earlier works, he went on, "I insisted maybe too much on . . . techniques of domination." For now he could see the importance of talking about "other types of techniques"—above all "techniques which permit individuals to effect a certain number of operations on their own bodies, on their souls, on their own thoughts, on their own conduct, and this in a manner so as to transform themselves, modify themselves, or to act in a certain state of perfection, of happiness, of purity, of supernatural power, and so on."[7]

It was these "techniques," or "technologies of the self," as he called them, that Foucault now proposed to study. He was particularly interested, he said, in tracing the origins of perhaps most important cluster of Western techniques of the self, "those oriented toward the discovery and formulation of the truth concerning oneself."[8]

Foucault devoted the remainder of his two lectures to examining the development in late antiquity of two different approaches to the self. The pagan approach to the self he interpreted through an account of Stoicism and the work of the Roman philosopher Seneca (c. 3 B.C.-A.D. 65); while the Christian techniques of self-examination he analyzed primarily through the work of John Cassian (360–435 A.D.), one of the founders of monasticism in the West. The two lectures together were designed to show how the positive Greek precept, "Know Thyself," had been transformed into the negative Christian injunction, "Renounce yourself."

The character and implications of this transition Foucault approached with some urgency. Frustrated in his efforts between 1976 and 1979 to elaborate a "new form of right" through a positive *political* philosophy, he had returned to the thought of pagan antiquity in hopes of finding some new positive "principle" that might yet inform the practice of "recent liberation movements." Of course, communing with the dead spirit of Greek and Hellenistic culture offered no immediate solution to contemporary political quandaries about how we ought to behave, and about what limits we ought to observe. Still, by analyzing pre-Christian ways of looking at the human being, one might be inspired to find some new way forward. As he explained in his first lecture at Berkeley, the pagan ethos of Stoicism, directive though it was, nevertheless "tended toward the autonomy of the directed." Unlike the Christian ethos of obedience to God's will, Stoicism was "centered on a problem of personal choice, of aesthetics." Its purpose was to shape one's self through a singular art of mnemotechnics, recollecting and reevaluating acts and events at the end of each day in order to draw up a "balance sheet of dependencies" still to be overcome. Seneca thus approached the self neither as a *fait accompli* nor as a locus of sinful impulses that had to be publicly renounced, but rather as an "ideal unity of the will and the truth," an *ethical* unity to be regulated independently of both organized religion and the laws of the state. [9]

"The idea of the *bios* as a material for an aesthetic piece of art is something which fascinates me," Foucault explained in one interview, summing up this aspect of his fascination with Stoicism. "The idea also that ethics can be a very strong structure of existence, without any relation with the juridical per se, with an authoritarian system, with a disciplinary structure. All that is very interesting." [10]

But it was also highly problematic, as Foucault's discussion of the Christian approach to the self made plain. Where a pagan thinker like Seneca evinced some confidence that the self could become a master in its own house, a Christian like Cassian regarded the self as a kind of groundless abyss from which dark powers constantly erupted, distracting us from the only sure source of salvation—a conversion in one's attitude toward one's self, summed up in one of the sayings of the desert saints: "The nearer a man draws to God, the more he sees himself a sinner." Unlike Stoicism, which had been oriented toward autarky and self-reliance, the Christian culture of the self thus stressed the need for a relentlessly suspicious form of self-examination, conducted under the watchful gaze of a spiritual guide. Weighing every impulse and idea, the Christian was enjoined to test which ones came from God—and which from "the work-shop of Demon." Discovering "the faults he may have committed," the Christian, as Foucault put it, was obliged to describe these things "to other people and hence to bear public witness against himself." [11]

And that was not the end of the Christian's "ordeal of truth." To bear witness against oneself properly, the Christian had to make all sins man-ifest, not only by confiding in a spiritual master, but also by punishing oneself through various somatic rites of mortification, submitting the self to a "kind of martyrdom." Foucault briefly enumerated some of the public rituals of penance—the hair shirt and ashes, the display of scars and wounds—through which the first Christians tried to understand who they were, and who, through the grace of God, they might yet become. Testing the soul like a moneychanger tested gold in a fire, the Christian ascetic struggled with a diabolical double, conjuring up this demonic other in order to defeat and drive out, through a kind of spiritual combat, this despicable self. [12]

In effect, the Christian thus had to *sacrifice* a part of who one was: and as Foucault went out of his way to stress, "we have to understand this sacrifice not only as a radical change in the way of life, but as the consequence of a formula. One renounces being the subject of one's will," in part by learning, and following, the will of God—and in part by disengaging from the lures and traps of this world through "the symbolic staging of one's own death."[13]

At first glance, Foucault's discussion of this Christian "hermeneutics of the self" may seem remote from the philosopher's own sense of who he was, or of what he wanted to become. In his view, the Christian techniques of "unconditional obedience, interminable examination, and exhaustive confession" formed a kind of unholy trinity. Self-mortification was not his style.[14]

Or was it? It is impossible, after all, to ignore the affinities between the ancient art of penance, as the philosopher described it at Berkeley, and the erotic theater of cruelty he was simultaneously exploring in San Francisco. Years before, writing about Georges Bataille, he had remarked on the similarities himself, suggesting that in "the Christian world of fallen bodies and of sin," the human being had once enjoyed a more "natural understanding" of the flesh. "All of mysticism and spirituality proves it, by knowing how not to divide the continous forms of desire, of rapture, of penentration, of ecstasy, of that outpouring which leaves us spent."[15]

Foucault had also long been fascinated by martyrdom and by the idea of self-sacrifice—one thinks of his enthusiasm for the revolution in Iran, and also of his famous remarks about the death of the author. "Writing is now linked to sacrifice, an actual sacrifice of life," he had declared in 1969. "The work that once had the duty of assuring immortality now attains the right to kill, to become the murderer of its author." "The negation of the self," he reaffirmed in a public discussion at Berkeley, "is the nucleus of the literary experience of the modern world."[16]

It is not surprising, then, that Foucault toward the end of his Howison lectures should have discerned in the Christian arts of self-sacrifice a genuine "richness": "No truth about the self is without the sacrifice of the self."[17]

Still, he concluded on a more ambiguous, almost wistful note. *If* he could demonstrate "that the self is nothing more than the correlate of [a] technology built into history," he speculated, *then* the "problem about the self" might yet disappear. Perhaps in a different kind of world, with a different set of techniques for approaching the self, a human being might no longer feel compelled to punish itself—and "sacrifice" itself—in order to become what one is.[18]

What such a world might look and feel like, nobody could say: for to inhabit such a world would require an all but unimaginable "change" in our way of thinking about our selves—and our way of being in the world. Or, as Foucault expressed this difficulty himself, in the final, halting words of his Howison lectures: "Maybe the problem now is to change those technologies [of the self], or maybe to get rid of those technologies, and then, to get rid of the sacrifice which is linked to those practices. In this case, one of the main problems would be, in the strictest sense of the word, politics—the politics of our selves."[19]

Near the end of his life, in 1984, Foucault tried to explain briefly the peculiarly personal resonance of his scholarly work in these years. "Considered from the standpoint of their 'pragmatics,' " he wrote, his lectures and texts on the Greeks and Romans were "the protocol of an exercise that was lengthy, groping, and often in need of renewal and correction." His research into ancient authors was not aimed at the mere acquisition of a certain fund of knowledge about the past for its own sake. A means to an end, his own scholarly research was rather "a philosophical exercise" in which he was struggling to understand—and to change—who *he* was: "At stake," as he laconically wrote, "was knowing to what extent the effort to think about one's own history can emancipate thought from what it silently thinks, and permit it to think differently."[20]

In effect, he explained, his study of the ancient world had been, for him, a peculiar kind of test, or "essay," using that word in its archaic alchemical sense, to indicate a trial, or an experiment, used to assay the value of something precious—in this case, one's self. "The 'essay'—which it is neccessary to understand as an ordeal [*épreuve*] that transfigures one's self in the play of truth, and not as an arrogation, appropriation, or conquest that simplifies for others in order to communciate—is the living body of philosophy, at least if the latter is still what it once was, namely an 'ascesis,' an exercise of the self, in thought."[21]

As Leo Bersani would lament shortly after Foucault's death, his old friend here resurrects one of the most hackneyed images in Western thought, that of "the philosopher as someone capable of thinking himself out of his own thought."[22]

This is true. But it is worth pausing to notice something that Bersani did not. Translating this hackneyed image into a living reality was no mean trick. As Foucault remarked in a 1983 lecture, one had to be ready to *convert* one's self and one's whole way of seeing the world, through "a kind of turning round on the spot." In order to pave the way for such "a rupture with one's self, with one's past, with the world, and with all previous life," it was necessary to jettison false opinions, evil masters, and old habits. And this entailed not only a kind of ongoing "critique," examining and evaluating every facet of experience, but also an ongoing combat and struggle in which the outcome was ambiguous, reversible, and always uncertain.[23]

This uncertainty was perhaps the ultimate agony. Plunged into an ordeal of self-doubt, one could never be sure that one had, finally, gotten free of one's despised self—or found the new self one was looking for.

"Such is the irony in those efforts one makes to alter one's way of looking, to transform the horizon of what one knows, and to try wandering a little," Foucault wrote in 1984, posing the crucial question—a question that it is perhaps best to leave open:

"Do such efforts actually lead to a different way of thinking?"[24]

Foucault's own struggle to "think differently" in these years unfolded in manifold, complex, and sometimes paradoxical ways. For a start, he changed his style of writing. Abandoning his former use of shocking vignettes, wild generalizations, and flashy neologisms, Foucault stripped his prose down to bare essentials, scrupulously qualifying his statements, carefully documenting every word in his historiographic works, eschewing trendy jargon. Like one of the classical "truth-tellers" he analyzed in these years, he used "the most direct words and forms of expression" he could find.[25]

In retrospect, it is easy to forget how risky this metamorphosis really was. Untrained in either Hellenistic or Latin studies, Foucault was speaking in unadorned language about difficult material that, as he admitted in 1983, "I had barely heard of six or seven years ago." In doing so, he opened himself to the possibility of committing a variety of blunders that would provoke the wrath of the academic specialists in classical thought—which duly happened. At the same time, he risked losing his own large audience of committed readers—which also duly happened: Leo Bersani was not the only one left disappointed, even bored, by Foucault's final works.[26]

Meanwhile Foucault was trying to change a number of other patterns in his everyday life and public behavior, some of them apparently trivial, others obviously not.

In Paris, he moved his base of research from his old haunts at the Bibliothèque Nationale to the Bibliothèque du Saulchoir, a quiet modern library, maintained by the Dominican order, where he could more easily immerse himself in early Christian texts. He talked about quitting his post at the Collège de France, and moving to the countryside. And he began to divide his time between France and North America. He visited Los Angeles in 1981; Toronto, Vermont, and New York City in 1982; and Berkeley twice in 1983. By the time of his death, he had made arrangements to spend several months each year at the University of California at Berkeley.[27]

In France, where he remained a figure of commanding public stature, he continued his efforts to moderate the character of his political commitments. He cautiously welcomed the electoral triumph of the French Socialist Party in May of 1981, when François Mitterrand was swept into offfice with a slogan borrowed from May '68, *Changer la vie* (Change life). Yet sooner than many, he realized that the Party was betraying its professed ideals; and by the end of 1981, he was protesting the Mitterrand government's tacit acquiescence in the Polish government's suppression of Solidarity, the nonviolent trade union and opposition movement. In the years that followed, while Paris was roiling with the usual quarrels and controversies, Foucault stood aside, trying to exercise his own "decisive will not to be governed" with a spirit of understated humility that he had learned the hard way. But he did not fall silent. Between 1980 and 1984, he spoke up against human rights violations in Vietnam and Poland, and helped establish a small political study group, comprised of Parisian activists, journalists, and intellectuals, to monitor and discuss abuses of power around the world. He forged links with France's largest non-communist trade union, the *Conféderation française et démocratique du travail* (CFDT), an organization committed to the democratic principle of *autogestion*, or worker's "self-management." And he quietly maintained his own ties to the Socialist Party.[28]

At the same time, in France and particularly in North America, Foucault participated in a quite different sort of social experiment, exploring a much more radical "politics" of the self. In these years, the philosopher became ever more deeply involved in the gay community. He publicly defended "the possibility—and the right—to choose your own sexuality," while in practice he continued to experiment actively with S/M as a way to discover "new forms of life." Through the suffering-pleasure of a "thinking that is shattered," one might "desexualize" the body in practice, thereby transforming murderous impulses and rendering "our selves infinitely more sensitive to pleasure." In the philosopher's eyes, such a "homosexual ascesis" was yet another way to "work on our selves" and perhaps even "to invent—I don't mean discover—a way of being that is still improbable."[29]

Muted in France, Foucault's most revolutionary hopes—for a total trans-figuration of life—thus remained vividly alive in America. Yet in both countries, whether writing as a modest scholar, articulating his concerns as a critic of power, or exploring new ways of experiencing pleasure, he was now working more openly and passionately than ever before toward a goal that was easy to state but—as the zigzag trajectory of his life so far confirmed—fiendishly difficult to reach. "I am not a great figure of intel-lectual life," he remarked to an American interviewer in 1982, expressing a modesty that, for once, does not ring entirely false. "The main interest in life and work is to become someone else that you were not in the beginning."[30]

Central to Foucault's effort to change who he was in these years was his exploration of what, for him, were new kinds of personal relationships. For the first time in his life, "friendship" became one of his explicit con-cerns. On more than one occasion, in interviews and composed texts, he returned to the theoretical possibility that two people, in spite of differences in age, status, and calling, might nevertheless be able to bridge the gaps between them through a reinvented "art" of friendship. By speaking frankly with someone who was neither a sycophant nor a coward, neither a lover nor a student, one might expand the reach of one's feelings, and test the value of one's own opinions, in the process confiding a part of who one was to the care of another.[31]

There is something poignant about Foucault's scattered comments on this topic: the range of intimate relationships that most human beings take for granted seemed, from the philosopher's point of view, to require a Herculean act of will. "Foucault was always very much alone," recalls one of his closest associates at the Collège de France. Like most of those who knew him, this associate often found Foucault inscrutable and melancholy, as if consumed by an unspeakable kind of *tristesse*. His legendary laugh and outward gaiety of manner, this witness suggests, "was a way to hide that sadness."[32]

Still, Foucault in the last years of his life went out of his way as never before to connect, to make contact, to breach the invisible walls that still separated him from most other people.

He became friendly with a coterie of younger Parisian artists, including the novelist Hervé Guibert. He drew close to the actress Simone Signoret, and also to Bernard Kouchner, a doctor and outspoken human rights advocate. He became an intimate of Paul Veyne, his colleague at the Collège de France, and also got to know Peter Brown, a colleague at Berkeley and one of the world's foremost authorities on early Christianity.[33]

But of all Foucault's new associations in these years, perhaps none is more improbable, or curiously revealing, than his relationship, after 1982, with Robert Badinter—at the time, France's minister of justice.

Foucault had first met Badinter in the 1970s. In those years, Badinter was in the midst of making a name for himself as France's most eloquent opponent of capital punishment. Born, like Foucault, in the 1920s, he was a writer, a law professor at the Sorbonne, and also a prominent lawyer. Allied with Foucault in the campaign against the death penalty, Badinter agreed with him about little else. An urbane and worldly scholar with a firsthand knowledge of French law, French courts, and French prisons, Badinter was a man of unabashedly liberal temperament. Deeply committed to reforming the system of justice, he had openly criticized Foucault's corrosive skepticism about the value of penal reform.[34]

In May of 1981, shortly after the Socialist Party gained control of the French government, Badinter became François Mitterrand's first minister of justice (he would serve until 1986, when he became the President of the country's *Conseil constitutionnel*). As minister, his top priority was ful-. filling the Socialist Party's pledge to abolish the death penalty, which duly happened before the year was over. It was the crowning moment of his public career.[35]

Foucault's response to this epochal event was utterly characteristic— and betrayed the extent to which, try as he might, certain habits of thought he simply could *not* change. "The oldest punishment in the world is in the midst of dying in France," wrote Foucault in a piece he contributed to *Libération* on the eve of the abolition. "It is necessary to rejoice; it is not necessary, however, to get lost in admiration. . . . To stop lopping off a few heads because the blood squirts out, because one no longer behaves in this manner in polite society and because there is always a risk of beheading an innocent—this is relatively easy. But to renounce the death penalty by proposing the principle that no public force . . . has a right to take away the life of *anyone*—that is when one joins an important and difficult debate." In the remainder of his piece, Foucault urged his readers to consider abolishing *all* forms of punishment. This, of course, was improbable; but given his "Nietzschean hypothesis," about the role of punishment in the infernal recurrence of guilt and transgression, it was perhaps the only honest position he could take.[36]

The minister of justice was dumbfounded. "I was a little surprised, and maybe a little bit hurt," Badinter recalls, "because this was a major success. And I knew that by writing this, he brought strength to people who would say, 'See, we're being led by intellectual crackpots. Not only do they want to save the lives of the worst criminals, but they want them set free to kill people.' "[37]

Oddly enough, Foucault's little essay sowed the seed from which his subsequent personal relationship with Badinter would soon grow. In an interview a few months later, the minister of justice, still smarting from the philosopher's barbed comments, took a swipe at Foucault. When the philosopher read the interview, he fired off an indignant personal letter to the minister.

At this point Badinter did something unusual: he invited Foucault to lunch. Thus began a sustained dialogue between the two men that was ended only by Foucault's death.

"Foucault wanted very much to be loved," recalls one of his closest associates, who would often see Foucault after his lunches with Badinter. "He craved a link," says this associate, "not with power, but a link of love: it was clear that he was waiting for the recognition of a political minister, waiting for someone to consult with him, for example about how to think about problems of justice." As this witness points out, it soon became evident that Foucault, through his association with the minister of justice, might obtain government money for various pet projects—and also wield some measure of influence on the government's thinking about the penal code. Still, what really mattered, he thinks, was that Badinter approached Foucault with respect, "as a man whose experience he might learn from."[38]

Badinter had reasons of his own to cherish their lunches. "Foucault was an exceptional man," he says—"and you don't meet many exceptional men when you're a minister. Free intellectual talk is an oxygen when you're in a government, because you have to restrain yourself so much— you're not free to talk freely."[39]

As time passed, their relationship seems to have deepened. About some things they agreed to disagree: the minister felt no sympathy at all for the philosopher's "demonic vision of power," and the philosopher often had trouble fathoming the minister's pragmatic point of view. About still other things, such as the nature of justice and the importance of change, they discovered some common ground. In order to understand better why repeated efforts to reform the French penal system had failed, they laid plans to teach a seminar together. Foucault talked as well about his admiration for the large American universities he had seen, and suggested that the socialists consider establishing a new kind of institution, bringing together scholars and students from different European countries. "We started working on the project," recalls Badinter. "I spoke to the president of the Republic about these views of Foucault's, and he was very interested."

Above all, the two of them began to talk more deeply about personal matters. "We talked of life, of death, of aging," recalls Badinter. "But I am a discreet man; I know that these are matters he would not have liked to have me discuss."

Their last lunch together occurred in the spring of 1984. The minister, who was scheduled to appear before the French Senate afterwards, asked whether the philosopher had ever gone for a visit. The great critic of "governmentality" admitted that he had never before seen the French government in action. "Oh," said the minister of justice, "they have a magnificent library, you must come along with me."

A limousine whisked the two men to their destination—the Luxembourg Palace, built originally by Marie de Médicis, and converted after the Revolution into a seat of the new republican government. With Badinter by his side, the philosopher toured the building with a twinkle in his eye, savoring the incongruity of the opulent furnishings and decor, most of them dating to the reign of Louis Philippe and the restored Bourbon monarchy. "The last remembrance I have of Foucault physically," recalls Badinter, "is of him leaving the Senate and laughing. 'Well,' he said, 'we'll have to visit another palace next time!' "

If nothing else, Foucault's association with Robert Badinter attests to his unflagging interest in understanding, and somehow affecting, the great political events of his own day. But this interest provoked in Foucault a paradoxically deepening sense of perplexity. Just as the nature of friendship emerged in these years as a topic of his reflections, so, too, did the origin and character of the modern philosopher's preoccupation with his own time. While on a practical level, Foucault was making an effort to pursue his own political commitments with a new thoughtfulness and restraint, on a theoretical level he began to treat his own cultural role, as an intellectual at grips with his era, as a source of astonishment—as it surely ought to have been. For why, and how, had *he*, of all people, come to function, like Sartre before him, as a model of avant-garde engagement?

As he often did in these years, Foucault pursued his puzzlement through abstraction and ponderous indirection, trying to unriddle a part of himself by writing about someone else entirely, someone with whom he could nevertheless identify: in this case, Immanuel Kant. His starting point was the same essay on enlightenment that had formed the basis for his 1978 lecture, "What is Critique?" In effect, the first paragraph of Kant's 1784 essay became a kind of Rorschach test. Every time Foucault interpreted it—as he did, repeatedly, in these months, in his first lecture at the Collège de France in 1983, and in a series of subsequent talks and texts—he revealed still another aspect of his puzzlement about himself, usually in the guise of some convoluted and gnomic question, phrased as if a character in a Beckett play had suddenly become consumed by a burning need to know whether he was a vessel of enlightenment, or simply a raving idiot: "How could we analyze the formation of our selves through the history of our thought?" "What is my present?" "What am I doing when I speak of my present?" "What is it in the present that produces meaning now for philosophical reflection?" "What is to be done with the will to revolution?" "Who are 'we' now?"[40]

Foucault's most telling examination of these questions appears in the laconic sequence of *pensées* he entitled, like Kant's original essay, "What is Enlightenment?" That this was, for Foucault himself, an important, even definitive text is indicated by the fact that it was published, at his behest, as a central document in the standard English-language anthology of his work, *The Foucault Reader*.[41]

His observations on enlightenment in this text fall into three parts. In the first part, he interprets Kant's essay as exemplifying a new and unprecedented ethos, which he calls the "attitude of modernity"; in the essay's second part, he goes on to discuss the poet Charles Baudelaire's vision of "the dandy," which he treats as still another model for the "attitude of modernity"; and in the third and final part, Foucault sums up his *own* philosophical ethos, describing it in terms that curiously combine themes to be found in Kant's ideal of the philosopher, on the one hand, and Baudelaire's vision of the dandy, on the other.

He starts by focusing on the word *Ausgang* in Kant's original text: "Enlightenment is man's exit [*Ausgang*] from his self-incurred tutelage." By using the term *Ausgang*, Foucault argues, Kant wants us to understand enlightenment as something almost "entirely negative." It is a way to escape, "an 'exit,' a 'way out.'" To take advantage of this exit, however, it is necessary to modify the "state of our will that makes us accept someone else's authority to lead us in areas where the use of reason is called for." Such a modification entails changes that are "at once spiritual and institutional, ethical and political." As an ideal, enlightenment has therefore to "be considered both as a process in which men participate collectively, and as an act of courage to be accomplished personally. Men are at once elements and agents of a single process. They may be actors in the process to the extent that they participate in it; and the process occurs to the extent that men decide to be its voluntary actors." The success of enlightenment hinges on a certain exercise of free will.[42]

By explicitly placing Kant's essay, thus interpreted, "at the crossroads of critical reflection and reflection on history," Foucault signals the extent to which his *own* reflections on history are colored by this distinctly modern "attitude." That Foucault started his 1983 course at the Collège de France by talking about Kant is thus of no small significance. Like Kant, Foucault regards free will as "the ontological condition of ethics"; ethics in turn he treats as "the deliberate form assumed by freedom." By importing these distinctly modern convictions into his subsequent accounts of Plato and Seneca, Foucault tended to minimize the movement of Platonism and Stoicism toward a consciousness of the self as a part of Nature, as a fragment of universal Reason. As one expert on Stoicism has acutely remarked, Foucault's study of antiquity may begin with an erudite interest in spiritual exercises—but it culminates in a "new form of dandyism."[43]

It was an association that Foucault himself drew in the second part of his essay, on Baudelaire's effort to express the poetry of modern life. As Foucault—following both Kant and Baudelaire—understood it, this effort required a "transfiguring play of freedom with reality." "To be modern," writes Foucault, "is not to accept oneself as one is in the flux of the passing moments"; it is rather to turn one's self into the object "of a complex and difficult elaboration: what Baudelaire, in the vocabulary of his day, calls *dandysme*." As Baudelaire had defined it in 1863, "dandyism" was "an institution beyond the laws" that nevertheless embodied "rigorous laws that all its subjects must strictly obey." Those who submitted to its regimen were "beings with no other calling but to cultivate the idea of beauty in their persons, to satisfy their passions, to feel and to think." Animated "first and foremost" by a "burning need to create for oneself a personal originality," the dandy was "a weird kind of spiritualist," devoted to a "kind of cult of the self." A poet of the flesh, he was exquisitely sensitive to the pleasures of the body, leading an erotic life animated by "passionate or poetical caprice."[44]

Foucault thus presented Baudelaire's dandy as an artist of everyday life at grips, like Kant's philosopher, with both free will and "modernity." It is a strange link to make: "poetical caprice" was not Kant's style at all—he wished rather to find, and fix, firm limits on thinking and acting. But "poetical caprice" *was* Foucault's style: like Baudelaire, he lived a life of erotic abandon, without inhibition testing his freedom "to pass beyond each and every specified limit." "If the Kantian question was that of knowing what limits knowledge has to renounce breaching," Foucault remarks, summing up his *own* ethos, "then it seems to me that the critical question today has to be turned back into a positive one. . . . The point, in brief, is to transform the critique conducted in the form of a necessary limitation into a practical critique that takes the form of a possible transcendence."[45]

Not that the transcendence of limits was an end in itself, either for Foucault, or for Baudelaire. For the dandy, as Foucault understands him, is a peculiarly modern kind of "ascetic." By pursuing the free play of imagination wherever it may lead, he tries to extract the "poetry within history." Searching for "something eternal that is not beyond the present instant, nor behind it, but within it," he lays his heart bare, making manifest (in Foucault's words) *"the essential, permanent, obsessive relation that our age entertains with death."* Revolting, in turn, against this fascination with death, he imposes on himself "a discipline more despotic than the most terrible religions," making "of his body, his behavior, his feelings and passions, his very existence, a work of art," struggling, in this way, to get free of himself—and then to "invent himself."[46]

In the final part of this terse, revealing text, Foucault briefly sums up his own "philosophical ethos." His work, he suggests, exemplifies a *"limit-attitude"* that issues in a "permanent critique of ourselves." "Modernity does not 'liberate man in his being,'" he concludes. "It compels him to face the task of producing himself," forcing him to carry forward, for better or worse—and in ways that Immanuel Kant would scarcely recognize— "the undefined work of freedom."[47]

Shortly after Foucault had finished his course at the Collège de France in the winter of 1983, the celebrated German philosopher Jürgen Habermas arrived in Paris to deliver four lectures of his own at the Collège. His topic, as it happens, was what he called "The Philosophical Discourse of Modernity."[48]

This visit came at the behest of Paul Veyne, Foucault's closest friend at the Collège de France. Indeed, Foucault later told Habermas that he, himself, had played a major role in arranging the visit.[49]

Foucault's evident eagerness to confront Habermas face-to-face was yet another symptom of Foucault's ongoing effort to think differently—and to change who he was. There had been a time in his life when he would have gone out of his way to *avoid* such a meeting. In 1967, for example, the phenomenologist Paul Ricoeur had delivered a series of lectures at the University of Tunis while Foucault was teaching there. At the time, the controversy over structuralism, and over Foucault's book, *The Order of Things*, was at its height. At one lecture that Foucault attended, he kept audibly poking fun at Ricoeur's remarks to a companion; yet when it came time for questions and open debate, Foucault refused to say a word. He had fallen similarly silent after hearing Jacques Derrida criticize *Madness and Civilization*. On one level, his way of thinking in these years was hermetic to the point of solipsism—a stance of icy solitude dissolved only by the events of 1968, and his subsequent emergence as a public figure. Even then, Foucault normally engaged his critics through polemic—one thinks of his savage 1971 attack on Derrida. It was only near the end of his life that his attitude softened, and Foucault took the further step of actively exploring the possibility of a mutual exchange of ideas. As Jean Lacouture once aptly summed up the outlines of this intellectual and existential trajectory, Foucault "wended his way from monologue to dialogue by way of combat."[50]

Dialogue was Habermas's philosophical forte: rarely has a thinker evinced such a principled eagerness to hold up his own ideas to free and open examination through conversation and contact with those who disagree with him. Born in 1929, three years after Foucault, Habermas was the foremost living representative of the "Frankfurt School" of "critical theory." An offshoot of Marxism, critical theory had first been formulated at the University of Frankfurt in the late 1920s and early 1930s by Max Horkheimer, Theodor Adorno, and Herbert Marcuse, all of whom were preoccupied with developing a new form of philosophical and cultural criticism that would contribute to the transformation of society. Taking up this project after World War II as Theodor Adorno's associate at Frankfurt, Habermas had broken with classical Marxism, and also with Adorno's efforts to elaborate a purely "negative dialectics," arguing instead that it was possible to discover a rationally justified normative basis for critique, through what he came to call a "discourse ethics." According to this ethics, there lies latent in our everyday use of language a possibility for uncoerced communication that, as a regulative principle, supplies a universal basis for rationally adjudicating the claims of competing values and interests: "Always, when we begin a discourse and carry it on long enough," as Habermas once formulated his frankly idealized supposition, "a consensus would have to result which would be per se a true consensus."[51]

Foucault was of two minds about critical theory in general and Habermas in particular. Though he became aware of the Frankfurt School's work only in the mid-1970s, he recognized immediately that Horkheimer and Adorno had been in many ways kindred spirits; he clearly admired aspects of Habermas's work as well. "The philosophers of this school posed problems that are still being worked on," he remarked in a 1978 interview, "for example, the problem of the effects of power on a [type of] rationality that has been historically and geographically elaborated in the West since the sixteenth century. . . . Now, how are we to separate this rationality from the mechanisms, procedures, techniques, and effects of power that define it, and that we no longer accept? . . . Couldn't we conclude that the promise of enlightenment, of realizing freedom through the exercise of reason, has been, on the contrary, subverted through the domination of reason itself, which increasingly usurps the place of freedom?" In his own work, Foucault had explored a similar set of issues by showing how subtle social mechanisms could sap the will and inhibit imagination, shackling the free spirit. [52]

On the other hand, Foucault sensed, even in Horkheimer and Adorno, a continuing commitment to a Marxist vision of the human essence. This vision he rejected. "For me, what must be produced is not man himself such as nature designed him, or such as his essence prescribes," he explained in 1978, trying to clarify where he most sharply disagreed with the critical theorists. "What must be produced is something that absolutely does not exist, about which we know nothing . . . the creation of something totally different, an innovation." [53]

The character of his disagreement became even sharper in the case of Habermas himself; for much as Foucault might admire his analytical acumen, and his continuing commitment to developing a theory of knowledge within a social and historical framework, the ideal of "a perfectly transparent communication" left him cold: "The thought that there could be a state of communication which would be such that the games of truth could circulate freely, without obstacles, without constraint, and without coercive effects, seems to me to be Utopia." Coming from Foucault, this was no compliment. [54]

Habermas, for his part, had been just as critical of Foucault, deploring his appeal to "the Dionysiac force of the poetical," and dismissing his genealogical histories as "cryptonormative" pseudo-science. Buoyed by such comments, disciples of Habermas in America often crossed swords with the acolytes of Foucault, jousting over the legacy of left-wing social criticism, and creating a furor that Foucault himself, particularly when he was in the United States, could scarcely ignore. On what basis, by what right, the followers of Habermas asked, could Michel Foucault pose as a critic of modern society? Why should his readers find resistance preferable to submission? "Only with the introduction of normative notions of some kind," wrote one such critic, "could Foucault begin to answer this question. Only with the introduction of normative notions could he begin to tell us what is wrong with the modern power/knowledge regime and why we ought to oppose it."[55]

This line of argument intensely irritated Foucault. In private, he vented his anger in no uncertain terms, fulminating against what he called "enlightenment blackmail." In public, on the other hand, he tried to strike a more diplomatic pose. He was "completely in agreement" with Habermas, he declared in an American interview in 1982: "If one abandons the work of Kant," one runs the risk "of lapsing into irrationality." However, the work of Kant, as Foucault went on to suggest, had perhaps been too narrowly interpreted: "I think that the central issue of philosophy and critical thought since the eighteenth century, has been, still is, and will, I hope, remain the question, *What* is this Reason that we use? What are its historical effects? What are its limits, and what are its dangers? How can we exist as rational beings, fortunately committed to practicing a rationality that is unfortunately crisscrossed by intrinsic dangers? One should remain as close to this question as possible, keeping in mind that it is extremely difficult to resolve."[56]

On March 6, 1983, Jürgen Habermas appeared at the Collège de France to deliver the first of his scheduled four lectures. Speaking in the famous "*salle 8*" where inaugural lectures at the Collège are traditionally delivered, the German guest found himself facing the kind of eager, overflow audience that only Foucault and a handful of other French philosophers could command.[57]

After a brief introduction by Paul Veyne, Habermas began to speak. A stunned silence settled over the crowd. The microphones were not working properly. His pronunciation was garbled. Worst of all—he was speaking in English!

No one understood a word—which is probably just as well. Supplied with a text, the reporter from *Libération* was shocked by the contents. Invited to speak at France's most prestigious institution of higher learning by two of the country's most famous living Nietzscheans—namely, Veyne and Foucault—Habermas had the audacity to deliver a talk that was, in part, about the fascist implications of Nietzsche's way of thinking. As the reporter acidly remarked, this was "a strange proposition" to be defending "in a place where two prominent Nietzscheans teach, neither of whom can be mistaken for anti-democrats."[58]

It was a disastrous beginning—and in fact, the audience for Habermas's next three Paris lectures shrank dramatically. But during his stay, Foucault and Habermas did, amazingly enough, manage to enter into a kind of dialogue.[59]

"We had several conversations," Habermas recalls. "The first evening I met him, there was a dinner in a restaurant." The two philosophers began by talking about German films, discovering that their taste in movies and directors was (as one might expect) almost completely divergent. "Another topic," says Habermas, "was the philosophical biography of each of us"— and here the differences between the two of them became illuminating. "He explained how important it was to break off from the phenomenological tradition, I remember his phrase, he 'emancipated himself from the grips of the transcendental subject,' that meant Husserl, Sartre, and so on, via structuralism on the one hand and Heidegger on the other hand. While I tried to tell him that I came under the sway of Heidegger and emancipated myself from his impact as soon as I realized the political implications of his philosophy, or at least of the particular thrust of Heidegger's work in the early 1930s, and turned to the young Hegelians, and to critical theory, and so on."[60]

Habermas remembers the exchange as "exciting"—and so, in an interview conducted a month later, did Foucault. "I was quite struck by his observation of the extent to which the problem of Heidegger and of the political implications of Heidegger's thought was quite a pressing and important one for him," said Foucault. "One thing he said has set me to musing, and it's something I'd like to mull over further. After explaining how Heidegger's thought indeed constituted a political disaster, he mentioned one of his professors who was a great Kantian, very well known in the thirties, and he explained how astonished and disappointed he had been when, while looking through card catalogues one day, he found some texts from around 1934 by this illustrious Kantian that were thoroughly Nazi in orientation."[61]

As Foucault points out, this was no isolated incident: he himself had just discovered that one of Germany's greatest twentieth-century students of Stoicism had also supported Hitler.

But what did it all mean? Did the association of these professors of philosophy with Nazism call into question the quite different kinds of ethical precepts each one had defended? Why should the thought of Nietzsche and Heidegger be impugned on political grounds, while the thought of Kant and Seneca was not? Presumably the Kantian Nazi had subscribed to a rational moral code; still, he had been a Nazi: what did this tell us about the limits of reason in a realm like politics? Was there not an invidious sort of inconsistency at work in Habermas's one-sided critique of the Nietzscheans and Heidegger?

"I do not conclude from this that one may say just anything within the order of theory," said Foucault, "but, on the contrary, that a demanding, prudent, 'experimental' attitude is necessary; at every moment, step by step, one must confront what one is thinking and saying with what one is doing, *with what one is.*" For Foucault in 1983, the key to appraising the values held dear by *any* philosopher was therefore "not to be sought in his ideas, as if it could be deduced from them, but rather in his philosophy-as-life, in his philosophical life, his ethos."[62]

Habermas continued to see matters quite differently. But the longer he talked with Foucault—they met a second time over lunch—the more impressed he became. "I had expected a bit more Parisian irony," says Habermas. "There was *nothing, absolutely nothing* of that about him. He complained to me about the Parisian style, the faddishness. Even apart from this remark I just realized how serious he was, how far from the 'circus' he was. I mean, he was a *philosopher.*"[63]

On a final visit to Foucault in his office at the Collège de France, Habermas, as he recalls, "tried to press him about his 'happy positivism.' I told him, 'look, it makes no sense to refrain from explaining normative premises if one proceeds in such a critical way as you do.'" Habermas spelled out a line of argument familiar from his writings.

Once more, he was surprised at Foucault's response. "He told me, 'Look, this is a question I'm thinking about just now. And you will have to decide, when I finish my History of Sexuality, how I will come out.'"[64]

The first fragments of Foucault's totally recast work on sexuality and the self had finally begun to appear. In 1982, he published an essay on "The Struggle for Chastity," followed a few months later by an essay entitled "Dreaming of One's Pleasures." In a spirit of "humbling serenity and un-affected craftsmanship," each of these essays examined relatively arcane classical texts: the *Institutions* and *Conferences* of John Cassian, and the *Oneirocritica* of the pagan philosopher Artemidorus of Daldis. Yet both texts were at the same time deeply personal, taking up, under the guise of the most rigorous erudition, areas of life in which the author himself had for some time now been struggling to "think differently." What, for example, was the relationship between a diagnosis of one's self, aimed at knowing "all the dark forces that can lurk behind the mask it may assume" and the effort, in practice, to escape (in Foucault's words) from "the austere monarchy of sex?" If our dreams, as he had argued in 1953, "throw into bright light the secret and hidden power at work in the most manifest forms of presence," was it "good or bad, favorable or ominous" to find pleasure in one specific type of dream?[65]

As Gilles Deleuze would later remark, Foucault's ongoing effort to change who he was now involved him, at a deeper level than ever before, in "thinking of the past as it is condensed on the inside, in the relation to oneself (there is a Greek in me, or a Christian . . .)." In examining himself in this way, his old friend was struggling, Deleuze suggested, to convert his way of thinking, from "a vitalism founded on mortalism," preoccupied with death in its singular negativity as the defining moment of existence, to a vitalism founded, instead, on aesthetics—that is, on an understanding of life, in its positivity, as a unique pattern of acts and ideas that, like a work of art, one might fashion for oneself. By analyzing how we, in the West, have historically approached our selves in Greek terms, in Christian terms (or in "modern" terms), the philosopher could sift through his own singular "dowry" of concepts and precepts, rejecting some, prizing others, in the process elaborating new concepts and precepts for himself. As Deleuze summed up Foucault's method, "Thought thinks its own history (the past), but in order to free itself from what it thinks (the present), and to be able finally to 'think differently' (the future)."[66]

The distant origins of this method Foucault himself traced back to the Stoics in a 1983 article he entitled "*L'écriture de soi*," or "The Scripting of the Self." In the body of this beautifully crafted essay, Foucault recounts some of the uses of writing commended by Seneca, Marcus Aurelius, and Plutarch. By routinely meditating on one's experience, and exploring certain ideas in writing and then putting these ideas to the test in practice, the aspiring Stoic could fashion a singular "script" for himself, one that enabled him to transform the truth, such as he understood it, into an *ethos*—a form of life that would meet both the claim of reason, and the need for courage. This "scripting" of the self the pagan philosophers had accomplished primarily through the exchange of letters with like-minded souls, and, above all, through the daily composition of diaries and journals, carefully recording thoughts about things read and ventures undertaken, compiling the raw material that a writer like Seneca would later work up into more systematic treatises, offering techniques and reasoned arguments for mastering personal flaws like anger, envy, and flattery.[67]

This, as it happens, bears more than a passing resemblance to how Foucault himself had long approached his own work. Throughout his life, according to Daniel Defert, Foucault kept a journal, largely devoted to extracts from what he was reading—usually works of fiction, says Defert. And according to Paul Veyne, "During the last eight months of his life, writing his two books played the same part for him that philosophical writing and personal journals played in ancient philosophy—that of work performed by the self on the self, of auto-stylization."[68]

But Foucault's essay on "The Scripting of the Self" does not confine itself to exploring the role of correspondence and personal journals in ancient philosophy. For he frames his comments about Stoicism in terms of the much darker Christian understanding of the same techniques, as a means of getting rid of "the Other, the Enemy, who hides behind seeming likenesses of oneself." "The Scripting of the Self" in fact begins with a long passage from Athanasius's *Life of Saint Anthony*, one of the founding documents of Christian monasticism. In this passage, reproduced verbatim by Foucault, in yet another of his inconspicuous commentaries "à la Borges," Anthony is quoted admonishing anyone who would "trample under foot the machinations of the Enemy" to bring his *body into subjection*," by keeping a daily record of his experience. "Let us each note and write down our actions and impulses of the soul as though we were to report them to each other," says Anthony, "and you may rest assured that from utter shame of becoming known we shall stop sinning and entertaining sinful thoughts altogether."[69]

For a hermit like Saint Anthony—who for years lived alone in the desert of Egypt, heroically courting, and withstanding, every temptation the Devil could devise—"composing a script for one's self alleviates the dangers of solitude." The kind of constraint imposed on conduct by the presence of others, the process of writing, in effect, imposes on "the interior movements of the soul"—though not without a furious struggle. The need for struggle, which demands the most agonizing kind of self-renunciation, is, for Foucault, precisely what defines the crucial difference between the Stoic and Christian "scripting" of the self. For by writing down *everything* one has experienced, one must come face-to-face, again and again, with one's diabolical double. Wielded as a weapon of war against a demonic power that may yet lead us astray, and fool us about who we are, writing becomes an "an ordeal [*épreuve*] and a touchstone," in Foucault's words, "bringing to light the movements of thought"—and so dissipating "the interior darkness where the webs of the enemy are spun."[70]

Foucault discovered the Stoic art of "scripting" the self relatively late in his life. And though the contemplative and calming *style* of an essay like "The Scripting of the Self" strongly suggests that Seneca had become a kind of model for him, just as Paul Veyne suggests, it was Saint Anthony—and Nietzsche's harrowing vision of the "self-chosen torture" of the ascetic philosopher—that haunted Foucault's imagination throughout his life. Try as he might, he had trouble seeing the self in any more positive light; even in his "ethics," he could not get beyond "Nietzsche's hypothesis." "Now, the problem is this," he remarked in an informal public discussion of his work at Berkeley: "Have we found a positive foundation, instead of self-sacrifice, for the hermeneutics of the self? I cannot say this, no. We have tried, at least from the humanistic period of the Renaissance till now. *And we can't find it.*"[71]

Preoccupied throughout his life by the origins and morbid implications of the negative, ascetic injunction to renounce oneself, Foucault composed no less than three different accounts of Saint Anthony and his ordeal, offering three different images of the hermit—and three different allegories of his *own* lifelong struggle, in the words of his last piece of writing, to get free of himself ("*se déprendre de soi-même*").[72]

Foucault's first account had appeared in 1961. Inspired by Hieronymus Bosch's famous painting *The Temptation of Saint Anthony*, it forms part of the first chapter of *Madness and Civilization*. Evoking the central panel of Bosch's Lisbon triptych, with its teeming mass of "hermetic, demented forms which have risen from a dream," Foucault lingers over the figure directly opposite the anchorite. The figure is of a head resting on two legs, a "wan smile" on its disembodied face. This, comments Foucault, "is one of those images born of madness." A figure of terrible "solitude," the disembodied face represents the involuntary "penitence" of the man who is mad—his unending reenactment, in an insane parody of Christ's Passion, of "all the glories of torture and its innumerable dreams." "Now it is exactly this nightmare silhouette"—of a *daimon* that has dropped its earthly body, dead to carnal lusts, or perhaps simply *dead*—"that is at once the subject and object of the temptation; it is this figure that fascinates the gaze of the ascetic—the one and the other are prisoners of a sort of interrogation in a mirror, which remains indefinitely unanswered, in a silence inhabited only by the monstrous swarm that surrounds them." A bleaker emblem would be hard to imagine: from this "interrogation in a mirror" there would seem to be no exit, no escape—no possible way for the madman to become enlightened. Still, in this very image—of the ascetic and his demonic double—"man finds," as Foucault portentously puts it, "*one of the secrets and one of the vocations of his nature.*" The disembodied figure "fascinates because it *is knowledge*"—a symbol promising to yield the "Great Secret" of a "difficult, hermetic, esoteric learning." And though what the demonic double appears to reveal is perhaps the most horrifying of imaginable truths—"the reign of Satan and the end of the world; ultimate bliss and supreme punishment; omnipotence on earth and the infernal fall"—Bosch's Saint Anthony, as Foucault here imagines him, is nevertheless tempted; drawn not by carnal lust, but rather "by the much more insidious lure of curiosity."[73]

Foucault's second account of Saint Anthony appeared in 1964. Inspired by Flaubert's novel *The Temptation of Saint Anthony*, it was originally published as a preface to a German translation of this book. Like Bosch's painting, Flaubert's novel uses the raw material of the anchorite's life as a pretext for organizing a "formal progression of unconfined reveries," as Foucault puts it, stressing how both artists (and, implicitly, the philosopher himself) have revived the imagery of ascetic struggle in order to give shape to "the fallen trees of a dream." In this context, the philosopher elaborates in greater detail the perverse origins of Anthony's ordeal. Besieged by hallucinations, and overwhelmed by monstrous apparitions, the ascetic turns to Holy Scripture, opening his Bible to compose his thoughts, to dissipate the phantasms—and to rekindle the divine spark within. His eyes come to rest, alas, on Esther 9: 5: "So the Jews smote all their enemies with the sword, slaughtering and destroying them, and worked their will on their opponents." Flaubert's Saint Anthony is aghast: "But now I'm plunging into thoughts of blood and murder!" It is one of the great comic moments in Flaubert's strange book—and Foucault in his 1964 essay lingers over it. "Evil is not embodied in individuals," he comments, but is "incorporated in words. A book that ought to lead to the threshold of salvation also opens the gates to Hell. All of the fantastic apparitions that are going to unfold before the eyes of the hermit—orgiastic palaces, drunken emperors, unfettered heretics, misshapen forms of the gods in agony, aberrant natures—this entire spectacle arises from the book opened by Saint Anthony."[74]

Foucault's final image of Anthony, inspired by Athanasius's canonic *Life*, appears in "The Scripting of the Self." Superficially, it seems as if the Pandora's Box opened up by imagination has been slammed shut: without a hint of irony, Foucault, drawing from Athanasius, offers a brief exegesis of Anthony's techniques of self-mastery. It is as if, through this gesture, the philosopher, turning to another possibility of the tradition inaugurated by the anchorite, were trying (just as Paul Veyne has cryptically written) "to settle a long-term debt to himself." Refusing the wages of delirious self-invention, he here recollects, with striking tranquility and painstaking fidelity to the documents he is working from, the kind of ascetic regimen practiced by the desert saint. [75]

In these years, as we have seen, Foucault came to think of himself as a kind of ascetic. But what kind of ascetic was he? Through the texts that he was writing, what kind of self was he "scripting"? By exercising the courage to "think differently," had he found a way out of a mad kind of "interrogation in a mirror"? Was he now headed towards "the gates of salvation"? Or, like the hapless anchorite in Flaubert's tale, was he fated to become a victim of his own morbid fantasies, perhaps led astray by a book that he hopes will save him? [76]

In the spring of 1983, shortly after Habermas's visit to Paris, Foucault returned to California. Thanks to the joint efforts of Leo Bersani, who at the time was chairman of Berkeley's French department, and Hans Sluga, then chairman of the philosophy department, Foucault had secured a standing offer to teach at Berkeley for two months every year.

"I saw quite a bit of him," recalls Sluga, who came to admire Foucault in these years for his intellectual daring and his readiness to leave earlier positions behind him. "When he was here, he always lived in San Francisco, and I lived in San Francisco. Very often I would give him a lift back home." [77] And while stuck in rush-hour traffic on the Bay Bridge from Berkeley to the city, the two of them would talk.

"We talked about lots of things," says Sluga. "I myself had been working on Wittgenstein, so we ended up talking quite a bit about Wittgenstein's critique of the self. He was also very interested in what his colleagues in the philosophy department stood for, what their interests were—it was clear that he was wondering how he fitted into their picture of what philosophy was.

"He was a very austere person. The way he lived was straightforward and simple, it was goal-directed, and determined, and meditative.

"Still, there was something about his personal life that he usually bracketed out, there was a whole attempt to bracket out the self. You could see it in his relationship to his own fame. He withdrew from it: he didn't want to be at the center of attention. I saw that withdrawal as an attempt to preserve himself for himself—and also as a way of escaping from his identity.

"We talked a lot about living in San Francisco. We had some long talks about the leather scene, which interested him, but which I knew very little about. He brought up the topic: he asked me what I thought about it. And I said, 'Look, I really think people have different needs and interests, and I can't personally say it's something close to my heart.' For him, the crucial point, I think, was that the leather scene had something to do with power relations and sexuality, it raised the possiblity of power relations that didn't simply run in one direction: the master and slave could reverse roles, it was an ambiguous relationship. He was also interested in the question of masculinity. I realized that the leather scene was something very important to him, and so we talked about it.

"I remember driving across the bridge one day and telling him about some strange disease that was appearing, and didn't even have a name at that time; and telling him, 'You'd better be careful.'

"He didn't believe it. He thought that Americans were basically puritanical and anti-sexual; and that it was all coming out in this sudden hysteria over this mysterious disease. I never brought it up again. Afterwards, I felt badly about it. I felt that I should have impressed this upon him more forcefully. I'm not sure it would have made a difference."[78]

Probably not. Too much was at stake in Foucault's ongoing exploration of "bodies and pleasures." Lured on by the most "insidious" of lusts, curiosity—and convinced that the kind of curiosity that "enables one to get free of oneself" even merited "the pain of being practiced with a little obstinacy"—Foucault remained desperately eager to unriddle the truth about himself. By discovering the truth, he might still be able to transfigure himself, and create "something that absolutely does not exist, about which we know nothing"—a different kind of man with a different kind of soul, and a different kind of body, "utterly new, utterly beautiful."[79]

Of course there were dangers. One needed courage. That was one point of Kant's motto for enlightenment: Dare to Know!

"We have reconquered our courage," Nietzsche wrote in a passage that Foucault had discussed in 1971. "And it is for precisely this reason that individuals and generations can now fix their eyes on tasks of a vastness that would to earlier ages have seemed madness, and a trifling with Heaven and Hell. We may experiment with ourselves! Yes, mankind has a right to do that! The greatest sacrifices have not yet been offered to knowledge. . . . "[80]

Comments Foucault: "Where religions once demanded the sacrifice of human bodies, knowledge now calls for experimentation on ourselves"—even if, as he ominously adds, such experimentation entails "the sacrifice of the subject of knowledge." The possibility of doing, or suffering, evil was no counter-argument. Neither was the prospect of death. If to become "what one is" unleashed a morbid compulsion—so be it: "Man needs what is most evil in him for what is best in him." If the attempt to unriddle the *daimon* of death seemed suicidal—so be it: "The secret for harvesting from existence the greatest fruitfulness and the greatest enjoyment is—to *live dangerously*."

In his 1971 essay, Foucault quoted Nietzsche again: "It may be a basic characteristic of existence that those who know it completely would perish."[81]

During his stay at Berkeley in the spring of 1983, Foucault taped a series of interviews with his colleagues and American expositors Paul Rabinow and Hubert Dreyfus. He had agreed to talk about his work in progress so that it might be covered in the paperback edition of Rabinow and Dreyfus's study of his philosophy, *Michel Foucault: Beyond Structuralism and Hermeneutics*.

In these conversations, he described his difficulty in starting over the History of Sexuality: "I first wrote a book about sex, which I put aside," he explained. "Then I wrote a book about the self and the techniques of the self; sex disappeared, and for the third time I was obliged to rewrite a book in which I tried to keep the equilibrium between one and the other."[82]

He also suggested one reason for his evident fascination with Hellenistic and Roman thought: "I don't think one can find any normalization in, for instance, the Stoic ethics. The reason is, I think, that the principal aim, the principal target of this kind of ethics was an aesthetic one. First, this kind of ethics was only a problem of personal choice. Second, it was reserved for a few people in the population; it was not a question of giving a pattern of behavior for everybody. It was a personal choice for a small elite. The reason for making this choice was the *will* to live a beautiful life"—the positive side, as it were, of the decisive will not to be governed. The aim, he went on, was "to leave to others memories of a beautiful existence. I don't think we can say that this kind of ethics was an attempt to normalize the population."[83]

At one point, Rabinow and Dreyfus asked him, "What will come next?"

"Well," exclaimed Foucault spontaneously, "I am going to take care of myself!"[84]

But how? Suggestive as much of his work on the genealogy of the modern subject is, it leaves characteristically blank the space that Foucault himself might occupy in his own "scripting" of the self.

Still, in his final lectures, essays, books, and interviews, Foucault offered a number of clues about how he now wanted to "take care" of himself. In order to organize these clues into a coherent pattern, it helps to recall the categories he used in his last books to analyze the "ethos" of the different schools of classical thought. As he explained in his conversations with Dreyfus and Rabinow, and in his introduction to *The Use of Pleasure*, he discerned four major aspects of the ethical "relationship to oneself":

—First, there was the substance that one cares for; "that is, the way in which the individual has to constitute this or that part of himself as the principal material of his moral conduct."[85]

—Second, there was the mode in which care is brought to bear on the substance; that is, "the way in which the individual establishes his relation to a rule and recognizes himself as obliged to put it to work."[86]

—Third, there was the means by which care is exercised; that is, the "ethical labor that one performs on oneself, not only in order to make one's conduct conform with a given rule, but also in order to try to transform oneself into the moral subject of one's behavior."[87]

—Fourth, and finally, there was the telos that one aimed at in taking such care; that is, the "mode of being" that served as the person's goal.[88]

For Foucault, the "substance" at stake in taking care of himself was neither his desires nor his thoughts, but, as he remarked to Dreyfus and Rabinow, one's *bios*—life in its chaotic, prepersonal flux. This substance he had glimpsed firsthand, at the limits of experience, by exploring without inhibition "bodies and pleasures."[89]

That he felt moved to exercise care at all was due neither to a divine law, nor a natural law, nor a rational rule, but rather to a passion for beauty, which led him to try to give to his existence, as he explained to Dreyfus and Rabinow, "the most beautiful form possible." By approaching one's life in such frankly aesthetic terms, one might turn one's self into a kind of existential artwork—a "work" (as Maurice Blanchot had once put it) that might enable the artist to transform "a part of himself from which he feels he is free, and from which the work has contributed to freeing him."[90]

The means by which Foucault expressed this aesthetic style of caring for himself was on one level relatively traditional. By undertaking an "analytics of truth," he had devoted his life to the discipline of critique, scripting his self in the historico-philosophical works that he wrote, trying to understand how he had become what he was, and at the same time making an effort to renew "the living body of philosophy, at least if the latter is still what it once was, namely an 'ascesis,' an exercise of the self in thought." But thinking and writing were not the only ways in which he had tried to take care of himself: for at the same time, he had pursued a "critical ontology," trying to transform and transfigure his self, by experimenting, sacrificing himself, putting his body and soul to the test directly, through an occult kind of ascesis, centered on the *daimonic* ordeals of S/M.[91]

His telos and ultimate aim, in entering into this hermetic, and highly ambiguous, "game" of truth, was not to become chaste, pure, or immortal—or even to become a master of himself. It was to "think differently"; it was to feel bathed in the "forgotten sparkle of the primitive light"; it was to feel attuned to a mysterious (and perhaps divine) spark within—what Kant called freedom; what Nietzsche called will to power; and what Heidegger called the "*transcendens* pure and simple."[92]

The day that he finished taping the last of his interviews with Hubert Dreyfus and Paul Rabinow, Foucault met another Berkeley colleague and friend, D.A. Miller, a professor of English, for lunch.

Walking toward Miller's car, Foucault suddenly seemed to wilt in the sun. He staggered onto a lawn, and sagged to the ground, crumpled up, as Miller recalls, like a kind of rag doll.[93]

Miller rushed to his side and asked whether he needed help. Foucault indicated he did not, and Miller ran to get his car. Racing back, he found the philosopher conscious, but still dazed. He helped Foucault into the front seat. "He said he was okay, but he obviously wasn't." Uncertain what to do next, Miller drove to an air-conditioned restaurant nearby: perhaps, he thought, the older man had been a victim of heat stroke; it was a relatively hot day; perhaps the cool air would make him feel better. In the car neither one of them said a word.

The change of scene worked: once inside the restaurant, Foucault's spirits lifted. He became his old self, urbane and animated. Falling into a certain gay lingua franca, he began to swap notes with Miller on the men in the room. The fabric of their friendship thus stitched back together, Foucault raised the issue of AIDS.

What did the acronym mean?, he asked Miller.

"It was a little bit like floating a balloon," says Miller, "a way of asking, 'What do you think of this subject?' "

They talked about the state of medical knowledge about the disease, and also about the idea of a "gay cancer."

" '*Je n'y crois pas*,' " Miller recalls the philosopher saying: 'I don't believe in it.'[94]

Foucault was not alone in his skepticism. The character of the plague was slowly becoming undeniable—and yet, particularly in these months, confusion, disbelief, and denial were still common responses among many gay men. "It wasn't as if people didn't know about AIDS," says Miller, "but everyone was unwilling to believe that it would attack you because you were gay."

As Miller himself stresses, such skepticism was perfectly justified, particularly given the long history of efforts by various medical "experts" to stigmatize homosexuality as pathological. That scientists had initially regarded AIDS as "a homosexual disease" was "an accident of social history," as one immunologist has put it. The epidemic had not broken out, as many people were prepared to believe, because homosexuals had "sinned against nature."[95]

But on still another level, the bitter truth of the matter—and it was becoming clearer and clearer—was that the most sexually adventurous gay subcultures that had evolved since the early 1970s formed ideal mediums for the emergence and spread of virulent strains of HIV.

On March 17, the *Bay Area Reporter*, San Francisco's gay newspaper, had run an editorial: "The position we have taken is to portray that each man owns his own body and the future he plots for it. And he retains ownership of the way he wants to die." But the pandemic had made it impossible to go on as before, acting as if AIDS was merely a pretext for scapegoating homosexuals: "We have made a very deliberate decision," the editorial announced, "to up the noise level on AIDS and the fatal furies that follow in its wake."[96]

This editorial was a bellwether: by that spring, the tide of opinion had begun to turn within the gay community itself. Convinced by the mounting medical evidence and mobilized by alarmed members of their own community, a small but growing number of gay men were changing the way they lived, improvising their own imaginative approach to "safe sex," using condoms, cutting down on sexual contacts—and, in a matter of months during the course of 1983, radically transforming the prevailing beliefs and practices of the male gay community.[97]

Miller himself was one of those already convinced that AIDS was a real menace. He now tried to convince Foucault: "I hazarded a bit of 'safe sex' propaganda."

The philosopher laughed.

" 'Are you afraid to die?,' " Miller remembers him asking.

"And I said, 'Yes,' even though I knew that this answer would disappoint him."

Whether he was disappointed or not is unclear: but Foucault sharply disagreed.

Death was nothing to fear, he assured Miller. Once, he explained, as Miller recalls the conversation, "he'd been walking across the street outside of his Paris apartment. He had been hit by a car. And he thought he was going to die. He compared it to a drug experience: it was a euphoric, ecstatic moment. He had a sense that he was leaving his body, that he was outside his own body."

The philosopher had hit his stride. He was now animated and affable— a far cry from the rag doll on the grass a few minutes before. Clinching his point, Foucault leaned toward the professor.

" 'Besides,' " he said, " 'To die for the love of boys: What could be more beautiful?' "[98]

At the close of his famous essay "On Providence," Seneca imagines god addressing a man fearful of what fate holds in store. "Scorn poverty," exhorts Seneca's imaginary god: "scorn pain," "scorn death"—and, finally, "scorn fate," for "I have given her no weapon with which she may strike your soul. Above all, I have taken pains that nothing should keep you here against your will; the way out lies open."[99]

Under most circumstances in life, the most useful way "out," for a philosophically inclined spirit, be it Seneca or Foucault, lay in the disciplined examination of one's existence: in this way, a thoughtful soul might escape from its self-imposed tutelage. One had only to bend one's will to the care of one's self—a process that Kant had defined in terms of "enlightenment."

But sometimes, forces beyond one's control threatened to overwhelm a person. Besieged by events, one was in danger of becoming a hostage of fortune.

Yet even under such harrowing circumstances, Seneca's imaginary god holds out a possiblity that a great many moralists (Kant, for one) simply rule out: namely, suicide.

"I have taken pains," says Seneca's imaginary god, "that nothing should keep you here against your will; the way out lies open. If you do not choose to fight, you may run away. Therefore of all things that I have deemed necessary for you, I have made nothing easier than dying."[100]

Hence the pagan god's advice: "Let every season, every place, teach you how easy it is to renounce Nature and fling her gift back in her face. In the very presence of the altars and the solemn rites of sacrifice, while you pray for life, learn well concerning death."[101]

Michel Foucault had learned early, and learned well.

"Suicide is not a way of cancelling the world or myself," he had written in 1953, inspired by Ludwig Binswanger's Stoic approach to the death of Ellen West: rather, suicide is a moment of potential "authenticity," a way of "rediscovering the original moment in which I make myself world."[102]

"I am a partisan of a true cultural struggle," Foucault reiterated nearly thirty years later: we must "teach people that there is not a piece of conduct more beautiful or, consequently, more worthy of careful thought than suicide. One should work on one's suicide throughout one's life."[103]

As Daniel Defert put it several years after Foucault's death, the philosopher "made an ascetic work of himself, and it was within this work that his death was inscribed."[104]

And from the standpoint of Foucault's own considered ethos—Why not?

After all: if one's *bios* had been fashioned like an artwork that would express "the *trancendens* pure and simple," there could be no more fitting capstone to this work, particularly in dark times, than the free embrace of a beautiful death.

On Foucault's last day in residence that spring at Berkeley, on a Friday afternoon at 5:00, he had arranged an unusual conference with a young Berkeley undergraduate.

The undergraduate's name was Philip Horvitz. He was studying to become an actor and a dancer, but, like so many ambitious young artists, he had also set out to master the main currents of avant-garde thought. Struck by the parts of *Discipline and Punish* that he had read, he had gone to hear the great man deliver a public lecture, before two thousand people, in Berkeley's largest auditorium. The lecture, about Kant, Socrates and Seneca, left him baffled and slightly bored. Still, there was something about Foucault's manner that drew him in, just as there had been something in his way of writing that piqued his curiosity; so he decided to take advantage of that institution customary in American universities, and scrupulously honored by Foucault, the "open office hour."[105]

He arrived to find Foucault looking wan and tired, surrounded by eager students peppering him with knowing questions, most in the form of 'What, exactly, did you mean on page 157 of the History of Sexuality when you wrote. . . .'

Horvitz patiently waited his turn, while Foucault fielded the erudite queries of the others, almost always with a laugh, "as if to say," as Horvitz recalls, " 'Are you kidding?' "

At last the master's gaze fell on him. Mustering his courage (and unwittingly revealing his limited command of the master's jargon), Horvitz popped his question: "Does the artist have an identity, or is he a powerless 'type,' who in the last fifty years has become more powerless than ever, due to the manipulation of technical media like television? Can the artist transcend 'The Structure?' Or is he doomed to commoditization, puppetization?"[106]

Foucault paused, sized up the earnest young man in front of him—and said, as Horvitz later recalled the conversation, " 'Come back tomorrow. . . . I need time to think.' "

He came back. Foucault was again surrounded by fawning young disciples. After waiting for some time, Horvitz explained that he had to go, and asked whether Foucault could please answer his question. " 'No,' " responded the philosopher—" 'But could you meet me Friday afternoon at five? We could have coffee.' "

Horvitz could not believe his ears. *He* was going to have *coffee* with *Michel Foucault*? The other students exchanged envious and puzzled glances.

At the appointed time, Horvitz appeared outside Foucault's office. A few minutes later, Foucault arrived. As they walked across campus toward a coffee shop, Foucault, clearly relishing the moment, spontaneously launched into a kind of sermon, inspired by Horvitz's original question.

Freedom can be found, he said—but always in a context. Power puts into play a dynamic of constant struggle. There is no escaping it. But there is freedom in knowing the game is yours to play. Don't look to authorities: the truth is in your self. Don't be scared. Trust your self. Don't be afraid of living. And don't be afraid of dying. Have courage. Do what you feel you must: desire, create, transcend—you can win the game.[107]

Foucault paused.

Horvitz summoned the nerve to press the philosopher further. What about the economic constraints on the artist?

" 'Well, you can't have a perfect world,' " responded Foucault. Revolution doesn't work. Still, it's an ideal. Playing *with* the structure—transforming and transfiguring its limits—is different from playing *inside* the structure. Artists have more freedom than ever. Once, the mere difference between artists and others in terms of attire and behavior was scandalous. But no more. See how much freedom you have: use it, to get still more.

They finally arrived at their destination. After ordering coffee, Foucault fixed his gaze on Horvitz: " 'You're gay, aren't you?' "[108]

The student was taken aback. Yes, he replied; he supposed he was, even though he hadn't yet "come out" in public.

The philosopher launched into another peroration.

Look at the gay community that has come into being, he said. And look at what AIDS is doing to it. It is terrible. It is absurd. A group that has risked so much, that has won so much, is now looking to outside authorities for guidance in a time of crisis. Relying on public health officials. Listening to doctors. It is unbelievable. The world, the play of power, the game of truth, all this " 'is *dangerous!*' " he exclaimed, his voice almost a shout: " 'But that's it! That's what you've got!' " Who could be scared of AIDS? You could be hit by a car tomorrow. Even crossing the street was dangerous! " 'If sex with a boy gives me pleasure' "—why renounce such pleasure?

We have the power, he said again: *we* shouldn't give it up.

Horvitz listened in silence. He was stunned. Deeply touched, he was also confused. At a loss for words, he said nothing.

Foucault indicated that he had to go. The student accompanied him to the local subway stop.

Entering the underground to go back to San Francisco, Foucault stopped and turned back to Horvitz. " 'Good luck,' " he said, " 'And don't be scared!' "

"You, too," ventured Horvitz: "Don't you be scared."

Foucault shrugged.

" 'Oh, don't cry for me if I die,' " he laughed.[109] And then he disappeared.

— *11* —

THE SECRETS

of

A M A N

ON JUNE 2, 1984, Foucault collapsed in the kitchen of his Paris apartment. In the previous months, he had been in and out of the hospital. He had developed a hacking cough, suffered bouts of crippling migraine, and steadily grown weaker. Warned by his doctors that he had little time to live, he had worked feverishly to complete his History of Sexuality, fighting through pain and fatigue. By the time he collapsed, two volumes were done, with a third almost finished.[1]

The next day, he was visited in the hospital by one of his closest friends, a young artist named Hervé Guibert. Years later, Guibert conjured up the scene in one of his autobiographical novels: "He avoided meeting my eyes," wrote Guibert, "and said, 'You always think that in a certain kind of situation you'll find something to say about it, and now it turns out there's nothing to say after all.' " The philosopher was exhausted and in visible pain, but "the worst blow," the novelist later wrote, was that "his mind was slipping." The doctors were preparing to do a spinal tap and the philosopher looked frightened: "You could see it in his eyes, that panic at suffering, no longer mastered inside the body, but provoked artificially by an outside intervention directed at the site of the illness."[2]

He would never go home again. And as the days slipped by, Foucault gradually sank into "a state of weakness and surrender that uncages the beast within," as Guibert later described the ravages of AIDS. "The microorganisms responsible for both *Pneumocystise carinii* pneumonia, that boa constrictor of the lungs, and the brain-destroying cysts of toxoplasmosis are present inside each one of us but are kept in check by a healthy immune system, whereas AIDS gives them the green light, opening the floodgates of destruction."[3]

Doctors in 1984 could do nothing to forestall the destruction, little to alleviate the pain. The end, however, came slowly. Foucault was able to read the first reviews of his new books, which appeared in the middle of June. He was able to arrange one last interview for publication. And in these last days of his life, as he lay in the hospital undergoing his final agony—long imagined, now a reality—he was also able to participate in an ambiguous but telling little drama that unfolded quietly at his bedside.

Illuminating one of the most paradoxical aspects of the philosopher's ethos—his tortuous personal approach to telling the truth—the drama revolved around Hervé Guibert. Virtually every day, for as long as words still came—and until the young artist was forbidden to visit—Guibert talked with Foucault. Virtually every day, for as long as the philosopher talked, the artist carefully listened, and later wrote down, all that he said. And if Guibert's subsequent accounts can be trusted, Foucault in their talks did something he rarely did: he confessed. Evoking his childhood and its dreams, he volunteered what he felt to be the deepest truths about himself.

His friendship with Guibert, witnesses agree, was the most intimate and classically chaste of his final years. Though only twenty-nine years old, Guibert had already won a reputation as a novelist, photographer, and screenwriter. In appearance, he was faintly angelic, with willowy blond hair, a whisper of a voice, and a gaze of piercing intensity. But his consuming passions were anything but celestial. Like Foucault, he was fascinated by transgression, by moments of madness, by the instability of the frontiers between fantasy and reality, pleasure and pain, life and death. One of his first novels, in fact, was a "sado-masochistic tale," written, he later confessed, in the hopes of impressing Foucault—to no avail: "I think he found the book fell short of his own sado-masochistic intensity."[4]

They had first met in 1977. Their friendship, in Guibert's words, developed "very bizarrely, very slowly." At the time, Foucault liked to hold court in his Paris apartment surrounded by a coterie of beautiful and brilliant gay young men. Within this circle, Guibert was perhaps the most beautiful, and certainly the most brilliant, a latter-day dandy who was also a cool master of surreal imagery freely drawn from firsthand experience.[5]

His artistry Foucault admired. In one essay, published in 1983, he linked Guibert with the novelist Malcolm Lowry, the painter René Magritte, and the photographer Duane Michals, all figures he held in high esteem. Each of them had created works that subtly transfigured the world, transforming experience into a phenomenon shot through with uncanny possibilities, hovering uncertainly between dream and reality—between the true and the false. To express such a "transfiguration does not entail an annulling of reality," Foucault wrote in 1983, "but a difficult interplay between the truth of what is real and the exercise of freedom; 'natural' things become 'more than natural,' 'beautiful' things become 'more than beautiful,' and individual objects appear 'endowed with an impulsive life like the soul of [their] creator.' "[6]

A letter Foucault wrote to Guibert in the same year offers a glimpse at the dreamy aura of their friendship—and also suggests the extent to which the philosopher and novelist inhabited the same imaginative universe. "I have a longing to recount to you," Foucault writes, "the pleasure that I find in watching, without stirring from my table, a boy who each day at the same hour comes to lean out a window on the rue d'Alleray. At nine o'clock he opens the window, he wears a small blue bathtowel, or similarly blue underwear; he leans his head on his arms, burying his face in his elbow . . . hunting for dreams extremely strong, intense, exhausting, leaving him in a great (flute, more blue paper) despondency. . . . And then briskly, he stands up, he sits down at a table where he must read? Write? Type? I do not know; I only see the naked elbow and shoulder; and I ask myself what dreams his eyes have drawn from the fold of his arms, what words or drawings can burst forth; but I tell myself that I am the only one to have seen, from the outside, taking shape and losing shape, the graceful chrysalis where they were born. This morning the window remained closed; in place of which I am writing to you."[7]

In June of 1984, such dreamy erotica was about the last thing on Hervé Guibert's mind. As the month wore on, it was obvious that Foucault was dying. After a lifetime spent trying to fathom the roots of his "experience" in both its positive and negative dimensions, probing the uncertain line between life and death, the philosopher was about, in earnest, to step once and for all over that line. And the artist, despite a morbid-mindedness that he had exquisitely refined in his fiction, discovered that nothing in his own previous experience had quite prepared him for the ordeal of his visits to the hospital.

In an effort, he later explained, to contain his anguish, Guibert secretly decided to keep a journal. With a growing conviction that "it was my own destiny that I was in the midst of writing down," he methodically recorded the thoughts, moods, gestures, and physiognomy of the man dying before his eyes, "point by point, gesture after gesture, and without omitting the slightest word of the rarified conversation, organized hideously around the situation."[8]

Guibert later admitted to feeling disgust at his behavior. His journal, he guessed, would have appalled Foucault—and so, perhaps, would have his later books and public interviews about their friendship.

As the artist well knew, Foucault was a man of supreme discretion, of deliberate reserve, of tensile silences. That the philosopher took a keen pleasure in keeping his distance is suggested by one of Guibert's most memorable photographs. It shows Foucault dressed in a kimono, a faint smile on his face, a brilliantly illuminated space behind him, standing at a threshold. His figure is flanked by an open door and polished dark panels, his image doubled and redoubled on the flat angled ebony surfaces in a distorted reflection of the man who wordlessly beckons from beyond.[9]

In the months before his death, Foucault had hurriedly destroyed hundreds of pages of notebooks, letters, and manuscripts, including an unpublished work on the painter Manet. In his will, he prohibited the posthumous publication of anything he might have missed. He wanted not simply to die, but to enjoy what he had called a few months before a "death-effacement," leaving behind, as Guibert later put it, "only polished bones around a black diamond, gleaming and impenetrable, securely closed in on its secrets."[10]

But if Guibert's own accounts are as truthful as they seem, Foucault at the end of his life relented, and in fact confided some of his secrets—precisely to Guibert. Why? Why reveal the truth about formative experiences he had a spent a lifetime concealing?

As it happens, Foucault himself, in the last lectures he had delivered at the Collège de France a few months before, had in effect addressed this very question. Why tell the truth? How do we come to feel *obliged* to tell the truth—particularly the truth about ourselves?

His explicit topic was *parrhesia*—the art of truth-telling, as this had been practiced by Socrates and the Cynics and Stoics who came after him. But implicitly Foucault was once again examining—and implicitly trying to change—deeply rooted habits of thought. That the approach to truth was a kind of game, the contingent product of changing rules, embodied in different social beliefs and practices, had long been one of his main contentions. But that struggling to tell the truth, particularly when death drew near, might be a game worth playing—this suggestion, conveyed through both the tone and content of these lectures, was something new for Foucault, something different. [11]

For years, Foucault had waged a kind of guerrilla war, in theory as well as in practice, against the imperative to tell the truth. The exemplary individual, he insisted, "is not the man who goes off to discover himself, his secrets, his hidden truth; he is the man who tries to invent himself," uninhibited by the constraints of conventional morality. Perhaps the most chafing of these constraints, in Foucault's mind, was the duty to confess— one of the most insidious legacies that Christianity had bequeathed to modern society. Fearful of being pinned down, the philosopher struggled throughout much of his life against this "pastoral power" that by "knowing the inside of people's minds . . . exploring their souls . . . [and] making them reveal their innermost secrets," threatened to tie "the individual to himself," and stifle his creative ability. "One confesses in public and in private," Foucault lamented in the first volume of his History of Sexuality. One avows "crimes," "sins," "one's thoughts and one's desires," memories of childhood, "the past and its dreams," in an infernal spiraling crescendo of words that flood us, find us, betray us, prompting us "to say that which is most difficult to say," confessing "to one's parents, to one's educators, to one's doctor, to those one loves"—and that is not all. For one whispers as well "to oneself, in pleasure and in pain, confessions impossible to make to anyone else, and one writes books about them." [12]

But when the philosopher confided on his deathbed in Hervé Guibert— a man obviously interested in the things "one writes books about"—just as when he delivered his last lectures at the Collège de France, Foucault, in effect, was conceding his own inability, when all was said and done, to escape from the duty to tell the truth—above all, the truth about who he was, and what he had become.

On one level, indeed, telling the truth about such matters had become easier than ever before, because *what* he was had become clearer than ever before. He was *not*, after all, so he decided, a historian of science like Bachelard, or an intellectual like Sartre, or a revolutionary like Marx, or an infamous man like Pierre Rivière, but rather something at first glance familiar, reassuring, obvious: for he was, so he now thought, a *philosopher*— a lover of wisdom, a seeker of truth.

"If I know the truth I will be changed," he said in 1982, in one of his most revealing interviews. "And maybe I will be saved. Or maybe I'll die"— he burst out laughing—"but I think that is the same for me anyway." [13]

Contemplating possible antecedents for the peculiar *style* of his own philosophical life, Foucault in his final lectures examined two quite different sorts of forerunners, two possible models, illustrating two divergent roads to truth: that taken by Socrates, on the one hand; and that explored by Diogenes the Cynic, on the other.[14]

Recounting the life of Socrates, Foucault lingered over a host of details with an autobiographical resonance. He recalled the enigma of the philosopher's *daimon*, the ghostly double that had plunged the first great apostle of reason into a kind of involuntary ordeal of truth (*épreuve*). He recollected the oracle Socrates received at Delphi, which had launched him on his lifelong philosophical quest (*recherche*) to try to verify whether there was anyone wiser than himself. And he described how Socrates exercised care (*souci*) by putting others to the question and his soul to the test, refining a new kind of art, of not being governed, exhibiting an admirable and unwavering kind of courage in his willingness to reason without direction from another. By devoting his life to "critique," as Foucault understood it, Socrates thus came to embody a just and pleasing balance of *logos* and *bios*, idea and existence.[15]

The capstone of this philosophical life, as Foucault now depicted it, came when Socrates decided to embrace death freely. He pondered the meaning of the martyr's last words, uttered after he had drunk the hemlock: "Crito, we ought to offer a cock to Asclepius." Following a suggestion made by his old friend Georges Dumézil, Foucault points out that Crito previously had tried to convince Socrates to escape from Athens rather than kill himself with the poison, arguing that popular opinion might be scandalized by the fact that the philosopher had not done everything he could to avoid death. Socrates, however, sharply disagreed with Crito, arguing that in all such matters, whether of death or of life, the philosopher should be governed not by popular opinion, but rather by the convictions he had forged for himself during his own search for truth. Moreover, in any life of unrelenting struggle against misleading opinions and false authorities, the philosopher will feel free of their grip, and at peace with himself, only as the hour of his death draws near. Hence the last words of Socrates, as Foucault understood them: welcoming death, the philosopher feels delivered from the travails of his lifelong struggle against falsehood; and therefore urges Crito to give thanks by paying tribute to Asclepius, the Greek god of healing and health.[16]

That Socrates was for Foucault (as for Nietzsche before him) one kind of model seems clear enough: he remains the first great thinker in the West to offer his own existence as an inexhaustible subject of philosophical investigation. But of course the Socratic method—his effort to elaborate a reasoned code of moral life, his search for the principles of universal justice, his unstinting struggle to purge his mind of "the follies of the body"—was not quite Foucault's own. [17] And in his final lectures, he soon enough turned away from the figure of Socrates, and away, as well, from the figure of Seneca and the tradition of the Stoics, which he discussed only in passing on this occasion. Instead, he focused on a far less familiar figure, and a much more obscure spiritual tradition: that of Diogenes and the Cynics.

Foucault devoted what turned out to be the last five lectures of his life to this topic. In these last lectures, delivered at the Collège de France between February 29 and March 28, 1984, he spoke emphatically and ranged widely—his rhetoric was powerful, his analysis bold and often surprising. He talked not just about the Cynics as a group of pagan phi-losophers, but also about Cynicism as a neglected current in the history of Western thought; about Diogenes as the greatest hero of Cynicism; and, implicitly, about what he, Foucault, had in fact become—a kind of ar-chetypal modern Cynic, following in the traces of Diogenes and those who came after.

He began by defining the classic tradition of pagan Cynicism as it flourished from roughly the end of the first century B.C. to the fourth century A.D. As philosophical schools go, it was very loosely organized, not around treatises and texts, but rather around the study of exemplars, figures the Cynics admired and treated as standards—for example, Her-acles, Odysseus, and also Diogenes. Such heroes, whether mythic or real, all illustrated an "extremely radical conception," according to which a "person is nothing else but his relation to truth"—and the truth "takes shape or is given form" *only* in a person's "own life." [18] The true life could only be embodied—never handed down in the form of commandment, prohibition, or law. In contrast with classical Platonism and classical Stoi-cism—and of course with Judaism and Christianity as well—pagan Cyn-icism thus involved the study of "no established texts," and "no settled, recognizable doctrine." Yet it was not an ingathering of solipsists; for the Cynics communicated their approach to the truth in three different ways, elaborating their own peculiar "game of truth":

—First, they resorted to "critical preaching," fashioning monologues addressed to large audiences. These diatribes, with their frequent use of aphorism and the gnomic aside, were meant to provoke auditors to action and revolt, moving them "to eliminate all of the dependencies introduced by culture." (The Cynical technique here stood in stark contrast to Socratic dialogue, which was addressed to a few select souls and was meant to produce a contemplative life devoted to sharing reasoned knowledge about unchanging and universal ideas.)[19]

—Second, the Cynics exploited the pedagogical possibilities of "scandalous behavior," turning their personal conduct into a source of public controversy by breaking laws, flouting customs, ignoring taboos. In this way, comments Foucault, the Cynic made of himself "a *blazon* of essential truths," often taking direct action in his own right.[20]

—Third, Cynics sometimes exploited what Foucault calls "provocative dialogue," an exchange of views in which the love and mutual trust that formed one ground of Socratic inquiry was replaced by something "like a fight, a battle, or a war, with peaks of great aggressivity and moments of peaceful calm." The Cynical hero here behaved toward others as he behaved toward himself, plunging his interlocutor into an unconcealed spiritual combat in which one might learn to grapple with another, be that other a foe in public life—or the *daimon* lurking within. Viewing life as an adventure to be lived in the spirit of Odysseus, the Cynics supposed that each might find his natural home, but only by resisting the blandishments of slavery, setting sail—and then drawing a line, stubbornly staying the course, ignoring the Song of the Sirens. "The main effect of this parrhesiastic struggle with power," comments Foucault, "is not to bring the interlocutor to a new truth, or to a new level of self-awareness; it is to lead the interlocutor to *internalize* this parrhesiastic struggle—to fight with himself against his own faults."[21]

The first great historical product of this agonizing and idiosyncratic approach to the truth, as Foucault reconstructs the Cynical strand in Western thought, was the early Christian ascetics. The desert saint, like the pagan Cynic, wrenched himself away from everyday life and ordinary society, cutting the normal ties that bind a human being to family and friends. The goal, in so doing, was not to achieve a pleasing balance between the *logos* and *bios*, as in the case of Socrates and the Stoics. The goal was rather to transfigure totally who one was and what one thought, creating, if necessary through the most immoderate and punishing of practices, a radically *other* sort of existence, manifest in one's body, unmistakable in one's style of life— turning one's *bios*, as such, into "the immediate, explosive, and savage presence of truth." A similarly radical approach to producing an equally personal sort of "truth" was resurrected—so Foucault goes on to suggest—in the Renaissance, by certain artists; in the Reformation, by certain radical Protestant sects; in the Age of Reason by "Rameau's nephew," Diderot's make-believe figure of enlightened folly; at the threshold of our own era by Faust, Goethe's mythic figure of diabolical genius; and in our own age of uncertainty by Sade and his erotic followers, by Nietzsche and his philosophical heirs, by the votaries of revolutionary nihilism most vividly depicted by Dostoyevsky in *The Possessed*, and by a series of intensely disquieting modern poets, painters, and artists, from Baudelaire to Beckett.[22]

This is a revealing genealogy. But with the exception of the desert saints, whom he discussed in some detail, Foucault spent little time in his lectures on the modern heirs of Cynicism, perhaps because he had already discussed so many of them in previous lectures, essays, and books. Instead, he focused in these final lectures on the life, and legend, of the arch-Cynic, Diogenes. The most storied of the ancient Cynics became, in effect, Foucault's hermetic touchstone, offering a standard by which to understand, and measure, a long history of thought—and his *own* singular approach to truth.

A contemporary of Plato, Diogenes of Sinope (413–327 B.C.) is said to have lived in a tub and to have carried a lit lamp in broad daylight, explaining that "I am looking for a man." Once asked what sort of man he was, Diogenes replied, "a Socrates gone mad." Rather than try to define clear ideas about an immortal soul and a transcendent good, or treat wisdom as the rational contemplation of an "other world," he strove to embody his own singular truth, by living an "other life."[23]

Like Socrates, Diogenes received an oracle at Delphi: "Change the value of the currency." Interpreting this oracle as a summons to transform the conventional wisdom, he set about transgressing every custom and law of society, "asserting that the manner of life he lived was the same as that of Heracles when he preferred liberty to everything." He called himself the "Dog," to emphasize the "recoining of values" that had led him to satisfy without shame his own animal needs. Unafraid to tell the truth, no matter how shocking, he was bold enough to offend the most powerful ruler of his day: humiliating Alexander the Great in a legendary encounter, the arch-Cynic personified the political paradox, said Foucault, of being "*le roi anti-roi*"—"an anti-sovereign sovereign," a ruler at war with rules.[24]

Fearlessly Diogenes explored the limits of reason, no matter how crazy his quest might seem. He notoriously condoned cannibalism, and incest as well: when Oedipus discovered that he had killed his father and married his mother, Diogenes, it is said, remarked that he should have taken it in stride, saying that "I see this happening everyday in my own hen-house!" But for Foucault, perhaps the paramount symbol of the Cynic's way of life was Diogenes' gesture of masturbating in the marketplace— defiantly "doing *everything* in public, the works of Demeter and Aphrodite alike."[25]

Diogenes, in other words, approached philosophy as a field of limit-experience, pushing thought to its breaking point—just like Michel Foucault. Putting truth to the test, he mocked, shocked, and provoked—just like Foucault. Above all, by living a life of bodily freedom, he issued a radical challenge to the society he criticized and rejected. In Foucault's words: "The *bios philosophicos* is the animality of being human, renewed as a challenge, practiced as an exercise—and thrown in the face of others as a scandal."[26]

But in one respect, at least, the archetypal Cynic issued Foucault himself a final challenge, presenting him with one last test, one last "ordeal of truth." For Diogenes, no less than Socrates, took seriously the injunction to "Know thyself." And Diogenes, no less than Socrates, believed such knowledge obliged the philosopher to tell the truth about himself. As Epictetus put it, the Cynic will not "wish to keep anything concealed that is his (otherwise he is lost, he has destroyed the Cynic within him, the man of outdoor life, the free man . . .)."[27]

"Why do we care for ourselves," Foucault wondered in one of his last interviews, "only through the care for truth?" Given his earlier views, his ultimate answer to this question has a poignant ring: "I think that we are touching on a question which is very fundamental and which is, I would say, the question of the Western world. What caused all Western culture to begin to turn around this obligation of truth, which has taken on a variety of different forms? *Things being what they are*"—this is the heart of the matter—"*nothing has, up to the present, proved that we could define a strategy exterior to it*"—a strategy, that is, beyond the "care for truth."[28]

The "obligation of truth," in short, was our unavoidable destiny—and Foucault's inescapable fate—like it or not. Try as we might, we creatures of Western culture cannot remain silent about who we really are. However unconventional our style of life may be, however vehemently we may reject the moral codes upheld in society and observed by others, we cannot—and should not—avoid communicating our selves, our secrets, our hidden mysteries, our most singular and personal "truth."

One is reminded of one of Foucault's favorite passages from Beckett: "I can't go on, you must go on, I'll go on, you must say words, as long as there are any, until they find me, until they say me, strange pain, strange sin"—strange and inescapable confession of the truth. [29]

And so, at the threshold of death, "before the door that opens on my story," it seems plausible that Foucault should have decided to emulate Diogenes and all those who, he now supposed, had already followed in his footsteps, from Saint Anthony to Sade, from Baudelaire to Samuel Beckett. Trying to "think differently," he would try to the tell the truth more directly. Picking at old wounds and ancient memories, recollecting the furies that had driven him to become what he was—a philosopher!— he would invite a friend (was Guibert the only one?) to gaze directly upon the "strange pain, strange sin" that up till then had silently haunted his inner experience, swirling anonymously in "this dust of words" that were his books. Rendering his own tribute to Asclepius, he would then talk at last about what Beckett had called this "wordless thing in an empty place, a hard shut dry cold black place, where nothing stirs, nothing speaks, and that I listen, and that I seek, like a caged beast born of caged beasts born of caged beasts born of caged beasts born in a cage. . . . " [30]

In fact, of course, he had been born in Poitiers fifty-seven years before. But that was a place, and a time long gone, that he had rarely discussed— until, apparently, that June of 1984. As death drew near, Foucault, re-assured perhaps by Guibert's attentiveness and professions of undying friendship, plunged deeper and deeper into the past. Spiraling back in time, he began to recall painful truths, confiding personal secrets, dredging up images from the sunken continent of his childhood—images in some cases that he had never before shared, even with Daniel Defert. [31]

What Foucault may have said in these conversations appears in two places: Guibert's novel, *To the Friend Who Did Not Save My Life*, largely about AIDS, published in 1990, when Guibert himself, afflicted with the disease, was facing death himself; and one of his short stories, entitled "The Secrets of a Man," written the day after Foucault was buried but first published in 1988. [32]

Of these two works, "The Secrets of a Man" is by far the more revealing— and, also, not coincidentally, the more macabre and fantastic. The novel, by contrast, contains, in Guibert's words, an "incomplete and partial"— but quite moving and often verifiably accurate—description of Foucault, mainly focused on his attitude towards AIDS and how he faced dying from the disease. [33]

In neither work is Foucault identified by his own name. In the novel, he appears as "Muzil," as if to evoke the Austrian novelist Robert Musil and his autobiographical hero Ulrich, the "man without qualities" in quest of his *daimon*, a self-effacing herald of Nietzsche's "overman."

In the short story, by contrast, the character modeled on Foucault appears, perhaps more aptly, as a nameless but notorious philosopher.

The short story starts with a passage typical of Guibert at his most ghoulish. It describes a neurosurgeon gleefully slicing open the skull of a genius, taking perverse pride in "assailing such a fortress." He is thrilled to be violating the inner sanctum of such a famous critic of modern psychiatry and medicine, and astonished by the beauty of the organ before his eyes, "luminescent," still teeming with life, despite the three lesions that it is his goal to remove in an effort to delay the onset of delirium and death. (Foucault in fact suffered from toxoplasmosis, which produces lesions on the brain; but these lesions were considered by his doctors to be inoperable—just as Guibert describes in his novel).[34]

The normally concealed nerves and vessels of the nameless thinker's brain remind the narrator of the subterranean complexities of his personality. "Digging a little, one found vast stores, reserves of secrets, memories of childhood, novel theories. The memories of childhood had been buried more deeply than anything else in order not to come up against the idiocy of interpretations, or the dubious craftsmanship of the large, deceptively luminous veil that would drape the work." Certain primal scenes nevertheless were too deeply etched to be easily effaced. And "in the sanctuary of his vessels lurked two or three images, like terrible dioramas."[35]

These, then, are the images that Foucault apparently shared on his deathbed with Guibert: the sunken continent of childhood revealed; the "secrets" of the story's title; the philosopher's most singular truths confessed, his "granite of spiritual *fatum*" at last revealed in primal scenes as dark and solid as the boulder in Magritte's painting *The Château of the Pyrénées*, as preternatural as the blue of the sea and the air around the chiseled stone, as disconcerting as the prospect of a previously hidden fortress, and the bedrock on which it sits, suddenly hoving into view, floating in midair, a hard shut dry cold black place bizarrely made visible.[36]

The first of the "terrible dioramas," writes Guibert, "shows the philosopher-child, led by his father, who was a surgeon, into an operating room in the hospital at Poitiers, to witness the amputation of a man's leg—this was to steel the boy's virility."[37]

In the second scene, we see the young philosopher walking past a nondescript courtyard. "But that courtyard was suffused with the thrill of infamy: it was there, on a straw mattress, in a kind of garage, that for decades had lived the woman the newspapers called 'the Sequestered of Poitiers.'"[38]

The third of the "terrible dioramas" is set in the war years. "At school, the little philosopher, always first in his class, is threatened by the sudden intrusion, at first unexplained, of a band of arrogant young Parisians, naturally smarter than everyone else. Dethroned, the philosopher-child is seized by hate, damns the intruders, invites every curse to rain down upon them: the Jewish children, refugees in the provincial city, did in fact disappear, spirited off to the camps."[39]

Nietzsche, a keen student of the anecdotal lore that surrounded ancient Greek sages like Diogenes, once remarked that "what is truly irrefutable" in any philosophy is what is "personal," adding that "with three anecdotes, it is possible to convey the image of a man."[40] Has Guibert offered us three such anecdotes? Do these "terrible dioramas" illuminate what is most personal—and "irrefutable"—in his work? Finally: Are they "true"?

The first story, of being forced by his father to witness an amputation, Foucault told to at least one other person before he died.[41] This, of course, does not mean that the story is "true," in the sense of accurately representing an event that actually occurred. The recollection of primal scenes from childhood, as Freud has taught us, often produces elaborations, omissions, strange and telltale ellipses, and fabrications, in which the scene summoned from the past quivers with "an impulsive life like the soul of [its] creator."

The image, certainly, has all the ingredients of a recurrent nightmare: the sadistic father, the impotent child, the knife slicing into flesh, the body cut to the bone, the demand to acknowledge the sovereign power of the patriarch, and the inexpressible humiliation of the son, having his manliness put to the test.

Like debris from a shipwreck, fragments of this scene keep bobbing up throughout Foucault's life and work. One thinks, for example, of Foucault's youthful dream of the floating surgeon's knife—and also of the young student slashing his chest with a razor. One is reminded, too, of the strange link the philosopher makes in *The Birth of the Clinic* between sadism and the scientific foundations of modern medicine. And then there is the truly terrible diorama that opens *Discipline and Punish*. In this passage, the philosopher forces us to watch as the regicide Damiens has his legs and arms carved up and pulled off by a team of six horses. Later in the same work, Foucault discusses the emotions of the people who witnessed such dismemberments. Evoking a bitter rage, he suggests that the spectators were constantly on the verge of erupting in an uncontrollable orgy of violence aimed at the hateful sovereign who had ordered this cruel display of power.[42]

The second and most cryptic of the images in Guibert's short story—where the young philosopher feels a *frisson* of curiosity as he passes by the place where a woman had been "sequestered"—Foucault seems to have shared with no one else. Whether the young philosopher ever felt such a *frisson* must remain in doubt.

One thing about the vignette is nevertheless not only verifiably true, but also richly suggestive, given Foucault's lifelong interest in the confinement of the mad, the sick, and the criminal in closed institutions. There really was a woman known as "the Sequestered of Poitiers." And it seems improbable that Foucault would *not* have known something about her, since her discovery provoked one of the greatest scandals in the history of modern Poitiers.

The story of this woman first came to light in 1901. In May of that year, the police of Poitiers, acting on an anonymous tip, discovered that a woman in her fifties named Melanie Bastian, the daughter of a family as impeccably haute-bourgeoise as Foucault's, had been locked up by her mother and brother and kept in a room with the windows boarded up, in complete darkness, with scarcely enough food to survive, living in excrement, covered with lice, maggots, and rats. A quarter century before, it was said, the daughter, then nearly twenty-five, had become pregnant out of wedlock, given birth, and killed the illegitimate child. The family, declaring that the girl had become mad, had her confined, first to a hospital, then to the care of a charitable religious order—and finally to the darkened room with the straw mattress where the poor woman was discovered in 1901. Surveying the room, officials discovered an inscription on the walls:

"To create beauty, not out of love or liberty, but solitude forever. You must live and die in a dungeon. . . . "[43]

In a city the size of Poitiers—an old Roman town that had a population of roughly forty-five thousand in the 1930s—a house where a terrible crime had been committed would remain a marked, haunted spot for years afterward. And though a court case was quickly resolved—the mother and brother, when brought to trial, were acquitted of any wrongdoing—the impressions left by the incident lived on, as did the woman herself (though she never recovered her sanity). The incident was shocking enough to capture the imagination of André Gide, who collected contemporary newspaper accounts and court documents, and published them in 1930 in a small book entitled *The Sequestered of Poitiers*. There is no direct evidence that Foucault read Gide's book. But there is a striking resemblance between the documentary format pioneered by Gide, and Foucault's own later dossier, containing newspaper accounts and court documents, about the similarly lurid trial of Pierre Rivière.[44]

And, of course, Foucault's own imagination was throughout his life haunted, as we have seen, by the prospects opened up by dark covered spaces; by dungeons and labyrinths; by cruel and unusual forms of punishment; by the intolerable and harrowing conditions inside French prisons, where men lived chained to beds, swimming in filth; by the agonizing conviction (expressed implicitly, powerfully, unmistakably in the pages of *Discipline and Punish*) that his own soul was such a place, a stinking cage and a prison, where his own animal instincts had been sequestered, branded, perverted, giving rise, in a kind of hideous reflux motion, to the most shocking sort of Cynicism—as if he, too, had been condemned "to create beauty, not out of love or liberty, but solitude forever. . . . "

As for the third "terrible diorama" in Guibert's short story, showing the young schoolboy wishing his newfound Parisian rivals dead—this, too, seems to contain at least a grain of truth. After an uncharacteristically poor year in school, Foucault in 1940 entered the Catholic collège Saint-Stanislas, where he began to excel in his studies, often ranking first or second in his class.

As Guibert implies, the war during these years was never far from Foucault's mind. Refugees from Paris poured into the city, making life difficult, even for young students like Foucault. The philosopher told at least one other friend of the confusion he felt when the influx of newcomers meant that suddenly he was no longer at the top of his class.[45]

In one of the few interviews in which he publicly discussed his childhood, Foucault recalled how, during this period, his "private life was really threatened." As a youngster, school had been "an environment protected from exterior menaces"—but with the coming of war, there was no safe haven. "Maybe that is the reason why I am fascinated by history and the relationship between personal experience and those events of which we are a part," he later speculated: "I think this is the nucleus of my theoretical desires."[46]

There is one crucial aspect of Guibert's third vignette that is impossible to verify. That the fate of the Jews in World War II preoccupied Foucault seems clear: he said so on more than one occasion. But had he really wished his refugee rivals *dead*?

Though it is impossible to confirm the accuracy of this detail, it is also hard to ignore the affinity between this last of Foucault's ostensible confessions and one of the most vexing of his "theoretical desires"—namely, to comprehend and to ferret out the lust for power and "fascism," wherever it occurred. By "fascism," as Foucault once explained, he meant "not only historical fascism, the fascism of Hitler and Mussolini," but also "the fascism in us all, in our heads and in our everyday behavior," in "our speech and our acts, our hearts and our pleasures," buried deep in "the body," its traces diabolically difficult to expunge, "the fascism that causes us to love power, to desire the very thing that dominates and exploits us."[47]

But power, as we know, is not the only thing that Foucault was worried about loving, not the only menacing desire he found buried in his speech, his acts, his heart, and his pleasures. Death, too, stood like an implacable sphinx at the threshold of his fondest dreams. And if, once upon a time, he had wished his rivals dead, then, at the end of his life, he had perhaps wished *himself* dead, casting his fate freely with a community he knew was doomed, doomed as surely as the Jews of Poitiers had been doomed forty years before, ending his life in a potentially suicidal gesture of solidarity by spiriting himself off to the bathhouses of San Francisco in the fall of 1983, putting his body on the line one last time in a shocking but strangely lyrical, strangely logical act of Passion, perhaps mad, perhaps tragic—yet also perfectly fitting. Perhaps.

Such are some of the facts surrounding the "terrible dioramas" described by Hervé Guibert, and a few of the related passages that spring to mind from the philosopher's life and work.

Taken together, the images described by Guibert form a kind of unholy trinity. They show an amputation, a dungeon, a fantasy of murder; a figure of wanton power, an erotic transgression, an implicit burden of crushing guilt: three eerily resonant images of cruelty, confinement, and death.

Has Guibert then truly revealed "the secrets of a man"?

In 1990, as Guibert himself was struggling with AIDS, a heated debate erupted in Paris over the artist's credibility and motives. The occasion was the publication of his *roman à clef* about AIDS, *To the Friend Who Did Not Save My Life*. Some commentators felt that the thinly veiled characterization of Foucault in this novel had violated not merely the trust of his dead friend but the unwritten code, still strong in France, that one simply does not talk in public about a person's private life. Critics seemed particularly upset by Guibert's account of the philosopher's dying delirium, and his description, even more scandalous, of his sado-masochistic erotic practices and his fondness for the gay bathhouses of San Francisco.

In a series of interviews, Guibert patiently defended himself. Making no effort to deny that the character called Muzil was in fact Foucault, he stressed how narrowly his novel had focused on the ordeal of AIDS, treating the philosopher's final agony as a preview of what Guibert knew to be his own imminent fate. His short story, he explained, also came from the heart, written in grief in the hours immediately after the philosopher had been buried. He had turned down, he pointed out, more than one offer to write a memoir of his friendship with Foucault, preferring to let his two fictions speak for themselves. (In the same spirit, he refused to be interviewed for this book.)[48]

At the height of the uproar, Guibert appeared on the television program *Apostrophes*. Looking wan and sallow, his beautiful, piercing gaze now sunken in a kind of death mask, Guibert confessed that yes, it was true, he *did* feel guilty while he was writing his secret journal as Foucault lay dying. He conceded that his behavior might well have made the philosopher "furious."[49]

The program's host, Bernard Pivot, bore down, reading out loud one of the novel's most controversial passages: " 'This afternoon, I was alone in the [hospital] room with Muzil.' Muzil, that's Foucault. 'I held his hand for a long time, as he sometimes had held mine in his apartment. Then I put my lips on his hand to kiss it. Returning home, I would wash these lips with shame and relief as if they had been contaminated. I was so happy, relieved.' It's terrible to write this!"

"Yes," Guibert agreed with Pivot, "it's terrible!" But, added the artist, "*it is the truth.*"

But why, wondered Pivot, did Guibert insist on revealing this *particular* truth? Because, the artist replied, in a phrase that harmonizes well with the sentiments of Foucault's final lectures at the Collège de France, "the truth has a virtue. . . . The truth, cruel though it may be, I don't know. . . . There is a certain delicacy, I find"—even in rehearsing the most scandalous facts and events. And besides: "Michel Foucault, here was someone who was evidently attentive to the notion of private life, but also someone who had a freedom in his life, who had an audacity, and who was anything but what one calls, in homosexual jargon, a 'closet queen' "— this last phrase Guibert spoke in English. The philosopher himself, the artist went on, "had given interviews on sado-masochism," he appeared in public wearing his leather clothes, he made no secret of his inclinations—he lived, in his own fashion, as freely and defiantly as Diogenes had in ancient Athens.

All of which, as we have seen, is true.

None of which, by itself, can resolve any lingering doubts about whether the "terrible dioramas" described by Guibert convey "the truth of what is real."

We are left, as Foucault once put it, "with a stubborn, perplexing indiscretion, a key itself bolted—a cipher deciphering and enciphered."[50]

In trying to weigh the significance of Guibert's apparent revelations about what Foucault felt to be the secret of his inner experience, one is constantly being reminded of what Foucault himself wrote about the novelist Raymond Roussel. Foucault was fascinated by Roussel's work, not least because of his ambiguous final gesture, a posthumously published essay explaining his literary method, entitled *How I Wrote Certain of My Books*. "At the moment of his death," writes Foucault, the author "sets *before* his work a mirror" possessed of "a bizarre magic: it pushes the central figure into the distance where the lines are blurred, moves further away the spot where the revelation occurs, but brings closer, as if from myopia, that which is most distant at the moment when the figure speaks. To the extent the figure draws near to itself, it deepens in secrecy. A double secret: the solemn finality of its form, the care with which this revelation had been, throughout the work, withheld to be delivered at the moment of death, transforms into an enigma the behavior it brings to light"—and leaves the reader baffled about "this form of reticence which maintained the secret in a reserve suddenly abandoned."[51]

It was perhaps with Roussel's final gesture in mind that Foucault confided in Guibert, of all people, expecting that his confession would be made public—and knowing as well that the artist would reveal the truth only after it had been veiled in "fiction."[52]

And it was perhaps also with Roussel in mind that Foucault arranged to give a final interview before he died, a kind of public coda to his private conversations with Guibert. For one last time, he would point out that *all* of his work amounted to a kind of autobiography; in effect, like Roussel, he would try to explain how he wrote certain of his books.

The first question had been carefully prepared in advance: "What strikes us upon reading your latest books is a clear, pure, and smooth writing, very different from the style we were used to. . . . In detaching yourself from a certain style, have you not become more of a philosopher than you ever were before?"[53]

"I admit it!" Foucault exclaimed. "The philosophical study I performed in *The Order of Things*, *Madness and Civilization*, and even in *Discipline and Punish*, was essentially based on a certain use of a philosophical vocabulary, game, and experience, to which I was, moreover, completely devoted." But now, the dying sage confides, "I am trying to detach myself" from this rhetorically evasive "form of philosophy," in order "precisely to use it as a field of experience to be studied, mapped out, and organized," in part by reinserting the previously occluded dimension—the subject, the self, the philosopher passionately interested in knowing the truth about himself.

There is a strange echo here of Nietzsche: "Gradually it has become clear to me what every great philosophy so far has been: namely, the personal confession of its author and a kind of involuntary and unnoticed memoir."[54]

And an echo, too, of Foucault's lament in the first volume of his History of Sexuality: "One makes to oneself, in pleasure and in pain, confessions impossible to make to anyone else, and one writes books about them."

The "obligation of truth," it seems, really was Foucault's unavoidable fate—just as he implied in his final lectures at the Collège de France. Try as he might, the philosopher could not remain silent about who he really was. That is why *all* of Foucault's books, from the first to the last, comprise a kind of involuntary memoir, an implicit confession.

And that is why, for all of the "games" that Foucault confessed to playing in these books, they express at least one serious and irrefutable truth—

thetruth about himself. The self that he spent a lifetime trying to unriddle, renounce, and reinvent, he was never quite able to escape: he is always there, right before our eyes, lurking in the pages of his books, swirling in their "dust of words," "a transitory existence doubtless confessed in order to be effaced," unleashing strange "powers and dangers," as Foucault once put it, leaving uncanny traces in the work of "struggles, victories, wounds, dominations, enslavements." And even if the writing itself "through long use" and familiarity may have lost its "harshness," dulling the "strange pain" still quietly held within, Foucault's singular truth has remained locked in the dark interior of this tortured language of disavowal, sequestered in a "hard shut dry cold black place," just waiting to be "mapped out," cut open, and examined—a unique field of inner experience, laden with philosophical significance.[55]

Near the end of his life, as Guibert later conjured up the scene, the philosopher had joked with the novelist about his fondest fantasy, a characteristic dream of making himself disappear. In his most famous books, he had, as he well knew, in effect accomplished this feat, not with a magical ring like that of Gyges, but rather through the alchemy of language. And though for nearly a decade he had been trying to "think differently" and struggling to tell the truth—if only by lecturing on *parrhesia* and suggesting how to read some of his books—the old dream had kept recurring.

One night, as Guibert writes, the philosopher had described the pleasure he took in imagining himself, not in an institution where a person would go to die—but rather in a place where he would only *seem* to die. " 'Everything would be splendid,' " Guibert later described his friend musing, " 'with sumptuous paintings and soothing music.' " The place would look like a hospital; but hidden behind one of the paintings at the rear of each room would be a small door, an escape hatch. At a suitable time, the "patient," dosed with a pleasurable drug, would slip behind the picture and open the door. Presto! " 'Off you would go, you would disappear, you would die in the eyes of the world, and reappear without a witness on the other side of the wall, in a rear courtyard, without bags, without anything in your hands, without a name, ready to invent your new identity.' "[56]

Never, say friends, had Foucault seemed so serene as he did in the final weeks of his life.[57]

And never, reports Hervé Guibert, had the philosopher laughed so madly as when he was dying, contemplating, one imagines, "the door that opens on my story," knowing that he would soon slip over to the other side of that threshold, just dust without words now, no longer speaking, no longer listening, no longer seeking, no longer caged, truly a "wordless thing in an empty place"—free of the need for truth at last.

POSTSCRIPT

WHILE WRITING THIS BOOK, *friends and acquaintances often asked me why I had chosen Foucault as a subject—and what I thought about the life I was recounting. I have explained some of my reasons for writing the book in my preface, and I have doubtless conveyed at least a hint of my feelings about Foucault by the way in which I have told his story. Still, since any historical account, no matter how strenuously one strives for a measure of objectivity, is going to be shaped, in part, by the author's personal interests and moral beliefs, it may be useful, now that my narrative is done, to describe in a little more detail some of the chance events, mixed emotions, and conscious judgments that informed its composition; and some of my own convictions about the value of Foucault's life and work.*

My research began with a rumor—one that I now believe to be essentially false.

One evening in the spring of 1987, an old friend who teaches at a university in Boston, where I live, relayed a shocking piece of gossip: knowing that he was dying of AIDS, Michel Foucault in 1983 had gone to gay bathhouses in America, and deliberately tried to infect other people with the disease.

At the time, I was no great admirer of so-called "poststructuralist" or "postmodernist" modes of thought; indeed, I still feel that a great many of the French names fashionable in the United States in the eighties—Baudrillard, for one—are minor figures. Foucault, however, had always seemed to me to be different. I took his work seriously, though I then knew relatively little about it. In the spring of 1987, I had a working command of Foucault's jargon, and could participate in cocktail conversations about the links between power and knowledge; I had been impressed by Madness and Civilization *in the 1960s, and had found*

Discipline and Punish *of value for thinking about certain issues I had explored in a previous book, on Jean-Jacques Rousseau and the French Revolution. Such was the extent of my knowledge and interest in Foucault's work.*

The night my friend told me his story about Foucault and AIDS, I thought little more about it. When I woke up the next day, however, I found that I could not get my friend's story out of my mind. What if the story were true? Mulling the matter over, I went to my shelves and pulled down the books by and about Foucault. As it happened, I had quite a few—certainly more titles than I had read. I quickly discovered, however, that my books told me little about who Foucault was. The same thumbnail biography ("Michel Foucault was born in Poitiers, France, in 1926. . . . He writes frequently for French newspapers and reviews. . . . ") was reprinted on the jacket of almost all of the English translations of his work; the same unforthcoming paragraph was even reprinted verbatim in the introduction to Hubert Dreyfus and Paul Rabinow's standard study, Michel Foucault: Beyond Structuralism and Hermeneutics.

Curious to learn more, I called up my friend, and asked him where he had heard the ghastly story about Foucault. He gave me the name of a well-known professor of French literature who also taught in Boston. I called up this professor, and asked the same question: Where had he heard the story? After three phone calls, I gave up for the day. The trail of gossip led back to Paris. And my head was now spinning with still more improbable stories about Foucault, a great many of them revolving around his fondness for sado-masochistic forms of eroticism.

At this point, I stopped wearing my journalist's hat, and sat down with Foucault's books. The idea of writing something had crossed my mind. But what, if anything, did the stories I was hearing have to do with Foucault's major works?

I decided to read his books in chronological order, starting with Madness and Civilization. *I was immediately struck by the fact that the stories were leading me to pay attention to aspects of Foucault's style and historical argument that I had previously ignored. The Marquis de Sade, for example, played a small but pivotal role in* Madness and Civilization—*a role I had never noticed before. Much of Foucault's prose now seemed to me suffused with a strange kind of aura, both morbid and vaguely mystical. I didn't know what to make of this aura, and I didn't understand how Foucault's language produced this effect. Perhaps I was reading something into him, though I doubted it. In order to be sure, I began to take notes, compiling an informal index of recurrent images and motifs, in my own crude way following the sort of method that the literary critic Jean Starobinski has perfected.*

Although I hadn't yet admitted it, I was already hooked on Foucault. Seduced by his literary style, I found myself grappling with topics that, until then, I had always shied away from. In ways that were unfamiliar and therefore interesting to me, I began to think about the meaning of death and the human capacity for cruelty, about the tractable character of pain, and the possible implications of embodying an ethos of deliberate irresponsibility.

After finishing all of Foucault's books, I was convinced that there was an essay, at least, to be written. But I was still unsure about the need for a book.

So I consulted several academic experts on Foucault, often talking to people who had known him personally. More than one reminded me that Foucault himself had attacked the myth of the "author." Most warned me that pursuing my curiosity about the man would violate the spirit of his philosophy. Almost everyone, nevertheless, volunteered still more stories about him.

I went forward, though with some trepidation. By now, I was all too cognizant of how much I didn't know. I didn't yet know whether the initial rumor was true, though I had begun to think not. I knew far too little about the wider French milieu that had produced Foucault. Most critically, I realized, I knew virtually nothing about America's gay community—and even less about its sado-masochistic subculture.

For the next two years, I immersed myself in the work of the Marquis de Sade, Antonin Artaud, Georges Bataille, Maurice Blanchot, Samuel Beckett, and René Char, reading book after book with Foucault's own concerns in mind, taking notes, trying to picture what had grabbed his imagination in the works of these very different kinds of writers.

At the same time, I tried to educate myself about gay politics, and also about consensual sado-masochism. Since I had written a previous book about American student radicalism in the 1960s, and had also participated actively in the radical "counter-culture" of that era, the gay liberation movement, which had also started in the sixties, seemed in many ways familiar to me, even though I was an outsider. The world of consensual S/M, on the other hand, tested my powers of sympathetic imagination. At first, I was shocked: I could not fathom how people could take pleasure in pain, particularly in suffering pain—I'm the kind of person who gets squeamish over having a tooth filled. But the more I read, the easier it became to understand what the appeal of S/M might be. (I had one ad-

vantage: like a lot of people in the 1960s, I had experimented with LSD. I knew from firsthand experience the appeal of deliberately dissociating one's consciousness; as I discovered, a deliberate dissociation of consciousness was one part of S/M's appeal.)

At a crucial juncture in my research, I discovered the work of the American psychoanalyst Robert J. Stoller. His theories of perversion and his ethnographic studies of consensual sado-masochism confirmed a great deal of what the practitioners of S/M had written themselves. Thanks to Stoller and to writers like Geoff Mains and Gayle Rubin, whose work became another one of my touchstones, I came to regard consensual S/M as a generally benign set of sexual practices. Its techniques no longer shocked me. And today I am persuaded that the various prohibitions and prejudices against it are unwarranted.

I also discovered that S/M as a practice cast a revealing light on some of the philosophical issues that reading Foucault had raised in my mind. For example, the apparently self-evident distinction between pleasure and pain—a distinction of some importance to a great many moral theorists, from Plato to Bentham and beyond—was anything but self-evident from the standpoint of consensual sado-masochistic practices. Such practices also suggested a far from self-evident way to express, and perhaps imaginatively master, fantasies of aggression and cruelty. In addition, S/M seemed to raise with special force a series of larger questions, of central importance to all of Foucault's work, but particularly salient when trying to understand and evaluate his idea of "limit-experience." Where do our most apparently ineluctable impulses come from? Are they voluntary, involuntary—or an uncertain mixture of both? Do the aggressiveness, hostility, and fascination with death so vividly dramatized in S/M's theater of cruelty testify to the existence of elemental and essentially immutable animal instincts, as Freud had suggested? Are the most erotically charged of our cruel impulses potentially transformable by-products of painful and humiliating childhood experiences, as Robert Stoller speculated? Or do our most compelling desires rather represent and reproduce a web of socially constructed aptitudes and inclinations that, as Foucault sometimes implied, might disappear—but only if our form of life could somehow be totally transfigured?

Similar questions were at stake in the works that I was reading, by Sade, Artaud, and Bataille—writers I had never seriously studied before reading Foucault. In addition, a set of closely related questions had been raised by Nietzsche, a philosopher whose work I knew—though I now began to read it in a different way.

By the summer of 1989, when this phase of my research drew to a close, I had come to regard Foucault with respect, even awe. Though I was not at all confident that I understood everything he had to say (even today, I am pretty sure that I do not), I felt certain that he was one of the most original—and daring—thinkers of the century. I had decided that I would, in fact, write some kind of book about his life and his work.

Turning back to Foucault's texts, I now read virtually everything I could find that he had written or said. The interviews, essays, and books, like the anecdotes I already knew, all seemed to be pieces in a larger puzzle. And this puzzle, I had become convinced, would be impossible to resolve by focusing exclusively either on the texts, or on tales about Foucault's life. His oeuvre rather seemed to incorporate both his books and his life; and the one could not be understood—least of all philosophically—apart from the other. Indeed, some kind of biographical approach seemed warranted by Foucault's own final thoughts on the unusual kind of "philosophical life" he had evidently led. As he reminded his audience in his last lectures at the Collège de France, to be a philosopher had once been a matter of living one's life in a certain way, and embodying a certain style of thought. "And it seems to me that it would be interesting to write a history," he remarked in one lecture, "starting from the problem of the philosophical life, a problem . . . envisaged as a choice which can be detected both through the events and decisions of a biography, and through the [elaboration of the] same problem in the interior of a system [of thought], and the place which has been given in this system to the problem of the philosophical life." In this particular lecture, Foucault went on to deplore, emphatically, our own modern "negligence" of the idea of the "philosophical life," which had gone into eclipse, he speculated, "because the relationship to truth can now be made valid and manifest only in the form of scientific knowledge."[1]

Intrigued by Foucault's own challenge, and hoping to conjure up an unfamiliar type of "philosophical life," I decided to try writing a work that would combine personal vignettes and the exegesis of doctrine, just as the ancient historian Diogenes Laertius had done in his Lives of Eminent Philosophers, but using modern critical methods to establish the facts and to open my interpretation to independent evaluation. My goal, to borrow a formula from Gilles Deleuze, was to "find vital Aphorisms which would also be Anecdotes of thought."[2]

In the fall of 1989, I began to search for the right anecdotes by conducting interviews. I started on the West Coast of the United States, and worked my way back to Paris. By now, I took it for granted that Foucault's *preoccupation with sado-masochism was an important key for unlocking some of the most challenging but commonly neglected aspects of his work. I also assumed—correctly, as it turned out—that Americans were far more likely than the French to talk freely about this aspect of Foucault's life.*

Meanwhile, I had become convinced that the rumor that had gotten me started was false. For one thing, the sexual geography of the rumor was suspicious: all my informants were straight. Furthermore, I had already gathered a great deal of evidence indicating that Foucault himself was never told that he in fact had AIDS. If this was true, then the notion that he had been some kind of "AIDS guerrilla," intent on killing others, seemed farfetched—a perverse tribute, I speculated, to an inchoate sense of paranoia and panic about AIDS, even among otherwise sensible people.

My trip to Paris in March of 1990 gave me a fresh jolt. For some months I had been trying to establish contact with Foucault's longtime companion, Daniel Defert. He was hard to reach. My initial letters to him went unanswered. When I arrived in Paris, I tried phoning Defert at his apartment, at first to no avail. Then, on a Sunday afternoon at 5:00 P.M. I caught him by his phone. I explained my project directly; he agreed to see me that night. I hurried to Foucault's old apartment, where Defert now lives.

We talked for nearly three hours. My line of questioning seemed to strike some nerve. It was, I suppose, clear that I had immersed myself in Foucault's texts. It was clear as well that I had done my homework about Foucault's experiences in America's gay community. Defert of course knew all about these experiences; and he clearly agreed that these experiences were important, indeed crucial, for a proper understanding of Foucault's work, and particularly his last books. That night, Defert talked at some length about Foucault's idea of "limit-experience." I felt instantly that Defert's focus on this idea was right—and the book I have written reflects this conviction.

Two hours into our conversation, the talk turned to AIDS. Defert explained that the looming threat of AIDS had played a key role in determining how Foucault had approached Greek and Roman thought. "It's quite possible," Defert remarked, "that he had a real knowledge of his near death, without making it a drama, but constructing, really everyday, a [new kind of] relationship with others. . . . Even if he was not certain about his own situation," the menace of AIDS was constantly on his mind. "He took AIDS very seriously," Defert continued. "When he went to San Francisco for the last time, he took it as a 'limit-experience.' "

I was stunned.

Our conversation continued for another hour. But as I left Foucault's old apartment that night, all I could think about was Defert's deceptively simple statement: He took AIDS very seriously; he took it as a limit-experience.

I now had to wonder whether the rumor that had gotten me started was closer to the truth than I had come to think possible.

When I returned from Paris, I immediately set to work writing. Unable to come to grips with Defert's sentence in any other way, I began with an effort to try to understand its meaning, to put it in some kind of context by piecing it together with other comments, about AIDS and death, that Foucault had made to other friends. As an experiment, I decided to follow Foucault's own instructions for reading another writer's life, by examining the way in which the author had died. Once underway, I discovered, to my own astonishment, that this (to me) improbable way of approaching a writer's life seemed, at least in the case of Foucault himself, to lead, step by step, and quite logically, to the major issues in his philosophy that I wanted to lay open for the scrutiny of my readers.

This put me in a quandary about how to handle the possibility that Foucault had embraced AIDS as a "limit-experience." Everything that I had learned, from Defert and others, persuaded me that it was highly unlikely that Foucault would (as the rumor depicted him) go around deliberately trying to infect—and hence, in effect, murder—innocent people. Evidently he had been uncertain, perhaps to the day he died, whether or not he actually had AIDS. Given the circumstances in San Francisco in the fall of 1983, as best I could reconstruct them, to have taken AIDS as a "limit-experience," it seemed to me, would have involved engaging in potentially suicidal acts of passion with consenting partners, most of them likely to be infected already; deliberately throwing caution to the wind, Foucault and these men were wagering their lives together; that, at least, is how I came to understand what may have happened.

There are, admittedly, other ways to interpret my evidence, all of which is indirect and circumstantial. As one skeptical interlocutor reminded me, it is possible that Foucault, even if he did visit the baths in the fall of 1983, practiced only "safe sex;" however, given his own lifelong convictions about suicide and death, as well as his evident disdain for "safe sex," this seems to me improbable. Then again, as still other readers have pointed out, it is possible that Foucault, if he returned to the baths, jeopardized unwitting partners; but this, too, seems to me improbable: despite lingering uncertainties about the nature of AIDS, virtually anyone still going to the baths in the fall of 1983 would surely have recognized the possible risks.

Still, it is important to remember that these risks were just that: risks—

not certainties. As Allan Bérubé has written, "even those few who know-ingly took the greatest risks" in these months were not, for all that, simply "choosing AIDS." Wagering one's life—and losing the wager—is not quite the same thing as deliberately killing oneself.[3]

I am reminded of what Foucault wrote about Raymond Roussel's lethal drug overdose in 1933. Had Roussel meant only "to liberate this death"? Or "perhaps also to rediscover the life from which he had furiously tried to free himself, but which he had also long dreamed of infinitely prolonging through his works and through the meticulous, fantastic and tireless ma-chinery of these very works?" Maybe Roussel in a fit of madness had deliberately tried to kill himself. Or—on the contrary—maybe he had died quite by accident, as an unintended consequence of his ongoing struggle, through the vital alchemy of "limit-experience," to get free of himself ("se déprendre de soi-même"). As Foucault put it in his commen-tary on Roussel's apparent suicide, the "impossibility, here, of determining" what the dead man had in mind means that "every discourse" about his work runs the risk of "being deceived less by a secret than by the awareness that there is a secret."[4]

In this regard, there is one last point worth making. Once the lethal character of HIV had been established beyond any reasonable doubt, the overwhelming majority of sexually active gay men dramatically changed their behavior. Members of the S/M subculture have been particularly imaginative in contriving new erotic games, altogether "safe" yet intensely pleasurable. As a result of the gay community's extraordinary transfor-mation of beliefs and behavior, there has been a heartening fall in the number of new sexually-transmitted infections within this community. It seems likely that Foucault, too, given enough time, would have ultimately changed his mind, and his behavior: after all, this is what happened once he began to ponder the practical implications of the murderous political fantasies he had shared with others on the French ultra-left. As one of Foucault's San Francisco friends, Gayle Rubin, put it in a letter she wrote after reading an early draft of this book: "Whatever romance of death, whatever notions of extremity, whatever courage of exploration informed his behavior, I think that his contracting AIDS was an unanticipated, accidental, unfortunate, and utterly tragic sequel. . . . If he had known what to do in time, so that he had would not have been infected, and would not have died this hideous death, I have no doubt that he would have taken whatever steps were necessary; at the same time, I think he would have regretted the loss of some very important, profound, soul-shaking experiences."[5]

Postscript

About one thing Rubin is certainly right: given the personal stakes of Foucault's "soul-shaking" involvement in the S/M subculture, he (like many other participants) had good reason to regret the loss of certain experiences. Indeed, the longer I pondered the risks, and tried to imagine in retrospect the grim alternatives facing any sexually adventurous gay man in 1983— an anxious restraint or a fatalistic abandon—the more I came to sympathize with those who chose what turned out to be the foolhardy course of action. In some respects, Foucault's effort at the end of his life to "think differently" had perhaps been unsuccessful. But in the context of Foucault's mature "ethos" as I had reconstructed it, his possible approach to AIDS as a "limit-experience" had a certain dignity. By apparently casting his fate in this way with the gay male S/M subculture, he tacitly affirmed, paradoxically, how positive, and how truly transformative, his experiences within this community had been. These views inform the last two chapters of my account.

I realize that my final views on this and some of the other controversial matters I have recounted will seem to some readers deplorable—yet another symptom of the kinds of vicious behavior that become acceptable once strict moral standards have been set aside. Perhaps the old saying is true: to understand is to forgive. Certainly, my sustained effort to achieve an empathic understanding at crucial junctures involved a conscious suspension of moral judgment—and this may well indicate a critical limitation in the kind of biographical approach I have taken. My work is also marked by my conviction, perhaps misguided, that what Nietzsche and Foucault have written about the genealogy of moral judgment is, in some broad sense, "true." For all of these reasons, I have felt neither able, nor inclined, to deliver a summary verdict on how Foucault chose to live his life—or on how he may have chosen to end it. Others will doubtless feel no such inhibition.

As these comments may suggest, the composition of my book involved a continuous struggle between sometimes conflicting impulses. No other topic I have written about has stirred up such a range of powerful emotions, from horror to pity. Since I wanted to write about Foucault's lifework with passion as well as objectivity (I do not believe these goals are necessarily in contradiction), I had to keep a close check on my feelings as well as my evidence. What emotions should I let color my language? How sympathetic should I be? Apart from an overriding commitment to telling the truth, what values did I hold dear? As I struggled with these questions, I tried to keep an open mind without succumbing to a blind reverence.

In the fall of 1990, I began to speak in public in the United States about my book. I quickly discovered that I was not the bearer of glad news—if, indeed, it was news that I was conveying: as one critic reminded me, there was always the possibility (she, indeed, seemed to regard it as a likelihood) that the character I was calling "Foucault" was a figment of my own pathological homophobia.

This initial reaction startled me; naturally, it gave me pause. There is always some danger that one's work is colored by unnoticed biases.

Still, after pondering the complaints of my most vociferous critics, I have decided to leave the fundamentals of my account largely unchanged. I nevertheless think that I now understand better why some people have been so upset by what I have to say. During the 1980s, a number of Americans working in a university setting enshrined Foucault as a kind of patron saint, a canonic figure whose authority they routinely invoked in order to legitimate, in properly academic terms, their own brand of "progressive" politics. Most of these latter-day American Foucauldians are high-minded democrats; they are committed to forging a more diverse society in which whites and people of color, straights and gays, men and women, their various ethnic and gender "differences" intact, can nevertheless all live together in compassionate harmony—an appealing if difficult goal, with deep roots in the Judeo-Christian tradition. Unfortunately, Foucault's lifework, as I have come to understand it, is far more unconventional—and far more discomfiting—than some of his "progressive" admirers seem ready to admit. Unless I am badly mistaken, Foucault issued a brave and basic challenge to nearly everything that passes for "right" in Western culture—including nearly everything that passes for "right" among a great many of America's left-wing academics.

So what, then—my friends often ask—is one to conclude about this discomfiting thinker?

A few things seem to me clear. Foucault took Nietzsche's injunction, to become "what one is," quite seriously—in some ways more seriously than Nietzsche himself. In the course of his own Nietzschean quest, Foucault struggled bravely: against conventional ways of thinking and behaving; against intolerable forms of social and political power; against intolerable aspects of himself. With a curiosity and courage that I find admirable, he persevered. Harboring his maddest impulses in the books that he wrote, he tried to understand these impulses, simultaneously explaining and expressing them, exorcising his desires while struggling to establish their innocence, in part by methodically documenting the historical origin of the divisions we customarily make between good and evil, true and false, the normal and the pathological. In this ambiguous way, he joined in the conversation of culture, contesting some of its key terms, and challenging widely held assumptions. At the same time, he offered his life as a model, not of truth, but of what the search for truth must involve. His own will to know was unflinching and unrelenting. Pushing his mind and body repeatedly to the breaking point, he set a standard for the philosophical life that would be dangerous, if not impossible, for most human beings to emulate. If nothing else, his lifework, I think, proves the wisdom of Nietzsche's adage that the "love of truth is terrible and mighty."[6]

It is in the spirit of this two-edged adage that I have tried to tell Foucault's story. And if my book were to succeed only in conveying something of the disturbing force of Foucault's central preoccupations—perhaps filling others with the mixed emotions I have felt while writing it—I would consider that I have achieved my goal.

A NOTE ON SOURCES
AND TRANSLATIONS

Complete information about my sources appears in the endnotes that follow. But one source of special interest should be pointed out. In 1978, Foucault gave the most revealing interview of his life to the Italian political militant and journalist Duccio Trombadori, who for many years worked for *L'Unita*, the daily newspaper of the Italian Communist Party. Until recently, Foucault's book-length conversation with Trombadori was available only in an Italian translation, under the title *Colloqui con Foucault*. First published in 1981, it had long been out of print and virtually impossible to find, especially in the United States. At the end of 1991, however, an English version (translated from the Italian) appeared under the title *Remarks on Marx*; a French text has also been announced. In preparing my own book, I was granted access to two different transcriptions of Foucault's conversations with Trombadori, which were conducted in French: one typescript had been edited for publication, the other had evidently not. In addition, as this book was going to press I was told that François Ewald and Daniel Defert, by combining passages from both of these transcripts, had prepared yet a *third* French version of Foucault's conversations with Trombadori: it is apparently this composite text that will appear in the Gallimard edition of Foucault's complete shorter works. Since the original transcripts should be available to scholars at the Centre Michel Foucault in Paris, in my endnotes I have cited the relevant page number of either the edited or unedited French typescript, as well as the corresponding passage in the English edition; in the case of the unedited French typescript, a roman numeral indicates the number of the cassette transcribed.

When referring to Foucault's essays and interviews, I have generally cited both the original French source and, if one exists—and it often does—an English translation. Ironically, Foucault's shorter works were, at the time I was writing, more easily available in English than in French. When Gallimard publishes its comprehensive edition of Foucault's shorter works, all this will change; since the contents of this collection will be arranged chronologically, I have included the original date of each essay and interview in my endnotes in order to help readers of this book find the appropriate reference in the definitive Gallimard edition.

The decision by Ewald and Defert to include all of Foucault's interviews as an integral part of his oeuvre is one that I agree with. As Gilles Deleuze once put it, Foucault staged "a theater of statements"—and his various interviews played a defining role in his public enactment of his thought. A number of these interviews were carefully edited, corrected—and in a few cases, substantially rewritten—by Foucault himself. Others were evidently impromptu, but no less important for that: speaking of one of Foucault's most revealing dialogues (with the German film director Werner Schroeter), Deleuze rightly remarks that "this is an extraordinary text, precisely because it is an improvised conversation. . . ."

Since Foucault's interviews and essays reveal a great deal about the externals of his life, and also about his inner experience, I have been able to use his published texts as a primary source for much of the information presented in my book. Many other biographical details, particularly about Foucault's visits to America, and also about his involvement in the S/M subculture, come from new interviews. In addition, I have relied on Didier Eribon's biography for some of the facts about Foucault's early life. I know that several of Foucault's intimates—Daniel Defert, for one—regard Eribon's work as deeply flawed. But in our conversations, Defert was willing to specify only a few passages in Eribon's book that he disagreed with, and in every case his disagreement seemed to me more a matter of interpretation than of fact. Furthermore, while conducting my own research, I was able to corroborate independently a great many of the facts contained in Eribon's biography; I have therefore treated his book as a trustworthy source of information.

In an effort to insure the accuracy of the new material in my own book, I submitted the relevant parts of my manuscript to many of the key people I interviewed, including (in alphabetical order) Leo Bersani, Daniel Defert, Bob Gallagher, Philip Horvitz, D.A. Miller, Hans Sluga, Simeon Wade, and Edmund White; with the exception of Defert, who did not respond, my final text reflects their comments and corrections.

All translations from the French are my own. I have relied to different degrees on the extant English translations, which vary considerably in quality, ranging from Richard Howard's rendering of *Madness and Civilization*, which is superb, to the standard English translation of *L'ordre du discours*, "The Discourse on Language," which is less helpful.

With one significant exception, I have used the standard English titles of Foucault's major books in my text: it would be too confusing to offer my own, more literal translations, and also needlessly confusing, I concluded, to leave the titles in French. The exception is *La volonté de savoir*, volume one of Foucault's History of Sexuality. In my view, Foucault's own Nietzschean title to this methodological prolegomenon is both elegant and revealing, while the main English title—*The History of Sexuality, Volume 1*—is perfectly anodyne, even subtly misleading: whatever else the book is, it is *not*, in fact, a history. I have therefore consistently referred to this book in my text as *The Will to Know*, while consistently referring to Foucault's larger *Histoire* as his History of Sexuality, without italics, to avoid possible confusion with *La volonté de savoir*.

I have tried on the whole to eliminate arbitrary references to gender, not always successfully. Foucault's French pronouns are relentlessly masculine, and my translations, and some of my adjacent text, reflect his usage. I have felt similarly obliged to retain Foucault's own use of the word *homme*, or "man," to designate humanity in the abstract.

In conducting my research, as I explain in my preface, I deliberately avoided immersing myself in the secondary literature on Foucault, which has become unmanageable. There are nevertheless a handful of texts that influenced my thinking more deeply than endnotes can acknowledge. One had nothing to do with Foucault at all, namely Alexander Nehamas's pathbreaking study *Nietzsche: Life as Literature*. As for essays about Foucault, I must single out "Le noir soleil du langage: Michel Foucault" by Michel de Certeau; "Vers la fiction" by Raymond Bellour; "Foucault révolutionne l'histoire" by Paul Veyne; "Michel Foucault, 1926–1984" by Edward Said; "Pedagogy and Pederasty" by Leo Bersani; and—above all—*Foucault* by Gilles Deleuze.

ABBREVIATIONS
USED IN NOTES

et   =   English translation.

int   =   Interview (when it is unclear from other matter in the endnotes, the date of the interview is given in parentheses).

AS   =   *L'archéologie du savoir* (Paris, 1969); et: *The Archeology of Knowledge*, trans. A.M. Sheridan Smith (New York, 1972).

CF   =   *Colloqui con Foucault* (Salerno, 1981); et: *Remarks on Marx*, trans. R. James Goldstein and James Cascaito (New York, 1991). All passages are translated, and cited, from either the typescript of the original edited French text, or (where a Roman numeral precedes the page number) from the typescript of the original unedited French transcript (as of early 1992, neither of these texts had been published, though a new, composite French text was being prepared for the forthcoming Gallimard edition of Foucault's complete shorter works).

CP   =   *Ceci n'est pas une pipe* (Paris, 1973); et: *This is Not a Pipe*, trans. James Harkness (Berkeley, Calif., 1982).

FD   =   *Folie et déraison* (Paris, 1961), reprinted without the original preface as *Histoire de la folie a l'âge classique* (Paris, 1972). With the exception of citations from the orignal preface, all quotes refer to the 1972 edition; partial et: *Madness and Civilization*, trans. Richard Howard (New York, 1965).

HB   =   *Herculine Barbin dite Alexina B* (Paris, 1978); et: *Herculine Barbin*, trans. Richard McDougall (New York, 1980).

MC   =   *Les mots et les choses* (Paris, 1966); et: *The Order of Things* (New York, 1970).

MM   =   *Maladie mentale et personnalité* (Paris, 1954).

MM*   =   *Maladie mentale et psychologie* (Paris, 1962); et: *Mental Illness and Psychology*, trans. Alan Sheridan (New York, 1976).

NC   =   *Naissance de la clinique* (Paris, 1972). This is a slight revision of the original edition, published in 1963—with the exception of a few passages quoted from the original edition, cited as "NC (1963)," all quotes refer to the 1972 edition; et: *The Birth of the Clinic*, trans. A.M. Sheridan Smith (New York, 1973).

OD   =   *L'ordre du discours* (Paris, 1971); et: "The Discourse on Language," trans. Rupert Swyer, in *The Archeology of Knowledge* (New York, 1972), pp. 215–237.

PD   =   *La pensée du dehors* (Paris, 1986), originally published as an essay in *Critique*, 229 (June 1966) pp. 523–46; et: "Maurice Blanchot: The Thought from Outside," trans. Brian Massumi, in *Foucault/Blanchot* (New York, 1987).

Abbreviations Used in Notes

PR = *Moi, Pierre Rivière, ayant égorgé ma mère, ma soeur et mon frère . . .* (Paris, 1973); et: *I, Pierre Rivière, Having Slaughtered my Mother, my Sister, and my Brother . . .*, trans. Frank Jellinek (New York, 1975).

RC = *Résumé des cours, 1970–1982* (Paris, 1989).

RE = "Introduction" to *Le rêve et l'existence* by Ludwig Binswanger (Paris, 1954), pp. 8–128; et: "Dream, Imagination and Existence," trans. Forrest Williams and Jacob Needleman, in *Review of Existential Psychology & Psychiatry* Vol. XIX, No. 1, (1984–85) pp. 31–78.

RR = *Raymond Roussel* (Paris, 1963); et: *Death and the Labyrinth*, trans. Charles Ruas (New York, 1986).

SP = *Surveiller et punir* (Paris, 1975); et: *Discipline and Punish*, trans. Alan Sheridan (New York, 1977).

SS = *Le souci de soi* (Paris, 1984); et: *The Care of the Self*, trans. Robert Hurley (New York, 1986).

UP = *L'usage des plaisirs* (Paris, 1984); et: *The Use of Pleasure*, trans. Robert Hurley (New York, 1985).

VS = *La volonté de savoir* (Paris, 1976); et: *The History of Sexuality*, trans. Robert Hurley (New York, 1978).

BSH = *Michel Foucault: Beyond Structuralism and Hermeneutics*, by Hubert L. Dreyfus and Paul Rabinow (Chicago, 1982).

FCR = *Foucault: A Critical Reader*, ed. David Couzens Hoy (Oxford, 1986).

FLI = *Foucault Live*, by Michel Foucault, ed. Sylvère Lotringer, trans. John Johnston (New York, 1989).

LCP = *Language, Counter-Memory, Practice*, by Michel Foucault, trans. Donald F. Bouchard and Sherry Simon (Ithaca, N.Y., 1977).

MFP = *Michel Foucault philosophe: Rencontre internationale, Paris, 9, 10, 11 janvier 1988* (Paris, 1989).

PKN = *Power/Knowledge*, by Michel Foucault, ed. Colin Gordon (New York, 1980).

PPC = *Politics, Philosophy, Culture*, by Michel Foucault, ed. Lawrence D. Kritzman (New York, 1988).

PTS = *Power, Truth, Strategy*, by Michel Foucault, ed. Meaghan Morris and Paul Patton (Sydney, 1979).

TFF = *The Final Foucault*, ed. James Bernauer and David Rasmussen (Cambridge, Mass., 1988).

TFR = *The Foucault Reader*, ed. Paul Rabinow (New York, 1984).

NOTES

PREFACE

1. "Le Mallarmé de J.-P. Richard," *Annales* (September-October 1964), pp. 997–98. My greatest methodological debt is to the critical work of Jean Starobinski, whose approach to reconstructing the imaginative universe of a figure like Jean–Jacques Rousseau I consider exemplary. My book is also deeply indebted to Alexander Nehamas's study of what it means "to become what one is" in *Nietzsche: Life as Literature* (Cambridge, Mass., 1985).

2. See Didier Eribon, *Michel Foucault* (Paris, 1989); et: *Michel Foucault*, trans. Betsy Wing (Cambridge, Mass., 1991). I could not have written my book without Eribon because a great many of the facts recounted in what follows I found first in the pages of his biography; because he personally helped me out at several junctures; and finally, because he inadvertently opened doors for me. My access to Foucault's longtime companion, Daniel Defert, grew, in part, out of his dislike of Eribon's portrait and his wish to correct it. David Macey's work, on the other hand, I did not see while I was writing; so it is likely that various parts of my own narrative may well have to be augmented, amplified, or revised almost as soon as my book appears. *Caveat lector.*

3. See Alasdair MacIntyre, *Three Rival Versions of Moral Enquiry* (Notre Dame, 1990), pp. 32–57, 196–215. The idea of a teleologically structured "quest," or *recherche*, that would combine aspects of the kind of *recherche* conducted by Proust, Borges, and Bachelard is articulated by Foucault as early as 1957: see "Le recherche scientifique et la psychologie," in Jean-Eduoard Morère, ed., *Des chercheurs français s'interrogent* (Paris, 1957). Cf. Foucault's final comments on the role of teleology in ethics: UP, pp. 34–35; et, pp. 27–28. The source of the popular misunderstanding of Foucault's position (if that is really what it is) doubtless is Foucault himself, whose (I believe) deliberately misleading assertions about the "death of the author" in the late 1960s served their purpose—of self-effacement and concealment—all too well. (I discuss some of these matters at greater length in chapter five.)

4. In my view, the best account of Foucault's philosophy of history is that of Paul Veyne: see "Foucault révolutionne l'histoire," in Veyne, *Comment on écrit l'histoire* (Paris, 1978).

5. I find my own struggle to elaborate, in practice, some notion of objectivity leavened by an appreciation for the literary dimension of historiographic inquiry mirrored in the pages of Lionel Gossman's elegant book *Between History and Literature* (Cambridge, Mass., 1990) That it is worth struggling for objectivity (problematic though this ideal obviously is) I take to be confirmed by the modern experience with unchecked myth-mongering: for example, in Russia between 1917 and 1989; and in Germany under Hitler.

6. D. A. Miller, *Bringing Out Roland Barthes* (Berkeley, 1992).

7. TFR, p. 374.

EPIGRAPHS

René Char, "Le mortel partenaire," in *Oeuvres complètes* (Paris, 1983), pp. 363–64: "Certains êtres ont une signification qui nous manque. Qui sont-ils? Leur secret tient au plus profond du secret même de la vie. Ils s'en approchent. Elle les tue. Mais l'avenir qu'ils ont ainsi éveillé d'un murmure, les devinant, les crée. O dédale de l'extrême amour!" An English version appears as "The Mortal Partner" in *The Poems of René Char*, trans. Mary Ann Caws and Jonathan Griffin (Princeton, N.J., 1976), p. 159.

Friedrich Neitzsche, *Werke*, ed. Naumann (Leipzig, 1894, ff.), Vol. X, p. 147: a note, not used, for his early and unfinished essay, also published only posthumously, in "Philosophy in the Tragic Age of the Greeks" (1873).

CHAPTER 1: THE DEATH OF THE AUTHOR

1. "The Subject and Power" (1982), in BSH, p. 211. See also Michael Donnelly, et. al., "La planète Foucault," *Magazine Littéraire*, 207 (May 1984), pp. 55–57.

2. For these and other obituaries, see: *Le Monde*, 27 June 1984 (Veyne); *Le Nouvel Observateur*, 29 June 1984 (Daniel, Braudel); *Libération*, 30 June–1 July 1984 (twelve-page supplement); and *Libération*, 26 June 1984.

3. "La folie n'existe que dans la société" (int), *Le Monde* (22 July 1961), p. 9. Cf. Robert Maggiori, "Michel Foucault: une pensée sur les chemins de traverse," *Libération* (26 June 1984), p. 2.

4. MC, p. 398; et, p. 387.

5. SP, pp. 22, 23; et, pp. 16, 18.

6. VS, p. 62; et, pp. 45.

7. NC, p. 176; et, p. 172.

8. MM, p. 54. Cf. MM* et, p. 83. My understanding of Sartre's generation has been informed by James D. Wilkinson, *The Intellectual Resistance in Europe* (Cambridge, Mass., 1981).

9. See "Qu'est-ce qu'un auteur?," *Bulletin de la Société française de philosophie* (July-September 1969), pp. 89, 92, 93; et in LCP, pp. 131, 135, 136. As Foucault points out, the inevitable "travesties" of the ideas of "fondateurs de discursivité" inevitably provoke a return to the work—*and* life—of the author.

10. Lawrence Stone, "An Exchange with Michel Foucault," *The New York Review of Books* (31 March 1983), p. 42. Gerald Weissmann, "Foucault and the Bag Lady," *Hospital Practice*, (August 1982).

11. J.G. Merquior, *Foucault* (London, 1985), p. 160. See Stone, "An Exchange with Michel Foucault," loc. cit., for a good summary of the concerns of a prominent American historian; for the French historians, see Arlette Farge, "Face à l'histoire," *Magazine Littéraire*, 207 (May 1984), pp. 40–42. For a demand for criteria, see Nancy Fraser, "Foucault on Power," in *Unruly Practices* (Minneapolis, 1989), p. 33. For Felix the Cat, see Michel de Certeau, "The Black Sun of Language: Foucault," in *Heterologies* (Minneapolis, 1986), p. 183.

12. "Qu'est-ce qu'un auteur?" (1969), loc. cit., p. 77; et in LCP, p. 115. AS, p. 28; et, p. 17. See also Michel de Certeau, "The Laugh of Michel Foucault," in *Heterologies*, pp. 193–98. The biography is Didier Eribon, *Michel Foucault* (Paris, 1989); et: *Michel Foucault*, trans. Betsy Wing (Cambridge, Mass., 1991).

13. "Qu'est-ce qu'un auteur?" (1969), loc. cit., p. 93; et in LCP, p. 136. "Politics and Ethics: An Interview" (1983), in TFR, p. 374. Cf. "Le Mallarmé de J.-P. Richard," *Annales* (September-October 1964), esp. pp. 997–98, 1000. In this telling defense of Richard's book *L'univers imaginaire de Mallarmé* (Paris, 1962), Foucault discusses the "new object" of literary analysis opened up by the new archival materials available since the nineteenth century, especially sketches and drafts of works, as well as biographical evidence about the author's life. The great achievement of Richard's book, in Foucault's view, is the deft way in which it handles the whole range of this new "documentary mass": "The Mallarmé to which he refers in his analyses is neither the pure grammatical subject, nor the deep psychological subject; but rather the one who says 'I' in the works, the letters, the drafts, the sketches, the personal secrets (*les confidences*). . . ."

14. "An Interview with Michel Foucault" (1983), in RR; et, p. 184 (emphasis added).

15. See RR, pp. 10–12; et, pp. 3–5. Cf. "Qu'est-ce qu'un auteur?" (1969), loc. cit., p. 78; et in LCP, p. 117: If we wish to decipher "the mark of the writer," we must "grasp the role of death in the play of writing." (This, as we shall see, is a conviction Foucault shares with Maurice Blanchot: see chapter three.)

16. RE, pp. 71–72; et, p. 54 (Foucault here explicitly talks about death and "authen-

ticity"). "The Ethic of Care for the Self as a Practice of Freedom" (int, 1984), in TFF, p. 9. NC, pp. 169, 170, 175–76; et, pp. 165, 166, 171. Cf. Martin Heidegger, *Being and Time*, trans. John Macquarrie and Edward Robinson (New York, 1962), pp. 302–3.

17. Gilles Deleuze, *Foucault* (Paris, 1986), pp. 102, 106; et: *Foucault*, trans. Sean Hand (Minneapolis, 1986), pp. 95, 99.

18. NC, p. 176; et, p. 171. Denis Hollier has written an essay that explores some of these themes: see "Le mot de Dieu: 'Je suis mort,'" in MFP, pp. 150–65.

19. *Le Monde* (27 June 1984), p. 10.

20. *Libération* (26 June 1984), p. 2.

21. Eribon, *Foucault*, p. 351; et, p. 327.

22. Mirko D. Grmek, *History of AIDS*, trans. Russell C. Maulitz and Jacalyn Dufflin (Princeton, 1990), p. 4, referring to J. Leibowitch, *Un virus étrange venu d'ailleurs* (Paris, 1984).

23. Grmek, *History of AIDS*, p. 70. I wish to thank my wife, Sarah Minden, a doctor who has herself been involved in AIDS research, for helping me to summarize the state of current medical knowledge about the HIV virus.

24. For the French media coverage of the early stages of the epidemic, see Michael Pollak, *Les Homosexuels et le SIDA: Sociologie d'une épidémie* (Paris, 1988), esp. pp. 144–51; the misconception of AIDS as a kind of "gay cancer" lingered longer in France than in America. The critic cited at the end of this paragraph is Rabbi Julia Neuberger, writing in the *Guardian* in 1985; quoted in Simon Watney, *Policing Desire: Pornography, AIDS and the Media* (Minneapolis, Minn, 1987), p. 3.

25. See "Discourse and Truth: The Problematization of *Parrhesia*," an unauthorized and unpublished transcription of Foucault's seminiar at Berkeley in fall, 1983, edited by Joseph Pearson (Evanston, Ill., 1985). In these seminars, as in his final lectures at the Collège de France in 1984 (discussed in more detail in chapter eleven), Foucault stresses the *danger* of telling the truth: particularly when truth-telling may offend those with political interests at stake; or those fearful of the dishonor and opprobrium truth-telling sometimes entails.

26. Hervé Guibert, *À l'ami qui ne m'a pas sauvé la vie* (Paris, 1990), p. 110; et: *To the Friend Who Did Not Save My Life*, trans. Linda Coverdale (New York, 1991), p. 97. For the value of Guibert's *roman à clef* as a source, see chapter eleven.

27. See Eribon, *Foucault*, pp. 348–49; et, pp. 325–26. Cf. Guibert, *À l'ami*, pp. 31–33; et, pp. 23–25.

28. Ibid., pp. 32–33; et, p. 24.

29. Edmund White interview, 12 March 1990. In public Defert has consistently denied any such emotions, and I did not feel it appropriate (or fruitful) to question him on this point. (For Defert's official position, notice the wording of his response to Jean-Paul Aron in 1987, reprinted below.) In my interview with him on 25 March 1990, however, Defert did make it plain that he did not know that Foucault had AIDS until *after* his death.

30. On Defert and AIDES, see Gerard Koskovich, "Letter From Paris," *The Advocate*, 4 (March 1986), pp. 31–32. For an instance of the most lurid of the rumors in public circulation, see Camille Paglia, "Junk Bonds and Corporate Raiders: Academe in the Hour of the Wolf," *Arion* (Spring 1991), p. 195: "The fruits of Foucault are wormwood. He was a Herod without a Salome. This was a man of mutilated psyche: if what I have reliably heard about his public behavior after he knew he had AIDS is true, then Foucault would deserve the condemnation of every ethical person." For more on the rumor—and its falsity—see the author's Postscript, above.

31. SP, p. 200; et, p. 198.

32. The journalist was Gerard Koskovich, whom I interviewed on 30 September 1989. Koskovich also kindly made available to me the tapes of his original interview with Jean Le Bitoux.

33. Koskovich, "Letter From Paris," *The Advocate* (4 March 1986), p. 31. Also Koskovich interview 30 September 1989.

34. Jean-Paul Aron, "Mon Sida," *Le Nouvel Observateur* (5 November 1987), p. 44. In his book *Les modernes* (Paris, 1984), pp. 216–33, Aron portrayed Foucault as a very nasty

piece of work, "ill-tempered," "capricious," constantly scheming to seduce beautiful young boys. See esp. pp. 219–20: "This critic of controls aspired to control [the world] in its essence. A born inquisitor, I imagine him in the fifteenth century . . . in the role of the monk [i.e., Savonarola] burning with anathemas and reclaiming for Christ the King, against the heretics, the government of Florence. . . ." Mean-spirited though it is, Aron's portrait is of some interest, since it is clearly the kind of caricature only an insider could draw.

35. Daniel Defert, " 'Plus on est honteux, plus on avoue,' " *Libération* (31 October–1 November 1987), p. 2. Notice how in his first sentence, Defert slides from "we" to "I"—if "we" had been ashamed, then "I" would never have created Association AIDES . . . ; but of course it is not Defert's sense of shame that is at issue. The bearing of his own posthumous gesture on Foucault's hypothetical shame is by no means obvious.

36. Jean Le Bitoux, "The Real Foucault," *New York Native* (23 June 1986), p. 5.

37. Defert interview, 25 March 1990. In an interview with Didier Eribon, Paul Veyne claimed to have seen after Foucault's death an entry in one of the journals that Foucault kept, dated November 1983: "I know I have AIDS, but my hysteria allows me to forget it" (see Eribon, *Foucault*, p. 348—this passage appears neither in the English translation of Eribon's book, nor in the revised second French edition). Defert vehemently denies that any such journal entry exists. This much seems clear: over the course of 1983, Foucault expressed his understandably mounting concerns about AIDS to a number of people, both in America and France. See, e.g., Foucault's conversations in Berkeley in the *spring* of 1983 with D. A. Miller and Philip Horovitz, recounted at the end of chapter ten.

38. As fate would have it, Foucault was surrounded between 1981 and 1984 by doctors and academic friends who were in a position to know the latest news about the mysterious new disease afflicting gay men. In the twelfth chapter of his *roman à clef* about AIDS (and Foucault), Hervé Guibert alludes to the study group that Foucault organized in 1983 with Bernard Kouchner and several other politically active doctors and intellectuals; the group met at the Tarnier hospital, where some of the first AIDS cases in France were being treated. He "would cough like mad at these meetings," writes Guibert; still, "he refused to see a doctor, finally giving in only when the head of the clinic voiced his concern over that persistent, hacking cough." This was apparently how the nature of Foucault's illness belatedly came to be diagnosed. (See Guibert, *À l'ami*, pp. 31–33; et, pp. 23–25.) For more on Foucault's reaction to the growing evidence of AIDS and its dangers, see the recollections of Hans Sluga and D. A. Miller, recounted in chapter ten. Guibert remembers talking to Foucault and raising the possibility of a new "gay cancer" as early as 1981: As soon as he raised the subject, Foucault burst into laughter: "A cancer that would hit only homosexuals, no, that's too good to be true, I could just die laughing!" (See Guibert, *À l'ami*, p. 21; et, p. 13. Appearing on the television program *Apostrophes* on 16 March 1990, Guibert told exactly the same story, this time citing Foucault by name. Edmund White recalls having a similar conversation with Foucault in Paris, also in 1981.)

39. For an extended discussion of the San Francisco gay community, and of Foucault's involvement with it, see chapter eight.

40. Katharina von Bülow, "Contredire est un devoir," *Le débat*, 41 (September–November 1986), p. 177.

41. For Foucault's most famous definition of "heterotopia" as a place (antithetical to a utopia) where "words are stopped in their tracks" and the comforting certainties of conventional knowledge dissolve, see MC, pp. 9–10; et, p. xviii. For the sorts of extreme experience that stop words in their tracks—"the overwhelming, the unspeakable, . . . the ecstatic," etc.—see "Le langage à l'infini," *Tel quel*, 15 (Autumn 1963), pp. 48–49; et in LCP, p. 60. For the welcome "limbo" of "those closed, narrow, and intimate societies where one has the strange happiness, which is at the same time obligatory and forbidden, of being acquainted with only one sex," see "Introduction" to et of HB, p. xiii. For S/M, see "An Interview: Sex, Power and the Politics of Identity" (1982), *The Advocate* (7 August 1984), p. 43.

42. "An Interview" (1982), in PPC, p. 12.

43. The most widely available source of information for the response of gay men to

AIDS in these months is, unfortunately, not entirely trustworthy, due to its author's partisan animus against the most sexually adventurous members of his community; even so, Randy Shilts, *And the Band Played On* (New York, 1987), remains an invaluable source, if approached critically. For one telling critique, see Douglas Crimp, "How to Have Promiscuity in an Epidemic," in Douglas Crimp, ed., *AIDS: Cultural Analysis, Cultural Criticism* (Cambridge, Mass., 1988), pp. 237–70. Crimp's essay usefully points out the leading role taken by the gay community in propagating "safe sex" practices. The chronology of these early "safe sex" efforts is unclear; but the efforts began informally in San Francisco among concerned gay activists early in 1983; and in May of that year, a group of Bay Area physicians issued their first set of public guidelines. On the mobilization of the gay community in these months, see also Cindy Patton's sharp early polemic, *Sex and Germs: The Politics of AIDS* (Boston, 1985), which contains an acute discussion of "erotophobia" as a key cultural factor in the wider public response to AIDS. In San Francisco, the most prominent gay activist campaigning from an early date (May 1983) to close the baths was Larry Littlejohn: for information on this (and for another source of use in corroborating and correcting Shilts), see the soberly analytic history of the debate over the baths in Ronald Bayer, *Private Acts, Social Consequences* (New York, 1989), pp. 20–71. (It is worth noting that Shilts was himself a relatively early and outspoken proponent of shutting the baths, which partially explains a certain "I-told-you-so" tone of self-righteousness that colors his account.) Last but not least, I must thank Gayle Rubin for checking her files and sharing with me her impressions, based on ten years of research on the history of the Bay Area S/M scene, of how the gay community generally, and the S/M subculture specifically, responded to AIDS in these grim months.

44. Shilts, *And the Band Played On*, p. 377.

45. SP, p. 199; et, p. 197.

46. "Un plaisir si simple," *Gai pied*, 1 (April 1979), p. 10; et: "The Simplest of Pleasures," *Fag Rag* 29, p. 3. NC, pp. 125, 175; et, pp. 124, 171.

47. SP, p. 38; et, p. 34. In my interview with him on 11 April 1991, D. A. Miller, one of Foucault's Berkeley friends, recalled talking to him in Paris in December of 1983 about his trips to the baths in San Francisco that fall. A similar conversation is recounted by Hervé Guibert in *À l'ami*—see the paragraph that follows. See also the anecdote reported, in passing, by Richard D. Mohr, *Gays/Justice* (New York, 1988), p. 268: "In the summer of 1983, two years after the first cases of AIDS came to light in New York City and well after condom dispensers began appearing in leather bars there, Michel Foucault gave a seminar at New York University's Humanities Institute. Every night of the seminar, he would go, I am told by the philosopher who served as a guide, to the gay baths which he enjoyed enormously."

48. See Guibert, *À l'ami*, p. 30; et, p. 22. Did Foucault ever express any such sentiments? Since Guibert is now dead, it is impossible to distinguish with any certainty fact from fiction in his account—although virtually every detail about Foucault that I have been able to check corroborates the factual accuracy of Guibert's portrait of Foucault in the novel. According to D. A. Miller, Foucault in their conversations evoked a rather different mood in the baths of San Francisco in the fall of 1983. Miller recalls Foucault remarking that on some nights, some of the baths were nearly deserted; and also lamenting that one of his favorite baths, the Hothouse, had gone out of business. (The Hothouse was the first important S/M establishment to shut down because of AIDS; at the time, its proprietor, Louis Gaspar— who closed his business voluntarily—explained that "considering the moral and ethical questions involved, I just couldn't stay open when I felt I might be somehow responsible for people getting it." See Randy Shilts, "A Gay Bathhouse Closes its Doors in S.F.," *San Francisco Chronicle* (11 July 1983), p. 3. My thanks to Gayle Rubin for tracking this article down.) In my conversation with Defert on 25 March 1990, immediately after Defert himself had said that Foucault took AIDS "very seriously" on his last trip to San Francisco—see the sentence quoted immediately below—I remarked that Guibert had said something similar about Foucault in his novel. "Yes," responded Defert, "I told him [i.e., Guibert]; he pretended that Michel told him that first." Defert went on to say that Foucault had summed up the experience with a pun, combining the words "SIDA" and "*décision*." He did not

explain the pun, but perhaps it involved a play on the verb "*décider*" (to decide), the past tense of which is "*décida*" (pronounced like de-sida); or perhaps the pun involved conflating the two words SIDA and "*décision*" ("de-sid-ion," i.e. to come to a decision about AIDS). The ethical issues raised by Foucault's possible behavior in the bathhouses of San Francisco in the fall of 1983—if this in fact is how he behaved—are complex. For a longer discussion, see the author's postscript.

49. Defert interview 25 March 1990 (emphasis added). Defert volunteered this comment in the course of responding to a question I had asked about what he had meant when he had written, in his *Libération* article (published in the issue of 31 October–1 November 1987), that Foucault "made an ascetic work of himself, and it was within this work that his death is inscribed." Earlier in our conversation, Defert had described at some length the importance of the idea of "limit-experience" for Foucault, and also discussed how Foucault had developed the notion out of his reading of Bataille—so the significance of the phrase "limit-experience" was plain to both of us. Indeed, when I prepared a verbatim transcription of our three-hour interview, I discovered that Defert himself had brought up the notion of limit-experience in the first minutes of our conversation, going out of his way to link Foucault's idea of experience with "madness, drugs, sexuality, and maybe I would say AIDS." At the time, I did not fully understand the possible implications of this comment. Two hours later, when Defert again linked AIDS and limit-experience, in the remark I have quoted in my text, I immediately asked him to explain what he meant. Unfortunately, Defert fell silent, shook his head, and declined to say anything more—just as he declined to comment on a typescript of an early draft of this book, which I gave him in November 1991. What Defert *wrote* in 1987—about Foucault inscribing his death within the ascetic work he made out of himself—is, I think, just as revealing, in context, as his comment to me about Foucault taking AIDS as a "limit-experience." For more on the philosophical context, see the discussion of Foucault's final views on death and asceticism in chapter ten. And compare, too, the suggestive portrait in Hervé Guibert's *À l'ami*, e.g., p. 39; et, p. 31: "At the very end of '83, when Muzil [Foucault] was coughing worse than ever, . . . I said to him, 'Actually, you hope you have AIDS.' He shot me a dark and peremptory glance."

50. UP, pp. 12–13; et, p. 6–7.

51. For "positivity," see, e.g., AS, p. 164; et, p. 125. The terms "positive" and "positivity" were used in a similarly ambiguous way by Auguste Comte, who meant to blur the scientific and moral connotations of "positive." My effort to define "positivity" here is indebted to Ian Hacking's account in "Language, Truth and Reason," in Martin Hollis and Steven Lukes, eds. *Rationalism and Relativism* (Oxford, 1982), p. 53.

52. CF (int, 1978), p. 2; et, p. 27. For "limit-experience" in *Madness and Civilization*, see the original preface, FD (1961), pp. i, iii–iv, also discussed below in chapter four. For the idea in Bataille, see esp. Georges Bataille, *L'expérience intérieure*, trans. Leslie Anne Boldt (Albany, N.Y., 1988). On the significance of literature and art for grasping the game of truth and "the game of signs," cf. RR, p. 209; et, p. 166.

53. "Qu'est-ce qu'un auteur?" (1969), loc. cit., p. 78; et in LCP, p. 117.

54. "Conversation" (int, 1981), in Gerard Courant, *Werner Schroeter* (Paris, 1981), pp. 39–40, 45.

55. OD, p. 37; et, p. 224. NC, p. 125; et, p. 124. MC, pp. 396, 398; et, pp. 384, 386.

56. VS, pp. 54–55; et, p. 39.

57. "Le retour de la morale" (int), *Les Nouvelles* (28 June–5 July 1984), p. 36; et in PPC, p. 243. "Est-il donc important de penser?" (int), *Libération* (30–31 May 1981), p. 21; et in PPC, p. 156. Eribon told me in an interview on 29 March 1990 that Foucault had handwritten the phrase about his books being "some fragment of autobiography" while correcting the transcript, as was his custom. "He was perfectly aware that this sentence would be quoted," says Eribon: "He wrote it down carefully." Cf. "Truth, Power, Self: An Interview with Michel Foucault" (1982) in Luther H. Martin, Huck Gutman, and Patrick H. Hutton, eds., *Technologies of the Self* (Amherst, Mass., 1988), p. 11: "Each of my works is a part of my own biography." Foucault's most famous public expression of misgivings about the philosophical

value of "experience" occurs in *The Archeology of Knowledge*: see AS, pp. 26–27, 64–65; et, pp. 16, 47.

58. CF (int, 1978), pp. 10, 35; et, pp. 38–39, 71.

59. Ibid., p. 35; et, p. 71 (emphasis added). Cf. ibid., p. 3; et, p. 29: "I don't construct a general method of definitive value for myself or for others. What I write does not prescribe anything. . . . At most its character is instrumental and visionary or dream-like."

60. UP, p. 13; et, p. 7.

61. RR, p. 210; et, p. 167.

62. Ibid., p. 11; et, pp. 4–5.

63. "An Interview with Michel Foucault" (1983), in RR, et, p. 182.

64. UP, p. 14; et, p. 8. On this phrase, cf. Deleuze, *Foucault*, p. 102–103; et, p. 95–96. Also see Leo Bersani, "Pedagogy and Pederasty," *Raritan*, V, No. 1 (Summer 1985), p. 15. There is still another context for understanding this phrase: In an anonymous interview on 22 March 1990, one of Foucault's closest associates recalled discussing this phrase with Foucault a few weeks before his death; when he was asked whether he had intended to replace the old Greek motto Know Thyself with the phrase Get Free of Oneself, Foucault answered, 'yes.'

65. Bersani, "Pedagogy and Pederasty," loc. cit., p. 21.

66. VS, p. 206; et, p. 156.

67. Cf. Deleuze, *Foucault*, p. 103; et, p. 96.

68. Daniel Defert, interviewed by Adam Block, October, 1989; Block, an American journalist, kindly supplied me with a tape of his interview (which was primarily about Defert's work with AIDES).

69. See *Libération* (30 June–1 July 1984), p. 18. Also see Eribon, *Foucault*, p. 353–54; et, pp. 329–30. And see Guibert, *À l'ami*, pp. 112–13; et, pp. 99–100. My description of the ceremony is also drawn from interviews with an anonymous associate (22 March 1990), Daniel Defert (25 March 1990) and André Glucksmann (26 March 1990).

70. Robert Badinter, "Au nom des mots," in *Michel Foucault: Une histoire de la verité* (Paris, 1985), p. 75.

71. UP, pp. 14–15; et, pp. 8–9.

CHAPTER 2: WAITING FOR GODOT

1. On Sartre's funeral, see Annie Cohen-Solal, *Sartre: A Life*, trans. Anna Cancogni (New York, 1987), pp. 523–24. And Ronald Hayman, *Sartre: A Biography* (New York, 1987), pp. 473–75.

2. Didier Eribon, *Michel Foucault* (Paris, 1989), p. 297; et: *Michel Foucault*, trans. Betsy Wing (Cambridge, Mass., 1991), pp. 278–79. See also Robert Maggiori, "Sartre et Foucault," *Libération* (30 June–1 July 1984), pp. 23–24.

3. Katharina von Bülow, "Contredire est un devoir," *Le débat* (September-October 1986), p. 177. Eribon, *Foucault*, p. 297; et, p. 280.

4. "Sexuality and Solitude," *London Review of Books* (21 May–3 June 1981), p. 3.

5. Otto Friedrich, "France's Philosopher of Power" (int, 1981), *Time* (16 November 1981), p. 148. See "An Interview" (1982), in PPC, p. 7. In Simeon Wade, *Foucault in California* (unpublished ms., 1990), p. 72, Foucault mentions his preoccupation with the fate of the Jews.

6. Daniel Defert, letter to author, 8 January 1991: Defert adds that the father of Foucault's brother-in-law fought in de Gaulle's Free French Force, and that the family on the whole was Gaullist in its political sympathies. For a more detailed account of Foucault's youth in Poitiers, based on extensive interviews, see Eribon, *Foucault*, pp. 19–31; et, pp. 3–14.

7. These phrases all appear in Wade, *Foucault in California*, p. 40, though they are the kinds of things Foucault seems to have said generally about his childhood, to judge only from the interviews I have conducted.

8. See Eribon, *Foucault*, p. 31; et, p. 14.

9. Arthur Goldhammer, review of Didier Eribon, *Michel Foucault* in *French Politics and Society*, 8, 1 (Winter 1990), p. 79.

10. On the "syncretic humanism" of Sartre's generation, see Jacques Derrida, "The Ends of Man," in *Margins of Philosophy*, trans. Alan Bass (Chicago, 1982), pp. 114–17. On the impact of Hegel, see Vincent Descombes, *Modern French Philosophy*, trans. L. Scott-Fox and J.M. Harding (Cambridge, England, 1980), esp. pp. 9–48. Cf. Thomas Pavel, *The Feud of Language: A History of Structuralist Thought* (New York, 1989), p. 3.

11. Michel Tournier, *The Wind Spirit: An Autobiography*, trans. Arthur Goldhammer (Boston, 1988), p. 131.

12. Jean Hyppolite, "Preface to the English Edition," *Studies on Marx and Hegel*, trans. John O'Neill (New York, 1969), pp. vii, x.

13. "Jean Hyppolite (1907–1968)," *Revue de Métaphysique et de Morale*, 74, 2 (April–June 1969), p. 133.

14. MC, p. 273; et, p. 261. RE, pp. 126–27; et, pp. 74–75. MM, p. 110.

15. Tony Judt, "Elite Formations," *Times Literary Supplement* (18–24 August 1989), p. 889. For the French education system generally, see the work of Pierre Bourdieu, especially *La noblesse d'état* (Paris, 1989) and *Homo Academicus*, trans. Peter Collier (Stanford, Cal., 1988). For philosophy in the postwar curriculum, see Descombes, *Modern French Philosophy*, pp. 5–6.

16. For information on Sartre's speech and its background, see Cohen-Solal, *Sartre*, pp. 249–52; for the Communists' unease with Sartre's fondness for Heidegger, see ibid., p. 221. I have drawn extensively from the dramatic description in Tournier, *The Wind Spirit*, p. 132.

17. Jean-Paul Sartre, "Existentialism is a Humanism," in Walter Kaufmann, ed., *Existentialism from Dosteovsky to Sartre* (New York, 1975), pp. 360, 361, 352, 353.

18. Cohen-Solal, *Sartre*, pp. 251–52.

19. Tournier, *The Wind Spirit*, pp. 131, 132.

20. Ibid., p. 133.

21. "Foucault répond à Sartre," *La Quinzaine Littéraire*, 46 (1–15 March 1968), p. 20; et in FLI, p. 35. "Une mise au point de Michel Foucault," *La Quinzaine Littéraire*, 46 (15–31 March 1968), p. 21.

22. See RE, p. 107–11; et, pp. 67–68: This early critique of Sartre is revealing, since it occurs at a time when Foucault was quite sympathetic to other brands of phenomenology and Marxism—for example, the work of Heidegger, Binswanger, Jaspers, Hyppolite, and (implicitly) Merleau-Ponty. Also see Eribon, *Foucault*, pp. 130, 141; et, pp. 105, 116. In my interview with Raymond Bellour, 30 March 1990 he recalled the explicit references to Sartre's *Critique* in the galleys of *Les mots et les choses*.

23. See Eribon, *Foucault*, pp. 42–44; et, pp. 25–27. The Goya etchings are mentioned in Daniel Rondeau, with Véronique Brocard, Annette Levy Willard, Dominique Nora, and Luc Rosenzweig, "Le Canard et le renard ou la vie d'un philosophe," *Libération* (30 June–1 July 1984), p. 17. The most vivid account of Foucault in these years remains Maurice Pinguet, "Les Années d'apprentissage," *Le débat*, 41 (September–November 1986), pp. 122–31.

24. Maurice Merleau-Ponty, *Phenomenology of Perception*, trans. Colin Smith (London, 1962), p. 309n.

25. "Le retour de la morale" (int), *Les Nouvelles*, 2937 (28 June–5 July 1984), p. 39; et in PPC, p. 250.

26. Hannah Arendt, "Martin Heidegger at Eighty," in Michael Murray, ed., *Heidegger and Modern Philosophy* (New Haven, 1978), p. 295.

27. Jean-Paul Sartre, *The War Diaries*, trans. Quintin Hoare (New York, 1984), pp. 185–86.

28. Martin Heidegger, *An Introduction to Metaphysics*, trans. Ralph Manheim (Garden City, N.Y. 1961), p. 166. On Heidegger and Nazism, the literature has become voluminous: in English, see in particular the fine special issue of *Critical Inquiry*, 15, 2 (Winter 1989),

containing essays by Arnold I. Davidson, Jürgen Habermas, and Jacques Derrida, among others.

29. Sartre, *The War Diaries*, pp. 186–87.

30. Martin Heidegger, "Letter on Humanism," trans. Frank A Capuzzi with J. Glenn Gray, in *Martin Heidegger: Basic Writings* (New York, 1977), p. 208.

31. Ibid., pp. 209, 216; cf. Martin Heidegger, *Being and Time*, trans. John Macquarrie and Edward Robinson (New York, 1962), p. 62.

32. See Heidegger, "Letter on Humanism," loc. cit., pp. 212 (on the mysteriousness of Being), 216–17 (on transcendence). Cf. Martin Heidegger, *The Essence of Reasons*, trans. Terrence Malick (Evanston, Ill., 1969), p. 127: *"Freedom is the reason for reasons."* Cf. Martin Heidegger, *An Introduction to Metaphysics*, trans. Ralph Manheim (New York, 1961), p. 128. Heidegger's debt to Kant is clearly recorded in his 1929 study on *Kant and the Problem of Metaphysics* (discussed in chapter five). Heidegger's debt to Nietzsche is, by contrast, more controversial, because it is harder to document. But I agree with David Farrell Krell, who has argued that Nietzsche's influence is simultaneously conveyed and "concealed on every printed page of *Being and Time*." Heidegger's great work avoids any overt discussion of the will, or willing: yet some years later, Heidegger summed up Nietzsche's idea of the will to power in terms that unmistakably evoke as well a central theme of *Being and Time*, by describing will to power as "resoluteness toward oneself." (See Martin Heidegger, *Nietzsche*, trans. David Farrell Krell, Vol. I, pp. 40, 48n., 247.) It is, of course, true that Heidegger in his famous lectures on Nietzsche, largely delivered between 1936 and 1946, elaborated an influential critique of Nietzsche's concept of the will to power—but this critique, which is linked to the "turn" in Heidegger's own thought, discussed directly below, I take to be, in part, a piece of veiled *self*-criticism, as well as a deepening of Heidegger's profound (if sometimes silent) dialogue with Nietzsche. (My interpretation here has been informed by that of Hannah Arendt and also by Reiner Schürmann, *Heidegger on Being and Acting: From Principles to Anarchy* [Bloomington, Inc., 1982], see esp. 245–50.)

33. Heidegger, *Being and Time*, pp. 47 (definition of *Dasein*), 340 (on taking action), 437 (on choosing a hero). In France, it was Alexandre Kojève who first made popular a synthesis of Hegel, Marx, and Heidegger. And it is worth stressing that Kojève, Hyppolite, and Merleau-Ponty were not alone in their views on the compatibility of Marx and Heidegger: an entire generation of radical thinkers, from Herbert Marcuse to Lucien Goldmann, felt Heidegger and Marx could be reconciled, thanks in part to the sheer abstractness of certain key formulations in *Being and Time*.

34. Hannah Arendt, *Willing* (New York, 1978), p. 173.

35. Derrida, "The Ends of Man," loc. cit., p. 130. Heidegger, "Letter on Humanism," loc. cit., p. 210.

36. Ibid, pp. 240, 199, 213, 222, 223, 238, 241, 237. Francisco Goya, *Caprichos* Plate 43, "El sueño de la razon produce monstruos."

37. Heidegger, "Letter on Humanism," loc. cit., pp. 232 (on tragedy), 201 and 219 (on Hölderlin), 223, 240, 242, 236. I take the reference to Hölderlin and the young Germans confronting death on p. 219 to be an oblique reference to the war; also compare the passing but pregnant reference to Sophocles on p. 232 with the full-blown treatment of *Antigone* in *An Introduction to Metaphysics*, pp. 122–38: these extraordinary pages in Heidegger's *Introduction* amount to an allegory of, and apology for, the tragic "violence" that alone can secure for a culture like the ancient Greek (and modern German?) "the fundamental condition of true historical greatness."

38. MC, pp. 336, 337, 339; et, pp. 325, 326, 328.

39. "Le Retour de la morale" (int, 1984), loc. cit., p. 39; et, in PPC, p. 250.

40. "Um welchen Preis sagt die Vernuft die Wahrhiet?" (int, 1983), *Spuren*, 1–2 (1983); et in PPC, p. 21.

41. "Sexuality and Solitude" (1981), loc. cit., p. 3. In the late 1940s, Merleau-Ponty was far more sympathetic to Marxism (and to the Soviet Union) than Sartre: see, e.g., his 1947 apology for the Moscow Trials, *Humanism and Terror*. Merleau-Ponty's *Phenomenology*

of Perception includes an implicit but sharp critique of Sartre's concept of freedom: see the book's last chapter, on "Freedom." For Merleau-Ponty's idiosyncratic understanding of transcendence as "operative intentionality," see *Phenomenology of Perception*, pp. xvii–xviii.

42. "An Interview" (1982), in PPC, p. 21. Merleau-Ponty began to lecture on Saussure in courses given (among other places, at the École Normale) between 1947 and 1950: see James Schmidt's illuminating account in *Maurice Merleau-Ponty: Between Phenomenology and Structuralism* (London, 1985), p. 105. Cf. Foucault's "Introduction" (1978) to the English edition of Georges Canguilhem, *The Normal and the Pathological*, trans. Carolyn R. Fawcett with Robert S. Cohen (New York, 1989), pp. 23–24: "Phenomenology could indeed introduce the body, sexuality, death, the perceived world into the field of analysis." Still, even for Merleau-Ponty (who is the philosopher evidently at issue in Foucault's remarks), "the cogito remained central" (which—if only as a matter of terminology—is true, at least in *Phenomenology of Perception*): "neither the rationality of science nor the specificity of the life sciences could compromise its founding role."

43. It is worth comparing Jacques Derrida's memoir of his own intellectual odyssey, which involved a much more sympathetic and sustained encounter with Husserl and phenomenology: see Derrida, "The time of a thesis: punctuations," in Alan Montefiore, ed., *Philosophy in France Today* (Cambridge, 1983), esp. pp. 38–39.

44. Jean-Paul Sartre, *Anti-Semite and Jew*, trans. George J. Becker (New York, 1948), p. 90.

45. Jean-Paul Sartre, *Being and Nothingness*, trans. Hazel E. Barnes (New York, 1956), p. 259.

46. Ibid., p. 260.

47. Ibid., pp. 260–261.

48. Eribon, *Foucault*, p. 43; et, p. 26.

49. Sartre, *Being and Nothingness*, p. 379; and cf. the passage on sadism, on p. 405.

50. SP, p. 202; et, p. 200. "On the Genealogy of Ethics: Overview of Work in Progress" (int, 1983), in TFR, p. 351. FD, p. 519; et, p. 265. The keyhole image appears, in passing (and for no clear reason), in Foucault's earliest published criticism of Sartre: see RE, p. 109; et. p. 68. Although I disagree with his conclusions, Martin Jay has published an interesting essay on "the gaze" in Foucault, "In the Empire of the Gaze: Foucault and the Denigration of Vision in Twentieth-Century French Thought," in FCR, pp. 175–204. In his 1983 remarks about authenticity, Foucault expressed hostility not simply toward Sartre's idea of authenticity, but toward Heidegger's idea in *Being and Time*. Since Heidegger's account of "authenticity" strongly emphasizes the call of conscience and the centrality of guilt, Foucault's hostility is not surprising. In his remarks, though, Foucault never discusses shame or guilt, rather charging both Heidegger and Sartre with trying to pin us down to a "true self"— which, in fact, Heidegger never did, though Sartre could certainly be read in this way. Oddly enough, the reference to Heidegger has been edited out of the published version of this tape, which is available in the Centre Michel Foucault in Paris.

51. See Eribon, *Foucault*, pp. 43–44, 55; et, pp. 26–27, 37. Louis Althusser was the teacher, and Jean Laplanche, later a well-known psychiatrist, was the person Althusser dispatched to make sure Foucault didn't kill himself.

52. "Un système fini face à une demande infinie" (int, 1983), in *Sécurité social: l'enjeu* (Paris, 1983), p. 63; et in PPC, p. 176. "Un plaisir si simple," *Gai Pied*, 1 (April 1979), p. 1, 10; et in *Fag Rag*, 29, p. 3.

53. Eribon, *Foucault*, p. 44; et, p. 26.

54. "Un plaisir si simple" (1979), loc. cit., p. 1; et, p. 3.

55. "Non aux compromis," *Gai Pied*, 43 (October 1982), p. 9. See also Wade, *Foucault in California*, p. 65.

56. Daniel Defert interview 25 March 1990; see also Pinguet, "Années d'apprentissage," loc. cit. After all (as Defert pointed out), a certain number of the École Normale's teachers and administrators were, themselves, gay.

57. Edmund White interview 12 March 1990.

58. Defert interview 25 March 1990.

59. See Jean-François Sirinelli, "Les Normaliens de la rue d'Ulm après 1945: une génération communiste?," *Revue d'histoire du monde moderne*, 32 (October–December 1986), p. 574.

60. "Pour une morale de l'inconfort," *Le Nouvel Observateur*, 754 (23 April 1979), p. 83. CF (int, 1978), p. 20; et, p. 52. Eribon's discussion of Foucault in the Party is excellent: see Eribon, *Foucault*, pp. 70–78; et, pp. 50–60.

61. CF (int, 1978), p. 19; et, p. 51. Foucault here gives the date of his joining the Party as 1950—a date that Eribon accepts. Daniel Defert, in a conversation on 4 November 1991, explained that Foucault's involvement with the Communists was a by-product of his personal opposition to the French Indochina War (which had begun in 1946 and would last until 1954).

62. CF (int, 1978), p. 21; et, p. 52. Friedrich, "France's Philosopher of Power" (int, 1981), loc. cit., p. 148.

63. CF (int, 1978), p. 22; et, p. 53. Cf. Eribon, *Foucault*, pp. 76–77; et, p. 56. In our conversation on 4 November 1991, Defert stressed the importance of Foucault's intolerance of anti-Semitism. For the "Doctors' Plot" and the eruption of anti-Semitism in the Soviet Union between 1952 and 1953, see Roy A. Medvedev, *Let History Judge*, trans. Colleen Taylor (New York, 1971), pp. 494–97.

64. Defert recalled Foucault's refusal to accompany him on a trip to China in our conversation on 4 November 1991.

65. See Eribon, *Foucault*, p. 78; et, p. 58.

66. "Introduction" (1978; to the English edition of Georges Canguilhem, *The Normal and the Pathological*), loc. cit., p. 8.

67. Ibid., p. 9.

68. For Foucault's regard for Cassirer and neo-Kantianism generally, see "Une histoire restée muette," *La Quinzaine Littéraire*, 8 (1 July 1966), his (highly favorable) review of a French translation of Cassirer's *The Philosophy of Enlightenment*. For Foucault on Cavaillès, see "Introduction" to Canguilhem (1978), loc. cit., pp. 8–9, 14–15; and "Politics and Ethics: An Interview" (1983), in TFR, 374.

69. Georges Canguilhem, *Le normal et le pathologique* (Paris, 1966), p. 139; et, *The Normal and the Pathological*, p. 209. Foucault explicitly calls attention to Canguilhem's vitalism in his "Introduction" (1978), loc. cit., pp. 18–19.

70. Ibid., p. 13.

71. CF (int, 1978), I, p. 35; cf. et, pp. 67–68.

72. RE, p. 126; et, p. 70. Cf. "Gaston Bachelard, le philosophe et son ombre: 'Pieger sa propre culture,'" *Le Figaro*, 1376 (30 September 1972), Litt, 16. See also FD, pp. 21–23; et, pp. 10–11.

73. Gaston Bachelard, *La Poétique de la rêverie* (Paris, 1960), p. 45. Bachelard, *La Terre et les rêveries du repos* (Paris, 1948), p. 51. Bachelard, *L'Eau et les rêves* (Paris, 1942), p. 24. Bachelard, *L'Air et les songes* (Paris, 1943), pp. 12, 13, 10.

74. See Thomas S. Kuhn, *The Structure of Scientific Revolutions* (Chicago, 1962), pp. v–vi (Alexandre Koyre, also esteemed by Foucault, was especially important for Kuhn). For Foucault on Kuhn and "normal science," see his "Introduction" to Canguilhem (1978), loc. cit., p. 16.

75. See Eribon, *Foucault*, p. 70; et, p. 50.

76. "An Interview" (1982), in PPC, p. 6. "Truth, Power, Self: An Interview with Michel Foucault" (int, 1982), in Luther H. Martin, Huck Gutman, Patrick H. Hutton, eds., *Technologies of the Self* (Amherst, 1988), p. 11. Friedrich, "France's Philosopher of Power" (int, 1981), loc. cit., p. 147. Also see Eribon, *Foucault*, pp. 67–69; et, pp. 48–49.

77. See Pinguet, "Années d'apprentissage," loc. cit., p. 126.

78. MC, p. 337; et, p. 326. MM, p. 54. Cf. MM* et, p. 83.

79. Pinguet, "Années d'apprentissage," loc. cit., p. 126.

80. Defert interview 25 March 1990. Cf. Wade, *Foucault in California*, p. 40.

81. Eribon, *Foucault*, p. 21.

82. See MM, p. 110, and also p. 104 . This text clearly reflects Foucault's overt com-

mitment to a kind of Marxist humanism, since Foucault goes out of his way here to state that mental illness "is the consequence of social contradictions within which man is historically alienated." At the same time, one of the most salient features of the book's Marxism is a recurrent stress on conflict and contradiction. And there are several passages that ill sort with the politically correct—and hopeful—character of the conclusion. See esp. MM, p. 87: "It is not by accident that Freud, while studying the neuroses caused by war, discovered a death-instinct that ran parallel to the life-instinct, which expressed the old bourgeois optimism of the nineteenth century. . . . Capitalism in this epoch was experiencing in a way that was clear for itself its own contradictions: it had to renounce the old theme of solidarity and admit that man can and must make of himself a negative experience, lived in the form of hate and aggression." When Foucault revised this text a decade later, he jettisoned all of the passages about the end of alienation. The passage about Freud's views on the death-instinct, by contrast, remained intact. Indeed, Foucault rephrased—and strengthened—his point about "negative experience" in a way that perhaps reveals the extent of his intellectual ambivalence, even in 1954. In the 1962 version, he states that Freud has shown that it is "man" in general—and not simply those who happen to live in a bourgeois society—who must "renounce the old dream of solidarity." This of course is the dream of Hegel, Marx, Hyppolite, and Merleau-Ponty in the late 1940s—but emphatically *not* the dream of Heidegger. In effect, by removing the Marxist rhetoric (and also by adding some of his own mature formulations), Foucault brings forward a Heideggerian stress that was there all along, underlining the possible value of madness as a form of "negative experience" in which the human being may explore a "thinking that is shattered." Cf. the observation of Hubert L. Dreyfus in his foreword to the 1987 University of California paperback version of MM*, p. xxxiii: "In the second version, he replaced the class struggle as the truth that is covered up with a historicized version of Heidegger's early claim that the truth that is covered up is strangeness, i.e., that there is no objective truth about the nature of human beings." For detailed accounts of the differences between the two versions of these texts, see Dreyfus's foreword and Pierre Macherey, "Aux sources de l'histoire de la folie: une rectification et ses limites," *Critique*, 471–72 (August–September 1986), pp. 753–74. And for an interpretation of Foucault that lays more stress than the present chapter on his youthful attachment to a kind of humanist philosophical anthropology, see Jerrold Seigel, "Avoiding the Subject: A Foucaultian Itinerary," *Journal of the History of Ideas* (1990), pp. 273–99. As the contents of this footnote may suffice to indicate—and as close readers will doubtless have already recognized—the available evidence for Foucault's early intellectual intinerary is sketchy, and open to different interpretations. What appears in this chapter (and the next) must remain, for the most part, a speculative reconstruction guided by a sympathetic reading of Foucault's influences, the memories of those who knew him then, and Foucault's own later recollections (which may or may not be accurate, memory being what it is—and Foucault's delight in playing games of hide-and-seek being what *it* was).

83. See Cohen-Solal, *Sartre*, pp. 90–91. Simone de Beauvoir recalls the drink being an apricot cocktail, while Aron recalls a beer.

84. "An Interview with Michel Foucault" (1983), in RR; et, p. 174.

85. Samuel Beckett, *Waiting for Godot* (New York, 1954), p. 7a. For the staging and first Paris performances of the play, see Ruby Cohen, *From Desire to Godot: Pocket Theater of Postwar Paris* (Berkeley, 1987), pp. 134–80.

86. Beckett, *Godot*, p. 12a.

87. Ibid., 15b.

88. Ibid., 28b.

89. See Alain Robbe-Grillet, "Samuel Beckett," in *For a New Novel*, trans. Richard Howard (New York, 1965), p. 111; this review was originally printed in *Critique* (February 1953). The detail about the solemnity of the audience I owe to Roger Shattuck, who recalls being the only person in the theater laughing at the first performance he saw of *Godot* in 1953.

90. Robbe-Grillet, "Beckett," loc. cit., p. 115.

91. "An Interview" (1983) in RR et, p. 174.

92. Charles Juliet, "Meeting Beckett," *TriQuarterly*, 77 (Winter 1989–90).

CHAPTER 3: THE HEART LAID BARE

1. Maurice Pinguet, "Les années d'apprentissage," *Le débat*, 41 (September–October 1986), p. 130.

2. "Truth, Power, Self: An Interview with Michel Foucault" (int, 1982), in Luther H. Martin, Huck Gutman, Patrick H. Hutton, eds. *Technologies of the Self* (Amherst, Mass., 1988), p. 13. "Le retour de la morale" (int), *Les Nouvelles* (28 June–5 July 1984), p. 37; et in PPC, p. 250. Cf. "Um welchen Preis sagt die Vernuft die Wahrheit?" (int), *Spuren*, 1–2 (1983); et in PPC, p. 23.

3. FD (1961) pp. iv–v.

4. Friedrich Nietzsche, "We Classicists," trans. William Arrowsmith, in *Unmodern Observations* [*Unzeitgemasse Betrachtungen*—I prefer the more familiar translation "Untimely Meditations," which I have used in my text], ed. William Arrowsmith (New Haven, 1990), pp. 338, 340–41 (I, §55, §64). Cf. Friedrich Nietzsche, *Ecce Homo*, trans. Walter Kaufmann (New York, 1967), pp. 270–75 (on *The Birth of Tragedy*). Biographical details here and elsewhere are drawn from Ronald Hayman, *Nietzsche: A Critical Life* (New York, 1980).

5. Nietzsche, *Ecce Homo*, p. 281 (on *Untimely Meditations*).

6. Friedrich Nietzsche, "Schopenhauer as Educator," trans. William Arrowsmith, in *Unmodern Observations*, p. 192 (§4). Daniel Defert allowed me, during our interview on 25 March 1990, to examine the copy of the book Foucault later added to his library: the cited passage was one of the few underlined boldly, and was also marked in the margin; it appears on p. 81 of the French edition, *Considérations intempestives III–IV*, trans. Genevieve Bianquis (Paris, 1954).

7. Nietzsche, "Schopenhauer as Educator," loc. cit., p. 163 (§1).

8. Ibid., p. 163 (§1).

9. Friedrich Nietzsche, *Beyond Good and Evil*, trans. Walter Kaufmann (New York, 1966), p. 26 (§19). Friedrich Nietzsche, *The Will to Power*, trans. Walter Kaufmann and R.J. Hollingdale (New York, 1967), p. 298 (§552). My discussion of Nietzsche here and elsewhere is deeply indebted to that of Alexander Nehamas in *Nietzsche: Life as Literature* (Cambridge, Mass., 1985), esp. pp. 170–99.

10. Nietzsche, *The Will to Power*, p.463 (§866).

11. Friedrich Nietzsche, *Thus Spoke Zarathustra*, trans. Walter Kaufmann, in *The Portable Nietzsche* (New York, 1954), p. 129 (Prologue, §5).

12. Nietzsche, *Thus Spoke Zarathustra*, p. 251 (II, §20). Cf. Friedrich Nietzsche, *The Gay Science*, trans. Walter Kaufmann (New York, 1974), pp. 232–33 (§290).

13. Nietzsche, "Schopenhauer as Educator," p. 165 (§1).

14. See Walter Burkert, *Greek Religion*, trans. John Raffan (Cambridge, Mass., 1985), pp. 179–81.

15. For the Pythagorean cult of the *daimon*, see Diogenes Laertius, *Lives of Eminent Philosophers*, trans. R. D. Hicks (Cambridge, Mass., 1925), VIII, 32. For Heraclitus, see the interesting discussion in Martin Heidegger, "Letter on Humanism," trans. Frank A. Capuzzi with J. Glenn Gray, in *Martin Heidegger: Basic Writings* (New York, 1977), pp. 233–34. For Socrates, see Paul Friedlander, *Plato: An Introduction*, trans. Hans Meyerhoff (New York, 1958), pp. 32–58; and Gregory Vlastos, *Socrates, Ironist and Moral Philosopher* (Ithaca, N.Y., 1991), pp. 280–88.

16. The *Oxford English Dictionary* tracks the evolution of the meaning of "demon." The notion of the good *daimon* does not disappear entirely in Christianity, but rather is transmuted into the idea that all persons have their own "guardian angel" watching over them.

17. In the context of this last quote from Nietzsche, the word "genius" is used in its old Latin sense, to connote the power of personal fate: it is, in effect, a translation of the Greek idea of the *daimon*. See William Arrowsmith's comments in the footnote to his translation of this passage from "Schopenhauer as Educator," pp. 163–64 (§1). The preceeding citations from Nietzsche come from *Thus Spoke Zarathustra*, p. 330 (III, §13) and *The Gay Science*, p. 228 (§283). Nietzsche's views on genius and the demonic suggest a strong debt to Johann Wolfgang von Goethe, for whose views see *Wahrheit und Dichtung*,

Book XX: "all which limits us seemed permeable to that . . . [which] I named the Dai-moniacal, after the example of the ancients. . . . It resembled chance, since it showed no sequel. It resembled Providence, since it pointed at connection." Goethe's understanding of the demonic figures implicitly in his staging of *Faust*. Also see Goethe's *Conversations with Eckermann*, trans. John Oxenford (San Francisco, 1984), pp. 202–3: Such things as "productiveness of the highest kind," Goethe here explains, "man must consider . . . as an unexpected gift from above, as pure children of God which he must receive and venerate with joyful thanks. They are akin to the *daemon*, which does with him what it pleases. . . ." See, too, Ralph Waldo Emerson's lecture on "Demonology," in *Lectures and Biographical Sketches* (Boston, 1896), pp. 9–32.

18. "La prose d'Acteon," *La Nouvelle Revue Française*, 135 (March 1964), pp. 444, 447; et: "The Prose of Acteon," introduction to Klossowski, *The Baphomet*, trans. Sophie Hawkes and Stephen Sartarelli (Hygiene, Colorado, 1988), pp. xxi, xxiv–xxv. Nietzsche, *The Gay Science*, pp. 273–74 (§341). Foucault maintained an interest in the demonic throughout his life. In 1961, in a footnote to *Folie et deraison,* he even promised a future inquiry into "the experience of the demonic" and its modern "reduction." (See FD, p. 39n.) The results (if any) of his inquiry he never published. But in his last lectures at the Collège de France, discussed in chapter eleven, Foucault returned to the role of the *daimon* in the philosophical life. In these years, he urged students curious to learn more to consult François Vanden-broucke, "Demon," in *Dictionnaire de spiritualité* (Paris, 1957), Vol. III, cols. 41–238. See "Discourse and Truth: The Problematization of *Parrhesia*," an unpublished and unauthorized transcription of Foucault's fall 1983 seminar at Berkeley, ed. by Joseph Pearson (Evanston, Ill., 1985), p. 88n.

19. Nietzsche, *The Gay Science*, pp. 273–74 (§341)—emphasis added by Foucault, in his discussion of the aphorism.

20. Nietzsche, *Thus Spoke Zarathustra*, p. 264 (III, §1). Cf. Nietzsche, *Beyond Good and Evil*, p. 162 (§231): "At the bottom of us, really 'deep down,' there is, of course, something unteachable, some granite of spiritual *fatum*"—and this, precisely, defines our unique "higher necessity."

21. Nietzsche, "Schopenhauer as Educator," loc. cit., p. 191 (§4).

22. The Binswanger quotes come from Ludwig Binswanger, *Being-in-the-World*, trans. and introduced by Jacob Needleman (New York, 1963), pp. 2, 3. For the importance of "love," see, e.g., Binswanger, "The Case of Ellen West," trans. Werner M. Mendel and Joseph Lyons, in Rollo May, Ernest Angel and Henri F. Ellenberger, eds., *Existence* (New York, 1958), pp. 268, 293, 312–13, 313–14. For biographical information, see *Being-in-the-World* and Ernest Jones, *The Life and Work of Sigmund Freud* (New York, 1953–57), and Herbert Spiegelberg, *The Phenomenological Movement: A Historical Introduction* (The Hague, 1969).

23. Didier Eribon, *Michel Foucault* (Paris, 1989), p. 64; et: *Michel Foucault*, trans. Betsy Wing (Cambridge, Mass., 1991), pp. 44–45.

24. Daniel Defert interview, 25 March 1990.

25. Binswanger, "The Case of Ellen West," loc. cit., p. 243. The details that follow are all drawn from Binswanger's case history: see pp. 238–67.

26. Ibid., pp. 254, 258, 255 (emphasis added by Binswanger).

27. Ibid., p. 256.

28. Ibid., p. 256.

29. See ibid., pp. 262, 267.

30. Ibid., p. 298.

31. Ibid., p. 298.

32. MM, p. 66; MM* et, pp. 54–55. RE, p. 94; et, p. 62.

33. Eribon, *Foucault*, p. 65; et, p. 45. Eribon, in his book, and in my conversations with him, has said that there is no certain way of knowing in what order Foucault wrote the Binswanger essay and his first book, also published in 1954, *Maladie mentale et personnalité*; Eribon's hunch is that the Binswanger was finished first. Even if he is right, and the Binswanger essay was *finished* first, I think there is both ample internal evidence as well as circumstantial external evidence that it was conceptualized and started *after* the book was

already well underway. Foucault himself never liked the book. He tried to salvage it for a reprinting in 1962 by rewriting the final chapters and retitling it *Maladie mentale et psychologie*; but he subsequently let the book go out of print in French and tried (unsuccessfully) to prevent it from appearing in an English translation. The Binswanger essay, on the other hand, he clearly regarded differently: when preparations were being made at the time of his death to translate it into English, he raised no objection. One other bit of circumstantial evidence: in his memoir of Foucault, Maurice Pinguet clearly recalls 1953 as the year when the focus of Foucault's interests "abruptly passed" from "conditioned reflexes to the analysis of *Dasein*, from Pavlov [a key figure in the book] to Binswanger." (Those puzzled by Foucault's youthful interest in Pavlov should remember, too, that 1953, not coincidentally, was also the year Foucault left the Communist Party.) See Pinguet, "Les années d'apprentissage," pp. 127–28.

34. RE, pp. 126–27; et, pp. 74–75. For Foucault's later views on the practice of "commentary," see NC, p. xii–xiii; et, p. xvi–xvii.

35. Binswanger, "The Case of Ellen West," loc. cit, p. 323. Ludwig Binswanger, "Dream and Existence," in *Being-in-the-World*, pp. 247, 244. Recent research has tended to lend more support to Binswanger's stress on the practical intelligibility of dreams than to Freud's emphasis on instinct and repression: see, e.g., J. Allan Hobson, *The Dreaming Brain* (New York, 1988).

36. RE, pp. 28, 40–41; et, pp. 38, 42–43.

37. RE, p. 64; et, p. 51. Surrealism is a constant presence in the background of Foucault's work, forming the "*épistémè*" he stands within, its influence communicated through figures like Maurice Blanchot, Georges Bataille, René Char, and Antonin Artaud, but also through the work of André Breton directly: see "C'était un nageur entre deux mots" (int), *Arts-loisirs*, 54 (5 October 1966), esp. p. 9, where Foucault hails Breton for his "discovery of the domain of experience" subsequently explored by Bataille and Blanchot.

38. RE, pp. 56, 114; et, p. 48, 69.

39. RE, p. 101; et, p. 65.

40. RE, pp. 85, 69, 52; et, pp. 59, 53, 47.

41. RE, pp. 64, 54, 69, 66, 70; et, pp. 51, 47, 53, 52, 54. Friedrich Nietzsche, *Daybreak*, trans. R. J. Hollingdale (Cambridge, England, 1982), p. 78 (§128).

42. RE, p. 66 ("*Le coeur mis à nu*"); et, p. 52.

43. Charles Baudelaire, "My Heart Laid Bare" (in French: "*Mon coeur mis à nu*"), trans. Christopher Isherwood, in *Intimate Journals* (San Francisco, 1983), pp. 100, 75, 57, 64.

44. RE, pp. 110–11; et, pp. 68.

45. RE, p. 70; et, p. 54.

46. RE, pp. 71–72; et, p. 54.

47. RE, pp. 114, 113, 73; et, pp. 69, 55.

48. Cf. RE, p. 128; et, p. 75: "happiness, in the empirical order, can only be the happiness of expression"—the problem, implicitly, then, is how to "express" the dream of death. Foucault's essay itself, of course, is a preliminary answer—it exemplifies one way, short of killing oneself, to express a dream of death.

49. "Conversazione con Michel Foucault" (int), *La Fiera Letteraria*, 39 (26 September 1967); I am translating from the original French transcript, p. 17. For Foucault and Barraqué, see Eribon, *Foucault*, pp. 85–90; et, pp. 64–68.

50. The details here and in what follows about Barraqué's life come from André Hodeir, *Since Debussy: A View of Contemporary Music*, trans. Noel Burch (New York, 1961), pp. 163–203; Hodeir's book also has useful chapters on Messiaen and Boulez (he knew all three composers personally).

51. Joan Peyser, *Boulez: Composer, Conductor, Enigma* (New York, 1976), pp. 37, 51, 33. On Foucault's friendship with Boulez, see Eribon's account in *Foucault*, pp. 85–87; et, pp. 64–65. Several of my sources indicate that the relationship between Foucault and Boulez was much closer than Eribon implies.

52. Jean Barraqué, "Propos impromptus," *Courrier musical de France*, 26 (1969), p. 78.

53. Barraqué's 1953 comment is quoted in Rose-Marie Janzen, "L'inachèvement sans

cesse," *Entretemps*, "Numéro spécial Jean Barraqué" (1987), p. 123. Arthur Rimbaud, Letter to Paul Demeny, 15 May 1871, in *Rimbaud: Complete Works, Selected Letters*, trans. Wallace Fowlie (Chicago, 1966), p. 307. Foucault discusses Barraqué's alcoholism in Simeon Wade, *Foucault in California* (unpublished ms., 1990), p. 21. Compare the photograph in Hodeir, *After Debussy*, with that on the cover of the Astrée recording of Barraqué's *Séquence* (AS 75).

54. Hodeir, *After Debussy*, pp. 194–95.

55. Beckett quoted in Charles Juliet, "Meeting Beckett," *TriQuarterly*, 77 (Winter 1989–90). "Um welchen Preis sagt die Vernuft die Wahrheit?" (int, 1983); et in PPC, p. 18.

56. In his first published interview, in *Le Monde*, after *Folie et déraison* had been published, Foucault, asked what were the influences on the book, responds "Above all, works of literature... Maurice Blanchot. . . ." See "La folie n'existe que dans une société," *Le Monde*, 5135 (22 July 1961), p. 9. Also see Eribon, *Foucault*, p. 79; et, pp. 58–59.

57. On Blanchot's mystique, see P. Adams Sitney, "Afterword," in Maurice Blanchot, *The Gaze of Orpheus*, trans. Lydia Davis (Barrytown, N.Y., 1981), pp. 163–69.

58. Eribon, *Foucault*, p. 79; et, p. 58. Daniel Defert interview 25 March 1990. The English translation of the Roussel book oddly enough omits the dash marks (—) that Foucault (following Blanchot's example) uses in the last chapter to indicate that he is staging an "interview" (or dialogue) with himself. (By contrast, the same convention is faithfully rendered in the English translation of the conclusion of *The Archeology of Knowledge*.)

59. See Sitney, ibid., and also Jeffrey Mehlman, "Maurice Blanchot," in *Dictionary of Literary Biography*, 72, pp. 77–82. For Levinas and Heidegger, see Maurice Blanchot, "Thinking the Apocalypse: A Letter from Maurice Blanchot to Cathérine David," trans. Paula Wissing, *Critical Inquiry*, 15, 2 (Winter 1989), pp. 479–80.

60. See Jeffrey Mehlman, "Blanchot at *Combat*: Of Literature and Terror," *MLN*, 95, 4 (May 1980), pp. 808–29.

61. Quoted in Mehlman, "Maurice Blanchot," loc. cit., p. 78.

62. John Updike, "No Dearth of Death," in *Hugging the Shore* (New York, 1983), p. 546.

63. PD, pp. 21–22; et, pp. 21–22.

64. Maurice Blanchot, *The Space of Literature*, trans. Ann Smock (Lincoln, Neb., 1982), pp. 52, 267, 54, 243 (this book was originally published as *L'Espace littéraire* in 1955, and contains material published between 1953 and 1955 in *Nouvelle Revue Français*).

65. Ibid., p. 107 (in a section entitled "Art, Suicide").

66. Ibid., p. 54.

67. For Blanchot's critical interests in these years, see *Faux pas* (Paris, 1943), *La part du feu* (Paris, 1949) and *Le livre à venir* (Paris, 1959). In one interview, Foucault pointed out that one of the most important things Blanchot did for him was to introduce him to Bataille and, through Bataille, to lead him back to Nietzsche. See "Um welchen Preis sagt die Vernuft die Wahrheit?" (int, 1983); et in PPC, p. 24: "I said earlier that I wondered why I had read Nietzsche [again in 1953]. But I know very well. I read him because of Bataille, and Bataille because of Blanchot."

68. Blanchot, *Le livre à venir*, p. 165. In my interview with Daniel Defert on 25 March 1990, he stressed to me the importance of Broch's book to both Foucault and Barraqué, suggesting it was one key to understanding the nature of their relationship.

69. Broch quoted in Hodeir, *After Debussy*, pp. 200–01. The reference to T. S. Eliot is made by Blanchot in his review, in a footnote about Broch's book in relationship to Nietzsche's doctrine of the eternal recurrence: see Blanchot, *Le livre à venir*, p. 170n.

70. See Hermann Broch, *The Death of Virgil*, trans. Jean Starr Untermeyer (New York, 1945), esp. pp. 200–203. My understanding of Broch has been informed by Hannah Arendt, "Hermann Broch, 1886–1951," in *Men in Dark Times* (New York, 1968), pp. 111–51.

71. See Hodeir, *After Debussy*, pp. 200–03.

72. Broch, *The Death of Virgil*, p. 482.

73. "Présentation," in Georges Bataille, *Oeuvres complètes I: Premiers écrits* (Paris, 1970), p. 5.

74. For Bataille's life, see Michel Surya, *Georges Bataille, la mort à oeuvres* (Paris, 1987), and also the special issue on Bataille of *Magazine Littéraire*, 243 (June 1987).

75. Georges Bataille, *Erotism*, trans. Mary Dalwood (New York, 1962), pp. 168, 185 (published in 1957 in France as *L'Erotisme*). Georges Bataille, *Guilty*, trans. Bruce Boone (Venice, Calif., 1988), p. 13 (originally published in 1944 in France as *Le coupable*, volume two of *La Somme Athéologique*).

76. The Dostoyevsky detail comes from Bataille's friend Michel Leiris; see his memoir of Bataille in *Brisées*, trans. Lydia Davis (San Francisco, 1990), pp. 238–47.

77. See Georges Bataille, "The Use Value of D.A.F. de Sade," in *Visions of Excess: Selected Writings, 1927–1939*, trans. Allan Stoekl (Minneapolis, 1985), p. 102. Claudine Frank, who is writing a dissertation about Bataille's friend Roger Callois, informs me that the "sacrifice" is discussed in letters from Bataille that she has examined. Surya's biography also has more details about this bizarre episode.

78. Bataille, "Use Value of Sade," loc. cit., p. 102. See also "Nietzschean Chronicle," where Bataille tries, quite unpersuasively to my mind, to explain why "his" exultation of violence is somehow different from and better than the fascist exultation of violence; in *Visions of Excess*, pp. 202–11.

79. "Préface à la transgression," *Critique*, 195–96 (August–September 1963), p. 754; et, LCP, p. 33. Cf. "Conversazione con Michel Foucault" (int, 1967), loc. cit., where Foucault identifies Bataille's importance for him as the "dissolution" of "the erotic subject" through "the experience of eroticism." (I am translating from the original French transcript, p. 19.)

80. "Préface à la transgression" (1963), loc. cit., pp. 754, 751; et in LCP, pp. 33, 29–30. MM, p. 54; MM* et, p. 83. For eroticism and "negative experience," see Bataille, *Erotism*, p. 23.

81. Georges Bataille, *Inner Experience*, trans. Leslie Anne Boldt (Albany, N.Y., 1988), pp. 43, 51, 54 (on *"la joie suppliciante"*). (This work was originally published in 1943 in France as *L'Expérience intérieure*, volume one of *La Somme Athéologique*.) The passage evoking *"la joie suppliciante"* is quoted in "Préface à la transgression" (1963), loc. cit., p. 762; et in LCP, p. 43. On Foucault's attitude toward "transgression" as a practice as well as a theory, see CF (int, 1978), pp. 15–16; et, p. 46. Foucault's fascination with sado-masochistic eroticism in these years became a problem in his relationship with Barraqué, as will be described.

82. Bataille, *Inner Experience*, p. 53. Bataille, *Erotism*, pp. 11, 23, 24.

83. "Préface à la transgression" (1963), loc. cit., pp. 755–56, 752; et in LCP, pp. 34–35, 30 (emphasis added). "La prose d'Acteon" (1964), loc. cit., p. 457; et in Klossowski, *The Baphomet*, p. xxxvi. The phrase about "the *transcendens* pure and simple" is Heidegger's definition of "Being" in *Being and Time*.

84. Bataille, *Erotism*, p. 11. The interpretation of sado-masochistic eroticism sketched here is informed, above all, by the work of Robert J. Stoller, see esp. *Perversion: The Erotic Form of Hatred* (New York, 1975); and also by the work of Gayle Rubin, Geoffrey Mains, and Leo Bersani. For a longer discussion, and more sources, see chapter eight.

85. "Préface à la transgression" (1963), loc. cit., p. 755; et in LCP, p. 34.

86. Georges Bataille, *Story of the Eye*, trans. Joachim Neugroschel (San Francisco, 1987), p. 33.

87. On the circumstances of the composition, see Hodeir, *After Debussy*, pp. 165–70. Foucault talks about his arrangement of the poems for Barraqué in Wade, *Foucault in California*, p. 21. Cf. Eribon, *Foucault*, p. 88; et, p. 66.

88. Gilles Deleuze, *Nietzsche et la philosophie* (Paris, 1962) , p. 199; et: *Nietzsche and Philosophy*, trans. Hugh Tomlinson (New York, 1983), p. 173. The poem appears in the section of Part IV of *Zarathustra* called "The Magician;" see Nietzsche, *Thus Spoke Zarathustra*, pp. 364–67 (IV, §5).

89. Friedrich Nietzsche, "Ariadne's Complaint," in *Dithyrambs of Dionysus*, trans. R. J. Hollingdale (Redding Ridge, Conn., 1984), p. 53.

90. Ibid., p. 59.

91. Hodeir, *After Debussy*, pp. 191, 172. Cf. Nietzsche, "Ariadne's Complaint," loc. cit., p. 55; my own translation here follows Foucault's arrangement of Henri Albert's French rendering—not Hollingdale's English.

92. PD, p. 28; et, p. 28. Charles Baudelaire, *The Painter of Modern Life and Other Essays*, trans. Jonathan Mayne (London, 1964), pp. 28, 27.

93. Nietzsche, *The Gay Science*, p. 232 (§290). Nietzsche, *The Will to Power*, p. 444 (§842).

94. Quoted in Eribon, *Foucault*, p. 89; et, p. 68. In my interview with him on 29 March 1990, Eribon explained that the passage quoted, in context, clearly refers to Barraqué's distress over Foucault's fascination with sado-masochistic eroticism. He also explained why he refrained from making this point explicitly in his biography: on the one hand (as he says in his book's preface), he did not wish to write a "sensational book," out of deference, in part, to surviving members of Foucault's family; and, on the other hand, he had to contend with France's strict libel laws, which allow a dead person's estate to sue. Eribon was frankly worried about the legal implications of revealing *anything* about the love affair between Foucault and Barraqué. His fears, happily, have proved to be unfounded. Still, the relevant documents have yet to be made fully accessible: Eribon himself was allowed only a few hours to consult Foucault's letters to Barraqué. His reconstruction of their important relationship, particularly under such difficult circumstances, must be accounted as one of his book's finest achievements.

95. See Wade, *Foucault in California*, p. 21. Wade here recounts Foucault talking explicitly about his preoccupation with Barraqué's alcoholism and eventual death from alcohol-related factors, a preoccupation Foucault alluded to often (though rarely mentioning Barraqué by name) when people in social situations would ask him why he rarely drank. Though the evidence in Eribon's book suggests that Foucault continued to drink in Sweden, Daniel Defert, in our conversation on 25 March 1990, asserted that Foucault "left France for Sweden to leave alcoholism."

96. Pinguet, "Les années d'apprentissage," loc. cit., p. 124. Foucault recalled his celibacy to Edmund White; interview, 12 March 1990. See also Eribon, *Foucault*, p. 100; et, pp. 77–78.

97. "Preface to *The History of Sexuality*, Volume II" (1983; a preface ultimately discarded), in TFR, p. 334.

98. Ibid.

99. "What is Enlightenment?" (1983), in TFR, pp. 46–47.

100. "Le recherche scientifique et la psychologie," in Jean-Eduoard Morere, ed., *Des chercheurs français s'interrogent* (Paris, 1957), p. 194.

101. Ibid., p. 194.

102. Ibid., p. 198. CF (int, 1978), pp. 15–16; et, p. 46.

103. "Le recherche scientifique et la psychologie" (1957), loc. cit., p. 199. "*L'homme de sac et de corde*" is an archaic French idiom dating from the seventeenth century, alluding to a punishment for theft in which the malefactor was tied up in a bag and drowned; the phrase, by extension, was later commonly used to refer to a thief, to a hangman, or to any disreputable person.

104. "Préface à la transgression" (1963), loc. cit., p. 760; et in LCP, p. 44.

105. "Le recherche scientifique et la psychologie" (1957), loc. cit., p. 201.

106. Nietzsche, *The Gay Science*, p. 269 (§338).

CHAPTER 4: THE CASTLE OF MURDERS

1. My description of Artaud's "Tête-à-tête" is drawn from the accounts cited in Ruby Cohn, *From 'Desire' to 'Godot': Pocket Theater of Postwar Paris* (Berkeley, 1987), pp. 51–63; and also from Roger Shattuck, *The Innocent Eye* (New York, 1984), pp. 169–70. The observer who thought of a drowning man was André Gide.

2. Antonin Artaud, *The Theater and Its Double*, trans. Mary Caroline Richards (New York, 1958), pp. 12, 92.

3. Antonin Artaud, "Artaud le Momo," in Artaud, *Selected Writings*, ed. Susan Sontag, trans. Helen Weaver (New York, 1976), p. 523.

4. Ibid., p. 523.

5. Shattuck, *Innocent Eye*, p. 170.

6. See Artaud, *Selected Writings*, p. 641.

7. "Artaud le Momo," in Artaud, *Selected Writings*, p. 529; "Indian Culture," in Artaud, *Selected Writings*, pp. 538–39.

8. Roger Blin (later the director of Beckett's *Waiting for Godot*), quoted in Cohn, *From 'Desire' to 'Godot'*, p. 60.

9. Jacques Audiberti, quoted in Cohn, op. cit., pp. 60–61.

10. Quoted in Cohn, op. cit., p. 59.

11. Ibid., p. 62.

12. Ibid., p. 54, 60.

13. Ibid., p. 61.

14. FD, p. 556; et, p. 287.

15. CF (int, 1978), p. 31; et, p. 66.

16. For a more detailed account of the externals of Foucault's life in these years, see Didier Eribon, *Michel Foucault* (Paris, 1989), p. 95–116; et: *Michel Foucault*, trans. Betsy Wing (Cambridge, Mass., 1991), pp. 73–91.

17. For Foucault in Uppsala, see Eribon, *Foucault*, p. 106; et, p. 83.

18. See FD, pp. 13–55 (the English translation, of an abridged French edition published in 1964, omits most of the footnotes).

19. "La folie n'existe que dans une société" (int), *Le Monde* 5135 (22 July 1961), p. 9.

20. FD, p. 13; et, p. 3.

21. FD, p. 13; et, p. 3. In this opening paragraph, as throughout the book, Foucault plays on the ambiguity in French of "*mal*"—a word that, depending on the context, can mean both a (moral) "evil" and a (physical) "disease."

22. FD, pp. 16, 26; et, pp. 7, 16.

23. FD, p. 26; et., p. 16.

24. FD, pp. 24, 26; et, p. 14, 16.

25. FD, p. 19; et, p. 8. OD, p. 37; et, p. 224.

26. FD, pp. 19–20; et, p. 9.

27. FD, pp. 18–19; et, pp. 7–8.

28. FD, p. 19; et, p. 8. In this context, Foucault cites figures from Nuremberg, where "in the first half of the fifteenth century, . . . thirty-one [madmen] were driven away." But of course this figure by no means proves that most (or even any) of these madmen were shipped out by boat.

29. FD, pp. 22, 23; et, pp. 11, 13. "L'eau et la folie," *Médecine et Hygiène*, 613 (23 October 1963), p. 901.

30. FD, pp. 22, 23, et, pp. 11, 12.

31. FD, pp. 20, 31, 30; et, pp. 9, 21, 20.

32. FD, pp. 31, 38; et, 21.

33. FD, pp. 32, 33; et, pp. 22, 23.

34. Cf. Foucault's evocation of the Last Judgment in FD, pp. 37– 38.

35. FD, p. 36; et, p. 28.

36. FD, pp. 38, 39, 47.

37. FD, pp. 39, 22; et, p. 11.

38. FD, p. 41.

39. FD, p. 117.

40. For a more detailed account of the Sorbonne jury and its reaction, see Eribon, *Foucault*, pp. 125–140; et, pp. 101–15.

41. "Rapport de M. Canguilhem sur le manuscrit deposé par M. Michel Foucault,

Directeur de l'Institut français de Hambourg, en vue de l'obtention du permis d'imprimer comme thèse principale du doctorat des lettres," p. 5. (I am quoting from the copy on deposit at the Centre Michel Foucault in Paris; the complete text now also appears in the revised second edition of Eribon, *Foucault* [Paris, 1991], pp. 358–61.)

42. Ibid., pp. 1, 3.

43. Ibid., pp. 3, 4.

44. "La folie, l'absence d'oeuvre" (1964), in FD (1972), pp. 577, 582.

45. See Eribon, *Foucault*, p. 126; et, p. 102.

46. Quoted in ibid., p. 137; et, p. 113.

47. Quoted in ibid., p. 139; et, p. 114.

48. For a convenient summary of the scholarly critiques, see J. G. Merquior, *Foucault* (London, 1985), pp. 26–34; in France, the most influential revision of Foucault's account has been Marcel Gauchet and Gladys Swain, *La pratique de l'esprit humain: L'institution asilaire et la révolution démocratique* (Paris, 1980). For a more sympathetic but equally firm critique based largely on the English experience, see Roy Porter, *Mind-Forg'd Manacles* (Cambridge, Mass., 1987), esp. pp. 279–80.

49. FD (1961), pp. iv, v, i, vii.

50. See Georges Bataille, *L'Expérience intérieure*, in Bataille, *Oeuvres complètes*, Vol. V (Paris, 1973); et: *Inner Experience*, trans. Leslie Anne Boldt (Albany, N.Y., 1988).

51. "La prose d'Acteon," *La Nouvelle Revue Francaise*, No. 135 (March 1964), p. 455; et: "The Prose of Acteon," trans. Sophie Hawkes and Stephen Sartarelli, in Pierre Klossowski, *The Baphomet*, trans. Hawkes and Sartarelli (Hygiene, Colorado, 1988), p. xxxiv. FD (1961), p. iv.

52. FD (1961), pp. iv–v. Foucault here announces his intention to follow up his history of madness with other studies of different "limit-experiences," starting with an account of the changing value accorded to dreams, and continuing with an inquiry into the changing limits of forbidden sexual behavior; the dream book he never finished and the History of Sexuality he left unfinished at his death.

53. FD (1961), p. v. Cf. Maurice Blanchot's own formula in *L'Entretien infini* (Paris, 1969), p. 46: "Le dehors, l'absence d'oeuvre." Blanchot's idea of *"le dehors"* ("the outside") Foucault discusses at length in his essay on Blanchot, "La pensée du dehors," *Critique*, no. 229 (June 1966): 523–546 (reprinted in PD). And compare, too, Foucault's "Introduction" to the Armond Colin edition of Jean-Jacques Rousseau, *Rousseau juge de Jean-Jacques* (Paris, 1962), pp. xxiii–xxiv. In the imaginary dialogue he stages with himself at the close of this introduction (as if to emulate both Rousseau *and* Blanchot), Foucault goes back and forth over the issue of whether or not Rousseau's writing bears the traces of his madness, one part of him insisting it does, the other part insisting it does not (since to produce a reasoned "work" proves that one is not, literally, "mad").

54. FD (1961), p. ii; et, p. x. Compare the exchange between Foucault and an interlocutor at a 1964 conference, quoted in Eribon, *Foucault*, p. 177; et, p. 151: "Concerning madness, you said that the experience of madness comes closest to absolute knowledge. . . . Is this really what you said?" Foucault: "Yes."—"You didn't mean 'consciousness,' or 'prescience,' or 'premonition' of madness? Do you really think that one can have . . . that great minds such as Nietzsche can have 'the experience of madness?' " Foucault: "Yes, yes."

55. FD (1961), p. ii; et, p. x.

56. FD (1961), p. vii.

57. FD (1961), p. vii.

58. FD (1961), p. vii. The rebel angels appear in the left panel of Bosch's triptych *The Hay Wain*, in the Prado, Madrid.

59. FD (1961), pp. vii, viii.

60. Ibid., pp. ix, x. The quote from Char is from the prose poem "Suzerain," in "Le poème pulverisé," reprinted in his collection *Fureur et mystère* (Paris, 1948).

61. RE, 114; et, p. 69.

62. For Char's life and work, and the connections between them, see now Paul Veyne, *René Char en ses poèmes* (Paris, 1990).

63. René Char, "Partage Formel," # XXII, reprinted in *Fureur et mystère*. I wish to thank Mary Ann Caws for her comments on the significance of this and other passages from Char, and also for her help with the translation.

64. Char, "Partage Formel," # XXII.

65. Daniel Defert interview, 25 March 1990.

66. Antonin Artaud, "Van Gogh, the Man Suicided by Society" (1947), in Artaud, *Selected Writings*, p. 491.

67. Maurice Blanchot, *The Space of Literature*, trans. Ann Smock (Lincoln, Neb., 1982), p. 54.

68. "Un 'Fantastique de bibliothèque'" (1964), reprinted, slightly abridged, as the introduction to the Le Livre de Poche edition of Gustave Flaubert, *La tentation de Saint Antoine* (Paris, 1971), p. 10; et in LCP, pp. 90–91. The same idea is expressed as well in "Distance, aspect, origine," *Critique*, 198 (November 1963), p. 938.

69. MC, pp. 142–43; et, pp. 130–31. FD, p. 536.

70. The Marquis de Sade, *Justine*, trans. Richard Seaver and Austryn Wainhouse (New York, 1965), p. 643 (in the castle of M. de Gernande).

71. Ibid., p. 675 (with M. de Corville and Roland).

72. The Marquis de Sade, *Juliette*, trans. Austryn Wainhouse (New York, 1968), p. 415 (at the outset of Part III, just before Juliette's induction into the "Sodality of the Friends of Crime").

73. FD, pp. 381, 554; et, pp. 209–10, 285.

74. FD, pp. 120, 121, 117.

75. FD, p. 381; et, p. 210. For an overview of Sade's life, see the chronology in the English translation of *Justine*, pp. 73–119; at first convicted of the alleged poisoning, Sade was eventually exonerated of this charge—though his family, trying to preserve its good name, made certain he remained in prison, using the power conferred under the ancien régime by the *lettre de cachet*.

76. This litany recurs at various junctures of *Folie et déraison*: see, e.g., FD, pp. 39–40, 120, 364, 371–72, 530, 554–557; et, pp. 278, 285–89. The litany itself has its orgins in Antonin Artaud, "Van Gogh, the Man Suicided by Society"; see Artaud, *Selected Writings*, pp. 483, 486. Jacques Derrida points out Foucault's debt to Artaud in his essay "La parole soufflée," in Derrida, *Writing and Difference*, trans. Alan Bass (Chicago, 1978), p. 326n.26. Foucault's genealogy differs from Artaud's in one crucial respect: unlike Artaud, he consistently places Sade (together with Kant) at the start of a tradition of thinking that reveals our own "modern" field of experience to be tragically divided—between those domains rationally regulated by modern science, and those "mad" realms explored only by certain daredevils of "literature."

77. FD, pp. 554, 550, 552; et, pp. 285, 280–281, 283. Hölderlin's description of his hero Empedocles is quoted in Wilhelm Dilthey, "Friedrich Hölderlin" (1910), in Dilthey, *Poetry and Experience*, ed. Rudolf A. Makkreel and Frithjof Rodi (Princeton, 1985), p. 352. Foucault's fascination with Nerval's suicide is expressed in "L'obligation d'écrire," *Arts*, 980, 11–17 November 1964, p. 7. The black crows swirling in Van Gogh's *Crows Over the Wheat Field* (1890; National Museum Vincent Van Gogh, Amsterdam) are discussed at length in Artaud, "Van Gogh, the Man Suicided by Society," loc. cit., and also in Meyer Schapiro, "On a Painting of Van Gogh," in Schapiro, *Modern Art: 19th and 20th Centuries* (New York, 1978), pp. 87–99. The description of Roussel evoking "the repetition of death" is Foucault's own: see MC, p. 395; et, p. 383. See also, of course, Foucault's book on Roussel, RR, discussed in chapter five. Besides the references to him in FD, Foucault devoted a separate essay to Hölderlin: see "Le 'non' du père," *Critique*, 178 (March 1962), pp. 195–209; et in LCP, pp. 68–86; and see, too, the role assigned Empedocles in the climax of *Birth of the Clinic*: NC, p. 202; et, p. 198.

78. FD, pp. 551, 554; et, pp. 281, 284–85.

79. FD, pp. 551, 552; et, pp. 281, 282 (emphasis added).

80. CF (int, 1978), pp. 4, 10; et, pp. 30, 38.

81. CF (int, 1978), p. 8; et, pp. 35–36.

82. The consensus among historians seems to be that Tuke was not nearly as important as Foucault implies; and that Pinel was a far more salutary figure in the history of the treatment of mental illness than Foucault will allow. See, e.g., Porter, *Mind-Forg'd Manacles*, p. 225.

83. FD, pp. 483–84; et, pp. 241–42.

84. FD, p. 523; et, p. 269.

85. FD, p. 504; et, p. 247.

86. FD, p. 509; et, p. 252.

87. FD, pp. 497, 500, 22; et, p. 11.

88. FD, pp. 516–17; et, pp. 260–61.

89. FD, pp. 517, 553; et, pp. 261, 284.

90. "Les déviations religieuses et le savoir médical" (1962), in Jacques LeGoff, ed., *Hérésies et sociétés dans l'Europe pré-industrielle 11e–18e siècles* (Mouton, 1968), p. 19.

91. "Préface à la transgression," *Critique*, 195–96 (August–September 1963), p. 757; et in LCP, p. 35.

92. FD, pp. 22, 115; et, p. 11.

93. FD, pp. 475, 553; et, p. 283. RE, p. 52; et, p. 47.

94. FD, p. 475. MC, p. 395; et, p. 384. Cf. "Préface à la transgression" (1963), loc. cit., p. 757; et in LCP, p. 35: "Since this existence [revealed through transgression] is both so pure and so complicated, it must be detached from its questionable association to ethics if we want to understand it and to begin thinking from it in the space that it denotes."

95. Friedrich Nietzsche, *Human, All Too Human*, trans. R. J. Hollingdale (Cambridge, England 1986), pp. 34–35 (I, §39, §41). Friedrich Nietzsche, *Twilight of the Idols*, trans. Walter Kaufmann, in *The Nietzsche Reader* (New York, 1954), p. 549 ("Skirmishes of an Untimely Man," §45). The same "ethical point of view" is expressed, as the title alone suggests, in Artaud's essay, "Van Gogh, the Man Suicided by Society"—a work constantly in the background of Foucault's argument in *Folie et déraison*.

96. FD, p. 556; et, p. 288. My discussion of tragedy here is informed by Nietzsche's *Birth of Tragedy*, and also by Heidegger's discussion of Sophocles in *An Introduction to Metaphysics*, trans. Ralph Manheim (Garden City, N.Y., 1961), pp. 122–38; the fact that Binswanger called Ellen West's a "tragic" existence is also relevant here.

97. FD, p. 557; et, p. 289.

98. For a more detailed account of the book's reception, see Eribon, *Foucault*, pp. 141–52; et, pp. 116–27.

99. Blanchot's review is reprinted in *L'Entretien infini*, pp. 291–99; Barthes's review is reprinted in Roland Barthes, *Critical Essays*, trans. Richard Howard (Evanston, Ill, 1972), pp. 163–70.

100. For a reconstruction of this lecture, see Eribon, *Foucault*, pp. 145–46; et, pp. 119–20.

101. For an autobiographical self-portrait, see Jacques Derrida, "The time of a thesis: punctuations," in Alan Montefiore, ed., *Philosophy in France Today* (Cambridge, 1983), pp. 34–50.

102. Jacques Derrida, *Of Grammatology*, trans. Gayatri Chakravorty Spivak (Baltimore, Md., 1976), p. 5.

103. Derrida, "Cogito and the History of Madness," in *Writing and Difference*, p. 61.

104. Ibid., p. 40.

105. Ibid., pp. 40, 55.

106. Gilles Deleuze, "Un portrait de Foucault" (int, 1986), in Deleuze, *Pourparlers* (Paris, 1990), p. 141.

107. See Eribon, *Foucault*, p. 145; et, p. 120.

108. AS, pp. 26–27, 64–65; et, pp. 16, 47.

109. "Mon corps, ce papier, ce feu" (1971), in FD (1972), pp. 584, 590, 591; et: "My Body, this Paper, this Fire," trans. Geoff Bennington, *Oxford Literary Review*, IV, 1 (Autumn 1979), pp. 10, 16, 17.

110. Ibid., in FD (1972), p. 603; et in loc. cit., p. 27.

111. See Eribon, *Foucault*, p. 147; et, p. 122.

112. See Gilles Deleuze, *Foucault* (Paris, 1986), p. 22; et: *Foucault*, trans. Sean Hand (Minneapolis, 1986), p. 13 (the translation misses the point entirely).

113. AS, pp. 64–65; et, p. 47. Foucault's lack of "repentence" on the subject of "experience" is particularly obvious in his 1978 interview with Trombadori; and, of course, by the end of his life, in his preface to the final volumes of the History of Sexuality, the idea of "experience" reappears: see, e.g., UP, p. 13; et, p. 7.

114. "La folie, l'absence d'oeuvre" (1964), in FD (1972), p. 575.

115. Ibid, p. 575.

CHAPTER 5: IN THE LABYRINTH

1. AS, p. 28; et, p. 17.

2. "Nietzsche, la généalogie, l'histoire," in *Hommage à Jean Hyppolite* (Paris, 1971), pp. 145–46; et in LCP, p. 140. Friedrich Nietzsche, *The Gay Science*, trans. Walter Kaufmann (New York, 1974), pp. 81–82 (§7). MC, p. 224; et, p. 211.

3. "Deuxième entretien: sur les façons d'écrire l'histoire" (int, 1967), reprinted in Raymond Bellour, *Le livre des autres* (Paris, 1971), pp. 201–02; et in FLI, pp. 25–26. NC, p. xii; et, p. xvi. In my interview with Bellour, 30 March 1990, he recalled his sense during his 1967 talk with Foucault that the story of the nightmare was significant—and that Foucault, in talking about it, was quite deliberately revealing something difficult and important, from his own perspective, about his work.

4. NC, p. xiii; et, p. xix. "L'Arrière-fable," *L'Arc*, 29 (1966), p. 11; et: "Behind the Fable," trans. Pierre A. Walker, in *Critical Texts*, V, 2 (1988), p. 4.

5. MC, pp. 13, 16; et, pp. xxi, xxiv.

6. Gilles Deleuze, *Foucault* (Paris, 1986), p. 22; et: *Foucault*, trans. Sean Hand (Minneapolis, 1988), p. 13.

7. On Foucault's work in this period as a kind of "game," see especially his final interview, "Le retour de la morale," *Les Nouvelles*, 2937 (28 June–5 July 1984), p. 37; et in PPC, p. 243. On the reception of *The Order of Things*, see Michel de Certeau, "The Black Sun of Language: Foucault," in *Heterologies*, trans. Brian Massumi (Minneapolis, 1986), p. 171.

8. See Didier Eribon, *Michel Foucault* (Paris, 1989), p. 164; et: *Michel Foucault*, trans. Betsy Wing (Cambridge, Mass., 1991), p. 138. Eribon's biography contains a wealth of detail about the externals of Foucault's life in these years.

9. See Eribon, *Foucault*, pp. 158, 164; et, pp. 138, 133. For the show with Ricoeur et. al., see "Philosophie et vérité," *Dossiers pédagogiques de la radio-télévision scolaire*, the transcript of a program broadcast on 27 March 1965.

10. See Eribon, *Foucault*, pp. 170–76; et, pp. 144–50.

11. G. S. Bourdain, "Robbe-Grillet on Novels and Films" (int), *New York Times* (17 April 1989), p. C13.

12. On Robbe-Grillet, see Bruce Morrissette, *Robbe-Grillet* (Paris, 1963).

13. Alain Robbe-Grillet, *For a New Novel*, trans. Richard Howard (New York, 1965), pp. 29, 44–45.

14. Ibid., p. 138.

15. Alain Robbe-Grillet, *Ghosts in the Mirror*, trans. Jo Levy (New York, 1991), pp. 5, 27, 98–102. On Robbe-Grillet as emptying the novel of interiority, see Roland Barthes, *Essais critiques* (Paris, 1964), p. 39; et: *Critical Essays*, trans. Richard Howard (New York, 1972), p. 23.

16. Robbe-Grillet, *Ghosts in the Mirror*, pp. 10, 21, 29. Robbe-Grillet, *For a New Novel*, p. 24.

17. "Distance, aspect, origine," *Critique*, 198 (November 1963), p. 931.

18. Roland Barthes, *Essais critiques*, p. 107; et, p. 98. The link with surrealism Barthes himself makes in the cited short essay (published in 1959, just before *Tel quel* came into

existence). For a short overview of the history of *Tel quel*, see Susan Rubin Suleiman, "1960: As Is," in Denis Hollier, ed., *A New History of French Literature* (Cambridge, Mass, 1989), pp. 1011–18.

19. Elisabeth Roudinesco, *Jacques Lacan & Co.*, trans. Jeffrey Mehlman (Chicago, 1990), p. 528. Despite its psychoanalytic focus, Roudinesco's is by far the most vivid single book on the 1960s theory explosion in France. On the *Tel quel* view of Sade, see Roland Barthes, *Sade/Fourier/Loyola*, trans. Richard Miller (New York, 1976), pp. 36, 170. For the glimpse of Foucault from a *Tel quel* perspective, see Julia Kristeva's roman à clef, *Les Samouraïs* (Paris, 1990), esp. p. 186—in this book, "Scherner" = Foucault. (My thanks to Arthur Goldhammer for pointing out the relevant passages.)

20. "Débat sur le roman, dirigé par Michel Foucault," *Tel quel*, 17 (Spring 1964), p. 12.

21. See ibid., p. 13.

22. Ibid., p. 13.

23. "Distance, aspect, origine" (1963), loc. cit., p. 940 (emphasis added). For a discerning treatment of Foucault's approach to literature, see Raymond Bellour, "Vers la fiction," in MFP, pp. 172–81. Cf. the enigmatic description of "philosophical thought," in "Jean Hyppolite (1907–1968)," *Revue de Métaphysique et de Morale*, 74, 2 (April–June 1969), p. 131: "This moment, so difficult to catch hold of, concealed as soon as its appearance, where philosophical discourse comes to a decision, snatches itself from silence, and distances itself from what before had appeared as nonphilosophical." In effect, "fiction" is the only kind of language capable of expressing the "distancing" proper to "philosophical thought." For an extended analysis of similar matters, readers will soon be able to consult the as yet unpublished *Mémoire de D.E.A.* by Judith Revel, "Littérature et philosophie dans l'oeuvre de Michel Foucault." (Though I have not seen this text, I have heard Revel deliver a paper based on her work, which promises to be of some importance.)

24. Cf. Denis Hollier, "Le mot de Dieu: 'Je suis mort,'" in MFP, pp. 150–65.

25. NC, p. v; et, p. ix. RR, p. 190; et, p. 150.

26. NC, pp. 1, 133, 128, 138, 139, 199, 175; et, pp. 3, 131, 127, 136, 137, 195, 170. Foucault's original phrase, "reorganisation syntactique" [NC (1963), p. 197] becomes "reorganisation épistémologique" in the 1972 edition purged of "structuralist" rhetoric. Here, as in *Madness and Civilization*, Foucault plays on the ambiguity of the French word "*mal*": see below, and also note 21 in chapter four.

27. NC, pp. 200, 175; et, pp. 196, 170. For Roussel's fascination with death, see, besides Foucault's own study, John Ashbery, "On Raymond Roussel," reprinted in RR et, p. xix. On Roussel's drug addiction and madness, see also Wayne Andrews, *The Surrealist Parade* (New York, 1990), pp. 124–25. (An interesting coincidence: at the time of his suicide, Roussel was on his way to consult a renowned specialist—the Swiss psychiatrist Ludwig Binswanger!)

28. RR, p. 209; et, p. 166. Cf. the preliminary explanation of the use of the word "game" in Ludwig Wittgenstein, *Philosophical Investigations*, trans. G.E.M. Anscombe (Oxford, 1958), I, §23. Foucault refers to Wittgenstein explicitly in AS, p. 36; et, p. 24; and also in "Entretien," *La Quinzaine Littéraire*, 5 (16 May 1966), p. 14; cf. Paul Veyne, "Le Dernier Foucault et sa morale," *Critique* (August–September 1986), p. 940n1. In "La verité et les formes juridiques," a transcription of lectures delivered in Brazil in 1974, Foucault also explicitly credits his own idea of language as a "game" to unnamed "Anglo-American philosophers" (I am translating from an unpublished French transcript, p. 6). It is perhaps of some relevance here to recall that Foucault's friend Pierre Klossowski translated Wittgenstein's *Tractatus* into French. On the other hand, Hans Sluga, a professor of philosophy at Berkeley, an expert on Wittgenstein, and also a friend of Foucault, reports that Foucault in the course of their conversations freely admitted that he had never studied Wittgenstein's work closely—though he was eager to learn more about it. (Sluga interview 28 September 1989.)

29. Ashbery, "On Raymond Roussel," in RR, et, pp. xxiv–xv. See also Andrews, *The Surrealist Parade*, p. 118.

30. Michel Leiris, *Brisées*, trans. Lydia Davis (Berkeley, Calif, 1990), p. 52. MC, 395; et, p. 383. RR, p. 210; et, p. 167.

31. RR, pp. 208, 209; et, pp. 165, 166.

32. MC, p. 395; et, p. 383. Cf. "Entretien: Michel Foucault, 'les mots et les choses'" (int, 1966), in Bellour, *Le Livre des autres*, p. 142; et in FLI, pp. 6–7: "Man would die from the signs that were born in him—that's what Nietzsche, the first one to see this, wanted to say."

33. NC (1963), p. xiv; et, p. xvii. (The 1972 edition changes "analyse structurale" to "l'analyse d'un type de discours.") For the jargon in its original formulation, see Ferdinand de Saussure, *Course in General Linguistics*, trans. Wade Baskin (New York, 1959), p. 67.

34. Edward Said, *Beginnings* (New York, 1975), p. 323. Said's path-breaking analysis of Foucault and the "structuralist moment" remains one of the best available in English. It should be said that French "structuralism" in fact had very little to do with the evolving science of structural linguistics—a point well made in Thomas Pavel, *The Feud of Language* (Oxford, 1989).

35. For Barthes, see now the biography by Louis-Jean Calvet, *Roland Barthes* (Paris, 1990). For Foucault and Barthes, cf. Eribon, *Foucault*, pp. 175–76; et, pp. 149–50. The connoisseur is Pierre Bourdieu: see his preface to the English edition of *Homo Academicus*, trans. Peter Collier (Palo Alto, Ca., 1981), p. xxii (applying to Barthes a description made by a contemporary of Theophile Gautier).

36. Claude Lévi-Strauss, *The Scope of Anthropology*, trans. Sherry Ortner Paul and Robert A. Paul (London, 1967), pp. 16, 21, 28—these are all quotes from Lévi-Strauss's 1960 inaugural lecture at the Collège de France. Throughout his life, Foucault made a practice of sending a copy of everything he published to Lévi-Strauss, though this seems to have been the extent of their relationship. See Claude Lévi-Strauss and Didier Eribon, *Conversations with Claude Lévi-Strauss*, trans. Paula Wissing (Chicago, 1991), p. 72.

37. For Foucault's professed incomprehension of Lacan, see Jacques-Alain Miller, "Michel Foucault et le psychoanalyse," in MFP, p. 81. Also on Lacan, see CF (int, 1978), p. 37; et, p. 73: "Lacan has certainly influenced me. But I haven't followed him in a way that would enable me to say that I've had an in-depth experience of his teaching." On Foucault and structuralism, cf. the account in Eribon, *Foucault*, pp. 195–97; et, pp. 167–69. As late as March, 1968, Foucault was playing the structuralist language game with brio: see "Linguistique et sciences sociales," *Revue Tunisienne de science sociales*, 19 (December 1969), p. 255: "To summarize, I would say that linguistics is currently articulating the epistemological structure proper to the social and human sciences. . . ." (from a conference paper delivered in March, 1968). Years later, Foucault would tell Hubert Dreyfus and Paul Rabinow that "he was not as resistant to the seductive advances of structuralist vocabulary as he might have been"; see BSH, p. viii. This sounds too disingenuous to be credible. One thing is clear: as the 1972 revision of his 1963 book *The Birth of the Clinic* suggests, Foucault's use of structuralist *jargon* was largely cosmetic: all the buzzwords were easily jettisoned in 1972, without touching the book's central argument.

38. Georges Dumézil, "Le Messager des dieux," *Magazine Littéraire*, 229 (April 1986), p. 19. For Dumézil, see also C. Scott Littleton, *The New Comparative Mythology* (Berkeley, Calif, 1966); and Arnaldo Momigliano, "Georges Dumézil and the Trifunctional Approach to Roman Civilization," *History and Theory*, XXIII, 3 (1984), pp. 312–30.

39. NC, p. 203; et, p. 199. "Revenir à l'histoire" (a lecture originally delivered in Kyoto, Japan, in October, 1970), transcribed in the Japanese journal *Représentations*, 2, (Autumn 1991), pp. v–vi (the passages quoted appear in the context of an extended—and highly sympathetic—discussion of Dumézil's comparative analysis of Irish and Roman myths). Foucault discussed Dumézil's work on the last words of Socrates in his Collège de France lecture of February 15, 1984 (described below in chapter eleven). See also his comments on Dumézil in "Entretien" (int, 1966), loc. cit., p. 14.

40. The manifesto appears in André Breton, *What is Surrealism?*, ed. and trans. Franklin Rosemont (London, 1978), pp. 346–48.

41. Daniel Defert recalled Foucault's attitude in a letter to the author, 8 January 1991. In his memoir, Maurice Pinguet remembers Foucault as being relatively uninterested in the Algerian conflict (as Sartre had been before 1960): see Maurice Pinguet, "Les années d'ap-

prentissage," *Le débat*, 41 (September–November 1986), p. 127. For a more detailed account of Foucault's political stance in these years, see chapter six.

42. For a detailed account of Sartre's (quite peripheral) involvement in the manifesto, see Annie Cohen-Solal, *Sartre: A Life*, trans. Anna Cancogni (New York, 1987), pp. 415–17.

43. Ibid., p. 415, see also pp. 426–31.

44. See ibid., pp. 387–88.

45. Jean-Paul Sartre, *Critique de la raison dialectique* (Paris, 1960), pp. 29, 142, 153; et: *Search for a Method*, trans. Hazel Barnes (New York, 1967), p. 30; *Critique of Dialectical Reason*, trans. Alan Sheridan-Smith (London, 1976), pp. 52, 65–66.

46. The topic of Foucault's thesis is a little offbeat: most students of Kant never look at his anthropology. It is revealing that an English translation appeared only in 1978. In his thesis, Foucault himself argues strenuously for the centrality of the Anthropology to Kant's work: see *Introduction à l'anthropologie de Kant*, Ier tome (*thèse complémentaire*, typescript available in the Bibliothèque de la Sorbonne, and xerox copy available in the Centre Michel Foucault, Paris). Ernst Cassirer, by contrast, offers a more cursory appraisal in his classic study *Kant's Life and Thought*, trans. James Haden (New Haven, Conn., 1982), pp. 52–55.

47. Immanuel Kant, *Werke*, ed. Ernst Cassirer (Berlin, 1923), Vol. VIII, p. 343; et: *Logic*, trans. Robert S. Hartman and Wolfgang Schwarz (New York, 1974), p. 29. See also Martin Buber, "What is Man?" (1938), trans. Ronald Gregor Smith, in Buber, *Between Man and Man* (New York, 1965), pp. 118–26.

48. Immanuel Kant, *Anthropology from a Pragmatic Point of View*, trans. Victor Lyle Dowdell (Carbondale, Ill., 1978), pp. 81– 82, 223, 100–01, 184. For Heidegger's views, see Martin Heidegger, *Kant and the Problem of Metaphysics* (originally published in Germany in 1929), trans. James S. Churchill (Bloomington, Ind., 1962), esp. pp. 212–26 (on "The Laying of the Foundation of Metaphysics as Anthropology"). Cf. Cassirer, *Kant's Life and Thought*, p. 408, which dismisses the *Anthropology* in one sentence. It is worth recalling here that Foucault studied Kant at the École Normale with Jean Beaufret—Heidegger's foremost disciple in postwar France. When I asked Daniel Defert if he knew whether Foucault had read Heidegger's *Kant and the Problem of Metaphysics*, he responded, "Why of course. He read it, I know, when he was working on his Kant thesis." (Defert, conversation with the author, 2 November 1991.)

49. MC, p. 396; et, p. 384. "Maurice Florence" (Foucault's pseudonym), "Michel Foucault," in Denis Huisman, ed., *Dictionnaire des philosophes* (Paris, 1984), p. 941; et: "(Auto)biography: Michel Foucault 1926–1984," trans. Jackie Ursla, *History of the Present*, 4 (Spring 1988), p. 13. Cf. Ian Hacking, "Self-Improvement," in FCR, pp. 238–39.

50. Immanuel Kant, *Critique of Pure Reason*, trans. Norman Kemp Smith (London, 1929), B1. Cassirer, *Kant's Life and Thought*, p. 151.

51. Kant, *Critique of Pure Reason*, A317/B374.

52. *Introduction à l'anthropologie de Kant*, loc. cit., p. 17.

53. Ibid., pp. 83–84, 89, 119, cf. p. 103.

54. Ibid., pp. 72, 42, 100, 101.

55. Ibid., p. 63.

56. Kant, *Critique of Pure Reason*, A800/B828. *Introduction à l'anthropologie de Kant*, p. 41.

57. Heidegger, *Kant and the Problem of Metaphysics*, pp. 173, 172, 140. Heidegger is not the only philosopher to make such charges. From a quite different perspective, the American analytic legal philosopher Joel Feinberg has similarly remarked, apropros of Kant's condemnation of suicide, that "Kant's language implies that we must cherish and protect a person's choice, not because it is *his*, simply, but because of something within him, quite independent of his will, a kind of internal Vatican City not subject to his sovereign control." (See Joel Feinberg, *Harm to Self* [New York, 1986], p. 94.) Foucault's analysis of the *Anthropology* suggests that Kant's own "Vatican City" grew out of the network of social practices he grew up within.

58. "Préface à la transgression," *Critique*, 195–96 (August–September 1963), pp. 757–

58; et in LCP, p. 38. *Introduction à l'anthropologie de Kant,* loc. cit., p. 117. Kant, *Anthropology from a Pragmatic Point of View,* p. 39. MC, p. 352; et, p. 341.

59. *Introduction à l'anthropologie de Kant,* loc. cit., p. 106–07. Cf. MC, pp. 336–37; et, p. 325–26. In order to distinguish his own use of "limit-experience" from that of Husserl and Merleau-Ponty (who is implicitly a target as well of these comments), Foucault in his French text invariably refers to experience of the life-world as *le vécu,* literally "the lived," usually rendered into English as "lived experience" or "actual experience" (which makes the distinction that Foucault wants to draw, between "limit-experience" and "the lived," even harder to grasp).

60. "Un cours inédit," *Magazine Littéraire,* 207 (May 1984), p. 39; et in PPC, p. 95.

61. *Introduction à l'anthropologie de Kant,* loc. cit., pp. 125–26.

62. Ibid., p. 128.

63. CF (int, 1978), p. 59; et, p. 101.

64. For the premodern "human sciences" as a source in Kant, see *Introduction à l'anthropologie de Kant,* loc. cit., p. 109. MC, 333; et, p. 322.

65. "Préface à la transgression" (1963), loc. cit., p. 766; et in LCP, p. 49. "La recherche scientifique et la psychologie," in Jean Eduoard Morere, *Des chercheurs français s'interrogent* (Paris, 1957), p. 197 (I take Foucault's idiosyncratic development of *recherche* here, as a kind of unscientific "quest," to amount to a virtual synonym for his equally idiosyncratic idea that "experience" is a kind of experiment, putting knowledge to the test).

66. MC, pp. 353, 334; et, p. 342, 323. Foucault here speaks of *"expériences non fondées"* (experiences without foundation) and "les expériences de la pensée non fondée." Cf. "Conversazione con Michel Foucault" (int), *La Fiera Letteraria,* 39 (28 September 1967), where Foucault explains that philosophy in our own age has disappeared—but not the philosopher.

67. "Distance, aspect, origine" (1963), loc. cit., p. 940. "Préface à la transgression" (1963), p. 760; et in LCP, p. 40. "L'Arrière-fable" (1966), loc. cit., p. 11; et: "Behind the Fable," loc. cit., p. 4. Cf. NC, xii; et, pp. xv–xvi: "For Kant, the possibility of a critique and its necessity were linked, through certain scientific contents, to the fact that there is such a thing as knowledge. In our time—and Nietzsche the philologist testifies to it—they are linked to the fact that language exists and that, in the innumerable words spoken by men—whether they are reasonable or insane, demonstrative or poetic—a meaning has taken shape that hangs over us."

68. MC, pp. 386–87; et, p. 375 (emphasis added). See also "Préface à la transgression" (1963), loc. cit., p. 762; et in LCP, pp. 43–44, where the possibility of "the mad philosopher" is discussed.

69. Ibid., pp. 761–62; et in LCP, p. 43.

70. The labyrinth is an important figure to Roussel himself, but given the use I am going to be making of Foucault's development of the image in his discussion of Roussel's work, it is worth pointing out that the novelist himself never elaborated the kind of fantasy of the Minotaur that Foucault does. Years later Foucault himself said of the Roussel book, "it's my secret affair. . . . My relationship to my book on Roussel, and to Roussel's work, is something very personal. . . . No doubt what could be said is that perhaps the same reasons which in my perverseness [laughs] and in my own psychopathological makeup made me pursue my interest in madness, on the one hand, made me pursue my interest in Roussel on the other." "An Intervew with Michel Foucault" (1983, by Charles Ruas), RR et, pp. 185, 176. See also in this interview Foucault's comments on Roussel's homosexuality, pp. 183–84.

71. "Un si cruel savoir," *Critique,* 182 (July 1962), p. 610. This essay is a comparison of two pornographic works, one by Claude Crébillon, first published in 1736–38, the other by J. A. Reveroni de Saint-Cyr, first published in 1798; in his essay, Foucault uses the two authors as evidence for his view that a sharp "break" separates, even in the genre of pornography, the classical epoch of *Les liaisons dangereuses* and the "modern" era marked by Sade as well as Reveroni.

72. "Un si cruel savoir" (1962), loc. cit., pp. 598, 609.

73. Ibid., p. 604.

74. Ibid., p. 609. "Ariane s'est pendue," *Le Nouvel Observateur*, 229 (31 March 1969), pp. 36–37 (the Ariadne image arises in the context of a review of Gilles Deleuze's *Différence et répétition*).

75. "Un si cruel savoir" (1962), loc. cit., pp. 609–10.

76. RR, p. 102; et, p. 80.

77. Ibid., p. 112; et, p. 87. Cf. "Un si cruel savoir" (1962), loc. cit., pp. 610–11, where the labyrinth is called "a space of transmutation; a cage, it makes of man a beast of desire— desiring like a wild animal, desiring like a victim."

78. "Theatrum philosophicum," *Critique*, 282 (November 1970), p. 905; et in LCP, p. 193: Foucault is here commenting on Deleuze's use of the labyrinth in *Logique du sens*— but, again, in phrases that express his own understanding of the myth.

79. MC, p. 393; et, p. 381. RR, p. 117; et, p. 91. Cf. PD, 34–35; et, p. 34–35: "Transgression endeavors to overstep prohibition in an attempt to attract the law to itself; it always surrenders to the attraction of the essential withdrawal of the law; it obstinately advances into the opening of an invisibility over which it will never triumph; insanely, it endeavors to make the law appear in order to be able to venerate it and dazzle it with its own luminous face. . . . [For] how could one know the law and truly experience it, how could one force it to come into view, to exercise its powers clearly, to speak, without provoking it? . . . How can one see its invisibility unless it has been turned into its opposite, punishment . . . ?"

80. RR, pp. 117, 120; et, pp. 91, 93. The star on the forehead was Roussel's personal emblem for his *daimon*. It appears in his play *L'étoile au front*, discussed by Foucault—and also in Roussel's conversations with Pierre Janet (a text that Foucault knew as well). Cf. Andrews, *The Surrealist Parade*, pp. 116, 122.

81. RR, p. 120; et, p. 93.

82. RR, p. 120; et, pp. 93–94.

83. RR, pp. 120–21; et, p. 94.

84. "Un si cruel savoir," loc. cit., pp. 610–11 (emphasis added).

85. On the labyrinth as a figure in Western culture, see Penelope Reed Doob, *The Idea of the Labyrinth from Classical Antiquity through the Middle Ages* (Ithaca, N.Y., 1990). And see, too, the discussion of mazes in Norman O. Brown, *Love's Body* (New York, 1966), pp. 38–48. It is worth recalling that Robbe-Grillet's fourth novel was titled *In the Labyrinth*, and also that Borges's first well-known collection of fictions (in both France and the United States) was titled *Labyrinths*.

86. RR, p. 203; et, p. 161. In Paolo Caroso's "Conversazione con Michel Foucault," in *La Fiera Letteraria*, 39 (28 September 1967), Foucault makes it plain that his own interest in Roussel was fueled in part by Pierre Janet's psychiatric interpretation of his patient's work as an expression of Roussel's psychopathology.

87. "Un si cruel savoir" (1962), loc. cit., p. 610. FD, p. 507; et, pp. 249–50.

88. See Jean-Paul Aron, *Les modernes* (Paris, 1984), p. 272.

89. See Madeleine Chapsal, "La plus grande révolution depuis l'existentialisme," *L'Express*, 779 (23–29 May 1966), pp. 119–22.

90. See Jacques Ehrmann, ed., *Structuralism* (Garden City, N.Y., 1968), a reprint of the 1966 special issue of *Yale French Studies*, and one of the first important English-language treatments of the subject.

91. See Chapsal, "La plus grande révolution," loc. cit., p. 119.

92. Aron, *Les modernes*, p. 272. For a similarly critical appraisal of the implications of the mass media brouhaha over *Les mots et les choses*, see Roudinesco, *Jacques Lacan & Co.*, p. 408.

93. Chapsal, "La plus grande révolution," loc. cit., pp. 119–20.

94. Ibid., p. 121.

95. Ibid., p. 121.

96. See Eribon, *Foucault*, p. 183; et, p. 156. And see "Les succes du mois," *L'Express*, 790 (8–14 August 1966), p. 32.

97. See de Certeau, "The Black Sun of Language: Foucault," in *Heterologies*, p. 171.

98. "Entretien: Michel Foucault, 'les mots et les choses' " (int, 1966), reprinted in Bellour, *Les livres des autres*, p. 137; et in FLI, p. 1

99. Ibid., p. 138; et in FLI, p. 2. MC, p. 13; et, pp. xi, xxii. See also "Entretien" (int, 1966), Foucault's interview with Madeleine Chapsal, published in *La Quinzaine Littéraire*, 5 (16 May 1966), pp. 14–15.

100. Ibid., pp. 14–15.

101. "Entretien: Michel Foucault" (int, 1966), reprinted in Bellour, *Le livre des autres*, p. 142; et in FLI, pp. 6–7. "Entretien" (int, 1966), *La Quinzaine Littéraire*, loc. cit., p. 15.

102. Georges Canguilhem, for one, wondered why the development of modern physics, crucial for Kant's thinking and hard to fit into Foucault's temporal (and epistemological) framework, is omitted: see Georges Canguilhem, "Mort de l'homme ou épuisement du cogito?," *Critique*, 242 (July 1967), pp. 612–13. For a useful summary of the scholarly criticisms, see J. G. Merquior, *Foucault* (London, 1985), pp. 56–75.

103. MC, pp. 38, 42, 48; et, pp. 23, 27, 33. That this is not a wholly fictive picture is indicated by the similar account of the transition from the Renaissance to the Classical Age recently offered by the estimable American philosopher of science, Stephen Toulmin.

104. MC, pp. 59, 129; et, pp. 44, 113.

105. MC, pp. 103, 119, 63; et, pp. 89, 103, 49.

106. Gilles Deleuze, "L'homme, une existence douteuse," *Le Nouvel Observateur* 81 (1–7 June 1966), pp. 32–34. MC, p. 274; et, p. 262.

107. Paul Veyne, "Foucault révolutionne l'histoire," in *Comment on écrit l'histoire* (Paris, 1978), p. 235. Cf. MC, p. 14; et, p. xxii: "We see that the system of positivities was transformed in a wholesale fashion at the end of the eighteenth and beginning of the nineteenth century. Not that reason made any progress: it was simply that the mode of being of things, and of the order that divided them up before presenting them to understanding, was profoundly altered."

108. See *Le Nouvel Observateur*, 81 (1–7 June 1966), loc. cit., p. 34.

109. Canguilhem, "Mort de l'homme," loc. cit., p. 612. Cf. MC, p. 13; et, p. xxii: "What I am attempting to bring to light is the epistemological field, the *épistémè* in which knowledge, envisaged apart from all criteria having reference to its rational value or to its objective forms, grounds its positivity, and thereby manifests a history which is not that of a growing perfection, but rather of its conditions of possibility." Among Anglo-American philosophers of science, perhaps Paul Feyerabend and Ian Hacking (with their "anarcho-rationalism") come closest to Foucault's views; both at least offer arguments that might allay the kind of uneasiness that Canguilhem's essay voices. For de Certeau's remark, see "The Black Sun of Language: Foucault," in *Heterologies*, p. 172.

110. PD, pp. 15–16; et, pp. 15–16.

111. PD, p. 16, et, p. 16.

112. PD, p. 17; et, p. 17.

113. "Conversazione con Michel Foucault" (int, 1967); I have translated from the edited typescript of the original French transcript of this interview by Paolo Caruso, p. 19.

114. MC, p. 224; et, p. 211.

115. PD, p. 18; et, p. 17. Cf. MC, p. 59; et, p. 44: "Literature [in our day] is appearing more and more as that which must be thought."

116. MC, p. 64; et, p. 50 (emphasis added)—the French phrase is "une érosion du dehors."

117. PD, p. 24; et, p. 23.

118. PD, p. 19; et, p. 19.

119. MC, pp. 16, 333, 31; et, pp. xxiv, 322, 16.

120. Friedrich Nietzsche, *The Gay Science*, p. 254 (§322).

121. Friedrich Nietzsche, *Thus Spoke Zarathustra*, in Walter Kaufmann, ed. and trans., *The Portable Nietzsche* (New York, 1954), p. 129 (Preface, §5).

122. MC, p. 275; et, p. 263.

123. Friedrich Nietzsche, *Daybreak*, trans. R. J. Hollingdale (Cambridge, 1982), p. 184 (§429). Cited in "Nietzsche, la généalogie, l'histoire" (1971), loc. cit., p. 170n.1; et in LCP, p. 163n.59.

124. Nietzsche, *Daybreak*, p. 175 (§174).

125. MC, p. 398; et, p. 387. SP, p. 21–22; et, p. 16. For Nietzsche's use of the ocean as an emblem, see *Thus Spoke Zarathustra*, loc. cit., p. 125 (Preface, §3): "Behold, I teach you the overman: he is this sea. . . ." Cf. CF (int, 1978), p. 77; et, pp. 123–24: "Men never cease to produce themselves, that is, they continually displace the plan of their subjectivity, constituting themselves in an infinite and multiple series of different subjectivities that have no end and never leave us face-to-face with something that would be 'man.' Man is an animal of [limit-] experience, he is ceaselessly engaged in a process that, by defining a field of objects, displaces him at the same time, deforming, transforming and transfiguring him as an object. In speaking of 'the death of man,' in however confused, simplifying, and prophetic a fashion, it was this that I wished to say. . . ."

126. MC, pp. 387–99; et, pp. 376 (emphasis added).

127. PD, p. 28; et, p. 28. MC, pp. 396–97; et, p. 385. "La prose d'Acteon," *La Nouvelle Revue Française*, 135 (March 1964), p. 444, 452; et: "The Prose of Acteon," trans. Sophie Hawkes, in Pierre Klossowski, *The Baphomet*, trans. Hawkes (Hygiene, Col., 1988), pp. xxi, xxx: "Everything in [such human beings in the grip of rapture] is breaking apart, bursting, presenting itself and then withdrawing in the same instant; they might well be living or dead, it matters little; oblivion in them oversees the Identical."

128. Nietzsche, *Thus Spoke Zarathustra*, p. 264 (III, §1). Cf. PD, p. 17; et, p. 16: "Although this experience involves 'going outside of oneself,' this is done ultimately in order to find oneself. . . ."

129. Eribon, *Foucault*, p. 197; et, p. 185.

130. "Nietzsche, la généalogie, l'histoire" (1963), loc. cit., p. 165; et in LCP, p. 158. Merquior, *Foucault*, p. 56.

131. Daniel Defert interview 25 March 1990. "Du pouvoir" (int, 1978), *L'Express*, 1722 (13 July 1984), p. 58; et in PPC, p. 99. CF (int, 1978), p. 57; et, pp. 99–100.

132. Jean Piaget, *Structuralism*, trans. Chaninah Maschler (New York, 1970), p. 134. The other critic is quoted in Gilles Deleuze, "Un nouvel archiviste," *Critique*, 274 (February, 1970): 195n1. These criticisms have in recent years been renewed in France by Luc Ferry and Alain Renaut in *La pensée 68* (Paris, 1985). Oddly enough (and in seeming obliviousness to the epistemological and ontological difficulties they are embracing) they wish to return to the political theory of Fichte (!) and the "humanism" of Jean-Paul Sartre (!!). On this score, see Ferry and Renaut, *Heidegger and Modernity*, trans. Franklin Philip (Chicago, 1990), pp. 95–98.

133. "Jean-Paul Sartre répond," *L'Arc*, 30 (1966).

134. CF (int, 1978), p. 45; et, p. 85.

135. See Eribon, *Foucault*, pp. 199–210; et, pp. 187–98.

136. AS, pp. 188, 37, 164; et, pp. 144, 25, 125. CF (int, 1978), p. 69; et, p. 113. The "mystery" of the eruption Foucault cleared up years later, during a 1983 seminar at Berkeley: "We have to understand very clearly, I think, that a given problematization [of a phenomenon like madness, crime, sex, etc.] is not an effect or consequence of a historical context or situation, but is an answer given by definite individuals (although you may find the same answer given in a series of texts, and at a certain point the answer may become so general it becomes anonymous)." See "On Problematization," *History of the Present* (Spring 1988), p. 17. And cf. AS, p. 261; et, p. 200 (quoted below).

137. Deleuze, *Foucault*, p. 27; et, p. 18.

138. AS, pp. 183, 268, 27, 148, 261, 41, 172–73, 274; et, pp. 140, 205, 16, 112, 200, 28, 130–31, 210 (the past participle of the verb *méconnaitre*, "*méconnu*," which I have translated as "ignored," could also be translated as "underrated," or "underestimated").

139. "Revenir à l'histoire" (1970), loc. cit., p. vii. Cf. AS, pp. 22–23, 20; et, pp. 13–14, 11. In his critique of Sartre, characteristically, the philosopher is not mentioned by

name, though Foucault's target is obvious. (In the *Critique of Dialectical Reason*, Sartre in fact refers to Braudel—but only in passing, and chiefly to demonstrate, in a swift and unconvincing series of assertions, how the kind of historical phenomena that interest Braudel square with Sartre's own ideas about freedom and "praxis.")

140. AS, p. 20; et, p. 11. MC et, p. xiv. That Foucault's disavowal of structuralism in this English-language preface is as "tactical" and misleading as his earlier *avowal* of structuralism is made plain by his comments in "Revenir à l'histoire," a lecture delivered in Japan in October, 1970: in this context, Foucault felt free to explain more candidly and less polemically the substance of his real interest in—and debt to—certain structuralists (Dumézil above all) and certain *Annales*-style historians. See "Revenir à l'histoire" (1970), loc. cit., p. viii: "I think that structuralism . . . facilitates the abandonment of [the] great biological myth of history" (as an organic process of gradual evolution).

141. AS, p. 27; et, p. 17.

142. Bellour interview, 30 March 1990.

143. "Deuxième entretien: sur les façons d'écrire l'histoire" (int, 1967), in Bellour, *Les livres des autres*, p. 197; et in FLI, p. 20.

144. Ibid., pp. 197, 199; et in FLI pp. 20, 22–23. Cf. AS, pp. 172–73, 274; et, pp. 130–31, 210: two critical passages in the *Archeology* where Foucault alludes to Blanchot and the "outside" with characteristic terseness. Cf. also Maurice Blanchot, "Où maintenant, qui maintenant?," in *Le livre à venir*, p. 290: "*The Unnameable* [by Beckett] is precisely an experience lived under the threat of the impersonal, the approach of a neutral voice that is raised of its own accord, that penetrates the man who hears it, that is without intimacy, that excludes all intimacy, that cannot be made to stop, that is the incessant, the *interminable*."

145. "Deuxième entretien: sur les façons d'écrire l'histoire" (int, 1967), in Bellour, *Les livres des autres*, pp. 201–02; et in FLI, p. 25.

146. Ibid., pp. 206, 203; et in FLI, pp. 30, 27.

147. "Le 'non' du père," *Critique*, 178 (March 1962), p. 200; et in LCP, p. 75.

148. "Deuxième entretien: sur les façons d'écrire l'histoire" (int, 1967), loc. cit., p. 204; et in FLI, p. 28.

149. Ibid., p. 203; et in FLI, p. 27. Hans Ulrich Gumbrecht has interesting things to say about Foucault's academic reception in his paper "Beyond Foucault/Foucault's Style," forthcoming in the proceedings of the conference "Le siècle de Foucault," held at Tokyo University, November 1991.

150. Nietzsche, *Daybreak*, p. 1 [Preface, §1].

151. Ibid., p. 1 [preface, §1].

152. AS, p. 28; et, p. 17.

153. See Robert Graves, *The Greek Myths* (Harmondsworth, England, 1960), Vol. I, pp. 285–86, on Trophonius. It is perhaps worth pointing out that Karl Jaspers, in his study *Nietzsche*, trans. Charles F. Wallraf and Frederick J. Schmitz (Chicago, 1969), pp. 225–227, argues that the labyrinth in Nietzsche, too, is a figure used to express "the final truth" of "*death*."

154. Cf. "Theatrum philosophicum" (1970), loc. cit., p. 905; et in LCP, p. 193: "Becoming leads into this great interior labyrinth. . . . Dionysus with Ariadne: you have become my labryinth."

CHAPTER 6: BE CRUEL!

1. For the account of the Night of the Barricades (and much else in the chapter that follows), I have depended on Hervé Hamon and Patrick Rotman, *Génération* (Paris, 1987–88), an epic and generally meticulous narrative history of the French student left: see Vol. I, pp. 476–88. I have also drawn upon the vivid brief account, full of firsthand memoirs, in Ronald Fraser, ed., *1968: A Student Generation in Revolt* (New York, 1988), pp. 203–30; René Viénet, *Enragés et situationistes dans le mouvement des occupations* (Paris, 1968), the most useful of the partisan contemporary accounts (Viénet was a situationist); and Patrick

Seale and Maureen McConville, *Red Flag, Black Flag: French Revolution 1968* (New York, 1968), an often unsympathetic but informed description by two British journalists who covered the May events for *The Observer*; and the coverage at the time in *Le Monde*.

2. Quoted in Fraser, ed., *1968*, p. 210.

3. See Hamon and Rotman, *Génération*, I, p. 477; Viénet, *Enragés et situationistes*, p. 58; Seale and McConville, *Red Flag, Black Flag*, p. 85; Fraser, ed., *1968*, pp. 210–11.

4. See the map in Viénet, *Enragés et situationistes*, p. 59.

5. Ibid, p. 57.

6. The importance of the radio broadcasts is brought out well in Fraser, ed., *1968*, pp. 212–13.

7. See Hamon and Rotman, *Génération*, I, p. 487.

8. See the photographs in Viénet, *Enragés et situationistes*, pp. 95, 97, 100, 99; and in Julien Besançon, *Les murs ont la parole* (Paris, 1968), p. 171; and the examples in Greil Marcus, *Lipstick Traces* (Cambridge, Mass., 1989), pp. 31–32.

9. "We Are On Our Way," reprinted in Alain Schapp and Pierre Vidal-Naquet, ed., *The French Student Uprising*, trans. Maria Jolas (Boston, 1971), p. 456. The report of a student "commission" on "culture and creativity" is cited in José Pierre, "Create!," in Charles Posner, ed., *Reflections on the Revolution in France* (Middlesex, England, 1970), p. 242.

10. On the "Revolutionary Pederasty Action Committee," see "Les quarantes insolences du FHAR, Quelques dates heroïques," in *Gai Pied*, 25 (April 1981), p. 34.

11. André Glucksmann, *Strategy and Revolution in France 1968*, trans. in *New Left Review*, 52 (November–December 1968), p. 101.

12. For a more detailed account of Foucault's stay in Tunisia, see Didier Eribon, *Michel Foucault* (Paris, 1989), pp. 199–210; et: *Michel Foucault*, trans. Betsy Wing (Cambridge, Mass., 1991), pp. 187–98.

13. Jean Daniel, "La Passion de Michel Foucault," *Le Nouvel Observateur*, 29 June 1984, p. 20.

14. Daniel Defert, letter to the author, 8 January 1991, p. 2.

15. "Michel Foucault, An Interview: Sex, Power and the Politics of Identity" (int, 1982), *The Advocate*, 400 (7 August 1984), p. 58, emphasis added, to bring out the distinction between a party and a "movement" commonly made in these years. Foucault says much the same thing, with a somewhat different emphasis, in CF (int, 1978).

16. I wish to thank Professor Clement Henry of the University of Texas at Austin for talking to me about the general contours of Tunisian politics after independence; see also Clement H. Moore and Arlie R. Hochschild, "Student Unions in North African Politics," *Daedalus*, 97, 1 (Winter 1968), pp. 21–50. Cf. Eribon, *Foucault*, pp. 204–08; et, pp. 192–95.

17. CF (int, 1978), V, p. 18; cf. et p. 133. See also Howard C. Reese, et. al., *Area Handbook for the Republic of Tunisia* (Washington, D.C., 1970), pp. 192–93.

18. See Foucault's 7 June 1967 letter to Georges Canguilhem, quoted in Eribon, *Foucault*, p. 205; et, pp. 192–93. That this letter accurately reflected Foucault's strong sentiments was confirmed by Daniel Defert in a letter to the author, 8 January 1991, p. 3.

19. CF (int, 1978), V, p. 20; cf. et, p. 134. Georges Sorel, *Reflections on Violence*, trans. J. Roth and T. E. Hulme (New York, 1961), p. 127 (from chapter four, on "The Proletarian Strike" as a myth).

20. See Eribon, *Foucault*, p. 206; et, pp. 193–94. Foucault's decision, and the Tunisian students' plea that he stay was described to me by Daniel Defert, letter to the author, 8 January 1991, p. 3.

21. CF (int, 1978), V, p. 19; cf. et, p. 134.

22. In this regard, I believe the impression left by Eribon in his biography is misleading. Foucault's 1968 essay, "Réponse à une question," lays out quite clearly the many threads that tie together his preoccupation with language in the mid-sixties and his growing interest in politics after May '68: see "Réponse à une question," *Esprit*, 371 (May 1968), esp. pp. 871–74; et: "Politics and the Study of Discourse," *Ideology and Consciousness*, 3 (Spring 1978), pp. 24–26. These pages summarize Foucault's "hypotheses" about the implications

of his work for "une politique progressiste"—a phrase that Foucault would never again use, for good reason: from a consistently Nietzschean perspective, the idea of a "progressive politics," far from being self-evident in its reference to liberal and socialist movements of the left, amounts to a virtual oxymoron. Indeed, the most interesting aspect of this essay is what is *missing* in it. The question Foucault responds to ran as follows: "Doesn't a thought which introduces discontinuity and the constraint of a system into the history of the mind remove all basis for a progressive political intervention? Does it not lead to the following dilemma: either the acceptance of the system; or the appeal to an untamed event (*l'événement sauvage*), to the eruption of an exterior violence which alone is capable of unsettling the system" (p. 850; et, p. 8). In his essay, Foucault declares "that I accept this diagnosis almost entirely" (p. 850; et, p. 8); he goes on to dissent from the idea that his way of thinking entails "an acceptance of the system;" but he does *not* say anything about his possible appeal to "*l'événement sauvage*"—for the simple reason that this is a perfectly accurate gloss of the most important (though not the only) basis for political change, from his point of view. The most succinct summary of his perspective on this issue he offered a decade later, in his essay, "Inutile de se soulever?," in *Le Monde*, 11 May 1979 (et: "Is it Useless to Revolt?," trans. James Bernauer, *Philosophy and Social Criticism*, VIII, 1 [Spring, 1981]): "There is no explanation for the man who revolts. His action is necessarily a tearing that breaks the thread of history and its long chain of reasons so that a man can genuinely give preference to the risk of death over the certitude of having to obey" (p. 1; et, p. 5). What renders this view sharply different from Hegel's account of the master-slave dialectic (which lays a similar stress on the willingness to die) is, precisely, Foucault's *anti*-dialectical emphasis on the "Untimely" (in Nietzsche's sense, "a tearing that breaks the thread of history") as the (ultimately irrational) milieu of revolt. The complex practical implications of this way of thinking about politics should become clear in what follows.

23. CF (int, 1978), V, pp. 19, 20; cf. et, pp. 134, 135. Also see Eribon, *Foucault*, pp. 201, 270; et, pp. 189, 255 for Dumézil's refusal to take Foucault's leftist politics seriously.

24. On Fouchet's reforms, see Schnapp and Vidal-Naquet, eds., *The French Student Uprising*, pp. 15–16; the authors of this collection of documents convincingly reject the claim sometimes made that Fouchet's reforms were the principle factor behind the student movement of May '68. For Foucault's comment on reforming education in 1966, see "Entretien," *La Quinzaine Littéraire*, 5 (16 May 1966), p. 15.

25. "Conversazione con Michel Foucault" (int), *La Fiera Letteraria*, 39, 28 September 1967; I am translating from the edited French transcript, p. 24 (emphasis added).

26. CF, V, p. 21; cf. et, p. 136.

27. Maurice Blanchot, *Michel Foucault tel que je l'imagine* (Paris, 1986), pp. 9–10; et: *Michel Foucault as I Imagine Him*, trans. Jeffrey Mehlman in *Foucault/Blanchot* (New York, 1987), p. 63. The circumstances of this encounter were recalled by Daniel Defert in a letter to the author, 8 January 1991, p. 4.

28. Eribon, *Foucault*, p. 204; et, p. 192 (emphasis added).

29. CF (int, 1978), p. 74; et, p. 121. In evoking Marx's vision of the "new man," I am paraphrasing perhaps its most lyrical expression, in his "Comments on James Mill, *Éléments d'économie politique*," in Karl Marx and Frederick Engels, *Collected Works* (Moscow, 1975), III, pp. 227–28.

30. CF (int, 1978), p. 75; et, pp. 121–22. For Nietzsche's vision, I am paraphrasing *Thus Spoke Zarathustra*, preface, §3, on the *übermensch*.

31. For the end of the revolutionary moment in France, see Fraser, ed., *1968*, pp. 226–30.

32. For more details about Foucault's involvement with Vincennes, see Eribon, *Foucault*, pp. 208–10; et, pp. 196–98.

33. See "Postface," in Schnapp and Vidal-Naquet, eds., *The French Student Uprising*, p. 597.

34. See Hamon and Rotman, *Génération*, II, p. 64; and Eribon, *Foucault*, p. 215; et, p. 203.

35. See Eribon, *Foucault*, pp. 215–16. Serres quickly fled, appalled by the disorder at

Vincennes, but Chatelet stayed: for Chatelet's views, see François Chatelet, "Le mai permanent de l'université," *Magazine Littéraire*, 112–13 (May, 1976), p. 27.

36. See ibid., p. 216; Glucksmann told me about Foucault's effort to hire him in an interview on 26 March 90. For another perspective on the Maoist faculty at Vincennes, see Elisabeth Roudinesco, *Jacques Lacan & Co.*, trans. Jeffrey Mehlman (Chicago, 1990), pp. 553–54

37. For the GP in general, and the size of its active membership in particular, see Bernard Kouchner and Michel-Antoine Burnier, *La France sauvage* (Paris, 1970), esp. p. 159. An informed short account in English is Belden Fields, "French Maoism," in Sohnya Sayres et. al., eds, *The Sixties Without Apology* (Minneapolis, 1984), pp. 148–77. The most exhaustive French source is Hamon and Rotman, *Génération*.

38. See *Chairman Mao Tse-tung on People's War* (Peking, 1967), p. 4.

39. For the raid on Fauchon, see Hamon and Rotman, *Génération*, II, pp. 169–71.

40. CF (int, 1978), V, p. 22; cf. et, pp. 138–39.

41. "Revenir à l'histoire," originally delivered as a talk in Kyoto Japan, in October, 1970, transcribed in the Japanese journal *Représentation*, 2 (Autumn 1991), p. iv. CF (int, 1978), V, p. 21; cf. et, p. 136.

42. CF (int, 1978), V, p. 23 (emphasis added); cf. et, p. 139.

43. Georges Bataille, "Propositions" (1937), in Bataille, *Visions of Excess: Selected Writings, 1927–1939*, ed. and trans. Allan Stoekl, with Carl R. Lovitt and Donald M. Leslie, Jr. (Minneapolis, 1985), p. 200; for the Bataille vogue among student radicals in France after May '68, see Hamon and Rotman, *Génération*, II, p. 112 (Gallimard began its publication of Bataille's collected works in 1970). Glucksmann, *Strategy and Revolution in France 1968*, loc. cit., p. 99. The leader of the GP is Pierre Victor, speaking with Foucault, in "Sur la justice populaire: Débat avec les maos," *Les temps modernes*, 310 (bis, 1972), p. 336; et in PKN, p. 3.

44. See "L'Agitation universitaire," *Le Monde* (January 25, 1969), p. 1.

45. See B. Frappat, "Vincennes: cinq milles etudiants se sont inscrit au centre expérimental," *Le Monde* (15 January 1969).

46. Hamon and Rotman, *Génération*, II, p. 62.

47. Ibid., II, p. 56.

48. Glucksmann interview, 26 March 1990.

49. Defert interview, 25 March 1990; for the use of Foucault's image by the *London Review*, see Alan Sheridan, "Diary," *London Review of Books* (19 July –1 August 1984), p. 21.

50. Glucksmann interview, 26 March 1990.

51. See Roudinesco, *Jacques Lacan & Co.*, p. 558. Eribon, *Foucault*, p. 221; et, p. 208.

52. "Le piège de Vincennes" (int), *Le Nouvel Observateur*, 274 (9 February 1970), pp. 35, 34.

53. "A Conversation with Michel Foucault," *Partisan Review*, 38, 2 (1971), p. 201. This passage is omitted from the truncated version of the interview reprinted in FLI.

54. Ibid., p. 201 (also omitted in FLI). My comments about Foucault's performance as a teacher sum up the impressions relayed to me by François Delaporte and Blandine Barret-Kriegel, two (of the very few) students who actually conducted a major piece of research under his supervision at the Collège de France; their experience is borne out by that of several Berkeley students who worked with Foucault in the 1980s. Foucault's "hands-off" approach presented certain problems, for it meant that his students had largely to fend for themselves; it also, of course, meant that Foucault in practice devoted a minimum amount of time to directing students outside of class.

55. Hamon and Rotman, *Génération*, II, p. 62.

56. See "A Conversation with Michel Foucault" (int, 1971), loc. cit., p. 195 (in FLI, pp. 67–68).

57. Eribon, *Foucault*, p. 222; et, p. 209.

58. Ibid., p. 219; et, p. 207.

59. "Nietzsche, la généalogie, l'histoire" in *Hommage à Jean Hyppolite* (Paris, 1971), pp. 154, 159; et in LCP, pp. 148, 153.

60. "Precisazioni sul potere. Riposta ad alcuni critici" (int), *Aut Aut*, 167–168 (September–December 1978); et in FL, p. 191 (emphasis added).

61. "Nietzsche, la généalogie, l'histoire" (1971), loc. cit., p. 163; et in LCP, p. 156.

62. Friedrich Nietzsche, *Human All Too Human*, trans. R. J. Hollingdale (Cambridge, England, 1986), p. 356 ("The Wanderer and His Shadow," §188); footnoted by Foucault in the passage cited above.

63. For a detailed account of the machinations behind Foucault's nomination to the Collège de France, see Eribon, *Foucault*, pp. 226–32; et, pp. 213–18.

64. See "Le Collège de France: Quelques données sur son histoire et son caractère propre," *Annuaire de Collège de France 1986–1987* (Paris, n.d.), pp. 5–8.

65. Jean Lacouture, "Le cours inaugural de M. Michel Foucault," *Le Monde* (4 December 1970), p. 8.

66. Edward Said, "Michel Foucault, 1926–1984," in Jonathan Arac, ed., *After Foucault* (New Brunswick, N.J., 1988), p. 7.

67. OD, pp. 10, 37; et, pp. 216, 224.

68. OD, pp. 11, 55, 37; et, pp. 216, 229, 224.

69. OD, p. 17; et, p. 218.

70. For an acute analysis of the self-cancelling aspects of Foucault's performance in this lecture, see Alasdair MacIntyre, *Three Rival Versions of Moral Enquiry: Encyclopaedia, Genealogy and Tradition* (Notre Dame, 1990), p. 219. The paradoxical aspects of Foucault's lecture were publicly noted at the time: see, e.g., Lacouture's report in *Le Monde* (4 December 1970), p. 8.

71. Pierre Bourdieu, "Preface to the English Edition" of *Homo Academicus*, trans. Peter Collier (Stanford, 1988), p. xix.

72. When the magazine *Actuel* devoted a story to the GIP, it was Defert, not Foucault, whom they interviewed: see Bernard Kouchner, "Un vrai samourai," in Robert Badinter et. al., *Michel Foucault: Une histoire de la verité* (Paris, 1985), p. 86. Yet in keeping with the behind-the-scenes role Defert played, he was not the focus of the article Kouchner actually wrote: see Bernard Kouchner, "Prisons: les petits matons blêmes," *Actuel*, 9 (June 1971), pp. 41–43.

73. Daniel Defert, letter to the author, 8 January 1991, p. 5.

74. Ibid., p. 6.

75. Ibid., p. 6. For Defert at Vincennes, see Eribon, *Foucault*, p. 218; et, p. 206.

76. Edmund White interview, 12 March 1990. Cf. Eribon, *Foucault*,; p 167; et, pp. 141–42.

77. "Conversation" (int, 1981), in Gerard Courant, *Werner Schroeter* (Paris, 1981), pp. 41, 43, 40.

78. Daniel Defert, letter to the author, 8 January 1991, p. 7.

79. Ibid., p. 8.

80. Ibid., p. 8.

81. For another overview of the activities of the GIP, cf. Eribon, *Foucault*, pp. 237–51; et, pp. 224–37.

82. See Hamon and Rotman, *Génération*, II, pp. 294–96.

83. "Création d'un groupe d'information sur les prisons," *Esprit*, 3 (March 1971), pp. 531–32.

84. "Entretien avec Michel Foucault," *Pro Justitia*, 3–4 (October 1973), p. 12. Cf. "Luttes autour des prisons," a retrospective conversation among three veterans of the struggle in the early 1970s—François Colombet (who had been a member of the court system), Antoine Lazarus (who had worked in the prisons), and "Louis Appert" (the pseudonym for a former GIP activist, in fact Foucault)—published in *Esprit*, 35 (November 1979), pp. 102–11. Although "Appert" in this context stresses the independence of the GIP from the Maoists (which surprises Lazarus, who remembers things quite differently), he does admit (on p. 105) that the GIP tried to keep people guessing about what it actually was: "it was important that the prison bureaucracy not know whether it was a [real] organization or not." A classic political "front" group, the GIP was indeed formally "independent"—*and* closely linked to

the Maoists. Cf. the remarks in G.I.P., "A propos de la justice populaire," *Pro Justitia*, 3–4 (October 1973), p. 116: "The Maoists have been the only political movement that has participated effectively in the actions of the GIP, and with which the GIP has held discussions on prison problems."

85. "Les intellectuels et le pouvoir," (int, 1982, with Gilles Deleuze), *L'Arc*, 49 (1972), p. 4; et in LCP, p. 207. "Foucault répond à Sartre" (int, 1968), *La Quinzaine Littéraire*, 46 (1–15 March 1968), p. 20; et in FLI, p. 35.

86. "Foucault: Non au sexe roi" (int, 1977), *Le Nouvel Observateur*, 644 (12 March 1977), p. 130; et in PPC, p. 124: at the risk of making the English sound more awkward than the French original I have translated the word "*peine*" here as "punishment" rather than "trouble" or "difficulty," in order to bring out the burden of *physical* sacrifice that Foucault elsewhere insists the revolutionary must bear.

87. Jean-Paul Sartre, "À propos de la justice populaire" (int, 1972), *Pro Justitia*, 2 (premier trimestre 1973), p. 26. The irony goes deeper still: for Sartre in fact would support the GIP itself! No matter how hard Foucault tried to distinguish his own *modus operandi*, it somehow invariably seemed to produce the same practical results: year after year, he and Sartre supported the same causes, signed the same manifestos, marched in the same demonstrations, apparently fought the same fight. For Sartre's links to the Maoist movement, see Annie Cohen-Solal, *Sartre: A Life*, trans. Anna Cancogni (New York, 1987), pp. 478–86.

88. "Creation d'un groupe d'information sur les prisons," *Esprit*, 3 (March 1971), p. 532.

89. Gilles Deleuze, "Foucault and the Prison" (int, 1986), *History of the Present*, 2 (Spring 1986), p. 1. G.I.P., "A propos de la justice populaire," loc. cit., p. 115.

90. "Les intellectuels et le pouvoir" (int, 1972), loc. cit., p. 6; et in LCP, p. 210.

91. Deleuze, "Foucault and the Prison," loc. cit., p. 1.

92. Michelle Perrot, "La leçon des ténèbres: Michel Foucault et la prison," *Actes* (Summer 1986), p. 76.

93. Deleuze, "Foucault and the Prison," loc. cit., p. 1.

94. On the importance of Attica, see G.I.P., "À propos de la justice populaire," loc. cit., p. 115.

95. For the revolt at Toul, see Hamon and Rotman, *Génération*, II, pp. 377–79. For Foucault on "*déculpabilisation*," see "Luttes autour des prisons" (int, 1979), loc. cit., p. 109.

96. See Hamon and Rotman, *Génération*, II, p. 381. This press conference—and the Maoist involvement in the Toul revolt generally—came only after further fierce debate within the movement, with André Glucksmann (and Foucault) in favor of continuing agitation around the prison issue, and Pierre Victor still against, on the grounds that most workers did not condone criminal behavior. See ibid., p. 380.

97. Edith Rose, "Je puis affirmer . . . ," *Le Nouvel Observateur*, 372, (27 December 1971–2 January 1972), p. 15.

98. "Le discours de Toul," *Le Nouvel Observateur* 372, (December 27, 1971–January 2, 1972), p. 15.

99. Ibid., p. 15.

100. *Suicides de Prison* (1972) (Paris, 1973), pp. 7–8.

101. See the biographical sketch of H.M. in ibid., pp. 15–16.

102. Ibid., pp. 21, 28, 29, 22, 39.

103. Ibid., pp. 39, 18, 22.

104. Ibid., p. 39.

105. Ibid., p. 38.

106. Ibid., p. 38.

107. "Nietzsche, la généalogie, l'histoire" (1971), loc. cit., p. 154; et in LCP, p. 148.

108. Deleuze, "Foucault and the Prison," loc. cit., p. 1.

109. See the "repères biographiques" in the special Deleuze issue of *Magazine Littéraire*, 257 (September 1988), p. 19; and the short sketch of his own philosophical generation in Gilles Deleuze, *Différence et répétition* (Paris, 1968), pp. 1–2.

164. Ibid., p. 340; et in PKN, p. 6: the Bastille's commanding officer on 14 July 1789, was de Launay, whose name is mistakenly transcribed as "Delaunay."

165. Ibid., pp. 360, 346; et in PKN, pp. 29, 13.

166. For a detailed account of this episode, which would prove pivotal for French Maoism, see Hamon and Rotman, *Génération*, II, pp. 383–422.

167. Ibid., p. 398.

168. See ibid., pp. 404ff.

169. In fact, the French Maoists, in their twilight years, long after Foucault and Defert and most of the other key figures of May '68 had given up on revolutionary gestures of direct action, did resort to murder once—to exact a final revenge for Overney's death. In 1977, after serving two years in prison for killing Overney, the Renault security officer responsible, Jean-Antoine Tramoni, was gunned down in turn by Maoist militants. See Fields, "French Maoism," loc. cit., p. 177n33.

170. Cf. Deleuze and Parnet, *Dialogues*, p. 137: "Politics is active experimentation, since we do not know in advance which way a line is going to turn. Draw the line, says the accountant: but one can in fact draw it *anywhere*."

CHAPTER 7: AN ART OF UNBEARABLE SENSATIONS

1. SP, p. 9; et, p. 3. "*Insoutenable*" was the word used by Max Gallo in his review, "La prison selon Michel Foucault," *L'Express*, 1233 (24 February–2 March 1975), p. 31.

2. SP, p. 11; et, p. 5.

3. Quoted in François Ewald, "Anatomie et corps politiques," *Critique*, 343 (December 1975), p. 1228n.

4. OD, pp. 25, 28; et, pp. 220, 221. On Foucault's description of Damiens' death as "*faites avec amour*," cf. Gilles Deleuze, *Foucault* (Paris, 1986), p. 31; et: *Foucault*, trans. Sean Hand (Minneapolis, 1986), p. 23. The Borges fiction that Foucault here alludes to is "Pierre Menard, Author of the *Quixote*," in which the "admirable intention" of the imaginary author is "to produce a few pages which would conicide—word for word and line for line—with those of Miguel de Cervantes," in this way reaching, and subtly transfiguring "the *Quixote* through the experiences of Pierre Menard," turning the words of the novel into a pragmatic doctrine of history as the origin of truth. See Jorge Luis Borges, *Labyrinths*, ed. Donald A. Yates and James E. Irby (New York, 1964), pp. 36–44.

5. SP, pp. 9–10; et, pp. 3–4.

6. SP, pp. 12, 13; et, pp. 6, 7.

7. SP, pp. 19–20; et, p. 14.

8. Perhaps the most important English-language critique of Foucault's work is Pieter Spirenburg, *The Spectacle of Suffering* (Cambridge, 1984), a very scholarly (and numbingly pedantic) effort to construct a "counter-paradigm" to that of Foucault. In addition, Daniel S. Milo has written a very interesting (though to my knowledge unpublished) paper on the book, "Dire-faire? La discontinuité: la machine(rie) métaphorique de *Surveiller et punir* de Michel Foucault." Among other things, Milo tabulates hot and cold metaphors in the text (hot for death-by-torture, as one would guess; cold for the regimen of prison); he also demonstrates how Foucault has taken the quote from Faucher out of its original polemical context, ignoring, apparently deliberately, Faucher's actual views (which were strongly critical of mechanical discipline in prisons); my thanks to Jerrold Seigel for bringing the Milo paper to my attention.

9. SP, p. 34; et, p. 30.

10. "Table ronde du 20 mai 1978," in Michelle Perrot, ed., *L'impossible prison: Recherches sur le système pénitentiaire au XIXe siècle* (Paris, 1980), p. 35; et: "Question of Method: An Interview with Michel Foucault," in Kenneth Baynes, James Bohman, and Thomas McCarthy, eds., *After Philosophy* (Cambridge, Mass., 1987), p. 111.

11. CF (int, 1978), p. 6; et, pp. 32–33.

12. "Les rapports de pouvoir passent à l'intérieur des corps" (int), *La Quinzaine Littéraire*, 247 (1–15 January 1977), p. 6; et in PKN, p. 193.

13. CF (int, 1978), p. 8; et, p. 37.

14. "Table ronde du 20 mai 1978," loc. cit., p. 31; et, loc. cit., p. 105. Deleuze, *Foucault*, p. 31; et, p. 23.

15. SP, pp. 21–22, 238, 302; et, pp. 16, 235, 297.

16. Edward Peters, in his exemplary short history of *Torture* (Oxford, 1985), p. 89, points out this double transvaluation. "L'éclat des supplices" is the title of chapter two of SP; Alan Sheridan translates it as "The Spectacle of the Scaffold," which takes away the paradoxical sting of the French.

17. For the theme of cruelty in Deleuze, see e.g. Gilles Deleuze and Félix Guattari, *Anti-Oedipus*, trans. Robert Hurley, Mark Seem, and Helen R. Lane (New York, 1972), pp. 144–45: "cruelty is the movement of culture that is realized in bodies and inscribed on them"—a point developed with reference to Nietzsche's *Genealogy of Morals*. Cf. SP, p. 29n.1; et, p. 309n.2: "In any case, I could give no notion by references or quotations what this book owes to Gilles Deleuze and the work he is undertaking with Félix Guattari."

18. "Entretien sur la prison," *Magazine Littéraire*, 101 (June 1975), p. 33; et in PKN, p. 53. Cf. his remarks about SP "reactivating the project of a 'genealogy of morals,'" in "Table ronde du 20 mai 1978," loc. cit., p. 40; et, loc. cit., p. 102. And also see the last line of his own précis of the book, on the back cover of the French edition of SP: "Can one produce a genealogy of modern morals through a political history of bodies?"

19. For the 1970 course, see Didier Eribon, *Michel Foucault* (Paris, 1989), p. 219; et: *Michel Foucault*, trans. Betsy Wing (Cambridge, Mass., 1991), p. 207. For the 1971 Collège de France course, see RC, pp. 9–16. While he was in the midst of composing SP, Foucault lectured again about Nietzsche's theory of knowledge, in May 1973, in Brazil: see the first of four lectures given under the title "La vérité et les formes juridiques." Here his starting point is the opening sentence of Nietzsche's early essay, "On Truth and Lying in an Extra-Moral Sense" (1873): "In some remote corner of the universe that is poured out in countless flickering solar systems, there once was a star on which clever animals invented knowledge. That was the most arrogant and the most untruthful moment in 'world history'. . . ." (See *Friedrich Nietzsche on Rhetoric and Language*, ed. Sander L. Gilman, Carole Blair, David J. Parent [Oxford, 1989], p. 246.)

20. RC, pp. 13–14 (translating "*intéresser*" as "to enthrall"). It is perhaps worth noting the way that Foucault tends to assimilate the insights of Canguilhem to his own Nietzschean perspective: see his comments on "error" as the "root of what makes human thought and its history," in his "Introduction" to Georges Canguilhem, *The Normal and the Pathological*, trans. Carolyn R. Fawcett (New York, 1989), p. 22.

21. SP, p. 143; et, p. 141. Cf. "Nietzsche, la généalogie, l'histoire," in *Hommage à Jean Hyppolite* (Paris, 1971), pp. 151–158; et in LCP, pp. 145–152.

22. Friedrich Nietzsche, *On the Genealogy of Morals*, trans. Walter Kaufmann (New York, 1967), pp. 61 (II, §3), 40 (I, §11). Friedrich Nietzsche, *Daybreak*, trans. R.J. Hollingdale (Cambridge, 1982), p. 16 (§18).

23. Nietzsche, *Genealogy of Morals*, pp. 60 (II, §3), 58 (II, §1), 59 (II, §2).

24. Ibid., pp. 61 (II, §3), 58 (II, §1).

25. "Nietzsche, la généalogie, l'histoire" (1971), loc. cit., p. 157; et in LCP, p. 151. Nietzsche, *Genealogy of Morals*, p. 62 (II, §3).

26. SP, pp. 38, 49; et, pp. 33–34, 46.

27. Nietzsche, *Genealogy of Morals*, pp. 67 (II, §6), 82, (II, §14).

28. Friedrich Nietzsche, *Ecce Homo*, trans. Walter Kaufmann (New York, 1967), p. 312 ("Genealogy of Morals").

29. Nietzsche, *Genealogy of Morals*, p. 83 (II, §15). "Nietzsche, la généalogie, l'histoire" (1971), loc. cit., p. 147; et in LCP, p. 151.

30. Nietzsche, *Genealogy of Morals*, p. 79 (II, §12). Nietzsche, *Daybreak*, p. 16 (§18).

31. Nietzsche, *Genealogy of Morals*, p. 84 (II, §16).

32. Ibid., p. 87 (II, §17).

33. Ibid, pp. 57–58 (II, §1), 59 (II, §2).

34. Nietzsche, *Daybreak*, p. 16 (§18).

35. Nietzsche, *Genealogy of Morals*, pp. 87–88 (II, §18).

36. Friedrich Nietzche, *Beyond Good and Evil*, trans. Walter Kaufmann (New York, 1966), p. 67 (§55).

37. Nietzsche, *Genealogy of Morals*, p. 96 (II, §24). "Nietzsche, la généalogie, l'histoire" (1971), loc. cit., pp. 170, 171; et in LCP, p. 163.

38. Nietzsche, *Beyond Good and Evil*, p. 161 (§230). Cf. Deleuze, *Foucault*, p. 31; et, p. 23.

39. SP, pp. 34, 228; et, pp. 29, 227.

40. SP, p. 84; et, p. 82.

41. "Entretien avec Michel Foucault à propos de l'enfermement pénitentiaire," *Pro Justitia*, 3–4 (October 1973), p. 7 (emphasis added).

42. Jeremy Bentham, *Panopticon; or, the Inspection House: Containing the Idea of a New Principle of Construction Applicable to Any Sort of Establishment, in Which Persons of any Description are to be kept under Inspection; and in particular to Penitentiary Houses, Prisons, Houses of Industry, Work-Houses, Poor-Houses, Manufactories, Mad-Houses, Lazarettos, Hospitals, and Schools: With a Plan of Management Adapted to the Principle: In a Series of Letters Written in the Year 1787, from Crecheff in White Russia, to a Friend in England*, in John Bowring, ed., *The Works of Jeremy Bentham* (New York, 1962), Vol. 4, p. 39. Bentham on the advantages of the Panopticon is quoted in Elie Halevy, *The Growth of Philosophic Radicalism*, trans. Mary Morris (London, 1955), p. 83; for the popular image of Bentham as a crank, also see Halevy, p. 251.

43. See the *Oxford English Dictionary* entry for "panopticon," for the evolution of the term.

44. "L'oeil du pouvoir" (int), in Jeremy Bentham, *Le panoptique* (Paris, 1977), p. 7; et in PKN, p. 147.

45. SP, pp. 201–02; et, p. 200.

46. Bentham, *Panopticon*, loc. cit., Vol. 4, pp. 64, 39.

47. Friedrich Nietzsche, *The Will to Power*, trans. Walter Kaufmann and R. J. Hollingdale (New York, 1967), p. 463 (§866). Friedrich Nietzsche, *Thus Spoke Zarathustra*, trans. Walter Kaufmann in *The Portable Nietzsche* (New York, 1954), p. 129 (Prologue, §5).

48. SP, p. 207; et, p. 205

49. SP, pp. 140, 202; et, pp. 138, 201.

50. CF (int, 1978), VIII, p. 18; cf. et, p. 167. SP, 309–10, 180, 228, et, pp. 303, 178, 227.

51. "L'oeil du pouvoir" (int, 1977), loc. cit., p. 19; et in PKN, p. 155.

52. Nietzsche, *Thus Spoke Zarathustra*, loc. cit., p. 130 (Prologue, §5). Nietzsche, *Genealogy of Morals*, p. 93 (II, §22).

53. VS, p. 65; et, p. 48. SP, p. 195; et, p. 193.

54. "Theatrum philosophicum," *Critique*, 282 (November 1970), pp. 888–89; et in LCP, 170. MC, p. 290; et, p. 278. SP, p. 195; et, p. 193. "La prose d'Acteon," *La Nouvelle Revue Française*, 135 (March 1964), p. 456; et in Pierre Klossowski, *The Baphomet*, trans. Sophie Hawkes and Stephen Sartarelli (Hygiene, Col., 1988), p. xxxv. The image of the "granite" is Nietzsche's: see *Beyond Good and Evil*, p. 162 (§231). "Phantasm" is a term of art for Gilles Deleuze, one that he links with Nietzsche's concept of eternal recurrence: see Deleuze, *Différence et répétition* (Paris, 1968), p. 165. Cf. Gilles Deleuze, *Logique du sens* (Paris, 1969), p. 249; et: *The Logic of Sense*, trans. Mark Lester (New York, 1990), p. 213: "What appears in the phantasm is the movement in which the ego opens itself to the surface and liberates the acosmic, impersonal, and preindividual singularities which had been imprisoned. It literally releases them like spores and explodes (*éclate*) as it gets unburdened."

55. FD, p. 381; et, p. 210.

56. "Les intellectuels et le pouvoir," *L'Arc*, 49 (1972), p. 5; et in LCP, pp. 210–11. SP, pp. 295–96; et, p. 289. The period of his greatest interest in crime was also the period when he was closest to Jean Genet: see Eribon, *Foucault*, pp. 255–56; et, pp. 240–41.

57. "La vie des hommes infâmes," *Les cahiers du chemin*, 29 (15 January 1977), p. 13; et in PTS, p. 77. He talked about this "vibration" to students and coworkers as well: both

Arlette Farge and François Delaporte at different times heard him speak in such terms.

58. "La vie des hommes infâmes" (1977), loc. cit., p. 13; et in PTS, p. 77.

59. RC, p. 24.

60. PR, pp. 10–11; et, pp. viii–ix.

61. PR, pp. 11, 14; et, pp. x, xiii.

62. PR, p. 27; et, p. 10.

63. PR, p. 129; et, p. 105.

64. PR, p. 68; et, p. 49.

65. PR, p. 21; et, p. 3.

66. "About the Concept of the 'Dangerous Individual' in 19th-Century Legal Psychiatry," *International Journal of Law and Psychiatry*, 1 (1978), reprinted in PPC, p. 131. On Sade's work as a "total contestation" of modern culture, see FD, p. 551; et, p. 281. Cf. PR, p. 11; et, p. x, where Foucault talks about the "beauty" of Rivière's life.

67. PR, p. 26; et, p. 8.

68. PR, pp. 34–35; et, p. 18.

69. PR, p. 132; et, p. 108.

70. PR, p. 148; et, p. 121.

71. SP, p. 64; p. et, p. 60.

72. PR, pp. 183, 202; et, pp. 145, 168–69.

73. PR, pp. 199, 225; et, pp. 160, 171.

74. PR, p. 13; et, p. xii.

75. PR, pp. 14, 271–72; et, pp. xiii, 206–07. "La vie des hommes infâmes" (1977), loc. cit., pp. 17, 13; et in PTS, pp. 80, 78. Foucault's transvaluation of the criminal, it is worth recalling, puts him in a distinguished French tradition that includes Fourierists, *fin-de-siècle* anarchists, the surrealists, and, of course, Jean Genet.

76. "Foucault, passe-frontières de la philosophie" (int, 1975), *Le Monde*, 6 September 1986.

77. "Entretien avec Michel Foucault" (int), *Cahiers du Cinéma*, 271 (November 1976), p. 52; et in FLI, p. 132.

78. FD, p. 556; et, p. 288.

79. "Entretien avec Michel Foucault à propos de l'enfermement pénitentiare" (int), *Pro Justitia*, 3–4 (October 1973), pp. 5–14. That Foucault by 1973 had already completed the theoretical backbone of SP is suggested by his lectures on the topic at the Collège de France in the winter of 1973, summarized in RC, pp. 29–51.

80. "Entretien avec Michel Foucault à propos de l'enfermement pénitentiare" (int, 1973), loc. cit., p. 5. SP, p. 72; et, p. 68. PR, p. 271; et, p. 206.

81. "Entretien avec Michel Foucault à propos de l'enfermement pénitentiare" (int, 1973), loc. cit., p. 6. Foucault's remarks here on the "normalizing" of popular violence during the course of the French Revolution are essentially accurate, at least if one accepts such standard historiographic accounts of the relationship between the sans-culottes and the Jacobins as Albert Soboul's and Richard Cobb's.

82. SP, pp 66–67, 64, et, pp. 63, 61. "L'esprit d'un monde sans esprit," in Claire Brière and Pierre Blanchet, *Iran: la révolution au nom de Dieu* (Paris, 1979), p. 229; et in PPC, p. 214 (Foucault's reference to the French Revolution comes in the context of explaining his fascination with the Iranian revolution). In *The Spectacle of Suffering*, Pieter Spirenburg reports that his own survey of the archival material suggests that Foucault has grossly exaggerated the "carnivalesque" and radicalizing aspects of public executions.

83. "Entretien avec Michel Foucault à propos de l'enfermement pénitentiaire," loc. cit., p. 8. Cf. SP, pp. 261–99; et, pp. 257–92.

84. "Entretien avec Michel Foucault à propos de l'enfermement pénitentiare," loc. cit., p. 6.

85. Ibid., p. 10.

86. Daniel Defert, in his letter to the author, 8 January 1991, tallied the revolts caused by the GIP. Gilles Deleuze recalls Foucault's feeling that the GIP had been a failure in "Foucault and the Prison" (int, 1986), *History of the Present*, 2 (Spring 1986), p. 1. Foucault

himself delivers a more sanguine verdict (and also a more "reformist" account of the organization) in his comments, under the pseudonym "Louis Appert," in the roundtable "Luttes autour des prisons," *Esprit*, 35 (November 1979), pp. 102–11. On the GIP and its disappearance, see Marc Kravetz, "Qu'est-ce que le GIP?," *Magazine Littéraire*, 101 (June 1975), p. 13; Daniel Defert and Jacques Donzelot, "La charnière des prisons," *Magazine Littéraire*, 112–13 (May 1976), pp. 33–35; and also Michelle Perrot, "La leçon des ténèbres: Michel Foucault et la prison," *Actes* (Summer 1986), pp. 74– 79.

87. For the quotes from Victor and *La Cause du peuple*, and for the Bruay affair generally, see Hervé Hamon and Patrick Rotman, *Génération* Vol II, (Paris, 1988), pp. 428–39; and also Eribon, *Foucault*, pp. 262–65; et, pp. 248–50.

88. In this and the preceding paragraph on Foucault's relation to events in Bruay, I have tried to sort out—and, in effect, reconcile—conflicting accounts of his views (which, based on the evidence, I have concluded were ambivalent). For Foucault's interest in Bruay, see Claude Mauriac, *Et comme l'esperance est violente* (Paris, 1977), pp. 373–74; and for one account of some of his reservations, as he expressed them at a meeting to establish the newspaper *Libération*, see ibid., pp. 418–19. Benny Lévy (a.k.a. Pierre Victor) recalls that Foucault "was very intrigued" by events in Bruay—see Hamon and Rotman, *Génération*, II, p. 439; this is the impression as well of some other witnesses (for example, Yves Cohen, another Maoist in these years, a friend of Lévy's who later came to know, and work with, Foucault). At the same time still other witnesses—including François Ewald, who was a Maoist leader in Bruay at the time—have emphasized Foucault's *distance* from events, stressing the fact that the philosopher was never directly involved in the agitation; which is true. Still, it is hard to imagine that Lévy's call, in 1972, to parade heads on a stake at Bruay, would *not* appeal, on some level, to Foucault, given the philosopher's strikingly similar comments on the virtues of parading heads on stakes, in his "debate" with Lévy (a.k.a. Pierre Victor), "Sur la justice populaire," *Les temps modernes*, 310 (bis 1972), p. 340; et in PKN, p. 6.

89. Lévy's comment comes from Hamon and Rotman, *Génération*, II, p. 439.

90. André Glucksmann interview, 26 March 1990.

91. "Foucault: non au sexe roi" (int), *Le Nouvel Observateur*, 644 (12 March 1977), p. 113; et in PPC, p. 122. Foucault's admission of having made a mistake about the lawyer in Bruay appears in Claude Mauriac, *Une certain rage* (Paris, 1977), p. 73. Foucault's political change of heart occurred slowly: he did not suddenly cease being involved in various kinds of activism. In 1973, for example, he joined in launching the new left-wing daily newspaper *Libération*; and in 1975, he participated in a tumultuous press conference at the airport in Madrid, where he had flown with Yves Montand, Regis Debray, and others to protest death sentences handed out by the Spanish government. For a more detailed account of Foucault's various political activities in these years, see Eribon, *Foucault*, pp. 265–73, 279–85; et, pp. 250–58; 263–69.

92. Foucault's comments came during a public question-and-answer session held at the University of California at Berkeley after his Howison lectures there in the fall of 1980; I have transcribed his remarks from the casette tape filed in the Centre Michel Foucault under the title "Talk with Philosophers, 23 October 1980," no. c16*.

93. See the annotated (and exhaustive Foucault) bibilography by Michael Clark, *Tool Kit for a New Age* (New York, 1983), p. 24.

94. See *Magazine Littéraire*, 101 (June 1975), pp. 6–33; *Critique*, 343 (December 1975), pp. 1207–76 (the three essays were by Gilles Deleuze, François Ewald, and Philippe Meyer).

95. An exemplary left-wing "reading" of the book, focused on the concept of power, is offered by François Ewald in "Anatomie et corps politiques," *Critique*, 343 (December 1975), pp. 1228–65. Though Ewald himself no longer holds the opinions expressed in this piece, Foucault himself liked the essay—indeed, it was primarily on the basis of the piece that he hired the young activist as his assistant at the Collège de France.

96. Gilles Deleuze, "Écrivain non: un nouveau cartographe," *Critique*, 343 (December 1975), p. 1212; this essay is reprinted, with slight modifications, in Deleuze, *Foucault*, p. 38; et, p. 30.

97. CF (int, 1978), I, p. 14; cf. et, p. 41. "Table ronde du 20 mai 1978," loc. cit., p. 37; et, loc. cit., p. 113. See also Gallo, "La prison selon Michel Foucault," *L'Express*, 1233 (24 February–2 March 1975), pp. 31–32. Interestingly enough, Foucault's closest ally in the GIP, Daniel Defert, though scarcely "paralyzed," had his own reservations about *Discipline and Punish*: the book, as he recalls, struck him as "too Nietzschean" (Defert interview, 25 March 1990: Defert was reading me a note he had written to himself in 1975).

98. Daniel Defert interview, 25 March 1990.

99. "An Exchange with Michel Foucault," *The New York Review of Books* (31 March 1983), p. 42. It is revealing, in itself, that Foucault would answer the criticisms of Lawrence Stone in such minute, even picayune detail; though, as we shall see in chapter ten, by the time of this letter, the "probity" of his own scholarly work had become a matter of some concern to Foucault. Arlette Farge, a younger scholar who collaborated with Foucault on a book compiling "*lettres de cachet*" from the French archives (*Le désordre des familles*, published in 1982), also noted Foucault's frustration that he was not taken more seriously by professional historians (Farge interview, 30 March 1990). See also Farge's essay on this theme, "Face à l'histoire," *Magazine Littéraire*, 207 (May 1984), pp. 40–42.

100. Ibid., p. 43.

101. See René Viénet, *Enragés et Situationistes dans le mouvement des occupations* (Paris, 1968), p. 99.

102. Georges Bataille, "The Use Value of D.A.F. de Sade," in *Visions of Excess*, trans. Allan Stoekl (Minneapolis, Minn., 1985), p. 102.

103. Georges Bataille, *Erotism: Death and Sensuality*, trans. Mary Dalwood (New York, 1962), p. 180.

104. The description of the works by Bosch (the Lisbon *Temptation of Saint Anthony*) and Goya (*Todos Caeran, Caprichos*, plate 19) is inspired by Foucault's reference to both artists in FD, p. 550; et, pp. 280–81. Leo Bersani has interesting things to say about sado-masochistic impulses in art in *The Freudian Body: Psychoanalysis and Art* (New York, 1986).

105. SP, p. 38; et, p. 34. "An Interview: Sex, Power and the Politics of Identity," *Advocate* (7 August 1984), pp. 27, 29. My description of S/M play is, in part, a paraphrase of that in Leo Bersani, "Is the Rectum a Grave?," in Douglas Crimp, ed., *AIDS: Cultural Analysis, Cultural Criticism* (Cambridge, Mass., 1988), p. 217.

106. For a sensible, if rather cautious, brief appraisal of Nietzsche's views on cruelty in politics, see Alexander Nehamas, *Nietzsche: Life as Literature* (Cambridge, Mass., 1985), pp. 215–17.

107. These categories are elaborately worked out in Gilles Deleuze, *Nietzsche et la philosophie* (Paris, 1962), see, e.g., pp. 148–49; et: *Nietzsche and Philosophy*, trans. Hugh Tomlinson (New York, 1983), pp. 129–30.

108. Martin Heidegger, *An Introduction to Metaphysics*, trans. Ralph Manheim (Garden City, N.Y., 1961), p. 137. Given the ongoing debate over Heidegger's relationship to the Nazi movement, it is worth noting that Heidegger himself nowhere explicitly advocates "total war," and in fact seems to have come to regard it, perhaps as early as 1936, as a baleful apotheosis of modern technology. His changing views on technology are linked to his evolving critique of Nietzsche's concept of will to power, briefly discussed above in chapter one, footnote 32. On the other hand, Ernst Jünger, a contemporary whose work Heidegger knew and valued, *did* advocate total war—even though, like Heidegger after 1936, Jünger remained aristocratically aloof from the Nazi leadership.

109. "Preface," to the American edition of Deleuze and Guattari, *Anti-Oedipus*, p. xiii. For the views of Deleuze and Guattari, see, e.g., p. 105, and also p. 277: they are not quite as emphatic as Foucault, though they do discuss the "oscillation" of the unconscious and unthought between "its reactionary charge and its revolutionary potential"; in this context, it is worth recalling that *Anti-Oedipus* first appeared in 1972, before the debate over violence on the left had come to a head. Glucksmann's first major critique of the "fascist" temptation on the left appeared in 1975, at roughly the same time as *Discipline and Punish*: see André Glucksmann, *La cuisinière et la mangeur d'hommes* (Paris, 1975).

110. Heidegger, *An Introduction to Metaphysics*, p. 111. "Discourse and Truth: The

Problematization of *Parrhesia*," ed. Joseph Pearson (an unauthorized 1985 transcription of Foucault's seminar at Berkeley in the fall of 1983), p. 14.

111. Nietzsche, *Genealogy of Morals*, pp. 54 (I, §16), 86–87 (II, §17).

112. Deleuze and Guattari, *Anti-Oedipus*, p. 277.

113. "Preface" to Deleuze and Guattari, *Anti-Oedipus*, p. xiii.

114. Quoted in Fons Elders, "Postscript" to Elders, ed., *Reflexive Water: The Basic Concerns of Mankind* (London, 1974), pp. 288–89.

115. Defert interview, 25 March 1990.

116. SP, p. 139; et, p. 138.

117. "Le jeu de Michel Foucault" (int), *Ornicar?*, 10 (July 1977), p. 90; et in PKN, p. 222.

118. VS, p. 181; et, p. 138.

119. VS, pp. 178–79; et, p. 136.

120. SP, 58; et, p. 55. VS, p. 182, 187; et, pp. 138, 142. See also the text of the last lecture of Foucault's course at the Collège de France in the winter of 1976—offering an early public version of the last chapter of *The Will to Know*—"Faire vivre et laisser mourir: la naissance du racisme," *Les temps modernes*, 535 (February 1991), pp. 49 and (on death) p. 53: "at the limit, sex is less taboo today than death." And cf. RC, p. 88.

121. VS, p. 182; et, p. 138. Heidegger, *An Introduction to Metaphysics*, p. 133.

122. VS, p. 182; et, pp. 138–39. One thinks, of course, of Durkheim's first major study, *Suicide*.

123. VS, p. 191; et, p. 145.

124. See VS, pp. 191–93; et, pp. 145–47. Cf. "Faire vivre et laisser mourir" (1976), loc. cit., pp. 49–50, where the concerns at issue in family supervision are more concretely spelled out.

125. VS, pp. 196, 206; et, pp. 149, 156.

126. Philippe Ariès, *L'Homme devant la mort*; et: *The Hour of Our Death*, trans. Helen Weaver (New York, 1981), p. 395. Cf. Foucault's glowing review of this book: "Une érudition étourdissante," *Le Matin*, no. 278, 20 January 1978, p. 25.

127. VS, p. 180; et, p. 137. Cf. "Faire vivre et laisser mourir" (1976), loc. cit., pp. 56–57.

128. VS, p. 197; et, pp. 149–50. "Fair vivre et laisser mourir" (1976), loc. cit., p. 59.

129. VS, p. 196; et, p. 149. A similar critique of Sade and the political implications of his thought appears in "Sade, sergeant du sexe," *Cinématographie*, 16 (December 1975–January 1976), pp. 3–5.

130. VS, p. 198; et, p. 150.

131. Cf. Foucault's remarks on repression and transgression, in "Pouvoirs et stratégies" (int), *Les révoltes logiques*, 4 (Winter 1977), p. 93; et in PKN, pp. 139–40.

132. VS, pp. 207–08; et, p. 157.

133. "Intervista a Michel Foucault" (int, 1976), in Alessandro Fontana and Pasquale Pasquino, *Microfisica del Potere* (Torino, 1977), et in PKN, p. 129.

134. VS, p. 208; et, p. 157. The phrase about dictatorial power is, of course, Foucault's own, uttered in the heat of his 1971 debate with Noam Chomsky: see "Human Nature: Justice versus Power," in Fons Elders, ed., *Reflexive Water*, p. 182.

135. VS, p. 208; et, p. 157.

CHAPTER 8: THE WILL TO KNOW

1. This paragraph and the account that follows is based on an unpublished 121-page typescript by Simeon Wade, *Foucault in California*. I met Wade and interviewed him on 3 October 1989, and have cleared up several details in subsequent phone calls. Daniel Defert, in my interview with him on 25 March 1990, confirmed that Foucault's LSD trip with Wade was pivotal. And so has Leo Bersani, who had dinner with Foucault the night that he returned to San Francisco after the acid trip. The Death Valley "limit-experience" was, in fact, *so* important to Foucault that he frequently mentioned it to friends and acquaintances,

both in the United States and France—it is perhaps the one episode in his personal life that virtually every person I interviewed had heard about from Foucault himself. (Foucault also kept in touch with Wade. And in 1981, when *Time* magazine published an article on Foucault, the photograph accompanying the piece showed Foucault sitting with Simeon Wade and Wade's friend Michael: see Otto Friedrich, "France's Philosopher of Power," *Time*, 118, 20 [6 November 1991], p. 147.) As for the veracity of Wade's account, this was for him the experience of a lifetime; he took mental notes throughout, as well as written notes; and so did his lover, Michael, with whom Wade still lives. There is, in addition, important circumstantial evidence that Wade's manuscript is accurate: for in the days that he spent with Foucault, he peppered him with personal questions, which the philosopher answered; and all of these answers (for example, about his affair with Jean Barraqué), as Wade has recollected them, are verifiably accurate. (It is relevant to note that Wade completed his manuscript before Didier Eribon's French biography made Foucault's life a matter of public record.) Another, perhaps more important indication that Wade's manuscript is reliable involves the crux of Foucault's epiphany, as he describes it. As I explain in note 16, Foucault was struck by something, apparently sexual, about his relationship to his sister: both Bersani and Defert have also told me that a personal revelation about his relation with his sister was crucial for Foucault. I have therefore decided to reproduce dialogue from Wade's manuscript—indicating that this is Wade's recollection, and always placing Foucault's comments, as Wade has remembered them, in double quotes: " '   .' "

2. "Qu'est-ce qu'un auteur?," *Bulletin de la Société française de philosophie*, 63 (July–September 1969), p. 78; et in LCP, p. 117. Gilles Deleuze, "Lettre à un critique sévère," in Deleuze, *Pourparlers* (Paris, 1990), pp. 15–16.

3. "Militant and professor at the Collège de France" is the by-line Foucault used for his first articles in *Libération*: see "Pour une chronique de la mémoire ouvrière," *Libération* (22 February 1973), p. 6.

4. Wade, *Foucault in California*, pp. 6–7.

5. Ibid., pp. 11–12.

6. Ibid., pp. 27–28. In Wade's mansuscript, he quotes himself using the circumlocution "powerful elixir," rather than telling Foucault they had brought along LSD; but in a subsequent phone call, Wade and his companion both agreed that they had been straightforward about what they had in mind; and that Foucault knew that dropping acid was on their Death Valley agenda.

7. "Theatrum philosophicum," *Critique*, 282 (November 1970), pp. 898, 904; et in LCP, pp. 183, 191. "Conversazione con Michel Foucault" (int), *La Fiera Letteraria*, 39 (28 September 1967); I am quoting from the original French transcript of this interview with Paolo Caruso, p. 5.

8. "Theatrum philosophicum" (1970), loc. cit., pp. 904, 903; et in LCP, pp. 191, 190. I am translating the French word "*bêtise*" in this context as "mute animality"—in other contexts, it might more appropriately be translated as "stupidity" or "folly."

9. Wade, *Foucault in California*, pp. 32, 47.

10. See Annie Cohen-Solal, *Sartre: A Life*, trans. Anna Cancogni (New York, 1987), pp. 102–03.

11. Wade, *Foucault in California*, pp. 5–6.

12. See ibid., pp. 45–47 (here and throughout, I have supplemented this written account with details gleaned from various conversations with Wade).

13. Ibid., p. 55. Foucault refers, in passing, to his love of *Under the Volcano* in "La pensée, l'émotion," in *Duane Michals: Photographie de 1958 à 1982* (Paris, 1982), p.iii.

14. Malcolm Lowry, *Under the Volcano* (New York, 1965), pp. 35–36.

15. Wade, *Foucault in California*, p. 55. Cf. Foucault's public comments, cited later in this chapter, about the virtues of anonymous sex.

16. Ibid., p. 56. Where the ellipses appear, Foucault went on to say: "It all goes back to my sister." Both Daniel Defert and Leo Bersani (see note 1, above) confirm that this was a crucial ingredient in Foucault's epiphany—and both refuse to say anything more about why. Circumstantial evidence—including a passing comment made to me by Bersani ("So

what if he had the hots for his sister? Lots of people do"; which is true)—suggests that the epiphany may have involved a memory of incestuous fantasies, and the guilt that accompanied these fantasies. Before his acid trip, the central focus of Foucault's critical remarks on sexuality had been the prohibitions surrounding masturbation; after it, the emphasis shifted—to the incest taboo. Cf. the remarks on incest in VS, pp. 143–47; et, pp. 109–11: "In a society such as ours, where the family is the most active site of sexuality, and where it is doubtless the exigencies of the latter which maintain and prolong its existence, incest . . . occupies a central place; it is constantly being solicited and refused; it is an object of obsession and attraction, a dreadful secret and an indispensable pivot. . . . Then these new personages made their appearance: the nervous woman, the frigid wife, the indifferent mother—or worse, the mother besest by murderous obsessions—the impotent, sadistic, perverse husband, the hysterical or neurasthenic girl, the precocious and already exhausted child, and the young homosexual who rejects marriage or neglects his wife. . . . The family was the crystal in the deployment of sexuality." As for Foucault's own family, Didier Eribon (apparently on the authority of Foucault's mother) reports that the young Michel was allowed to enter the lycée in Poitiers prematurely, because "he did not want to be separated from his sister." (See Didier Eribon, *Michel Foucault* [Paris, 1989], p. 22; et: *Michel Foucault*, trans. Betsy Wing [Cambridge, Mass., 1991], p. 6.) Foucault's sister, for her part, was informed by Defert after her brother's death of the importance he had ascribed to her in his self-understanding; but she showed little interest in pursuing the matter. (Defert interview, 25 March 1990.) This much is clear: Foucault's LSD epiphany about his "own sexuality" was tied to a fresh understanding of feelings first kindled, early in life, within his own family. But this kind of self-understanding is of course a banal commonplace in our own society; and given the lack of further details, nothing much can be said with any confidence about this aspect of Foucault's epiphany, which must therefore remain an enigma—and not on this count alone.

17. Wade, *Foucault in California*, p. 56.

18. "Michel Foucault: à bas la dictature du sexe!," *L'Express*, 1333 (24–30 January 1977), p. 56.

19. Daniel Defert interview, 25 March 1990. Parts of Foucault's draft privately circulated: for example, the American philosopher Arnold I. Davidson, a student of the history of sexuality in his own right, was permitted by Foucault to read a part of his unfinished volume on "the perversions." The part that he read, he reports, was roughly eighty typed pages long, and composed in a style that roughly resembled that of *Discipline and Punish*; the text focused largely on a nineteenth-century case of homicidal monomania; and it was evidently this kind of raw material that would have become the basis for Foucault's final, full-blown "fictive" treatment. (Communication to the author from Arnold Davidson.)

20. Stephane Mallarmé, "The Book: A Spiritual Instrument," in Mallarmé, *Selected Poetry and Prose*, ed. Mary Ann Caws (New York, 1982), p. 84. Cf. Hervé Guibert, *À l'ami qui ne m'a pas sauvé la vie* (Paris, 1990), p. 36; et: *To the Friend Who Did Not Save My Life*, trans. Linda Coverdale (New York, 1991), p. 23, on Foucault's "dream of an endless book that would raise every possible question, that nothing could bring to an end save death or exhaustion, the most powerful and fragile book in the world, a treasure-in-progress whose creator holds it out toward—or snatches it back from—the abyss with every twist and turn of his thoughts, toying with the idea of consigning it to the flames with each fit of dejection, a bible destined for hell."

21. For the original plan, see Eribon, *Foucault*, p. 290; et, pp. 273–74.

22. Defert interview, 25 March 1990: in my conversation with him, Defert was emphatic about the fact that Foucault, even though he announced the plan of the work, had already abandoned this plan. Wade, *Foucault in California*, p. 7. Cf. Guibert, *À l'ami*, p. 36; et, p. 22. And see "Le retour de la morale" (int), *Les Nouvelles*, 2937 (28 June–5 July 1984), p. 36; et in PPC, pp. 242–43: "the rupture did not occur progressively. It was very abrupt. Starting in 1975–76, I completely abandoned this style" of thinking about the History of Sexuality.

23. For a vivid journalistic survey of the boom years on Castro Street, see the first

chapter of Frances Fitzgerald, *Cities on a Hill* (New York, 1986), pp. 25–119. Despite a certain puritanism (and a certain "I-told-you-so" self-righteousness) that colors his account, Randy Shilts also conjures up the heyday in *And the Band Played On* (New York, 1987). For a more buttoned-down (and sympathetic) account of the golden age of the San Francisco bathhouses, see Alan Bérubé, "The History of Gay Bathhouses," *Coming Up*, 6, 4 (December 1984), pp. 15–19. I owe the Bérubé reference, and much else in what follows, to Gayle Rubin, who has patiently answered questions, corrected factual errors, and supplied fresh information based on her wealth of knowledge as an anthropologist who has spent years studying the gay community of San Francisco; and also on her firsthand experience as one of the most eloquent partisans of S/M as a reasonable and legitimate sexual practice.

24. Edmund White, *States of Desire: Travels in Gay America* (New York, 1983), p. 30.

25. Defert interview 25 March 1990. Cf. "Le jeu de Michel Foucault" (int), *Ornicar?*, 10 (July 1977), p. 86; et in PKN, p. 220. Speaking about the movement for "desexualization," Foucault mentions the women's movement and the American gay movement and their "inventive element. The American homosexual movements make that challenge [of invention] their starting point. Like women, they begin to look for new forms of community, coexistence, pleasure. But, in contrast with the position of women, the fixing of homosexuals to their sexual specificity is much stronger, they reduce everything to the order of sex"— except, as Foucault acknowledged (see his comments later in the chapter), for those homosexuals interested in the radical "ascesis" of S/M.

26. Wade, *Foucault in California*, pp. 64–65.

27. Ibid., p. 65.

28. The only article I know of that discusses this issue is Ed Cohen, "Foucauldian necrologies: 'gay politics'? politically gay?," *Textual Practice*, 2, 1 (Spring 1988), pp. 87–101. Despite the philosopher's central importance to current theorizing in gay studies, the literature on Foucault and gay liberation is, oddly enough, almost nonexistent. Perhaps this is a perverse tribute to a lingering homophobia in the American and European academies: as I was researching my book, straight Foucauldians kept telling me that I *could not* and *should not* write about this "purely personal" facet of the philosopher's life; one well-known American Foucault specialist refused to talk to me at all, on the grounds that my curiosity about the possible role of S/M in Foucault's way of thinking was "disgusting." Even in putatively "liberated" intellectuals, a surprisingly old-fashioned sense of what is "shameful" obviously runs deep.

29. I am following the usefully condensed account in John D'Emilio and Estelle B. Freedman, *Intimate Matters: A History of Sexuality in America* (New York, 1988), pp. 318–22, which also quotes the GLF manifesto. D'Emilio sketches out the historical background in much greater detail in *Sexual Politics, Sexual Communities: The Making of a Homosexual Minority in the United States, 1940–1970* (Chicago, 1983).

30. For FHAR, see the commemorative set of essays, under the general title "FHAR, le coup d'éclat" in *Gai Pied*, 25 (April 1981), pp. 33–35. Cf. Hervé Hamon and Patrick Rotman, *Génération* (Paris, 1988), Vol II, pp. 327–30. Thanks to Edmund White for his thoughts about "*pudeur*" as a central part of the French sexual ethos.

31. See Guy Hocquenghem, *Homosexual Desire*, trans. Daniella Dangoor (London, 1978), p. 81. I have drawn biographical details from the memoir of Hocquenghem by René Scherer that appears in the 1989 publication of the annual directory of the Association Amicale des Anciens Élèves de L'École Normale Supérieure," pp. 96–98. Hocquenghem entered the ENS in 1966; he died from AIDS on 28 August 1988.

32. Quoted in D'Emilio and Freedman, *Intimate Matters*, p. 322. Cf. the account in D'Emilio, *Sexual Politics, Sexual Communities*, pp. 235–36.

33. "An Interview: Sex, Power, and the Politics of Identity" (int, 1982), *The Advocate*, 400 (7 August 1984), p. 28.

34. Bersani interview 6 November 1989.

35. Bersani interview 6 November 1989.

36. "Histoire et homosexualité" (int), *Masques*, 13 (Spring 1982), p. 24.

37. See "La loi de la pudeur" (int), *Recherches*, 37 (April 1979), pp. 69–82; et in PPC,

pp. 271–85 (see esp. pp. 285, 284, 277). Foucault's alliance with Hocquenghem did not last long: by the early 1980s, Hocquenghem had broken bitterly with Foucault over political disagreements. And in private, Hocquenghem became scornful of Foucault's continuing anguish over how to address gay issues (communication to the author from Mark Blasius, a young American political theorist and gay activist who talked in these years with both Foucault and Hocquenghem about their positions on gay political issues).

38. "Enfermement, pyschiatrie, prison," *Change*, 32–33 (1977), p. 97; et in PPC, p. 200. The occasion for Foucault's comments was a roundtable that included the English anti-psychiatrist David Cooper, the French editor Jean-Pierre Faye, his editorial assistant Marie-Odèle Faye, and Cooper's collaborator Marine Zecca—the two women took strong exception to Foucault's proposal.

39. "Sexualité et politique," *Combat*, 9274 (27–28 April 1974), p. 16: the occasion for this short article was a French trial after the courts had banned the collective work entitled *La grande encyclopedie des homosexulatiés, ou 3 milliards de pervers*, edited by Félix Guattari, and published in 1973.

40. The biographical details about Jean Le Bitoux are gleaned from a résumé he prepared for a piece by Gerard Koskovich on the gay liberation movement in France for *The Advocate*; my thanks to Koskovich for supplying a copy of this résumé.

41. Jean Le Bitoux, "The Real Foucault," *New York Native* (23 June 1986), p. 5.

42. "De l'amité comme mode de vie" (int), *Gai Pied*, 25 (April 1981), p. 39; et in *Gay Information*, 7 (Spring 1981), p. 6.

43. "De l'amité comme mode de vie" (int, 1981), loc. cit., p. 38; et, p. 4 (emphasis added). Foucault's formulation about "becoming homosexual" was sufficiently odd that it prompted a follow-up question in his interview for the gay French quarterly *Masques*: see "Histoire et homosexualité" (int, 1982), loc. cit., p. 24.

44. "De l'amité comme mode de vie" (int, 1981), loc. cit., pp. 38–39; et, p. 5. The idea of "homosexual ascesis" I take to be central to Foucault's final understanding of his History of Sexuality: see chapter ten.

45. Ibid., p. 39; et, p. 6. Foucault's French translation of "coming out" is "*se manifester.*"

46. Ibid., p. 39; et, p. 6. Apart from the interview with *Masques*, and the two interviews about S/M, to be discussed later, Foucault also gave an interview to the American gay monthly *Christopher Street*: see "The Social Triumph of the Sexual Will," *Christopher Street*, 64 (Fall 1982), pp. 36–41. Under much more peculiar circumstances—he was interviewed by a straight man, whose line of questioning Foucault had trouble taking seriously—he also spoke about gay issues in an interview for the American intellectual quarterly *Salmagundi*: see "Sexual Choice, Sexual Act," *Salmagundi*, 58–59 (Fall–Winter 1983)—special issue on "Homosexuality: Sacrilege, Vision, Politics," edited by George Steiner—pp. 10–24; reprinted in PPC, pp. 286–303.

47. Leo Bersani, "Is the Rectum a Grave?," *AIDS: Cultural Analysis, Cultural Activism* (Cambridge, Mass., 1988), pp. 219–20.

48. My account of Foucault's fascination with Folsom Street is drawn, in the main, from interviews with four of his colleagues at Berkeley: in alphabetical order, Leo Bersani (6 November 1989); Leonard Johnson (28 September 1989); D. A. Miller (11 April 1991); and Hans Sluga (30 September 1989). On a more general level, in my interview with him on 25 March 1990, Daniel Defert stressed the importance to Foucault of his California experiences—though I suspect, judging from our subsequent conversations, that he may not agree with my own interpretation of what these experiences may have meant to Foucault as a philosopher. Other crucial pieces of information were supplied by Edmund White (interview 12 March 1990) and—most crucially for the S/M parts of the puzzle—Bob Gallagher (interview 9 October 1989), whose candid remarks, though I have only directly cited him once in what follows, informed my whole way of thinking about this aspect of Foucault's life. And cf. the texture of Hervé Guibert's thinly fictionalized portrait in *À l'ami qui ne m'a pas sauvé la vie*.

49. My account of the Folsom Street scene is drawn from: Gayle Rubin, "Valley of the Kings," *Sentinel USA* (13 September 1984), pp. 10–11; idem, "Requiem for the Valley of

the Kings," *Southern Oracle* (Fall 1989), pp. 10–15; and idem, "The Catacombs: A Temple of the Butthole," *Drummer*, 139, pp. 28–34. A crucial source has been Geoff Mains, *Urban Aboriginals: A Celebration of Leathersexuality* (San Francisco, 1984). For the techniques of gay S/M in these years, I have relied on Larry Townshend, *The Leatherman's Handbook II* (New York, 1983); and idem, *The New Leatherman's Workbook: A Photo Illustrated Guide to SM Sex Devices* (Los Angeles, 1984). I also have used Edmund White's *States of Desire*, and—though it concerns a New York City S/M haunt—Leo Cardini's memoir, *Mineshaft Nights* (Teaneck, N.J., 1990) See also Bérubé, "The History of the Baths," loc. cit.; and John Rechy, *The Sexual Outlaw* (New York, 1977), pp. 263–81.

50. White, *States of Desire*, p. 52. This club first opened in 1978.

51. I thank Edmund White for sharing his impressions of the difference between the gay (and S/M) subcultures of the United States and France (where he has lived for several years).

52. Wade, *Foucault in California*, pp. 38–39. The description of poppers comes from Townshend, *The Leatherman's Handbook II*, p. 283.

53. Wade, *Foucault in California*, p. 39.

54. Bersani interview 16 November 1989.

55. Bersani interview 16 November 1989.

56. For more on the legal status of S/M, and police harassment of the subculture, see Gayle Rubin, "The Leather Menace: Comments on Politics and S/M," in SAMOIS, ed., *Coming to Power* (Boston, 1981), pp. 194–229, esp. 199–200. I should add that S/M, at its outer limits, is obviously a risky business. Accidents do happen; in the course of S/M play, some people have been hurt—and some people have died. For obvious reasons, the organized S/M subculture carefully polices it own ranks to weed out madmen and murderers. Despite the precautions, it is always possible, particularly when drugs are involved, to make a fatal mistake—as cops and coroners in any major city can attest.

57. In addition to the interviews on S/M described in detail later in this chapter, S/M is also discussed in the *Salmagundi* interview, see PPC, pp. 298–99; and, more obliquely, in the 1975 interview "Sade sergent du sexe," and the 1982 conversation with the German film director Werner Schroeter: see note 104 of this chapter.

58. This account of the circumstances of the *Mec* piece is drawn from taped interviews with Le Bitoux conducted by Gerard Koskovich (22 September 1985) and Adam Block (October 1989); my thanks to both Koskovich and Block for supplying me with cassette copies of their interviews.

59. Bob Gallagher interview, 9 October 1989.

60. "An Interview: Sex, Power and the Politics of Identity" (int, 1982), loc. cit., p. 27.

61. Ibid, pp. 28 (on good drugs), 29 (on role-reversal). "Le gai savoir" (int, 1978), *Mec*, 5 (June 1988), p. 36 (on the anonymity of the baths).

62. "An Interview: Sex, Power and the Politics of Identity" (int, 1982), loc. cit., pp. 29–30. VS, pp. 66–67; et, p. 48.

63. "Le gai savoir" (int, 1978), loc. cit., p. 36.

64. Townshend's book has been through multiple editions since 1972; despite its popularity, the book must be taken with a grain of salt, since Townshend delights in describing the most extreme fantasies and practices. According to Simeon Wade (letter to the author, 1 May 1992), Foucault's favorite American writer on S/M was John Preston, whose fictional saga of masters and slaves, *Mr. Benson*, was serialized in the S/M magazine *Drummer* in the early 1980s.

65. Townshend, *The Leatherman's Handbook II*, p. 43.

66. See the list in Robert J. Stoller, M.D., *Pain and Passion: A Psychoanalyst Explores the World of S&M* (New York, 1991), pp. 10–14. My approach to S/M has been influenced by Stoller's work on the dynamics of sexual excitement, most classically expressed in *Perversion: The Erotic Form of Hatred* (New York, 1975).

67. Stoller, *Pain and Passion*, p. 21. Gayle Rubin has made the point about the relatively higher number of heterosexual S/M players both in her letters to me, and in the course of several of our conversations; her point, coincidentally, is corroborated by *Pain and Passion*,

in which Stoller presents detailed interviews with the owners, dominatrixes, and customers of two predominatly heterosexual bondage-and-discipline clubs in West Hollywood.

68. White, *States of Desire*, p. 54. See also Stoller, *Pain and Passion*, p. 19.

69. White, *States of Desire*, p. 54. Cf. Stoller, *Pain and Passion*, esp. p. 28: "Sado-masochistic perversions, then, are not just frank expressions of hostility, such as cruelty or guilt (as some psychoanalytic theories tend to state), but, superficial appearances to the contrary, pretty successful defenses against such impulses."

70. Stoller, *Pain and Passion*, pp. 28, 19.

71. White, *States of Desire*, p. 55. Stoller's research tends to support this hypothesis.

72. Townshend, *The Leatherman's Handbook II*, pp. 40, 45.

73. Ibid., p. 31.

74. Mains, *Urban Aboriginals*, p. 58. An S/M player describes the adjustable clamps in Stoller, *Pain and Passion*, p. 116.

75. Rubin, "The Catacombs," loc. cit., p. 30. Mains, *Urban Aboriginals*, p. 58.

76. Townshend, *The Leatherman's Handbook II*, p. 165 (see also p. 22, on S/M in general as essentially "asexual": "You may have noticed that I have not leaned heavily on the word 'sex' as an important part of either the definitions or escape activities"). Mains, *Urban Aboriginals*, p. 172. And cf. John Rechy, quoted in Stanley Crouch, *Notes of a Hanging Judge* (New York, 1990), p. 124: "There are the hoods, the leather gloves, the face is hidden, and quite often, many of the acts have nothing to do with sex. . . . There are very few hard cocks in the orgy room."

77. I am quoting from a footnote in Stoller's original manuscript of his paper on "Consensual Sado-Masochistic Perversions" that does not appear in the version published in *Pain and Passion*.

78. Townshend, *The Leatherman's Handbook II*, p. 127.

79. Ibid., p. 128.

80. Ibid., p. 139.

81. Ibid., pp. 186–87, 140. In the original manuscript of his paper "Consensual Sado-Masochistic Perversions," Stoller also documents a case of acting out a castration fantasy by driving a nail through the foreskin.

82. Townshend, *The Leatherman's Handbook II*, p. 277.

83. Mains, *Urban Aboriginals*, pp. 137–38.

84. Stoller, *Pain and Passion*, pp. 29, 24. Mains, *Urban Aboriginals*, p. 55. The pain research currently being done by neuropsychiatrists like Howard Fields at the University of California at Berkeley certainly does not rule out Mains's hypothesis. (Personal discussion between Fields and the author, 25 January 1990, at the American Neuropsychiatric Association's annual meeting; my thanks to Barry Fogel of Brown University for making possible this discussion.)

85. "Le gai savoir" (int, 1978), loc. cit., p. 34 (emphasis added).

86. RC, pp. 13–14.

87. "L'occident et la verité du sexe," *Le Monde*, 9885 (5 November 1976), p. 24; et: "The West and the Truth of Sex," *Sub-Stance*, 20 (1978), pp. 5, 7.

88. See "La verité et les formes juridiques," four lectures delivered in Brazil from 21–25 May 1973; and cf. the seminar on "L'épreuve et l'enquête" conducted in Montreal a year later, noted in PCP, pp. 124–25n. In the first of the Brazilian lectures, Foucault actually works with a tri-partite classificatory scheme, adding "*l'examen*" ("the examination") to his categories (cf. the pages on the practice of conducting examinations in SP: pp. 186–94; et, pp. 184–92). The binary opposition (between "ordeal," and "inquiry") nevertheless seems to have been sufficient from a strictly epistemological point of view. See the indicative treatment of "l'épreuve et l'enquête," extracted from Collège de France lectures delivered in 1974, and reprinted as "La maison des fous," in Franco Basaglia and Franca Basaglia-Ongaro, eds., *Les criminels de paix* (Paris, 1980), pp. 145–60.

89. "La maison des fous" (1974), loc. cit., p. 149.

90. Ibid., p. 145.

91. See ibid., pp. 145–46.

92. Ibid., p. 146.

93. SP, pp. 44, 45; et, pp. 40, 41. Cf. "La maison des fous" (1974), loc. cit., p. 147.

94. Ibid., p. 146. For the early Christian ascetics, the somatic rituals of penance produced a similar kind of "crisis" in the soul: see Foucault's remarks in his Berkeley Howison lectures of 1980, discussed below, chapter ten.

95. "La maison des fous" (1974), loc. cit., p. 146.

96. Ibid., pp. 146–47.

97. Gilles Deleuze, *Masochism*, trans. Jean McNeil (New York, 1971), p. 88.

98. VS, pp. 205–06; et, pp. 155–56.

99. VS, p. 208; et, p. 157.

100. VS, pp. 54, 62, 67; et, pp. 39, 45, 49.

101. VS, p, 205; et, p. 155.

102. "Les rapports de pouvoir passent à l'intérieur des corps" (int), *La Quinzaine Littéraire*, 247 (1–15 January 1977), p. 6; et in PKN, p. 191. One indication of Foucault's radicalism is the perfectly understandable unwillingness of most sexual "social constructionists" to go all the way with their philosophical forerunner. Consider, for example, David M. Halperin, in *One Hundred Years of Homosexuality* (New York, 1990), p. 53: "I can't imagine deacculturating myself any more than I can imagine desexualizing myself." But de-sexualization is, I believe, precisely—and *literally*—the improbable goal that Foucault has in mind in the final pages of *The Will to Know*.

103. "Les rapports de pouvoir passent à l'intérieur des corps" (int, 1977), loc. cit, p. 6; et in PKN, p. 191.

104. "Sade, sergent du sexe" (int), *Cinématographe*, 16 (December 1975–January 1976), pp. 3–5. The pretext for these comments was the German director Werner Schroeter's film, then new, *Der Tod der Maria Malibran* ("The Death of Maria Malibran"). Several years later, Foucault would discuss "the Passion" of "suffering-pleasure" with Schroeter directly: see "Conversation," in Gerard Courant, ed., *Werner Schroeter* (Paris, 1982), pp. 38–47.

105. VS, pp. 14, 198–200; et, pp. 7, 150–51.

106. VS, pp. 200, 205; et, pp. 152, 155.

107. "Sade, sergent du sexe" (int, 1975), loc. cit., p. 5. The metaphor of the "mirage" is Foucault's own: see VS, p. 207; et, p. 157.

108. Peter Brown, *The Body and Society* (New York, 1988), p. 168.

109. Antonin Artaud, "From *A Voyage to the Land of the Tarahumara*," in Artaud, *Selected Writings*, ed. Susan Sontag, trans. Helen Weaver (New York, 1976), p. 383.

110. Antonin Artaud, *To Be Done with the Judgment of God*, in Artaud, *Selected Writings*, pp. 570–71. The phrase "Dionysian castration" appears in "Un si cruel savoir," *Critique*, 182 (July 1962), p. 598.

111. Gilles Deleuze and Félix Guattari, *A Thousand Plateaus*, trans. Brian Massumi (Minneapolois, Minn., 1987), p. 150 (from chapter six, "November 28, 1947: How Do You Make Yourself a Body without Organs?," originally published in 1974 in France as an independent essay). For Foucault's admiration of *Anti-Oedipus*, see SP, p. 29n.; et, p. 308n.2: "I could give no notion by references or quotations what this book [namely, *Discipline and Punish*] owes to Gilles Deleuze and the work he is undertaking with Félix Guattari." For a typical example of what Deleuze and Guattari, writing in *Anti-Oedipus*, suggest that it means to be "a body without organs," see Gilles Deleuze and Félix Guattari, *Anti-Oedipus*, trans. Robert Hurley, Mark Seem, and Helen R. Lane (New York, 1977), p. 369: the image of the crucified Christ in Renaissance paintings, they declare, plays "the role of a full body without organs, a locus of connection for all the machines of desire, a locus of sado-masochistic exercises where the artist's joy breaks free."

112. Deleuze and Guattari, *A Thousand Plateaus*, p. 151.

113. "Nietzsche, la généalogie, l'histoire," in *Hommage à Jean Hyppolite* (Paris, 1971), pp. 159, 154; et in LCP, pp. 153, 148.

114. If this interpretation is right, then S/M would be among the most important of the practices that Foucault alludes to in "What is Enlightenment?" (1983), in TFR, pp. 46–47, where he praises "the very specific transformations that have proved to be possible in the

last twenty years in a certain number of areas that concern our ways of being and thinking, relations between authority, relations between the sexes, the way in which we perceive insanity or illness. . . ."

115. One of the most profound (and radical) critiques of S/M as a quintessentially *masculine* construction of sex and sexuality is that delivered by Catherine A. MacKinnon in *Feminism Unmodified* (Cambridge, Mass.); see esp. pp. 146–62. As Leo Bersani has pointed out, correctly in my view, the inner logic of the critique made by MacKinnon and her ally Andrea Dworkin points to "*the criminalization of sex itself until it has been reinvented.*" (See Bersani, "Is the Rectum a Grave?," loc. cit., p. 214.) As Bersani also points out, there is at the same time a paradoxical similarity in the thinking of MacKinnon and Foucault: for both in fact agree on the desirability—and possibility—of "reinventing" sex, and also on the desirability of "desexualizing" and "devirilizing" the body. But of course, the means they advocate in order to approach these (perhaps utopian) ends could not be more different, since the inner logic of Foucault's (Nietzschean) critique points to the *decriminalization* of *all* sex (in principle including even incest, boy-love, and rape), in order to lift the burden of guilt until such time as the body and its pleasures have been reinvented. Cf. Foucault's comments on rape (cited above) in "Enfermement, pyschiatrie, prison" (int, 1977), loc. cit., p. 97; et in PPC, p. 200.

116. RC, p. 14.

117. "Le jeu de Michel Foucault" (int, 1977), loc. cit, p. 76; et in PKN, p. 208 (emphasis added).

118. See chapter seven.

119. "Un Dibattito Foucault-Preti" (int), *Il Bimestre* (1973); et in FLI, pp. 83, 84.

120. "Sade, sergent du sexe" (int, 1975), loc. cit., p. 5.

121. Ibid., p. 5.

122. Ibid., p. 4. "Conversation" with Werner Schroeter (int, 1982), loc. cit., p. 40. "An Interview: Sex, Power and the Politics of Identity" (int, 1982), loc. cit., p. 27. In his book on *Masochism*, Gilles Deleuze draws a similarly sharp distinction between "sadism" (which he regards as a fearfully coercive and dictatorial "idea of demonstrative reason") and "masochism" (which he regards as consensual—and welcomes as "visionary"): see Deleuze, *Masochism*, esp. pp. 112–16.

123. FD, p. 372.

124. "What is Enlightenment?" (1983), in TFR, p. 50. I am citing from p. 26 of a typescript that evidently served as the basis for the English translation of this text ("*un vie philosophique où la critique de ce que nous sommes est à la fois analyse historique des limites qui nous sont posées et épreuve de leur franchissement possible*"). The word "*franchissement,*" which I have translated as "transcendence," in other contexts can be used to evoke "clearing" or "jumping over" a hurdle, or "crossing" a river, or "spanning" a canyon.

125. See the Marquis de Sade, *Justine,* trans. Richard Seaver and Austryn Wainhouse (New York, 1965), p. 643 (in the castle of M. de Gernande).

126. "Sept propos sur le septième ange," preface to Jean-Pierre Brisset, *La grammaire logique* (Paris, 1970), p. xix. FD, p. 26; et, p. 16. The phrase "perverse mysticism" appears in Deleuze, *Masochism,* p. 105.

127. NC, p. vii; et, p. xi.

128. Gallagher interview 9 October 1989. It is worth remembering that "scenes" is a term of art in the S/M subculture, referring to specific erotic scripts, such as the "crucifixion" and "castration" scenes described earlier.

129. Pierre Klossowski, "The Marquis de Sade and the Revolution," in Denis Hollier, ed., *The College of Sociology,* trans. Betsy Wing (Minneapolis, Minn., 1988), p. 230 (emphasis dropped). Klossowski himself makes the connection between his reading of Sade and "the Manichean gnosis of Marcion": see Pierre Klossowksi, *Sade My Neighbor,* trans. Alphonso Lingis (Evanston, Ill, 1991), p. 7. Foucault's subterranean link, via his affinities with Klossowski, to a Manichean kind of gnosticism, forms an unspoken subtext to the interpretation I will offer in chapter ten, of Foucault's peculiar brand of "asceticism."

130. Ibid., p. 222 (emphasis added). In the first edition of *Sade, mon prochain*, where Klossowski reprinted this talk in 1947, he added a footnote, making explicit the relevance of Sade for understanding—and struggling against—the Nazi experience. See *The College of Sociology*, p. 417n.5; and cf. Foucault's idea that a turn to bodies-and-pleasures will root out the fascism within.

131. "Le gai savoir" (int, 1978), loc. cit., p. 36. Cf. Foucault's comment on the ancient art of penance in the second of his 1981 Howison lectures: "The showing forth of the sinner should be efficient to efface the sins." (I am quoting from the bootleg transcription, II, p. 7, corrected against an audiotape of the lecture as delivered.)

132. Edmund White interview, 12 March 1990.

133. The account that follows is drawn from Wade, *Foucault in California*, pp. 67–88.

134. Ibid., p. 73.

135. Wade interview, 3 October 1989. Daniel Defert showed me the photograph when I talked to him in Foucault's old apartment: it was still hanging up near the bookcases in the living room on 25 March 1990.

136. Wade, *Foucault in California*, p. 79 (emphasis added).

137. Ibid., p. 81 (emphasis added).

138. Friedrich Nietzsche, *Human, All Too Human*, trans. R.J. Hollingdale (Cambridge, 1986), p. 35 (I, §39). Cf. Friedrich Nietzsche, *Philosophy in the Tragic Age of the Greeks*, trans. Marianne Cowane (Chicago, 1962), p. 63: "Man is necessity down to his last fibre, and totally 'unfree,' that is if one means by freedom the foolish demand to be able to change one's *essentia* arbitrarily, like a garment—a demand which every serious philosopher has rejected with the proper scorn."

139. Nietzsche, *Human, All Too Human*, pp. 34–35 (I, §39).

140. "Theatrum Philosophicum" (1970), loc. cit., p. 904; et in LCP, p. 191.

141. "What is Enlightenment?" (1983), in TFR, p. 47 (silently glossing one of Kant's definitions of free will).

CHAPTER 9: THE DISTANT ROAR OF BATTLE

1. The description of Foucault at the Collège de France is gleaned from interviews with a variety of people who heard him speak there, and also from published accounts: see, e.g., Thomas Flynn, "Foucault as Parrhesiast: His Last Course at the Collège de France (1984)," in James Bernauer and David Rasumussen, eds., *The Final Foucault* (Cambridge, Mass., 1988), p. 102.

2. "Corso del 7 gennaio 1976" and "Corso del 14 gennaio 1976," in Alessandro Fontana and Pasquale Pasquino, *Microfisica del Potere* (Turin, 1977); et (as "Two Lectures") in PKN, p. 78. Since his election to the Collège de France, Foucault had in fact delivered lectures on a relatively wide range of topics: "The Will to Know," on Aristotle and Nietzsche, was delivered in 1971; "Penal Theories and Institutions and 'The Punitive Society,'" in 1972 and 1973, introduced material that would appear in *Discipline and Punish*; "Psychiatric Power" in 1974, harked back to *Madness and Civilization*, but linked the material to Foucault's latest vision, of a "disciplinary" society of "normalized" individuals; and "The Abnormal," in 1975, was a series of lectures on one of the key categories in all of Foucault's work—and a concept crucial for his planned History of Sexuality.

3. "Course of Jaunary 7, 1976," in PKN, pp. 78–79. Nietzsche, "Schopenhauer as Educator," trans. William Arrowsmith, in *Unmodern Observations*, p. 165 (§1).

4. "Course of January 7, 1976," in PKN, p. 79.

5. Ibid., in PKN, pp. 85, 86, 87.

6. Ibid., in PKN, pp. 91, 90, 95. SP, p. 315; et, p. 308. "Nietzsche, la généalogie, l'histoire," in *Hommage à Jean Hyppolite* (Paris, 1971), p. 157; et, pp. 150–151. In his 1976 lecture, Foucault uses Clausewitz, the nineteenth-century German theorist of war, to develop, in part, the "Nietzschean hypothesis"; given the argument that follows in this lecture course (and in this chapter), it should be noted that Clausewitz was held in high esteem by Frederick

Engels, by Mao Tse-tung—and also by a number of French Maoists, above all André Glucksmann, whose first book was a neo-Marxist analysis of Clausewitz.

7. "Course of January 7, 1976," in PKN, p. 92. "Course of January 14, 1976," in PKN, p. 108.

8. Gilles Deleuze, "Un portrait de Foucault" (int), in Deleuze, *Pourparlers* (Paris, 1990), pp. 142–43.

9. Hervé Guibert, *À l'ami qui ne m'a pas sauvé la vie* (Paris, 1990), p. 36; et: *To the Friend Who Did Not Save My Life*, trans. Linda Coverdale (New York, 1991), p. 22.

10. " 'Il faut defendre la société," in RC, p. 87; et: "War in the Filigree of Peace Course Summary," trans. Ian Mcleod, *The Oxford Literary Review*, 4, 2 (1980), p. 16.

11. Ibid., p. 87 (this question is omitted from the English translation).

12. See RC, p. 88; et, p. 16.

13. RC, p. 89; et, p. 17.

14. RC, pp. 90–91, et, pp. 17–18.

15. RC, p. 90; et, p 17.

16. See RC, pp. 92–94; et, pp. 18–19. Karl Marx to Frederick Engels, 27 July 1854, in Karl Marx and Frederick Engels, *Collected Works* (New York, 1975), XXXIX, p. 473.

17. See "Faire vivre et laisser mourir: la naissance du racisme," *Les temps modernes*, 535 (February 1991), pp. 37–61. This is a transcription of the last lecture Foucault gave in the 1976 course at the Collège de France; much of the lecture covers material I have already summarized in chapter seven, in my discussion of "The Right of Power and Death over Life," the last chapter of *La volonté de savoir*.

18. Ibid., p. 53. VS, p. 196; et, p 149.

19. "Faire vivre et laisser mourir," loc. cit., p. 60. Racist ideas—and a willingness to countenance genocide—also surface in Frederick Engels's notorious remarks about "reactionary peoples," such as the Slavs, and the desirability of their defeat and annihilation in war. See Frederick Engels, "The Magyar Struggle" (first published in *Neue Rheinische Zeitung* in January, 1849), in Marx and Engels, *Collected Works*, VIII, pp. 238.

20. "Faire vivre et laisser mourir," loc. cit., p. 61. Foucault goes on to compare these "racist" forms of socialism with the more pacific (and hence less "racist") types, such as "the social democrats," the socialists of "the Second International," and even "Marxism itself."

21. "Course of January 14, 1976," in PKN, p. 108.

22. Some of the possible political implications of the last chapter of *The Will to Know* I have already summarized at the end of chapter seven. I suspect (though this is only speculation) that the "the 'right' to rediscover what one is and all that one can be" that Foucault refers to in *The Will to Know* roughly indicated where he thought he might a find a "new form of right." See VS, p. 191; et, p 145.

23. VS, pp. 53, 65, 15 ("une autre cité"); et, pp. 38–39, 47, 7–8. One of the key paradoxes underlined by Foucault—that attempts to study, supervise, and control sex in fact produce (or "incite") sexual variance and "perversity"—he could have found in the great *Allgemeine Psychopathologie* of Jaspers, first published in 1913. See Karl Jaspers, *General Psychopathology*, trans. J. Hoening and Marian W. Hamilton (Chicago, 1963), p. 628: "In all these active enquiries there is more than mere scientific research. This is indicated by the extensive circulation of medical books on sex and the fact that the whole subject has become a matter of wide concern. The obscurantism of the Christian occident on all matters of sex kindled a curiosity when faith deteriorated, though the conventions from the time of faith were still observed. . . . *This whole trend of investigation has itself become a historical factor in the mode of realisation of the sexual life*. Division, deception, new kinds of gratification, an uncurbing of instinct and a modifying of impulse . . . have been linked with this literature. . . ." The possible influence of Jaspers on Foucault is a subject for further research: it is perhaps relevant to recall here, as well, Jaspers's concept of "*Grenzsituationen*" ("limit-situation"), and his neo-Kantian brand of existentialism, with its emphasis on "the enigma" of "*individuality* as such" (see ibid., pp. 330, 754). Cf. Foucault's comment in 1954: "It was

Jaspers who showed that understanding may be extended beyond the frontiers of the normal and that intersubjective understanding may reach the pathological world in its essence." See MM, p. 55; MM*, et, p. 43. Foucault's claims about the historical novelty of perversions and sexuality have been elaborated (and in part corrected) by the American philosopher Arnold I. Davidson in two important articles: "Closing up the Corpses: Diseases of Sexuality and the Emergence of the Psychiatric Style of Reasoning," in George Boolos, ed., *Meaning and Method: Essays in Honor of Hilary Putnam* (Cambridge, 1990), pp. 295– 325; and "Sex and the Emergence of Sexuality," *Critical Inquiry*, 14 (Autumn 1987), pp. 16–48.

24. "Non au sexe roi" (int), *Le Nouvel Observateur*, 644 (12 March 1977), p. 92; et in PPC, pp. 110–11.

25. "Michel Foucault: à bas la dictature du sexe!" (int), *L'Express*, 1333 (24 January 1977), pp. 56–57. The claim, in this interview, that "power has made man into a sexual monster," nicely sums up the book's central (and more sober) set of claims about "the perverse implantation."

26. Ibid., pp. 56–67.

27. In "Non au sexe roi" (int, 1977), loc. cit., p. 126; et in PPC, p. 120, Foucault makes explicit his desire to dismantle "leftist *doxa*," and to make difficult "simple cheers (long live insanity, delinquency, sex)." He lamented the inattention to the last chapter in "Le jeu de Michel Foucault" (int), *Ornicar?*, 10 (July 1977), p. 90; et in PKN, p. 222. And he expressed his disappointment with the public's reaction to the book most vividly in an interview that served as a preface to the German translation: see the passages quoted in Didier Eribon, *Michel Foucault* (Paris, 1989), p. 292; et: *Michel Foucault*, trans. Betsy Wing (Cambridge, Mass., 1991), pp. 275–76.

28. "L'occident et la verité du sexe," *Le Monde*, 9885 (5 November 1976), p. 24; et: "The West and the Truth of Sex," *Sub-Stance*, 20 (1978), p. 7.

29. The transition to the television era of French intellectual life is vividly captured in a 1980 *New Yorker* essay, "Paris: Le Discours," reprinted in Jane Kramer, *Europeans* (New York, 1988), pp. 148–68. On the uses of intellectual products as status symbols in France, see also the work of Pierre Bourdieu and his concept of "cultural capital" (as elaborated, e.g., in Bourdieu, *Distinction*, trans. Richard Nice [Cambridge, Mass., 1984]).

30. "Um welchen Preis sagt die Vernuft die Wahrheit?" (int), *Spuren* 1–2 (1983); et in PPC, pp. 44–45.

31. For Foucault's surreal appearance on *Apostrophes*, see Eribon, *Foucault*, pp. 294–95; et, pp. 277–78. For the re-broadcast clip from the show, see Guibert, *À l'ami*, p. 35; et, p. 21.

32. See Kramer, *Europeans*, p. 150.

33. Ibid., p. 152.

34. André Glucksmann, *Les maîtres penseurs* (Paris, 1977), p. 310; et: *The Master Thinkers*, trans. Brian Pearce (London, 1980), p. 287.

35. Ibid., p. 309; et, p. 286.

36. See Gilles Deleuze, "À propos des nouveau philosophes et d'un problème plus général," 5 June 1977, supplement to *Minuit*, 24 (May 1977).

37. "La grande colère des faits," *Le Nouvel Observateur*, 652 (9 May 1977), reprinted in Sylvie Bouscasse and Denis Bourgeois, *Faut-il brûler les nouveaux philosophes?* (Paris, 1978), pp. 66, 67. In this context, Foucault explicitly mentions, and endorses, the work of François Furet on the French Revolution; which is ironic, given the subsequent hostility to Foucault evinced by Furet and his younger neo-liberal colleagues Luc Ferry and Alain Renault.

38. Ibid., p. 70. Cf. "Sur la justice populaire" (int), *Les temps modernes*, 310 (bis 1972), p. 340; et in PKN, p. 6.

39. This information comes from an interview with one of Foucault's closest associates at this time, who wishes to remain anonymous; in these months this friend was often a courier for Foucault and Deleuze. Anonymous interview, 22 March 1990. Cf. Eribon, *Foucault*, p. 292; et, p. 275. What Deleuze's letter may have said is not known, since this correspondence has never been made public.

40. Anonymous interview, 22 March 1990.

41. Edward Said interview, 7 November 1989. Said mentioned Middle-Eastern politics as a source of friction, based on a conversation he had had with Deleuze. I wrote and asked Deleuze about this; he did not deny it. Since Deleuze's review of Glucksmann's book appeared a few weeks after Foucault's review, his attack on Glucksmann amounted to a public parting of the ways with Foucault over the legacy of May '68.

42. For more details about the Croissant case, see Eribon, *Foucault*, pp. 275–76; et, pp. 259–60.

43. "Va-t-on extrader Klaus Croissant?," *Le Nouvel Observateur*, 679 (14 November 1977), pp. 62–63. Foucault's opposition to terrorism, it is worth noting, was essentially tactical— not moral. See "La securité et l'État" (int), *Tribune socialiste*, 24 November 1977: "When it comes as an expression of a nationality that has neither independence nor state structures and demands them, terrorism is ultimately accepted: Jewish terrorism before the creation of the state of Israel, Palestinian terrorism, Irish terrorism also; even if one is hostile to one or another of these types of action, the very principle of terrorism is not fundamentally impugned. By contrast, what is fundamentally impugned is a terrorist movement in which one speaks in the name of a class or political group or avant-garde or marginal group, saying '*I am rebelling . . . I am threatening to kill someone in order to gain one or another goal.*'" It is hard to see, in practice, how one might draw Foucault's distinction, though it is clear enough that he wants somehow to rule out ultra-left terrorism of the sort practiced by the Baader-Meinhof gang, without ruling out terrorism and political violence *tout court*. Foucault's evident ambivalence, even confusion, on this score is reflected as well in his enthusiasm for the revolution in Iran, which he expressed at the same time that he was expressing his newfound admiration for certain aspects of classical liberalism. In both cases, he was drawn to moments of revolt, and features of the economy and the law, that might allow individuals and groups to challenge and limit the exercise of power. For more on these matters, which Foucault never quite succeeded in clarifying, at least in terms of his own social and political theory, see the rest of this chapter.

44. Gilles Deleuze, letter to the author, 7 February 1990.

45. Anonymous interview, 22 March 1990.

46. Anonymous interview, 22 March 1990.

47. Anonymous interview, 22 March 1990.

48. "*Omnes et Singulatim*: Towards a Criticism of 'Political Reason'," The Tanner Lectures on Human Values, delivered at Stanford University on 10 and 16 October 1979; reprinted in PPC, p. 59. "Governmentality," *Ideology and Consciousness*, 6 (Autumn 1979), p. 5. The Tanner Lectures, delivered at the end of this phase of Foucault's work, conveniently summarize the major themes he was exploring in 1978 and 1979. "Governmentality" is an English translation of the fourth lecture of the 1978 sequence at the Collège de France, delivered on 1 February 1978; a slightly truncated French version (omitting the opening remarks that appear in the English version) has appeared as "La gouvernementalité," *Magazine Littéraire*, 269 (September 1989), pp. 97–103.

49. "Governmentality" (1978), loc. cit., pp. 5–6.

50. See "*Omnes et Singulatim*" (1979), in PPC, passim.

51. See "La gouvernementalité" (1978), loc. cit., passim. In the second of his Tanner Lectures, Foucault discusses at some length the equally obscure work *AristoDemocratic Monarchy* by Turquet de Mayenne.

52. "La gouvernementalité" (1978), loc. cit., p. 103; et, loc. cit., p. 21. "*Omnes et Singulatim*" (1979), in PPC, pp. 77, 82. "Un état de gouvernement" in effect describes the regime of power that Foucault had formerly tried to define in terms of "biopolitics."

53. "Conversation with Michel Foucault" (int), *The Threepenny Review*, 1 (Winter–Spring 1980), pp. 4–5 (this interview with Millicent Dillon was originally published in the fall of 1979 as a press release for the Tanner Lectures at Stanford).

54. For an indication of the kind of research performed by others that grew out of this phase of Foucault's work, see the essays in Graham Burchell, Colin Gordon, and Peter Miller, eds., *The Foucault Effect* (Chicago, 1991).

55. Anonymous interview, 22 March 1990. Augustine is treated at some length in the manuscript for volume four of the History of Sexuality.

56. See "Qu'est-ce que la critique?," *Bulletin de la Sociétié francaise de philosophie*, 84th year, 2 (April–June 1990), pp. 35–63, a transcription of a lecture delivered on 27 May 1978, at the Sorbonne.

57. Ibid., p. 36. Karl Marx, *Capital: A Critique of Political Economy*, trans. Ernest Untermann (Chicago, 1906), p. 87.

58. "Qu'est-ce que la critique?" (1978), loc. cit., pp. 36, 38.

59. Ibid., p. 39.

60. Immanuel Kant, "What is Enlightenment?," trans. Lewis White Beck, in Kant, *On History*, ed. Beck (Indianapolis, Ind., 1963), p. 3.

61. Friedrich Nietzsche, *The Will to Power*, trans. Walter Kaufmann and R.J. Hollingdale (New York, 1967), pp. 220–21 (§409).

62. "Qu'est-ce que la critique?" (1978), loc. cit., pp. 47, 45.

63. Ibid., p. 48. "Table ronde du 20 mai 1978," in Michelle Perrot, ed., *L'impossible prison: Recherches sur le système pénitentiaire au XIXe siècle* (Paris, 1980), p. 43; et: "Questions of Method," in Kenneth Baynes, James Bohman, and Thomas McCarthy, *After Philosophy* (Cambridge, Mass., 1987), p. 104. Foucault's comments to the French historians, coming a week before his lecture to the society of French philosophers, are worth comparing; in both cases, he was in effect trying to explain, and legitimate, his work before a jury of skeptical peers.

64. "Qu'est-ce que la critique?" (1978), loc. cit., p. 50.

65. Ibid., p. 51.

66. Ibid., p. 53.

67. Ibid., p. 55.

68. Ibid., p. 56. Immanuel Kant, *Critique of Judgement*, trans. J.H. Bernard (New York, 1968), p. 116 (I, §29).

69. "Qu'est-ce que la critique?" (1978), loc. cit., pp. 58–59.

70. Ibid., p. 59.

71. Ibid., p. 59.

72. "An Interview" (conducted in 1982 by Stephen Riggins), *Ethos*, I, 2 (Autumn 1983); reprinted in PPC, p. 12. Eribon, *Foucault*, p. 337; et, p. 315: he later told Paul Veyne that he had been smoking opium.

73. D. A. Miller interview, 11 April 1991. Foucault specifically told Miller about having an "out-of-body" limit-experience on this occasion. I will return to Foucault's remarks to Miller in chapter ten.

74. Writing about Pierre Klossowski in 1964, Foucault imagined the character in one of his novels as in the grips of a kind of profane rapture in which "everything" in the human being "is breaking apart, bursting, presenting itself and then withdrawing in the same instant." At such a moment, he had written, a man "might be living or dead, it matters little"—for "oblivion" here "oversees the Identical," "the Same," "the Double," bringing a soul face to face with its *daimon*. See "La prose d'Acteon," *La Nouvelle Revue Française*, 135, (March, 1964), p. 452; et: "The Prose of Acteon," in Pierre Klossowski, *The Baphomet*, trans. Sophie Hawkes (Hygiene, Colorado, 1988), p. xxx.

75. "An Interview" (1982), in PPC, p. 12.

76. Ibid., p. 12.

77. Foucault refers to Savonarola, John of Leyden, and the English Civil War in "Teheran: la fede contro lo Scia," one of his reports from Iran for *Corriere della Sera*: 103, 237 (8 October 1978), p. 11. He mentions the detail of the cassette recorders with the disembodied voices in "La rivolta dell'Iran corre sui nastri delli miniscasette," *Corriere della Sera*, 103, 273 (19 November 1978), pp. 1–2.

78. See "L'esprit d'un monde sans esprit" (int), in Claire Brière and Pierre Blanchet, *Iran: la révolution an nom de Dieu* (Paris, 1979), pp. 33–34; et in PPC, pp. 217–18. The title of this interview alludes to Karl Marx's famous comment that religion is "the heart of a heartless world."

79. Richard Cottam, "Inside Revolutionary Iran," in R.K. Ramazani, ed., *Iran's Revolution* (Bloomington, Indiana, 1990), p. 3.

80. For my account of the Iranian revolution, I am indebted to Edward Mortimer, *Faith and Power: The Politics of Islam* (New York, 1982), pp. 296–376; and, more generally, Roy Mottahedeh, *The Mantle of the Prophet: Religion and Politics in Iran* (New York, 1985).

81. On the forty day cycle of death, see Mottahedeh, *The Mantle of the Prophet*, pp. 373–76; and James A. Bill, *The Eagle and the Lion: The Tragedy of American-Iranian Relations* (New Haven, 1988), p. 236.

82. CF (int, 1978), dernière cassette [VI?], p. 2. The circumstances of Foucault's visits to Iran are recounted in greater detail in Eribon, *Foucault*, pp. 298–309; et, pp. 281–91.

83. "L'esprit d'un monde sans esprit" (int, 1979), loc. cit., p. 237; et in PPC, p. 220.

84. CF (int, 1978), V, p. 21; cf. et, p. 136.

85. "Taccuino Persiano: L'esercito, quando la terra trema," *Corriere della Sera*, 103, 228 (28 September 1978), pp. 1–2. "Teheran: la fede contro lo Scia" (1978), loc. cit., p. 11.

86. "A quoi rêvent les Iraniens?," *Le Nouvel Observateur*, 726 (9–16 October 1978), pp. 48–49. Perhaps the most important figure to mistake Khomeini as a figurehead was Abol Hassan Bani-Sadr: see Mortimer, *Faith and Power*, p. 348. Foucault never met Khomeini; he did go with François Ewald and (as Eribon reports) Pierre Blanchet, and Claire Brière to Neauphles-le-Château outside Paris, where Khomeini was in exile between 7 October 1978, and his eventual return to Iran the following year; but all the group got to see was Khomeini walking in the distance. Of all the Iranian religious leaders, Foucault's articles for *Corriere della Sera* express the greatest sympathy for Shari'ati, who had died in exile in England shortly before the revolution had begun. A defiantly modern thinker, influenced by Frantz Fanon and Christian mysticism, Shari'ati was harshly critical of the traditional *ulama*; apart from Khomeini, he was probably the most influential single thinker during the revolution, suggesting to secular Iranian intellectuals that it was possible to combine fighting for Islam with a movement of genuine national liberation and enlightenment. See Mortimer, *Faith and Power*, pp. 335–46. For Foucault on Shari'ati, see "Retour au prophète?," *Corriere della Sera*, 22 October 1978: Shari'ati for him exemplified the possiblity of a spiritual politics—and an enlightened mysticism.

87. "Il mitico capo della rivolta nell'Iran," *Corriere della Sera*, 103, 279 (26 November 1978), pp. 1–2. "L'esprit d'un monde sans esprit" (int, 1979), loc. cit., p. 230; et in PPC, p. 214. There is a Heideggerian flavor to Foucault's most apocalyptic comments about Iran. Cf. Martin Heidegger, *An Introduction to Metaphysics*, trans. Ralph Manheim (Garden City, N.Y., 1961), p. 166, on "the inner truth and greatness" of the German revolution of 1933 as "the encounter between global technology and modern man." I am *not* implying that Foucault was a crypto-Nazi in his comments about Iran; but I am suggesting that Foucault, like Heidegger, was deeply attracted to the possibility of a decisive struggle-to-the-death over "the weight of the order of the entire world."

88. Immanuel Kant, *The Strife of the Faculties*, II, §6; in Kant, *On History*, p. 144. Foucault would devote part of the first lecture of his 1983 course at the Collège de France to an analysis of this passage: see "Un cours inédit," *Magazine Littéraire*, 207 (May 1984), pp. 35–39; et in PPC, pp. 86–95.

89. For Kant's apparent views, see *Religion Within the Bounds of Reason Alone*, trans. Theodore M. Greene and Hoyt H. Hudson (New York, 1934), Bk. IV, Pt. 2, §4, pp. 176–77n: "To proceed on the principle that those who are once subjected to . . . bonds are essentially unfit for freedom . . . is to usurp the perogatives of Divinity itself, which created man for freedom."

90. Anonymous interview, 22 March 1990. Cf. "Une esthétique de l'existence" (int, 1984), *Le Monde Aujourd'hui* (15–16 July 1984), p. xi; et in PPC, p. 50.

91. RC, p. 111.

92. Ibid., pp. 111, 112.

93. See ibid., pp. 112–14.

94. "L'oeil du pouvoir" (int) in Jeremy Bentham, *Le panoptique* (Paris, 1977), p. 14; et

in PKN, p. 152. Foucault here explicitly refers to Jean Starobinski's great study of Rousseau's thought, *La transparence et l'osbstacle*—a silent influence, one suspects, on *Surveiller et punir*.

95. FD, p. 521, 513, 516; et, pp. 267, 257, 261 (the French phrase I have translated as "ethical uniformity" is in fact a more awkward neologism, "uniformisation éthique"—a forerunner of the idea of "normalization").

96. Isaiah Berlin, *Four Essays on Liberty* (Oxford, 1969), p. 123.

97. See "Inuitle de se soulever?," *Le Monde*, 10, 661 (11 May 1979), pp. 12; et: "Is It Useless to Revolt?," trans. James Bernauer, *Philosophy and Social Criticism*, VIII, 1 (Spring 1981), pp. 1–9.

98. See Mottahedeh, *The Mantle of the Prophet*, p. 376. The next day, Foucault commented on the change of regime in "Una polveriera chiamata Islam," *Corriere della Sera*, 104, 36 (13 February 1979). It was a "decisive" moment, he wrote. "A people without weapons" had risen up and overthrown with its own hands, and with the power of Shiah scripture, a regime regarded as "all-powerful." And now "this outcome, so infinitely rare in the twentieth century," had led to the installation of a new regime, a new power—raising the prospect, as Foucault warned, of a new "force of expansion" liable to change radically the balance of Middle-Eastern politics.

99. See Mortimer, *Faith and Power*, p. 353. In an issue of *Le Nouvel Observateur* dated 14 April 1979 (p. 46), Foucault published a "Lettre ouverte à Mehdi Bazargan," reiterating his hope that Iran's new "Islamic government" might yet imbue the "rights of man" with a welcome new spiritual force. Like most such open letters from famous intellectuals to distant potentates, it was a wan prayer.

100. "Inuitle de se soulever?" (1979), loc. cit., p. 1; et, p. 5.

101. Ibid, p. 1; et, p. 5.

102. Ibid., p. 2; et, p. 6. "L'esprit d'un monde sans esprit" (int, 1979), loc. cit., p. 236; et in PPC, p. 219. This is a rare event in Foucault's prose: a passage evoking "light," rather than darkness. It is as if he supposed a people, by facing death in concert, through revolt, somehow miraculously opened themselves to "that distant and lofty space of light" that a quarter century before he had imagined bathing Ellen West, Binswanger's suicidal patient, as she stood, on the threshold of death, in authentic communion with her self.

103. "Inutile de se soulever?" (1979), loc. cit., p. 1; et, p. 5. Cf. Foucault's comments on the "plebs" in "Pouvoirs et stratégies" (int), *Les révoltes logiques*, 4 (Winter 1977), p. 92; et in PKN, p. 138.

104. See Eribon, *Foucault*, p. 296–97; et, pp. 278–79.

105. André Glucksmann, "En horreur de la servitude," *Libération* (30 June–1 July 1984), p. 22. Blandine Barret-Kriegel, "De l'État de police a l'Etat de droit," *Le Monde* (13 October 1989), p. 43, also discusses Foucault's paradoxical impact on young French liberals (such as herself).

106. "Course of January 14, 1976," et in PKN, p. 96. CF (int, 1978), pp. 119–20; et, pp. 180–81. RC, p. 90; et: "War in the Filigree of Peace," p. 17.

107. RC, p. 89; et, p. 17. In a discussion after his Howison lectures at Berkeley in 1980, Foucault had this to say about human rights: "When you are confronted with the totalitarian phenomenon, first everybody can agree that . . . recourse to the [judicial] code, to a legal system, to the reference to human rights is something quite important; but I think that people would agree to say [that this] is just now—what could I say?—a *tactical* recourse. Maybe it's useful, maybe it's possible just now, but I don't think that coming back to juridical structures of government would be the solution of our problems now." I am transcribing from a cassette tape in the collection of the Centre Michel Foucault in Paris, titled "Talk with philosophers, 23 October 1980," c16*. On revolt as the anchor of right, see "Inutile de se soulever?" (1979), loc cit., p. 1; et, p. 5.

108. "The Social Triumph of the Sexual Will" (int), *Christopher Street*, 64 (May 1982), p. 38.

109. Cf. Blandine Barret-Kriegel, "Michel Foucault et l'État de police," in MFP, p. 225. The paradox of the Nietzschean democrat, and his vocation of withholding consent, is

beautifully elaborated by the American philosopher Stanley Cavell in *Conditions Handsome and Unhandsome* (Chicago, 1990), pp. 33–63.

110. "Face aux gouvernements, les droits de l'Homme," a document written and read by Foucault at a press conference in June, 1981, on the plight of the Vietnamese boat people; first printed in *Libération* (30 June–1 July 1984), p. 22.

111. "Qu'est-ce que la critique?" (1978), loc. cit., p. 60.

112. "The Subject and Power," in BSH, p. 209.

113. Ibid., in BSH, p. 222.

114. Ibid., in BSH, p. 212.

115. *Introduction à l'anthropologie de Kant*, Ier tome, pp. 125–26.

CHAPTER 10: THE SCRIPTING OF THE SELF

1. On the labyrinth and the "rediscovered origin," see "Theatricum philosophicum," *Critique*, 282 (November 1970), p. 905; et in LCP, p. 193. Cf. Hervé Guibert, *À l'ami qui ne m'a pas sauvé la vie* (Paris, 1990), p. 35; et: *To the Friend Who Did Not Save My Life*, trans. Linda Coverdale (New York, 1991), p. 22: "In the same way that he subverted in this new work the foundations of sexual consensus, he had begun to dynamite the tunnels of his own labyrinth." Friedrich Nietzsche, *Schopenhauer as Educator*, trans. William Arrowsmith, in *Unmodern Observations*, ed. Arrowsmith (New Haven, 1990), p. 191 (§4).

2. "Preface to *The History of Sexuality*, Volume II," in TFR, pp. 338–39: this text was set aside by Foucault in the spring of 1984, when he composed the preface that actually appears in volume II of the History of Sexuality.

3. "Le philosophe masqué," *Le Monde Dimanche*, 10,945 (6 April 1980), pp. I and XVII; et in PPC, pp. 330, 324.

4. Edmund White told me of Foucault's inability to go out at night in Paris without being mobbed—yet another reason he enjoyed his time in the United States (White interview 12 March 1990). The account given here of American college students and their perception of Foucault is based largely on my own contact with students teaching at various American universities between 1975 and the present.

5. See Michael Bess, "Foucault lecture packs Wheeler," *The Daily Californian* (10 November 1980), p. 15.

6. Transcribed from a tape recording of the first Howison lecture on "Truth and Subjectivity," 20 October 1980.

7. I am quoting from a bootleg transcription of the Howison lectures, corrected against the tape recording: I, pp. 6, 8. Cf. "The Subject and Power," in BSH, p. 208. Foucault's first important public enunciation of his new research interests had occurred in his Collège de France lectures the previous winter: see RC, pp. 123–29; these lectures, however, were almost exclusively devoted to the early Christian understanding of the self, whereas at Berkeley, nine months later, Foucault had broadened his inquiry to include Socrates and Seneca—thinkers he would treat in his next sequence of lectures at the Collège de France.

8. Howison lectures, I, p. 8.

9. Ibid., I, p. 10; II, p. 1. On the need for an ethic for "recent liberation movements," see "On the Genealogy of Ethics: An Overview of Work in Progress" (int, 1983), in TFR, p. 343. Cf. the more deeply skeptical view of the possibility of morality enunciated in MC, pp 338–39; et, p. 328: "Modern thought has never, in fact, been able to propose a morality. . . . since any imperative is lodged within thought and its movement toward the apprehension of the unthought. . . ." A footnote indicates that Foucault here sees Kant as the last classical thinker, since he articulates a universal law of morality—and also as the first modern thinker, since the subject must "give to itself its own law."

10. "On the Genealogy of Ethics: An Overview of Work in Progress" (int, 1983), in TFR, p. 348.

11. Howison lectures, II, p. 2. The saying of the desert saints is quoted in Peter Brown, *The Making of Late Antiquity* (Cambridge, Mass., 1978), p. 92. The confidence of the Stoics

in comparison with the Christians and gnostics is evoked in Hans Jonas, *The Gnostic Religion* (Boston, 1958), p. 283.

12. Howison lectures, II, pp. 5, 7, 3.

13. Ibid., p. 17.

14. RC, p. 128.

15. "Préface à la transgression," *Critique*, 195 (August–September 1963), p. 751; et in LCP, p. 29.

16. "Qu'est-ce qu'un auteur?" *Bulletin de la Société française de philosophie*, 63 (July–September 1969), p. 78; et in LCP, p. 117. Foucault elaborated the link betwen asceticism and writing in a public discussion in 1980 after his Howison lectures: "Modern literature began, I think, when hermeneutics of the self gave place to a kind of *écriture*, of scripting, for instance beginning with Montaigne. . . . Since literature is *in a way* a sacrifice of the self, or is *both* sacrifice of the self *and* the transposition of the self in the order of things, and another time, another light, and so on, so the modern writer is in a sense related and linked and similar to the first Christian ascetics, or the first Christian martyrs. When I say that, of course, it is with pointed irony"—Foucault here laughs; his audience, evidently having no idea what he is talking about, maintains a stony silence. Foucault continues: "I think the same problem of the relation between hermeneutics of the self and the *disappearing* of the self—sacrifice, the negation of the self—is the nucleus of the literary experience of the modern world." I have transcribed Foucault's remarks verbatim from the cassette tape filed in the Centre Michel Foucault under the title "Talk with philosophers 23 October 1980" c16*.

17. Howison lectures, II, p. 19.

18. Ibid., II, p. 20.

19. Ibid., II, p. 20.

20. UP, p. 15; et, p. 9.

21. UP, p. 15, et, p. 9. Cf. the entry on "essay" in the *Oxford English Dictionary*.

22. Leo Bersani, "Pedagogy and Pederasty," *Raritan*, V, 1 (Summer 1985), p. 20.

23. "The Culture of the Self," a lecture given at Berkeley on April 12, 1983; I have transcribed the passage on converting the self from a tape recording of this lecture. Howison lectures, II, p. 8.

24. UP, p. 17; et, p. 11.

25. "Discourse and Truth: The Problematization of *Parrhesia*," Notes to the Seminar given by Foucault at the University of California at Berkeley, Fall Term, 1973, transcribed and edited by Joseph Pearson , p. 2. This is another Foucault bootleg that has circulated in the United States.

26. "Preface to *The History of Sexuality*, Vol. II," in TFR, p. 339. On the reaction of academic specialists in the United States, see David Halperin's comments on Foucault in *One Hundred Years of Homosexuality* (New York, 1990), pp. 62–71: a case in point is Martha Nussbaum, who registered her misgivings in "Affections of the Greeks," *The New York Times Book Review* (10 November 1985), pp. 13–14.

27. For the externals of Foucault's life in these years, see Didier Eribon, *Michel Foucault* (Paris, 1989), pp. 329–55; et: *Michel Foucault*, trans. Betsy Wing (Cambridge, Mass., 1991), pp. 309–32.

28. For a more detailed rendering of Foucault's political activity in these years, see Eribon, *Foucault*, pp. 314–28; et, pp. 296–308. This is not, alas, one of the better chapters in Eribon's book: it leaves a misleading impression, in my view, of the real complexity and ambiguity of Foucault's links with the Socialist party. And some future biographer will want to investigate more fully the Académie Tarnier, the study group that Foucault organized with Bernard Kouchner, as Foucault's last experiment in politics as a vehicle for "critique." It is perhaps worth noting, finally, that one member of this study group was André Glucksmann—making him perhaps the most prominent figure (apart from Daniel Defert) to have been an ally at every stage of Foucault's political odyssey after May '68.

29. "Michel Foucault, An Interview: Sex, Power and the Politics of Identity" (int, 1982),

The Advocate, 400 (7 August 1984), p. 27. "De l'amitié comme mode de vie," *Gai pied*, 25 (April 1981), p. 39; et in FLI, p. 206.

30. "Truth, Power, Self" (int, 1982), in Luther H. Martin, Huck Gutman, and Patrick H. Hutton, eds., *Technologies of the Self* (Amherst, Mass., 1988), p. 9.

31. See "De l'amitié comme mode de vie" (int, 1981), loc. cit., pp. 38–39; et in FLI, pp. 203–09. "The Social Triumph of the Sexual Will" (int), *Christopher Street*, 64 (Fall 1982), pp. 36–41. And see also "On the Genealogy of Ethics: An Overview of Work in Progress" (int, 1983), in TFR, p. 345. Most of Foucault's comments about friendship occur in the context of discussing new modes of being gay; but he also refers in various public lectures, perhaps most pointedly in his final lecture course at the Collège de France, to the philosophical value of the friend as someone to confide in. Friendship, of course, played an important philosophical role in the Stoic conduct of life, as witness Seneca's famous correspondence with Lucilius: in these letters, the Roman sage was at pains to admonish Lucilius on the value of friendship, especially for those men "who have shrunk so far into dark corners that objects in bright daylight seem quite blurred to them." See Seneca, *Letters from a Stoic*, trans. Robin Campbell (London, 1969), p. 36 (*Epistulae Morales ad Lucilium*, III).

32. Anonymous interview, 22 March 1990.

33. For Foucault's crucial friendship with Guibert, see chapter eleven.

34. See Badinter's remarks in a roundtable discussion on the death penalty, "L'angoisse de juger," *Le Nouvel Observateur*, 655 (30 May 1977), pp. 92–126; et in FLI, pp. 176, 169: "How could [a humane judge] discard the idea that one was going to change the criminal by bringing him back to the norm? What else was there to do? Throw him into a hole for twenty years? It's not possible any longer. Cut him in half? It's not possible. What then? Reintegrate him by normalizing him." Anything else, concluded Badinter, would be "a frightful regression." Another sign of how remote Badinter's political interests and convictions were from Foucault's: after the philosopher's death, the lawyer collaborated with his wife (Elisabeth Badinter, a well-known scholar and feminist in France) on a study of Condorcet, the pioneering liberal and Enlightenment *philosophe*.

35. Robert Badinter interview, 29 March 1990.

36. "De la nécessité de mettre un terme à toute peine," *Libération*, 185 (18 December 1981), p. 12.

37. Badinter interview, 29 March 1990.

38. Anonymous interviews, 22 March 1990, 21 May 1991.

39. This, and all subsequent Badinter quotes, come from my interview with him on 29 March 1990.

40. See: "Un cours inédit," *Magazine Littéraire*, 207 (May 1984), pp. 35–39; et in PPC, pp. 86–95 (a partial transcription of Foucault's lecture at the Collège de France on 5 January 1983; Foucault went on to talk, in very erudite terms, about the circumstances in which Kant's essay came to be written). "What is Enlightenment?" (1983), in TFR, esp. p. 32. The question "Who are 'we' now?," I have transcribed from Foucault's lecture on "The Culture of the Self" at Berkeley on 12 April 1983, which opened with comments on Kant's essay, before taking up Socrates and Seneca. Foucault's lifelong fascination with Rorschach tests is mentioned in Eribon, *Foucault*, pp. 62–63; et, p. 43. It is worth noting that Kant's essay in these years became a central medium through which Foucault worked out his own ambivalent relationship to modern philosophy. When he first talked about Kant's essay in public, in 1978, he had gone out of his way to insist that he, himself, was *not* a philosopher (see "Qu'est-ce que la critique?," *Bulletin de la Société française de philosophie*, 84, 2 [April–June, 1990], p. 41); but five years later, he spoke in quite different terms, suggesting in fact that his own work should be situated in the tradition of modern philosophy that Kant inaugurates. The idea that modern philosophy is asking the question "What is happening right now?," dates back to the same period in Foucault's life: see "Non au sexe roi," *Le Nouvel Observateur*, 644 (12 March 1977), p. 113; et in PPC, p. 121.

41. See "What is Enlightenment?" (1983), in TFR, pp. 32–50. This text originates in a

lecture that Foucault delivered at least once, in the fall of 1983 at a philosophy seminar at Berkeley: see Hans Sluga, "Foucault, the Author, and the Discourse," *Inquiry*, 28, p. 403. Paul Rabinow says that Foucault had a personal hand in selecting materials for *The Foucault Reader*, which Rabinow was editing for Pantheon books; and that Foucault gave him the text of "What is Enlightenment?" expressly for inclusion in this volume (Rabinow interview, 26 August 1991). Just as this book was going to press, I obtained a copy of Foucault's original French text; fortunately, the English translation by Catherine Porter is excellent, and I have slightly modified only two passages: see note 124 in chapter eight, and note 45 in this chapter.

42. "What is Enlightenment?" (1983), in TFR, pp. 34, 35. Immanuel Kant, "What is Enlightenment?," trans. Lewis White Beck, in Kant, *On History*, ed. Beck (Indianapolis, Ind., 1963), p. 3.

43. "What is Enlightenment?" (1983), in TFR, pp. 38, 39. "L'éthique du souci de soi comme pratique de liberté" (int), *Concordia*, 6 (1984), p. 100; et in TFF, p. 4. Pierre Hadot, "Réflexions sur la notion de 'culture de soi,' " in MFP, p. 267. Hadot's remarks are revealing: along with Paul Veyne and Peter Brown, Hadot inspired Foucault to take the approach that he did; furthermore, Hadot deciphered the link to dandyism without having read Foucault's text on Kant's essay. (I wish to thank Arnold I. Davidson for sharing his extensive knowledge of Hadot's work, and of Hadot's personal links with Foucault: see also Davidson's short essay, "Spiritual Exercises and Ancient Philosophy: An Introduction to Pierre Hadot," *Critical Inquiry*, 16 [Spring 1990], pp. 480–82.)

44. "What is Enlightenment?" (1983), in TFR, pp. 42, 41. Charles Baudelaire, "The Painter of Modern Life," in *The Painter of Modern Life and Other Essays*, trans. Jonathan Mayne (London, 1964), pp. 27, 28, 29 ("IX, The Dandy").

45. "What is Enlightenment?" (1983), in TFR, p. 45: I am translating "*franchissement*" here as "transcendence," while Porter prefers "transgression"—a plausible choice, though Foucault had stopped using the French word "*transgression*" after criticizing Georges Bataille in *La volonté de savoir*. The definition of freedom as the ability "to pass beyond each and every specified limit" is, of course, Kant's own: see *Critique of Pure Reason*, A317/B374.

46. Charles Baudelaire, "The Painter of Modern Life," loc. cit., p. 12 ("IV, Modernity"). "What is Enlightenment?" (1983), in TFR, pp. 39, 40, 41, 42 (emphasis added in the passage about death). For Baudelaire's own struggle with fantasies of cruelty, torture, and death, see the poet's famous journal, "My Heart Laid Bare," discussed in chapter three.

47. "What is Enlightenment?" (1983), in TFR, pp. 46, 43, 42, 46. Cf. "Le philosophe masqué" (int, 1980), loc. cit., p. I; et in PPC, p. 326: "I can't help but dream about a critique that would not try to judge, but bring an oeuvre, a book, a sentence, an idea to life; it would light fires, watch the grass grow, listen to the wind, and catch the sea-foam in the breeze and scatter it. It would multiply, not judgments, but signs of existence; it would summon them, drag them from their sleep. Perhaps it would invent them some-times—all the better. All the better."

48. See Jürgen Habermas, *The Philosophical Discourse of Modernity: Twelve Lectures*, trans. Frederick Lawrence (Cambridge, Mass. 1987), p. xix: "I delivered the first four lectures at the Collège de France in Paris in March 1983."

49. Jürgen Habermas interview, 16 April 1991. Cf. D.E. (Didier Eribon), "Habermas le 'moderne,' " *Libération* (9 March 1983), p. 33.

50. Jean Lacouture, "Trois images de Michel Foucault," *Libération* (26 June 1984), p. 6. The episode with Ricoeur is recounted in Eribon, *Foucault*, p. 202; et, pp. 189–90.

51. Jürgen Habermas, "Summation and Response," trans. Matesich, *Continuum*, 8, 1–2 (Spring–Summer 1970), p. 132. This is an early formulation that (as Habermas came to see) may be misleading, since by itself the passage quoted can be understood as implying a real temporal expectation rather than a purely idealized supposition. For an authoritative study of the nuances in Habermas's "practical hypothesis" of "an ideal speech situation," see Thomas McCarthy, *The Critical Theory of Jürgen Habermas* (Cambridge, Mass., 1978), esp. pp. 291–310.

52. CF (int, 1978), pp. 71–72; et, pp. 117–18. Cf. "Um welchen Preis sagt die Vernuft

die Wahrheit?," *Spuren*, 1–2 (1983): et in PPC, p. 26: "Now, obviously, if I had been familiar with the Frankfurt School, I would not have said a number of stupid things that I did say and I would have avoided many of the detours which I made while trying to pursue my own humble path." Foucault once told Martin Jay that it was a reading of the 1976 French translation of Jay's classic study of the Frankfurt School, *The Dialectical Imagination*, that spurred Foucault's belated interest in Horkheimer and Adorno; Marcuse's work, by contrast, he already knew. (Martin Jay interview, 26 September 1989.) Foucault told Habermas directly of his admiration for *The Dialectic of Enlightenment* by Max Horkheimer and Theodor Adorno—a central work in the canon of critical theory (Habermas interview, 16 April 1991). Foucault also evidently knew Habermas's inaugural lecture at Frankfurt University, delivered in 1965 under the title "Knowledge and Human Interests" (and reprinted as an appendix to the English translation of the book of the same name: see Jürgen Habermas, *Knowledge and Human Interests*, trans. Jeremy J. Shapiro [Boston, 1971], pp. 301–17). In his first Howison lecture, Foucault refers to Habermas by name (and, implicitly, to this text), explaining that, beyond the three areas of human endeavor analyzed by Habermas (which, as Foucault describes them, involve respectively "techniques of production," "techniques of signification," and "techniques of domination") he wishes to analyze a fourth area, involving "techniques of the self." See the Howison lectures, I, p. 7. Foucault rarely built upon the work of a contemporary philosopher—so this reference to Habermas, trivial though it may seem, is not without significance.

53. CF (int, 1978), V, p. 5; cf. et, p. 121.

54. "L'éthique du souci de soi comme pratique de liberté" (int, 1984), loc. cit., p. 114; et in TFF, p. 18.

55. Jürgen Habermas, "Modernity versus Postmodernity," trans. Seyla Ben-Habib, *New German Critique*, 22 (Winter 1981), p. 13 (this is a translation of Habermas's Adorno Prize lecture, delivered in Frankfurt in September of 1980; this talk became one basis for the lectures he later delivered at the Collège de France). Habermas, *The Philosophical Discourse of Modernity*, pp. 275–76. Nancy Fraser, "Foucault on Modern Power: Empirical Insights and Normative Confusions," in Fraser, *Unruly Practices* (Minneapolis, Minn., 1989), p. 29; Habermas himself cites this passage with evident approval in one of his later lectures on Foucault: see Habermas, *The Philosophical Discourse of Modernity*, p. 284. In my conversations with one of Foucault's closest associates at the Collège de France, this associate emphasized how the issue of Habermas had come to the fore for Foucault at Berkeley. The literature on the "debate" (if that is the right word) between Foucault and Habermas is large, and growing: an especially astute analysis is offered by Thomas McCarthy in "The Critique of Impure Reason: Foucault and the Frankfurt School," *Political Theory*, 18, 3 (August 1990), pp. 437–69; and also by Richard J. Bernstein in "Foucault: Critique as a Philosophic Ethos," in Axel Honneth et al., eds., *Zwischenbetrachtungen, Im Prozess der Aufklärung: Jürgen Habermas zum 60. Geburtstag* (Frankfort, 1989), pp. 395–425.

56. "Space, Knowledge and Power" (int), *Skyline* (March 1982), pp. 18–19; in TFR, pp. 248–49.

57. The account of this first lecture is drawn from Eribon, "Habermas le 'moderne'," *Libération* (9 March 1983), p. 33.

58. Ibid. The article goes on to attack Habermas as a narrow pedant who has betrayed the original promise of the Frankfurt School. It is rumored in Paris that Foucault himself had a hand in Eribon's acidulous account; which, given the friendship between the philosopher and the reporter (and given Foucault's penchant for being wickedly devious), is not impossible.

59. Though Habermas, with characteristic honesty, would later concede that, in his encounter with Foucault, "perhaps I did not understand him well." See Jürgen Habermas, "Taking Aim at the Heart of the Present," in FCR, p. 103.

60. Habermas interview, 16 April 1991.

61. "Politics and Ethics: An Interview" (1983), in TFR, p. 373.

62. Ibid., in TFR, p. 374.

63. Habermas interview, 16 April 1991. During these talks, in a gesture that reveals

how much their conversations were framed by issues raised, most pressingly, in an *American* context, Foucault invited Habermas to join him and some American colleagues in Berkeley for a private conference in 1984, to mark the bicentennial of Kant's essay, "What is Enlightenment?" with a renewed debate of the question.

64. Habermas interview, 16 April 1991. A terse summary of Foucault's own final response appears in "L'éthique du souci de soi comme pratique de liberté" (int, 1984), loc. cit., p. 114; et in TFF, p. 18: "Relations of power are not something bad in themselves, from which one must free one's self. . . . The problem is not of trying to dissolve them in the utopia of a perfectly transparent communication"—Foucault is explicitly referring here to Habermas—"but to give one's self the rules of law, the techniques of management, and also the ethics, the *ethos*, the practice of self, which would allow these games of power to be played with a minimum of domination." ("Domination" Foucault in this context defines as reified and asymmetrical power relations; by this criterion, S/M, for example, is not an instance of domination, since the power relations in this consensual game are fluid and reversible.) Habermas's final verdict is delivered in *The Philosophical Discourse of Modernity*, p. 294: "His theory tries to rise above . . . pseudo-sciences to a more rigorous objectivity, and in doing so gets caught all the more hopelessly in the trap of a presentist historiography, which sees itself compelled to a relativist self-denial and can give no account of the normative foundations of its own rhetoric."

65. "Le combat de la chasteté," *Communications*, 35 (May 1982), p. 24: et: "The Battle for Chastity," trans. Anthony Foster, in Philippe Ariès and André Bejin, eds., *Western Sexuality* (Oxford, 1985), p. 24. "Rêver de ses plaisirs: sur l'onirocritique d'Artemidore," *Recherches sur la philosophie et le langage*, no. 3 (1983); incorporated into Part One of *Le souci de soi*: see SS, p. 29; et, p. 16. VS, p. 211; et, p. 159. RE, p. 114; et, p. 69. The characterization of Foucault's spirit in these years comes from Peter Brown, *The Body and Society* (New York, 1988), p. xvii.

66. Gilles Deleuze, *Foucault* (Paris, 1987), p. 127; et: *Foucault*, trans. Sean Hand, p. 119. Gilles Deleuze, "Fendre les choses, fendre les mots" (int), in Deleuze, *Pourparlers* (Paris, 1990), p. 135.

67. "L'écriture de soi," *Corps écrit*, 5 (1983), pp. 6–7.

68. Daniel Defert interview, 25 March 1990. Paul Veyne's remarks are quoted in Eribon, *Foucault*, p. 349; et, p. 325. According to Defert, Foucault's journal in the final days of his life is filled with passages from Franz Kafka—a revealing though unsurprising writer to be studying. For Foucault, after all, every conceivable society was fated to function, openly or covertly, as an engine of almost unspeakable suffering, much like the one Kafka had depicted in his short story, "In the Penal Colony"—a hideous instrument of mnemotechnics, inscribing The Law in blood, writing arbitrary and baffling sentences on the bodies of its hapless victims, forcing them to unriddle what sentence they had received by reading wounds so complicated and so deep that they became intelligible, if at all, only on the threshold of death.

69. See "L'écriture de soi" (1983), loc. cit., pp. 3–5, 23. "Le combat de la chasteté" (1982), loc. cit., p. 25; et, p. 25. For the passage Foucault reproduces, see Saint Athanasius, *The Life of Saint Antony*, trans. Robert T. Meyer (New York, 1950), pp. 67–68 (§55).

70. "L'écriture de soi" (1983), loc. cit., p. 4.

71. Emphasis added. I have transcribed Foucault's remarks from the cassette tape filed in the Centre Michel Foucault under the title "Talk with philosophers 23 October, 1980," c16*.

72. UP, p. 14; et, p. 8. James Bernauer points out the link between Foucault's interpretation of Christian self-sacrifice and his own quest to get free of himself in "Michel Foucault's Ecstatic Thinking," in TFF, p. 69.

73. FD, pp. 29, 30, 31; et, pp. 19, 20, 21 (emphasis added). Cf. "La prose d'Acteon," *La Nouvelle Revue Française*, 135 (March 1964), p. 444; et: "The Prose of Acteon," in Pierre Klossowksi, *The Baphomet*, trans. Sophie Hawkes (Hygiene, Colorado, 1988), p. xxii: "Dualism and gnosticism, in spite of all the denials and persecutions, have weighed heavily on

the Christian conception of Evil. . . . But what if the Devil, what if the Other, were the Same? And if the Temptation were not one episode in a great antagonism, but the meager insinuation of the Double?" As should be clear by now, I take *all* of Foucault's work to be an effort to issue a license for exploring this *daimonic* possibility—and also as a vehicle for expressing, "fictively," his own Nietzschean understanding of this harrowing vision of a gnosis beyond good and evil, glimpsed at the limits of experience.

74. "La bibliothèque fantastique," originally published in German in 1964, reprinted, slightly abridged, in French as the introduction to the 1971 Livre de Poche edition of Gustave Flaubert, *La tentation de Saint Antoine*, pp. 8, 15; et in LCP, p. 89, 95. Gustave Flaubert, *The Temptation of Saint Anthony*, trans. Kitty Mrosovsky (London, 1983), p. 67 (I).

75. Veyne, quoted in Eribon, *Foucault*, p. 349; et, p. 325.

76. As if to point out the possible use of the Temptation of Saint Anthony as an allegorical fragment in an autobiographical script, see FD, 30n, where Foucault remarks that some experts believe that Bosch, in rendering the bodiless face tempting Saint Anthony in the Lisbon triptych, painted a portrait of himself.

77. Hans Sluga interview, 28 September 1989.

78. Hans Sluga interview, 28 September 1989. Sluga recalls the date of the AIDS conversation as 1981, though Foucault was not formally in Berkeley that year; the fall of 1980, when he was at Berkeley, is too early for such a conversation.

79. UP, p. 14; et, p. 8. CF (int, 1978), V, p. 5; cf. et, p. 122. VS, 14; et, p. 7.

80. Friedrich Nietzsche, *Daybreak*, trans. R. J. Hollingdale (Cambridge, 1982), p. 204 (§501). Cited (and glossed) by Foucault in "Nietzsche, la généalogie, l'histoire," in *Hommage à Jean Hyppolite* (Paris, 1971), p. 171; et in LCP, p. 163. It is worth comparing Foucault's apparent response to the AIDS epidemic with Georges Bataille's response to the outbreak of World War II, recorded in the second volume of his *Summa Atheologica*, entitled *Guilty*— a Nietzschean journal as pitilessly self-flagellating, in its way, as anything one will find in the early church fathers. "I wanted to accept responsibility for this, myself," Bataille wrote some days after Germany had invaded Poland (and put an end to his plan to offer a human sacrifice to Dionysus): "Sitting on the edge of the bed at night," he writes, explaining how he imaginted expiating his bad conscience in 1939, "I practiced, determined to become a war zone myself. The urge to sacrifice and the urge to be sacrificed meshed like gears when a drive-shaft starts up and teeth interlock." See Georges Bataille, *Guilty*, trans. Bruce Boone (Venice, Calif., 1988), p. 15 (I, i. "Nighttime").

81. "Nietzsche, la généalogie, l'histoire" (1971), loc. cit., p. 171; et in LCP, pp. 163–64. Friedrich Nietzsche, *Beyond Good and Evil*, trans. Walter Kaufmann (New York, 1966), p. 49 (§39): I have quoted Kaufmann's English, which is much closer to the sense of the German text than Foucault's French (which, rendered into more or less literal English, has Nietzsche saying that "to perish from absolute knowledge may well form part of the foundation of being"—*être* being the French rendering of Nietzsche's German term, *Dasein*, which Kaufmann translates as "existence"). The previous citations from Nietzsche come from *Thus Spoke Zarathustra*, III, §13; and *The Gay Science*, §283.

82. "On the Genealogy of Ethics: An Overview of Work in Progress" (int, 1983) in TFR, p. 341.

83. Ibid., in TFR, p. 341.

84. Ibid., in TFR, p. 342.

85. UP, p. 33; et, p. 26.

86. UP, p. 34; et, p. 27.

87. UP, p. 24; et, p. 27.

88. UP, pp. 34–35; et, pp. 27–28. For all of these categories, cf. "On the Genealogy of Ethics: An Overview of Work in Progress" (int, 1983), in TFR, pp. 352–55. The secondary literature in English on Foucault's final "ethics" is surprisingly meager. But see Arnold I. Davidson, "Archeology, Genealogy, Ethics," in FCR, pp. 221–33.

89. "On the Genealogy of Ethics: An Overview of Work in Progress" (int, 1983), in TFR, p. 348.

90. Ibid., p. 353. Maurice Blanchot, *The Space of Literature*, trans. Ann Smock (Lincoln, Neb., 1982), p. 54.

91. UP, p. 15; et, p. 9.

92. UP, p. 14; et, p. 8. Howison lectures, II, p. 3: In evoking the "forgotten sparkle," Foucault is speaking of "the gnostic self" described in the "Manichean texts" of Thomas the Apostle. Cf. Kant's inscrutable freedom as a "kind of glimmering" that Foucault says he has "been trying to make appear" in his works (in "Qu'est-ce que la critique?" [1978], loc. cit., p. 56). By approaching Foucault's later work with an interest in its possible affinities with Sufi spiritual exercises, Christian Jambet also brings out its strain of mysticism: see Jambet, "Constitution du sujet et pratique spirituelle," in MFP, pp. 271–86.

93. D. A. Miller interview, 11 April 1991.

94. Ibid.

95. The immunologist, Anthony Pinching of St. Mary's Hospital in London, is quoted in Mirko D. Grmek, *History of AIDS*, trans. Russell C. Maulitz and Jacalyn Duffin (Princeton, 1990), p. 168.

96. Quoted in Randy Shilts, *And the Band Played On* (New York, 1987), p. 250. In Part V of his book, "Battle Lines: January–June 1983," Shilts offers a vivid though problematic account of the debate over AIDS within the gay community in these months; see my comments in note 43 in chapter one.

97. Another bellwether was Larry Kramer's call to arms, "1,112 and Counting," published in the *New York Native* issue dated 14–27 March 1983, and subsequently distributed and widely discussed in the Bay Area as well. In *And the Band Played On*, Randy Shilts leaves a somewhat misleading impression of the gay community's own "safe sex" initiatives (see, e.g., p. 239). As Douglas Crimp has written—and my own limited research suggests that his assertion is plausible—"gay people invented safe sex. We knew that the alternatives—monogamy and abstinence—were *unsafe*, unsafe in the latter case because people do not abstain from sex, and if you only tell them 'just say no,' they will have unsafe sex. We were able to invent safe sex because we have always known that sex is not, in an epidemic or not, limited to penetrative sex. Our promiscuity taught us many things, not only about the pleasures of sex, but about the great multiplicity of those pleasures. It is that psychic preparation, that experimentation, that conscious work on our own sexualities that has allowed many of us to change our sexual behaviors—something that brutal 'behavioral therapies' tried unsuccessfully for over a century to force us to do—very quickly and very dramatically." See Douglas Crimp, "How to Have Promiscuity in an Epidemic," in Crimp, ed., *AIDS: Cultural Analysis, Cultural Criticism* (Cambridge, Mass., 1988), pp. 252–53.

98. Miller interview, 11 April 1991.

99. Seneca, "On Providence," trans. John W. Basore, in Seneca, *Moral Essays* (Cambridge, Mass., 1928), p. 45. So far as I know, Foucault never discussed this passage. But he *did* discuss the Stoic practice of meditating on one's own death as "a manner of making death real within life." See RC, p. 164 (summarizing the course given at the Collège de France in the winter of 1982).

100. Seneca, "On Providence," loc. cit., p. 45.

101. Ibid., p. 46.

102. RE, p. 113; et, p. 69.

103. "Conversation" (int) in Gerard Courant, ed., *Werner Schroeter* (Paris, 1982), p. 45.

104. Daniel Defert, " 'Plus on est honteux, plus on avoue,' " *Libération* (31 October–1 November 1987), p. 2.

105. The account that follows comes from Philip Horvitz, "Don't Cry for Me Academia," *Jimmy & Lucy's House of 'K'*, 2 (August 1984), pp. 78–80; from the notes Horvitz took at the time of his encounter with Foucault; and also from several conversations with Horvitz, including one face-to-face interview on 29 September 1989.

106. Horvitz, "Don't Cry for Me Academia," p. 78.

107. I am largely transcribing Horvitz's notes. My use of quotation is governed by Horvitz's own: "Everything in quotes is actually a direct quote," he wrote me (letter to the

author, 11 August 1987); that is, a "direct quote," to the best of his recollection, as expressed in the note to himself he wrote the day of his meeting with the philosopher.

108. This question—a key moment, obviously—Horvitz omitted from his published memoir of the incident; though five years later, having forgotten that he had omitted it, he could not believe he had left it out. (Horvitz interview, 29 September 1989.)

109. Horvitz, "Don't Cry for Me Academia," p. 80.

CHAPTER 11: THE SECRETS OF A MAN

1. For another account of Foucault's final days, see Didier Eribon, *Michel Foucault* (Paris, 1989), pp. 347–53; et: *Michel Foucault*, trans. Betsy Wing (Cambridge, Mass, 1991), pp. 324–27.

2. Hervé Guibert, *À l'ami qui ne m'a pas sauvé la vie* (Paris, 1990), pp. 94, 100, 96; et: *To the Friend Who Did Not Save My Life*, trans. Linda Coverdale (New York, 1991), pp. 85, 89, 86. The general characterization in this chapter of Foucault's dying days and of his relationship with Guibert is drawn from several sources: first, interviews with several associates, above all Edmund White and Raymond Bellour, who knew both Foucault and Guibert; second (and there is an evident circularity here that cannot be avoided, for reasons I hope become clear in the course of this chapter), Hervé Guibert's own public interviews and fictions, above all *À l'ami*; and last but not least, Bellour's incisive (and persuasive) comments on the implicit "pact" between Foucault and Guibert, in his review of the novel, "Trompe-la-mort," *Magazine Littéraire* (April 1990), pp. 54–56. Guibert himself refused to be interviewed for my book.

3. Guibert, *À l'ami*, p. 17; et, p. 9.

4. Didier Eribon, "Hervé Guibert et son double," *Le Nouvel Observateur* (22 March 1991), p. 75 (the novel was *Les chiens*, or "The Dogs").

5. Hervé Guibert interviewed by Bernard Pivot on "Apostrophes," Antenne 2, 16 March 1990. (Thanks to Daniel Charbonnier for transcribing for me the relevant parts of this interview.) Cf. Guibert, *À l'ami*, p. 34; et, p. 26.

6. "What is Enlightenment?" (1983), in TFR, p. 41 (quoting Baudelaire). Also see "La pensée, l'émotion," in *Duane Michals: Photographies de 1958 à 1982* (Paris, 1982), p. iii, et p. ix: "I love forms of work that do not develop like an oeuvre, but rather open themselves up because they are drawn from experiences: Magritte, Bob Wilson, *Under the Volcano*, *The Death of Maria Malibran*, and, of course, H.G."—i.e., Hervé Guibert. Defert recalls that Foucault used to say of Guibert, with a laugh: " 'True things never happen to him—only false things!' " (Defert interview 25 March 1990.)

7. Foucault to Guibert, 28 July 1983, reprinted in Hervé Guibert, "L'autre journal d'Hervé Guibert," *L'Autre Journal*, (December 1985), p. 5.

8. François Jonquet, "Vie à credit," *Globe* (April 1990), p. 44. Guibert, *À l'ami*, p. 97; et, p. 87.

9. The photograph appears in *Michel Foucault: Une histoire de la verité* (Paris, 1985), pp. 112–13.

10. Guibert, *À l'ami*, pp. 26–27, 98; et, pp. 18–19, 88. "Un système fini face à une demande infinie" (int), in *Sécurité social: l'enjeu* (Paris, 1983), p. 63; et in PPC, p. 177.

11. For a description in English of these last lectures, see Thomas Flynn, "Foucault as Parrhesiast: His Last Course at the Collège de France (1984)," in TFF, pp. 102–18.

12. "What is Enlightenment?" (1983), in TFR, pp. 41–42. "The Subject and Power" (1982), in BSH, p. 214. VS, p. 79; et, p. 59.

13. "An Interview" (1982), in PPC, p. 14.

14. At Berkeley in the fall of 1983, Foucault in his seminar broached many of the themes he would explore the following winter at the Collège de France, but without such a strongly autobiographical aura: see "Discourse and Truth: The Problematization of *Parrhesia*," ed. Joseph Pearson, an unpublished and unauthorized transcription of a tape-recording of

Foucault's lectures to this seminar. In what follows, I will draw from Foucault's remarks about Cynicism to this seminar, as well as from his last lectures in the Collège.

15. Collège de France lecture, 15 February 1984 (I wish to thank Michael Behrent for transcribing this and the other lectures). At Berkeley the previous fall, Foucault had closed his seminar by pointing out that Socrates and those who came after represented "the roots of what we could call the 'critical' tradition in the West." See "Discourse and Truth," p. 114.

16. Collège de France lecture, 15 February 1984.

17. Plato, *Phaedo*, 67a. For the complicated and profoundly ambivalent relationship between Nietzsche and Socrates, see Alexander Nehamas, *Nietzsche: Life as Literature* (Cambridge, Mass., 1985), pp. 24–34.

18. "Discourse and Truth," p. 77.

19. Ibid., pp. 78, 79.

20. Ibid., p. 77.

21. Ibid, pp. 86, 88. Cf. Maurice Blanchot on "Le chant des Sirènes," in *Le livre à venir* (Paris, 1959), pp. 9–37.

22. The "tradition" of Cynicism is an explicit topic of the Collège de France lecture given on 29 February 1984; and Foucault added some names to his idiosyncratic genealogy at the outset of the following session, on 7 March 1984 (in this context, Foucault also mentions the work of André Glucksmann, who in his 1981 book *Cynisme et passion* laid claim to a very similar sort of intellectual patrimony). In his final Collège de France lecture, delivered on 28 March 1984, Foucault talked at some length about the relationship between Cynicism and Christianity, suggesting that early Christian asceticism was a fusion of Cynical techniques of the self with a Platonic ontology, replacing the Cynic's stress on elaborating, through a natural way of life, an "other world" (*autre monde*), beyond artificial social norms, with the Platonic hope of communing with a supernatural world, entirely beyond our own earthly one (*monde autre*).

23. For Diogenes, see Diogenes Laertius, *Lives of Eminent Philosophers*, trans. R. D. Hicks (Cambridge, Mass., 1929), VI, 23, 41, 54. The phrases about an "other world" vs. living an "other life" are Foucault's own, from the Collège de France lecture delivered on 14 March 1984.

24. Diogenes Laertius, *Lives of Eminent Philosophers*, VI, 71. Foucault analyzed the meaning of the Delphic oracle in the Collège de France lecture delivered on 14 March 1984. The political character of "le roi anti-roi" Foucault discussed in the lecture delivered on 21 March 1984. In his legendary encounter with Alexander, Diogenes says, "Stand out of my way, you are blocking the sun."

25. Diogenes Laertius, *Lives of Eminent Philosophers*, VI, 69. Foucault discussed Cynical views on incest and cannibalism in his Collège de France lecture of 14 March 1984. He adverts to "the scandalous gesture" of Diogenes masturbating in the marketplace twice in the text of the History of Sexuality: see UP, p. 64; et, p. 54; and SS, p. 164; et, p. 139.

26. The quote is from Foucault's Collège de France lecture of 14 March 1984. In the course of this lecture, he analyzes Cynicism as a "bringing to the limit" of the traditional understanding of living a "true life."

27. Epictetus, *The Discourses as Reported by Arrian*, trans. W. A. Oldfather (Cambridge, Mass., 1935), III, xxii, 16.

28. "L'éthique du souci de soi comme pratique de liberté" (int), *Concordia*, 6 (1984), p. 110; et in TFF, p. 15 (emphasis added).

29. Samuel Beckett, *The Unnameable*, in *Three Novels*, trans. Samuel Bowles, with Beckett (New York, 1965), p. 414. The same passage figures prominently in the beginning of Foucault's inaugural lecture at the Collège de France: see OD, p. 8; et, p. 215.

30. Beckett, *The Unnameable*, pp. 414, 386. Foucault, UP, p. 14; et, p. 8.

31. Daniel Defert interview 25 March 1990. On the inescapable importance to Foucault himself of his own childhood experiences, compare his gnomic comment during his LSD epiphany in Death Valley: "We must go home again."

32. For the composition of "Les secrets d'un homme," see Guibert's 1990 interview with Jonquet, "Vie à credit," *Globe*, p. 44.

33. Hervé Guibert, "La vie sida," *Libération* (1 March 1990), p. 20. Didier Eribon has said to me that the novel is, so far he can determine, truthful—an accurate account of what actually happened to Foucault in his final months. This is the impression, as well, of Edmund White. Even Daniel Defert, who (as the character Stephane) is portrayed very uncharitably in the novel, volunteered that despite many (mostly unspecified) factual errors (for an example of one specific "error," see note 48 in chapter one), the novel's "interpretations are not so bad." The specific details about the death and burial in the short story, by contrast (as Eribon emphasized), are often pure fantasy—naturally casting into doubt the verisimilitude of the "secrets" discussed later in this chapter.

34. Hervé Guibert, "Les secrets d'un homme," in *Mauve le Vierge* (Paris, 1988), pp. 103–4; et: "A Man's Secrets," trans. Arthur Goldhammer, *Grand Street*, 39 (1991), pp. 67–68. Cf. Guibert, *À l'ami*, p. 100; et, p. 90.

35. Guibert, "Les secrets," p. 105; et, p. 68.

36. Friedrich Nietzsche, *Beyond Good and Evil*, trans. Walter Kaufmann (New York, 1966), p. 162 (§231). According to Foucault's American friend Simeon Wade (interview 3 October 1989), Magritte's *Le château des Pyrénées* was one of Foucault's favorite paintings by the artist, and he was thrilled to be able to see it, during a visit to New York in 1975, in the personal collection of Harry Torczyner (who had been an adviser and friend of Magritte's). See also Wade, *Foucault in California* (unpublished ms., 1990), p. 51.

37. Guibert, "Les secrets," pp. 105–6; et, p. 68.

38. Ibid., p. 106; et, p. 68.

39. Ibid., p. 106; et, pp. 68–69.

40. Friedrich Nietzsche, *Philosophy in the Tragic Age of the Greeks*, trans. Marianne Cowan (South Bend, Ind., 1962), "A Later Preface," p. 25.

41. Paul Rabinow recalled Foucault telling the amputation story; interview 26 September 1989.

42. See SP, pp. 9–11, 64, 66–67, 75; et, pp. 3–5, 61, 63, 73. Also see NC, p. 175; et, p. 171—where Foucault links Bichat and (without mentioning him by name) Sade.

43. All of these details are drawn from André Gide, ed., *La Séquestrée de Poitiers* (Paris, 1930), see esp. pp. 10–15, 31.

44. *La Séquestrée de Poitiers* appeared as part of a Gallimard series, edited by Gide, called "Ne jugez pas"—it was planned, apparently, to document abuses of the legal code. *La Séquestrée de Poitiers* was first published in an edition limited to fifteen hundred numbered copies, and is known among book collectors as among the rarest (and most rarely read) of Gide's works.

45. See Eribon, *Foucault*, pp. 22–23; et, p. 6.

46. "An Interview" (1982) in PPC, p. 7. It is worth comparing the possible role played by the Nazi death camps in Foucault's experience with the role they certainly did play in Alain Robbe-Grillet's experience: see chapter five.

47. Foucault, "Preface," to Gilles Deleuze and Félix Guattari, *Anti-Oedipus*, trans. Robert Hurley, Mark Seem, and Helen R. Lane (New York, 1977), p. xiii.

48. The most important of Guibert's interviews about his books appeared in the *Libération* and *Globe* articles cited above. Guibert died in Paris on 27 December 1991.

49. All quotes here and in what follows come from a transcription of Guibert's interview with Bernard Pivot on *Apostrophes*, 16 March 1990.

50. RR, p. 12; et, p. 5.

51. RR, pp. 8–9; et, pp. 2–3.

52. This is Raymond Bellour's conjecture: see "Trompe-la-mort," *Magazine Littéraire* (April 1990), p. 56.

53. "Le retour de la morale" (int), *Les Nouvelles* (28 June–5 July 1984), p. 36; et in PPC, 243. I discussed the circumstances of this interview with Daniel Defert and Gilles Barbadette, one of Foucault's younger friends who, along with Gilles Deleuze's former pupil

André Scala, conducted the interview at Foucault's bedside; the philosopher was so sick by then that he could not correct and edit the transcript, as was his custom, entrusting the task to Defert who, following Foucault's instructions, tried (without success) to get the interview into print before his death. Barbadette, for one, felt that this was certainly intended to be Foucault's "last will and testament"—and also that Foucault may well have had Roussel's gesture in the back of his mind.

54. Friedrich Nietzsche, *Beyond Good and Evil*, trans. Walter Kaufmann (New York, 1966), p. 13 (§6).

55. Foucault, OD, p. 10; et, p. 216. These passages from Foucault's inaugural lecture at the Collège de France—they amount to an oblique confession in their own right—occur in the context of an implicit commentary on the passage from Beckett's *The Unnameable* cited in note 29 of this chapter.

56. Guibert, *À l'ami*, pp. 24–25; et, p. 16–17.

57. For example, one of Foucault's closest associates, in an anonymous interview with me on 3 March 1990, asserted that "He had attained serenity. Absolute serenity." Cf. Paul Veyne's portrait, quoted in Eribon, *Foucault*, p. 349; et, p. 326.

POSTSCRIPT

1. Collège de France lecture, 14 March 1984.

2. Gilles Deleuze, *Logique du sens* (Paris, 1969), p. 153; et: *The Logic of Sense*, trans. Mark Lester (New York, 1990), p. 128.

3. Allan Bérubé, "Caught in the Storm: AIDS and the Meaning of Natural Disaster," *Out/Look* (Fall 1988), p. 16. It is also worth pointing out that Foucault's behavior in 1983—whatever it was—almost certainly had little or no bearing on his death in 1984, since it is likely that he had become infected long before, at a time when nobody knew anything at all about either AIDS or safe sex. Current studies of HIV suggest an average incubation to "full-blown AIDS" of roughly ten years. The evidence suggests that Foucault probably was infected sometime in the 1970s.

4. RR, pp. 11, 10; et, pp. 4, 3. UP, p. 14; et, p. 8.

5. Gayle Rubin, letter to the author, 24 January 1992.

6. Friedrich Nietzsche, "Schopenhauer as Educator," trans. William Arrowsmith, in *Unmodern Observations*, ed. Arrowsmith (New Haven, 1990), p. 226.

ACKNOWLEDGMENTS

My colleague and friend James Schmidt got me started on this project. He also let me try out my ideas in the summer seminars he has been teaching on the Enlightenment and its critics, under the auspices of the National Endowment for the Humanities.

Another friend, Greil Marcus, was instrumental in convincing me to go forward, and also in spurring me on as I worked, encouraging me to explore yet another episode in what he has called the "secret history of the twentieth century." When I was done, he carefully read a draft of the entire manuscript, offering detailed editorial advice. That a profound student of Dylan, Dada, and Debord should have become the book's co-conspirator seems only fitting.

In the early stages of my project, I received critical support from several scholars who, after hearing me rehearse my hypotheses about the links between Foucault's life and philosophy, encouraged me to continue my research. Particularly important to me were conversations with Jean Starobinski, whose interpretive approach and generosity of spirit I consider exemplary; with Susan Sontag, whose impassioned essays on Roland Barthes and Artaud offered me another kind of model; and with Leonard Michaels, whose gift for evoking dark passions with loving precision I often had cause to envy.

Given my initial ignorance about the gay community, and also about consensual sado-masochism, I was lucky to have my friend, journalist Adam Block, as an early guide: leave it to Adam to show me a "dungeon" in San Francisco with throw pillows cozying up a make-believe cellblock. Adam also generously shared interview material he had gathered on his own with Daniel Defert, with Jean Le Bitoux, and Edmund White, and also offered detailed comments on several critical passages in early drafts of my manuscript.

As my research continued, I got to meet a variety of other journalists and scholars working on gay issues, including Richard Mohr, Jeffrey Escoffier, John D'Emilio, Robert Dawidoff, Edmund White, David Halperin, and D. A. Miller. Each of them in different ways helped alleviate my ignorance, often by offering frank criticism.

On the more specialized subject of consensual sado-masochism, I owe much to Gayle Rubin, who supplied me with information and advice at several junctures, and also took the time to read, and comment on, the entire manuscript. The rise of gay studies in the American university has created a space where scholars like Rubin can do pathbreaking research; without such research, my own work would have been very different, and certainly less informed.

In dating the spread of "safe sex" information, and in verifying the chronology and correcting the mistakes in Randy Shilts's invaluable AIDS history, *And the Band Played On*, I had the help not only of Rubin, but also of Ted Hammett and Michael Gross of Abt Associates; both Ted and Michael were able to draw on their own research on the official response to the AIDS crisis.

To the late Robert J. Stoller, I owe special thanks. A brave and original thinker in a field not generally notable for bravery and originality, this great American psychoanalyst took time off from his busy schedule to meet with me, and discuss my work. In the letters we subsequently exchanged, I was able to benefit from his broad clinical experience and insatiable sense of curiosity, not only about consensual sado-masochism and the dynamaics of sexual excitement generally, but also about human nature and the intractable difficulties in drawing a line between the normal and the "pathological."

Other psychological aspects of my work I was lucky to be able to discuss with my wife, Sarah Minden, and a number of her colleagues in the fields of psychiatry and clinical psychology in the Boston area: Justin Newmark, Paul Barreira, Stephanie Engel, Leston Havens, and, above all, Bennett Simon, whose work on Samuel Beckett offered interesting parallels to what I was trying to do.

I also learned much from my conversations with a variety of philosophers, particularly Stanley Cavell, whose Emersonian reflections on Nietzsche have left their mark on my text; Amélie Rorty, whose genial doubts about my project made me think twice; John Rajchman, whose sober understanding of Foucault I used as one of my points of reference;

Tom McCarthy, who helped put me in touch with Jürgen Habermas; and my mentor Alasdair MacIntyre, who again was generous in his support. Above all, I must thank Arnold I. Davidson: his extensive knowledge of Foucault's work and extraordinary willingness to entertain—and react to— my most farfetched flights of interpretive fancy made him into one of my most important sounding boards.

At different points in my research, I was fortunate to be able to discuss the broader context of Parisian intellectual life with Roger Shattuck, who was there in the early fifties; with Jeffrey Mehlman, who was there in the sixties; and with Edward Said, whose essays on French theory have always been incisive, original—and wonderfully free of cant.

I owe an even larger debt to Jerrold Seigel, whose work on French bohemia influenced my thinking about the *poètes maudits*—and whose discerning and detailed comments on my manuscript persuaded me to change my mind about a number of substantive points, particularly in the book's early chapters.

Others with whom I discussed various aspects of my book include Lindsay Waters, an invaluable reader and friend; Paul and Wini Breines, who were sympathetic and responsive, as always; Judy Vichniac, who put me in touch with a variety of helpful contacts in France; Martha Zuber, who showed me the ropes in Paris; Robert Scholes, a personable critic and scintillating interlocutor; Harvey Goldman, who was exploring similar themes in his own work on Max Weber and Thomas Mann; Tracy B. Strong, who helped me out on matters concerning Nietzsche, and much else; and Daniel Charbonnier, the most gracious of hosts—his guided tour of the *École Normale* was a highpoint of one visit to Paris.

Jay Cantor was one of my first readers, and also one of my most constant companions in conversation about Foucault and related topics.

In the early phases of my work, Siddharta Mitter helped track down various obscure articles by Foucault. Later, I was able to obtain the *really* obscure articles thanks to James Bernauer, a longtime student of Foucault's work who shared his large archive of material with me, as well as his impressions of the man and his philosophy, despite misgivings about the approach I was taking. Without his generosity, my research would have taken months longer.

Michael Behrent transcribed Foucault's final lectures at the Collège de France for me, and also read a draft of the entire manuscript.

Various early versions of the manuscript were read by my father James E. Miller, Jr., Sarah Minden, Kathleen Farley, and also Diane Brentari, whose enthusiasm cheered me up. In addition, I got helpful responses to different parts of the maunscript from David Halperin, D. A. Miller, and Arnold I. Davidson. Leonard Michaels, Tom McCarthy, Bert Dreyfus, Edmund White, and Paul Berman all took the time to read, and to comment on, the entire manuscript, as did Hans Sluga, who convinced me to change several passages about Heidegger's philosophy.

My favorite critic was perhaps Leo Bersani, who was simultaneously supportive and—as always—mordantly skeptical. After reading the manuscript, Bersani suggested in a letter to me that I was "too fixated, but from the outside, on the 'extreme' elements in Foucault's sexuality," and that my prose style, though it evoked "some *very* sympathetic dad-scholar-doctor," nevertheless tended to make the subject of Foucault's sexuality "even more impenetrable than it might be," needlessly complicating "something which, finally, may not be that difficult to understand, may not be as mysterious as '*expérience-limite*' tends to suggest." Impressed by Bersani's acuity, I shared his letter with Edmund White, who said, "That's very interesting. Do you think it's true? I'm not sure." Neither am I. Readers will have to judge for themselves.

At the appropriate points in my manuscript and endnotes, I have cited the people whom I interviewed for this book. But Simeon Wade did something more: he let me both read, and quote extracts from, his unpublished manuscript, *Foucault in California,* the basis for a great deal of chapter eight.

Papers based on my research were presented, starting in 1989, to audiences at Harvard's Center for European Studies, at New York University, at Columbia University, at the Humanities Institute of the University of Michigan, at the 1991 meeting of the American Political Science Association, and at an international conference at Tokyo University that same year on "Le siècle de Michel Foucault." The responses of my commentators and critics on these different occasions (particularly, in Japan, the responses of Daniel Defert, François Ewald, Paul Rabinow, Hubert Dreyfus, and Hans Ulrich Gumbrecht) have in a number of ways, both large and small, informed my final text.

The final text has also been shaped, in part, by the editorial acumen of Jean Stein and her colleagues at *Grand Street*, especially Lee Smith, who also helped copyedit the book. From start to finish I was helped even more by my dear friends Robert and Peggy Boyers of *Salmagundi,* whose interest has been unflagging.

A fellowship from the National Endowment for the Humanities supported me in the final stages of my writing.

Last but not least, I must acknowledge the contribution of Arthur

Goldhammer. Art is not only one of America's most gifted English translators of French historiography; he is also a longtime student of the philosophy of Gaston Bachelard and Georges Canguilhem; a profoundly perceptive aficionado of almost every aspect of French history and culture; and a gifted writer in his own right. At every stage, he was my first reader. As I was writing, he pointed out countless infelicities of style, mistakes in translation, and errors about facts, helping me to write more clearly and accurately about a wide variety of matters, particularly the quirky French worlds of higher education and cultural life. Along with Bob Asahina, my editor at Simon and Schuster, it is Art who has most deeply affected the character of my text. I cannot thank him enough for our conversations and his friendship.

J.M.
West Roxbury, Massachusetts
February 28, 1992

INDEX